# Health Economics: Theories, Insights, and Industry Studies

# Health Economics: Theories, Insights, and Industry Studies

**Rexford E. Santerre**
*Professor of Economics*
*Bentley College*

**Stephen P. Neun**
*Professor of Economics*
*Utica College of Syracuse University*

| | |
|---|---|
| **Acquisitions Editor** | Gary Nelson |
| **Market Strategist** | Debbie K. Anderson |
| **Developmental Editor** | Amy Porubsky |
| **Project Editor** | Colby Alexander |
| **Art Director** | Bill Brammer |
| **Production Manager** | Anne Dunigan |

Cover Photo: © Mark Humphries

ISBN: 0-03-025629-1
Library of Congress Catalog Card Number: 98-89949

*Address for Domestic Orders*
The Dryden Press, 6277 Sea Harbor Drive, Orlando, FL 32887-6777
800-782-4479

*Address for International Orders*
International Customer Service
The Dryden Press, 6277 Sea Harbor Drive, Orlando, FL 32887-6777
407-345-3800
(fax) 407-345-4060
(e-mail) hbintl@harcourtbrace.com

*Address for Editorial Correspondence*
The Dryden Press, 301 Commerce Street, Suite 3700, Fort Worth, TX 76102

*Web Site Address*
http://www.hbcollege.com

THE DRYDEN PRESS, DRYDEN, and the DP LOGO are registered trademarks of Harcourt Brace & Company.

Printed in the United States of America

9  0  1  2  3  4  5  6  7  8  0  3  9  9  8  7  6  5  4  3  2  1

The Dryden Press
Harcourt Brace College Publishers

*Dedicated to the memory of our parents:*

M. L. M.
C. N.
E. N.
R. E. S.

# The Dryden Press Series in Economics

When we first discussed the notion of writing a textbook in early 1988, only one health economics textbook essentially existed in the market. One book was not surprising for the time because interest in health economics had not yet taken off but was beginning to "rev" its engine. One book could easily satisfy the modest demands of the marketplace. Things changed, however, as interest in health economics exploded soon thereafter.

From the late 1980s onward, issues pertaining to health care economics captured the front pages of major newspapers and news magazines on a regular basis. Indeed, it seemed that not a day passed without a newspaper writer, a radio broadcaster, or a television news reporter updating us about where health care expenditures stood as a percentage of gross domestic product: "It's at 10 percent!, . . . 11.2 percent!, . . . 12.9 percent!, . . . 13.3 percent! . . . when will the vicious spiral end?" *The Wall Street Journal* ran numerous opinion pieces, editorial columns, letters to the editor, and voices from the trenches citing the root causes of and necessary reforms to alleviate many problems relating to the health economy. Even Bob, the owner of Bob's Barbershop in Thompson, Connecticut, was seen bending (not cutting, fortunately) a few ears of his customers as he talked incessantly about the plight of the uninsured. He wasn't alone. Stan, a retired electrician, and Mary, a former high school science teacher, couldn't pass up a conversation or two about the questionable behavior of managed care companies while they waited for their cars to be serviced at the Mercury dealership in Mohawk, New York.

As interest in health economics burgeoned, and because necessity (and profit) is the mother of invention, a number of new health economics books eventually entered the market. A quick count puts the current number of health economics textbooks at seven or so. Each book uniquely presents health economics theory and its application to real-world problems. Each textbook does a fine job of presenting the relevant material and communicating the information to the reader. You see, that's what happens in a competitive market. Competition is good because it produces variety and innovation. Competition forces suppliers to satisfy consumer demands and, in a pluralistic society like ours, a "one-size-fits-all" textbook is unlikely to satisfy everyone.

Our textbook, now in its revised edition, is one of the "lucky" seven. The fact that our textbook has been revised reflects that it has survived the tough test of the marketplace. Educators and students have found our textbook to enhance their teaching efforts and learning processes. Indeed, we are very appreciative of all the professors at colleges throughout the world who have adopted our textbook. Many business schools, liberal arts schools, medical schools, and schools of public health, pharmacy, and health administration, at both the undergraduate and graduate levels, have chosen to use our textbook. We are also happy that the national Certified Employee Benefits Specialist (CEBS) program, cosponsored by the International Foundation of

Employee Benefit Plans and the Wharton School of the University of Pennsylvania, has chosen our book for their program.

## Why Our Textbook Has Been So Successful

We believe the relative success of our textbook is dependent on several factors. First, we take a fresh, contemporary approach to health economics. Rather than use the scarce time of the students and space in the book to discuss the historical origins of various concepts, tools, and principles of health economic analysis, we typically adopt analyses currently and widely used by health economists. Although, as educators, we recognize that the historical evolution of ideas is important, as economists we realize that prioritization is necessary because of time and space constraints. Hence, contemporary health economic analysis is given priority over the evolution of health economic ideas. This frees more time and space to apply the analysis to a variety of health economic issues and problems that are relevant to today's students. As a result, the book is relatively self-contained, simultaneously teaching health economic analysis and its application to many health care topics.

Second, we keep the analysis at a level that will be understood by most students. We both teach at relatively small colleges. Our classes tend to be of a size that we can assign essay exams in all our classes. Because we read and grade each question on the essay exams, we are keenly aware of the various problems faced by students in economics courses. In the book, we take particular care to explain the analysis and provide many real-world examples so the relevance of the analysis is readily apparent to the student. Admittedly, we have purposely sacrificed some theoretical rigor for a deeper, more fundamental, and intuitive understanding of health economics. Nevertheless, the ideas, principles, and concepts developed in this book remain theoretically consistent and challenging to most students. More important, we believe the book will be read!

Third, we try to present the material in a very lively and inviting manner and provide numerous real-world examples throughout the text. Let's face it, economics can be very dull and technical at times. In the book, we try to keep the material upbeat by keeping the discussion complete but brief on any one topic, and by citing current examples that students may have heard about. Just as we referred to Bob, Stan, and Mary earlier, we use various characters throughout the text to make the topics more meaningful. After all, health economics is about people and we shouldn't forget that. (Keep an eye out for our good friend Joe throughout the text.)

Fourth, we resist the temptation to become overly encyclopedic, and we try to avoid purely technical issues that only interest academics and not students. Although we briefly present and summarize the different sides, we attempt to conclude with a mainstream view concerning various issues and problems when possible.

Fifth, many Insight boxes are provided throughout the book. Usually the Insights concern a detailed account of an article that empirically estimates or measures a concept discussed in the text, such as economies of scale and scope in hospitals or the price elasticity of demand for medical services. Some Insights discuss health economic issues pertaining to other countries, such as Canada and Japan. All the Insights help to extend and reinforce the analysis. Our goal in the book is for the students to achieve maximum understanding.

## Organization of the Text

The textbook contains five parts. Part I, Chapters 1 through 7, deals with basic health economics concepts, such as trade-offs, the production of health, health care systems and institutions, the demands for medical care and health insurance, the health insurance product, production and cost theory, and cost-benefit analysis. The different views that people adopt regarding health care, the so-called theories X and Y of health economics, are introduced in Chapter 1. Chapter 2, unlike other health economics textbooks, provides an overview of the structural features of the U.S. health care system to familiarize students with such institutions as HMOs, PPOs, DRGs, Medicare, and Medicaid. It also examines the health care systems in Canada, Germany, and the United Kingdom as a way of introducing various health care institutions. Chapter 5 discusses at length the differences between managed care and traditional insurance plans with regard to numerous criteria.

Part II, Chapters 8 through 10, analyzes the likely behavior of health care providers in a number of different settings based on alternative objectives of the firm and the competitiveness of the market environment. Profit maximization, perfect competition, imperfect competition, and nonprofit objectives are among the many topics covered. More advanced students of economics should be able to cover the material in Chapters 8 and 9 quite quickly. Even those students, however, should find the health care applications and insights enlightening because they reinforce understanding of how medical markets operate under different conditions.

Part III, Chapters 11 and 12, focuses on the important role of government in health matters and medical care markets. Chapter 11 provides an overview of government functions, such as regulation, antitrust, and redistribution as applied to health and medical care issues. Chapter 12 discusses government's ever-increasing role as a producer of health insurance and examines the Medicaid and Medicare programs in considerable detail. Again, the Insights offer a lively illustration of health economics in action.

Part IV includes Chapters 13 through 17. Chapters 13 through 16 use the concepts and theories developed in earlier chapters to extensively analyze specific health care industries by applying the structure, conduct, and performance paradigm of industrial organization. The private health insurance, physician, hospital, and pharmaceutical industries are covered in great depth, and the analysis is kept as current as possible. Chapter 17 deals with health care reform. Some of the more popular plans for reforming the U.S. health care system at the federal and state levels are discussed and evaluated. The book ends with an appendix and a glossary. The book appendix contains a brief exposure to econometrics and provides useful information because some of the Insights present the actual regression results of various empirical studies. Also, the book refers to a host of studies that have quantified economic relationships by using regression analysis. The glossary is provided at the end of the book for those students who forget a definition from time to time.

## What Is New in the Revised Edition

You may be wondering what changes have been made in the revised edition. You should know that a number of significant improvements have been made in response to the suggestions of our readers. First, we now discuss the theories X and Y of health economics in the first rather than last chapter so students will immediately learn that people view health care and health economics in fundamentally different ways. This obvious difference in opinion should motivate some interesting discussions throughout the course. Second, an appendix on regression analysis is now provided at the end of Chapter 1. The discussion is elementary so students without any previous exposure to statistics will understand and have a better appreciation for the estimation of empirical relationships when they are discussed in the text. As before, more advanced students can consult the book's appendix for an in-depth treatment of regression analysis.

Third, the material on health care systems and institutions, which was in the sixth chapter of the original edition, has been moved to the second chapter. Fourth, a new Chapter 5 on the demand for health insurance has been added. As mentioned earlier, this chapter also includes a critical examination of the health insurance product and discusses the many differences between traditional and managed care insurance plans. Fifth, in the chapter on competitive markets, Chapter 8, we now also examine the markets for medical inputs.

Sixth, material on monopolistic competition and oligopoly is now included in the noncompetitive chapter, Chapter 9. Seventh, we added some discussion concerning the conversion of nonprofit into for-profit organizations in Chapter 10. Eighth, all the data and Insights have been updated when necessary, and institutional changes, such as physician-hospital integration, have been incorporated into the industry chapters. Ninth, we have greatly enhanced the discussion on managed care throughout the text. Finally, a number of new review questions and problems have been added. In fact, you will notice a number of questions designed for the CEBS program have been included at the end of selected chapters.

## The Certified Employee Benefits Specialist (CEBS) Program

The International Foundation of Employee Benefit Plans (IFEBP) and the Wharton School of the University of Pennsylvania cosponsor the CEBS Program. Founded in 1954, the IFEBP is a not-for-profit educational association dedicated to the education of and exchange of information among individuals responsible for the administration of employee benefits. The Wharton School, the world's first collegiate school of management, was founded in 1881 and is today widely regarded as a leader in preparing students to succeed in a globally competitive business environment. The IFEBP and Wharton established the CEBS Program in 1974 by creating a ten-course curriculum in health and welfare and retirement employee benefit programs. The curriculum covers fundamental concepts and principles of insurance, law, accounting, finance, human resources management, and economics and their applicability to the employee benefits field.

Candidates earn the CEBS designation by successfully completing an exam after studying each of the following ten courses:

| | |
|---|---|
| Course I | Employee Benefits: Concepts and Health Care Benefits |
| Course II | Employee Benefits: Design, Administration and Other Welfare Benefits |
| Course III | Retirement Plans: Basic Features and Defined Contribution Approaches |
| Course IV | Retirement Plans: Defined Benefit Approaches and Plan Administration |
| Course V | Contemporary Legal Environment of Employee Benefit Plans |
| Course VI | Financial Concepts and Practices |
| Course VII | Asset Management |
| Course VIII | Human Resources and Compensation Management |
| Course IX | Health Economics |
| Course X | Contemporary Benefit Issues and Practices |

The candidate can prepare for the exams by self-study or by enrolling in classes that are offered at over 80 educational institutions, including the Wharton School.

CEBS candidates are a diverse group, holding such positions as: human resource manager, benefits consultant, insurance agent, trust plan administrator, and health care provider. The CEBS designation is the most widely recognized and respected designation in the employee benefits field and has been earned by about 8,000 individuals as of January 1999. CEBS graduates combine academic education with professional experience to fulfill employers' and clients' needs at the highest level. Upon completing the CEBS program, graduates continue their professional development by joining the International Society of Certified Employee Benefit Specialists and participating in educational activities sponsored by local chapters. As members of the Society, graduates can build on their employee benefits knowledge through continuing education courses and examinations on emerging benefit issues and statutory changes.

A CEBS Program Catalog of Information can be obtained by contacting the IFEBP or the Wharton School at the following addresses:

CEBS Program
IFEBP
18700 W. Bluemound Road
P.O. Box 1270
Brookfield, WI 53008-1270
(414) 786-6710, Ext. 8579

CEBS Program
The Wharton School
3700 Market Street
Suite 100
Philadelphia, PA 19104-3147
(215) 898-2678

The Review Questions and Problems sections of selected chapters in the textbook include sample Questions on Subject Matter from the CEBS Study Manual for Course IX and sample CEBS Exam Questions.

# Acknowledgments

Our goal is to create the best possible learning device for students and teaching tool for professors. We are especially grateful to all the reviewers for helping us bring this goal to fruition by providing us with many helpful suggestions for improving the book. Specifically, we thank Andrew Foster of Brown University, Glenn Graham of SUNY-Oswego, and Robert Jantzen of Iona College for reviewing the revised edition and offering their advice. Every attempt was made to incorporate their recommendations into the text. We also thank Steven Andes, Mary Ann Baily, Laurie Bates, Sylvester Berki, Partha Deb, Randall Ellis, A. Mark Freeman, Dennis Heffley, Donald Kenkel, Frank Musgrave, Albert Oriol, James Thornton, Gary Wyckoff, Donald Yett, and the graduate health economics students at the University of Connecticut for their detailed comments on the initial manuscript. The exhaustive appraisal of the original manuscript by Steven Andes, Mary Ann Baily, and Gary Wyckoff is, and always will be, greatly appreciated. Our greatest thanks goes to Bruce Carpenter of Mansfield University for developing the book's appendix, "A Brief Exposure to Econometrics." His succinct yet comprehensive appendix alone, is worth the price of this book.

At Dryden Press, we thank Gary Nelson, the senior economics acquisitions editor, for his continued encouragement, Amy Porubsky, the developmental editor, for keeping us on schedule and for directing traffic, and the entire production and marketing staff for their professional support. We also thank our wives and children for their love, patience, and understanding. Finally, we thank Bentley College and Utica College for providing us with concurrent sabbaticals when we worked on the first edition of this book. Without the opportunity to work closely together, our task would have been much more difficult.

If any of our readers, students, or colleagues have any comments or suggestions for improving the book, please bring them to our attention. We are only an e-mail message away. We thank you in advance.

Rex Santerre
rsanterre@bentley.edu

Stephen Neun
sneun@utica.ucsu.edu

# CONTENTS

## Chapter 3

# Chapter 4

# Chapter 7

**PART II**

Alternative Objectives
and Environments
Facing Health Care
Providers
201

# Chapter 8

## Chapter 10

**PART III**

**Government and Health**
**301**

## Chapter 11

# Chapter 12

# Chapter 13

**PART IV**

Health Industry
Studies
373

# Chapter 15

# Chapter 16

# Chapter 17

# I

# Basic Health Care Economic Tools and Institutions

# 1

# Introduction

L ike millions of Americans at some point in their lives, Joe awoke one
night feeling a crushing weight on his chest. As the pain spread down his
arm, he realized he was experiencing his worst dread: a heart attack. His wife,
Angela, called the paramedics. While the ambulance was rushing Joe to the
hospital, she anguished over the kind of care he would receive.

Angela's anxiety starkly illustrates the basic questions any health care system faces:

1. Who should receive the medical goods and services? Would a person
   like Joe receive care merely because he is a citizen, or would he receive
   care only if he worked for a large company that provides health
   insurance for its employees?

2. What types of medical goods and services should be produced? Should
   the most expensive tests (such as angiograms) be performed without
   regard to cost? What treatments (such as balloon angioplasties) should
   be provided?

3. What inputs should be used to produce the medical goods and
   services? Should the hospital use high-tech medical equipment, a large
   nursing staff, or both?[1]

This chapter examines these fundamental questions. In addition, the chapter

- Introduces the discipline of health economics.

- Discusses the design and purpose of models and analysis in health
  economics.

---

[1] We are indebted to Gary Wyckoff of Hamilton College for providing us with this example.

- **Explains how economic decisions are typically driven by a cost-benefit calculation.**
- **Examines the X and Y theories of health economics.**

## What Is Health Economics?

For many of you, this textbook provides your first exposure to the study of health economics. Perhaps the ongoing controversy regarding health care reform or the prospect of a career in the health care field motivated you to learn more about health economics. Or perhaps you need only three more credits to graduate. Whatever the reason, we are sure you will find health economics to be challenging, highly interesting, and personally rewarding.

The study of health economics involves the application of various microeconomics tools, such as demand or cost theory, to health issues and problems. The goal is to promote a better understanding of the economic aspects of health care problems so that corrective health policies can be designed and proposed. A thorough understanding of microeconomic analysis is essential for conducting sound health economics analyses. If you lack a background in microeconomics, don't worry. This textbook is intended to help you learn and apply basic microeconomic theory to health economic issues. Before long, you will be thinking like a health economist!

The tools of health economics can be applied to a wide range of issues and problems pertaining to health and health care. For example, health economics analysis might be used to investigate why 57 of every 1,000 babies born in Turkey never reach their first birthday, whereas all but 4 of every 1,000 babies born in Japan live to enjoy their first birthday cake (Schieber, Poullier, and Greenwald, 1994). The tools of health economics analysis might also be used to examine the economic desirability of a hotly contested merger between two large hospitals in a major metropolitan area. The burning question is: Will the merger of the two hospitals result in lower hospital prices due to overall cost savings or higher prices due to monopoly power?

Health economics is difficult to define in a few words because it encompasses such a broad range of concepts, theories, and topics. The *Mosby Medical Encyclopedia* (1992, p. 361) defines *health economics* as follows:

> **Health economics** . . . studies the supply and demand of health care resources and the impact of health care resources on a population.

Notice that health economics is defined in terms of the determination and allocation of *health care resources*. This is logical, because medical goods and services cannot exist without them.[2] Health care resources consist of *medical supplies* like pharmaceutical goods, latex rubber gloves, and bed linens; *personnel*, such as physicians and lab

---

[2]Even health care services produced in the home, like first aid (therapeutic services) or home pregnancy tests (diagnostic services), require resources.

assistants; and *capital inputs*, including nursing home and hospital facilities, diagnostic and therapeutic equipment, and other items that provide medical care services. Unfortunately, health care resources, like resources in general, are limited or scarce at a given time, and wants are limitless. Thus, trade-offs are inevitable and a society, whether it possesses a market-driven or a government-run health care system, must make a number of fundamental but crucial choices. These choices are normally couched in terms of four basic questions, discussed next.

## The Four Basic Questions

As just noted, resources are scarce. Scarcity means that each society must make important decisions regarding the consumption, production, and distribution of goods and services as a way of providing answers to the four basic questions, which are

1. What combination of nonmedical and medical goods and services should be produced in the macroeconomy?

2. What particular medical goods and services should be produced in the health economy?

3. What specific health care resources should be used to produce the final medical goods and services?

4. Who should receive the medical goods and services?

How a particular society chooses to answer these four questions has a profound impact on the operation and performance of its health economy.

The first two questions deal with **allocative efficiency:** What is the best way to allocate resources to different consumption uses? The first decision concerns what combination of goods and services to produce in the overall economy. Individuals in a society have unlimited wants regarding nonmedical and medical goods and services, yet resources are scarce. As a result, decisions must be made concerning the best mix of medical and nonmedical goods and services to provide, and this decision-making process involves making trade-offs. If more people are trained as doctors or nurses, fewer people are available to produce nonmedical goods like food, clothing, and shelter. Thus, more medical goods and services imply fewer nonmedical goods and services, and vice versa, given a fixed amount of resources.

The second consumption decision involves the proper mix of medical goods and services to produce in the health economy. This decision also involves trade-offs. For example, if more health care resources, such as nurses and medical equipment, are allocated to the production of maternity care services, fewer resources are available for the production of nursing home care for elderly people. Allocative efficiency in the overall economy and the health economy is achieved when the best mix of goods is chosen given society's underlying preferences.

The third question—what specific health care resources should be used?—deals with **production efficiency.** Usually resources or inputs can be combined to produce

FIGURE 1–1    PRODUCTION POSSIBILITIES CURVE FOR MATERNITY
AND NURSING HOME SERVICES

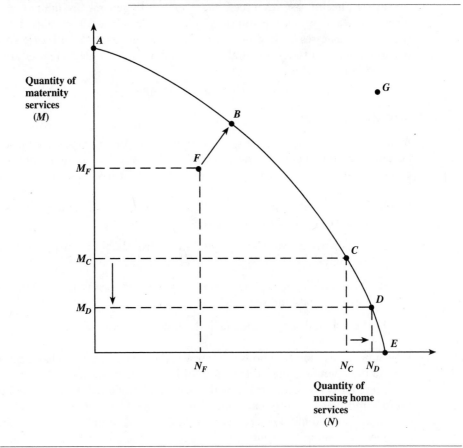

a particular good or service in many different ways. For example, hospital services can be produced in a capital- or labor-intensive manner. A large amount of sophisticated medical equipment relative to the number of patients served reflects a capital-intensive way of producing hospital services, whereas a high nurse-to-patient ratio indicates a labor-intensive process. Production efficiency implies that society is getting the maximum output from its limited resources because the best mix of inputs has been chosen to produce each good.

*Production and Allocative Efficiency and the Production Possibilities Curve*

The most straightforward way to illustrate production and allocative efficiency is to use the **production possibilities curve (PPC).** Figure 1–1 displays a PPC. The quantities of maternity services, $M$, and nursing home services, $N$, are shown on the vertical and horizontal axes, respectively.[3] Points on the bowed-out PPC depict the various combinations of maternity and nursing home care services that can be efficiently produced within a health economy assuming the amounts of health care resources and technology are fixed at a given point in time.

Every point on the PPC implies production efficiency, since all health care resources are being fully utilized. For example, notice points $A$, $B$, $C$, $D$, and $E$ on the PPC. At each of these points, medical inputs are neither unemployed nor underemployed (e.g., a nurse involuntarily working part time rather than full time) and are being used in the most productive manner so that society is getting their maximum use. If a movement along the curve from one point to another occurs, units of one medical service must be forgone to receive more units of the other medical service.

Specifically, assume the health economy is initially operating at point $C$ with $M_C$ units of maternity care services and $N_C$ units of nursing home services. Now suppose health care decision makers decide that society is better off at point $D$ with one more unit of nursing home services, $N_D - N_C$. The movement from point C to point $D$ implies that $M_C - M_D$ units of maternity care services are given up to receive the additional unit of nursing home services. Because medical resources are fully utilized at point $C$, a movement to point $D$ means that medical inputs must be drawn or reallocated from the maternity care services market to the nursing home services market. As a result, the quantity of maternity care services must decline if an additional unit of nursing home services is produced. The forgone units of maternity care services, $M_C - M_D$, represent the **opportunity cost** of producing an additional unit of nursing home services.[4] Generally, opportunity cost is the value of the next best alternative that is given up.

The bowed-out shape of the PPC implies that opportunity cost is not constant but increases with a movement along the curve. Imperfect substitutability of resources is one reason for this so-called **law of increasing opportunity cost.** For example, suppose the nursing home services market expands downward along the PPC. To produce more nursing home services, employers must bid resources away from the maternity care services market. Initially, the least productive inputs in the maternity care services market are likely to be bid away, because they are available at a lower cost to nursing home employers. Consequently, very few maternity care services are given up at first. As the nursing home services market continues to expand, however, increasingly productive inputs in the maternity care services market must be drawn away. The implication is that society gives up ever-increasing units of maternity care services. Thus, the law of increasing opportunity cost suggests that ever-increasing amounts of one good must be given up to receive successively more equal increments of another good.

If medical inputs are not fully utilized because some inputs are idle or used unproductively, more units of one medical service can be produced without decreasing

---

[3]We assume society has already made its choice between medical and nonmedical goods.

[4]As economists are fond of reminding noneconomists, "There is no such thing as a free lunch!"

the amount of the other medical service. An example of an underutilization of resources is indicated by point $F$ in the interior of the PPC. At point $F$, the health care system is producing only $M_F$ units of maternity services and $N_F$ units of nursing home services. Notice that by moving to point $B$ on the PPC, both maternity care services and nursing home services can be increased without decreasing the other. The quantities of both goods increase only because some resources are initially idle or underutilized at point $F$. Health care resources are inefficiently employed at point $F$.

A point outside the current PPC, such as $G$, is attainable in the future if the stock of health care resources increases or if a new, productivity-enhancing technology is discovered. If so, the PPC shifts out and passes through a point like $G$. For example, technological change may enable an increased production of both maternity and nursing home services from the same original stock of health care resources. Alternatively, a greater quantity of maternity and nursing home services can be produced and the PPC shifts outward if more people enter medical professions (possibly at the expense of all other goods and services).

Production efficiency is attained when the health economy operates at any point on the PPC, since medical inputs are producing the maximum amount of medical services and no unproductive behavior or involuntary unemployment exists. Allocative efficiency is attained when society chooses the best or most preferred point on the PPC. All points on the PPC are possible candidates for allocative efficiency. The ideal, or optimal, point for allocative efficiency depends on society's underlying preferences for the two medical services.

### The Distribution Question

The answer to the fourth question—who should receive the medical goods and services?—deals with *distributive justice*, or *equity*. It asks whether the distribution of output is equitable, or fair, to everyone involved. In a pure market system, the marketplace distributes output based on willingness and ability to pay. It follows that in a pure market system, those individuals without sufficient income face a financial barrier to obtaining goods and services. On the other hand, in a perfect egalitarian system, the government ensures that everyone receives an equal distribution of the output produced.

In the mixed-capitalistic system of the United States, many goods and services are distributed by both the market and the government. Yet many allege that an unfair distribution of output remains. For example, on an average day, about 14 percent of the U.S. population lacks public (e.g., Medicare or Medicaid) or private health insurance coverage. The uninsured typically face a financial barrier when obtaining medical services and often are forced to acquire the needed medical care, usually after it is too late and more costly, in the emergency room of a public hospital. As a result, equity advocates argue that health insurance coverage should be made available for all U.S. residents.

In contrast, nearly all individuals have health insurance coverage or free access to medical care services in the health care systems of Canada, the United Kingdom, and some other nations. Regardless of willingness and ability to pay, all people essentially pay a zero out-of-pocket price for medical treatment because medical costs are financed through taxes. This does not mean that medical services are not rationed. Any good that is scarce must be rationed in some manner. The difference between a market-directed system and a system that provides free medical care, like the Canadian system, lies in *how* medical services are rationed. In a market system, price rations scarce goods among consumers. In a system where price to consumers is essentially zero at the point of access, medical services must be rationed on some nonprice basis, such as the amount of waiting time, age, or severity of illness.

## Implications of the Four Basic Questions

Given a scarcity of economic resources, a society generally wishes to produce the best combination of goods and services by employing least-cost methods of production. Trade-offs are inevitable. As the production possibilities curve illustrates, some amount of one good or service must be given up if the production and consumption of another good or service increases. As a result, each society must make hard choices concerning consumption and production activities because scarcity exists. Choices may involve sensitive trade-offs, for example, between the young and the old, between prevention and treatment, or between men (prostate cancer) and women (breast cancer).

In addition, for various reasons, some individuals lack financial access to necessary goods and services like food, housing, and medical care. Because achieving equity is a desirable goal, a society usually seeks some redistribution of income. Normally, the redistribution involves taxation. However, a tax on labor or capital income tends to create a disincentive for employing resources in their most efficient manner.[5] Inefficient production suggests that fewer goods and services are available in the society (production inside the PPC). Thus, a trade-off often exists between equity and efficiency goals, and, consequently, hard choices must be made between the two objectives. The design of a nation's health care system normally reflects the way the society has chosen to balance efficiency and equity concerns.

A simple example will help to clarify how a trade-off might occur between efficiency and equity. In any classroom, some people learn more easily than others. The teacher can give every student the same amount of personal attention, or she or he can spend most of the time with the slow learners and leave the others to manage on their own. The second strategy will probably result in less variation in final performance across class members, but might mean a smaller increase in knowledge and skills for the class as a whole. That is because the faster learners may have learned much more with additional personal attention from the teacher. If efficiency is defined in relation to the total increase in knowledge and equity is defined in relation to variation in final knowledge levels, the efficiency and equity goals can be in conflict.[6]

---

[5]This point is discussed in more detail in later chapters after we develop the appropriate tools of economic analysis.

[6]We thank Mary Ann Baily of George Washington University for providing this insightful example.

# Economic Models and Analysis

*Economic Models*

The production possibilities curve is an example of an **economic model.** Models are abstractions of reality and are used in economics to simplify a very complex world. Economic models can be stated in descriptive (verbal), graphical, or mathematical form. Usually an economic model like the PPC describes a hypothesized relation between two or more variables. For example, suppose the hypothesis is that health care expenditures, *E*, are *directly* (as opposed to *inversely*) related to consumer income, *Y.* That hypothesis simply means that expenditures on health care services tend to rise when consumer income increases. Mathematically, a health care expenditure function can be stated in general form as

**(1–1)**   $E = f(Y)$.

Equation 1–1 implies that health care spending is a *function* of consumer income. In particular, health care expenditures are expected to rise with income.

An assumption underlying economic models is that all factors, other than the variables of interest, remain unchanged. For instance, our hypothesis that health care expenditures are directly related to income assumes that all other likely determinants of health care spending, such as prices, tastes, and preferences, stay constant. As another example, notice in the above analysis that the stocks of resources and technology are held constant when constructing the PPC. Indeed, economists normally qualify their hypotheses with the Latin phrase *ceteris paribus*, meaning "all other things held constant." By holding other things constant, we can isolate and describe the pure relation between any two variables.

The expenditure function in equation 1–1 is expressed in general mathematical form, but a hypothesis or model is often stated in a specific form. For example, the following equation represents a linear expenditure function for health care services:

**(1–2)**   $E = a + bY$,

where *a* and *b* are the fixed parameters of the model. This equation simply states that health care expenditures are directly related to consumer income in a linear (rather than nonlinear) fashion. Mathematically, the parameter *a* reflects the amount of health care expenditures when income is zero, whereas *b* is the slope of the expenditure function. The slope measures the change in health care expenditures that results from a one-unit change in income, or $\Delta E/\Delta Y$.

For example, let us assume the parameter *a* equals $1,000 per year and *b* equals one-tenth, or .1. The resulting health care expenditure function is thus

**(1–3)**   $E = 1,000 + .1Y$.

Equation 1–3 implies that health care expenditures rise with income. In fact, the slope parameter of .1 suggests that each $1,000 increase in consumer income raises health care spending by $100.

## We Should Address Some Basic Questions

Following is an excerpt from an opinion piece written by Samuel J. Tibbitts in 1988, well before the National Health Security Act of 1993 was proposed by the Clinton administration. Tibbitts was inducted into the Health Care Hall of Fame in 1997. When he wrote this article, Tibbitts was chair of the board of Unihealth of America, a health care company that owned 14 hospitals. In this essay, he expands on the four basic questions and offers some normative insights into health care policy in the United States.

We are in a health-care crisis that has never before been seen in this country. The public has come to believe that health care is a basic right. The government has fostered this belief. But neither government, employers, insurance carriers nor the people themselves are willing to pay the cost.

While it is not legally guaranteed, as a society we have come to expect access to health care as something highly desirable and important to our well-being. Without health we have nothing. But no one in this country has ever identified a national policy that describes how much health care should be everyone's right, how should it be provided and who should pay for it.

We must have state and national policies. A top-level, knowledgeable and bipartisan commission should be formed to address some very weighty and politically sensitive health care issues:

- Is health care a right for all Americans?

- Is there a limit on the resources that our society is willing to pay for health care?

- Is the financial responsibility for health care properly proportioned among government, employers, health-care providers and the individual citizen?

- Should health services be the same for all people regardless of income?

- If resources are limited, where should the money be spent in terms of health education, preventive health services, acute health care, home health care, mental health care, skilled nursing facilities and hospice?

- Should there be age limits or other criteria to ration the provision of highly expensive health services such as open heart surgery or liver transplants to those who would benefit the least? Bioethical issues such as the individuals' right to die must also be addressed.

This nation certainly has the capability to handle the health-care crisis. However, we have not yet found the political will to solve it. If we don't solve it soon, issues such as the national debt and trade imbalances will pale by comparison. The people without adequate access to needed health care will become weak and demoralized; an unhealthy nation will be a weak nation. We simply cannot afford the consequences.

SOURCE: Excerpt from Samuel J. Tibbitts, "Health Care Denied Makes a Weak Nation," *Los Angeles Times*, August 21, 1988, part 5, p. 5. Reprinted by permission of Audrey Tibbitts (widow of Samuel J. Tibbitts).

The health care expenditure function in equation 1–3 is represented graphically in figure 1–2. Yearly consumer income per household is shown on the horizontal axis, and annual health care spending per household is shown on the vertical axis. According to the function, health care spending equals $3,000 when household income is $20,000 per year. Consumers earning $50,000 per year spend $6,000 per

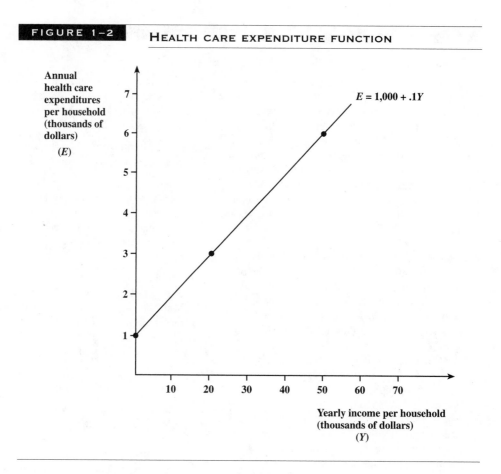

**FIGURE 1–2**    HEALTH CARE EXPENDITURE FUNCTION

Annual health care expenditures per household (thousands of dollars) (E)

$E = 1,000 + .1Y$

Yearly income per household (thousands of dollars) (Y)

year on health care services. Note that the expenditure function clearly represents our hypothesis concerning the direct relation between income and health care spending.

Now suppose some other determinants of health care expenditures change. Although this assumption violates our implicit *ceteris paribus* condition, we can incorporate changes in other factors into the health care expenditure model fairly simply. For instance, suppose people generally become sicker than before, perhaps because households have become older on average. Obviously, this change tends to increase health care spending. Assuming the "aging" effect influences only the intercept term and not the value of the slope parameter, the expenditure function shifts upward by the yearly increase in health care spending due to the aging population. Figure 1–3 shows an example of this effect.

Yearly medical costs are assumed to increase by $500 for the typical household. Thus, the health care expenditure function shifts upward at each level of income by $500 to $E_1$. If the aging effect also influences the percentage of additional income that

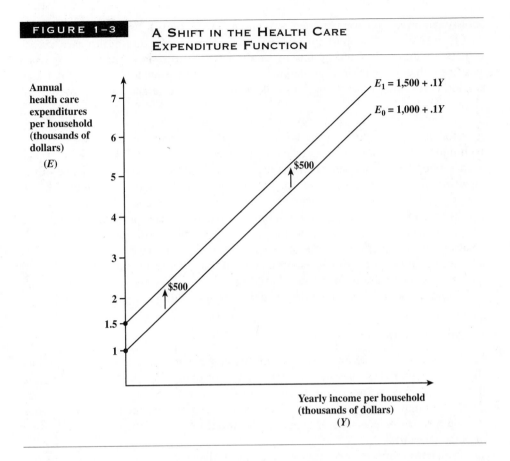

**FIGURE 1-3**  A SHIFT IN THE HEALTH CARE EXPENDITURE FUNCTION

people spend on health care services, the slope of the function changes as well. An increase (decrease) in the marginal propensity to spend out of income raises (lowers) the slope and rotates the expenditure function to the left (right).[7]

In sum, models are used in economics to simplify a complex world and to isolate the relation among a few important variables. Models can be stated descriptively, mathematically, or graphically.

## Empirical Testing of Health Economic Theories

Health economists often use statistical methods to test their theories. Statistical tests are conducted either to verify the theories or to quantify the magnitude of the relation among economic variables. For instance, empirical methods might be used

---

[7]A problem at the end of the chapter asks you to complete an exercise of this type.

to estimate values for the parameters, *a* and *b*, in equation 1–2. A statistical study of this type could lend support for our hypothesis that income and health care expenditures are directly related by finding empirically that the slope parameter, *b*, has a positive value. In addition, an empirical study could provide some useful information concerning how strongly income affects health care spending. Is *b* equal to .1 or 1.2?

Throughout this book, we refer to a host of empirical studies using multiple regression analysis. In the simplest terms, **multiple regression analysis** is a statistical technique used to estimate lines or curves such as equation 1–2. The only difference is that a number of independent variables are specified on the right-hand side of the equation—hence *multiple* regression. Reviewing multiple regression studies should give you a better understanding of the underlying theories and also help you learn how to interpret multiple regression findings. Most of you have probably studied multiple regression analysis in your statistics classes; an elementary discussion of regression analysis is provided in an appendix at the end of this chapter. For those desiring a more advanced treatment of regression analysis, an additional appendix is included at the end of the book for reviewing purposes. The material provides a general overview of the technique and some pitfalls commonly encountered in multiple regression studies.

## Positive and Normative Analysis

Health economists perform two types of analysis. **Positive analysis** uses economic theory and empirical analysis to make statements or predictions concerning economic behavior. It seeks to answer the questions "What is?" or "What happened?" For example, we might investigate the exact relation between income and health care spending. Because positive analysis provides explanations or predictions, it tends to be free of personal values.

**Normative analysis,** on the other hand, deals with the appropriateness or desirability of an economic outcome or policy. It seeks to answer the questions "What ought to be?" or "Which is better?" For example, an analyst might conclude that households with incomes below $30,000 per year should be subsidized by the government because they are unable to maintain a proper level of health care spending. Naturally, this implies that the analyst is making a value judgment. Because opinions vary widely concerning the desirability of any given economic outcome and the role government should play in achieving outcomes, it is easy to see why normative statements generally spark more controversy than positive ones. For instance, when 518 health economists were asked whether the Canadian health care system is superior to the U.S. system, there was much disagreement. Fifty-two percent of the economists agreed and 38 percent disagreed with the statement. The remaining 10 percent had no opinion or lacked the information needed to respond to the question (Feldman and Morrisey, 1990).

The following sets of positive and normative economic statements should give you a better understanding of the difference between the two. Notice that the positive statements deal with what is or what will be, whereas the normative statements concern what is better or what ought to be.

*Positive:* According to Becker and Murphy (1988), a 10 percent increase in the price of cigarettes leads to a 6 percent reduction in the number of cigarettes consumed.

*Normative:* The government should increase the tax on cigarettes to prevent people from smoking.

*Positive:* A study by Hellinger (1991) estimates that the average yearly cost of treating someone with AIDS is $38,300, while the lifetime costs equal $102,000.

*Normative:* It is in our country's best interests that the federal government take a more active role in the prevention of AIDS.

*Positive:* National health care expenditures per capita in the United States equaled $3,759 in 1996 (Levit et al., 1997).

*Normative:* To control health care expenditures, the United States should adopt a national health insurance program similar to Canada's.

# The Net Benefit Calculus

As we saw from the PPC analysis, resource scarcity forces society to make choices. For example, an entire economy must collectively decide how much medical care to produce and who is to receive it, while each health care provider must determine the most appropriate method to produce health care services. Even the consumer who has complete medical insurance coverage faces scarcity and choices because time is a finite commodity. In this situation, the consumer must consider the opportunity cost of time. The consumer must decide whether the time needed to make a doctor's appointment, travel to the physician's office, and receive medical services is worth the value of forgone activities. Thus, scarcity necessitates choice, and economics is the social science that analyzes the process by which society makes these choices.

Economists treat people as *rational* decision makers. **Rationality** means people know how to rank their preferences from high to low or best to worst. It also means people never purposely choose to make themselves worse off. Consequently, it stands to reason that people will make choices based on their self-interests and choose those activities they expect will provide them with the most net satisfaction. Pursuing self-interests does not mean people are always selfish, however. For example, giving money to charity or volunteering one's time at a local hospital gives even the most devout good samaritan a considerable amount of pleasure.

The decision rule people follow when choosing activities is straightforward and involves an assessment of the expected benefits and costs associated with each choice. If expected benefits exceed expected costs for a given choice, it is in the economic agent's best interest to make that choice. In formal terms, the optimizing rule looks like this:

**(1–4)**    $NB^*(X) = B^*(X) - C^*(X)$

where $X$ represents a particular choice or activity under consideration, $B^*$ stands for the expected benefits associated with the choice, $C^*$ equals the expected costs resulting from the choice, and $NB^*$ represents the expected net benefits.

Expected values take both the probability of occurrence and the magnitude of the loss or gain into consideration. For example, the expected benefit of activity $X$ can be expressed in the following manner:

**(1–5)**    $B^*(X) = Pr(X) \cdot B(X)$, where $0 \leq Pr(X) \leq 1$.

$Pr(X)$ measures the probability or degree of certainty that activity $X$ will provide actual benefits, and $B(X)$ reflects the dollar magnitude of the actual benefits. If $Pr(X)$ equals 1, the actual benefits of activity $X$ are known with perfect certainty. Oppositely, if $Pr(X)$ equals zero, the true benefits of $X$ are completely unknown. Intermediate values for $Pr(X)$ mean the benefits of $X$ are uncertain to some degree. For instance, in deciding whether to purchase an over-the-counter cold remedy, a person implicitly considers both the probability that the cold remedy will be effective and the benefit of being relieved of cold symptoms.

Expected costs are calculated in an analogous manner. In the decision to purchase a cold remedy, the monetary costs are known, a priori, so the probability of occurrence is 100 percent, or 1. In that case, the expected cost equals the actual cost of the cold remedy. In some instances, however, the true costs may be unknown when the activity initially takes place, so expected costs are either implicitly or explicitly estimated. For example, actual physician charges are never known until after the episode of care is completed. One office visit may result in numerous tests and many follow-up visits.

If $NB^*$ is larger than zero, the economic agent's well-being is enhanced by choosing the activity. Your reading of this textbook indicates that the book's expected benefits outweigh its expected costs (unless, of course, your professor forced you to buy and read it). That is, you expect this book to provide benefits in excess of the money you spent on it, plus the forgone use of your time. Nonreaders of this book obviously believe the costs outweigh the benefits.

Health care providers, government agencies, and individual consumers employ cost-benefit analysis on either an informal or a formal basis to guide them in the decision-making process. The formal approach is to estimate the monetary value of the expected costs and benefits associated with a policy proposal. If the benefits exceed the costs, the policy may warrant adoption. More likely, however, several proposals are under consideration, so the best proposal is associated with the highest net benefit or payoff. Chapter 7 discusses formal cost-benefit analysis in detail.

Medical care providers use cost-benefit analysis when deciding whether to produce an additional unit of medical services. For example, the expected benefits to a physician of performing one more office visit are the added revenues plus the psychic value that she or he places on helping an additional person. The incremental expected costs equal the amount of money and time needed to perform the additional office

## The Opportunity Cost of 1 Million Medical Dollars

Economists generally prefer to look at opportunity costs when judging whether a given medical expenditure is generating the maximum amount of output. Recall that the opportunity cost of any medical good or service equals the benefits forgone from not pursuing the next best alternative. If the opportunity cost, or benefits forgone, is compared with the benefits generated from a particular medical intervention, a decision can be made concerning the appropriateness of the expenditure. For example, if the benefits generated from a medical program exceed its opportunity cost, medical expenditures enhance net welfare. If the opposite occurs, net benefits can be increased by adopting the alternative medical program.

Table 1 illustrates the opportunity cost of $1 million spent on various medical interventions.[1] For example, $1 million spent on monitoring low-risk patients in coronary units buys 3 life-years, while a Pap smear every three years for women between 20 and 75 years of age buys 52 life-years.[2] Bypass surgery for middle-aged men with symptoms of left-main coronary artery disease buys the greatest number of life-years (134).

Based solely on the results presented, the opportunity cost of spending $1 million to monitor low-risk heart patients is 134 life-years. This represents the life-years that could be saved if this $1 million were spent on bypass surgery rather than on monitoring low-risk heart patients. If the objective is to maximize the number of life-years saved, the results indicate that more money should be spent on bypass surgery and less on monitoring low-risk patients. Information such as this helps decision makers spend medical care dollars more wisely.

SOURCE: Based on Louise B. Russell "Opportunity Costs in Modern Medicine, *Health Affairs* (summer 1992), pp. 162–69.

[1] The estimates consider the number of units of a medical service that $1 million can buy and the effectiveness, in terms of life-years saved, of an individual unit, or medical procedure.

[2] A Pap smear is a medical procedure that tests for cervical cancer.

| TABLE 1 | YEARS OF LIFE PURCHASED PER $1 MILLION (1990 DOLLARS) | |
| --- | --- | --- |
| **Procedure** | | **Life-Years** |
| Monitoring low-risk patients in coronary care units | | 3 |
| Pap smear every 3 years | | 52 |
| Bypass surgery for left-main coronary artery disease in middle-aged men | | 134 |

visit. The difference between the two is the net benefit generated from the office visit. Naturally, if incremental net benefits are expected to be positive, it is in the physician's best interest to treat the patient.

Consumers also use cost-benefit analysis to make allocation decisions, although they generally do not go to the trouble of calculating the monetary value of the expected benefits and costs associated with the various choices. Consider the individual who is deciding whether to visit a physician for an annual physical exam. The cost equals the direct out-of-pocket expense the consumer incurs after the impact of health insurance has been taken into account, plus the opportunity cost of the individual's time spent in making the appointment, traveling to and from the doctor's office, and receiving the physical exam. Although difficult to quantify, the benefits equal the potential decrease in out-of-pocket medical care costs that result from preventing an illness, plus the monetary value attached to any increase in life-years or restoration of good health that the visit generates. If the benefits exceed the costs, it is in the consumer's best interest to have the physical exam.

Equation 1–4 can also be used to illustrate how government policies sometimes attempt to alter behavior by manipulating the expected costs or benefits associated with a health care decision. For example, the primary purpose of "sin taxes" on cigarettes and alcohol is to discourage the consumption of both products by increasing their actual costs. Government warnings on cigarette packages and alcoholic beverages aim to lower the expected benefits associated with these consumption practices and thereby reduce the amount of medical care services directed toward alcohol- and tobacco-induced illnesses.

## The Theories X and Y of Health Economics

Discussions concerning health economics often spark considerable debate. Controversy abounds because people tend to have different views about such matters as the primary determinants of good health, the practice of medicine, the uniqueness of medical care, and the proper role of economics and government in health care affairs. Musgrave (1995) provides a useful conceptual framework in which different views can be contrasted. He refers to the framework as the theories X and Y of health economics. Table 1–1 summarizes Musgrave's dichotomy, presenting theories X and Y as they pertain to five dimensions of health economics. Notice the essential differences.

On the one hand, theory X views illnesses as occurring randomly. That is, some people get sick or become involved in accidents, and others do not: some live long and healthy lives, whereas others live abnormally short lives plagued with illness. On the other hand, theory Y treats illnesses and accidents as being determined largely by lifestyle choices. Choices concerning cigarette smoking, excessive drinking, safe sex, wearing safety belts, occupation, and the like can affect the probability of entering a state of sickness or suffering a harmful accident. Those individuals who choose healthy lifestyles enjoy long lives free of sickness, according to theory Y.

Theory X treats medical care as being special. Necessity, consumer ignorance, the dominance of nonprofit hospitals and other medical institutions, highly inelastic demand, and the preponderance of government intervention all make medical care unique. Theory X says that because of uniqueness, medical care "is not and cannot be treated in the same fashion as other economic commodities whose allocation is left to relatively unregulated markets" (Aaron, 1991, p. 6). In fact, greedy, profit-oriented doctors, insurance companies, and pharmaceutical companies as well as the unfettered forces of the marketplace are the root cause of rising health care costs, according to theory X.

| TABLE 1-1 | THE X AND Y THEORIES OF HEALTH ECONOMICS | |
|---|---|---|
| **View of** | **Theory X** | **Theory Y** |
| Health | Health and disease occur randomly | Health is determined by people's lifestyle choices |
| Medical care | Special | No different than any other good or service |
| The practice of medicine | A science | An art |
| Economics | Financial rewards reduce the quality of caring | Financial rewards are responsible for generating high-quality medicine |
| Policy | Regulations are needed to mitigate economic forces | Reduce regulations and encourage market forces |
| | Tax the healthy; subsidize the sick | Tax the sick, not the healthy |
| | Discourage new medical technologies | Encourage new medical technologies |

SOURCE: Based on Gerald L. Musgrave, "Health Economics Outlook: Two Theories of Health Economics," *Business Economics* (April 1995), pp. 7–13.

Theory Y, in contrast, perceives medical care to be no different from any other good or service. Health care is not more important than food, clothing, or shelter. Consumers probably know more about health care than they do about the engines in their cars, Musgrave asserts, because the benefit of possessing information is greater. Just as no one blames carpenters for homelessness, according to theory Y, health care providers should not be held responsible for the failure of the U.S. health care system. High profits in the health care sector reflect success, not failure. Theory Y'ers believe that markets have not been allowed to work because of excessive government regulations.

Theory X also views medicine as a science. Someday experts will arrive at the best way to treat each and every illness. Conversely, theory Y treats medicine as an art. Health care providers will never find the best cure for a given illness, especially because many illnesses are patient specific and newer, less painful, and lower-cost treatments will always be in demand.

Regarding economics, theory X proposes that financial rewards diminish the quality of care. Economics and medicine, like oil and water, do not mix. Profit seeking gets in the way of proper patient care. For example, theory X'ers claim that personal investments in MRI facilities create an incentive for physicians to overprescribe their diagnostic services to patients. Theory Y, in contrast, views financial rewards as the reason for high-quality medicine in the United States. Health care providers are in the best position to determine the true needs for health care capital. Ownership provides health care providers with an incentive to ensure that needed capital is supplied.

Given the difference between the two views regarding health, medical care, the practice of medicine, and the role of economics, it should not be surprising that theories X and Y take a different stance on policy as well. Table 1–1 lists three policy stances. According to theory X, because financial rewards are the source of system failure, further regulations are needed to curb the profit appetites of health care providers. Government planning is necessary to control the number of hospitals, physicians, and other health care providers and establishments. Government requires more information on health care markets for planning purposes.

Theory Y asserts that health care markets are already overregulated as mentioned earlier. Excessive regulations are partly accountable for some of the observed health care problems. Competitive economic forces should be allowed to function such that health care providers have incentives to produce with least-cost methods and satisfy consumer wants. Consumers need information to make more informed decisions.

Theory X further proposes that taxes should be levied on healthy individuals to pay for the health care costs of unhealthy ones. Because bad health or illness occurs randomly, it is fair to tax the lucky and not the unlucky. In contrast, theory Y argues that subsidizing sickness rewards it. Taxing health reduces the number of people who will remain healthy. It is not efficient to tax the healthy to subsidize the unhealthy.

Finally, theories X and Y differ on their positions concerning medical technology. New technology and health care spending are undesirable, according to theory X. Global budgets and other spending controls are necessary to curb technologies offering high-cost, low-benefit medicine. Theory Y asserts just the opposite. New technologies advance medical care. More health care services, just like more clothing or food, are good. When expenditures rise in the computer or automobile industry, for example, people point to success, not failure.

Given these two extreme views, it should not be surprising that many issues pertaining to health economics are hotly debated. Of course, it is constructive to remember that most issues, especially as they pertain to a social science field like health economics, are never truly black or white, but, as Billy Joel reminds us, are only different "shades of grey."[8] Hence, many people adopt an intermediate view of health economics somewhere in the XY theory plane. Indeed, you may wish to return to this section as your understanding of health economics progresses for some introspection to determine where your overall perspective falls in the XY theory plane of health economics.

## SUMMARY

Health economics is concerned with the determination and allocation of health resources and distribution of medical services in a society. Because resources are scarce, society must determine what amounts of medical services to produce, what kinds of

---

[8]"Shades of Grey," written by Billy Joel, © 1992 Impulsive Music (ASCAP).

medical services to produce, what mix of health resources should be used, and who should receive the output of health care services. Answering these four basic questions involves tough trade-offs.

Essential to the study of health economics is the use of microeconomic models. Economic models are necessary to simplify a very complex world. Models or hypotheses can be expressed in descriptive, mathematical, or graphical form and can be used to conduct positive analysis or draw normative conclusions.

A major assumption in economics is that people are rational; that is, people are able to rank their preferences from high to low and never purposely make themselves worse off. People choose activities that offer the greatest benefits at the lowest possible cost.

Most health economics issues are sharply debated, in part, because people adopt different views concerning, for example, the uniqueness of medical care and whether economics and medicine mix in practice. These alternative views were couched in terms of the theories X and Y of health economics.

## Review Questions and Problems

1. Draw a bowed-out production possibilities curve (PPC) with an *aggregate* measure of medical services, Q, on the horizontal axis and an *aggregate* measure of all other goods (and services), Z, on the vertical axis. Discuss the implications of the following changes on the quantities of medical services and all other goods.

    a. A movement down along the curve.

    b. A movement from the interior of the curve to a northeasterly point on the curve.

    c. An increase in the quantity of labor in the economy.

    d. A technological discovery that increases the production of Z.

    If it were your choice, where would you choose to produce on the PPC? Why?

2. Determine whether the following statements are based on positive or normative analysis. Be sure to substantiate your answers.

    a. Prices of physician services should be controlled by the government because many citizens cannot afford to pay for a visit to a physician.

    b. According to Tosteson et al. (1990), a 25 percent drop in the number of people who smoked in 1990 would reduce the incidence of coronary heart diseases by .7 percent by the year 2015.

    c. Rising health care costs have forced numerous rural hospitals to close their doors in recent years.

    d. According to government statistics, in 1989 7.2 deaths per 100,000 residents were alcohol induced. To decrease this number, the government should impose higher taxes on alcohol.

3. According to Louise B. Russell (1992), $1 million spent on the two medical interventions below yield the following life-years for elderly persons.

| | |
|---|---|
| Pneumococcal pneumonia vaccine | 100 life-years |
| Influenza vaccine | 11,100 life-years |

Given this information, what is the opportunity cost of $1 million spent on the pneumococcal pneumonia vaccine? What is the opportunity cost of $1 million worth of influenza vaccine? If $1 million were available to spend on medical care for elderly persons, how should it be spent based on the data provided if the goal is to save the greatest number of life-years?

4. Suppose a health expenditure function is specified in the following manner:

$$E = 500 + .2Y,$$

where $E$ represents annual health care expenditures per capita and $Y$ stands for income per capita.

a. Using the slope of the health expenditure function, predict the change in per capita health care expenditures that would result from a $1,000 increase in per capita income.

b. Compute the level of per capita health care spending when per capita income takes on the following dollar values: 0; 1,000; 2,000; 4,000; and 6,000.

c. Using the resulting values for per capita health care spending in part b, graph the associated health care expenditure function.

d. Assume the fixed amount of health care spending decreases to $250. Graph the new and original health care functions on the same graph. What is the relation between the original and new health care expenditure functions?

e. Now assume the fixed amount of health care spending remains at $500 but the slope parameter on income decreases to .1. Graph both the original and new health care expenditure functions. Explain the relation between the two lines.

5. Assume the following facts at a particular point in time:

a. There is a 20 percent, or .20, probability that the appropriate dosage of a painkiller will relieve your headache.

b. Headache relief provides you with $30 worth of actual benefits.

c. The monetary cost of the appropriate dosage is $7.50. Would you purchase the painkiller? Why or why not?

6. Victor Fuchs (1996) lists the following questions in an article in *The Wall Street Journal.* Identify whether the following questions involve positive or normative analysis. All the questions deal with a Republican plan to reform Medicare, the public health insurance program for the elderly.

a. How many Medicare beneficiaries will switch to managed care?

b. How much should the younger generation be taxed to pay for the elderly?

c. Should seniors who use less care benefit financially, or should they subsidize those who use more care?

*d.* How many Medicare beneficiaries will switch to medical savings accounts (see Chapter 18)?

*e.* What effect will these changes have on utilization?

*f.* How much should society devote to medical interventions that would add one year of life expectancy for men and women who have already passed the biblical "three score and ten"?

*g.* Will senior citizens' choices about types of coverage depend on their health status?

*h.* If the rate of spending growth is reduced to 6 percent from 10 percent a year, what will happen to the growth of medical services? To physician incomes?

7. At this early juncture in the learning process, would you consider yourself more of a theory X'er or theory Y'er? What are the main reasons why you are leaning toward that particular theory? Are your cited reasons based on gut instincts or sound empirical analysis?

## References

Aaron, Henry J. *Serious and Unstable Condition: Financing America's Health Care*. Washington, D.C.: The Brookings Institution, 1991.

Becker, Gary S., and Kevin M. Murphy. "A Theory of Rational Addiction." *Journal of Political Economy* 96 (August 1988), pp. 675–700.

Feldman, Roger, and Michael A. Morrisey. "Health Economics: A Report on the Field." *Journal of Health Politics, Policy and Law* 15 (fall 1990), pp. 627–46.

Fuchs, Victor R. "The Tofu Triangle." *The Wall Street Journal*, January 26, 1996, A16.

Hellinger, Fred J. "Forecasting the Medical Care Costs of the HIV Epidemic: 1991–1994." *Inquiry* 28 (fall 1991), pp. 213–25.

Levit, Katharine R., et al. "National Health Expenditure, 1996." *Health Care Financing Review* 19 (fall 1997), pp. 161–200.

Musgrave, Gerald L. "Health Economics Outlook: Two Theories of Health Economics." *Business Economics* (April 1995), pp. 7–13.

*The Mosby Medical Encyclopedia*. New York City: C. V. Mosby, 1992.

Russell, Louise B. "Opportunity Costs in Modern Medicine." *Health Affairs* 11 (summer 1992), pp. 162–69.

Schieber, George J., Jean-Pierre Poullier, and Leslie M. Greenwald. "DataWatch: Health System Performance in OECD Countries, 1980–1992." *Health Affairs* 13 (fall 1994), pp. 100–112.

Tibbitts, Samuel J. "Health Care Denied Makes a Weak Nation." *Los Angeles Times*, August 21, 1988, part 5, p. 5.

Tosteson, Anna, et al. "Long-Term Impact of Smoking Cessation on the Incidence of Coronary Health Disease." *The American Journal of Public Health* 80 (December 1990), pp. 1481–86.

APPENDIX TO CHAPTER 1

# Regression Analysis

As mentioned in Chapter 1, empirical testing of economic theories is important for two reasons. First, economic hypotheses require empirical validation, especially when there are a number of competing theories for the same real world occurrence. For example, those who prescribe to the theory X of health economics believe medical illnesses occur randomly whereas theory Y'ers believe medical illness is largely a function of lifestyle. The "random" and "lifestyle" explanations represent two competing theories for medical illnesses. Empirical studies can potentially ascertain which theory does a better job of explaining illnesses.

Second, even well-accepted theories are unable to establish the magnitude of the relation between any two variables. For example, suppose we accept the theory that lifestyle is a very important determinant of health status. A question remains about the magnitude or strength of the impact lifestyle has on health status. Does a young adult who adopts a sedentary lifestyle face a 10, 20, or 50 percent chance of dying prematurely than an otherwise comparable individual? Empirical studies can help provide the answer to that question.

There are many different ways for researchers to conduct an empirical analysis. The method we emphasize in this book, which most economists also use, is **regression analysis.** Regression analysis is a statistical method used to isolate the cause-and-effect relation among variables. Our goal in this appendix is to provide the reader with an elementary but sufficient understanding of regression analysis so the regression results discussed in this book can be properly interpreted. Regression analysis is explained through an example.

The example used concerns the relation between health care expenditures, $E$, and consumer income, $Y$, which was briefly introduced in Chapter 1. Suppose we hypothesize that health care expenditures rise with household income and want to test our theory. Health care expenditures represent the dependent variable and income is the independent variable. Furthermore, suppose we expect a linear (or straight line) relationship between income and health care expenditures, or

**(A1–1)** $E = a + bY$,

where $a$ is the constant or intercept term and $b$ is the slope parameter. If you recall, the slope parameter in this case identifies the change in health care expenditures that results from a one-unit change in income.

Because we are interested in the actual or real-world magnitudes of the parameters $a$ and $b$, we now collect a random sample of observations relating information on both medical expenditures and income. The data might be series observations on income and expenditures for a particular household over time or cross-sectional

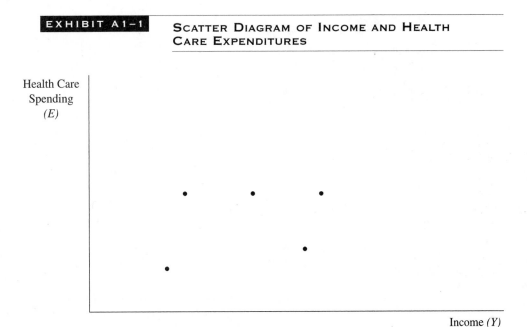

**EXHIBIT A1–1**   SCATTER DIAGRAM OF INCOME AND HEALTH CARE EXPENDITURES

Health Care Spending *(E)*

Income *(Y)*

observations on income and expenditures across different households at a particular point in time, for instance. In this case we collect cross-sectional data on income and medical expenditures from a random survey of 30 households.

Exhibit A1–1 shows a scatter diagram illustrating our random sample of observations (only 5 of the 30 observations are illustrated for easier manageability). Notice that the scatter diagram of observations does not automatically show a linear relation between income and health care expenditures because of omitted factors that also influence spending on health care, some randomness to economic behavior, and measurement error. Our objective is to find the line that passes through those observations and provides the best explanation of the relation between $Y$ and $E$. One can imagine numerous lines passing through the set of observations. What we want is the line that provides the best fit to the data.

A criterion is necessary to determine which line constitutes the best fit. One popular criterion is ordinary least squares, or OLS. OLS finds the best line by minimizing the sum of the squared deviations, $e_i$, from the actual observations and a fitted line passing through the set of observations, or

**(A1–2)**  Minimize $\Sigma\, e_i^2 = \Sigma\, (E_a - E_f)^2 = \Sigma\, (E_a - a - bY)^2$,

where $E_a$ is the actual observation on medical expenditures and $E_f$ is fitted (or predicted) expenditures from the estimated regression line, $a + bY$. In exhibit A1–2, we show an example of a fitted line and the resulting deviations between actual and fitted

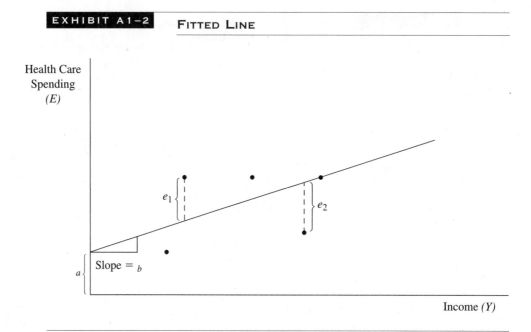

**EXHIBIT A1-2**    **FITTED LINE**

expenditures. Based upon the sample of observations, a computer program (like SAS, SPSS, or TSP) searches for the best line using the OLS procedure. In the process of finding the best line, the intercept and slope are determined and thus we estimate the best magnitudes for $a$ and $b$ that minimize the sum of the squared deviations from the actual observations.

Let's suppose the following results are obtained from the regression analysis.

**(A1–3)**  $E = 2,000 + .2Y.$

The results would tell us that the best fitted line to the data has an intercept of $2,000 and a slope of .2. Although the fitted or estimated regression line provides the "best" fit compared to all other lines, we do not know yet whether it represents a "good" fit to the actual data. Fortunately, the computer estimation procedure also provides us with some goodness of fit information that we can use to determine if the best fit is also a reasonably good one.

The two most common and elementary goodness of fit measures are the coefficient of determination, $R^2$, and the t-statistic, $t$. The coefficient of determination identifies the fraction of the variation in the dependent variable that is explained by the independent variable. Thus, the $R^2$ ranges between 0 and 1. Researchers tend to place more faith in a regression line that explains a greater proportion of the variation in the dependent variable.

The values for the parameters $a$ and $b$ are average estimates rather than true values because they are based on a sample instead of all possible observations; thus, they are associated with some error. Accordingly, there will be some deviations around the average estimate for $a$ and also around the average estimate for $b$. In fact, if the deviations are very large, we cannot place much faith in the estimated value for the parameters. Indeed, the true value for $b$ may be zero. If so, no relationship exists between income and health care expenditures.

The computed $t$-statistic helps us identify how much deviation occurs around the estimated average value for the parameters of the model. A $t$-statistic of 2 or more means that the value of the estimated parameter was at least twice as large as its average deviation. A rule of thumb is that when the $t$-statistic is 2 or more, we can place about 95 percent confidence in the estimated average value for the parameter, meaning that only a 5 percent likelihood exists that the relationship could have occurred by chance. Another rule of thumb is that when the $t$-statistic is 3 or more, we can place 99 percent confidence in our estimated value for the parameter. In this case, only a 1 percent likelihood exists that the relation occurred by chance.

Regression results are generally reported something like the following:

**(A1–4)** $E = 2{,}000 + .2Y.$     $R^2 = .47$
            $(2.52)\quad(3.40)$      $N = 30$

The $t$-statistics are reported in parentheses below the parameter estimates. Because the $t$-statistic associated with income is greater than 3, we can place a high degree of confidence in the parameter estimate of .2. Also according to the regression results, income explains about 47 percent of the variation in health care expenditures. The number of observations, $N$, is 30.

Before we move on we need to interpret the parameter estimates for equation A1–4. The intercept term of 2,000 tells us the level of health care expenditures when income is zero. The parameter estimate of .2 on the income variable is much more telling and suggests that expenditures on health care will increase by twenty cents if income increases by one dollar. If the estimated parameter was instead $-.2$, it would mean that a one dollar increase in income causes health care expenditures to decrease by twenty cents. Thus, both the sign and value of the parameter estimate convey important information to the researcher.

The regression analysis we have been discussing thus far is an example of a simple regression because there is only one independent variable. Multiple regression refers to an analysis when more than one independent variable is specified. For example, theory might tell us that price or tastes and preferences should also be included in an expenditure equation. The OLS procedure behind multiple regression is the same as that for simple regression and finds the best line that minimizes the squared deviations between the actual and fitted values. The computed $R^2$ identifies the variation in the dependent variable, say, health care expenditures, explained by the set of independent variables, which in our example would be price, income, and tastes and preferences. Each independent variable would be associated with an estimated parameter and $t$-statistic. For example.

**(A1–5)** $E = 1{,}000 - .2P + .13Y + .8A$     $R^2 = .75$
            $(2.32)\quad(.42)\quad(3.23)\quad(4.00)$      $N = 30$

where $P$ represents the price of medical services and $A$ represents the average age in the household as a proxy for tastes and preferences. According to the regression results, the independent variables explain 75 percent of the variation in health care expenditures. Also, the regression results suggest that income and age both have a statistically significant direct impact on health care expenditures. Price, on the other hand, has no impact on health care expenditures according to the regression findings.

## CEBS Questions

CEBS Sample Question on Subject Matter from CEBS Course IX Study Manual

1. Using the mathematical terminology in the text and the model, $E = a + bY$, how much will health care expenditures change when income increases from $30,000 to $50,000 if when income is zero health care expenditures equal $2,000 and the slope is .05? (pages 10–12)

CEBS Sample Exam Questions

1. The "XY theory plane" of health economics refers to:
   A. The "excellent income" hypothesis
   B. The level of production that could be achieved if both labor and capital were utilized perfectly.
   C. A theory of health economics that considers illnesses as not being solely determined by lifestyle choices
   D. The level of theory that is too theoretical to be of practical value
   E. The opposite of the "YX" theory of health economics

2. Which of the following statements regarding a production possibilities curve is (are) correct?
   I. Points on the curve show the combinations of production that can be efficiently produced.
   II. Points under the curve illustrate combinations with the highest opportunity cost.
   III. Points above the curve can be achieved in the future with better technology.
   A. I only
   B. II only
   C. I and II only
   D. I and III only
   E. I, II, and III

3. All the following statements regarding regression analysis are correct EXCEPT:
   A. The purpose of regression analysis is to isolate the cause and effect among variables.
   B. The "ordinary least squares" is a popular method of fitting a line to data in a scatter diagram.

C. T-statistics identify the fraction of the variation in the dependent variable that is explained by the independent variable.

D. Multiple linear regression has more than one independent variable.

E. A rule of thumb is that when the t-statistic is 2 or more we can place about 95% confidence in the estimated average value of the estimated parameter.

*Answer to Sample Question from Study Manual*

At an income level of $30,000 expenditures will be: ($2,000 + .05 ($30,000)) or $3,500. At an income level of $50,000, expenditures will be ($2,000 + .05 ($50,000)) or $4,500. The difference, or increase, is $1,000, i.e., $3,500 − $2,500.

*Answers to Sample Exam Questions*

1. C. See pages 18–21 of the text.
2. D. See pages 6–8 of the text.
3. C. The coefficient of determination, $R^2$, shows the percentage of the variation in the dependent variable that is explained by the independent variable. See pages 24–28 of the text.

# 2

# Health Care
# Systems and Institutions

**P** POs, HMOs, and DRGs are just a few of the many health care acronyms bandied around in the popular press. To the uninformed, they are simply the ingredients in an alphabet soup. Those familiar with them know they stand for preferred provider organizations, health maintenance organizations, and diagnosis-related groups. They, like many other health care institutions, have evolved over the last two decades and have greatly contributed to the ongoing and wide-sweeping transformation of the U.S. health care system.

This chapter introduces and explains the structure and purpose behind various institutions and payment systems that typically comprise a health care system. The knowledge you gain will help you better understand how the different parts of a health care system are interrelated. In addition, the material will provide you with a greater appreciation for the remaining chapters of the book and help make you a more informed consumer or producer of health care services. Specifically, this chapter:

- Constructs a general model of a health care system.

- Discusses the reasoning for and responsibilities of third-party payers.

- Introduces and explains some of the different reimbursement methods used by third-party payers.

- Identifies some structural features associated with the production of medical services and the role of health care provider choice.

- Uses the general model to describe the health care systems in Canada, Germany, and the United Kingdom.

- Provides an overview of the U.S. health care system.

# Elements of a Health Care System

A **health care system** consists of the organizational arrangements and processes through which a society makes choices concerning the production, consumption, and distribution of health care services. How a health care system is structured is important because it determines who actually makes the choices concerning the basic questions, such as what medical goods to produce and who should receive the medical care. At one extreme, the health care system might be structured such that choices are decided by a centralized government, or authority, through a single individual or an appointed or elected committee. At the other extreme, the health care system might be decentralized. For example, individual consumers and health care providers, through their interaction in the marketplace, may decide the answers to the basic questions.

From a societal point of view, it is difficult to determine whether a centralized or decentralized health care system is superior. A normative statement of that kind entails value judgments and trade-offs are inevitably involved. On the one hand, a centralized authority with complete and coordinated control over the entire health care system may be more capable of distributing output more uniformly and have a greater ability to exploit any economies associated with large size. At the same time, a single centralized authority may lack the competitive incentive to innovate or respond to varied consumer-voter demands. A central authority may also face high costs of collecting information about consumer needs.

On the other hand, a health care system with a decentralized decision-making process, such as the marketplace (or a system of local governments), may provide more alternatives and innovation but may result in high costs in the presence of economies of size, nonuniformity, or lack of coordination. Determining the best structure for a health care system involves quantifying the value society places on a number of alternative and sometimes competing outcomes, such as choice, innovation, uniformity, and production efficiency, among other things. A study of that kind is difficult at best because it involves so many normative decisions. Indeed, alternative health care systems exist throughout the world because people place different values on each of the various outcomes (Reinhardt, 1996). Reflecting the trade-offs involved, most health care systems today are neither purely centralized nor decentralized but rather take on elements of both systems of decision making. In any case, as we discuss the elements of various health care systems, it is important to keep in mind that understanding how and at what level decisions are made is critical to grasping how any health care system works.

Health care systems are huge, very complex, and constantly changing as they respond to economic, technological, social, and historical forces. For example, the structure of the U.S. health care system involves a seemingly endless list of participants, some of which were foreign to us only a decade ago, such as preferred provider organizations. The list includes over 800,000 physicians and dentists, about 2 million nurses, nearly 7,000 hospitals, and over 80,000 nursing homes and mental retardation facilities, not to mention the many millions of people who purchase medical care, the thousands of health insurers, and the multitude of government agencies involved in health care issues.

Because of the vastness and complexity of health care systems, many people have trouble understanding how they function. With that problem in mind, figure 2–1 presents a general model of a health care system. Notice that the diagram is triangular to reflect the three major players in any health care system: patients or consumers, health care providers or producers, and third-party payers or financial intermediaries. The figure also illustrates the three elements common to all health care systems: financing, reimbursement, and production or delivery.

In a typical market transaction, only the bottom flow of money paid out and services rendered takes place between the individual consumer and the producer. In that instance, the consumer's out-of-pocket price equals the full cost of the service provided. Buyer and seller are equally well informed, and the buyer pays the seller directly for the good or service. For example, the purchase of a loaf of bread at a local convenience store involves a normal market transaction. Both consumer and seller have the same information regarding the price and quality of the bread, and the transaction is anticipated and planned by the consumer. An unexpected outcome is not likely to occur, and, if it did, it could be easily rectified (for example, stale bread can be easily returned).

In a medical market, the corresponding situation is a prespecified patient fee paid directly to a doctor or a hospital for some predetermined and expected quantity and quality of medical services. In the case of medical services, however, the transaction is often not anticipated, and the price, quantity, and quality of medical services are unknown until after the medical event occurs. The transaction is unanticipated because medical illnesses occur irregularly and unexpectedly (Arrow, 1963). The price, quality, and quantity of medical services are not known initially because much uncertainty surrounds the diagnosis and proper treatment of a medical problem. In addition, health care providers possess a greater amount of information relative to patients regarding the provision of medical services, giving rise to an asymmetry of information. Because no simple relation exists between diagnosis and treatment, and much is left to the discretion of health care providers, possibilities for opportunistic behavior arise. That is, health care providers may produce more treatments or a higher-quality treatment than economic considerations warrant.[1]

## The Role and Financing Methods of Third-Party Payers

Because the timing and amount of medical treatment costs are uncertain from an individual consumer's perspective, third-party payers, such as private health insurance companies or the government, play a major role in medical care markets. Third-party payers often serve as intermediaries between the consumer and the health care producer and monitor the behavior of health care providers as a means of controlling medical costs.

Also, third-party payers are responsible for managing the financial risk associated with the purchase of medical services. A third-party payer faces a much lower level of

---

[1]This so-called **supplier-induced demand theory** is explained in great detail in Chapter 10.

| FIGURE 2–1 | A MODEL OF A HEALTH CARE SYSTEM |
| --- | --- |

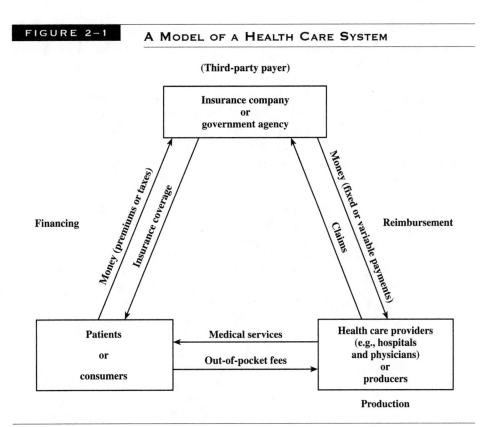

SOURCE: Developed from Stahl (1990) and Reinhardt (1990).

risk than does an individual consumer because it can pool its risk among various subscribers by operating on a large scale. The law of large numbers implies that whereas single events may be random and largely unpredictable, the average outcome of many similar events across a large population can be predicted fairly accurately. For example, it is difficult for one individual to predict whether he or she will experience a heart attack. An insurance company, on the other hand, can be reasonably sure about the heart attack rate by judging from past experiences involving a large number of individuals. Third-party payers can use actuarial tables to forecast medical care costs in the aggregate. A risk-averse consumer is made better off by making a certain preset payment to an insurer for coverage against an unforeseen medical event rather than facing the possibility of paying some unknown medical costs. Essentially, consumers receive a net benefit from the financial security that third-party payers supply.[2]

Third parties make the health care system much more complex because the source of third-party financing and the method of reimbursement must be worked into the

---

[2]Health insurance principles are developed more fully in Chapters 4 and 5.

model. If the third-party payer is a private health insurance company, the consumer pays a premium in exchange for some amount of medical insurance coverage. As part of the health insurance plan, the consumer may be responsible for paying a deductible portion as well as a copayment amount. The deductible provision requires the consumer to pay the first $X of medical costs, after which the health insurance company is responsible for reimbursement. With a copayment provision, the consumer pays a fixed percentage of the cost each time he or she receives a medical service.

When a government agency (or a public health insurance company) acts as a third-party payer, the financing of medical care insurance usually comes from taxes. Premiums and taxes differ in the way risk is treated and the voluntary nature of the payment.[3] Premiums are paid voluntarily and often depend on the risk category of the buyer of health insurance. Tax payments are mandatory and represent a single fee without reference to risk category.

Some alternative ways to finance health care can be gleaned by examining the different methods used in Canada, Germany, and the United Kingdom.[4] We chose these particular countries because their health care systems possess highly unique features. In addition, most proposals for health care reform in the United States are based to some extent on the health care systems of these three countries.

Canada has a compulsory **national health insurance (NHI)** program administered (somewhat differently) by each of its 10 provinces. The NHI program provides first-dollar coverage, and no limit is imposed on the level of medical benefits an individual can receive during his or her lifetime. **First-dollar coverage** means complete health insurance coverage in that the health insurer reimburses for the first and every dollar spent on medical services (i.e., there is no deductible or copayment amount). For all practical purposes, taxes finance the NHI program in each province.[5] In addition, the Canadian government provides up to 40 percent in direct cost sharing and makes hospital construction grants available to provinces. Private insurance is available for some forms of health care in Canada, although private coverage is prohibited for services covered by the NHI plan. Because the public sector rather than the private sector insures against medical costs, there are no marketing expenses, no administrative costs of estimating risk status or determining whom to cover, and no allocation for profits.

The **socialized health insurance (SI)** program in Germany is based on government-mandated financing by employers and employees. The premiums of unemployed individuals and their dependents are paid by former employers or come from various public sources (the Federal Labor Administration and public pension funds). Private not-for-profit insurance companies, called **Sickness Funds,** are

---

[3]See Bodenheimer and Grumbach (1992) for an in-depth comparison of taxes and premiums for financing universal health insurance.

[4]See Raffel (1997) for discussion on the health care systems in various industrialized countries. For manageability, we confine the discussion to the insurance, physician, and hospital services industries. No mention is made of the existing systems in the pharmaceutical and long-term care markets, for example.

[5]Three provinces charge insurance premiums that are related to family size rather than risk. These premiums are not compulsory for coverage and will be paid by the province if individuals are unable to pay. Because these premiums are not adjusted for risk, they are essentially taxes.

responsible for collecting funds from employers and employees and reimbursing physicians and hospitals. The statutory medical benefits are comprehensive, with a small copayment share for some services. Affluent and self-employed individuals are allowed to go outside the system and purchase private health insurance coverage.

Mechanic (1995) and others refer to the health care system in the United Kingdom (UK) as a **public contracting** model because the government contracts with various providers of health care services on behalf of the people. The UK health care system, under the auspices of the National Health Service (NHS), offers universal health insurance coverage financed through taxation. The NHS provides global budgets to district health authorities (DHAs). Each DHA is responsible for assessing and prioritizing the health care needs of about 300,000 people and then purchasing the necessary health care services from public and private health care providers. Hospital services are provided by nongovernmental trusts, which compete among themselves and with private hospitals for DHA contracts. Community-based primary care givers also contract with the DHAs. In addition, general practitioner (GP) fundholders apply for budgets from the DHAs, and, with the budgets, service a minimum group of 5,000 patients by providing primary care and purchasing elective surgery, outpatient therapy, and specialty nursing services. There is some limited competition among GP fundholders for patients.

## Reimbursement Method of Third-Party Payers

Another important element of a health care system is the way third-party payers reimburse health care providers for medical services rendered. As figure 2–1 indicates, public or private health insurers may reimburse health care providers with a *fixed* or a *variable* payment, although in practice the payments are sometimes combined. With a **fixed payment,** reimbursement is predetermined at a fixed lump-sum rate, sometimes prepaid and independent of the amount of medical services provided to the patient. When reimbursed on a fixed-payment basis, *net* provider income—the difference between the fixed payment and the costs of production—is a function of the quantity of services delivered and actual costs incurred. In particular, a fixed-payment plan implies that net provider income falls (rises) with greater (lower) costs of production. The higher costs of production may result from more services supplied or greater input prices, for example. A prospective budget to a hospital or nursing home, a prepaid health insurance plan such as a health maintenance organization (HMO), and a salary paid to a physician or an employee of a staff HMO are examples of fixed-payment systems.[6]

Under a **variable-payment** system, the reimbursement amount varies with either the quantity of medical services delivered to patients and/or the actual per-unit costs of production. Retrospective reimbursement, in which the health care provider bills

---

[6]An HMO is a type of managed-care institution and is discussed later in a brief overview of the U.S. health care system. Notice that although the monetary value of a physician's fixed salary does not decline with more services rendered, the effort the physician expends may subtract from his or her on-the-job leisure time and result in less utility or "psychic income."

FIGURE 2-2     THE LIKELIHOOD OF A LARGE VOLUME OF MEDICAL SERVICES FOR DIFFERENT REIMBURSEMENT AND CONSUMER COPAYMENT SCHEMES

Type of reimbursement scheme

|  |  | Fixed prepayment | Variable payment |
|---|---|---|---|
| Out-of-pocket price to consumer | Low | Low likelihood (1) | High likelihood (2) |
|  | High | Very low likelihood (3) | Moderate likelihood (4) |

SOURCE: Based on Aaron (1981) and Reinhardt (1975).

for actual costs incurred, and fee-for-service reimbursement, in which a price is paid for each individual medical service, are two common examples of a variable-payment system. A few state governments reimburse nursing homes on a retrospective basis for servicing Medicaid patients (Swan et al., 1993). The price paid for a physician office visit is an example of a fee-for-service payment. When reimbursement is on a variable-payment basis, *total* provider income increases with either more medical services supplied and/or greater per-unit costs of production.

The matrix in figure 2–2 illustrates how the two reimbursement schemes just discussed and the consumer's out-of-pocket price interact and affect the likelihood that a large volume of medical services will be supplied and demanded. The probability of a high volume of medical services is given inside each cell of the matrix for each combination of reimbursement method and consumer out-of-pocket price.

We can identify the opportunity for a large volume of medical services per patient by considering how the different provider reimbursement schemes and consumer copayment plans affect the incentives of health care providers and consumers. For instance, a health care provider that is reimbursed on a fixed-payment basis is very unlikely to supply a large volume of medical services to a patient unnecessarily. The cost of additional medical services immediately subtracts from the fixed payment and translates into lower net income. In contrast, for the variable-payment schemes, a financial incentive exists for health care providers to offer a greater amount of medical services per patient compared to the fixed-payment system. More medical services mean greater provider income under a variable-payment scheme.

We can conduct a similar analysis for the consumer. Consumers who face a low out-of-pocket price of obtaining medical services are more likely to seek out additional medical services (this is referred to as the moral hazard problem in Chapter 4). On the other hand, consumers who face a high out-of-pocket price are less inclined to seek out medical services given the greater opportunity cost of their money.

Combining the reimbursement and copayment schemes, the likelihood of a large volume of medical services per patient is the greatest in cell 2, where a variable-payment scheme interacts with a low consumer copayment plan. Neither party loses much financially in the exchange of dollars for medical services, and one party, the health care provider, actually gains more income. Conversely, a large volume of medical services is least likely in cell 3, where a fixed-payment plan coexists with a large consumer copayment scheme. Both parties in the exchange lose financially. Cell 4 offers a moderate likelihood of a large volume of medical services, since the provider is financially rewarded for providing additional services. For this to happen, however, either the consumer's out-of-pocket price must not be too high or the consumer must be relatively insensitive to price (i.e., highly inelastic demand). Finally, in cell 1, the health care provider is made worse off while the consumer is relatively unaffected by additional medical services, so the probability of a large volume of medical services is low.

A major current concern of health care policymakers is that a variable reimbursement system, when combined with a modest consumer copayment plan, results in excessive medical services that provide low marginal benefits to patients but come at a high marginal cost to society. For example, medical care providers may offer expensive diagnostic tests to low-risk patients. The tests come at a high marginal cost to society but yield only small marginal benefits to patients given their low-risk classification. Small marginal medical benefits coincide with the "flat-of-the-curve" medicine observed in several empirical studies, as discussed later in Chapter 3.

As a result, many health policy analysts believe that fee-for-service or retrospective payments and small consumer copayments are responsible for high-cost, low-benefit medicine. Policymakers typically argue that some cost sharing is needed on the supply and/or demand side of the market to reduce the potential for excess medical services (Ellis and McGuire, 1993). That is, they believe fixed-payment reimbursement plans and nontrivial consumer copayments are required to control unnecessary medical services.

We can appreciate the importance of the reimbursement method by examining and contrasting the countrywide reimbursement schemes practiced in Canada, Germany, and the United Kingdom. In Canada, everyone is eligible for the same medical benefits, and there are no copayments for most medical services. Patients essentially drop out of the reimbursement picture, and reimbursement exclusively takes place between the public insurer (the government) and the health care provider. In terms of figure 2–1, this means that the monetary exchange is virtually nonexistent between patient and health care provider. The ministry of health in each province is responsible for controlling medical costs. Cost control is attempted primarily through fixed global budgets for hospitals and predetermined fees for physicians. Specifically, the operating budgets of hospitals are approved and funded entirely by the ministry in each province, and an annual global budget is negotiated between the ministry and each individual hospital. Capital expenditures must also be approved by the ministry, which funds the bulk of the spending.

Physician fees are determined by periodic negotiations between the ministry and provincial medical associations (the Canadian version of the American Medical Association). With the passage of the Canada Health Act of 1984, the right to **extra billing** was removed in all provinces. Extra billing or balance billing refers to a situation in which the physician bills the patient some dollar amount above the predetermined fee set by the third-party payer. For the profession as a whole, negotiated fee increases are implemented in steps, conditional on the rate of increase in the volume of services. If volume per physician rises faster than a predetermined percentage, subsequent fee increases are scaled down or eliminated to cap gross billings—the product of the fee and the volume of each service—at some predetermined target. The possible scaling down of fee increases is supposed to create an incentive for a more judicious use of resources. Physicians enjoy nearly complete autonomy in treating patients (e.g., there is no mandatory second opinion for surgery) because policymakers believe there is no need for intrusive types of controls given that the hospital global budgets and physician expenditure targets tend to curb unnecessary services.

The Sickness Funds in Germany, which collect employer and employee insurance premiums, pay negotiated lump-sum funds equal to the product of a capitation (per-patient) payment and the number of insured individuals to regional associations of ambulatory care physicians. These regional associations, in turn, reimburse individual physicians for services on the basis of a fee schedule. The fee schedule is determined through negotiation between the regional associations of Sickness Funds and physicians. To determine the fee schedule, each physician service is assigned a number of points based on relative worth. The price per point is established by dividing the lump-sum total budget by the actual number of points billed within a quarter by all physicians. The income to an individual physician equals the number of points billed times the price per point.

The Sickness Funds that operate in a given state also negotiate fixed prices for various procedures (based on the diagnosis-related group, or DRG) with local hospitals. Because hospitals can make profits or incur losses because of the fixed prices, there is an incentive for hospitals to save resources and specialize in certain procedures. For some procedures, hospital accommodations are reimbursed on a per diem basis but funds are limited by an overall budget. Hospital-based physicians are paid on a salary basis. Most of the hospital funds for capital acquisitions come from state and local governments and are reviewed and approved through a state planning process.

In the UK, the district health authorities are allocated funds by the NHS on a weighted capitation basis, which considers age, sex, and health-risk factors as well as geographical cost differences. Independent community-based family practitioners contract with the NHS and are uniformly paid throughout the UK, primarily on a capitation basis. The DHAs prospectively reimburse individual hospital trusts based on the actual cost of providing the services. All hospital-based physicians and consultants are paid on a fixed salary basis by the trusts. Trusts are required to earn a

# Physician Utilization Rates in Salary- and Fee-Based Reimbursement Systems

As discussed in this section, the reimbursement method influences the quantity of services supplied to patients. Because a fee-for-service reimbursement scheme pays a set amount for each unit of services, physician income increases with a greater number of services provided. Thus, a fee-for-service reimbursement system may create an incentive for physicians to deliver more services, some of which may be excessive or wasteful (column 2 in figure 2–2). In contrast, if physicians are paid on a salary basis, they receive a predetermined amount of income that is independent of the amount of services provided. In this type of reimbursement system, physicians could actually face the opposite incentive: to discourage office visits and reduce workloads as a way to receive on-the-job leisure time (column 1 in figure 2–2).

Most empirical studies attempting to sort out any behavioral differences between salary- and fee-for-service-based reimbursement systems have compared medical utilization rates in the salaried physician practices of health maintenance organizations to conventional fee-for-service practices. These studies may have been flawed, however, because the results could have been affected by other factors, such as the organizational form of the practice setting, types of physicians, and patient behavior. In particular, observed medical utilization rates depend on both the provider net benefits and the patient costs associated with additional services. Because consumer out-of-pocket costs are typically higher in a fee-for-service setting than in a prepaid practice, it is difficult to compare any utilization differences that arise solely from the health care provider reimbursement scheme.

A study by Hickson, Altemeier, and Perrin (1987) overcomes this problem. Specifically, nine pairs of closely matched medical residents at a Vanderbilt pediatric clinic were randomly assigned to a fee-for-service or salary-based reimbursement group over a nine-month period. The common clinic setting and random assignment of physicians controlled for the organizational form, patient payment methods, and physician characteristics, so any utilization differences could be attributed solely to the method of reimbursing physicians. Residents in the fee-for-service group received $2 per patient visit, while the others received a monthly salary of $20. At the end of the nine months, records were consulted to determine the utilization rates of the residents in the two groups. Table 1 displays some of the results of the experiment.

Although the average number of patient visits per physician did not differ significantly between the fee-for-service (111.6) and salaried (104.8) physician groups, the results show that fee-for-service patients are more likely to see their regular physicians. In the study, almost 87 percent of fee-for-service visits were attended by the primary physician, whereas the comparable figure for the salaried group was only about 78 percent. In addition, fee-for-service patients were less likely to visit the emergency room than those patients assigned to salaried physicians, supporting the contention that fee-for-service physicians direct their patients away from the emergency room to their offices, where it is easier for them to personally treat their patients. Thus, Hickson, Altemeier, and Perrin noted that a fee-for-service reimbursement scheme may provide more "continuity" of care given that patients are more likely to see their regular doctors.

The results also suggest that fee-for-service physicians schedule and attend more visits than salaried physicians. In fact, there were 22 percent more visits per capita among patients assigned to fee-for-service physicians than for salaried physicians. The difference was due to well-child visits and not initial or follow-up visits. Further investigation by Hickson, Altemeier, and Perrin found that the number of well-child visits was higher because fee-for-service physicians miss fewer recommended visits (due to the financial incentive) and

*(continued)*

*(continued)*

make more visits in excess of the American Academy of Pediatrics' guidelines.

Interestingly, the authors found that patient satisfaction did not differ significantly in the two groups, although for some unknown reason, parents in the salary group perceived that they had better access to their physicians. From an eco-nomic perspective, Hickson, Altemeier, and Perrin concluded that the potential benefits from greater continuity of care and fewer emergency room visits must be weighed against the likely higher costs associated with excessive services under a fee-for-service reimbursement scheme.

**TABLE 1**     PHYSICIAN UTILIZATION RATES IN FEE-FOR-SERVICE AND SALARY-BASED REIMBURSEMENT SYSTEMS

| Volume of Services | Physician Group | | Statistical Significance |
|---|---|---|---|
| | Fee-for-Service | Salary | |
| Average number of patient visits attended per physician | 111.60 | 104.80 | |
| Percentage of visits attended by patients' primary care physician | 86.60 | 78.30 | * |
| Emergency room visits per enrolled patient per physician | 0.12 | 0.22 | * |
| Average number of visits per enrolled patient per physician | | | |
|   Scheduled | 3.69 | 2.83 | * |
|   Completed | 2.70 | 2.21 | * |
|     Sick, primary | 0.95 | 0.98 | |
|     Sick, follow-up | 0.33 | 0.24 | |
|     Well child | 1.42 | 0.99 | * |

\* = Figures for the two groups were statistically different at the 5 percent level or better. This means there was only a 5 percent or less chance that the figures are really the same.

SOURCE: Gerald B. Hickson, William A. Altemeier, and James M. Perrin, "Physician Reimbursement by Salary or Fee-for-Service: Effect on Physician Practice Behavior in a Randomized Prospective Study," *Pediatrics* 80 (September 1987), Table 2.

6 percent return on assets and the residual is returned to the DHA. Capital funding for the trusts is determined by the DHA and is based on its regional allocation.

Any funds allocated to GP fundholders are deducted from the DHA's allocation. GP fundholders annually negotiate funds to purchase elective and nonemergency services for their subscribers. About 41 percent of the population in England is served by GP fundholders. Any savings made by a fundholder may be reinvested in the practice or new services but cannot directly increase the GPs personal income. GP fundholders are not at personal financial risk as they are protected against any legitimate cost overruns by the DHAs.

In sum, these three countries have shied away from relying on an uncontrolled fee-for-service reimbursement scheme because of the concern that it creates incentives for high-cost, low-benefit medicine. The payment is on either a per diem, per-person, or negotiated fee-for-service basis. In addition, the payment for medical services is determined by a single payer—the government in Canada and the United Kingdom and representatives of the Sickness Funds in Germany. Policymakers in these countries believe that a single-payer, controlled-payment system can reduce the incentive to provide high-cost, low-benefit medicine and better contain health care costs.

## The Production of Medical Services

The mode of production also differs across health care systems. Several distinguishing features of production are worth mentioning. We normally think of health care services as being produced on an inpatient care basis in hospitals or nursing homes or on an outpatient (ambulatory) care basis at physician clinics or in the outpatient department of a hospital. However, health care services are also produced in the home. Preventive care (e.g., exercise, dieting, and flossing) and first aid are two prime examples of home-produced health care services. In addition, long-term or chronic care services are often produced in the home rather than in an institution, such as a nursing home. Although acute care services can also be produced in the home, the cost of producing these services is usually prohibitive for the individual consumer because of the high per-person labor and capital expenses.[7] As a result, it is almost always cheaper for the individual consumer to purchase acute care services at a hospital because such an organization can exploit various economies associated with large size.

Outside the home, health care services may be produced in the private or public sector from health care providers in the medical services industry. If produced in the private sector, the health care provider may offer medical services on a not-for-profit or a for-profit basis. A not-for-profit organization is required by law to use any profits exclusively for the charitable, educational, or scientific purpose for which it was formed. For example, a hospital may use profits to lower patient prices or finance medical equipment or hospital expansion. Not-for-profit health care providers are normally granted an exemption from paying certain taxes.

In addition to the form of ownership, the health care provider may be organized in a number of other ways. For example, a hospital may be a freestanding, independent institution or part of a multihospital chain. Similarly, a physician may operate in a solo practice or belong to a group practice. Usually the size and scope of the

---

[7]According to the *Mosby Medical Encyclopedia*, long-term care is "the provision of medical care on a repeated or continuous basis to persons with chronic physical or mental disorders" (p. 471). Acute care is "treatment for a serious illness, for an accident, or after surgery. . . . This kind of care is usually for only a short time" (p. 11).

# Medical Technology in Canada, Germany, and the United States

The availability of medical technologies undoubtedly has a powerful impact on the production of medical care services and health care costs. Medical technologies, such as drugs, medical devices, and procedures, may offer cost savings or higher-quality services.

Four stages are associated with the development and diffusion of medical technology. According to the National Science Foundation, the first stage, *basic research*, is defined as "original investigation for the advancement of scientific knowledge without specific commercial objectives." Basic medical research produces new knowledge about various biological mechanisms or malfunctions involving the human body. In the second stage, *applied research*, the basic knowledge is applied to yield solutions for the prevention, treatment, or curing of diseases. At the *clinical investigation and testing* stage, new medical technologies are tested on human subjects. The benefit and safety of the medical technology are usually demonstrated at this point. The final stage, *diffusion* (or imitation), involves the commercial introduction, adoption, and spreading of medical technologies.

Recently health policy analysts (e.g., Aaron, 1991) have expressed concern that unconstrained health care markets result in medical technologies that offer low benefits at high costs. As a result, many countries have adopted policies to either directly or indirectly control the adoption and diffusion of medical technologies to contain costs. Public control may occur at any one or all four of the stages associated with the invention and diffusion of medical technology (Banta and Kemp, 1982).

For example, hospital budgets are limited in Canada and Great Britain partly to indirectly control the proliferation of expensive medical technologies. It is argued that the limited budgets create a financial incentive for hospital administrators to economize on medical technologies offering low benefits at a high cost. At the other extreme, the adoption and diffusion of technology are determined largely by the unfettered forces of supply and demand in the United States. A fee-for-service system with minimal consumer cost sharing may create an incentive for low-benefit, high-cost medical technologies to be adopted in the United States. Germany, on the other hand, has taken a middle position between these two extremes with some limited control over the proliferation of new medical technologies (Rublee, 1989).

Table 1 shows the comparative availability of several medical technologies in Canada, Germany, and the United States. The number of units per 1 million persons is shown for six medical technologies: open-heart surgery, cardiac catheterization, organ transplantation, radiation therapy, extracorporeal shock wave lithotripsy, and magnetic resonance imaging (MRI). Open-heart surgery and organ transplantation are self-explanatory, but the other four technologies may require some explanation. With cardiac catheterization, a long, fine tube is placed into the arteries of the heart to withdraw any deposits that are blocking blood circulation. Radiation therapy attempts to destroy cancerous cells in the body. Extracorporeal shock wave lithotripsy disintegrates kidney stones and gallstones through the use of shock waves and does not require an incision. An MRI takes a cross-sectional picture of a human body and therefore provides much more detailed information than an X ray does.

We can draw several conclusions from table 1. First, the data show a greater availability of medical technologies in the United States than in

medical organization depend on whether any economies exist from operating on a small or large scale. In addition, some physicians, such as radiologists and anesthesiologists, may be employees of the hospital. In contrast, some physicians on the medical staff may not be employees of the hospital but instead are granted admitting privileges.

## (continued)

either Canada or Germany. For example, the United States has more than twice the number of open-heart surgery, radiation therapy, and MRI units per person than Canada or Germany. The greater availability of medical technologies in the United States is most likely a function of the greater predominance of fee-for-service medicine. Second, technology appears to be equally restricted in Canada and Germany compared to the United States. In particular, while Canada has more open-heart surgery, organ transplantation, and radiation therapy units than Germany, Germany possesses a greater number of cardiac catheterization, lithotripsy, and MRI units than Canada. Third, it is difficult to conclude from the information available whether medical technologies are overprovided in the United States or underprovided in the other two countries. In fact, a different level of medical technology could be optimal for each country because of differing social values (Rublee, 1994). Cost-benefit analysis, cost effectiveness studies, or outcomes research would be necessary to draw any definitive conclusions on this issue (see Chapter 7). Finally, the availability of medical technology in itself indicates little about the overall effectiveness of the health care system. To determine overall health care system effectiveness, a host of factors must also be considered, including the quantity and quality of other medical inputs.

**TABLE 1**  AVAILABILITY OF MEDICAL TECHNOLOGY IN CANADA, GERMANY, AND UNITED STATES

| | Units per 1 Million People | | |
|---|---|---|---|
| **Type of Technology** | **Canada (1993)** | **Germany (1993)** | **United States (1992)** |
| Open-heart surgery | 1.3 | 0.8 | 3.7 |
| Cardiac catheterization | 2.8 | 3.4 | 6.4 |
| Organ transplantation | 1.2 | 0.5 | 2.4 |
| Radiation therapy | 4.8 | 4.6 | 10.3 |
| Extracorporeal shock wave lithotripsy | 0.5 | 1.4 | 1.9 |
| Magnetic resonance imaging | 1.1 | 3.7 | 11.2 |

SOURCE: Dale A. Rublee, "Medical Technology in Canada, Germany, and the United States: An Update," *Health Affairs* 13 (fall 1994), Exhibit 1.

The organization of production in the three health care systems we have been discussing have some slight differences. In Canada, medical services are produced in the private sector. Most hospitals in the private sector are organized on a not-for-profit basis and are owned by either charitable or religious organizations. In Germany, medical services are produced primarily in the private sector, because most physicians operate in private practices. Public hospitals control about 51 percent of all hospital beds in Germany. The remaining beds are managed by not-for-profit (35 percent) and for-profit hospitals (13 percent). Office-based physicians are normally prohibited from treating patients in hospitals, and most hospital-based physicians are not allowed to provide ambulatory care services in Germany.

The structure of production in the UK now largely takes place in the private, although mostly not-for-profit, sector. The present situation in the UK is in stark contrast to the method of production that prevailed before the passage of the National Health Service and Community Act of 1990. Up to 1990, almost all hospitals were publicly owned and operated and most doctors were employees of the NHS. Even before 1990, however, family practitioners were community-based in solo or small group practices and simply contracted with the NHS.

## Physician Choice and Referral Practices

Important differences in the availability and utilization of medical services can also result from the degree of physician choice the health care consumer possesses and the types of referral practices used within the health care system. More choice typically provides consumers with increased satisfaction (Schmittdiel et al., 1997). However, greater choice may come at a cost if it leads to a large number of fragmented health care providers that are unable to sufficiently coordinate care or exploit any economies that come with large size (Halm et al., 1997).

In some health care systems, patients have unlimited choice of and full access to any physician or health care provider within any type of setting (e.g., clinic or hospital). For example, at one time in the United States, insured individuals could directly seek out any general practitioner or specialist without financial penalty. Moreover, at one time in the United States, it was not unusual for a general practitioner to review the care of a patient referred for hospital services. We will see below that conditions regarding physician choice and referral practices have changed a great deal in the United States.

Other countries have adopted different referral practices. Although the Canadian and German health care systems allow free choice of provider, general practitioners in the UK act as "gatekeepers" and must refer patients to a specialist or a hospital. Once the patient is referred to a hospital, the patient–general practitioner relationship is severed for any particular illness in both the UK and Germany. Unlike in Germany, however, patients are allowed to go directly to a family practitioner or a hospital for primary care in the UK, unless they are registered with a GP fundholder.

## The Three National Health Care Systems Summarized

Based on our generalized model of a health care system, table 2–1 provides a capsulized summary of the current national health care systems in the three countries we have been discussing. Each national health care system is differentiated according to

| TABLE 2-1 | A COMPARISON OF HEALTH CARE SYSTEMS |

| Feature | Canada (NHI)* | Germany (SI)† | United Kingdom (PC)‡ | United States (Pluralistic) |
|---|---|---|---|---|
| Health insurance coverage | Universal | Near universal | Near universal | 84 percent |
| Financing | General taxes | Payroll and general taxes | General taxes | Voluntary premiums or general taxes |
| | Single-payer system | Single-payer system§ | Single-payer system | Multipayer system |
| Reimbursement | Global budgets to hospitals | Fixed payments to hospitals | Global budgets to hospitals | Mostly fixed payments to hospitals |
| | Negotiated fee-for-service to physicians | Negotiated point-fees-for-service to physicians | Salaries and capitation payments to physicians | Mostly fee-for-service to physicians |
| Consumer copayment | Negligible | Negligible | Negligible | Positive, but generally small |
| Production | Private | Private | Private but public contract | Private |
| Physician choice | Unlimited | Unlimited | Limited | Relatively limited |

*NHI = national health insurance program.
†SI = socialized insurance.
‡PC = public contracting.
§Multiple third-party payers are responsible for paying representatives of the health care providers, but the universal fees are collectively negotiated by the third-party payers.

the degree of health insurance coverage, type of financing, reimbursement scheme, consumer copayment, mode of production, and degree of physician choice. The essential features of the Canadian health care system are national health insurance, free choice of health care provider, private production of medical services, and regulated global budgets and fees for health care providers. The dominating features of the German health care system include socialized health insurance financed through Sickness Funds, negotiated payments to health care providers, free choice of provider, and private production of health care services. In the case of Great Britain, the distinguishing characteristics include restrictions on choice of provider, public contracting of medical services, global budgets for hospitals, fixed salaries for hospital-based physicians, and capitation payments to family practitioners.

The U.S. health care system is discussed in detail in the next section, and the last column in table 2–1 gives a quick preview. The pluralistic U.S. health care system contains some structural elements found in most of the other three systems (e.g., private production) but relies more heavily on a fee-for-service reimbursement scheme. In addition, health care providers are reimbursed through multiple payers, including the government and thousands of private insurance companies, in contrast to the single-payer system in Canada (government), Germany (Sickness Funds), and the UK (government).

# An Overview of the U.S. Health Care System

Some analysts argue that the multifaceted nature of the health care system accounts for the relatively high expenditures devoted to medical care in the United States. Although this may be true and is a topic of discussion throughout this book, it most certainly is true that this diversity makes it very difficult to describe the U.S. health care system in sufficient detail. This section presents a brief overview of the current system in the United States based on the generalized model of a health care system. The remainder of the book discusses the operation and performance of the U.S. health care system in much greater detail, albeit on a piecemeal basis.

## Financing of Health Care in the United States

The United States has no single nationwide system of health insurance. Health insurance is purchased in the private marketplace or provided by the government to certain groups. Private health insurance can be purchased from various for-profit commercial insurance companies or from nonprofit insurers, such as Blue Cross/Blue Shield (hereafter referred to as the Blues). About 84 percent of the population is covered by either public (26 percent) or private (70 percent) health insurance.[8]

Approximately 61 percent of health insurance coverage is employment related, largely due to the cost savings associated with group plans that can be purchased through an employer. Employers voluntarily sponsor the health insurance plans. Rather than purchasing an insurance policy from an external party, such as a commercial insurance company or the Blues, employer and employee premiums sometimes fund an internal health insurance plan. The fully self-insured firm assumes all the risk for its employees' health care costs. A partially self-insured firm limits the risk it assumes by purchasing "stop-loss" insurance coverage, which protects it from incurring costs over a specified maximum amount. In either case, the firm usually contracts with a third party to administer the health insurance program.

---

[8]These are estimates rather than actual figures based on recent issues of the *Statistical Abstract of the United States*, and the *Source Book of Health Insurance Data*. The figures for private and public insurance coverage do not sum to 84 percent because of double-counting. For example, some people receiving public insurance coverage also purchase private health insurance.

A **conventional health insurance plan,** which allows unrestricted choice of health care provider and reimburses on a fee-for-service basis, presently covers less than 30 percent of all employees. Even these plans now provide some type of **utilization management program** (e.g., preadmission certification, concurrent review of length of stay, and mandatory second opinions for surgery). Traditional plans differ depending on the medical services that are covered and the copayment and deductible amounts.

Rather than enroll employees in a traditional insurance plan, most employers have turned to managed-care health insurance plans. According to the *Source Book of Health Insurance Data* (1994), **managed-care organizations (MCOs)** are

> systems that integrate the financing and delivery of appropriate health care services to covered individuals by means of: arrangements with selected providers to furnish a comprehensive set of health-care services to members; explicit criteria for the selection of health-care providers; formal programs for ongoing quality assurance and utilization review; and significant financial incentives for members to use providers and procedures associated with the plan (p. 167).

Although the distinction is becoming blurred in practice, there are essentially two major types of MCOs: the **health maintenance organization (HMO)** and the **preferred provider organization (PPO).** About 70 percent of employees are currently enrolled in MCOs. HMOs are of two distinct types: the staff model and the individual practice association (IPA). The staff HMO provides insurance and also delivers medical care internally. As a result, physicians are typically paid on a salaried basis. In terms of figure 2–l, an HMO collapses the insurer and provider functions into one by integrating the financing and delivery of care. Although at one time the staff HMO was the dominant form, today less than 4 percent of HMO subscribers belong to a staff HMO. The IPA/HMO, on the other hand, contracts with an independent group of physicians on a fee-for-service or capitation basis. HMOs either own or contract with a community hospital. The HMO is a type of prepaid health plan because consumers pay a fixed annual capitation fee to the HMO and, in return, receive comprehensive medical care services exclusively from the HMO upon request. Financial risk essentially passes from consumer to provider under a prepaid plan. Choice of provider is restricted, and treatments received from other health care providers are typically not reimbursed by the HMO without prior authorization. Analysts argue that an HMO has an incentive to minimize the costs of servicing a patient because it can make higher profits (i.e., cells 1 and 3 of figure 2–2).

A PPO, the other main type of MCO, provides typical insurance coverage to the consumer and receives a discount from participating providers, both hospitals and physicians, that have contracted with the PPO. The chosen hospitals and physicians have usually proven to be low utilizers of high-cost treatments. Unlike the HMO, the PPO reimburses for medical care services received from health care providers that have not contracted with the PPO, although the consumer typically must pay a higher copayment. The higher copayment serves as a disincentive to go outside the group of participating health care providers. PPOs are said to promote both price competition and cost effectiveness (Frech, 1988).

In addition to private health insurance, nearly 26 percent of the U.S. population is covered by public health insurance. The two major types of public health insurance, both of which began in 1966, are **Medicare** and **Medicaid**.[9] Medicare is a uniform, national public health insurance program for aged and disabled individuals (e.g., those with kidney failure). Administered by the federal government, Medicare is the largest health insurer in the country, covering about 13 percent of the population.

The Medicare plan consists of two parts. Part A is compulsory and provides health insurance coverage for inpatient hospital care, very limited nursing home services, and some home health services. Part B, the voluntary or supplemental plan, provides benefits for physician services, outpatient hospital services, outpatient laboratory and radiology services, and home health services. Part A of Medicare is funded by a Medicare tax that is similar to the Social Security tax, and part B is financed by monthly premiums (25 percent) and general taxes (75 percent). The Medicare patient is also responsible for paying a deductible and a copayment for most part B services and for long-term hospital services under part A. Many Medicare recipients also choose to purchase **Medigap** insurance, a private health insurance plan offered by commercial insurance companies and the Blues, that pays for medical bills not fully reimbursed by Medicare.

The second type of public health insurance program, Medicaid, provides coverage for certain economically disadvantaged groups. Medicaid is jointly financed by the federal and state governments and is administered by each state. The federal government provides state governments with a certain percentage of matching funds ranging from 50 to 77 percent, depending on the per capita income in the state. Coverage under Medicaid varies because states have established different requirements for eligibility. Individuals who are elderly, blind, disabled, or members of families with dependent children must be covered by Medicaid for states to receive federal funds. In addition, although the federal government stipulates a certain basic package of health care benefits (i.e., hospital, physician, and nursing home services), some states are more generous than others. Consequently, in some states individuals receive a more generous benefit package under Medicaid than in others. Medicaid is the only public program that finances long-term nursing home care. Approximately 12 percent of the population is covered by Medicaid.

In summary, the financing of health care falls into three broad categories: private health insurance (e.g., traditional free choice/fee-for-service insurance, HMOs, and PPOs), Medicare, and Medicaid. However, another category of individuals exists: those who are uninsured. Approximately 16 percent of the U.S. population is estimated to lack health insurance coverage at any point in time. This does not mean these individuals are without access to health care services. Many uninsured people receive health care services through public clinics and hospitals, state and local health

---

[9]See Chapter 12 for a more detailed discussion on the Medicare and Medicaid programs. The federal government is also responsible for providing health insurance to individuals in the military and to federal employees.

programs, or private providers that finance the care through charity and by shifting costs to other payers. Nevertheless, the lack of health insurance can cause uninsured households to face considerable financial hardship and insecurity. Furthermore, the uninsured often find themselves in the emergency room of a hospital, sometimes after it is too late for proper medical treatment.

## Reimbursement for Health Care in the United States

As mentioned earlier, the reimbursement scheme has a considerable impact on the behavior and performance of health care markets. For example, fixed-payment schemes may create incentives for a more judicious use of health care resources. With a fixed payment, health care providers have less incentive to overproduce medical services and more incentive to produce with least-cost methods of production. Fee-for-service reimbursement, in contrast, often leads to a large volume of medical services. Given this consideration, we now describe the various ways in which health care providers are reimbursed in the United States.

Unlike in Canada and Europe, where a single-payer system is the norm, the United States possesses a multipayer system in which a variety of third-party payers, including the federal and state governments, commercial health insurance companies, and the Blues, are responsible for reimbursing health care providers. Naturally, reimbursement takes on various forms in the United States, depending on the nature of the third-party payer. The most common form of reimbursement is fee-for-service, although prospective payment and prepaid health plans are becoming more popular. For example, most traditional health insurance plans reimburse health care providers on a fee-for-service basis. In addition, health care providers contracting with most MCOs are paid on a fee-for-service basis; the fee is usually discounted, however.

Physician services under Medicare (and most state Medicaid plans) are also reimbursed on a fee-for-service basis, but the fee is fixed by the government. Historically, the fees were based on the usual, customary, and reasonable fee. This means the fee was limited to the lowest of three charges: the actual charge of the physician, the customary charge of the physician, or the prevailing charge in the local area. Since January 1992, physician services to Medicare patients are reimbursed according to a point system called the **Resource-Based Relative-Value Scale** system (see Chapter 12). Various physician services are assigned points based on resource costs, such as the time and intensity of the physician's work, practice expenses (e.g., office rent, salaries, equipment, and supplies), and malpractice insurance expenses. The total number of points, or relative-value scale (RVS) indicates the value of each service relative to others. The RVS is transformed into a schedule of fees when it is multiplied by a dollar conversion factor and a geographic adjustment factor that allows fees to vary in different locations.

Under both of the public programs, the physician can choose to accept assignment of patients. For example, if the physician accepts assignment under Medicare, he or she agrees to accept the government-determined fee in full and cannot charge the patient an additional amount beyond the normal 20 percent copayment. The physician must also agree to treat all Medicare patients for all services. A physician who does not accept assignment can charge patients a price higher than the Medicare fee and accept patients on a case-by-case basis. Without assignment, a patient pays the actual physician charge and receives reimbursement for 80 percent of the Medicare fee.

In contrast to the fee-for-service method, some health care providers are paid on a fixed-fee or prospective basis. For example, the staff HMO is prepaid by the consumer, and physicians are paid on a salary basis. While the IPA/HMO is prepaid by the consumer, health care providers are usually paid on a fee-for-service or capitation basis.

Since 1983, the federal government has reimbursed hospitals on a prospective basis for services provided to Medicare patients. This Medicare reimbursement scheme, called the **diagnosis-related group (DRG)** system, contains 500 or so different payment categories based on the characteristics of the patient (age and sex), primary and secondary diagnosis, and treatment.[10] A prospective payment is established for each DRG. The prospective payment is claimed to provide hospitals with an incentive to contain costs (cells 1 and 3 of figure 2–2).

Beginning in the early 1980s, many states, such as California, instituted **selective contracting,** in which various health care providers competitively bid for the right to treat Medicaid patients. In fact, much of the favorable experience with selective contracting in the United States led to the adoption of the public contracting model in the United Kingdom (Mechanic, 1995). Under selective contracting, recipients of Medicaid are limited in the choice of health care provider. In addition, to better contain health care costs and coordinate care, the federal government and various state governments have attempted to shift Medicare and Medicaid beneficiaries into MCOs. As of 1997, about 48 percent of all Medicaid recipients and roughly 15 percent of all Medicare beneficiaries are enrolled in MCOs.

### Production of Health Services and Provider Choice in the United States

We mentioned previously that the method of production is an important aspect of a health care system. We will learn later that the production method may matter because many economists argue that for-profit organizations operate more efficiently than nonprofit enterprises. Their argument is based on a property rights theory that in a for-profit setting, the owners, or, as economists refer to them, the residual claimants, put pressure on the organization to maximize profits and to thereby minimize the costs of production. The property rights theory will be discussed more fully later. For now we will simply describe the organization of production in the United States.

Like the financing and reimbursement schemes, the U.S. health care system is very diversified in terms of production methods. Government, not-for-profit, and for-profit institutions all play an important role in health care markets. For the most

---

[10]The DRGs are based on 23 major diagnostic groups centered on a different organ of the body.

## Consumer Satisfaction with the Health Care Systems in 11 Countries

We mentioned in Chapter 1 how any health care system must concern itself with the allocation of medical resources and distribution of medical services because economic resources are so scarce. The people in various nations count on their governments to choose and support the health care system that best promotes efficiency and equity given their historical background, cultural system, and political beliefs. One interesting question is whether people in various nations are satisfied with their current health care system. In an attempt to answer this question, a number of public opinion polls have tried to estimate the degree of consumer satisfaction with the present health care system in a number of nations.

The public opinion polls cited by Blendon et al. (1990, 1991), involved telephone and in-home interviews of a random sample of approximately

1,000 households in 11 countries, including the United States, Canada, 7 European countries, Australia, and Japan. The households were asked to answer *yes* or *no* to the following three statements:

1. On the whole, the health care system works pretty well, and only minor changes are necessary to make it work better.

2. There are some good things in our health care system, but fundamental changes are needed to make it work better.

3. Our health care system has so much wrong with it that we need to completely rebuild it.

The poll findings on this topic yielded some very interesting insights. Table 1 shows the results of the 11-nation survey. Several conclusions are worth

| TABLE 1 | CONSUMER SATISFACTION WITH HEALTH CARE SYSTEM IN 11 COUNTRIES | | |
|---|---|---|---|
| | **Minor Changes Needed** | **Fundamental Changes Needed** | **Completely Rebuild System** |
| Canada | 56% | 38% | 5% |
| Netherlands | 47 | 46 | 5 |
| West Germany | 41 | 35 | 13 |
| France | 41 | 42 | 10 |
| Australia | 34 | 43 | 17 |
| Sweden | 32 | 58 | 6 |
| Japan | 29 | 47 | 6 |
| United Kingdom | 27 | 52 | 17 |
| Spain | 21 | 49 | 28 |
| Italy | 12 | 46 | 40 |
| United States | 10 | 60 | 29 |

SOURCES: Robert J. Blendon, Robert Leitman, Ian Morrison, and Karen Donelan, "Satisfaction with Health Systems in 10 Nations," *Health Affairs* 9 (summer 1990), Exhibit 2; Robert J. Blendon et al., "Spain's Citizens Assess Their Health Care System," *Health Affairs* 10 (fall 1991), Exhibit 2.

*(continued)*

INSIGHT 2–3

## (continued)

noting. The first is that Canadians are most satisfied with their health care system. Remember that among other characteristics, the Canadian health care system offers national health insurance financed by taxes, private production of health care services, and regulated budgets and fees for health care providers. Approximately 56 percent of the respondents in Canada believed the health care system requires only minor changes, and only 5 percent thought the system needs complete rebuilding.

The second conclusion to be drawn is that people in the United States are the least satisfied with their current health care system. Only 10 percent of the respondents believed that the present health care system could be improved with minor changes, and an overwhelming 60 percent thought the system needs fundamental changes. Moreover, almost 3 out of every 10 respondents in the United States believed the health care system requires a complete restructuring! Blendon, Leitman, Morrison, and Donelan speculated that the dissatisfaction with the present U.S. health care system is due to the financial insecurity caused by inadequate insurance protection and high out-of-pocket costs.

The third conclusion is that the presence of a national health care plan does not guarantee high levels of consumer satisfaction. Except for the United States, all the countries in the table have some type of national health care program that provides universal or near universal access to medical care. But except for Canada, over 50 percent of the poll respondents in the other nine countries believed their health care system requires more than minor changes. Consequently, a national health care program may not provide the cure for all health care system woes.

Of course, public opinion polls may not accurately reflect the success or failure of a health care system or provide a complete representation of the quality of life in a nation. For example, low levels of education and income may cause individuals to be generally dissatisfied with their environment. How people feel about the operation of the health care system relative to the functioning of the overall economic system (or job market) might provide a more accurate indicator of public satisfaction. In addition, unknown to the public, the structure of the health care system may not account for the poor performance of the medical sector. Instead, the poor performance of the health care sector may be due to insufficient resources and income or adverse lifestyles. Finally, from a general welfare perspective, consumer dissatisfaction with the health care system may be sufficiently balanced by high levels of satisfaction with other sectors of the economy. These trade-offs should be considered when assessing the general quality of life across nations.

part, primary care physicians in the U.S. function in the private for-profit sector and operate in group practices, although some physicians work for not-for-profit clinics or in public organizations. In the hospital industry, the not-for-profit is the dominant form of ownership. Specifically, not-for-profit hospitals control about 70 percent of all hospital beds. The ownership structure is quite the reverse in the nursing home industry, however. More than 70 percent of all nursing homes are organized on a for-profit basis. One should also keep in mind that mental retardation facilities, dialysis facilities, and most other medical care facilities, even insurance companies and MCOs, have different ownership forms. These different ownership forms most likely lead to variations in the operation and performance of medical organizations. (This is discussed much more fully below.) Moreover, the variety of ownership forms helps to make health care a very difficult, but challenging and interesting, industry to analyze.

In addition, we mentioned above that provider choice matters. Consumers typically receive greater satisfaction from facing more choices. We also discussed, however, that more choices may come at greater costs if small, differentiated providers are unable to fully exploit any economies associated with size. Hence, it is important to know how much choice consumers have over health care providers in the United States.

Up to the early 1980s most insured individuals had full choice of health care providers in the United States. Consumers could choose to visit a primary care giver or the outpatient clinic of a hospital, or see a specialist if they chose to. The introduction of various MCOs and such new government policies as selective contracting have limited the degree to which consumers can choose their own health care provider. For example, those individuals belonging to a staff HMO must receive their care exclusively from that organization, otherwise they are fully responsible for the ensuing financial burden. Furthermore, the primary care giver acts as a gatekeeper and must refer the patient for additional care. Of course, the lower premiums of a staff HMO compensate consumers at least to some degree for the restriction of choice. Even those individuals belonging to the less restrictive PPO face a financial penalty when choosing health care providers outside the network. There are arguments for and against free choice of provider and once again trade-offs are involved. This issue will be discussed below in more depth. For now let us just say that these trade-offs must be given serious thought when determining what degree of consumer choice is best from a societal point of view.

## SUMMARY

Every health care system must answer the four basic questions concerning the allocation of medical resources and the distribution of medical services. Some systems rely on centralized decision making whereas others answer the basic questions through a decentralized process. Health care systems are complex largely because third-party payers are involved. Third-party payers help to reduce the financial risk associated with the irregularity and uncertainty of many medical transactions. Third-party payers also help monitor the behavior of health care providers.

The financing, reimbursement, and production methods and the degree of choice over the health care provider are important elements that make up a health care system. Medical care is financed by out-of-pocket payments, premiums, and/or taxes. Medical care providers are reimbursed on a fixed or variable basis. The production of medical care may take place in a for-profit, a not-for-profit, or a public setting, and medical care providers may operate in independent or large group practices. Choice of provider may be limited. All these features are important because they often influence the operation and performance of a health care system. For example, many economists predict that fee-for-service insurance plans provide an incentive for medical care providers to produce a large volume of services.

The U.S. health care system is very pluralistic. For instance, considerable variation exists in the financing, reimbursement, and production of medical care. The remainder of this book provides a better understanding about how each of these elements affects the functioning of the U.S. health care system.

## Review Questions and Problems

1. Answer the following questions pertaining to health care systems.

   a. Why isn't the market for health care services organized according to a typical consumer (patient) and producer (health provider) relationship?

   b. What are the basic differences between insurance premiums and taxes as sources of medical care financing?

   c. How might the reimbursement method differ among health care providers? Why might the reimbursement method make a difference?

   d. Identify the four basic kinds of health care systems discussed in the chapter.

   e. Point out some unique institutions (compared to the United States) associated with the health care systems of the various countries discussed in the chapter.

2. Suppose you had the opportunity to organize the perfect health care system. Explain how you would organize the financing method, reimbursement scheme, mode of production, and physician referral procedure.

3. Which of the following reimbursement and consumer copayment schemes would have the greatest and lowest likelihood of producing high-cost, low-benefit medicine? Explain your answers.

   a. Fee-for-service plan with 40 percent consumer copayment.

   b. Prepaid health plan with 40 percent consumer copayment.

   c. Fee-for-service plan with no consumer cost sharing.

   d. Fixed-salary plan with no consumer cost sharing.

   e. Prepaid health plan with no consumer cost sharing.

   f. Fixed-salary plan with 40 percent consumer cost sharing.

4. Answer the following questions regarding the U.S. health care system.

   a. What are the basic differences between conventional health insurance and managed-care health insurance in terms of type of insurance offered and reimbursement practice?

   b. What is the difference between Medicare and Medicaid? How is Medicare financed? How is Medicaid financed?

   c. What is the DRG system? How are physicians currently reimbursed under the Medicare system?

## References

Aaron, Henry J. *Serious and Unstable Condition: Financing America's Health Care*, Washington, D.C.: The Brookings Institution, 1991.

———. "Economic Aspects of the Role of Government in Health Care." In *Health, Economics and Health Economics*, ed. J van der Gaag and M. Perlman. Amsterdam: North Holland, 1981.

Arrow, Kenneth J. "Uncertainty and the Welfare Economics of Medical Care." *American Economic Review* 53 (December 1963), pp. 941–73.

Banta, H. David, and Kerry Britten Kemp, eds. "Introduction." In *The Management of Health Care Technology in Nine Countries*. New York: Springer, 1982, pp. 1–9.

Blendon, Robert J., Robert Leitman, Ian Morrison, and Karen Donelan. "Satisfaction with Health Systems in Ten Nations." *Health Affairs* 9 (summer 1990), pp. 185–92.

Blendon, Robert J., et al. "Spain's Citizens Assess Their Health Care System." *Health Affairs* 10 (fall 1991), pp. 216–28.

Bodenheimer, Thomas, and Kevin Grumbach. "Financing Universal Health Insurance: Taxes, Premiums and the Lessons of Social Insurance." *Journal of Health Politics, Policy and Law* 17 (fall 1992), pp. 439–62.

Ellis, Randall P., and Thomas G. McGuire. "Supply-Side and Demand-Side Cost Sharing in Health Care." *Journal of Economic Perspectives* 7 (fall 1993), pp. 135–51.

Frech, H. E., III. "Preferred Provider Organizations and Health Care Competition." In *Health Care in America*, edited by H. E. Frech III. San Francisco: Pacific Research Institute for Public Policy, 1988, pp. 353–70.

Halm, Ethan A. Nancyanne Causino, and David Blumenthal. "Is Gatekeeping Better Than Traditional Care?" *Journal of the American Medical Association*, 278 (November 1997), pp. 1677–81.

Hickson, Gerald B., William A. Altemeier, and James M. Perrin. "Physician Reimbursement by Salary or Fee-for-Service: Effect on Physician Practice Behavior in a Randomized Prospective Study." *Pediatrics* 80 (September 1987), pp. 344–50.

Mechanic, David. "Americanization of the British NHS." *Health Affairs* 14 (summer 1995), pp. 51–67.

*Mosby Medical Encyclopedia*. New York: C. V. Mosby, 1992.

Raffel, Marshall W., ed. *Health Care and Reform in Industrial Countries*. University Park, PA: Pennsylvania State University Press, 1997.

Reinhardt, Uwe. "Economics," *Journal of the American Medical Association* 275 (June 1996), pp. 23–25.

———. "What Can Americans Learn from Europeans: A Response." In *Health Care Systems in Transition*. Paris: OECD, 1990, pp. 105–12.

———. "Alternative Methods of Reimbursing Noninstitutional Providers of Health Services." In *Controls on Health Care*. Washington DC: National Academy of Science, 1975.

Rublee, Dale A. "Medical Technology in Canada, Germany, and the United States: An Update." *Health Affairs* 13 (fall 1994), pp. 113–17.

———. "Medical Technology in Canada, Germany, and the United States." *Health Affairs* 8 (fall 1989), pp. 178–81.

Schmittdiel, Julie, Joe V. Selby, Kevin Grumbach, and Charles P. Quesenberry. "Choice of Personal Physician and Patient Satisfaction in a Health Maintenance Organization. *Journal of the American Medical Association* 278 (November 1997), pp. 1596–99.

*Source Book of Health Insurance Data*, 1994. Washington, DC: Health Insurance Association of America, 1995.

Stahl, Ingemar. "Sweden." In *Advances in Health Economics and Health Services Research, Supplement 1: Comparative Health Systems*, ed. Richard M. Scheffler and Louis F. Rossiter. Greenwich, CT: JAI Press, 1990, pp. 197–210.

Swan, James H., et al. "Trends in Medicaid Nursing Home Reimbursement: 1978–89." *Health Care Financing Review* 14 (summer 1993), pp. 111–32.

## CEBS Questions

CEBS Sample Question on Subject Matter from CEBS Course IX Study Manual

1. Why does a third-party payer face a much lower level of risk than an individual health care consumer does? (pp. 32–33.)

CEBS Sample Exam Questions

1. In the Canadian health care system cost containment is accomplished primarily through:
   A. Copayments
   B. High deductibles
   C. Cost sharing with the government
   D. Voluntary restraint in raising prices
   E. Fixed budgets for hospitals and predetermined fees for physicians

2. Which of the following statements regarding health insurance systems in foreign countries is (are) correct?
   I. Canada has a national health insurance program that provides first-dollar coverage with no limit on lifetime benefits.
   II. Germany has socialized health insurance financed by employers and employees.
   III. The primary health service in the United Kingdom is much the same as the Medicaid program in the United States.
   A. II only
   B. III only
   C. I and II only
   D. II and III only
   E. I, II, and III

3. The four stages associated with the development and dissemination of medical technology include all the following EXCEPT:
   A. Basic research
   B. Applied research
   C. Clinical investigation and testing
   D. Comparative analysis
   E. Diffusion

*Answer to Sample Question from Study Manual*

Third-party payers face much lower risk than individual consumers because of the law of large numbers. That is, third-party payers can pool the experience of many individuals and use actuarial tables to predict aggregate medical costs.

*Answers to Sample Exam Questions*

1. E is the correct answer. See pages 37–38 of the text.
2. C is the correct answer. The primary health care system in the United Kingdom is not only for the economically disadvantaged. See pages 34–35 of the text.
3. D is the answer. See page 42 of the text.

# 3

# Health, Medical Care, and Medical Spending: An Economic Perspective

N ot too long ago, a newspaper article reported that the residents of Glasgow, Scotland, pursue such an unhealthy lifestyle that their average life expectancy is one of the lowest in the Western world (Horwitz, 1992). Their diets generally lack fruits and vegetables and consist primarily of high-fat-content foods, such as "greasy cannonballs" (deep-fried, hard-boiled eggs wrapped in sausage). In addition, the per capita consumption of cigarettes and alcohol is extremely high in Glasgow. For instance, eighty-three percent of all middle-aged men in Glasgow have regularly smoked cigarettes at some time in their lives.

Economic and environmental factors also contribute to the low life expectancy rate in Glasgow. A lack of job opportunities over the years has forced many residents to live in very unhealthy surroundings, including crowded, damp tenements and heavy smog. At one point, the smog was so bad and the "slums so foul that a parliamentarian branded Glasgow earth's nearest suburb to hell" (Horwitz, 1992).

The situation in Glasgow illustrates the important roles lifestyle, socioeconomic conditions, and the environment play in the overall health of a community. This chapter explores these relationships by establishing the theoretical and empirical connection between health and various factors such as medical care. In particular, this chapter

- Discusses the concepts of health and medical care.

- Introduces utility analysis to explain why people desire health.

- **Utilizes production theory to explain the making of health.**

- **Reviews the empirical results concerning the factors that influence health.**

- **Examines health care spending in the United States.**

- **Reviews the sources and uses of health care funds in the United States.**

## What Is Health?

The *Mosby Medical Encyclopedia* (1992, p. 360) defines **health** as "a state of physical mental and social well-being and the absence of disease or other abnormal condition." Economists take a radically different approach. They view health as a durable good, or type of capital, that provides services. The flow of services produced from the stock of health "capital" is consumed continuously over an individual's lifetime (see Grossman, 1972a, 1972b). Each person is assumed to be endowed with a given stock of health at the beginning of a period, such as a year. Over the period, the stock of health depreciates with age and may be augmented by investments in medical services. Death occurs when an individual's stock of health falls below a critical minimum level.

Naturally, the initial stock of health, along with the rate of depreciation, varies from individual to individual and depends on a great many factors, some of which are uncontrollable. For example, a person has no control over the initial stock of health allocated at birth, and a child with a congenital heart problem begins life with a below-average stock of health. However, we will learn later that medical services may compensate for any deficiencies, at least to some degree. The rate at which health depreciates also depends on many factors, such as the individual's age, physical makeup, and, lifestyle; environmental factors; and the amount of medical care consumed. For instance, the rate at which health depreciates in a person diagnosed with high blood pressure is likely to depend on the amount of medical care consumed (is this person under a doctor's care?), environmental factors (does he or she have a stressful occupation?), and lifestyle (does the person smoke or have a weight problem?). All these factors interact to determine the person's stock of health at any point in time, along with the pace at which it depreciates.

Regardless of how you define it, health is a nebulous concept that defies precise measurement. In terms of measurement, health depends as much on the quantity of life (i.e., number of life-years remaining) as it does on the quality of life. Quality of life has become an increasingly important issue in recent years due to the life-sustaining capabilities of today's medical technology. The issue gained national prominence in 1976 when, in a landmark court decision, the parents of Karen Ann Quinlan were given the right to remove their daughter, who was in a persistent vegetative state, from a ventilator. Because the quality of life is a relative concept that is open to wide interpretation, researchers have wrestled with developing an instrument that accurately measures health. As we will see, health economists often use the (inverse of) mortality or morbidity rates as a measure of health.

# Why Good Health? Utility Analysis

Now that we have a working definition of health, the next step is to introduce some fundamental economic principles to illustrate why an individual desires health. As mentioned earlier, the stock of health generates a flow of services as other durable goods do. The services yield satisfaction, or what economists call **utility.** Your television set is another example of a durable good that generates a flow of services. It is the many hours of programming, or viewing services, that your television provides that yield utility, not the set itself.

As a good, health is desired for consumption and investment purposes. From a consumption perspective, an individual desires to remain healthy because she or he receives utility from an overall improvement in the quality of life. In simple terms, a healthy person feels great and thus is in a better position to enjoy life. The investment element concerns the relation between health and time. If you are in a positive state of health, you allocate less time to sickness and therefore have more healthy days available in the future to work and enhance your income or to pursue other activities, such as leisure. Economists look at education from the same perspective. Much as a person invests in education to enhance the potential to command a higher wage, a person invests in health to increase the likelihood of having more healthy days to work and generate income.

The investment element of health can be used to explain some of the lifestyle choices people make. A person who puts a high value on future events is more inclined to pursue a healthy lifestyle to increase the likelihood of enjoying more healthy days than a person who puts a low value on future events. A preference for the future explains why a middle-aged adult with high cholesterol orders a salad with dressing on the side instead of a steak served with a baked potato smothered in sour cream. In this situation, the utility generated by increasing the likelihood of having more healthy days in the future outweighs the utility received from consuming the steak dinner. In contrast, a person who puts a much lower value on future events and prefers immediate gratification may elect to order the steak dinner and ignore the potential ill effects of high cholesterol.

Naturally, each individual chooses to consume that combination of goods and services, including the services produced from the stock of health, that provides the most utility. The isolated relation between an individual's stock of health and utility is captured in figure 3–1, where the quantity of health, $H$, is measured on the horizontal axis and the level of utility, $U$, is represented on the vertical axis.[1] The positive slope of the curve indicates that an increase in a person's stock of health directly enhances total utility. The shape of the curve is particularly important because it illustrates the fundamental economic principle of the **law of diminishing marginal utility.** This law states that each successive incremental improvement in health generates smaller and smaller additions to total utility; in other words, utility increases at a decreasing rate with respect to health.

---

[1] To simplify matters, we ignore the intermediate step between the health stock, the services it provides, and the utility received from these services and assume that the stock of health directly yields utility.

| FIGURE 3–1 | THE TOTAL UTILITY CURVE FOR HEALTH |

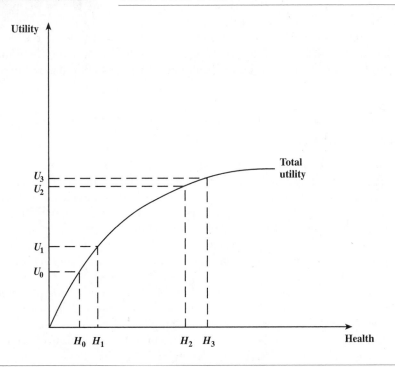

For example, in figure 3–1 an increase in health from $H_0$ to $H_1$ causes utility to increase from $U_0$ to $U_1$, while an equal increase in health from $H_2$ to $H_3$ generates a much smaller increase in utility, from $U_2$ to $U_3$. In the second case, the increase in utility is less when the stock of health is greater because of the law of diminishing marginal utility. The implication is that a person values a marginal improvement in health more when sick (i.e., when having a lower level of health) than when healthy. This does not mean that every individual derives the same level of utility from a given stock of health. It is possible for two or more people to receive a different amount of utility from the same stock of health. The law of diminishing marginal utility requires only that the addition to total utility decreases with successive increases in health.

Another way to illustrate the law of diminishing marginal utility is to focus on the marginal utility associated with each unit of health. Marginal utility equals the addition to total utility generated by each successive unit of health. In mathematical terms,

**(3–1)** $\quad MU_H = \Delta U / \Delta H,$

where $MU_H$ equals the marginal utility of the last unit of health consumed and $\Delta$ represents the change in utility or health. In figure 3–1, equation 3–1 represents the slope of the tangent line at each point on the total utility curve. The bowed shape of the total utility curve implies that the slope of the tangent line falls as we move along the curve, or that $MU_H$ falls as health increases.

Figure 3–2 captures the relation between marginal utility and the stock of health. The downward slope of the curve indicates that the law of diminishing marginal utility holds because each new unit of health generates less additional utility than the previous one.

## What Is Medical Care?

Medical care is composed of myriad goods and services that maintain, improve, or restore a person's physical or mental well-being. For example, a young adult might have shoulder surgery to repair a torn rotator cuff so that he can return to work, an elderly woman may have hip replacement surgery so that she can walk without pain, and a parent may bring a child to the dentist for an annual cleaning to prevent future medical problems. Prescription drugs, wheelchairs, and dentures are examples of medical goods, while surgeries, annual physical exams, and visits to physical therapists are examples of medical services.

Because of the heterogeneous nature of medical care, units of medical care are very difficult to measure precisely. Units of medical care are also hard to quantify because most represent services rather than tangible products. As a service, medical care exhibits the four *I*s that distinguish it from a good: intangibility, inseparability, inventory, and inconsistency (Berkowitz, Kerin, and Rudelius, 1989).

The first characteristic, **intangibility,** means a medical service is incapable of being assessed by the five senses. Unlike a new car, a steak dinner, or a new CD, the consumer cannot see, smell, taste, feel, or hear a medical service.

**Inseparability** means the production and consumption of a medical service take place simultaneously. For example, when you visit your dentist for a checkup, you are consuming dental services at the exact time the dentist is producing them. In addition, a patient often acts as both producer and consumer. Without the patient's active participation, the medical product is likely to be poorly produced.[2]

**Inventory** is directly related to inseparability. Because the production and consumption of a medical service occur simultaneously, health care providers are unable to stockpile or maintain an inventory of medical services. For example, a dentist cannot maintain an inventory of dental checkups to meet demand during peak periods.

Finally, **inconsistency** means the composition and quality of medical services consumed vary widely across medical events. Although everyone visits his or her physician at some time or another, not every visit to a physician is for the same reason. One person may go for a routine physical, while another may go because she or he needs heart bypass surgery. The composition of medical care provided or the intensity at which it is consumed can differ greatly among individuals.

---

[2]Educational services, like medical services, require the consumer's active participation; that is, education is likely to be poorly provided when the student plays a passive role in the process.

| FIGURE 3-2 | THE MARGINAL UTILITY CURVE FOR HEALTH |

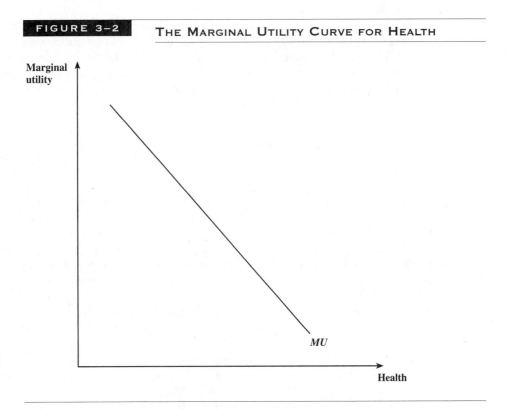

The quality of medical services may also be inconsistent. Quality differences are reflected in the structure, process, and/or outcome of a medical care provider (Donabedian, 1980, 1988). **Structural quality** is reflected in the physical and human resources of the medical care provider, such as the facilities (level of amenities), medical equipment (type and age), personnel (training and experience), and administration (organization structure). **Process quality** reflects the specific actions health care providers take on behalf of patients in delivering and following through with care. Process quality might include access (waiting time), data collection (background history and testing), communication with the patient, and diagnosis and treatment (type and appropriateness). **Outcome quality** refers to the impact of care on the patient's health and welfare as measured by patient satisfaction, work time lost to disability, or postcare mortality rate. Because it is extremely difficult to keep all three aspects of quality constant for every medical event, the quality of medical services, unlike that of physical goods, is likely to be inconsistent.

As you can see, medical care services are extremely difficult to quantify. In most instances, researchers measure medical care in terms of either availability or use. If medical care is measured on an availability basis, such measures as the number of physicians or hospital beds available per 1,000 people are used. If medical care is measured in terms of use, the analyst employs data indicating how often a medical service is actually delivered. For example, the quantity of office visits or surgeries per capita is often used to represent the amount of physician services rendered, whereas the number of inpatient days is frequently used to measure the amount of hospital or nursing home services consumed.

## The Production of Good Health

Health economists take the view that the creation and maintenance of health involves a production process. Much as a firm uses various inputs, such as capital and labor, to manufacture a product, an individual uses medical inputs and other factors, such as lifestyle, to produce health. The relation between medical inputs and output can be captured in what economists call a production function. A **production function** is simply a mathematical expression that shows how the level of output (in this case, health) depends on the quantities of various inputs, such as medical care. A generalized health production function for an individual takes the following form:

**(3–2)**     Health = $H$(Profile, Medical Care, Lifestyle, Socioeconomic Status,
                         Environment),

where *health* reflects the level of health at a point in time; *profile* captures the individual's mental and physical profile as of a point in time; *medical care* equals the quantity of medical care consumed; *lifestyle* represents a set of lifestyle variables, such as diet and exercise; *socioeconomic status* reflects the joint effect of social and economic factors, such as education and poverty; and *environment* equals a vector of environmental factors, including air and water quality.

To focus on the relation between health and medical care, we assume initially that all other factors in the health production function remain constant. Figure 3–3 depicts this relation with the quantity of medical care, $q$, measured on the horizontal axis and the level of health, $H$, measured on the vertical axis. The intercept term represents the individual's level of health when zero medical care is consumed. As drawn, the **total product curve** implies that an individual's level of health is positively related to the amount of medical care consumed.[3] The shape of the curve is very similar to that in figure 3–1 and reflects the **law of diminishing marginal productivity.** This law implies that health increases at a decreasing rate with respect to additional amounts of medical care, holding other inputs constant. For example, suppose an individual makes an initial visit and several follow-up visits to a physician's office for a specific illness or treatment over a given period of time. It is very likely that the first few visits

---

[3]However, we should not rule out the possibility that poor health status or an illness might be created by additional medical services. An illness created by a medical care encounter is referred to as an *iatrogenic disorder,* "a condition caused by medical personnel or procedures or through exposure to the environment of a health-care facility" (*Mosby Medical Encyclopedia,* p.401). For example a physician may accidentally harm a patient by prescribing the wrong medicine for a given medical condition.

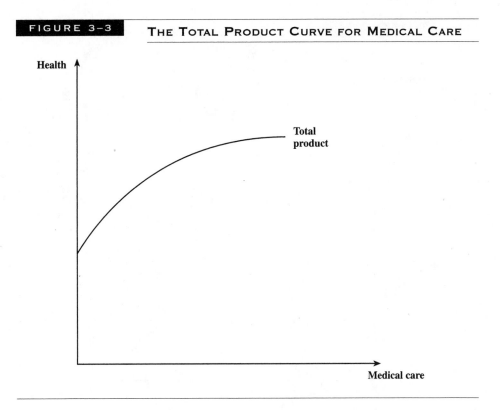

FIGURE 3-3   THE TOTAL PRODUCT CURVE FOR MEDICAL CARE

have a much more beneficial impact on the individual's stock of health than the later visits. Thus, each successive visit generates a smaller improvement in health than the previous one.

The relation between health and medical care can also be viewed from a marginal perspective, where the marginal product of medical care represents the incremental improvement in health brought about by each successive unit of medical care consumed, or

(3–3)   $MP_q = \Delta H/\Delta q,$

where $MP_q$ equals the marginal product of the last unit of medical care services consumed. The law of diminishing marginal productivity holds that the marginal product of medical care diminishes as the individual acquires more medical care. A graph of this relationship appears as a negatively sloped curve in figure 3–4.[4]

---

[4]As in utility analysis, the marginal product of medical care equals the slope of the tangent line drawn to every point on figure 3–3.

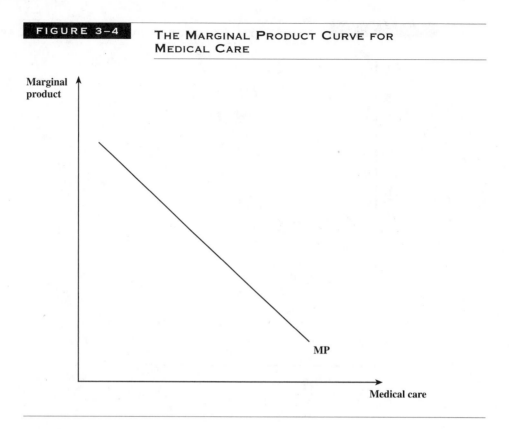

**FIGURE 3–4**     THE MARGINAL PRODUCT CURVE FOR MEDICAL CARE

The other variables in the health production function can also be incorporated into the analysis. In general terms, a change in any of the other variables in the production function shifts the total product curve. The slope of the total product curve may also change if the marginal product of medical care has been affected.

The profile variable in equation 3–2 depends upon a host of variables and controls for such items as the person's genetic makeup, mental state, age, gender, and race/ethnicity as of a given point in time (e.g., the beginning of the year). Any change in the profile variable affects both the intercept term and the slope of the health production function. For example, an individual's genetic makeup may make him or her a candidate for prostate or breast cancer. If this individual gets cancer, then his or her total product curve shifts downward. That is because overall health has decreased regardless of the amount of medical care consumed. The total product curve is also likely to rotate downward at the same time because the marginal product of medical care should decrease as health diminishes. The total product curve rotates downward because an otherwise healthy person is likely to respond more favorably to medical treatments *for a given medical complication* than one who is less healthy. Both of these changes are represented in figure 3–5, where the total product curve shifts and

FIGURE 3-5    A SHIFT IN THE TOTAL PRODUCT CURVE
FOR MEDICAL CARE

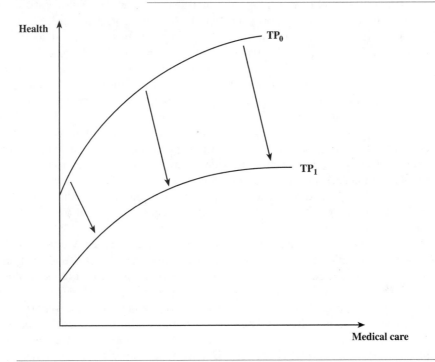

rotates downward at the same time from $TP_0$ to $TP_1$. The marginal product curve for medical services also shifts to the left, because each incremental unit of medical care now brings about a smaller improvement in health.

The effect of age on the production of health is relatively straightforward. Age affects health through the profile variable. As an individual ages and deteriorates physically, both health and the marginal product of medical care are likely to fall. In addition, the rate at which health depreciates over the period is also likely to increase with age. This causes the total product curve to shift downward and flatten out. The decrease in the marginal product of medical care also causes the marginal product curve to shift to the left.[5]

Lifestyle variables consider the impact of personal health habits on the production of health. Personal habits include such things as whether the person smokes, drinks excessively, leads a sedentary lifestyle, is overweight, or has an improper diet. For example, consider a newly health-conscious individual who decides that a change

---

[5]The impact of gender on the total and marginal product curves is left to the reader and is the focus of a review question at the end of this chapter.

in lifestyle is in order. After a regimen of diet and exercise, this person loses some weight and improves his physical conditioning. As a result of this change in lifestyle, the individual's level of health and the marginal product of medical care should increase. This causes the total product curve to shift and rotate upward.

As is the case with improvements in personal habits, improved socioeconomic conditions cause the intercept term and the marginal product of medical care to increase. For instance, since education is likely to make the individual a more efficient producer of health independently of the amount of medical care consumed, the total product curve shifts upward. An individual with more education is likely to better understand the positive impact of a healthy diet on health. The total product curve also steepens, or the marginal product of medical care increases, because education allows the person to utilize each unit of medical care consumed more effectively. For example, an educated individual may be more inclined to understand and follow a physician's advice concerning diet and exercise after undergoing a heart bypass operation. In addition, she may be able to recognize a medical problem early and seek medical care quickly when the effectiveness of medical treatment is generally at its maximum.

Some analysts have hypothesized that the relation between education and health is far more complex. For example, Fuchs (1979) has argued that the acquisition of education and health depends on the value people place on future events, or the rate at which they discount future events. Individuals who place a high value on future benefits and are willing to postpone gratification are inclined to acquire more education and pursue a healthier lifestyle when they are young. This is because they want to reap the rewards of a higher income and a longer life that more education and a healthier lifestyle can bring. On the other hand, individuals who place a low value on future events and desire immediate gratification are not likely to acquire significant amounts of education or to follow a healthy lifestyle because they have adopted a "live for today" attitude. Thus, according to Fuchs, higher levels of education may be associated with better health not because there is a direct link between the two variables but because both variables are directly correlated with a third factor, the degree to which future events are valued.

An adjustment in a person's physical environment is also likely to affect the total product curve. For example, an individual with an asthmatic condition might move from Los Angeles, where smog is intense, to a community on the far outskirts of the city. Or the person's spouse may give up smoking to decrease the level of secondhand smoke in the home. As a result, the probability that this person will succumb to a respiratory ailment diminishes. Both of these changes cause the total product curve to shift and rotate upward.

In short, health production theory suggests that a variety of factors, such as the individual's profile, medical care, lifestyle, socioeconomic status, and environment, interact to determine health. The theory also suggests that health increases at a diminishing rate with respect to greater amounts of medical care consumed, provided all other inputs remain constant. If any other inputs in the production process change, the impact of medical care on health is also likely to change.

# Empirical Evidence on the Production of Health in the United States

The production of health has been the focus of numerous empirical studies. In most instances, a formula similar to equation 3–2 is estimated using multiple regression analysis. Health is usually represented by (the inverse of) an age-, gender-, and race-adjusted mortality rate. Using the literature as our guide, we will review the empirical evidence concerning the characteristics associated with the production of health for adults and infants.

## *The Determinants of Health among Adults*

To no one's surprise, the literature has found that the consumption of medical care has a positive impact on the production of adult health. However, the results also indicate that quantitatively, the impact is relatively small. For example, Hadley (1982) found that a 10 percent increase in per capita medical care expenditures results in only a 1.5 percent decrease in the adult mortality rate. These estimates confirm those of an earlier study conducted by Auster, Leveson, and Sarachek (1969), who estimated that a 10 percent increase in medical services leads to a 1 percent drop in the age-adjusted mortality rate. Enthoven (1980) has referred to the small marginal impact of medical care services on the health status of adults as "flat-of-the-curve" medicine. In the context of figures 3–3 and 3–4, this means that the typical adult consumes medical services at the point where the slope of the total product curve or marginal product of medicine is near zero.

If, as the empirical evidence indicates, the overall contribution of medical care to health is rather modest at the margin, what determines marginal improvements in health? The answer lies in the other factors associated with the production of health, with education, lifestyle, the environment, and income being the major contributing factors.

Specifically, a positive relation between education and health has been well documented in the literature. For instance, employing four alternative measures of health (disability, functional limitations, and systolic and diastolic blood pressure), Berger and Leigh (1989) investigated the impact of education on health. They found the number of school years completed to be associated with lower blood pressure and lower probabilities of reporting functional limitations or disabilities.[6] In addition, Guralnik et al. (1993) found education positively impacted life expectancy among older adults. Those adults 65 years of age with 12 years' or more education had a life expectancy approximately three years longer than those of similar age with less than 12 years' education.

---

[6]Other studies have found similar results. Auster, Leveson, and Sarachek (1969) estimated that a 10 percent increase in education causes the age-adjusted mortality rate to fall by 2 percent. Newhouse and Friedlander (1980) found that every additional four years of education causes the probability of experiencing hypertension to decrease by one percentage point.

# The Impact of Specific Medical Services on Life Expectancy

In an attempt to obtain a more precise measure of the impact of medical care on overall health in the United States, Bunker et al. (1995) estimate the increases in life expectancy that can be attributed to a select group of preventive and curative medical services. A total of 26 chosen medical services were equally divided among preventive and curative services. These services were chosen primarily because they have made "the greatest contributions to increased life expectancy and improved quality of life" (p. 308) in industrialized countries.

The top half of table 1 provides an abbreviated list of 6 of the 13 preventive medical services the authors examined.[1] The second column in the table lists the increase in life expectancy for each individual receiving the preventive medical service, while the last column gives the average increase in life expectancy for the entire population of the country. For example, screening for hypertension adds an average of three months to the life expectancy of anyone receiving the medical service and has caused the average life expectancy in the United States to increase from between 1.5 and 2 months for the entire population, while childhood immunization for diphtheria in the United States has increased life expectancy by 10 months. In total the authors estimate that the 13 preventive medical services examined increased the average life expectancy in the United States by approximately 1.5 years.

The lower half of table 1 provides a look at 6 of the 13 curative medical services the authors examined. According to their work, treatment for cancer of the cervix increases the life expectancy of the individual receiving the medical care by 21 years and has improved the average life expectancy in the country by two weeks. Treatment for diabetes improves the life expectancy of the average recipient by 25 years while adding six months to the average life expectancy of the general population. When all is said and done, the authors estimate that the 13 medical interventions improved life expectancy by a total of between 3.5 and 4 years for the entire country. These results are somewhat surprising in that they suggest curative medical services have a much greater impact on life expectancy than do preventive medical services. The reader is cautioned not to conclude that emphasis should be placed on curative at the expense of preventive medical interventions, however. Such conclusions can be arrived at only after the cost of medical services has been factored into the analysis. This issue is treated in more detail in Chapter 7 when we discuss cost-benefit analysis.

Bunker et al. conclude that the preventive and curative medical services reviewed have improved the average life expectancy by a total of approximately 5 years as of 1990. These results represent a sizable contribution to longevity given that the average life span in the United States increased by a little more than 12 years from 1940 to 1990 (62.9 years to 75.4 years). These results somewhat contradict those of other studies by suggesting that medical services have had a significant impact on health as measured by length of life. Obviously, much more work needs to be done in this area as researchers untangle the complex relationship between medical care and health.

[1]The other seven include counseling to stop smoking, immunization for poliomyelitis, immunization for tetanus, immunization for influenza, hepatitis B immunization, hormone replacement, and aspirin prophylaxis for heart attack.

Lifestyle also appears to significantly influence the production of health. For instance, poor health habits, such as cigarette smoking and alcohol consumption, have been found to negatively affect health. Hadley (1982) estimated that a decrease in the consumption of cigarettes by 10 percent caused the mortality rate for black men and white men between ages 45 and 64 to decrease by 2.3 and 1.4 percent, respectively.

INSIGHT 3–1

**(continued)**

TABLE 1   IMPACT OF SPECIFIC MEDICAL SERVICES ON LIFE EXPECTANCY

| Preventive Medical Service | Gain in Life Expectancy per Individual Receiving Medical Care | Average Gain in Life Expectancy across Entire U.S. Population |
| --- | --- | --- |
| Screening for hypertension | 3 months | 1.5–2 months |
| Screening for cancer of cervix | 96 days | 2 weeks |
| Screening for colorectal cancer | 2 weeks | unknown |
| Immunization for diphtheria | 10 months | 10 months |
| Immunization for smallpox | 3–6 months | 3–6 months |
| Pneumococcal immunization | 6 weeks | 1 week |

| Medical Condition Treated | Gain in Life Expectancy per Individual Receiving Successful Treatment | Average Gain in Life Expectancy across Entire U.S. Population |
| --- | --- | --- |
| Hypertension | 10 years | 3.5–4 months |
| Cancer of the cervix | 21 years | 2 weeks |
| Colorectal cancer | 12 years | 2 weeks |
| Kidney failure | 11 years | 2–3 months |
| Diabetes | 25 years | 6 months |
| Pneumonia and influenza | 9 years | 3 months |

SOURCE: Bunker et al., "The Role of Medical Care in Determining Health: Creating an Inventory of Benefits," in *Society and Health*, edited by Benjamin C. Amick et al., 1995, tables 10.1 and 10.2.

The same decrease in consumption caused the mortality rate for both black and white women to fall by 1.1 percent. In another study of almost 1,600 Bank of America retirees, Leigh and Fries (1992) estimated that the typical one-pack-a-day smoker experiences 10.9 more sick days every six months than a comparable nonsmoker, while a person who consumes two or more drinks a day has 4.6 more sick days than a comparable light drinker (one or fewer drinks a day).

Other lifestyle traits, such as weight and sleeping and eating habits, also appear to affect health. Breslow and Enstrom (1980) discovered that men and women who follow seven beneficial health habits have, respectively, mortality rates 28 percent and 43 percent lower than men and women who follow three or fewer of these health habits. The seven habits include never smoking cigarettes, regular physical activity, moderate or no use of alcohol, seven to eight hours of sleep per day, maintaining proper weight, eating breakfast, and not eating between meals. Taken together, these studies illustrate the fundamental role lifestyle plays in the production of health for adults.

The relation between environmental factors and health is mixed and, as a result, it is difficult to draw overall conclusions from the literature. Auster, Leveson, and Sarachek (1969) included two variables in the regression equation to capture the impact of environmental factors on health: an index of industrialization and a variable that measured the extent of urbanization. Both measures were hypothesized to be positively associated with such factors as air and water pollution, and therefore negatively related to health. The index of industrialization was found to cause higher mortality, but the level of urbanization had no influence.

Hadley (1982) undertook one of the more comprehensive assessments of the impact of environmental factors on health. Included in the regression analysis were variables representing water quality, air quality, climate, and occupational hazards. The results were inconclusive, which Hadley attributed mainly to "the lack of good quality data" (p. 73). Clearly more refined data must be analyzed before any definitive conclusions can be drawn regarding the importance of environmental factors on the production of health.

The impact of income on health is far from clear. Auster, Leveson, and Sarachek (1969) uncovered a negative relation between income and health, while Grossman (1972a) found no relation between them. Hadley (1982), on the other hand, observed a weak relation between income and health as measured by adult mortality rates. Specifically, Hadley found that a 10 percent increase in income leads to a one-half of 1 percent reduction in the adult mortality rate.

The lack of consensus concerning the impact of income on health may occur partly because the relation between the two variables has changed over time. According to Fuchs (1975), increases in real income in the United States had a decidedly positive impact on health from the middle of the 18th century to the middle of the 20th century. Since that time, however, income has had little impact on the health status of adults in the United States. Fuchs offered two reasons for these results. First, by the middle of the 20th century, average real income in the United States had grown to the point where most citizens were able to afford adequate nutrition, running water, and sewage disposal, all of which improve overall health. At this point, incremental improvements in real income are likely to have little impact on health. Second, higher incomes brought a wider diffusion of medical care throughout the economy. Once medical care is sufficiently diffused throughout the economy, access to such care is less dependent on income.

More current research seems to have established a positive relation between income and health. For example, Ettner (1996) found increases in income enhanced both mental and physical health,[7] while Pappas et al. (1993) found income to

[7]Ettner also found higher income to be correlated with increased alcohol consumption, which suggests that higher income may adversely impact lifestyle.

## A Look at the Major Causes of Death in the United States in 1996

As mentioned in the text, lifestyle factors play a significant role in the production of health. If so, one might suspect that national disease-specific mortality rates would reflect the importance of lifestyle. That is, mortality rates should be high for diseases that are more sensitive to adverse lifestyle behavior. With this in mind, table 1 lists the top 10 causes of death in the United States for 1996. Over the course of the year, a little over 2.3 million individuals died in the United States from all causes. Of this number, approximately 81 percent succumbed to the 10 most common causes of death listed in the table. By far the number one cause of death was diseases of the heart. It accounted for almost one-third of all deaths in the United States in 1996. Although researchers are still unclear as to what determines an individual's risk for heart disease, they are certain that the blood level of cholesterol, smoking, level of physical activity, and obesity play a major role in determining the risk of heart disease. Each one of these factors is influenced by lifestyle to a large degree.

The second leading cause of death is malignant neoplasms, or cancers. Lifestyle choices often have an impact on this type of illness as well. For example, Edlin and Golanty (1988, p. 296) point out that approximately 80 percent of all lung cancer deaths, the most common form of cancer, can be attributed to smoking. The remaining 20 percent may in part result from environmental factors, such as air pollution.

It is interesting to note that two of the ten categories, accidents and adverse effects and suicide, deal with deaths related to individual behavior rather than natural causes. A total of 124,736 people died from violent deaths in 1996. Together, these causes represent the number four reason for deaths in the United States.

Human immunodeficiency virus infection was the eighth leading cause of death. This accounts for those individuals who died from complications stemming from AIDS. Since the large majority of individuals with the AIDS virus become infected through sexual contact or intravenous drug use, it is apparent that the spread of AIDS is dependent upon socioeconomic factors and lifestyle. Finally, chronic liver disease and cirrhosis was the tenth leading cause of death. Social factors also play a role here as cirrhosis can be alcohol induced and brought about by years of heavy drinking.

Clearly, these data point to the importance of lifestyle in determining deaths in the United States. Of course, some social scientists would argue that lifestyle itself is strongly influenced by environment and socioeconomic conditions. That is a topic beyond the scope of this book.

*(continued)*

positively impact health as measured by a decrease in mortality rates for adults between the ages of 24 and 65. For a comprehensive review of the impact of income and other socioeconomic factors on health, consult Feinstein (1993).

Other variables found to contribute to health are age and marital status. The impact of marital status on health is interesting and merits a brief discussion. Married adults appear to experience better health than their single counterparts, everything else held constant. Most likely, this is because a spouse augments the production of health within the home. Marriage may also have a positive effect on health by altering preferences for risky behavior.

**INSIGHT 3-2**

**(continued)**

**TABLE 1**     THE LEADING CAUSES OF DEATH IN THE UNITED STATES IN 1996

| Cause | Number | Percent of Total |
|---|---|---|
| 1. Diseases of the heart | 733,834 | 31.9% |
| 2. Malignant neoplasms (cancerous tumors) | 544,278 | 23.4% |
| 3. Cerebrovascular diseases (diseases associated with the blood vessels and the supply of blood to the brain) | 160,431 | 6.9% |
| 4. Chronic obstructive pulmonary disease (obstructive breathing diseases) | 106,146 | 4.6% |
| 5. Accidents and adverse effects | 93,874 | 4.0% |
| 6. Pneumonia and influenza | 82,579 | 3.6% |
| 7. Diabetes mellitus | 61,559 | 2.7% |
| 8. Human immunodeficiency virus infection | 32,655 | 1.4% |
| 9. Suicide | 30,862 | 1.3% |
| 10. Chronic liver disease and cirrhosis | 25,135 | 1.1% |
| Total—All Causes | 2,322,421 | 80.9% |

SOURCE: *Monthly Vital Statistics Report*, United States Department of Health and Human Services, vol. 46 (September 11, 1997), table 17.

## The Determinants of Health among Infants

Numerous health production studies have investigated the factors that influence infant mortality rates. For brevity's sake, our discussion will concentrate on two studies conducted by Corman and Grossman (1985) and Hadley (1982).

Employing county-level data, Corman and Grossman regressed the neonatal mortality rates for blacks and whites on the average education of the mother, the prevalence of poverty (a measure of income), and the availability of public programs.[8] Among the public programs included in the analysis were the existence of neonatal intensive care facilities, the availability of abortion services, organized family planning, Bureau of Community Health Services (BCHS) projects, Women, Infants, and

---

[8]The infant mortality rate equals the number of deaths from the first to the 364th day of life per 1,000 live births. The neonatal mortality rate represents the number of deaths from the first to the 27th day of life per 1,000 live births.

| TABLE 3-1 | THE CONTRIBUTIONS OF VARIOUS FACTORS TO THE DECREASE IN U.S. NEONATAL MORTALITY RATES, 1964–1977 |

| Factor | Number of Infant Lives Saved per 1,000 Births | |
| --- | --- | --- |
| | **Blacks** | **Whites** |
| Schooling | .721 | .451 |
| Poverty | .229 | .335 |
| Neonatal intensive care | .631 | .426 |
| Availability of abortion services | .984 | .182 |
| Family planning | .126 | .156 |
| BCHS Projects | .243 | −.051 |
| WIC | .170 | .414 |
| Medicaid | .632 | .359 |
| Total reduction explained | 3.735 | 2.272 |
| Percentage explained | 32.5 | 30.3 |

SOURCE: Hope Corman and Michael Grossman, "Determinants of Neonatal Mortality Rates in the United States," *Journal of Health Economics* (September 1985), table 4.

Children (WIC) program availability, and Medicaid. BCHS projects measure the number of maternal and infant care projects and community health centers, while WIC assesses the impact of the Special Supplemental Food program for Women, Infants, and Children.

Overall, the results are robust and very enlightening. Lack of schooling and the existence of poverty were found to raise the neonatal mortality rate for both whites and blacks. Moreover, the results indicated that various government programs are associated with a reduced mortality rate for black as well as white children. Using the empirical estimates, the authors determined the relative contribution each independent variable made to the decrease in black and white neonatal mortality rates in the United States from 1964 to 1977. Over this period, the neonatal mortality rate for whites fell from 16.2 to 8.7 per 1,000 live births, and for blacks it fell from 27.6 to 16.1.

An abbreviated version of these results appears in table 3–1. The first column contains an abridged list of the independent variables; the second and third columns contain the individual contribution each variable made to the decrease in neonatal mortality rates for blacks and whites from 1964 through 1977. According to the figures, the factors collectively caused the neonatal rate to fall by 3.735 and 2.272 deaths per 1,000 live births for blacks and whites, respectively. Together they accounted for slightly more than 30 percent of the reduction in the neonatal death rate during this period.

For the black population, the availability of abortion services appears to have played the greatest role in reducing the neonatal death rate. Specifically, abortion availability accounted for a decline of almost 1 death per 1,000 live births. Schooling, the availability of neonatal intensive care, and Medicaid also played a major role in decreasing the neonatal mortality rate among blacks; each caused the rate to fall by approximately .7 deaths per 1,000 live births. The prevalence of poverty and BCHS projects seem to have played a lesser role, and family planning and the WIC program had the smallest impact.

The primary difference between the white and black mortality rates was in the impact of abortion services availability. According to table 3–1, the availability of abortion services lowered the neonatal death rate for whites by only .182 deaths per 1,000 live births, compared to .984 for blacks. The individual impacts of the other factors are reasonably similar across the two populations. As in the case of blacks, the schooling of the mother, the presence of neonatal care facilities, and Medicaid played an important role in lowering the white neonatal mortality rate. However, the reduction in poverty and the WIC program seem to have played a slightly greater role in reducing the neonatal death rate for whites than for blacks. For both groups, family planning played only a minor role, whereas the BCHS projects had a positive impact on white infant mortality rates for some unexplained reason.

Hadley's (1982) findings complement those of Corman and Grossman rather nicely. Employing race-specific infant mortality rates as the dependent variable, Hadley also found that public policy initiatives played a significant role in decreasing the infant death rate. In addition, Hadley discovered that the consumption of medical care reduced the infant mortality rate. In particular, a 10 percent increase in medical spending per capita reduced the mortality rate among white children by 1.5 percent. For blacks, the relation was less clear-cut.

These two studies combined indicate that public policies have a major impact on the infant death rate in the United States. Higher levels of schooling among mothers and less poverty also favorably influence the health status of infants, especially among the white population.

Some researchers have used multiple regression analysis to investigate the causes of health status differences across countries. For instance, Santerre, Grubaugh, and Stollar (1991) looked at the factors explaining variations in the infant mortality rate among 20 member countries of the OECD over the period from 1960 to 1985. Included in their health production function were explanatory variables that captured the quantity of medical services, income, environment (urbanization), education, the female labor force participation rate, the percentage of health care expenditures financed by the government, a time trend variable, and a series of country dummy variables to control for other country-specific effects, such as climate and diet.

The empirical findings are interesting and, to a large extent, mirror the results of domestic studies. Specifically, a greater availability of medical services was found to inversely affect the infant mortality rate, although the impact was moderate. A 10 percent increase in medical care caused the infant death rate to fall by 3.3 percent. Income was

## The Impact of Drug Use on Number of Newborns with Low Birthweight in New York City

A study by Joyce et al. (1992) illustrates in rather dramatic fashion the impact of lifestyle on health. Realizing that birthweight is one major predictor of neonatal and infant morbidity and mortality, the authors examined the causes of the dramatic increase in low-birthweight infants in New York City during the mid-1980s. In particular, they used regression analysis to focus on the impact of prenatal illicit substance abuse on the proportion of low-birthweight infants in various districts across New York City from 1980 through 1986.

The dependent variable in the regression equation was the proportion of low-birthweight infants across districts in New York City. The dependent variables included, among other items, the proportion of births to a woman out-of-wedlock, the proportion of mothers who smoked, the proportion of women who received inadequate medical care, and, most important, the proportion of women who used illicit substances during pregnancy.

The authors ran separate regressions for blacks, Hispanics, and whites and found that the impact of illegal drug use on the proportion of low-birthweight infants varied significantly across race. They found almost no impact for whites and only some impact for Hispanics. They found a much stronger relation between illicit drug use and the proportion of low-birthweight babies among blacks. In fact, the authors estimated that illicit drug use accounted for between 1,500 and 3,400 low-birthweight babies, which equaled between 3.2 and 7.3 percent of all low-birthweight infants in New York City from 1980 to 1986. They also estimated the neonatal costs of these births to be between $18 million and $41 million over the period in question.

This study clearly points out that the lifestyle of pregnant women plays a critical role in determining the initial endowment of health for newborns.

also found to be inversely related to the mortality rate; a 10 percent increase in real income caused a 6.5 to 8.9 percent drop in the infant mortality rate. Finally, Santerre, Grubaugh, and Stollar determined that increased urbanization caused a higher infant mortality rate, while education and the female labor force participation rate inversely influenced the infant death rate.

In summary, health production studies have left little doubt that at the margin, socioeconomic conditions and lifestyle factors play a greater role in determining health than medical care does. These results have some rather interesting policy implications. They suggest that any public policy aimed at improving health should be directed toward raising education levels, reducing the number of children who live in poverty, or improving lifestyles rather than simply providing additional medical care. Naturally, the specifics of any policy should be based on sound cost-benefit analysis.

## Health Care Spending in the United States

Continually rising health care costs are certainly one of the most glaring problems associated with the U.S. health care system. According to table 3–2, nominal national

| TABLE 3–2 | HEALTH CARE EXPENDITURES IN THE UNITED STATES, 1960–1996 | | | | | | | |
|---|---|---|---|---|---|---|---|---|
| | **1960** | **1970** | **1980** | **1990** | **1993** | **1994** | **1995** | **1996** |
| **Nominal Health Expenditures (billions of dollars)** | $26.9 | 73.2 | 247.3 | 699.5 | 895.1 | 945.7 | 991.4 | 1,035.1 |
| **Annual Rate of Growth (average annual percentage change from previous period shown)** | — | 10.6% | 12.9 | 11.0 | 8.6 | 5.6 | 4.8 | 4.4 |
| **Nominal Per Capita Health Expenditures** | $141 | 341 | 1,052 | 2,691 | 3,341 | 3,497 | 3,633 | 3,759 |
| **Health Expenditures as a Percent of GDP** | 5.1% | 7.1 | 8.9 | 12.2 | 13.6 | 13.6 | 13.6 | 13.6 |

SOURCE: Katherine R. Levit et al., "National Health Spending Trends in 1996," *Health Affairs* (January/February 1998), exhibits 2 and 4.

health care expenditures totaled $26.9 billion in 1960 and by 1996 had grown to $1,035.1 billion. This represents an increase of over 3,700 percent in 36 years.

The annualized rates of growth, also provided in table 3–2, indicate that the increase in medical expenditures was sustained throughout the entire period. The average annual rate of increase topped 10 percent between 1960 and 1970 and increased to 12.9 percent during the 1970s. In more recent years, the annual rate of growth in national medical care expenditures decreased substantially. From 1980 through 1990, the average annual rate of growth was 11.0 percent and fell to 8.6 percent over the period 1990 to 1993. The rate fell again from 1993 to 1996 to an annual average of 4.9 percent. The rise in total national health care expenditures was accompanied by an increase in per capita national medical expenditures. In 1960 the typical American consumed $141 worth of medical care, and by 1996 per capita consumption grew to $3,759 (see table 3–2). This equals an increase of more than 2,500 percent.

Although these statistics clearly indicate that health care expenditures have risen substantially in the United States, they tell only part of the story, because the U.S. economy also grew over the same period. A more telling statistic is the ratio of medical spending to national income, because it measures the portion of the economic pie allocated to the production of medical care. These figures appear in the bottom row of table 3–2. In 1960, health care expenditures as a percentage of GDP equaled

5.1 percent, and by 1980 this number had grown to 8.9 percent.[9] The ratio continued to grow throughout the 1980s and by 1993 reached 13.6 percent. Since that time it has remained constant, suggesting that from 1993 through 1996, health care expenditures have grown at the rate of the overall economy. Before 1993, however, health care expenditures in the United States grew at a much faster pace than the economy as a whole. As a result, the portion of GDP allotted to the production of health care services increased significantly.

### Sources and Uses of Medical Funds in the United States in 1993

Table 3–3 provides detailed figures regarding the sources and uses of health care funds in the United States in 1996. The sources of funds tell us where the health care dollars came from, while the uses indicate how the funds were spent. In 1996, 53.3 percent of the funds spent on national health care came from the private sector, down from approximately 76 percent in 1960. The bulk of this decrease took place in the mid-1960s, when the Medicare and Medicaid programs were first introduced. Since 1990, the share of national health expenditures emanating from the private sector has dropped slightly from 59 percent to slightly more than 53 percent.

The mix between private insurance and out-of-pocket payments has also changed in recent years. Private insurance expanded its role as a source of funds and substituted partially for out-of-pocket payments. Specifically, in 1980, private health insurance provided the funding for 28 percent of total national health expenditures, and out-of-pocket payments accounted for 24.4 percent. By 1996, approximately one-third of total national health care expenditures came from private health insurance, while out-of-pocket payments fell to about 17 percent. Other private expenditures, which included funds from business to provide health care services directly to employees, philanthropic sources, private construction, and nonpatient revenue sources (i.e., revenue from hospital gift shops), accounted for 4.2 percent of the total in 1996, and this percentage has remained relatively stable over time.

Public sources accounted for the remaining 46.7 percent of total national health care expenditures in 1996. The single largest source of public funds in 1996 was the Medicare program that provides medical insurance to disabled individuals and those 65 years of age and older, with 19.6 percent of the total; this was up from 14.6 percent in 1980. The Medicaid program that provides insurance to some segments of the poor accounted for 14.3 percent of the total, an increase of approximately four percentage points since 1980. Other government expenditures, which reflected spending on other state and local public assistance programs, expenditures by the Department of Veterans Affairs, and outlays for state and local hospitals made up 12.8 percent of the total expenditures in 1996.

The single largest use of medical funds in 1996 was hospital services, which accounted for 34.6 percent of the total. The next largest use of funds was physician services (19.5 percent). Together these two uses of medical dollars made up

---

[9]GDP stands for *gross domestic product* and equals the total value of goods and services produced within a country's borders over a particular period of time. GDP is measured on an annual basis in this case.

| TABLE 3-3 | A BREAKDOWN OF THE SOURCES AND USES OF HEALTH CARE FUNDS IN THE UNITED STATES, 1996 |

## Sources of Funds

| Revenue Source | Amount (in billions of dollars) | Percentage of Total |
|---|---|---|
| **Private** | $552.0 | 53.3% |
| Private health insurance | 337.3 | 32.6 |
| Out-of-pocket payments | 171.2 | 16.5 |
| Other private payments | 43.5 | 4.2 |
| **Public** | $483.1 | 46.7 |
| Medicare | 203.1 | 19.6 |
| Medicaid | 147.7 | 14.3 |
| Other government programs | 132.2 | 12.8 |
| **Total** | 1,035.1 | 100 |

## Uses of Funds

| Spending Category | Amount (in billions of dollars) | Percentage of Total |
|---|---|---|
| Hospital care | $358.5 | 34.6% |
| Physician services | 202.1 | 19.5 |
| Dentist services | 47.6 | 4.6 |
| Other professional services | 58.0 | 5.6 |
| Home health care | 30.2 | 2.9 |
| Nursing home care | 78.5 | 7.6 |
| Drugs and other nondurable products | 91.4 | 8.8 |
| Program administration and net cost of private insurance | 60.9 | 5.9 |
| Government public health | 35.5 | 3.4 |
| Research and construction | 31.5 | 3.0 |
| Other | 40.9 | 4.0 |
| **Total** | 1,035.1 | 100 |

SOURCE: Katherine R. Levit et al., "National Health Spending Trends in 1996." *Health Affairs* (January/February 1998), exhibits 3 and 4.

approximately 54 percent of the total. It is interesting to note that this percentage has remained relatively constant over the years. In fact, in 1980, the two categories combined to make up 57.7 percent of the total national health care expenditures. The next two largest uses of medical funds in 1996 were drugs and other nondurable products, along with nursing home care, accounting for 8.8 and 7.6 percent of total medical expenditures, respectively. Expenditures in the remaining, smaller categories are also shown in table 3–3.

### SUMMARY

Health, like any other good or service, is desired because it generates utility. Also like other goods and services, health is subject to the law of diminishing marginal utility. This law stipulates that each additional unit of health provides less marginal utility than the previous unit.

The making, or production, of health is influenced by a variety of factors, including the amount of medical care consumed. The positive relation between health and medical care, however, is nonlinear due to the law of diminishing marginal productivity. This law underlies a fundamental production relation that states that health increases at a decreasing rate with additional amounts of medical care, holding other inputs constant. Some of the other factors determining health are the individual's initial endowment of health, socioeconomic status, lifestyle, and environmental factors.

The empirical evidence for both infants and adults indicates that good health depends only moderately on the consumption of medical care. Socioeconomic status and lifestyle appear to play a much greater role in the production of good health.

Medical expenditures in the United States have grown rapidly in recent decades. In 1960 nominal per capita health expenditures equaled approximately $140, and overall health expenditures accounted for 5.1 percent of GDP. By 1996 per capita expenditures equaled almost $3,759, while total health expenditures accounted for 13.6 percent of GDP.

## Review Questions and Problems

1. Describe the factors that make it difficult to measure output in medical care markets.

2. As mentioned at the beginning of the chapter, the life expectancy rate for Glasgow is low primarily because of the residents' lifestyle. Use health production theory to explain what would happen to the relationship between good health and medical care for those residents of Glasgow who improved their lifestyle. Provide a graph to illustrate your explanation.

3. Use health production theory to explain the role gender plays in the production of health during pregnancy. Provide a graph to illustrate your answer.

4. In your own words, use utility analysis to explain why people demand health. How does the law of diminishing marginal utility fit into the analysis?

5. Explain how an increase in income would affect the level of health in a relatively affluent country like the United States compared to a relatively poor country like Haiti.

6. You have just been appointed to the post of surgeon general of the United States. The president wants you to develop an advertising campaign called "A Healthy America by the Year 2000" that encourages Americans to lead a healthier lifestyle. What types of behavior would you try to influence? Why?

7. You have just been hired by a major metropolitan city as a health policy analyst. Your assignment is to devise a plan that city authorities could implement to lower the infant mortality rate. Based on the results cited in this chapter, what types of policies would you recommend? Substantiate your answer.

8. Explain how a change in each of the following factors would alter the shape of the total product curve for medical care.

   *a.* An increase in education.

   *b.* An improvement in lifestyle.

   *c.* An improvement in the environment.

9. Discuss the major sources and uses of medical care funds in the United States.

10. Some people believe cigarette and alcohol advertisements should be banned completely in the United States. If this were the case, what would likely happen to the shapes of the total and marginal product curves for medical care?

## References

Auster, Richard, Irving Leveson, and Deborah Sarachek. "The Production of Health: An Exploratory Study." *Journal of Human Resources* 9 (fall 1969), pp.411–36.

Berger, Mark C., and J. Paul Leigh. "Schooling, Self-Selection, and Health." *Journal of Human Resources* 24 (summer 1989), pp. 433–55.

Berkowitz, Eric N., Roger A. Kerin, and William Rudelius. *Marketing*, 2d ed. Homewood, IL: Richard D. Irwin, 1989.

Breslow, Lester, and James E. Enstrom. "Persistence of Health Habits and Their Relationship to Mortality." *Preventive Medicine* 9 (July 1980), pp. 469–83.

Bunker, John P., et al. "The Role of Medical Care in Determining Health: Creating an Inventory of Benefits." In *Society and Health*, edited by Benjamin C. Amick et al. New York: Oxford University Press, 1995, pp. 305–40.

Corman, Hope, and Michael Grossman. "Determinants of Neonatal Mortality Rates in the U.S." *Journal of Health Economics* 4 (September 1985), pp. 213–36.

Donabedian, Avedis. *The Definition of Quality and Approaches to Its Assessment*. Ann Arbor, MI: Health Administration Press, 1980.

———. "The Quality of Care: How Can It Be Assessed?" *Journal of the American Medical Association* 260 (September 23–30,1988), pp. 1743–48.

Edlin, Gordon, and Eric Golanty. *Health and Wellness: A Holistic Approach*. Boston: Jones and Bartlett Publishers, 1988.

Enthoven, Alain C. *Health Plan*. Reading, MA: Addison-Wesley, 1980.

Ettner, Susan L. "New Evidence on the Relationship between Income and Health." *Journal of Health Economics* 15 (1996), pp. 67–85.

Feinstein, Jonathan S. "The Relationship between Socioeconomic Status and Health: A Review of the Literature." *Milbank Quarterly* 71 (1993), pp. 279–322.

Feldman, Roger, and Michael A. Morrisey. "Health Economics: A Report on the Field." *Journal of Health, Politics, Policy and Law* 15 (fall 1990), pp. 627–46.

France, Kern Russo, and Rajiv Grover. "What Is the Health Care Product?" *Journal of Health Care Marketing* 12 (June 1992), pp. 31–38.

Fuchs, Victor R. *Who Shall Live?* New York: Basic Books, 1975.

———. "Economics, Health and Post-Industrial Society." *Millbank Memorial Fund Quarterly* 57 (1979), pp. 153–82.

Grossman, Michael. *The Demand for Health: A Theoretical and Empirical Investigation.* New York: National Bureau of Economic Research, 1972a.

———. "On the Concept of Health Capital and the Demand for Health." *Journal of Political Economy* 80 (March–April 1972b): pp. 223–55.

Guralnik, Jack M., et al. "Education Status and Active Life Expectancy among Older Blacks and Whites. *New England Journal of Medicine* 329 (July 8, 1993), pp. 100–116.

Hadley, Jack. *More Medical Care, Better Health.* Washington, DC: The Urban Institute Press, 1982.

Horwitz, Tony. "Lethal Cuisine Takes High Toll in Glasgow, West's Sickest City." *The Wall Street Journal*, September 22, 1992, p. A1.

Joyce, Theodore, Andrew D. Racine, and Naci Mocan. "The Consequences and Costs of Maternal Substance Abuse in New York City." *Journal of Health Economics* 11 (1992), pp. 297–314.

Leigh, Paul J., and James F. Fries. "Health Habits, Health Care Use and Costs in a Sample of Retirees." *Inquiry* 29 (spring 1992), pp. 44–54.

Levit, Katherine R., et al. "National Health Spending Trends in 1996." *Health Affairs* 17 (January/February 1998), pp. 35–51.

*Mosby Medical Encyclopedia.* New York City: C. V. Mosby, 1992.

Newhouse, Joseph P., and Lindy J. Friedlander. "The Relationship between Medical Resources and Measures of Health: Some Additional Evidence." *Journal of Human Resources* 15 (Spring 1980), pp. 200–218.

Pappas, Gregory et al. "The Increasing Disparity in Mortality between Socioeconomic Groups in the United States, 1960 and 1986." *New England Journal of Medicine* 329 (July 8, 1993), pp. 103–109.

Santerre, Rexford E., Stephen G. Grubaugh, and Andrew J. Stollar. "Government Intervention in Health Care Markets and Health Care Outcomes: Some International Evidence." *Cato Journal* 11 (spring–summer, 1991), pp. 1–12.

Ventura, Stephanie J. et al. "Births and Deaths: United States, 1996." *Monthly Vital Statistics Report* 46 (Supplement 2, September 11, 1997).

# 4

# The Demand for Medical Services

**M**any people have the misconception that economic theory has little relevance to the demand for medical care because economic factors are not important when an individual needs urgent medical attention. Recall Joe in Chapter 1, who awoke one night with a pain in his chest and realized he was having a heart attack. It is highly unlikely that he and his wife considered the price of medical care as Joe was rushed to the hospital.

However, most visits to a physician's office and the majority of visits to a hospital emergency room are not of a life-threatening nature. Thus, for many medical care transactions, there is sufficient time to make conscious choices, and price often plays an important role in the determination of choices. Results of a recent survey of various types of health care providers and insurers substantiate the critical role price plays in determining the demand for medical care (Winslow, 1994). According to the survey, price was ranked as more important than patient satisfaction or access to doctors, among other factors, in determining the economic success of health care providers.

This chapter explores the demand side of the medical care market. The chapter highlights

- The theoretical derivation of the demand curve for medical services.

- Economic and noneconomic variables that influence the demand for medical services.

- The impact of health insurance on the demand for medical services.

- The concept of elasticity of demand.

- A review of the empirical literature concerning the factors that determine the demand for medical care.

# The Demand for Health Care Services and the Law of Demand

To derive the demand curve for medical services, we must first establish the relation between the quantity of medical services and utility. Recall from Chapter 3 that the stock of health can be treated as a durable good that generates utility and is subject to the law of diminishing marginal utility.[1] This means that each incremental improvement in health generates successively smaller additions to total utility. We also know that medical services are an input in the production of health because a person consumes medical care services for the express purpose of maintaining, restoring, or improving health. However, the law of diminishing marginal productivity causes the marginal improvement to health brought about by each additional unit of medical care consumed to decrease.

From this discussion, it follows that medical care indirectly provides utility. Specifically, medical care helps to produce health, which in turn generates utility. Consequently, utility can be specified as a function of the quantity of medical care. Figure 4–1 depicts the relation between the level of medical care consumed and utility. Utility is specified on the vertical axis, and the quantity of medical care ($q$) is measured on the horizontal axis. The shape of the total utility curve indicates that utility increases at a decreasing rate with respect to medical care, or that medical care services are subject to diminishing marginal utility. Marginal utility decreases because (1) each successive unit of medical care generates a smaller improvement in health than the previous unit (due to the law of diminishing marginal productivity) and (2) each increase in health, in turn, generates a smaller increase in utility (due to the law of diminishing marginal utility).

## The Utility-Maximizing Rule

Given market prices at a point in time, consumers must decide which combination of goods and services, including medical care, to purchase with their fixed incomes. According to microeconomic theory, each consumer chooses the bundle of goods and services that maximizes utility. Without working through the mathematics underlying the process, logic dictates that consumer utility is maximized when the marginal utility gained from the last dollar spent on each product is equal across all goods and services purchased.[2] This condition is known as the **utility-maximizing rule,** and it basically states that total utility reaches its peak when the consumer receives the maximum "bang for the buck" in terms of marginal utility per dollar of income from each and every good. In mathematical terms, the rule states that utility is maximized when

**(4–1)** $MU_q/P_q = MU_z/P_z$

---

[1] As a reminder, note that we continue to ignore the intermediate step between the stock of health, the services it provides, and utility.

[2] That is, assuming all prices are known, income is spent over the period in question, and all products are subject to the law of diminishing marginal utility.

**FIGURE 4–1**    THE RELATIONSHIP BETWEEN UTILITY AND
MEDICAL SERVICES

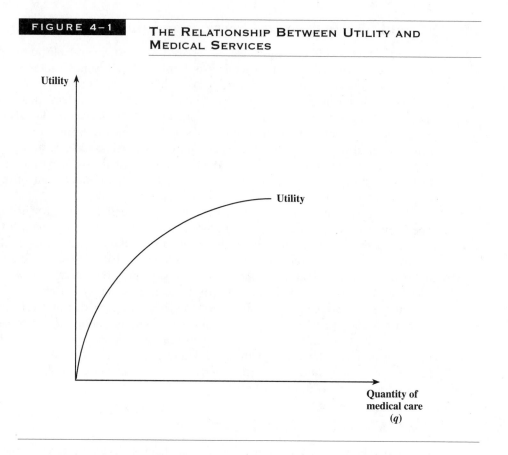

where $MU_q$ represents the marginal utility received from the last unit of medical care purchased, $q$, and $MU_z$ equals the marginal utility derived from the last unit of all other goods, $z$. The latter good is often referred to as a *composite good* in economics. To illustrate why the utility-maximizing rule must hold, suppose that

**(4–2)**    $MU_q/P_q > MU_z/P_z.$

In this instance, the last dollar spent on medical care generates more additional utility than the last dollar spent on all other goods. The consumer can increase total utility by reallocating expenditures and purchasing more units of medical care and fewer units of all other goods. As the consumer purchases more medical services at the expense of all other goods (remember that the consumer's income and the composite good's price are fixed), the marginal utility of medical care falls and the marginal utility of other goods increases. This, in turn, causes the value of $MU_q/P_q$ to fall and the value of $MU_z/P_z$ to increase. The consumer purchases additional medical services until the equality in equation 4–1 again holds, or the last dollar spent on each product generates the same amount of additional satisfaction. At this point, total utility is maximized and any further changes in spending patterns will negatively affect total utility.

## The Law of Demand

The equilibrium condition specified in equation 4–1 can be used to trace out the demand curve for a particular medical service, such as physician services. For simplicity, assume the prices of all other goods and income remain constant and initially the consumer is purchasing the optimal mix of physician services and all other goods. Now assume the price of physician services increases. In this case, $MU_q/P_q$ is less than $MU_z/P_z$ (where $MU_q$ and $P_q$ now specifically represent the marginal utility and price of physician services, respectively). Consequently, the consumer receives more satisfaction per dollar from consuming all other goods. In reaction to the price increase, the consumer purchases fewer units of physician services and more units of all other goods. This reallocation continues until $MU_q/P_q$ increases and $MU_z/P_z$ decreases and the equilibrium condition of equation 4–1 is again in force such that the last dollar spent on each good generates an equal amount of utility. Thus, an inverse relation exists between the price and the quantity demanded of physician services.

If the price of physician services continually changes, we can determine a number of points representing the relation between the price and the quantity demanded of physician services. Using this information, we can map out a demand curve like the one depicted in figure 4–2, where the horizontal axis indicates the amount of physician services consumed as measured by the number of visits and the vertical axis equals the price of physician services. The curve is downward sloping and reflects the inverse relation between the quantity demanded and the price of physician services, *ceteris paribus*.[3] For example, if the price of physician services equals $P_0$, the consumer is willing and able to purchase $q_0$. Notice that if the price falls to $P_1$, the consumer purchases $q_1$ amount of physician services.

In this case, price represents the per-unit out-of-pocket expense the consumer incurs when purchasing medical services from a physician. As such, it equals the amount the consumer must pay after the impact of third-party payments has been taken into account. Naturally, if the visit to the physician is not covered by a third party, the actual price of the visit equals the out-of-pocket expense.

Another way to illustrate the inverse relation between price and the quantity demanded of physician services is with the substitution and income effects of a price change. Both of these effects predict that a higher price will lead to a smaller quantity demanded and, conversely, a lower price will result in a greater quantity demanded. According to the substitution effect, a decrease in the price of physician services causes the consumer to substitute away from the relatively higher-priced medical goods, such as hospital outpatient services, and purchase more physician services. That is, lower-priced services are substituted for higher-priced ones. As a result, the quantity demanded of physician services increases as price decreases.

---

[3]Recall from Chapter 1 that *ceteris paribus* is a Latin phrase meaning "all other things held constant."

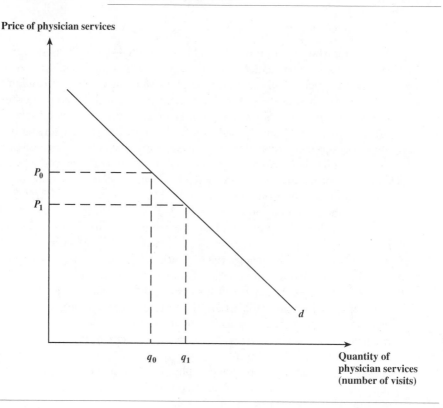

FIGURE 4-2

### THE INDIVIDUAL DEMAND CURVE FOR PHYSICIAN SERVICES

According to the income effect, a lower price also increases the real purchasing power of the consumer. Because medical care is assumed to be a normal good (i.e., the quantity demanded of medical services increases with income), the quantity demanded of physician services increases with the rise in purchasing power. That also generates an inverse relation between price and quantity demanded because as price falls, real income increases and quantity demanded rises. Taken together, the substitution and income effects indicate that the quantity demanded of physician services decreases as price increases.

In summary, figure 4–2 captures the inverse relationship between the price the consumer pays for medical care (in this instance, physician services) and the quantity demanded. The curve represents the amount of medical care the consumer is willing and able to purchase at every price. Utility analysis, or the income and substitutions effects, can be used to theoretically generate this relationship. This negative relationship is sometimes referred to as the **law of demand.** It is important to note that the demand for medical care is a *derived* demand, because it depends on the demand for

| FIGURE 4–3 | SHIFTS IN THE INDIVIDUAL DEMAND CURVE FOR PHYSICIAN SERVICES |

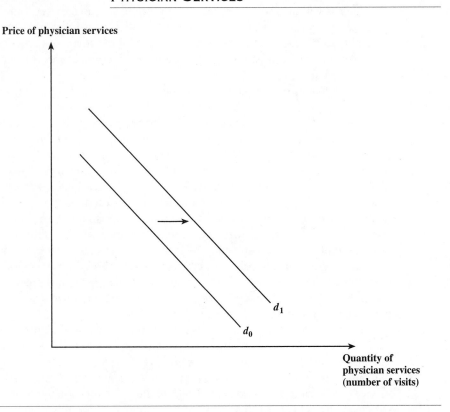

good health. A visit to a dentist illustrates this point quite nicely. An individual receives no utility directly from having a cavity filled. Rather, utility is generated from an improvement in dental health.

Of course, other economic and noneconomic variables also influence the demand for health care. Unlike price, which causes a movement along the demand curve, other factors influence quantity demanded by altering the position of the demand curve. These other economic and noneconomic determinants of demand are the topic of the next section.

### Other Economic Demand-Side Factors

Real income is another economic variable that is likely to affect the demand for medical services. Because medical care is generally assumed to be a normal good, any increase in real income, which represents an increase in purchasing power, should cause the demand for medical services to rise. Figure 4–3 illustrates what happens to the demand for physician services when real income increases. The increase in income causes the demand curve to shift to the right, from $d_0$ to $d_1$, because at each price the consumer is willing and able to purchase more physician services. Similarly, for each quantity of medical services, the consumer is willing to pay a higher price. This is attributable to the fact that at least some portion of the increase in income is spent on physician services. Conversely, a decrease in real income causes the demand curve to shift to the left.[4]

The demand for a specific type of medical service is also likely to depend on the prices of other goods, particularly other types of medical services. If two or more goods are jointly used for consumption purposes, economists say that they are *complements* in consumption: Because the goods are consumed together, an increase in the price of one good inversely influences the demand for the other. For example, the demand for eyewear (i.e., glasses or contact lenses) and the services of an optometrist are likely to be highly complementary. Normally, an individual has an eye examination before purchasing eyewear. If these two goods are complements in consumption, the demand for optometric services should increase in response to a drop in the price of eyewear. As a result, the demand curve for optometric services shifts to the right. Another example of a complementary relation exists between obstetric and pediatric services. An increase in the price of pediatric services should inversely influence the demand for obstetric services. If, for example, a woman postpones pregnancy because of the high cost of pediatric services, her demand for obstetric services also falls. The demand curve for obstetric services shifts to the left.

It is also possible for two or more goods to satisfy the same wants or provide the same characteristics. If that is the case, economists say that these goods are *substitutes* in consumption: The demand for one good is directly related to a change in the price of a substitute good. For example, suppose physician services and hospital outpatient services are substitutes in consumption. As the price of outpatient services increases, the consumer is likely to alter consumption patterns and purchase more physician services because the price of a visit to the doctor is cheaper in relative terms. That causes the demand curve for physician services to shift to the right. Generic and brand-name drugs provide another example of two substitute goods. The demand for brand-name drugs should decrease with a decline in the price of generic drugs. If so, the demand curve for brand-name drugs shifts to the left. Finally, eyeglasses and contact lenses are likely to be substitutes in consumption.

Time costs also influence the quantity demanded of medical services. Time costs include the monetary cost of travel, such as bus fare or gasoline, plus the opportunity cost of time. The opportunity cost of an individual's time represents the dollar value of the activities the person forgoes when acquiring medical services. For example, if a plumber who earns $50 an hour takes two hours off from work to visit a dentist, the

---

[4]Some goods are referred to as *inferior* goods. This is because the demand for these goods decreases as income increases. A classic nonmedical example is hamburger. As real income increases, the consumer may prefer to buy more expensive cuts of meat and purchase less hamburger. In the medical sector, hospital outpatient services may be an example of an inferior good. As income increases, the consumer may prefer to visit a private physician to receive individual care rather than outpatient services. As a result, the demand for outpatient services may decrease as income increases. Some researchers have found that tooth extractions represent an inferior dental service.

opportunity cost of the time equals $100. The implication is that the opportunity cost of time is directly related to a person's wage rate. Given time costs, it is not surprising that children and elderly people often fill doctors' waiting rooms. Time costs can accrue while traveling to and from a medical provider, waiting to see the provider, and experiencing delays in securing an appointment. In other words, travel costs increase the farther an individual has to travel to see a physician, the longer the wait at the doctor's office, and the longer the delay in getting an appointment. It stands to reason that the demand for medical care falls as time costs increase (i.e., the demand curve shifts to the left).

### The Relationship between Health Insurance and the Demand for Medical Services

The growth of health insurance coverage is one of the most significant developments in the health care field over the past several decades. It has had a profound influence on the allocation of resources within the medical care market, primarily through its impact on the out-of-pocket prices of health care services. Insight 4–1 illustrates how dramatic this change has been. Out-of-pocket payments for health care dropped from almost half of total expenditures in 1960 to approximately one-sixth in 1996. Even more striking, out-of-pocket payments for hospital care fell from 20.7 percent in 1960 to a mere 2.6 percent in 1996. Given that various features are associated with health insurance policies, it is impossible to discuss the economic implications of each one. Here we will focus on three of the more common features of health insurance policies: coinsurance, indemnity insurance, and deductibles.

**Coinsurance.** Many health insurance plans, particularly private plans, have a **coinsurance** component. Under a coinsurance plan, the consumer pays some fixed percentage of the cost of health care and the insurance carrier picks up the other portion. For example, under a plan with a coinsurance rate of 20 percent (a common arrangement), the consumer pays 20 cents out of every dollar spent on health care and the carrier picks up the remaining 80 cents. As you can imagine, an insurance plan like this one has a significant impact on the demand for health care because it effectively lowers the out-of-pocket price of health care by 80 percent.

Let's begin our discussion of coinsurance coverage by looking at the demand curve for medical care from an alternative perspective. We normally think of the demand curve as revealing the amount of a good that a consumer is willing and able to buy at various prices. However, a demand curve also shows the consumer's willingness to pay (or marginal benefit) for each unit of a good. The negative slope of the curve indicates that the willingness to pay falls as more of the good is consumed due to the law of diminishing marginal utility.

For instance, the demand curve $d_{WO}$ (WO = without insurance) in figure 4–4 stands for the consumer's demand or willingness-to-pay curve without insurance coverage. This demand curve reveals that the consumer is willing to pay $50 for the fifth unit of medical services. If $50 is the actual price paid for medical services, the consumer purchases five visits in the process of maximizing utility. Notice, however, that the consumer's willingness to pay for the first four units, as revealed

| FIGURE 4-4 | THE DEMAND CURVE FOR MEDICAL SERVICES WITH COINSURANCE |
| --- | --- |

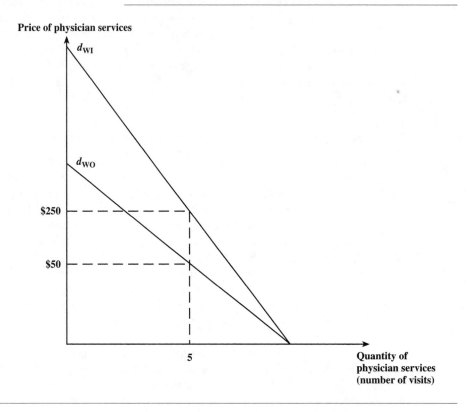

by the demand curve, exceeds the actual price of $50. The difference is referred to as **consumer surplus** and reflects the net benefits received from consuming the physician services.

Now suppose the consumer acquires a health insurance plan that calls for her to pay a certain fraction, $C_0$, of the actual price, $P$, of medical services. In this case, the insurance coverage drives a wedge between the willingness to pay and the actual price paid for the medical services. Because this utility-maximizing consumer determines the appropriate amount of medical services to buy by equating her willingness to pay (marginal benefit) to the out-of-pocket price (marginal cost), the relationship between the actual and out-of-pocket price can be specified by the following equation:

**(4–3)** $\quad P_w = C_0 P.$

Here $P_w$ stands for the consumer's willingness to pay for the last unit, and $C_0$ represents the coinsurance amount. If we solve equation 4–3 for the actual price, we get

**(4–4)**   $P = P_w/C_0.$

Because the coinsurance, $C_0$, is less than 1, it follows that the actual price paid for medical services is greater than the out-of-pocket price the consumer pays. For example, if she is willing to pay $50 for five visits to a doctor and the coinsurance is 20 percent of the full price, the actual price equals $250 per visit, or $50/.2.

The demand curve labeled $d_{WI}$ (WI = with insurance) in figure 4–4 reflects the total demand curve for medical services that takes into account the coinsurance paid by the insured. The vertical distance between $d_{WI}$ and the horizontal axis represents the total price for units of medical services. That can be broken down into the amount the consumer pays and the amount the insurance carrier pays. The portion of the total price the consumer pays as an out-of-pocket payment, or *copayment*, equals the distance between the horizontal axis and the $d_{WO}$ demand curve. The remaining distance between the two curves represents the amount the insurance carrier pays. It represents the wedge that coinsurance drives between the consumer's willingness to pay and the total price for medical services.[5]

It is easy to see from this analysis that a reduction in the coinsurance rate causes $d_{WI}$ to rotate clockwise and pivot off the point where $d_{WO}$ crosses the horizontal axis. At a zero willingness-to-pay price, insurance has no bearing on quantity demanded because medical care is a free good to the individual. In addition, $d_{WI}$ becomes steeper as the coinsurance, $C_0$, decreases in value as indicated by equation 4–4. That makes intuitive sense, because we expect the consumer to become less sensitive to changes in the total price as the coinsurance declines.

In the case where the consumer has full coverage ($C_0 = 0$), the demand curve $d_{WI}$ rotates out to its fullest extent and becomes completely vertical. This is shown in figure 4–5. Because the consumer faces a zero price, she consumes medical care as though it were a free good, when in reality it has a nonzero price. Equation 4–4 can be used to illustrate that point. As $C_0$ approaches zero, the total price is potentially infinity even when $P_w$ equals zero.

**Indemnity Insurance.**   With **indemnity insurance,** the insurance carrier pays a fixed amount for various types of medical services purchased. For example, the insurance may pay $150 for each overnight visit to a hospital. If the bill exceeds this amount, the consumer picks up the difference in the form of an out-of-pocket payment. Figure 4–6 shows the impact of indemnity insurance on the demand for health care. Let $d$ represent a linear noninsured demand curve for hospital services and $A$ the fixed payment received for each overnight stay. The indemnity insurance shifts the demand curve for hospital services upward in a parallel fashion by the amount $A$. The

---

[5] *Coinsurance* refers to the percentage, while *copayment* refers to the amount of costs paid by the insured consumer.

**FIGURE 4-5**   THE DEMAND CURVE FOR MEDICAL SERVICES WITH 100 PERCENT COVERAGE

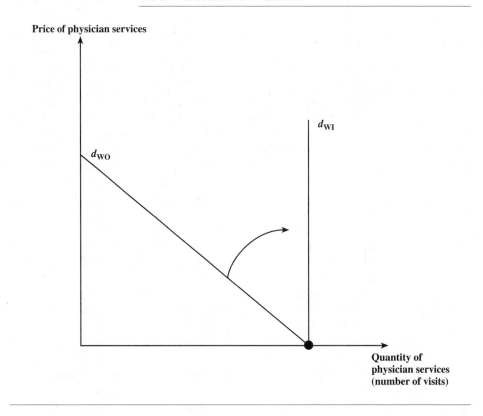

new demand curve, $d_*$, considers the impact of indemnity insurance on the demand for hospital services. An increase in the level of payment, $A$, causes the demand curve to shift upward even farther.

**Deductibles.**   Many insurance policies have a deductible whereby the consumer must pay out of pocket a fixed amount of health care costs per calendar year before coverage begins. For example, the plan may call for the individual to pay the initial $100 of health care expenses with a limit of $400 per family per year. Once the deductible is met, the insurance carrier pays all or some portion of the remaining medical bills, depending on how the plan is specified. From the insurance carrier's perspective, the purpose of a deductible is to lower costs. This is accomplished in two ways.

First, the deductible is likely to lower administrative costs because fewer small claims will be filed over the course of a year. Second, the deductible is likely to have a negative impact on the demand for health care. The extent to which this is true, however, is difficult to determine and depends on such factors as the cost of the medical

FIGURE 4-6    THE DEMAND CURVE FOR MEDICAL SERVICES WITH INDEMNITY IINSURANCE

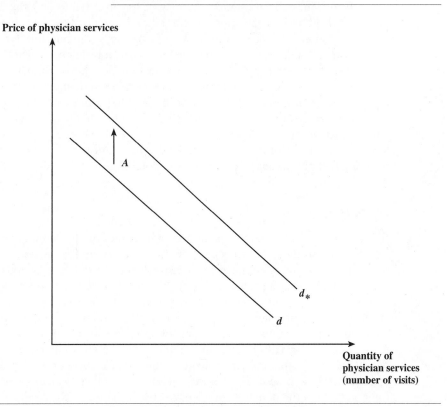

episode, the point in time when the medical care is demanded, and the probability of needing additional medical care for the remainder of the period. To illustrate, assume a new deductible is put in place at the beginning of each calendar year and once the deductible is met, the consumer has full medical coverage. It is easy to see that the extent to which a deductible influences the demand for medical services for any one medical episode is likely to be negatively related to the cost of the medical services involved. For instance, if the consumer faces a potentially large medical bill for an operation, the existence of a deductible is likely to have very little impact on demand. This is because in relative terms, the deductible represents very little money. On the other hand, a deductible may play a crucial role in the decision to purchase medical care if the cost of such care is relatively inexpensive. In this case, the out-of-pocket cost is substantial relative to the total cost, and the consumer may elect not to purchase the medical care or postpone the purchase to a later date.

It is slightly more difficult to understand how the health of the individual, along with the time of the year, influences the impact of a deductible on demand. The best way to explain this is with an example. Consider a normally healthy individual who contracts the flu late in November and has incurred no medical expenses up to this point. Under these circumstances, he may be less inclined to visit the doctor. This is because he will have little opportunity to take advantage of the fact that health care is a free good after he makes his initial visit to the physician and fulfills the deductible. On the other hand, this same individual is much more likely to visit the physician if he catches the flu early in February and his overall health is such that he can expect to visit the physician three or four more times over the remainder of the year. By visiting the doctor and meeting the deductible, he lowers the cost of any future visits to zero for the rest of the year. Therefore, a deductible is likely to have the greatest negative impact on the demand for medical care when the cost of the medical episode is low, the need for care is late in the calendar year, and the probability of needing future care is slight because the person is in good health.

## Moral Hazard

Before we leave the subject of the impact of insurance on the demand for medical care, we need to introduce the concept of moral hazard. **Moral hazard** refers to the situation where consumers alter their behavior when provided with health insurance. For instance, health insurance may induce consumers to take fewer precautions to prevent illnesses or to shop very little for the best medical prices. In response to health insurance, consumers may act in a fashion that leads to an increase in the consumption of medical care. Let's illustrate this point by referring to figure 4–4. According to the graph, a consumer without insurance purchases five units of medical services at a price of $50 per unit. If that consumer acquires full medical coverage such that the insurer's coinsurance rate, $C_0$, equals zero, the quantity demanded of medical care increases to the point where the demand curve crosses the horizontal axis. At this point, the consumer consumes medical care as though it were a free good because she faces a zero price. Thus, any extension of medical insurance coverage has the potential to increase the consumption of medical care because consumers no longer pay the full price. The availability and extensiveness of health insurance may have a profound effect on medical care expenditures. Chapter 13 examines the implications of moral hazard in more detail in a discussion of the private health insurance industry.

## Noneconomic Determinants of the Demand for Medical Services

Four general noneconomic factors influence the demand for medical services: tastes and preferences, physical and mental profile, state of health, and quality of care.

*Taste and preference* factors include such personal characteristics as marital status, education, and lifestyle, which might affect how people value their healthy time (i.e., their marginal utility of health), or might lead to a greater preference for certain types of medical services. Marital status is likely to impact the demand for health care in the marketplace primarily through its effect on the production of health care in the home. A married individual is likely to demand less medical care, particularly hospital

# Out-of-Pocket Health Expenditures in 1996

Table 1 indicates that total health care expenditures were rising at the same time that the percent financed directly by consumers as out-of-pocket payments was falling. In 1960 consumers directly financed almost half (48.7 percent) of health care expenditures. This percentage dropped continuously throughout the period and by 1996 consumers financed slightly less than one-fifth (16.5 percent) of total health care expenditures as out-of-pocket payments. This percentage decrease in out-of-pocket expenditures can be attributed to a simultaneous growth in private and public health insurance coverage.

The lower portion of table 1 also presents the portion of health care costs financed by out-of-pocket payments for various categories of

expenditures in 1996. The data indicate that the percentage of out-of-pocket payments varied widely across categories. Out-of-pocket payments accounted for only 2.6 percent of hospital expenditures and 14.6 percent of physician expenditures. At the other extreme, less than half of dentist expenditures and 55 percent of drug and other medical nondurable expenditures were the result of out-of-pocket expenditures. Out-of-pocket payments account for almost one-third of nursing home care expenditures.

It is interesting to note that there appears to be a strong inverse correlation between the amount spent on health care and the percent financed by out-of-pocket payments. This is true not only over time but also across types of medical expenditures.

| TABLE 1 | PERCENT OF OUT-OF-POCKET PAYMENTS IN THE UNITED STATES FROM 1960 TO 1996 |
|---|---|

### National Health Expenditures and Percent of Out-of-Pocket Payments for Selected Years

| | 1960 | 1970 | 1980 | 1990 | 1993 | 1994 | 1995 | 1996 |
|---|---|---|---|---|---|---|---|---|
| National health expenditures (Billions of current dollars) | $26.9 | $73.2 | $247.3 | $699.5 | $895.1 | 945.7 | $991.4 | $1,035.1 |
| Percent out-of-pocket | 48.7% | 34.0% | 24.4% | 20.6% | 18.3% | 17.4% | 16.8% | 16.5% |

### Percent of Out-of-Pocket Payments for Selected Categories of Health Care Expenditures in 1996

| | 1996 |
|---|---|
| Total | 16.5% |
| Hospital care | 2.6% |
| Physician services | 14.6% |
| Dentist services | 46.4% |
| Drugs and medical nondurables | 55.0% |
| Nursing home care | 31.5% |

SOURCE: *Health Care Financing Administration*, "1996 National Health Expenditures," table 11. http:/www.hcfa.gov/stats/stats.htm.

*(continued)*

## (continued)

From 1960 to 1996 when total medical expenditures grew almost fortyfold, out-of-pocket payments fell from just under 50 percent to approximately one-sixth of total expenditures. Also, the single largest category of medical expenditures in 1996 was hospital care with $358.5 billion. It had the lowest percentage of out-of-pocket payments. Expenditures on physician services was the next largest category and in this case only 14.6 percent of the expenditures were directly financed by consumers. Two of the smaller categories were dentist services and drugs and other nondurables, and in these two instances out-of-pocket payments equaled 46.4 percent and 55 percent, respectively. This cursory evidence is consistent with the hypothesis that a lower out-of-pocket price increases the quantity demanded of medical services. However, it could also reflect just the opposite—that the demand for third-party insurance coverage increases with the magnitude of health care costs. That possibility is discussed further in Chapter 5.

care, because of the availability of a spouse to care for him at home, such as when recuperating from an illness.

The impact of education on the demand for medical care in the marketplace is difficult to predict. On the one hand, a consumer with additional education may be more willing to seek medical care to slow down the rate of health depreciation because that consumer may have a better understanding of the potential impact of medical care on health. In other words, an individual with a high level of education may be more inclined to visit a dentist for periodic examinations. As a result, we should observe a direct relation between education and demand.

On the other hand, an individual with a high level of education may make more efficient use of home-produced health care services to slow down the rate of health depreciation and, as a result, demand less medical care services in the marketplace. For instance, such an individual may be more likely to understand the value of preventive medicine (e.g., proper diet, exercise). In addition, the individual may be more likely to recognize the early warning signs of illness and be more apt to visit a health care provider when symptoms first occur. As a result, health care problems are addressed early when treatment has a greater probability of success and is less costly. That means that we should observe an inverse relation between the level of education and the demand for medical care, particularly acute care.

Finally, lifestyle variables, such as whether the individual smokes cigarettes or drinks alcohol in excessive amounts, affect health status and consequently the amount of health care demanded. For example, a person may try to compensate for the detrimental health impact of smoking by consuming more health care services. That translates into an increased demand for medical care.

The *profile* variable considers the impact of such factors as gender, race/ethnicity, and age on the demand for medical services. For instance, females generally demand more health care services than males primarily because of childbearing. In addition, certain diseases, such as cardiovascular disease, osteoporosis, immunologic diseases (e.g., thyroid disease and rheumatoid arthritis), mental disorders, and Alzheimer's disease, are more prevalent in women than men (Miller, 1994). Age also plays a vital role in determining the demand for medical care. As we stated in the preceding chapter, as an individual ages, the overall stock of health begins to depreciate. To compensate for this loss in health, the demand for medical care is likely to increase with age, at least beyond the middle years (the demand curve shifts to the right). Thus, we should observe a direct relation between age and the demand for medical care.

*State of health* controls for the fact that sicker people demand more medical services, everything else held constant. As you might expect, health status and the demand for health care are also likely to be directly related to the severity of the illness. For instance, a person who is born with a medical problem, such as hemophilia, is likely to have a much higher than average demand for medical care. In economics jargon, an individual who is endowed with less health is likely to demand more health care in an attempt to augment the overall stock of health.

Finally, although nebulous and impossible to quantify, the *quality of care* is also likely to impact the demand for medical care. Because quality cannot be measured directly, it is usually assumed to be positively related to the amount and types of inputs used to produce medical care. Feldstein (1967, pp. 158–62) defines the quality of care as "a catch-all term to denote the general level of amenities to patients as well as additional expenditures on professional staff and equipment." For instance, a consumer may feel that larger hospitals provide better quality care than smaller ones because they have more specialists on staff along with more sophisticated equipment. Or, that same individual may think that physicians who have graduated from prestigious medical schools provide a higher quality of care than those who have not. It matters little whether the difference in the quality of medical care provided is real or illusory. What matters is that the consumer perceives differences in quality actually exist.

With regard to the example above, it is certainly not the case that larger hospitals provide better care for all types of hospital services. However, if the consumer generally feels that larger hospitals provide better services, the demand for medical services at larger hospitals will be higher than at smaller ones. As Feldstein's definition indicates, quality can also depend upon things that have little to do with the actual production of effective medical care. For example, the consumer may have a preference for a physician who has a pleasant office with a comfortable waiting room along with courteous nurses. Thus, any increase in the quality of care provided is likely to increase that consumer's demand for medical care regardless of whether it affects the actual production of health care.

Before we move on, we must make a distinction between a movement along the demand curve and a shift of the curve. A change in the price of medical services generates a change in the quantity demanded, and this is represented by a movement along the demand curve. If any of the other factors change, such as income or time costs, the demand curve for medical services shifts. This shift is referred to as a change in demand. Thus, a change in the quantity demanded is illustrated by a movement along the demand curve, while a change in demand is illustrated by a shift of the curve.

In summary, let's review the variables we expect to influence an individual's demand for medical care. Economic theory indicates that the demand equation should look something like the following:

**(4-5)**  Quantity  = *f*(out-of-pocket price, real income, time costs,
demanded    prices of substitutes and complements, tastes and
preferences, profile, state of health, and quality of care)

Equation 4–5 states that the quantity demanded of medical services is a function of, or depends upon, the general factors listed.

## The Market Demand for Health Care

Up to now, we have been discussing the individual's demand for medical care services. The market demand for medical care, such as physician services, equals the total demand by all consumers in a given market. In graphical terms, we can construct the market demand curve for medical care services by horizontally summing the individual demand curves. This curve represents the amount of medical services that the entire market is willing and able to purchase at every given price. For example, if the average price of a visit to a doctor is $50 and at this price consumer A is willing to see a physician three times over the course of a year while consumer B is willing to make four visits, the total, or market, demand for physician services is seven visits per year at $50 per visit. The market demand curve is downward sloping for the same reasons the individual demand curves are downward sloping. In addition, the factors that shift the individual demand curves also shift the overall market demand curve, providing the changes take place on a marketwide basis. The market demand curve also shifts if the overall number of consumers in the market increases or decreases. For instance, the demand for medical care in a particular community may increase if an influx of new residents occurs. This causes the market demand curve to shift to the right.

## The Fuzzy Demand Curve

Up to this point, we have assumed the market demand curve for medical care is a well-defined line, implying a precise relation between price and quantity demanded. In reality this is usually not the case, and we need to refer to the derivation of the demand curve for medical care to see why. Recall that the demand for medical care is a derived demand and depends on the demand for health and the extent to which medical care influences the production of health. The relation between medical care and health, however, is far from exact. That is because there is a considerable lack of medical knowledge concerning the efficacy of certain types of medical interventions. As a result, health care providers disagree about the treatment of some types of medical problems, and the demand for medical services becomes fuzzier. For example, there is debate among physicians concerning when surgery is necessary for elderly males with prostate cancer.

## INSIGHT 4 – 2

# Chicken Soup or Physician Care for the Common Cold?

When health insurance coverage allows consumers to pay a zero out-of-pocket price, they tend to consume large amounts of medical services because of the moral hazard problem. This economic relation has presented some problems for the Canadian health care system, because all citizens are covered by a national health insurance program and receive free medical care. The following article explains how free care, or the zero price for medical services, may have led some Canadian consumers to unnecessarily seek professional help for the common cold.[1]

Ontario's socialized health-care system has a new prescription for patients with a cold or flu: Don't bother your doctor; eat chicken soup. Ontario residents get free medical coverage. But officials here complain that frequent snifflers go to the doctor too much, clogging up the health-care system and costing the province about 200 million Canadian dollars (US $148 million) a year. So now the government is trying to convince cold and flu sufferers that they can cure themselves without professional advice.

"A cold lasts a week, and if you see a doctor it lasts seven days," goes one government advertisement. The campaign to reduce doctor visits is being tested in London, Ontario, where residents were mailed brochures extolling the virtues of chicken soup. To clear a stuffed nose, the brochure relates, "Egyptians favor mustard, Greeks use vinegar and pepper, Russians swear by horseradish. And South Asians drink a ginger and coriander tea." "We don't deny a cold is a miserable thing. But we're trying to conserve

dollars and physician time. It's like getting people to turn off the lights to conserve energy," says Eleanor Brownridge, who's leading the Ontario program. If successful, the campaign could spread across the province by next fall's flu season. Weaning patients from free medical care will take more than soup and horseradish, some say. "Most people go to the doctor too much. If they had to pay for it they'd go much less," says Brenda Willis, a registered nurse in London.

People visit a doctor for more reasons than just being sick. Some people are lonely. "They like to come and schmooze. Their appointment's at 3 P.M., they come at 1 P.M. There's more to do here than at home," says Steve Gottesman, a family practitioner in Toronto. Still others are scared. An elderly patient of Dr. Gottesman, otherwise healthy, used to come in every Friday "to make sure he was OK for the weekend," when the office was closed. The visits ended after a neighbor began checking on the man over the weekend. Under any health-care system, doctors and nurses sometimes treat more than their patients' illnesses. Says Ms. Willis: "Some of their lives are pretty poor. Maybe it's the only sympathy they get."

SOURCE: Larry M. Greenberg, "Take Two Tablespoons of Mustard and Call if You Don't Feel Better," *The Wall Street Journal*, February 22, 1994, p. B1. Reprinted by permission of *The Wall Street Journal*, © (1994) Dow Jones and Company, Inc. All Rights Reserved Worldwide.

[1]The article refers to "Ontario's socialized health-care system." But in Chapter 2, you discovered that the Canadian provinces have a "private" health care system coupled with a national health insurance program.

In addition, in some instances consumers may lack the information or medical knowledge they need to make informed choices. Consequently, consumers tend to rely heavily on the advice of their physicians when making such decisions as when a particular medical test or surgery is necessary. The implication is that physicians rather than consumers choose medical services, which makes the demand curve

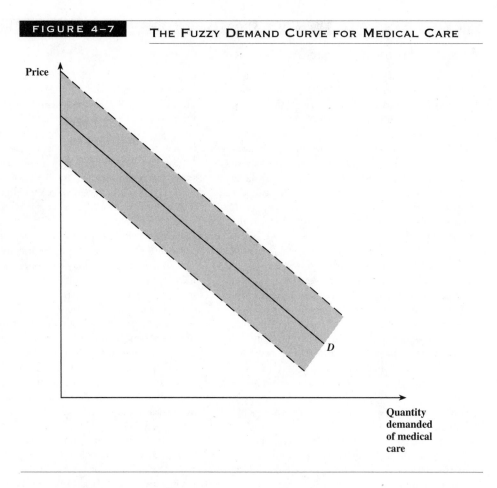

FIGURE 4–7 THE FUZZY DEMAND CURVE FOR MEDICAL CARE

fuzzier. Further complicating matters is the inability to accurately measure medical care, an issue we touched on earlier. For example, how do we measure the quantity of medical care produced during a one-hour therapy session with a psychiatrist?

All these factors combined make it extremely difficult to accurately delineate the relation between the price and the quantity demanded of medical care. In other words, the relation between price and quantity demanded is rather fuzzy (Aaron, 1991). A more accurate depiction of the relation between price and quantity may not be a well-defined line but a gray band similar to the one depicted in figure 4–7.

Two implications are associated with the fuzzy demand curve. First, for a given price, we may observe a wide variation in the quantity or types of medical services rendered. Indeed, researchers have well documented the wide variation in physician practice styles across geographical areas (e.g., Phelps, 1992); we take up that discussion in Chapter 14. Second, for a given quantity or type of medical service, we are likely to witness a wide variation in prices. For example, Feldstein (1988) reported a substantial variation in physician fees for similar procedures in the same geographical area. We must stress, however, that the existence of the band is unlikely to detract from the inverse relation between the price and the quantity demanded of medical care.

# Elasticities

Economic theory gives us insights into the factors that influence the demand for medical care, along with the direction of their influence. For example, we know that if the price of physician services increases by 15 percent, the quantity demanded falls. But by how much does it fall? Is there any way to determine whether the decrease is substantial or negligible? The answer is yes, with the help of a measure economists call an *elasticity*. Elasticity measures the responsiveness of quantity demanded to a change in an independent factor.

## Own-Price Elasticity of Demand

The most common elasticity is the **own-price elasticity of demand.** This measure gauges the extent to which consumers alter their consumption of a good or service when its own price changes. The formula looks like this:

**(4–6)**  $E_D = \%\Delta Q_D / \%\Delta P$

where $E_D$ denotes the price elasticity of demand, $\%\Delta Q_D$ represents the percentage change in quantity demanded, and $\%\Delta P$ stands for the percentage change in price. As you can see from the formula, $E_D$ is a simple ratio that equals the percentage change in quantity demanded divided by the percentage change in price. Because elasticity is specified as a ratio of two percentage changes, it is scale free. This makes it much easier to compare elasticities across different goods. For instance, we can compare the price elasticity of demand for physician services with that for nursing home care and not have to concern ourselves with the fact that the demand for physician services is usually measured in terms of the number of visits while the demand for nursing home care is measured in terms of the number of inpatient days.[6]

The value of $E_D$ is negative and reflects the inverse relationship between price and quantity demanded. In economics, the normal practice is to take the absolute value of the price elasticity of demand measure, or $|E_D|$, and eliminate the minus sign. If the price elasticity of demand is greater than 1 in absolute terms ($|E_D| > 1$), the demand for the product is referred to as **price elastic.** In arithmetic terms, $|E_D| > 1$ if the absolute value of the percentage change in price is smaller than the absolute value of the change in the quantity demanded, or $|\%\Delta P| < |\%\Delta Q_D|$. For instance, if the price

---

[6]The *point elasticity* formula can be used to actually calculate the elasticity of demand if the changes in the variables are small. The formula equals $(\Delta Q_D/Q_D)/(\Delta P/P)$. For readers with a background in calculus, it equals $(dQ_D/Q_D)/(dP/P)$ if the changes are infinitesimally small.

---

**I N S I G H T   4 – 3**

## Those Pointy-Headed Economists

McMenamin (1990) questions whether the theory of demand can be realistically applied to health care. He asks, "If patients' demand for health care services were responsive to price, at a price sufficiently low such patients should be expected to ask for two or more, say, appendectomies." Because many health care purchases, such as operations, are one-time events, it seems absurd to think that price plays a role in the decision. Do economists deserve their reputation for being pointy-headed?

As McMenamin points out, the idea that consumers respond to the price of health care is not as absurd as you might imagine if you consider the fact that decisions to purchase health care take place at either the intensive or the extensive margin. Most of the time, economists focus on the intensive nature of demand. Thus, as the price of a product falls, consumers purchase more of it, or consume it more intensively. That is basically the approach we have taken in this chapter. For example, as the price of physician services falls, consumers visit their physicians more frequently—that is, use their services more intensively.

To explain many of the "one-shot" purchases that take place on an either-or basis in health care, economists rely on the notion of the *extensive demand* for a product. Although each individual consumer can elect to purchase certain types of health care only once, in the aggregate more consumers may elect to purchase that particular type of health care if its price falls. Therefore, we may still observe an inverse relationship between price and quantity demanded. For example, an individual can have a particular tooth pulled only once. This is a one-shot purchase that either happens or does not happen. If the price of tooth extractions falls, however, we may still observe an inverse relationship between the price and number of teeth extracted. That is because at the extensive margin, more consumers elect to purchase this one-time form of dental service as price falls.

Thus, the notion of using traditional demand theory to explain the role of price in the consumption of health care is less absurd than it first appears. It seems that economists are not as pointy-headed as many imagine.

---

elasticity of demand for dental services equals 1.2, this means the quantity consumed falls by 12 percent if the price of dental care increases by 10 percent, *ceteris paribus*.

The price elasticity of demand is referred to as **inelastic** if $|E_D| < 1$ but greater than zero. In this case, $|\%\Delta P| > |\%\Delta Q_D|$, or the percentage change in price is greater than the percentage in quantity demanded in absolute value terms. For example, if the elasticity of demand for physician services equals .6, a 10 percent decrease in price leads to a 6 percent increase in quantity demanded. If $|E_D|$ happens to equal 1 because $|\%\Delta P|$ equals $|\%\Delta Q_D|$, the price elasticity of demand is **unit elastic.** This implies that a 1 percent decrease in the price of the product leads to a 1 percent increase in the quantity demanded.

A demand curve that is vertical is said to be **perfectly inelastic** because no change occurs in the quantity demanded when the price changes. In mathematical terms, $E_D$ equals zero because $\%\Delta Q_D$ equals zero. At the other extreme, if the demand curve is horizontal, it is referred to as being **perfectly elastic** and $|E_D|$ equals infinity ($\infty$). Any change in price leads to an infinite change in the quantity demanded.

| FIGURE 4-8 | THE ELASTICITY OF DEMAND AND THE SLOPE OF THE DEMAND CURVE |
| --- | --- |

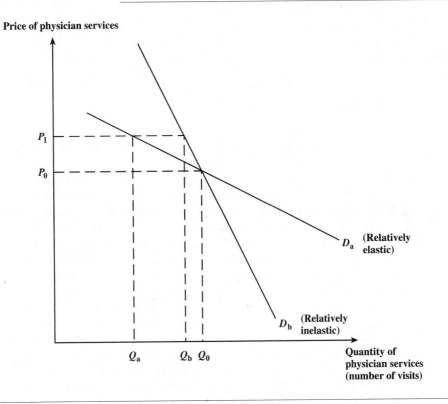

It stands to reason that the more elastic the demand for the product, the greater the response of quantity to a given change in price. Compare the effects of a 10 percent decrease in price on two goods—one with a price elasticity of $-.1$ and another with a price elasticity of $-2.6$. In the first case, the quantity demanded increases by only 1 percent, while in the second case, it increases by 26 percent. We can also use the elasticity of demand to make inferences regarding the slope of the demand curve. Generally, the more elastic the demand for the product, the flatter the demand curve at any given price. This also means the curve is relatively steep at any given point for an inelastic demand. Consider the two linear demand curves that intersect at point $P_0$, $Q_0$ in figure 4–8. If the price of the product increases to $P_1$, the quantity demanded decreases to $Q_a$ off the flat curve ($D_a$) and to $Q_b$ off the steep curve ($D_b$). Therefore, the same percentage increase in price generates a smaller percentage decrease in the quantity demanded for the steeper curve $D_b$ than for the flatter curve $D_a$ at a similar price of $P_0$. This means demand must be more price elastic for curve $D_a$ than for curve

| TABLE 4–1 | A SUMMARY OF THE OWN-PRICE ELASTICITY OF DEMAND | | | |
|---|---|---|---|---|

| Perfectly Inelastic | Inelastic | Unitary | Elastic | Perfectly Inelastic |
|---|---|---|---|---|
| $\left\vert E_D \right\vert = 0$ | $0 < \left\vert E_D \right\vert < 1$ | $\left\vert E_D \right\vert = 1$ | $1 < \left\vert E_D \right\vert < \infty$ | $\left\vert E_D \right\vert = \infty$ |
| $\%\Delta Q_D = 0$ | $\left\vert \%\Delta Q_D \right\vert < \left\vert \%\Delta P \right\vert$ | $\left\vert \%\Delta Q_D \right\vert = \left\vert \%\Delta P \right\vert$ | $\left\vert \%\Delta Q_D \right\vert > \left\vert \%\Delta P \right\vert$ | $\%\Delta P = 0$ |

$D_b$ over the range $P_0$ to $P_1$. Table 4–1 summarizes our discussion thus far on price elasticity of demand.

The own-price elasticity of demand varies greatly across products, and economists point to several factors that determine its value. Among the factors most often mentioned are the portion of the consumer's budget allocated to the good, the amount of time involved in the purchasing decision, the extent to which the good is a necessity, and the availability of substitutes. Briefly, as the portion of a consumer's budget allocated to a good increases, the consumer is likely to become much more sensitive to price changes. Demand should therefore become more elastic. An increase in the decision-making time frame is also likely to make demand more elastic. If the consumer has more time to make informed choices, he or she is likely to react more strongly to price changes. Because the consumer typically pays a small portion of the cost of medical services because of insurance, and because medical services are sometimes of an urgent nature, these two considerations suggest that in many cases, the demand for medical services is inelastic with respect to price.

If a good is a necessity, such as a basic foodstuff, the own-price elasticity should be relatively inelastic. The product is purchased with little regard for price because it is needed. Basic phone service might be considered another example of a necessity. Because our society depends so heavily on the phone as a form of communication, it is difficult to imagine a household functioning effectively without one. Naturally, basic health care falls into the same category. If an individual needs a particular medical service, such as an operation or a drug, and if not having it greatly affects the quality of life, we can expect that person's demand to be inelastic with respect to price. In addition, when a person needs a particular medical service in a life-or-death situation, demand is likely to be perfectly inelastic because the medical service must be purchased regardless of price if the person has sufficient income.

Given that many medical services are necessities, we expect the overall demand for medical services to be somewhat inelastic. A word of caution, however: This does not mean the amount of health care demanded does not react to changes in price. Rather, it means a given percentage change in price generates a small percentage change in the quantity demanded of medical services. For some types of medical care, however, demand may be more elastic. Elective medical care, such as cosmetic surgery, may fall into this category, because in most instances it is considered a luxury rather than a necessity. As a result, price may play an important role in the decision to have the surgery. To a lesser degree, dentist services and eyewear might fall into this category. In fact, any medical service that can be postponed is likely to display some degree of price elasticity.

The availability of substitutes is another determinant of price elasticity. As we saw earlier, various types of medical services may serve as substitutes for one another. The larger the number of substitutes, the greater the opportunity to do some comparison shopping. As a result, the quantity demanded of any medical service is likely to be much more sensitive to price changes when alternative means of acquiring medical care are available. The own-price elasticity of demand for any given product should be directly related to the number of substitutes available. Stated another way, demand should become more price elastic as the number of substitutes expands. One implication is that the demand for an individual medical service or an individual medical care provider is likely to be more elastic than the overall demand for medical care.

One more point concerning the elasticity of demand needs to be discussed before we leave this subject. The own-price elasticity of demand can be used to predict what happens to total health expenditures if price increases or decreases. Total revenues (or total expenditures, from the consumer's perspective) equal price times quantity. In mathematical notation,

$$(4\text{–}7) \quad \text{TR} = PQ_D$$

where TR stands for total revenue. Demand theory tells us that as the price of a product increases, the quantity demanded decreases, or that $P$ and $Q_D$ move in opposite directions. Whether total revenue increases or decreases when the price changes is dictated by the relative rates at which both variables change, or the elasticity of demand. Consider an increase in the price of physician services where demand is inelastic. This means that $|\%\Delta Q_D| < |\%\Delta P|$, or that the percentage increase in price is larger than the percentage decrease in quantity demanded in absolute value terms. In terms of equation 4–7, $P$ increases faster than $Q_D$ falls. This means total revenue must increase with a higher price. If demand happens to be elastic, the opposite occurs: Quantity demanded falls faster than price increases, and, as a result, total revenue decreases. No change occurs in total revenue when demand is unitary because the increase in price is matched by the same percentage decrease in quantity demanded. We leave it to you to work out the implications of a price decrease on total revenue when demand is elastic, inelastic, and unitary.

## Other Types of Elasticity

The concept of elasticity can be used to measure the sensitivity of quantity demanded to other demand-side factors as well. The **income elasticity of demand** represents the percentage change in quantity demanded divided by the percentage change in income, or $E_Y = \%\Delta Q_D / \%\Delta Y$, where $\%\Delta Y$ equals the percentage change in real income. It quantifies the extent to which the demand for a product changes when real income changes. If $E_Y$ is positive, the good is referred to as a *normal good* because any increase in real income leads to an increase in quantity demanded. For instance, if $E_Y$

equals .78, this means a 10 percent increase in income causes the quantity consumed to increase by 7.8 percent. An *inferior good* is one for which $E_Y$ is negative and an increase in income leads to a decrease in the amount consumed. For most types of medical care, the income elasticity of demand should be larger than zero.

The **cross-price elasticity** $(E_C)$ measures the extent to which the demand for a product changes when the price of another good is altered. In mathematical terms, $E_C = \%\Delta Q_X / \%\Delta P_Z$, where the numerator represents the percentage change in the demand for good X and the denominator equals the percentage change in the price of good Z. If $E_C$ is negative, we can infer that the two goods are complements in consumption. Returning to our earlier example, the cross-price elasticity between the demand for optometric services and the price of eyewear should be negative. If the price of eyewear increases, the demand for optometric services should drop. Two goods are substitutes in consumption when the cross-price elasticity is positive. For example, the cross-price elasticity of the demand for physician services with respect to the price of hospital outpatient services may turn out to be positive. Naturally, if $E_C$ equals zero, the demand for the product is independent of the price of the other product.

## Empirical Estimation

Numerous studies have attempted to empirically quantify how various factors influence the demand for medical care. Although the studies varied widely in terms of methodology and scope of analysis, certain broad conclusions emerged. Generally, some form of equation 4–5 was estimated with the use of regression analysis. Unfortunately, the dependent variable representing the amount of medical services consumed is very difficult to measure. Ideally, quantity demanded should capture both the utilization and the intensity of medical services. Data of these kinds are unavailable, so usually only some utilization measure, such as number of physician visits or hospital patient days, is used to measure the quantity demanded of medical services. Proxy variables are then included as independent variables to control for variations in quality. A failure to properly control for quality biases the results. That is because changes in demand may be attributed to changes in other variables when in fact they are the result of differences in the quality of care provided.

The measurement of the out-of-pocket price of medical care also presents a problem for economists. This problem has become more severe in recent years given the increasing role of third-party payers. In a perfect world, the out-of-pocket price of medical services should equal the amount the consumer pays after the impact of insurance has been considered. Unfortunately, such data are rarely available, and economists often have to resort to using such variables as the average price of medical services rendered. An additional variable is then included in the equation to control the presence of health insurance. The price variable should negatively affect the demand for medical care, while the presence of insurance should positively influence quantity demanded.

A real income variable is included to capture the impact of purchasing power on demand, while time cost variables control for the effects of travel and waiting costs on demand. We expect the real income variable to have a positive effect on demand and

## An International Look at the Relationship between Income and Health Care Spending

A group of researchers has looked at the relation between real income and health care expenditures to ascertain how economic growth impacts national health care expenditures. This is generally done by regressing real per capita health expenditures on some measure of real per capita income along with a number of other control variables. The samples usually include most of the more developed countries of the world. The estimates are then used to calculate the aggregate income elasticity, which gives the extent to which health care expenditures increase as national income expands.

The intercountry estimates suggest that the aggregate income elasticity generally approaches or exceeds +1.0. For example, Newhouse (1977) finds the income elasticity to range between 1.13 and 1.31, while Parkin et al. (1987) estimate the rate to be slightly below +1. Finally, Leu (1986) and Gerdtham et al. (1992) agree with Newhouse and find the aggregate income elasticity to be above one. The intercountry income elasticity estimates are in direct contrast to intracountry estimates. Income elasticity estimates for the United States are generally well below +1.0. This difference is interesting and deserves explanation. According to Newhouse, the difference exists because, for example, within the United States at any point in time the average consumer pays only a small portion of the price of medical care (approximately 16.5 percent in 1996), while over time the country as a whole must pay the full price of health care. As the out-of-pocket price of health care falls for the average consumer, the income elasticity should also fall because the consumer is less conscious of price. For example, if the out-of-pocket price of health care falls to zero, then the average individual is going to consume health care regardless of income. The income elasticity in the extreme equals zero. The country as a whole, however, must face the entire burden of the cost of health care and, as a result, is going to be much more sensitive to price and income.

One of the more interesting questions concerning this research has to do with whether health care is a luxury good. Economists define a luxury good as one that has an income elasticity above +1.0. In this case, an increase in income leads to an even larger increase in the quantity consumed of the good. For example, assume that the income elasticity of a good equals 1.5. A 10 percent increase in income leads to a 15 percent increase in consumption of the good. Naturally, this means that the portion of one's budget allocated to the consumption of the good also increases with income.

If the aggregate income elasticity of health care is above +1.0, this may provide a demand-side explanation as to why health care expenditures in the United States as a portion of GDP have increased over the past few decades. As the U. S. economy grew over the past few decades and real per capita income expanded, the nation allocated a greater portion of GDP health care because it is a luxury good. Consequently, the health care sector received a larger and larger slice of the economic pie. A simple example will illustrate that point. Let's assume that a fictitious country with 100 inhabitants has a GDP of $1 million and a per capita income of $10,000. Let's also assume that the aggregate income elasticity equals 1.2, and this country presently spends 10 percent of its income on health care services ($100,000). Now, let's assume that per capita income grows by 20 percent ($12,000) over the next five years and the size of the population remains constant. GDP would equal $1.2 million, while expenditures on health care services would expand to $124,000. That represents 10.33 percent of GDP, or an increase of one-third of a percent in just five years.

the time cost variables to have a negative impact. The prices of various substitutes and complements in consumption should also be included in the regression equation. This has become even more important in recent years as medical markets have become more interrelated. For example, if we are trying to assess the quantity demanded of inpatient services at a hospital, we should control for the prices of hospital outpatient services (potentially a substitute service) and physician services (potentially a complementary service). The remaining factors (tastes and preferences, rate of health depreciation, stock of health, and quality of care) are referred to as *control variables* and capture the impact that various noneconomic factors may have on the demand for health care services. Theoretically, a change in any one of these independent factors should affect the demand for medical care.

### Own-Price, Income, Cross-Price, and Time Cost Elasticity Estimates

In general, the literature has found that the demand for primary care services is price inelastic. For example, Newhouse and the Insurance Experiment Group (1993) found the overall own-price elasticity for medical care to be $-.22$, while Eichner (1998) estimated it to lie between $-.62$ and $-.75$. Although the estimates vary, they tend to be in the $-.1$ to $-.7$ range. In more specific terms, Manning et al. (1987) estimated the own-price elasticity of hospital admissions to be between $-.1$ and $-.2$, while Cromwell and Mitchell (1986) found the own-price elasticity for total and elective surgery to be $-.14$ and $-.17$, respectively. To round things out, Stano (1985) found the price elasticity of physician visits to equal $-.06$. Taken as a whole, the estimates suggest that a 10 percent increase in the out-of-pocket price of hospital or physician services leads to a 1 to 7 percent decrease in the quantity demanded. The inelastic estimates also imply that total expenditures on hospital and physician services increase with a greater out-of-pocket price, *ceteris paribus*.[7]

In general, the research indicates that the demand for other types of medical care is slightly more price elastic than the demand for primary care. That is not at all surprising given that the percentage of out-of-pocket payments is the lowest for hospital and physician services (see Insight 4–1). Everything else held constant, consumers should become more price sensitive as the portion of the bill paid out of pocket increases. For example, Manning and Phelps (1979) found the demand for dental services to be slightly more price elastic and to vary by type of service provided and the sex and age of the patient. The price elasticity of demand for dental services by adult females appears to vary between $-.5$ and $-.7$, and the demand for dental services by adult males and children seems to be slightly more price elastic. The demand for nursing home services also appears to be more price elastic than primary medical services. Chiswick (1976) found the own-price elasticity for nursing home services to be between $-.73$ and $-2.40$, and Lamberton, Ellingson, and Spear (1986) estimated that it equals $-.76$. Finally, Headen (1993) found the own-price elasticity for the probability of entering a nursing home to be $-.7$.

---

[7]Here is an abbreviated list of selected results from other studies. Davis and Russell (1972) found price elasticity for outpatient visits to equal $-1.0$ and inpatient visits to vary between $-.32$ and $-.46$; Phelps and Newhouse (1974) found the elasticity of demand for physician visits to equal $-.14$; and Feldman and Dowd (1986) found the price elasticity of demand for patient days to vary between $-.74$ and $-.80$ and admissions to equal $-1.1$.

Overall, the empirical evidence indicates that health care is a normal good with an income elasticity below +1.0. Time costs also appear to have a significant impact on the demand for medical services. In fact, research indicates that the travel time elasticity of demand is approximately equal to the own-price elasticity of demand. According to Acton (1975) and Phelps and Newhouse (1974), the travel time elasticity of demand ranges from −.14 to −.51. This means a 10 percent increase in travel time reduces the quantity demanded of medical services by roughly 3.3 percent, on average. It also appears that consumers put a value on the time spent waiting for medical services. McCarthy (1985) found the wait time elasticity to range from −.36 to −1.14. This same study also indicated that an appointment delay does not appear to influence the demand for physician services. At the extensive margin, time costs also influence the decision to acquire medical care. For instance, Frank et al. (1995) found the elasticity of travel time costs on the probability of a timely completion of childhood immunization to be roughly −.08.

The extent to which various types of medical services serve as substitutes or complements in consumption is not clear at this time. For example, there appears to be little consensus as to whether inpatient and outpatient hospital services are substitutes or complements. Davis and Russell (1972) found that the cross-price elasticity between the price of inpatient services and number of outpatient visits to vary between .85 and 1.46, indicating that they are substitutes. These results were later qualitatively confirmed by Gold (1984). Thus, as the price of inpatient services at a hospital increases, consumers rely more on outpatient services to save money. Freiberg and Scutchfield (1976), on the other hand, found that no substitution occurs between these two types of hospital services. At the other extreme, Manning et al. (1987) suggested that they are complements in consumption. A similar debate in the literature concerns whether physician and hospital inpatient or outpatient services are substitutes or complements.

## The Impact of Insurance on the Demand for Medical Services

The growth of health insurance, both public and private, has had a profound impact on the demand for health care. Instead of reviewing the results from the many studies that analyzed the impact of insurance on the demand for health care, we will focus on a study conducted by the RAND Corporation (Manning et al., 1987). The RAND Health Insurance Study (HIS) is without doubt the most comprehensive study to date. Families from six sites (Dayton, Ohio; Seattle, Washington; Fitchburg, Massachusetts; Charleston, South Carolina; Georgetown County, South Carolina; and Franklin County, Massachusetts) were enrolled in various types of health insurance plans in a controlled experiment to test the impact of differences in insurance coverage on the demand for medical care.[8]

---

[8]The present discussion focuses on the results published by Manning et al. (1987). However, a number of other articles analyze the data from the RAND HIS study. Among them are Newhouse et al. (1981), Keeler and Rolph (1983), O'Grady et al. (1985), Manning et al. (1985), Leinowitz, Manning, and Newhouse (1985b), Leibowitz et al. (1985a), and Manning et al. (1986). For a summary of the entire RAND HIS study, consult Newhouse and the Insurance Experiment Group (1993).

| TABLE 4-2 | | SAMPLE MEANS FOR ANNUAL USE OF MEDICAL SERVICES PER CAPITA | | | |
|---|---|---|---|---|---|

| Plan* | Face-to-Face Visits | Outpatient Expenses (1984 $) | Inpatient Dollars (1984 $) | Total Expenses (1984 $) | Probability of Using Any Medical Services |
|---|---|---|---|---|---|
| Free | 4.55 | $340 | $409 | $749 | 86.8 |
| 25% | 3.33 | 260 | 373 | 634 | 78.8 |
| 50% | 3.03 | 224 | 450 | 674 | 77.2 |
| 95% | 2.73 | 203 | 315 | 518 | 67.7 |
| Individual deductible | 3.02 | 235 | 373 | 608 | 72.3 |

*The *chi*-square test was used in test the null hypothesis of no difference among the five plan means. In each instance, the *chi*-square statistic was significant to at least the 5 percent level. The only exception was for inpatient dollars.

SOURCE: Willard G. Manning et al., "Health Insurance and the Demand for Medical Care: Evidence from a Randomized Experiment," *American Economic Review* 77 (June 1987), table 2.

In one phase of the study, families were enrolled in 14 different fee-for-service plans. The plans varied in terms of the consumer coinsurance rate (0.25 percent, 50 percent, or 95 percent) and the upper limit on annual out-of-pocket expenses. Every plan had a *maximum* limit of $1,000 in out-of-pocket expenses per year. Table 4–2 presents selected results for five of the plans: free (0 coinsurance rate), 25 percent coinsurance rate, 50 percent coinsurance rate, 95 percent coinsurance rate, and individual deductible. The individual deductible plan had a 95 percent coinsurance rate for outpatient services, subject to a limit of $150 per person or $450 per family, and free inpatient care. Essentially, an individual or a family with this plan receives free medical care after meeting the deductible for outpatient expenditures. In table 4–2, face-to-face visits equal the number of per capita visits per year to a medical provider, such as a physician. The category excludes visits for radiology, anesthesiology, or pathology services. The third, fourth, and fifth columns list, respectively, total per capita expenditures for outpatient, inpatient, and all medical services, excluding dental care and psychotherapy. The sixth column indicates the probability of using any medical services over the course of the year.

The results largely confirm our expectations concerning the impact of coinsurance on the demand for health care. As the level of coinsurance rises, or the out-of-pocket price of medical care increases, consumers demand less medical care. The number of face-to-face visits decreased from 4.55 per year when health care was a free good to 2.73 when the consumer paid 95 percent of the bill. This represents a decrease in visits of 40 percent. The largest drop in visits took place between the free plan and the 25 percent coinsurance plan. This overall decrease in visits was matched by an identical drop in outpatient expenses from $340 to $203 per year. According to

# Time Is Money: It Was Then and Still Is Now[1]

In the mid-nineteenth century the average income for most physicians in the United States was quite modest and many were forced to find a second income to make ends meet. One major factor that contributed to the low demand for physician services, and therefore the low income, was the high cost of transportation. During the mid-1800s, the United States was primarily a rural society without a modern transportation system. Since most families lived in rural settings and travel was slow, a trip into town to visit a physician was in all likelihood an all-day affair. For a farmer, that meant losing a day's labor, making the opportunity cost of travel very high for most families.

When an individual was ill and could not be moved, it was up to the physician to travel to the individual's house or farm to administer care. Most physician fee schedules at that time reflected the high cost of travel, which included the opportunity cost of the physician's time along with the explicit cost of a horse or horse and buggy. In many cases the transportation costs outweighed the direct cost of medical care. For instance, in Addison County, Vermont, in 1843, "the fee for each visit by a doctor was 50 cents at less than half mile; $1.00 between a half mile and two miles; $1.50 between two and four miles; $2.50 between four and six miles and so on" (Starr, p. 67). As you can imagine, physicians did not have to travel far out of town before the proportion of the bill resulting from travel exceeded the direct cost of medical services. The historical evidence clearly indicates the important role time costs played in determining the price of physician services in the mid-1800s.

A study by Whitney et al.[2] illustrates that time costs still play a role in the pricing behavior of medical care providers. In this case, however, the time costs are not related to travel but rather to the time associated with scheduling an appointment and waiting in the reception room to see a dentist. According to the results of the study, the price of dental services "decreased by $4.86 per day wait for a new-patient appointment and by $5.20 per minute wait in the reception room" (p. 783). Anyone who has nervously waited in the dentist's reception room can attest to the willingness of consumers to pay a premium for shorter waiting times.

[1]This insight is based primarily on Chapter 2 of Paul Starr's *The Social Transformation of American Medicine* (New York: Basic Books, 1982).

[2]Coralyn Whitney et al., "The Relationship between Price of Services, Quality of Care, and Patient Time Costs for General Dental Practice," *Health Services Research* 31 (February 1997), pp. 773–90.

Manning et al., this indicates that as the out-of-pocket price of medical care increases, consumers reduce medical expenditures largely by cutting back on the number of visits to health care providers and not on the amount spent on each visit. It is interesting to note that the authors reported no significant differences in the amount spent on inpatient services across plans. This, they concluded, was the result of the $1,000 cap put on out-of-pocket expenditures. In 70 percent of the cases where people were admitted for inpatient services, the cost exceeded the $1,000 limit.

The last two columns in table 4–2 also largely support our expectations regarding the impact of insurance on the demand for medical services. In every case, as the level of coinsurance increased, the probability of using any medical services, along with total medical expenditures, diminished. The only exception occurred between the 25 and 50 percent coinsurance rates for total medical expenditures.

Finally, the results from the individual deductible plan illustrate the negative impact of deductibles on the consumption of medical care. In every instance, less medical care was consumed with the deductibles than would have been the case if medical care was a free good. It seems that individuals with this plan consumed medical services at a rate somewhere between the 25 and 95 percent coinsurance rate.

The results also indicate that the own-price elasticity of demand is sensitive to the level of insurance. When the level of coinsurance ranged from 25 to 95 percent, the elasticities of demand for all care and outpatient care were calculated as −.14 and −.21. These numbers decreased to −.10 and −.13 when the level of coinsurance ranged from 0 to 25 percent. This makes economic sense. As the level of coinsurance drops, consumers are likely to become less sensitive to price changes due to lower out-of-pocket payments.

In conclusion, the results from the RAND HIS study point to the significant impact of health insurance on the demand for medical care. It is apparent that if either the rate of coinsurance or the deductible falls, the amount of health care consumed increases.

### The Impact of Noneconomic Factors on the Demand for Medical Services

The empirical research also indicates that a host of other factors, such as tastes and preferences or the stock of health, affect the demand for medical care. Researchers generally agree that age and severity of illness positively influence the demand for medical care, while the overall health of the individual negatively affects the demand for care. There does not, however, appear to be a consensus concerning the impact of education on the demand for health care. This may indicate that the positive impact of education on the demand for medical care (a greater willingness to seek care) is offset by the negative effect (a greater ability to produce health care at home) or that more research needs to be done in this area.

It is interesting to note that a few researchers have focused specifically on the effect of medical knowledge on the demand for medical care. Unlike the results for general education, a positive relationship appears to exist between consumers' medical knowledge and the demand for medical care. This means that consumers with a more extensive background in medicine tend to consume more medical services. For example, Kenkel (1990) found that consumers' medical knowledge is positively related to the probability of visiting a physician for medical care, while Hsieh and Lin (1997) uncovered that those elderly who had a greater understanding of health were more likely to acquire preventive medical care. Both studies suggest that consumers with a lack of medical knowledge tend to underestimate the impact of medical care on overall health, and, as a result, fail to consume an appropriate amount. It may also be the case that more medical information enhances the ability of an individual to effectively consume medical care, causing the marginal product of medical care to increase (consult Chapter 3). As a result, the demand for various types of medical care increases with consumer information.

It is interesting to note that Hsieh and Lin (1997) found that years of schooling, whether the individual worked in the health care field, medical insurance, and income positively influenced the level of health information. They also found that age and whether the individual drank or smoked inversely affected the quantity of health information. It appears that older people acquire less new knowledge because they have fewer years to live and reap any reward from that knowledge, while individuals who drink or smoke receive less utility from any good health that may result from added medical knowledge.

**SUMMARY**

Economic theory suggests that the demand for medical care is a derived demand because it is but one input in the production of health. As a result, the utility received from consuming medical care is in the form of the satisfaction that accrues from improvements in the stock of health. Utility analysis also indicates that the demand for health care is negatively related to price because improvements in health are subject to diminishing returns. The demand for medical care, like the demand for many other services, depends on the out-of-pocket price, income, the prices of substitutes and complements, and time costs, along with a host of noneconomic factors, such as tastes and preferences, quality of care, and the state of health.

Economists use the concept of elasticity to measure the degree to which an economic agent, such as a consumer, adjusts to a change in the value of an independent variable. The most common elasticity is the own-price elasticity of demand, which measures the extent to which consumers react to a change in the price of a good or service. In mathematical terms, it equals the percentage change in quantity demanded divided by the percentage change in price. If the demand for a product is elastic, the consumer's willingness to purchase the product is very sensitive to a price change. On the other hand, if the demand for the product is inelastic, price changes play a less significant role in determining overall demand. From a graphical perspective, the more elastic the demand for a product, the flatter the demand curve. Additional types of elasticities, such as the income elasticity of demand, have also been employed to assess how demand reacts to changes in variables other than own price.

The empirical evidence indicates that the demand for medical care is inelastic with respect to price. Medical care also appears to be a normal good in that the demand for medical care increases with real income. In addition, time costs along with many noneconomic variables, such as age, gender, severity of illness, education, and consumer knowledge, influence demand. The evidence from the RAND HIS study verifies that health insurance plays a major role in determining the demand for medical care. As economic theory suggests, when the level of health insurance rises, the amount of medical care demanded increases while the price elasticity of demand becomes more inelastic.

## Review Questions and Problems

1. In your own words, use utility analysis and production theory to explain why the demand curve for medical care is downward sloping.

2. After reading the chapter on demand theory, a classmate turns to you and says, "I'm rather confused. According to economic theory, people demand a good or service because it yields

utility. This obviously does not apply to medical services. Just last week I went to the dentist and had a root canal, and you can't tell me I received any utility or satisfaction from that!" Explain to your classmate how utility analysis can be used to explain why she or he went to the dentist.

3. Use a graph to illustrate how the following changes would affect the demand curve for inpatient services at a hospital in a large city.

   *a.* Average real income in the community increases.

   *b.* In an attempt to cut costs, the largest employer in the area increases the coinsurance rate for employee health care coverage from 10 percent to 20 percent.

   *c.* The hospital relocates from the center of the city, where a majority of the people live, to a suburb.

   *d.* A number of physicians in the area join together and open up a discount-price walk-in clinic; the price elasticity of demand between physician services and inpatient hospital services is −0.50.

4. In recent years, many elderly people have purchased Medigap insurance policies to cover a growing Medicare copayment. These policies cover some or all of the medical costs not covered by Medicare. Use economic theory to explain how the growth of these policies is likely to influence the demand for health care by elderly people.

5. If you are covered by a private or a public insurance plan, obtain a pamphlet outlining the benefits provided and the cost of the plant. Are there any copayments or deductibles? If so, use economic theory to explain how they may influence your demand for medical care.

6. In your own words, explain what a fuzzy demand curve means. Why does it exist? What are its implications?

7. In reaction to higher input costs, a physician decides to increase the average price of a visit by 5 percent. Will total revenues increase or decrease as a result of this action? Use the concept of price elasticity to substantiate your answer.

8. You have just been put in charge of estimating the demand for hospital services in a major U.S. city. What economic and noneconomic variables would you include in your analysis? Justify why each variable should be included in the study, and explain how a change in each variable would likely affect the overall demand for hospital services.

9. Define *own-price elasticity of demand,* and explain how it is related to the demand curve. Provide four reasons why the demand for medical services is likely to be inelastic with respect to its price.

10. You are employed as an economic consultant to the regional planning office of a large metropolitan area, and your task is to estimate the demand for hospital services in the area. Your estimates indicate that the own-price elasticity of demand equals −.25, the income elasticity of demand equals +.45, the cross-price elasticity of demand for hospital services with respect to the price of nursing home services equals −.1, and the elasticity of travel

time equals −.37. Use this information to project the impact of the following changes on the demand for hospital services.

 a. Average travel time to the hospital diminishes by 5 percent due to overall improvements in the public transportation system.

 b. The price of nursing home care decreases by 10 percent.

 c. Average real income decreases by 10 percent.

 d. The hospital is forced to increase its price for services by 2 percent.

11. A recent study estimates the demand for over-the-counter cough and cold medicines to be:

$$\text{Log } Q = .885 - .744 \log(P) - .50 \log(INC) + .253 \log(ADV) - .30 \log(PHYSP)$$
$$\quad (5.52)\ (4.92) \qquad (1.40) \qquad (6.64) \qquad (0.99)$$
$$\text{Adj. } R^2 = .30$$
$$N = 243$$

where  $Q$ = Annual dosages demanded of cough and cold medicines

  $P$ = Price per dosage of cough and cold medicines

  INC = Average income of buyers

  ADV = Advertising expenditures on cough and cold medicines

  PHYSP = Market price of a physician visit

  $t$-statistics shown in parentheses below the estimated coefficient

  All variables expressed in logarithms so the coefficient estimates can be interpreted as elasticities.

 a. Which of the estimated coefficients have signs contrary to theoretical expectations? Explain. Be very specific in your explanation.

 b. Which coefficient estimates are statistically significant from zero at the 5 percent level or better? Explain.

 c. What percentage of the variation in dosages demanded remains unexplained? Explain.

 d. Suppose the price per dosage increased by 10 percent. By how much would dosages demanded change? Explain. Would total revenues to cold medicine producers increase or decrease? Explain.

## References

Aaron, Henry J. *Serious and Unstable Condition: Financing America's Health Care*. Washington, DC: The Brookings Institution, 1991.

Acton, Jan Paul. "Nonmonetary Factors in the Demand for Medical Services: Some Empirical Evidence." *Journal of Political Economy* 83 (June 1975), pp. 595–614.

Chiswick, Barry. "The Demand for Nursing Home Care." *Journal of Human Resources* 11 (summer 1976), pp. 295–316.

Cromwell, Jerry, and Janet B. Mitchell. "Physician-Induced Demand for Surgery." *Journal of Health Economics* 5 (1986), pp. 293–313.

Davis, Karen, and Louise B. Russell. "The Substitution of Hospital Outpatient Care for Inpatient Care." *Review of Economics and Statistics* 54 (May 1972), pp. 109–20.

Eichner, Matthew J. "The Demand for Medical Care: What People Pay Does Matter." *American Economic Review Papers and Proceedings* 88 (May 1998), pp. 117–121.

Feldman, Roger, and Bryan Dowd. "Is There a Competitive Market for Hospital Services?" *Journal of Health Economics* 5 (1986), pp. 272–92.

Feldstein, Martin S. "Hospital Cost Inflation: A Study of Nonprofit Price Dynamics." *American Economic Review* 61 (December 1971), pp. 853–72.

———. *Economic Analysis for Health Services Efficiency.* Amsterdam: North-Holland Publishing Co., 1967.

Feldstein, Paul. *Health Care Economics.* New York: John Wiley & Sons, 1988.

Frank, Richard G., et al. "The Demand for Childhood Immunizations: Results from the Baltimore Immunization Study." *Inquiry* 32 (summer 1995), pp. 164–73.

Freiberg, Lewis, Jr., and F. Douglas Scutchfield. "Insurance and the Demand for Hospital Care: An Examination of the Moral Hazard." *Inquiry* 13 (March 1976), pp. 54–60.

Gerdtham, Ulf-G, et al. "An Econometric Analysis of Health Care Expenditure: A Cross-Section Study of the OECD Countries." *Journal of Health Economics* 11 (1992), pp. 63–84.

Greenberg, Larry M. "Take Two Tablespoons of Mustard and Call if You Don't Feel Better." *The Wall Street Journal*, February 22, 1994, p. B1.

Gold, Marsha. "The Demand for Hospital Outpatient Services." *Health Services Research* 19 (August 1984), pp. 384–412.

Grossman, Michael. "On the Concept of Health Capital and the Demand for Health." *Journal of Political Economy* 80 (March–April 1972), pp. 223–55.

Headen, Alvin E. "Economic Disability and Health Determinants of the Hazard of Nursing Home Entry." *Journal of Human Resources* 28 (1993), pp. 80–110.

*Health Care Financing Administration.* "1996 National Health Expenditures." http://www.hcfa.gov/stats/stats.htm

Hsieh, Chee-ruey, and Shin-jong Lin. "Health Information and the Demand for Preventive Care among the Elderly in Taiwan." *Journal of Human Resources* 32 (1997): pp. 308–33.

Keeler, Emmett B., and John E. Rolph. "How Cost Sharing Reduced Medical Spending of Participants in the Health Insurance Experiment." *Journal of the American Medical Association* 249 (April 22–29, 1983), pp. 2220–22.

Kenkel, Don. "Consumer Health Information and the Demand for Medical Care." *Review of Economics and Statistics* 72 (1990), pp. 587–95.

Lamberton, C. E., W. D. Ellingson, and K. R. Spear. "Factors Determining the Demand for Nursing Home Services." *Quarterly Review of Economics and Business* 26 (winter 1986), pp. 74–90.

Leibowitz, Arleen, et al. "Effects of Cost-Sharing on the Use of Medical Services by Children: Interim Results from a Randomized Controlled Trial." *Pediatrics* 75 (May 1985a), pp. 942–50.

Leibowitz, Arleen, Willard G. Manning, and Joseph P. Newhouse. "The Demand for Prescription Drugs as a Function of Cost-Sharing." *Social Science and Medicine* 21 (1985b), pp. 1063–69.

Leu, Robert E. "The Public-Private Mix and International Health Care Costs." In *Public and Private Health Services*, edited by A. J. Culyer and B. Jonsson. Oxford: Basil Blackwell, 1986.

Levit, Katherine R., et al. "National Health Spending Trends, 1960–1993." *Health Affairs* 13 (winter 1994), pp. 14–31.

Manning, Willard G., Howard L. Bailit, Bernadette Benjamin, and Joseph P. Newhouse. "The Demand for Dental Care: Evidence from a Randomized Trial in Health Insurance." *Journal of the American Dental Association* 110 (June 1985), pp. 895–902.

Manning, Willard G., et al. "Health Insurance and the Demand for Medical Care: Evidence from a Randomized Experiment." *American Economic Review* 77 (June 1987), pp. 251–77.

Manning, Willard, et al. "How Cost Sharing Affects the Use of Ambulatory Mental Health Services." *Journal of the American Medical Association* 256 (October 10, 1986), pp. 1930–34.

Manning, Williard G., and Charles E. Phelps. "The Demand for Dental Care." *Bell Journal of Economics* 10 (autumn 1979), pp. 503–25.

McCarthy, Thomas. "The Competitive Nature of the Primary-Care Physicians Service Market." *Journal of Health Economics* 4 (1985), pp. 93–118.

McMenamin, Peter. "What Do Economists Think Patients Want?" *Health Affairs* 9 (winter 1990), pp. 112–19.

Miller, Lisa. "Medical Schools Put Women in Curricula." *The Wall Street Journal*, May 24, 1994, p. B1.

Newhouse, Joseph P. "Medical-Care Expenditures: A Cross-National Survey." *Journal of Human Resources* 12 (winter 1977), pp. 115–24.

Newhouse, Joseph P., et al. "Some Interim Results from a Controlled Trial of Cost Sharing in Health Insurance." *New England Journal of Medicine* 305 (December 17, 1981), pp. 1501–07.

Newhouse, Joseph P. and the Insurance Experiment Group. *Free for All? Lessons from the RAND Health Insurance Experiment.* Cambridge, Mass.: Harvard University Press, 1993.

O'Grady, Kevin F., Willard G. Manning, Joseph P. Newhouse, and Robert H. Brook. "Impact of Cost Sharing on Emergency Department Use." *New England Journal of Medicine* 313 (August 22, 1985), pp. 484–90.

Parkin, David, Alistair Mcquire, and Brian Yule. "Aggregate Health Care Expenditures and National Income: Is Health a Luxury Good?" *Journal of Health Economics* 6 (1987), pp. 109–27.

Phelps, Charles E. "Diffusion of Information in Medical Care." *Journal of Economic Perspectives* 6 (summer 1992), pp. 23–42.

Phelps, Charles E., and Joseph P. Newhouse. "Coinsurance, the Price of Time, and the Demand for Medical Service." *Review of Economics and Statistics* 56 (August 1974), pp. 334–42.

Stano, Miron. "An Analysis of the Evidence on Competition in the Physician's Services Market." *Journal of Health Economics* 4 (1985), pp. 197–211.

Starr, Paul. *The Social Transformation of American Medicine.* New York: Basic Books, 1982.

Whitney, Coralyn W., et al. "The Relationship between Price of Services, Quality of Care, and Patient Time Costs for General Dental Practice." *Health Services Research* 31 (February 1997), pp. 773–90.

Winslow Ron. "In Health Care Low Cost Beats High Quality." *The Wall Street Journal*, January 18, 1994, p. B1.

## CEBS Questions

CEBS Sample Question on Subject Matter from CEBS Course IX Study Manual

1.  What effect does each of the following have on the demand curve for medical services? (pages 91–95)
    a.  Coinsurance
    b.  Indemnity insurance (defined in the textbook as the insurance carrier pays a fixed amount for various types of medical services)

CEBS Sample Exam Questions

1. When a demand curve for medical care is described as "fuzzy" this refers to the fact that:
   A. Demand is less important than supply
   B. The concept of a demand curve cannot be applied to medical care
   C. It is extremely difficult to accurately delineate the relation between the price and the quantity demanded of medical care
   D. The demand for medical care is a derived demand
   E. The demand curve for medical care, unlike typical demand curves, does not slope downward to the right

2. Which of the following statements regarding a demand curve is (are) correct?
   I. In a demand curve illustration the vertical axis is "quantity"
   II. A demand curve normally slopes downward to the right
   III. A demand curve shows that a greater quantity will be demanded at a higher income
   A. II only
   B. III only
   C. I and II only
   D. II and III only
   E. I, II, and III

3. All the following statements regarding elasticity are correct EXCEPT:
   A. If elasticity is negative, the good is called a normal good
   B. Total revenue decreases when the price increases and the demand is elastic
   C. When the price elasticity is greater than one, the demand for the product is said to be elastic
   D. A horizontal demand curve is perfectly elastic
   E. The availability of substitutes is a determinant of price elasticity

*Answer to Sample Question from Study Manual*
   a. Coinsurance makes the demand curve for medical services rotate clockwise and become steeper. When the price is zero, without coinsurance, a certain amount of medical services will be demanded. With coinsurance, this same amount will be demanded. Thus, the quantity demanded is the same with or without coinsurance but only when the price is zero. At a higher and higher price the demand curve rotates more. When the coinsurance percentage is zero (the insurance carrier pays all), the demand curve becomes perfectly vertical.
   b. The existence of indemnity insurance shifts the demand curve for medical services upward. The greater the amount paid by insurance, the more the demand curve will shift.

*Answer to Sample Exam Questions*

1. C is the correct answer. The demand curve for medical care is "fuzzy" because the exact relationship between price and quantity demanded is difficult to determine. See page 102 of the text.

2. A is the correct answer. The vertical axis for a demand curve is "price" not quantity. Statement III is incorrect because a demand curve shows the relationship between price and quantity demanded, not income. See pages 87–90 of the text.

3. The correct answer is A. If elasticity is positive, the good is a normal good. All the other statements are correct. See pages 103–108 of the text.

# 5

# The Demand for Medical Insurance: Traditional and Managed Care Coverage

R emember Joe, who suffered a heart attack at the beginning of Chapter 1? Things turned out quite well, both medically and financially, for our friend Joe. You see, Joe's medical bills were covered by a Blue Cross indemnity insurance plan he had obtained through his employer. Joe could thus afford the best and fastest hospital care money could buy, and the triple bypass surgery he received at the prestigious private teaching hospital was highly successful. Angela, his wife, and the two children are tickled pink now that Joe is back to his former self.

But, how might events have differed if Joe had not been covered by medical insurance, or if Joe was enrolled in a managed care plan? Would Joe have been unduly delayed in the busy emergency room of a public hospital? Would Angela be inordinately stressed out because she was concerned about the unknown financial consequences associated with Joe's illness or worried that the managed care plan may not cover the cost of the care because the hospital did not participate in the plan, or because she did not receive prior authorization for the hospital services? These are among the questions for which we search for answers in this chapter.

Specifically, this chapter

- Looks at the factors influencing the demand for health insurance.

- Examines empirical estimates of the price and income elasticities of the demand for health insurance.

- Discusses the health insurance product, contrasting traditional and managed care coverage.

- Reviews the literature concerning the health care costs and quality of care associated with managed care plans.
- Addresses the regulation of managed care organizations.

# The Demand for Private Health Insurance

Because of imperfect information, many of the choices individuals make as health care consumers or providers involve a substantial amount of uncertainty. For example, for an individual consumer, many medical illnesses occur randomly, and therefore the timing and amount of medical expenditures are uncertain. Likewise, from the health care provider's perspective, patient load and types of treatment are unknown before they actually occur. Since these events are unpredictable, they involve a substantial degree of risk. Because most people generally dislike risk, they are willing to pay some amount of money to avoid it.

For the medical care consumer, health insurance mitigates some of the risk involved in purchasing medical care services. Consumers pay an insurer a certain amount of income (i.e., a premium), and the insurer covers some or all of the medical costs in the event an illness actually occurs. For any given year, the dollar value of the medical services the insurer pays for any single consumer may be higher or lower than the premiums received from that consumer. By operating on a large scale, an insurer pools or spreads the risk among many subscribers so that, on average, the total premiums received *at least* compensate for the total cost of paying for medical services, particularly in the long run. In addition, given some amount of competition in the health insurance market, the difference between total premiums and total benefits paid out to all subscribers (or the loading fee) should approximate a "normal" amount.

Consumers differ in terms of the amounts and types of health insurance coverage they buy, and these differences are reflected in such items as the deductible amount, the coinsurance rate, and the number of events covered. (We will examine the health insurance product more closely later on in the chapter.) In general, a high deductible and a high coinsurance rate reflect less extensive or less complete health insurance coverage. For instance, some consumers purchase health insurance plans that offer first-dollar coverage for all types of medical services, including routine care. Others purchase health insurance plans with large deductibles and copayments that cover only catastrophic illnesses. Differences in health care coverage can be explained by a host of factors, including the price of obtaining health insurance, the individual's degree of risk aversion, the perceived magnitude of the loss relative to income, and information concerning the likelihood that an illness will actually occur.

## Deriving the Demand for Private Health Insurance

We can get a better understanding about how these factors individually influence the quantity demanded of health insurance by focusing on figure 5–1, where the actual utility, $U$, associated with different levels of income, $Y$, is shown for a representative

| FIGURE 5-1 | EXPECTED UTILITY MODEL |
| --- | --- |

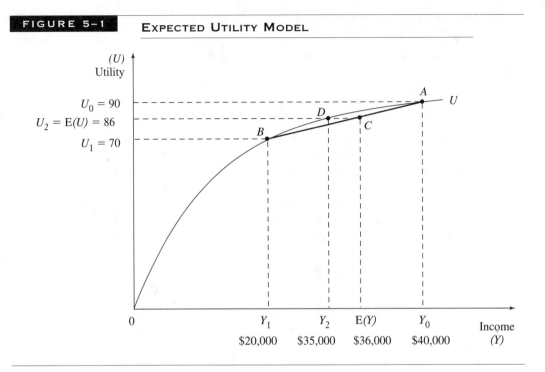

consumer (ignore the chord *AB* for now). The slope of this utility function at any point is $\Delta U / \Delta Y$ and represents the marginal utility of income. The declining slope, or marginal utility of income, is based on the premise that the individual is risk averse. This means the risk-averse person is opposed to a fair gamble where there is a 50–50 chance of losing or gaining one dollar because a dollar loss is valued more highly than a dollar gain. That is, for any given level of income, the pain of losing an incremental dollar exceeds the pleasure associated with gaining an additional dollar.[1]

Suppose a person has an income of $Y_0$ equaling \$40,000. As indicated in the figure, this income level yields actual utility of $U_0$, which amounts to 90 utils.[2] Further, suppose the person faces a choice concerning whether or not to purchase health insurance. The decision is based partly on a belief that if an illness occurs, the medical services will cost \$20,000. Consequently, if the illness occurs and the consumer pays the entire medical bill, income declines to \$20,000 and the level of actual utility falls to $U_1$, or 70 utils.

The two outcomes that can occur if the consumer does not purchase health insurance are represented by points *A* and *B*. At point *A*, no illness occurs and income

---

[1] If the marginal pain equals the marginal pleasure, the slope of the utility curve is constant (a straight line through the origin) and the person is risk neutral. For a risk lover, the pleasure of an additional dollar gained exceeds the pain of an incremental dollar loss, and the slope is increasing in value.

[2] For expository purposes, we assume utility can be measured directly in units called *utils*.

remains at $40,000 such that actual utility equals $U_0$. At point $B$, an illness occurs and (net) income falls to $20,000 such that actual utility equals $U_1$. Because the resulting outcome is unknown before it actually occurs, the individual forms expectations concerning the probability of each outcome occurring. With these subjective probabilities, the expected (rather than actual) levels of utility and income can be determined. Specifically, the individual's expected level of utility, $E(U)$, can be determined by weighing the actual utility levels associated with the two possible outcomes by their subjective probabilities of occurrence, $Pr_0$ and $Pr_1$:

(5–1)   $E(U) = Pr_0 \cdot U_0(Y_0 = \$40,000) + Pr_1 \cdot U_1(Y_1 = \$20,000),$

or

(5–2)   $E(U) = Pr_0 \cdot 90 + Pr_1 \cdot 70,$

where $Pr_0$ and $Pr_1$ sum to 1. Based on equation 5–2, the chord $AB$ in figure 5–1 shows the level of expected utility for various probabilities that the illness will occur. As the probability of getting ill increases, expected utility declines, and this outcome is associated with a point closer to $B$ on the chord. The precise probability value that the individual attaches to the illness occurring is based on his or her best personal estimate. It is likely to depend on such factors as the individual's stock of health, age, and lifestyle.

Suppose the consumer attaches a subjective probability of 20 percent to an illness actually occurring. Following equation 5–2, the expected utility is

(5–3)   $E(U) = .8 \cdot 90 + .2 \cdot 70 = 86$

and the expected level of income, $E(Y)$, is

(5–4)   $E(Y) = Pr_0 \cdot Y_0 + Pr_1 \cdot Y_1 = .8 \cdot 40,000 + .2 \cdot 20,000 = 36,000.$

Equation 5–4 represents the weighted sum of the two income levels with the probability values as the weights. Thus, expected income equals $36,000 and the expected level of utility is 86 utils if insurance is not purchased (and full risk is assumed) given a perceived probability of illness equal to .2 and a magnitude of the loss equal to $20,000. The levels of expected income and expected utility are also shown in figure 5–1.

Notice in the figure that the person is just as well off in terms of actual utility by paying a third party a "certain" income of $5,000 to insure against the expected loss of $4,000. The certain loss of $5,000 reduces net income to $35,000 and provides the consumer with an actual utility level of 86 utils, which equals the expected utility level without insurance. To the consumer, the $1,000 discrepancy, or distance $CD$, represents the maximum amount he or she is willing to pay for health insurance above the expected loss. It reflects the notion that a risk-averse consumer always prefers a known amount of income rather than an expected amount of equal value. This preference reflects the value the consumer places on financial security. It is for this reason that the typical person faces an incentive to purchase health insurance.

It is easy to see from this analysis why an insurance company is willing to insure against the risk. Assuming this person is the average subscriber in the insured group and the probability of an illness occurring is correct from an objective statistical perspective, the insurance company could potentially receive premium revenues of $5,000 to pay the expected medical benefits of $4,000 with enough left over to cover administrative expenses, taxes, and profits. To the insurer, the difference between the premium and medical benefits paid out is referred to as the *loading fee*. In the economics of insurance literature, the loading fee is also referred to as the *price of insurance*.

## Factors Affecting the Quantity Demanded of Health Insurance

The model in figure 5–1 can be used to explain how the price of insurance affects the quantity demanded of health insurance. Under normal circumstances, the consumer purchases health insurance if the actual utility with health insurance exceeds the expected utility without it. In figure 5–1, that happens whenever the loading fee leads to an income level associated with a point between *D* and above *C* on the actual utility curve for the given set of circumstances (i.e., probability values, degree of risk aversion, and magnitude of loss). In terms of the present example, the consumer demands health insurance if the loading fee is less than $1,000 because actual utility exceeds expected utility. If expected utility exceeds actual utility, the consumer does not purchase health insurance coverage because the price is too high (a loading fee producing actual utility between points *D* and *B*). This happens if the loading fee exceeds $1,000 in our example. Finally, if actual and expected utility are equal due to the loading fee, the individual is indifferent between buying and not buying health insurance (point *D* or a loading fee of $1,000). Both options make the consumer equally well off. Therefore, it follows that the loading fee, or the price of health insurance, helps to establish the completeness of insurance coverage and the number of people who insure against medical illnesses. Specifically, as the price of insurance declines, actual utility increases relative to expected utility and the quantity demanded of health insurance increases, *ceteris paribus*.

At this point, it is useful to note that the employer contribution to health insurance premiums, unlike cash income, is presently exempt from federal and state income taxes even though it is a form of in-kind income. For example, if an employer pays cash wages of $800 and provides health insurance benefits equal to $200 per month to an employee, only the $800 is subject to taxes even though total compensation equals $1,000. Assuming a 20 percent marginal tax rate, the individual pays $160 in taxes on $800 of cash income rather than $200 on $1,000 of total compensation.

Thus, relative to cash income (or all other goods purchased out of cash income), health insurance is effectively subsidized by the government because of its tax exemption status. We can view this tax subsidy on health insurance benefits in another way. Each time the employer raises the employee's wage by $1, the employee receives only 100– *t* percent of that $1 as after-tax income, where *t* percent is the marginal tax rate.

However, if employer health insurance contributions increase by \$1, the employee receives the entire dollar as benefits. In effect, the government picks up $t$ percent of the price of the health insurance in forgone taxes and the employee pays the remaining $(100 - t)$ percent in forgone wage income (since both wages and in-kind benefits are substitute forms of compensation).[3] Given $t = 20$, the government implicitly pays 20 cents and the employee pays 80 cents of the marginal dollar spent on health insurance. If we allow for the possibility that not all health insurance premiums are tax exempt (e.g., the health insurance premiums of self-employed people), the effective, or user, price of health insurance can be written as $(1 - et/100)P_{HI}$, where $e$ is the fraction of health insurance premiums exempted from taxes and $P_{HI}$ is the price of health insurance (the loading fee). The user price of health insurance obviously decreases with a higher marginal income tax rate and tax-exempt fraction.

The model in figure 5–1 can also help explain other factors affecting the demand for health insurance. First, the subjective probability of an illness occurring affects the amount of health insurance demanded. In terms of the figure, as the probability of an illness increases from zero to 1, the relevant point on chord $AB$ moves from $A$ toward $B$. Given the shapes of the two curves, the horizontal distance between the actual utility curve and the expected utility line, which measures the willingness to pay for health insurance beyond the expected level of medical benefits, at first gets larger, reaches a maximum, and then approaches zero with a movement from $A$ to $B$. Therefore, holding the loading fee constant, the quantity demanded of health insurance first increases, reaches a maximum amount, and then decreases with respect to a higher probability of an illness occurring. The implication is that individuals insure less against medical events that are either highly unlikely (closer to $A$) or most probable (closer to $B$). In the latter case, it is cheaper for the individual to self-insure (i.e., save money for the "rainy day") and avoid paying the loading fee. For example, assume the probability of illness is 1. In this case, the expected and actual levels of utility are equal at point $B$ in figure 5–1. In this situation, it is cheaper for the individual to self-insure than to pay the loading fee. The probability of an illness occurring is one reason more people insure against random medical events than against routine medical events, such as periodic physical and dental exams, which are expected.

Another factor affecting the amount of insurance coverage is the magnitude of the loss relative to income. Assuming the same probabilities as before, the expected utility line (chord $AB$) in figure 5–1 rotates down and pivots off point $A$ if the magnitude of the loss increases. In this case, the new expected utility line meets the actual utility curve somewhere below point $B$. For the same probability values as before, the horizontal distance between the expected and actual utility curves increases. Thus, the willingness to purchase health insurance increases with a greater magnitude of a loss. This implies that a greater number of people insure against illnesses associated with a large loss, at least relative to income. Insurance coverage is also more complete. The potential for a greater loss is one reason more people have hospital insurance than dental or eye care insurance coverage.

---

[3] In other words, the opportunity cost of \$100 of nontaxable benefits is $(100 - t)$ dollars of wage income.

| TABLE 5-1 | PRICE AND INCOME ELASTICITIES OF THE DEMAND FOR HEALTH INSURANCE | |
|---|---|---|
| **Study** | **Price Elasticity** | **Income Elasticity** |
| Taylor and Wilensky (1983) | −.21 | .02 |
| Farley and Wilensky (1984) | −.41 | .04 |
| Holmer (1984) | −.16 | .01 |
| Short and Taylor (1989) | −.32 | .13 |
| Manning and Marquis (1989) | −.54 | .07 |
| Marquis and Long (1995) | −.03 | .15 |

The final factor affecting the amount of health insurance demanded is the degree of risk aversion. Obviously, people who are more risk averse have more insurance coverage than otherwise identical people who are less risk averse. In fact, according to the theory, a risk lover does not choose to purchase health insurance coverage.

In sum, we can specify the quantity demanded of health insurance, $Q_{HI}$, as a function of the following factors:

**(5–5)**    $Q_{HI} = f[(1 - et/100) \cdot P_{HI},$ Degree of risk aversion, Probability of an illness occurring, Magnitude of loss, Income].

With suitable data, equation 5–5 can be estimated to determine the user price and income elasticities of the demand for health insurance. In practice, however, it is very difficult to measure the user price and quantity demanded of health insurance. Therefore, various proxies are used depending on data availability. For example, the price of health insurance, $P_{HI}$, is sometimes proxied by the size of the insured group. The expectation is that the loading fee, or the price of health insurance, will fall with a larger group size due to administrative and risk-spreading economies. Some studies assume the price of health insurance is the same for all individuals and allow only marginal tax rates, $t$, and the tax-exempt fraction, $e$, to vary.

Proxy measures for the quantity of health insurance must also be employed. The quantity of health insurance is usually measured by either total insurance premiums, some measure of insurance coverage completeness, or a coverage option (e.g., an HMO versus a fee-for-service plan). Table 5–1 displays some of the estimated price and income elasticities of the demand for health insurance reported in various studies. The studies reveal that individuals possess a price-inelastic demand for health insurance. Furthermore, while health insurance is considered to be a normal good (i.e., an income elasticity greater than zero), the studies found a relatively small income

# The Demand for Employer Contributions to Health Insurance Premiums

Voluntary private employer contributions to health insurance premiums as a percentage of total wage and salary compensation grew from 1.47 in 1965 to 6.56 in 1995.[1] Economic theory suggests that the proportion of health care benefits in total compensation can be attributed to a variety of factors. First, given the tax-exempt status of employer contributions to health insurance, higher marginal tax rates on wage income reduce the user price of health insurance and lead to a greater quantity demanded of employer contributions to health insurance. Thus, the marginal tax on wage income and, correspondingly, the user price of health insurance partly account for employer contributions to health care benefits.

Second, the size of the insured group affects the price of health care benefits. As the size of the group increases and administrative and risk-bearing costs fall, the price of health care benefits declines. The lower price raises the demand for employer contributions. Therefore, the number of employees at the typical firm may be partly responsible for the amount of employer contributions to health care benefits.

Third, changes in real income can affect the demand for employer-provided health care benefits. The exact relationship depends on the relative income elasticities of the demand for wage and non-wage compensation. Higher income leads to an increased demand for employer contributions to health insurance if the income elasticity of demand for health care benefits is greater than that for wage compensation.

Fourth, health care benefits increase relative to wage compensation as a result of unionization. Unions provide information to employees about the tax and group size advantages of health care benefits, which serves to increase the demand for health care benefits relative to wage income.

Finally, demographic factors, such as the age and gender composition of the workforce and the distribution of job characteristics, cause the demand for employer-provided health care benefits

to change given potential differences in risk aversion and medical utilization rates. For example, the labor force participation rate of women age 16 years and older increased from 37.7 percent in 1960 to 57.9 percent in 1993 (*Statistical Abstract of the United States, 1994,* table 616). Given that women generally consume more medical services than men, it is easy to see why the demand for employer-provided medical insurance changes when the female labor force participation rate adjusts.

Using time series data, a study by Long and Scott (1982) determined how these various factors individually affected the demand for employer-provided health care benefits in the United States over the period 1947 to 1979. The authors specified a linear multiple regression equation linking the percentage of compensation as health insurance (PCTHLTINS) to the average marginal tax rate (MTR), average real family income (RFAMINC), union membership as a fraction of the total labor force (UNION), the percentage of total employees who are female (PCTFEM), and the percentage of employment found in the service industries (PCTSERV).[2] They obtained the following results (*t*-statistics in parentheses):

(5–6)  PCTHLTINS =
   $-8.64 + .0284$ MTR
   (6.22)  (3.98)

   $+ .0498$ RFAMINC $- .0094$ UNION
   (1.14)        (.57)

   $+ .088$ PCTFEM $+ .1283$ PCTSERV
   (3.72)        (5.52)

   Adj. $R^2 = .9968, N = 32$

The coefficient estimate on MTR was found to be positive and statistically significant, lending strong support for the premise that higher marginal

*(continued)*

INSIGHT 5-1

**(continued)**

tax rates reduce the price and increase the quantity demanded of employer contributions to health insurance. Using sample averages, Long and Scott computed the elasticity to be .41, implying that a 10 percent increase in the marginal tax rate increases the health insurance percentage by 4.1 percent.

The coefficient estimate on real family income, RFAMINC, was found to be positive but statistically insignificant. The result suggests that the income elasticities of demand are approximately equal for wage income and health care benefits. No empirical evidence was found for the expected direct relation between unionization and employer-sponsored health care benefits given that the coefficient estimate on UNION was not statistically different from zero. However, some cross-sectional findings in this same study and a paper by Woodbury (1983) did report a positive relation be-

tween the degree of unionization and total fringe benefits. Finally, the last two variables, reflecting demographic (PCTFEM) and employment (PCT-SERV) differences over time in the United States, were both shown to lead to a higher percentage of compensation paid as employer contributions to health insurance.

[1]Estimates are drawn from Cowan and Braden (1997).

[2]Due to limited data availability, Long and Scott were unable to examine the relation between firm size and the demand for health care benefits in a time series context. In their cross-sectional study of total fringe benefits, they found a positive relation between firm size and the demand for total fringe benefits (also see Woodbury [1983]). Long and Scott also specified a variable reflecting the labor turnover rate. Labor turnover did not seem to be a likely determinant of health care benefits, however, and proved to be statistically insignificant; hence, the results for this variable are not discussed above.

effect.[4] Even the demand for long-term care insurance is found to be inelastic, with price and income elasticities of about $-.39$ and $.18$, respectively (Kumar et al., 1995).

The importance of the elasticity estimates becomes apparent later when we discuss how public policies might be used to influence the quantity demanded of health insurance. For instance, it is argued that complete health insurance coverage provides an incentive for excessive spending on medical services. To counteract the "moral hazard" problem, government can reduce the completeness of insurance coverage by removing part or all of the tax exemption on health insurance. According to the preceding demand analysis, the partial or full loss of the tax exemption raises the user price and thereby reduces the quantity demanded of health insurance.

---

[4]These studies generally assume the individual is able to make marginal changes in the insurance policy. But employer-sponsored group insurance policies are largely beyond the control of the single individual employee. Typically, the employer or union representatives make decisions concerning the insurance package by taking into consideration the welfare of the overall group rather than that of any one individual employee. See Goldstein and Pauly (1976) or Pauly (1986) for further discussion on this point. When employees can select from multiple similar plans offered by the employer, demand is much more responsive to price. For example, Dowd and Feldman (1994/95) found that the demand for a health plan is highly elastic with respect to price at about $-7.9$ when multiple similar plans are offered.

**FIGURE 5-2**  MODEL OF THE INSURER RELATION

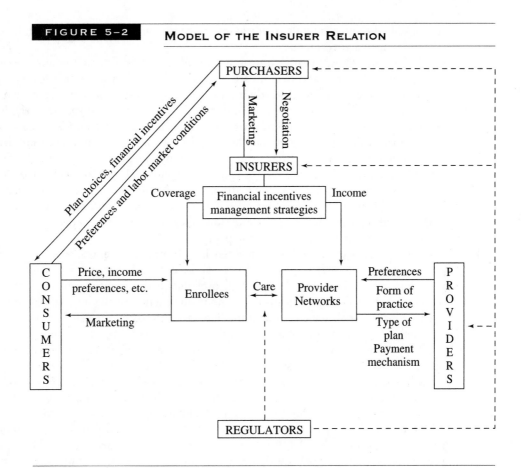

Adapted from Gold et al., "Behind the Curve," *Medical Care Research and Review* 52 (September 1995) figure 1. Reprinted by permission of Sage Publications, Inc.

## The Health Insurance Product: Traditional versus Managed Care Insurance

One way to begin our discussion of the health insurance product is by focusing on the nexus of relationships between the insurer and the other main actors upon whom insurers are dependent: purchasers, consumers, providers, and regulators. To help us focus, figure 5–2, which is actually a more elaborate version of figure 2–1, provides a diagram depicting the relationship between these major players. Notice that the insurer is in the center of the figure, which makes much sense given that the insurer, at least in today's world, has the important responsibilities of designing the payment system and coordinating the care that takes place between enrollees and provider networks, among other obligations. The figure also demonstrates that someone else is often responsible for purchasing the medical insurance for enrollees, such as an employer, a labor union, or a government.

Before the 1980s, the health insurance product was fairly easy to define because the consumer, insurer, and health care provider relationship was much less complicated. Most consumers, through their employers, purchased conventional indemnity insurance that allowed for free choice of health care provider. Insurance premiums were largely determined by **community rating,** where the premium is based on the risk characteristics of the entire membership. In contrast, when premiums are determined using **experience rating,** insurers place individuals, or groups of individuals, into different risk categories based on various identifiable personal characteristics, such as age, gender, industrial occupation, and prior illnesses. The main difference among health insurance plans before the 1980s was simply the amount of the deductible and copayment, if any, that the subscriber had to pay for medical services and the specific benefits covered under the plan.

Because physicians typically operated in solo practices, enrollees dealt directly with individual physicians or local hospitals for care rather than with a network of providers before the 1980s. Health care providers had full autonomy and practiced medicine as they deemed appropriate. The main function of the insurer was to manage the financial risk associated with medical care and to pay the usual, customary, or reasonable (UCR) charge for any medical services rendered by physicians.

Since 1980, however, managed care organizations (MCOs) have exploded on the health care scene. The phrase "managed care" has been assigned to these organizations because, by design, they are supposed to emphasize cost-effective methods of providing comprehensive services to enrollees in exchange for a prepaid premium. As mentioned in Chapter 2, MCOs integrate the financing and delivery of medical care. The integration often involves such practices as a network of providers, reimbursement methods other than UCR charges, and various review mechanisms. MCOs also rely to a greater degree on experience rating of enrollees because of the price competition that results.

The main types of MCOs are the health maintenance organization, the preferred provider organization, and the point of service plan. A **health maintenance organization (HMO),** like other MCOs, combines the financing and delivery of care into one organization by providing medical care to enrollees in exchange for a prepaid premium. A distinguishing feature of an HMO is that the assigned or chosen primary care provider acts as a gatekeeper and refers the patient for specialty and inpatient care. Four distinct types of HMOs are generally recognized:

**Staff Model.** In this type of HMO, physicians are directly employed by the organization on a salary basis. In terms of figure 5–2, a staff HMO merges the insurer and provider functions. Because medical care is not reimbursed on a fee-for-service basis, physicians have little if any incentive to overutilize medical services.

**Group Model.** This type of HMO provides physician services by contracting with a group practice. Normally the group is compensated on a capitation basis.

As a result, physicians in the group face a strong disincentive to overutilize medical services.

**Network Model.** The only difference between the group model and the network model is that in the latter case, the HMO contracts with more than one group practice for physician services. As is the case with the group model, compensation is generally on a capitation basis.

**Individual Practice Association (IPA) Model.** This form of HMO contracts with a number of physicians from various types of practice settings for medical services. In this situation, physicians generally provide care in a traditional office setting and are normally compensated on a fee-for-service basis, but at a discounted rate. In return, the HMO promises a large and continuous volume of patients.

A **preferred provider organization (PPO)** is a different type of insurer and health care provider arrangement. A PPO exists when a third-party payer provides financial incentives to enrollees to acquire health care from a predetermined network of physicians and hospitals. The incentive can be in terms of a higher copayment or a higher deductible when someone acquires medical care outside the network of health care providers. To participate in a PPO network, physicians agree to accept a lower fee for services rendered. In return for a lower fee, physicians are promised a steady supply of patients. Normally, patients can directly seek out specialty or inpatient care if they belong to a PPO.

Like PPOs, **point-of-service (POS)** plans provide generous coverage when enrollees use in-network services and cover out-of-network services at reduced reimbursement rates. Unlike PPOs but similar to HMOs, POS plans assign each enrollee a primary caregiver who acts as a gatekeeper and authorizes specialty and inpatient care.

Jensen et al. (1997) estimate that nearly three-fourths of insured workers in 1995 were covered by MCOs. Traditional indemnity insurance, which covered nearly 49 percent of insured workers in 1993, fell to a 27 percent coverage rate in 1995. HMOs continued their dominance of MCO plans, covering 27 percent of the insured employees, but PPOs and POS plans were not far behind, covering 25 percent and 20 percent of insured workers, respectively, in 1995. Although possessing the lowest share, POS plans enjoyed the fastest growth rate, increasing from 9 percent of insured employees in 1993.

Landon, Wilson, and Cleary (1998), among others, argue that the traditional distinction among health insurance products, such as conventional insurance and MCOs, or even the distinction among MCOs, has become very blurred in practice. For instance, even the so-called conventional insurance plans now involve some type of utilization review program. Given that the traditional taxonomy of insurance plans may no longer adequately describe the differences among organizations, it is better to differentiate among health insurance products based on the types and restrictiveness of the financial incentives and management strategies facing patients and health care providers. Let us elaborate.

*Financial Incentives and Management Strategies Facing Consumers/Patients*

Depending on the precise nature of the health insurance product, consumers/patients face different financial incentives to use medical care. As mentioned in Chapter 2 and examined theoretically in Chapter 4, the consumer's out-of-pocket price, as captured by the size of the deductible and copayment, inversely affects the quantity demanded of medical care. Some health insurance plans may contain high deductibles and co-payments as a way of containing medical costs. In addition, some plans may set their premiums on an experience-rated basis as an incentive for subscribers to adopt more healthy lifestyles.

In addition to indirect financial incentives, insurers may also adopt various management strategies to directly affect the consumer's utilization of medical care. First, the insurer may require prior medical screening to avoid insuring high-risk patients or exclude coverage for preexisting conditions. Insurers may also restrict the choice of provider by building provider networks in which the consumer must participate. In addition, the insurer may employ a primary care gatekeeper to determine whether further services are medically warranted. Pre-authorization of medical services, a type of utilization review practice, is another management strategy affecting the consumer's direct use of medical care.

By combining the financial incentives and management strategies facing patients, we can get a better understanding of the underlying health insurance product. For instance, a health insurance plan with a high deductible and copayment and experience-rated premiums, combined with limits on choice of physician and pre-authorization, offers much less insurance than one with no out-of-pocket costs or pre-authorization, community-rated premiums, and full choice of provider. The latter situation aptly describes the conventional insurance offered by the Blues back in the 1970s. A POS plan comes close to an example of the former situation as far as financial incentives and management strategies facing consumers are concerned.

*Financial Incentives and Management Strategies Facing Health Care Providers*

The health insurance product may also contain financial incentives and/or management strategies to affect the delivery of medical care by health care providers. As a result, the health insurance product can also be differentiated based on the types and restrictiveness of the financial incentives and management strategies facing health care providers. In terms of financial incentives, the health insurance product may adopt different provider reimbursement practices, such as fee-for-service, capitation, bonuses, and/or withholds. Withholds occur when the insurer withholds part of the health care provider's reimbursement until after a stipulated period at which the appropriate use of medical care has been evaluated. Inappropriate use of medical care results in the physician not receiving all or part of the withheld money. The prospect of incomplete reimbursement payments presumably acts as an incentive for health care providers to offer the truly medically necessary care.

As we saw in Chapter 2, fixed payment systems, such as capitation, can discourage the delivery of high-cost, low-benefit medicine. Capitation places the health care providers financially at risk for any cost overruns. When properly designed, performance-based measures, such as bonuses and withholds, can accomplish that same goal.

Insurers can also directly influence the delivery of medical care through various management strategies. Selective contracting, deselection of providers, physician profiling, utilization review, practice guidelines, and formularies are among the more common management strategies facing health care providers. **Selective contracting** occurs when managed care plans contract solely with an exclusive set of providers. The selection and **deselection** of providers involves the establishment of the criteria and process by which health care providers will be included in or terminated from the network. For example, insurers may include physicians in their network who are of high quality and/or utilize cost-effective practice patterns. **Physician profiling** may be used to monitor performance in the selection or deselection process. The profiling may only include information, for example, on the primary care physician's track record regarding referrals to specialty and inpatient care as a way to identify high-cost providers, or it may include information on quality of care or patient satisfaction.

**Utilization review** programs "seek to determine whether specific services are medically necessary and whether they are delivered at an appropriate level of intensity and cost" (Ermann, 1988, p. 683). **Practice guidelines** provide information to health care providers about the appropriate medical practice in certain situations. A **formulary** contains a list of pharmaceutical products that physicians must prescribe whenever necessary. All these management strategies are designed to directly affect how a physician behaves in a specific clinical circumstance.

Consequently, the health insurance product also differs based on the type of provider reimbursement method and the existence and restrictiveness of various management strategies. For example, a capitation reimbursement scheme in conjunction with utilization review and practice guidelines means a much different insurance product than one with a fee-for-service payment system in which the health care provider has full autonomy over patient care. The former situation resembles the staff HMO whereas the latter reflects the traditional BC/BS or commercial insurance of the 1970s.

The first column in table 5–2 provides a summary of the four basic features of any health insurance product: patient financial incentives, consumer management strategies, provider financial incentives, and provider management strategies. Below each feature is a list of specific policies aimed at altering the behavior of either consumers or health care providers. As you can see, health insurance is a complex and multidimensional product. At one extreme, you have the perfectly unrestricted health insurance plan, the basic characteristics of which are provided in the second column of table 5–2. With this type of insurance consumers pay no out-of-pocket prices; health care providers are reimbursed based on the usual, customary, and reasonable fee-for-service; and there are no consumer or provider management strategies. At the other extreme, the basic characteristics of a perfectly restrictive insurance plan are shown in the third column of table 5–2. In this case, significant financial incentives and management strategies face both consumers and health care providers. In terms

| TABLE 5–2 | SPECTRUM OF HEALTH INSURANCE PRODUCTS | | |
|---|---|---|---|
| **Basic Features (Examples)** | **Unrestricted or Complete Insurance Plan** | **Restrictive Insurance Plan** |
| Patient Financial Incentives<br>  Deductibles<br>  Copayment<br>  Premiums | no or low deductible with no copayment<br><br>community rated | significant deductible with a high copayment<br><br>experience rated |
| Consumer Management Strategies<br>  Prior medical screening<br>  Restrictions on choice<br>  Gatekeeper<br>  Pre-authorization | no restrictions | consumers must receive care exclusively from the network of providers |
| Provider Financial Incentives<br>  Risk-sharing and/or bonus arrangements | none—UCR charges | capitation with bonuses or withholds |
| Provider Management Strategies<br>  Selective contracting<br>  Deselection<br>  Physician profiling<br>  Utilization review<br>  Practice guidelines<br>  Formularies | none | An array of management strategies are employed to control costs. |

of examples, the traditional Blue Cross/Blue Shield insurance plan of the 1970s compares quite closely to the unrestricted plan described in table 5–2, while the staff HMO, except for the significant out-of-pocket price, fits the insurance plan described in the last column of table 5–2.

Although table 5–2 provides a good framework for defining and conceptualizing the health insurance product, some caveats are in order. For one, it is important to realize that any one health insurer may offer multiple health insurance products. For example, a health insurer may offer both a staff HMO and a traditional indemnity plan. Of course, the prices of the two plans should differ significantly. It is also important to realize that health care providers may deal with various health insurance products. A large physician practice may treat some patients who belong to a PPO plan and others who subscribe to HMO plans, for example. An additional complexity is that a group physician practice may be reimbursed on a capitation basis by the insurer whereas the individual physician within the practice is compensated on a salary basis. It is also important to mention that financial incentives and management strategies may serve as complementary or substitute methods of controlling the behavior of consumers and providers. As Gold et al. (1995, p. 315) point out:

> For example, plans that capitate primary care physicians and place them at risk for specialty referrals and inpatient care through a withholding account

may be expected to place particular emphasis on monitoring physicians to ensure that the financial incentives do not result in underservice. On the other hand, plans operating in areas where physicians are resistant to accepting much financial risk may rely particularly heavily on nonfinancial mechanisms such as utilization management to influence practice patterns.

## MCOs and the Cost and Quality of Medical Care

There has been considerable debate in the academic literature and the popular press concerning the effect of managed care plans on the cost and quality of medical care. By design, MCOs are supposed to employ cost-effective methods of delivering a comprehensive set of services to enrollees for a fixed premium. The original proponents of managed care thought that MCOs would encourage preventive and coordinated primary care as a way of reducing the need for more expensive specialty and inpatient care. Also, advocates thought that MCOs would eliminate the high-cost, low-benefit medicine associated with traditional fee-for-service indemnity insurance (i.e., the moral hazard problem). As a result, high quality of care and low operating costs were expected from MCOs.

However, critics argue that the main interest of MCOs is the bottom line. Because lower quality of care translates into lower costs and higher profits, critics claim that MCOs face an incentive to reduce the quality of care, perhaps by denying or skimping on costly but necessary medical treatments. Health care providers have no recourse but to follow the wishes of the MCOs given the restrictive financial incentives and management strategies they face, according to the critics.

Not surprisingly, the debate has led to a considerable amount of empirical studies devoted to the relation between managed care organizations and the cost and quality of medical care. The findings, though too voluminous to cite in sufficient detail, have been conveniently summarized by Miller and Luft (1994, 1997). Specifically, Miller and Luft (1994) find that MCOs, largely HMOs, provide medical cost savings of about 15 to 20 percent primarily through a reduced hospital-intensive practice style.

Schwartz and Mendelson (1992) argue that the cited cost savings represent only a one-time reduction and that MCOs will be incapable of continually lowering how quickly health care costs rise over time. They argue that MCOs have simply squeezed out the excess in the health care system. Once all the excess or slack is eliminated, future attempts by MCOs to lower costs will be impossible at some point unless rationing of services takes place, according to Schwartz and Mendelson.

In response to Schwartz and Mendelson's argument, some health economists point out that medical care providers, in a health economy characterized by fee-for-service indemnity insurance, face an incentive to compete on the basis of quality through cost-enhancing technologies (e.g., Weisbrod, 1991). If so, MCOs might slow the growth of health care costs if the proper financial incentives are created for health care providers to demand and adopt less cost-enhancing or more cost-saving technologies. As proof, Teplensky et al. (1995) find that expected net revenue is an important determinant behind the adoption of MRIs and conclude that "mechanisms such as global budgeting and capitation, which force hospitals to make trade-offs among alternative investments, appear to offer particular promise for slowing the rate of technology diffusion" (p. 461). The General Accounting Office (1994) provides some corroborating evidence by reporting that "officials from most of the 17 hospitals [in Texas] stated that managed care creates incentives for their hospitals to limit expenditures on new technologies that increase costs because hospitals may have difficulty recouping their investments where revenue is based on discounted or fixed rates rather than costs or charges" (p. 25). It remains to be seen whether MCOs will affect the adoption of medical technology on a much broader scale and permanently slow the growth of health care costs.

In terms of the quality of care provided by MCOs, the evidence is mixed. For example, in Miller and Luft's (1997) extensive review of the literature, quality of care evidence from 15 studies showed an equal number of significantly better and worse HMO results compared with non-HMO plans. However, Miller and Luft point out that in several instances, HMO enrollees with chronic conditions received worse quality of care.

A number of empirical and theoretical factors may account for the quality of care similarity in MCO and non-MCO plans. First, empirically it is very difficult to distinguish among health plans in practice, as described above, especially when health insurers have multiple plans and health care providers treat patients belonging to a number of alternative plans. Quality of care may appear similar because the observations are wrongly assigned into MCO and non-MCO plans.

Second, some MCOs are structured as not-for-profit institutions. For example, 42 percent of all HMO enrollees received their care from organizations that were structured as not-for-profit in 1994 (Corrigan et al., 1997). Many researchers argue that not-for-profit institutions pursue goals other than profit maximization, as we will see in Chapter 10. Researchers often assume that not-for-profit enterprises maximize the quantity and quality of care subject to a breakeven level of profits. If not-for-profit MCOs attempt to maximize the quantity and quality of care rather than the "bottom line," it is not theoretically apparent why the quality of care in those MCOs should differ from that of traditional indemnity insurers.

Third, like traditional indemnity plans, MCOs often invest huge sums of money establishing brand names that can be tarnished by offering inferior care. The prospect of losing repeat buyers and not receiving a proper return on investment can place a considerable amount of pressure on MCOs to provide the proper level of care. Of course, well-informed consumers are necessary for that kind of pressure to materialize. In this regard, it would be interesting to know if the constant attention given MCOs in the popular press and political arena has had any effect on the behavior and performance of MCOs.

Fourth, physicians that contract with MCOs most likely subscribe to the same basic ethical code of conduct (like the Hippocratic Oath) as the doctors that deal with indemnity insurers. In fact, many physicians simultaneously contract with both types of insurers. Although doctors may find themselves pressured by the financial incentives and management strategies of MCOs at the margin, it is not clear theoretically if these pressures dominate over ethical concerns, on average.

These four considerations make it very difficult to determine if MCOs and non-MCOs deliver different levels of care. Better-developed empirical analyses are

# Satisfaction with Managed Care in Switzerland

Not a day goes by, it seems, without a popular press article describing the experience of managed care in the United States. But do we know anything about how managed care has fared in other countries? To some extent we do. Perneger, Etter, and Rougemont (1996) were able to conduct a natural experiment on the effect of switching enrollees from indemnity health insurance to a managed care plan in Switzerland. It all began in the fall of 1992 when the University of Geneva automatically transferred the members of its indemnity plan into a managed care plan. Some of the characteristics associated with the managed care plan were restricted choice of primary care provider, gatekeeper referral to specialty care, gatekeepers paid on a salary basis, and no consumer copayment.

Employees semi-voluntarily joined the managed care program because they had only two choices. One choice was to switch to managed care and receive the benefit of a university-negotiated group insurance premium. The other was to opt out of the university plan and find a new indemnity insurance plan. Because the monthly premium was about 25 percent higher for the indemnity plan than for the managed care plan, 88 percent of the university's former plan members switched to managed care.

Perneger et al. performed a before-and-after evaluation of health status and satisfaction with care in the managed care and indemnity plans. Specifically, they compared three groups of enrollees: 332 managed care joiners, 186 nonjoiners who opted out and purchased an indemnity plan on their own, and a control group of 296 persons who continuously enrolled in other indemnity plans. Health status and satisfaction with care in-formation was collected at the time of the switch and one year later.

The researchers found that health status over the one-year period remained unchanged in the three groups. Satisfaction with health insurance coverage increased for those belonging to the MCO but satisfaction with health insurance coverage declined for both the nonjoiners and the continuous indemnity plan enrollees. In addition, they found that the nonjoiners and the continuous indemnity plan members both experienced an increase in their satisfaction with health care, particularly with continuity of care, whereas the joiners suffered a loss in satisfaction with health care.

The main implication of the study is that the semi-voluntary change from an indemnity plan to a managed care plan had a mixed effect on global indicators of care: health status remained unchanged and satisfaction with insurance coverage increased but satisfaction with health care decreased for those in the managed care plan. While the basic limitation of the study is the one-year follow-up period, the authors point out that their results are consistent with those of the RAND Health Insurance Experiment of the 1970s (see Chapter 4). The RAND study also found that health status remained unchanged but satisfaction with health care worsened for a group of individuals who were randomly assigned to a managed care plan. The general dissatisfaction with health care in MCOs should not come as too much of a surprise given that economic theory predicts that people receive generous amounts of care, perhaps too much care, in a fee-for-service indemnity plan. If MCOs force individuals to consume the appropriate amount of care, obviously some will be disappointed.

necessary. Until these analyses are forthcoming, Miller and Luft (1997, p. 22) warn:

> Nonetheless, in the absence of better information, the policy debate will use available research results. When research is limited or absent, anecdote prevails. The reliance in policy debate on anecdotes more than research results

biases the debate against managed care, because not all studies will produce results favorable to HMOs, but nearly all anecdotes will be unfavorable to HMOs. This bias can affect health policy and therefore ultimately affect competition among plans and providers.

## The Regulation of MCOs

Although little systematic evidence exists to support the hypothesis that MCOs reduce the quality of care, many states and the federal government have introduced or enacted various regulations to influence the behavior of MCOs. Miller (1997, p. 1102) notes that the regulatory actions taken to control managed care practices have been "referred to as 'patient protection' or 'patient bill of rights' acts by proponents and as 'anti-managed' bills by those opposed." The legislation has attempted to extend the rights of patients and physicians and also improve the patient/physician relationship under managed care. According to Miller, in just six months from January to July 1996, more than 400 bills were introduced in the various states to control managed care practices. Most of the laws concern such issues as anti-gag rules, limits on financial incentives, continuity of care, and expanding the rights of health care professionals. Let's examine each of these issues more closely.

**Gag rules** prohibit doctors in a managed care plan from discussing treatment options not covered under the plan, from providing information on plan limitations, or from commenting unfavorably upon the plan. Opponents of managed care argue that gag rules cause physicians to deny care by suppressing useful information on alternative treatments that the managed care plan may not find cost-effective to provide. Managed care representatives claim that the so-called gag rules are designed to prevent physicians from disparaging the plan or releasing proprietary information concerning compensation and similar issues.

Critics further argue that managed care payment systems, such as capitation or performance-based systems like bonuses or withholds, create a financial incentive for physicians to deny medically appropriate or useful treatments. Indeed, much mention has been made in the popular press of "drive-through medicine," involving short maternity stays in hospitals or mastectomies taking place in outpatient rather than inpatient facilities because of managed care financial arrangements. Laws limiting financial incentives are designed to prevent denial of care from taking place. Managed care representatives, on the other hand, argue that the financial incentives of MCOs are necessary to control the moral hazard problem.

Miller notes that state policies offer little concrete guidance about how the general prohibition against financial incentives applies to the myriad financial arrangements set by MCOs. As a result, she claims that without additional clarification, regulatory actions against managed care financial arrangements will have to be argued on a case-by-case basis, creating much uncertainty for the various parties involved.

Medical experts argue that continuity of care is an important consideration for the patient/physician relationship and for patient well-being, especially for certain groups, such as pregnant women or the severely ill. Critics of MCOs claim that continuity of care is at stake because some employers subscribe to only one managed care plan, because a managed care plan may change its networks of physicians, or because physicians may be deselected. In all these cases, consumers have to pay more to visit a physician of their own choice and the continuity of care is compromised. Although proponents argue that MCOs can only provide the desired health care cost savings for society by directing patients to selected physicians, laws have been introduced in many states to extend the option of continued care from primary care givers.

In addition, numerous laws have been introduced across the states that aim to expand the rights of health care professionals. With the growth of MCOs, many health care professionals feel the pressure from market demands and also the loss of autonomy brought on by contracts with managed care plans. For example, some physicians find themselves unable to participate in or are deselected from managed care plans without cause.

The first laws introduced concerned any willing provider (AWP) or freedom of choice (FOC) laws. According to Hellinger (1995, p. 297), "AWP laws require managed care plans to accept any qualified provider who is willing to accept the terms and conditions of a managed care plan." According to the law, MCOs do not have to contract with all providers but must explicitly state evaluation criteria and ensure "due process" for providers wishing to contract with the plan. Due process rights provide professionals with access to information regarding MCO standards, termination decisions, and physician profiling. FOC laws allow a patient to be reimbursed for medical services received from qualified physicians from outside the network. FOC laws do not guarantee that the patient will incur the same out-of-pocket cost, however (Hellinger, 1995). Proponents of AWP and FOC laws argue that they increase the continuity of care by offering a fuller choice of provider. Opponents argue that without selective contracting, managed care plans are unable to obtain volume discounts because they are powerless to channel patients to selected providers. In addition, it is alleged that these laws lead to a diminished quality of care because of the higher monitoring costs brought on by a greater number of health care providers (Hellinger, 1995).

In sum, anti-gag laws, laws restricting the financial incentives of MCOs, laws promoting continuity of care, and laws extending the rights of health care professionals are among the various regulations advanced by various states to control the practices of MCOs. The basic hypothesis is that MCOs face an incentive to restrict the quality of care because increased profits can be made. Critics claim that various financial incentives and management strategies help MCOs achieve their objective of maximum profits. Interestingly, all these laws essentially attempt to transform MCOs into indemnity plans. The superiority of indemnity and managed care plans remains a controversial issue and is the subject of ongoing theoretical and empirical debates.

## SUMMARY

As for any good or service, a demand exists for private health insurance that can be derived theoretically from a utility maximization model. As a result, the quantity demanded of health insurance can be specified as a function of user price, income, and other factors. Empirical studies have found that an individual's demand for health insurance is inelastic with respect to both price and income.

The health insurance product is multidimensional and very complex because many attributes, such as benefits covered, out-of-pocket payments, choice of provider, and the provider payment scheme, must be considered. Most of the insured in the United States today are covered by some type of managed care plan. Managed care plans are found to lower the cost of providing health care and seem not to have seriously compromised the quality of care. Many states have enacted various regulations to control the financial incentives and management strategies adopted by managed care plans.

## Review Questions and Problems

1. Joe is currently unemployed and without health insurance coverage. He derives utility ($U$) from his interest income on his savings ($Y$) according to the following function:

$$U = 5Y^{1/2}.$$

Joe presently makes about $40,000 of interest income per year. He realizes that there is about a 5 percent probability that he may suffer a heart attack. The cost of treatment will be about $20,000 if a heart attack occurs.

   *a.* Calculate Joe's expected utility level without any health insurance coverage.

   *b.* Calculate Joe's expected income without any health insurance coverage.

   *c.* Suppose Joe must pay a premium of $1,500 for health insurance coverage with ACME insurance. Would he buy the health insurance? Why or why not?

   *d.* Suppose now that the government passes a law that allows all people—not just the self-employed or employed—to have their entire insurance premium exempted from taxes. Joe is in the 33 percent tax bracket. Would he buy the health insurance at a premium cost of $1,500? Why or why not? What implication can be drawn from the analysis?

   *e.* Suppose Joe purchases the health insurance coverage and represents the average subscriber, and his expectations are correct. Calculate the loading fee the insurance company will receive.

2. During the Reagan administration, the marginal tax rate on wage income fell dramatically. For example, the top rate was sliced from 70 to 33 percent. Use the demand theory of health insurance to predict the effect of this change on the quantity demanded of employer-sponsored health insurance.

3. Explain the effect of the following changes on the quantity demanded of health insurance.

   *a.* A reduction in the tax-exempt fraction of health insurance premiums

   *b.* An increase in buyer income

   *c.* An increase in per capita medical expenditures

   *d.* New technologies that enable medical illnesses to be predicted more accurately

   *e.* A tendency among buyers to become less risk averse, on average

4. What are the primary differences between the HMO, PPO, and POS plans?

5. Explain the following terms:

   *a.* Community rating

   *b.* Experience rating

   *c.* Selective contracting

   *d.* Utilization review

   *e.* Physician profiling

   *f.* Practice guidelines

   *g.* Formulary

   *h.* Gatekeeper

   *i.* Gag rules

   *j.* Any Willing Provider law

   *k.* Freedom of Choice law

6. Briefly summarize the evidence regarding managed care and the cost and quality of medical care.

7. If you had the choice between a traditional unrestricted indemnity plan with a 10 percent copayment and a staff HMO with no copayment, at what percentage difference in premiums (i.e., 10 percent, 20 percent, 30 percent) would you be indifferent between the plans? Do you think your choice of the percentage difference is a function of your age and/or health status? If you were elderly and/or sickly, which plan would you prefer if they cost you the same amount? Why?

8. Would a theory X'er or Y'er want increased regulation of MCOs? Why?

## References

Cowan, Cathy A., and Bradley R. Braden. "Business, Households and Government: Health Care Spending, 1995." *Health Care Financing Review* 18 (spring 1997), pp. 195–206.

Corrigan, Janet M., Jill S. Eden, Marsha R. Gold, and Jeremy D. Pickreign. "Trends Toward a National Health Care Marketplace." *Inquiry* 34 (spring 1997), pp. 11–28.

Dowd, Bryan, and Roger Feldman. "Premium Elasticities of Health Plan Choice." *Inquiry* 31 (winter 1994/95), pp. 438–44.

Ermann, Dan. "Hospital Utilization Review. Past Experience, Future Directions." *Journal of Health Politics, Policy, and Law* 13 (winter 1989), pp. 683-704.

Farley, Pamela J., and Gail Wilensky. "Household Wealth and Health Insurance as Protection Against Medical Risks." In *Horizontal Equity, Uncertainty, and Economic Well-Being*, edited by David Martin and Timothy Smeeding. Chicago: University of Chicago Press for the NBER, 1984, pp. 323–54.

General Accounting Office. *Hospital Costs: Cost Control Efforts at 17 Texas Hospitals.* GAO-AIMD–95–21. Washington DC, December 1994.

Gold, Marsha, Lyle Nelson, Timothy Lake, Robert Hurley, and Robert Berenson. "Behind the Curve: A Critical Assessment of How Little Is Known about Arrangements between

Managed Care Plans and Physicians." *Medical Care Research and Review* 52 (September 1995), pp. 307–41.

Goldstein, Gerald S., and Mark V. Pauly. "Group Health Insurance as a Local Public Good." In *The Role of Health Insurance in the Health Services Sector,* edited by Richard Rossett. New York: NBER, 1976, pp. 73–110.

Hellinger, Fred J. "Update: Any-Willing-Provider and Freedom-of-Choice Laws: An Economic Assessment." *Health Affairs* 14 (winter 1995), pp. 297–302.

Holmer, Martin. "Tax Policy and the Demand for Health Insurance." *Journal of Health Economics* 3, no. 3 (1984), pp. 203–21.

Jensen, Gail A., Michael A. Morrisey, Shannon Gaffney, and Derek K. Liston. "The New Dominance of Managed Care: Insurance Trends in the 1990s." *Health Affairs* 16 (January/February 1997), pp. 125–36.

Kumar, Nanda, Marc A. Cohen, Christine E. Bishop, and Stanley S. Wallack. "Understanding the Factors Behind the Decision to Purchase Varying Coverage Amounts of Long-Term Care Insurance." *Health Services Research* 29 (February 1995), pp. 653–78.

Landon, Bruce E., Ira B. Wilson, and Paul D. Cleary. "A Conceptual Model of the Effects of Health Care Organizations on the Quality of Medical Care." *Journal of the American Medical Association* 279 (May 6, 1998), pp. 1377–82.

Long, James E., and Frank A. Scott. "The Income Tax and Nonwage Compensation." *Review of Economics and Statistics* (May 1982), pp. 211–19.

Manning, William G., and M. Susan Marquis. "Health Insurance: The Trade-off between Risk Pooling and Moral Hazard." (R-3729–NCHSR) Santa Monica, CA: RAND, 1989.

Marquis, M. Susan, and Stephen H. Long. "Worker Demand for Health Insurance in the Non-Group Market." *Journal of Health Economics* 14 (1995), pp. 47–63.

Miller, Robert H., and Harold S. Luft. "Does Managed Care Lead to Better or Worse Quality of Care?" *Health Affairs* 16 (September/October 1997), pp. 7–25.

Miller, Robert H. and Harold S. Luft. "Managed Care Performance since 1980." *Journal of the American Medical Association* 271 (May 18, 1994), pp. 1512–19.

Miller, Tracy E. "Managed Care Regulation: In the Laboratory of the States." *Journal of the American Medical Association* 278 (October 1, 1997), pp. 1102–09.

Pauly, Mark V. "Taxation, Health Insurance, and Market Failure in the Medical Economy." *Journal of Economic Literature* 24 (June 1986), pp. 629–75.

Perneger, Thomas V., Jean-François Etter, and Andre Rougemont. "Switching Swiss Enrollees from Indemnity Health Insurance to Managed Care: The Effect on Health Status and Satisfaction with Care." *American Journal of Public Health* 86 (March 1996), pp. 388–93.

Schwartz, William B., and D. N. Mendelson. "Why Managed Care Cannot Contain Hospital Costs—Without Rationing." *Health Affairs* 20 (summer 1992) pp. 100–107.

Short, Pamela F., and Amy K. Taylor. "Premiums, Benefits, and Employee Choice of Health Insurance Options." *Journal of Health Economics* 8 (1989), pp. 293–311.

Taylor, Amy K., and Gail R. Wilensky. "The Effect of Tax Policies on Expenditures for Private Health Insurance." In *Market Reforms in Health Care*, edited by Jack Meyer. Washington, DC: American Enterprise Institute, 1983.

Teplensky, Jill D., Mark V. Pauly, John R. Kimberly, Allan L. Hillman, and J. Sanford Schwartz. "Hospital Adoption of Medical Technology: An Empirical Test of Alternative Models." *Health Services Research* 30 (August 1995) pp. 437–65.

Weisbrod, Burton A. "The Health Care Quadrilemma: An Essay on Technological Change, Insurance, Quality of Care, and Cost Containment." *Journal of Economic Literature* 20 (June 1991), pp. 523–52.

Woodbury, Stephen A. "Substitution between Wage and Nonwage Benefits." *American Economic Review* (March 1983), pp. 166–82.

# 6

# Medical Care Production and Costs

In October 1993, Mease Health Care, a 378–bed hospital in Dunnedin, Florida, announced that it planned to merge with Morton Plant Hospital, a larger hospital in nearby Clearwater, Florida. Executives at the two hospitals claimed the proposed merger had the potential to save as much as $80 million over five years (Anders, 1993). Similarly, Lahey and Hitchcock, two of New England's largest specialty physician clinics, agreed to merge in September 1994. The newly created organization would result in a large "medical-services powerhouse, with 5,400 employees, about 800 physicians, more than 140,000 patients and $600 million in annual revenue" (Stecklow, 1994). Spokespersons for the two physician clinics argued that the merger would help contain the costs of providing medical care.

These are just two examples of the many mergers that take place in the health care sector. Recent combinations among firms in other health care markets, such as the insurance, pharmaceutical, and nursing home industries, also testify to the assertion that larger firm size confers significant cost advantages. But are there any plausible economic reasons to support the claim that cost savings are associated with larger organizational size? If so, sound economic reasoning can justify a merger among two or more firms in the same industry. On the other hand, might operating costs actually increase as a firm gets too large? If that is the case, a merger among firms is not desirable if cost savings are the overriding concern.[1]

This chapter introduces various microeconomic principles and concepts that can be used to analyze the cost structure of medical firms and thereby

---

[1]Another concern relating to mergers among firms in the same industry is that the newly combined companies will attain monopoly power because of their larger size. As noted in Chapter 9, monopoly power results in higher prices and a reduction in consumer well-being. In fact, federal officials allowed only a partial merger between Morton Plant Hospital and Mease Health Care, citing the potential for monopoly pricing as the reason for denying the full merger (see Davidson, 1994).

determine the true relation between firm size and costs of production. In addition, the chapter

- Discusses various production characteristics, including marginal and average productivity and the elasticity of substitution among inputs.

- Uses the resulting production theory to derive short-run and long-run costs of production.

- Examines economies and diseconomies of scale and scope.

# The Short-Run Production Function of the Representative Medical Firm

All medical firms, including hospitals, physician clinics, nursing homes, and pharmaceutical companies, earn revenues from producing and selling some type of medical output. Production and retailing activities occur regardless of the form of ownership (i.e., for-profit, public, or not-for-profit). Because these activities take place in a world of scarce resources, microeconomics can provide valuable insights into the operation and planning processes of medical firms. In this chapter, we focus on various economic principles that guide the production behavior of medical firms. We begin by analyzing the short-run production process of a representative medical firm.

To simplify our discussion of short-run production, we make five assumptions. First, we assume a hospital produces a single, homogeneous output, $q$. Second, we initially assume only two homogeneous medical inputs exist: nurse-hours, $n$, and a composite capital good, $k$. We can think of the composite capital good as an amalgamation of all types of capital, including any medical equipment and the physical space in the hospital building. Third, since the short run is defined as a period of time over which the level of *at least* one input cannot be changed, we assume the quantity of capital is fixed at some amount. This assumption makes intuitive sense, because it is usually more difficult to change the stock of capital than the number of nurse-hours, at least in the short run. Fourth, we assume for now that medical firms face an incentive to produce as efficiently as possible. Finally, we assume medical firms possess perfect information regarding the demands for their products. We relax the last two assumptions at the end of the chapter.

As we know from Chapter 3, a production function identifies how various inputs can be combined and transformed into a final output. In the present example, the short-run production function for hospital services can be mathematically generalized as

**(6–1)**  $q = f(n, k_*)$.

The short-run production function for hospital services in equation 6–1 indicates that the level of hospital services is a function of a variable nurse input and a fixed (denoted with an asterisk) capital input. The production function identifies the different ways nurse-hours and capital can be combined to produce various levels of hospital services. The production function allows for the possibility that each level of output may be produced by several different combinations of the nurse and capital inputs (similar to the adage "There is more than one way to skin a cat"). Each combination is assumed to be **technically efficient,** since it results in the maximum amount of output that is feasible given the state of technology. Later we will see that both technical and economic considerations determine a unique least-cost, or economically efficient, method of production.

We begin our analysis by examining how the level of hospital services, $q$, relates to a greater quantity of the variable nurse input, $n$, given that the capital input, $k*$, is assumed to be fixed. Various microeconomic principles and concepts relating to production theory are used to determine the precise relation between the employment of the variable input and the level of total output. As mentioned in Chapter 3, one important microeconomic principle from production theory is the law of diminishing marginal productivity. This is not really a law; rather, it is a generalization about production behavior and states that total output at first increases at an *increasing* rate, but after some point increases at a *decreasing* rate, with respect to a greater quantity of a variable input, holding all other inputs constant.[2]

Figure 6–1 applies the law of diminishing productivity. It shows a graphical relation between the quantity of hospital services on the vertical axis and the number of nurse-hours on the horizontal axis. The curve is referred to as the *total product curve,* TP, because it depicts the total (rather than the marginal or average) output produced by different levels of the variable input, holding all other inputs constant. Notice that the quantity of hospital services first increases at an increasing rate over the range of nurse-hours $0n_1$. The rate of increase is identified by the slope of the curve at each point. As you can see, the slope of the total product curve increases in value as the tangent lines become steeper over this range of nurse-hours.

Beyond point $n_1$, however, further increases in nurse-hours cause hospital services to increase, but at a decreasing rate. That is the point at which diminishing productivity sets in. Notice that the slope of the total product curve gets smaller as output increases in the range $n_1 n_2$ (as indicated by the flatter tangent lines). At $n_2$, the slope of the total product curve is zero, as reflected in the horizontal tangent line. Finally, beyond $n_2$, we allow for the possibility that too many nurse-hours will lead to a reduction in the quantity of hospital services (similar to the adage "Too many cooks spoil the broth"). The slope of the total product curve is negative beyond $n_2$.

In terms of the production decision at the firm level, we have not yet accounted for the specific reasoning underlying the law of diminishing marginal productivity. Economists point to the fixed short-run inputs as the basis for diminishing productivity. For example, when nurse-hours are increased at first, there is initially a considerable amount of capital, the fixed input, with which to produce hospital services. The

---

[2]In Chapter 3, we assumed for simplicity that the law of diminishing marginal returns sets in immediately; that is, the marginal product of medical services was always declining. In this chapter, we take a less restrictive approach to allow for the theoretical possibility that the marginal product of the variable input may increase initially. The fundamental idea remains the same, however. Eventually a point is reached where additional units of an input generate smaller marginal returns.

---

| FIGURE 6–1 | THE TOTAL PRODUCT CURVE |
| --- | --- |

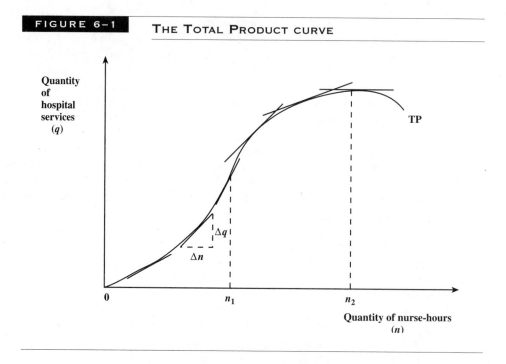

abundance of capital enables increasingly greater amounts of hospital services to be generated from the employment of additional nurses. In addition, a synergy effect may dominate initially. The synergy effect means that nurses, working cooperatively as a team, are able to produce more output collectively than separately because of labor specialization, for example.

At some point, however, the fixed capital becomes limited relative to the variable input (e.g., too little medical equipment and not enough hospital space), and additional nurse-hours generate successively fewer incremental units of hospital services. In the extreme, as more nurses are crowded into a hospital of a fixed size, the quantity of hospital services may actually begin to decline as congestion sets in and creates unwanted production problems.

In general, any physical constraint in production, such as the fixed size of the hospital or a limited amount of medical equipment, can cause diminishing productivity to set in at some point. In fact, if it weren't for diminishing productivity, the world's food supply could be grown in a single flowerpot and the demand for hospital services could be completely satisfied by a single large hospital. What a wonderful world it would be! Unfortunately, however, diminishing productivity is the rule rather than the exception.

### Marginal and Average Products

We can also use marginal and average product curves rather than the total product curve to illustrate the fundamental characteristics associated with the production

**FIGURE 6–2**   THE MARGINAL PRODUCT CURVE

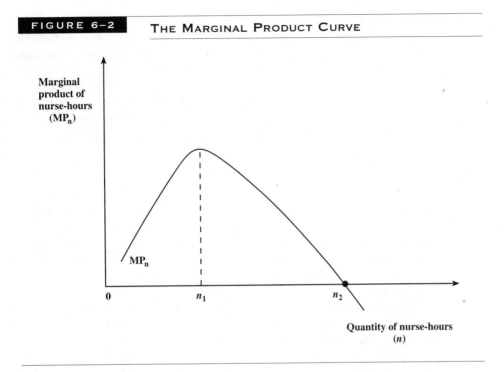

process. In general, the marginal product is the change in total output associated with a one-unit change in the variable input. In terms of our example, the marginal product or quantity of hospital services associated with an additional nurse-hour, $MP_n$, can be stated as follows:

**(6–2)**   $MP_n = \Delta q / \Delta n.$

The magnitude of the marginal product of a nurse-hour reveals the additional quantity of hospital services produced by each additional nurse-hour. It is a measure of the marginal contribution of a nurse-hour in the production of hospital services.

In figure 6–1, the slope of the total product curve at every point represents the marginal product of a nurse-hour, since it measures the rise (vertical distance) over the run (horizontal distance), or $\Delta q / \Delta n$. Consequently, we can determine the marginal product of an additional nurse-hour by examining the slope of the total product curve at each level of nurse-hours. Figure 6–2 graphically illustrates the marginal product of a nurse-hour. Initially, the $MP_n$ is positive and increases over the range $0n_1$ due to increasing marginal productivity. In the range $n_1n_2$, the marginal product is positive but decreasing, because diminishing marginal productivity has set in. At $n_2$, the marginal product of a nurse-hour is zero and becomes negative thereafter. The marginal product curve suggests that each additional nurse-hour cannot be expected to generate the same marginal contribution to total output as the previous one. The law of diminishing marginal productivity dictates that in the short run, a level of output is eventually reached where an incremental increase in the number of nurse-hours leads to successively fewer additions to total output (because some other inputs are fixed).

In addition to the $MP_n$, the average product of a nurse-hour can provide insight into the production process. In general, the average product equals the total quantity of output divided by the level of the variable input. In terms of the present example, the average product of a nurse-hour, $AP_n$, is calculated by dividing the total quantity of hospital services by the total number of nurse-hours:

**(6–3)** $\quad AP_n = q/n.$

The average product of a nurse-hour measures the average quantity of hospital services produced within an hour. For example, suppose we (crudely) measure total hospital services by the number of daily patient-hours at the hospital (i.e., the product of the number of patients and the average length of stay in hours during the entire day). In addition, suppose 200 nurse-hours are employed to service 300 daily patient-hours. In this example, the average product of a nurse-hour equals 300/200 or $1\frac{1}{2}$ patient hours.

We can also derive the average product of a nurse-hour from the total product curve, as shown in figure 6–3*a*. To derive the $AP_n$, a ray from the origin is extended to each point on the total product curve. The slope of the ray measures the $AP_n$ for any given level of nurse-hours, since it equals the rise over the run, or $q/n$. In figure 6–3*a* three rays, labeled 0*A*, 0*B*, and 0*C*, emanate from the origin to the total product curve. The slope of ray 0*A* is flatter than that of 0*B* and therefore is of a lower magnitude. In fact, as it is drawn, ray 0*B* has a greater slope than any other ray emanating from the origin. At this level of nurse-hours, the average product is maximized. The slope of ray 0*C* is flatter and of a lower magnitude than that of 0*B*. The implication is that average product initially increases over the range $0n_3$ reaches a maximum at $n_3$, and then decreases, as shown in figure 6–3*b*. It is the law of diminishing marginal productivity that accounts for the shape of the $AP_n$.

In figure 6–4, the marginal and average product curves are superimposed to illustrate how they are related. Some characteristics of the relation between these two curves are worth mentioning. First, the marginal product curve cuts the average product curve at its maximum point. In fact, it is a common mathematical principle that the marginal equals the average when the average is at its extreme value.[3] Second, the $MP_n$ lies above the $AP_n$ whenever the $AP_n$ is increasing. This too reflects a common

---

[3]*Proof:* For simplicity, suppose the production function relates the quantity of output, $q$, to a single input of nurse-hours, $n$, such that $q = f(n)$. The average product of nurse-hours, $AP_n$, can be written as $f(n)/n$. To determine where $AP_n$ reaches a maximum point, we can take the first derivative of $AP_n$ and set it equal to zero. Following the rule for taking the derivative of a quotient of two functions (see Chiang, 1984), it follows that

**(6–1*a*)** $\quad f'(n) = \dfrac{f(n)}{n}.$

Since $f'(n)$ equals $MP_n$ and $f(n)/n$ equals $AP_n$, $MP_n = AP_n$ when $AP_n$ is maximized.

FIGURE 6-3

## DERIVING THE AVERAGE PRODUCT CURVE FROM THE TOTAL PRODUCT CURVE

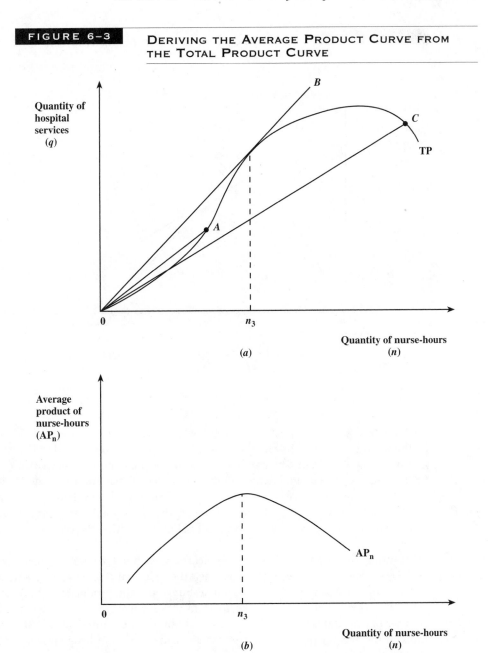

| FIGURE 6-4 | RELATION BETWEEN THE MARGINAL AND AVERAGE PRODUCT CURVES |

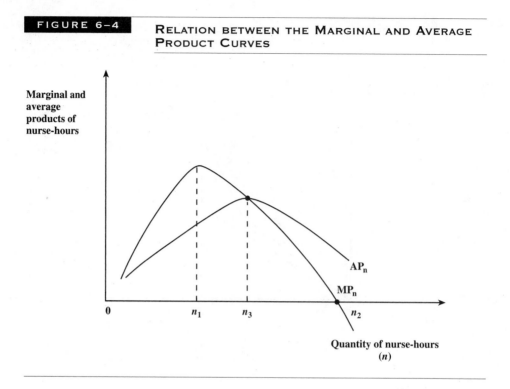

mathematical principle and should come as little surprise to the reader. For example, if your average grade in a course is a B+ until the final and you receive an A on the final exam, this incremental higher grade pulls up your final average grade. Third, the $MP_n$ lies below the $AP_n$ whenever the $AP_n$ is declining. This relation between marginal and average values also should not be surprising. As you know, your course grade slips if you receive a lower grade on the final exam relative to your previous course average.

Putting the grades aside (because learning is more important than grades—right?), we can discuss the relation between the marginal and average product curves in terms of our example concerning nurse-hours and the production of hospital services. For this discussion, it helps to think of the marginal product curve as the amount of hospital services generated hourly by the next nurse hired. Also, we can think of the average product curve as the average quantity of hospital services generated by the existing team of nurses within an hour—that is, the "team" average.

Looking back at figure 6–4, notice that the next nurse hired always generates more hospital services per hour than the team average up to point $n_3$. Consequently, up to this point, each additional nurse helps to pull up the team's average level of output. Beyond $n_3$, however, the incremental nurse hired generates less hospital services per hour than the team average; as a result, the team average falls. It is important to realize that any increase or decrease in the marginal product has nothing to do with the individual talents of each additional nurse employed. Rather, it involves the law of diminishing marginal productivity. At some point in the production process, the incremental nurse becomes less productive due to the constraint imposed by the fixed input. The marginal productivity, in turn, influences the average productivity of the team of nurses.

At first glance, it seems logical to assume that a medical firm desires to produce at a point like $n_1$ or $n_3$ in figure 6–4. After all, they represent the points at which either the marginal or the average product is maximized. In most cases, however, a medical firm finds it more desirable to achieve some financial target, such as a maximum or break-even level of profits. As a result, we need more information concerning the revenue and cost structures the medical firm faces before we can pinpoint the desired level of production. In later chapters we will see that under normal conditions, the relevant range of production in figure 6–4 is between $n_3$ and $n_2$.

## Elasticity of Input Substitution

Up to now, we have assumed only one variable input. Realistically, however, the medical firm operates with more than one variable input in the short run. Thus, there may be some possibilities for substitution between any two variable inputs. For example, licensed practical nurses often substitute for registered nurses in the production of inpatient services, and physician assistants sometimes substitute for physicians in the production of ambulatory services. The actual degree of substitutability between any two inputs depends on technical and legal considerations. For example, physician assistants are prohibited by law from prescribing medicines in most states. In addition, licensed practical nurses normally lack the technical knowledge needed to perform all the duties of registered nurses.

In general terms, the elasticity of substitution between any two inputs equals the percentage change in the input ratio divided by the percentage change in the ratio of the inputs' marginal productivities, holding constant the level of output, or

$$\textbf{(6–4)} \quad \sigma = \frac{\Delta(I_1/I_2)}{I_1/I_2} \div \frac{\Delta(MP_2/MP_1)}{MP_2/MP_1}$$

$I_i$ ($i = 1,2$) stands for the quantity employed of each input. The ratio of marginal productivities, $MP_2/MP_1$, referred to as the *marginal rate of technical substitution*, illustrates the rate at which one input substitutes for the other in the production process, at the margin. For example, suppose the marginal product of a registered nurse-hour is four patients and the marginal product of a licensed practical nurse-hour is two patients. It follows that two licensed practical nurse-hours are needed to substitute completely for one registered nurse-hour.

Theoretically, $\sigma$ (Greek letter sigma) takes on values between 0 and $+\infty$ and identifies the percentage change in the input ratio that results from a 1 percent change in the marginal rate of technical substitution. The magnitude of $\sigma$ identifies the degree of substitution between the two inputs. For instance, if $\sigma = 0$, the variable inputs

## A Production Function for Hospital Admissions

Jensen and Morrisey (1986) provide one of the more interesting empirical studies on the production characteristics of hospital services. In keeping with equation 6–1, Jensen and Morrisey estimated a production function for admissions at 3,540 non-teaching hospitals in the United States as of 1983 in the following general form:[1]

**(6–5)**  Case-mix-adjusted = $f$(Physicians,
hospital          nurses, other
admissions        nonphysician staff,
hospital beds, X).

Notice that hospital admissions serve as the measure of output. Given the heterogeneous nature of hospital services, however, this output measure was adjusted for case-mix differences across hospitals by multiplying it by the Medicare patient index. This index is the weighted sum of the proportions of the hospital's Medicare patients in different diagnostic categories where the weights reflect the average costs per case in each diagnostic group. The number of physicians, nurses (full-time equivalent [FTE] units), and other nonphysician staff (FTE) represented the labor inputs, the number of beds constituted the capital input, and $X$ stood for a number of other production factors not central to the discussion.

To put equation 6–5 in a form that can be estimated with a multiple regression technique, Jensen and Morrisey specified a translog production function. The form and properties of this particular mathematical function are too complex to describe briefly; it suffices to note that the translog is a flexible functional form that imposes very few restrictions on the estimated parameters.[2]

From the empirical estimation, Jensen and Morrisey were able to derive estimates of each input's marginal product. Table 1 shows the estimated marginal products of the four medical inputs. As expected, the marginal products were all positive. Jensen and Morrisey noted that the marginal product of each input declined in magnitude with greater usage, as the law of diminishing

marginal product suggests. The estimated marginal product of a physician implied that an additional doctor generated 6.05 additional case-mix-adjusted annual admissions. The nurse input was by far the most productive input. In particular, the marginal nurse was responsible for producing about 20.3 additional case-mix-adjusted annual admissions. The marginal products of other nonphysician staff and beds were found to be 6.97 and 3.04 case-mix-adjusted annual admissions, respectively.

| TABLE 1 | ANNUAL MARGINAL PRODUCTS FOR ADMISSIONS |
|---------|------------------------------------------|

| Input | MP (at the means) |
|-------|-------------------|
| Physicians | 6.05 |
| Nurses | 20.30 |
| Other staff | 6.97 |
| Beds | 3.04 |

SOURCE: Gail A. Jensen and Michael A. Morrisey, "The Role of Physicians in Hospital Production," *Review of Economics and Statistics* 68 (1986), table 4.

The estimation procedure also generated sufficient information to enable Jensen and Morrisey to measure the input substitution possibilities available to hospitals. Table 2 lists the estimated substitution elasticities reported by Jensen and Morrisey. The positive substitution elasticities mean that each input was a substitute for the others in production. The relatively large elasticity of .547 between physicians and nurses tells us that the average hospital can more easily substitute between these two inputs. This particular input elasticity estimate can be interpreted to mean that a 10 percent increase in the marginal productivity of

INSIGHT 6-1

**(continued)**

a doctor causes a 5.47 percent increase in the ratio of nurses to doctors, *ceteris paribus.* These positive substitution elasticities suggest that hospital policymakers can avoid some of the price (wage) increase in any one input by substituting with the others. For example, to maintain a given level of admissions, a wage increase for nurses might be partially absorbed by increasing the number of hospital beds.

[1]For the sake of brevity, we do not discuss their results for the sample of teaching hospitals.

[2]In a translog function, (the natural log of) each independent variable enters the equation in both linear and quadratic form. In addition, a cross-product linear term is created between any two independent variables and specified in the function. Similar cross-product terms are eliminated from the specification. To ensure a well-behaved function, restrictions are normally imposed on the parameter estimates.

| TABLE 2 | ELASTICITIES OF SUBSTITUTION BETWEEN INPUTS |
|---------|---------------------------------------------|

| Input pair | $\sigma$ |
|------------|----------|
| Physicians with nurses | 0.547 |
| Physicians with beds | 0.175 |
| Nurses with beds | 0.124 |

SOURCE: Gail A. Jensen and Michael A. Morrisey, "The Role of Physicians in Hospital Production," *Review of Economics and Statistics* 68 (1986), table 5.

cannot be substituted in production. In contrast, when $\sigma = \infty$, the two variable inputs are perfect substitutes in production. In practice, it is more common for $\sigma$ to take on values between these two extremes, implying that limited substitution possibilities exist.

## Short-Run Cost Theory of the Representative Medical Firm

Before we begin our discussion of the medical firm's cost curves, we need to address the difference between the ways economists and accountants refer to costs. In particular, accountants consider only the *explicit costs* of doing business when determining the accounting profits of a medical firm. Explicit costs are easily quantified because a recent market transaction is available to provide an accurate measure of cost. Wage payments to the hourly medical staff, electric utility bills, and medical supply expenses are all examples of the explicit costs medical firms incur because disbursement records can be consulted to determine the magnitudes of these expenditures.

Economists, unlike accountants, consider both the explicit and implicit costs of production. *Implicit costs* reflect the opportunity costs of using any resources the medical firm owns. For example, a general practitioner (GP) may own the physical assets (e.g., clinic and medical equipment) used in producing physician services. In this case, a recent market transaction is unavailable to determine the cost of using these assets.

Yet an opportunity cost is incurred when using them because the physical assets could have been rented out for an alternative use. For example, the clinic could be remodeled and rented as a beauty salon, and the medical equipment could be rented out to another physician. Thus, the forgone rental payments reflect the opportunity cost of using the physical assets owned by the GP.[4]

Consequently, when determining the economic (rather than accounting) profits of a firm, economists consider the total costs of doing business, including both the explicit and implicit costs. Economists believe it is important to determine whether sufficient revenues are available to cover the cost of using all inputs, including those rented and owned. For example, if the rental return on the physical assets is greater than the return on use, the GP might do better by renting out the assets rather than retaining them for personal use.

### The Short-Run Cost Curves of the Representative Medical Firm

Cost theory is based on the production theory of the medical firm outlined above and relates the quantity of output to the cost of production. As such, it identifies how (total and marginal) costs respond to changes in output. If we continue to assume the two inputs of nurse-hours, $n$, and capital, $k_*$, the short-run total cost, STC, of producing a given level of medical output, $q$, can be written as

**(6–6)** $\quad STC(q) = w \cdot n + r \cdot k_*,$

where $w$ and $r$ represent the hourly wage for a nurse and the rental or shadow price of capital, respectively. Input prices are assumed to be fixed, which means the single medical firm can purchase these inputs without affecting their market prices. This is a valid assumption as long as the firm is a small buyer of inputs relative to the total number of buyers in the marketplace.[5]

Equation 6–6 implies that the short-run total costs of production are dependent on the quantities and prices of inputs employed. The wage rate times the number of nurse-hours equals the total wage bill and represents the total variable costs of production. Variable costs respond to changes in the level of output.[6] The product of the rental price and the quantity of capital represent the total fixed costs of production. Obviously, this cost component does not respond to changes in output, since the quantity of capital is fixed in the short run.

The total product curve not only identifies the quantity of medical output produced by a particular number of nurse-hours but also shows, reciprocally, the number of nurse-hours necessary to produce a given level of medical output. With

---

[4]The general practitioner's labor time should also be treated as an implicit cost of doing business if he or she independently owns the clinic. As an entrepreneur, the GP does not receive an explicit payment but instead receives any residual profits that are left over after all other costs are paid. If the physician does not receive an appropriate rate of return, he or she may leave the area or the profession to get a better rate of return.

[5]If the single firm were a large or an influential buyer, it would possess some monopsony power and could affect the market prices of the inputs. We will examine this case in Chapter 9.

[6]For simplicity, we assume the wage rate represents total hourly compensation, including any fringe benefits.

| FIGURE 6–5 | THE SHORT-RUN TOTAL COST CURVE |

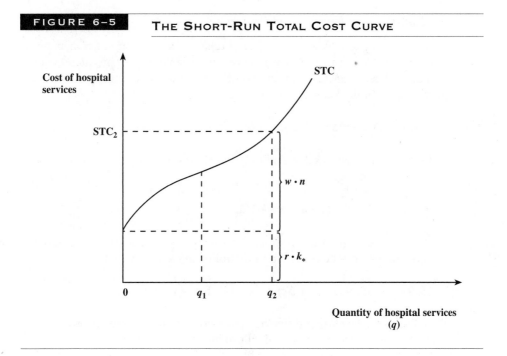

this information, we can determine the short-run total cost of producing different levels of medical output by following a three-step procedure. First, we identify, through the production function, the necessary number of nurse-hours, $n$, for each level of medical output. Second, we multiply the quantity of nurse-hours by the hourly wage, $w$, to determine the short-run total variable costs, STVC, of production, or $w \cdot n$. Third, we add the short-run total fixed costs, STFC, or $r \cdot k_*$, to STVC to derive the short-run total costs, STC, of production. If we conduct this three-step procedure for each level of medical output, we can derive a short-run total cost curve like the one in figure 6–5.

Notice the reciprocal relation between the short-run total cost function in figure 6–5 and the short-run total product curve in figure 6–1. For example, when total product is increasing at an *increasing* rate up to point $n_1$ in figure 6–1, short-run total costs are increasing at a *decreasing* rate up to point $q_1$ in figure 6–5. This is because the increasing productivity in this range causes the total costs of production to rise slowly. Output increases at a *decreasing* rate immediately beyond point $n_1$ in figure 6–1 (as shown by the slope of the total product curve), and, as a result, short-run total costs increase at an *increasing* rate beyond $q_1$ in figure 6–5. Also notice that total costs increase solely because additional nurses are employed as output expands. Figure 6–5 also shows how short-run total cost can be decomposed into its variable and fixed components for the level of output $q_2$.

### Short-Run Per-Unit Costs of Production

Another way to look at the reciprocal relation between production and costs is to focus on the short-run marginal and average variable costs of production. The short-run marginal costs, SMC, of production are equal to the change in total costs associated with a one-unit change in output, or

**(6–7)** $\quad \text{SMC} = \Delta \text{STC}/\Delta q.$

In terms of equations 6–6 and 6–7, the short-run marginal costs of production look like the following:

**(6–8)** $\quad \text{SMC} = \Delta(w \cdot n + r \cdot k_*)/\Delta q.$

Because the wage rate and short-run fixed costs are constant with respect to output, equation 6–8 can be rewritten in the following manner:

**(6–9)** $\quad \text{SMC} = w \cdot (\Delta n/\Delta q) = w \cdot (1/\text{MP}_n) = w/\text{MP}_n.$

Notice on the right-hand side of equation 6–9 that short-run marginal costs equal the wage rate divided by the marginal product of nurse-hours.

The short-run average variable costs, SAVC, of production equal the short-run total variable costs, STVC, divided by the quantity of medical output. Because STVC is the total wage bill (i.e., $w \cdot n$),

**(6–10)** $\quad \text{SAVC} = \text{STVC}/q = (w \cdot n)/q = w \cdot (1/\text{AP}_n) = w/\text{AP}_n$

such that SAVC equals the wage rate divided by the average product of a nurse-hour. Notice that the short-run marginal and average variable costs are inversely related to the marginal and average products of labor, respectively. Thus, marginal and average variable costs increase as the marginal and average products fall, and vice versa. Figure 6–6 shows the graphical relation between the per-unit product and cost curves.

The two graphs in figure 6–6 clearly point out the reciprocal relation between production and costs. For example, after point $n_1$ in figure 6–6a, diminishing productivity sets in and the marginal product begins to decline. As a result, the short-run marginal costs ($= w/\text{MP}_n$) increase beyond output level $q_1$ given a fixed wage. Similarly, the average product of a nurse-hour declines beyond $n_3$, so the average variable costs of production increase beyond $q_3$. Obviously, the shapes of the marginal cost and average variable cost curves reflect the law of diminishing marginal productivity. Because of this reciprocal relation, production and costs represent dual ways of observing various characteristics associated with the production process.

It is apparent from equations 6–9 and 6–10 that the maximum points on the marginal and average product curves correspond directly to the minimum points on the marginal and average variable cost curves. Note in figure 6–6b that the short-run marginal cost curve passes through the minimum point of the short-run average variable

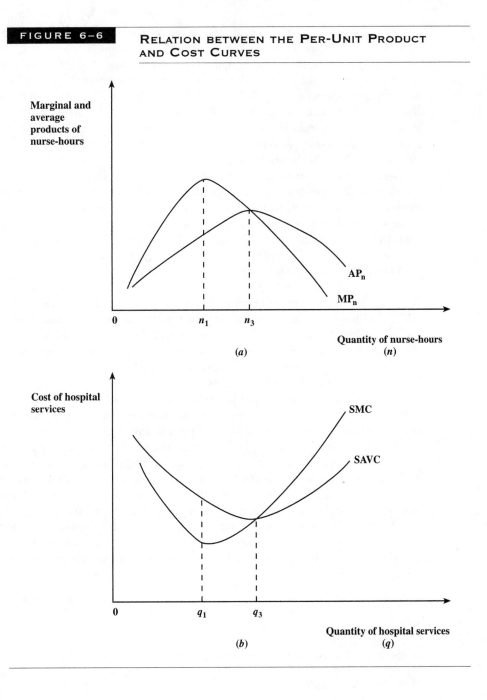

FIGURE 6–6

RELATION BETWEEN THE PER-UNIT PRODUCT
AND COST CURVES

cost curve. In addition, the SMC curve lies below the SAVC curve when the latter is decreasing and above the SAVC curve when it is increasing.

In simple terms, the graph in figure 6–6b identifies how costs behave as the medical firm alters output in the short run. Initially, as the medical firm expands output and employs more nurse-hours, both the marginal and average variable costs of production decline. Eventually, diminishing productivity sets in due to the fixed inputs, and both marginal and average variable costs increase. It follows that the marginal and average variable costs of production depend in part on the amount of output a medical firm produces in the short run.

Besides the marginal and average variable costs of production, decision makers are interested in the short-run average total costs of operating the medical firm. Following equation 6–6, we can find the short-run average total costs of production by summing the average variable costs and average fixed costs.[7] Short-run average fixed costs (SAFC) are simply total fixed costs (STFC) divided by the level of output, or

**(6–11)** SAFC = STFC/$q$.

Because by definition the numerator in equation 6–11 is fixed in the short run, the SAFC declines as the denominator, hospital services, increases in value. Consequently, the average fixed costs of production decline with greater amounts of output because total fixed costs (or overhead costs) are spread out over more and more units.

Figure 6–7 shows the graphical relation among SMC, SAVC, and SATC. Note that the marginal cost curve cuts the average total cost curve at its minimum point. (The minimum SATC lies to the right of the minimum SAVC. Why?) Also, note that the vertical distance between the average total and variable cost curves at each level of output represents the average fixed costs of production. This should not be surprising, since total costs include both variable and fixed costs. The vertical distance between the two curves gets smaller as output increases because the SAFC approaches zero with increases in output. One implication of the model is that average total costs increase at some level of output because eventually the cost-enhancing impact of diminishing productivity outweighs the cost-reducing tendency of the average fixed costs.

The unwitting reader may think that the medical firm should choose to produce at the minimum point on the SATC curve because average costs are minimized. As mentioned earlier, however, the level of output the medical firm chooses depends on

---

[7]Equation 6–6 can be rewritten as

**(6–6a)**   STC = STVC + STFC.

Dividing both sides of equation 6–6a by the level of output gives

**(6–6b)**   STC/$q$ = STVC/$q$ + STFC/$q$.

Thus, by definition;

**(6–6c)**   SATC = SAVC + SAFC.

| FIGURE 6-7 | RELATION AMONG SHORT-RUN MARGINAL, AVERAGE VARIABLE, AND AVERAGE TOTAL COSTS |

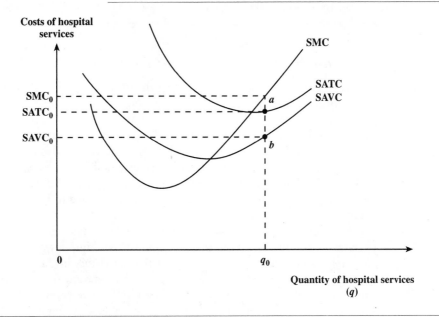

the firm's objective (e.g., to achieve maximum or break-even level of profits). Hence, a proper analysis requires some knowledge of the revenue structure in addition to the cost structure. In later chapters, we entertain some alternative objectives that may motivate the production behavior of medical firms. For now, however, assume for pedagogical purposes that the firm has chosen to produce the level of medical output, $q_0$, in figure 6–7. Let's identify the various costs associated with producing $q_0$ units of medical output.

The identification of the per-unit cost of producing a given level of output is a fairly easy matter. We can determine the per-unit cost by extending a vertical line from the appropriate level of output until it crosses the cost curves. For example, the average total cost of producing $q_0$ units of output is $SATC_0$, while the average variable cost is $SAVC_0$. The average fixed cost of producing $q_0$ units of output is represented by the vertical distance between $SATC_0$ and $SAVC_0$, or distance *ab*. In addition, $SMC_0$ identifies the marginal cost of producing one more unit assuming the medical firm is already producing $q_0$ units of medical services.

Now suppose that instead of the per-unit costs, we want to identify the various total costs (i.e., STC, STVC, and STFC) associated with producing $q_0$ units of output. We can do this by multiplying the level of output by the per-unit costs of production. For example, the rectangle $SAVC_0-b-q_0-0$ in figure 6–7 measures the total variable costs of producing $q_0$ units of output, since it corresponds to the area found by multiplying the base of $0-q_0$ by the height of $0-\text{SAVC}_0$. Following similar logic, the total fixed costs are represented by rectangle $\text{SATC}_0-a-b-\text{SAVC}_0$, and total costs can be measured by area $\text{SATC}_0-a-q_0-0$. The ability to interpret and read these cost curves is useful for the discussion that follows.

## Factors Affecting the Position of the Short-Run Cost Curves

A variety of short-run circumstances affect the positions of the per-unit and total cost curves.[8] Among them are the prices of the variable inputs, the quality of care, the patient case-mix, and the amounts of the fixed inputs. Whenever any one of these variables changes, the positions of the cost curves change through either an upward or a downward shift depending on whether costs increase or decrease. For example, if input prices increase in the short run, the cost curves shift upward to reflect the higher costs of production (especially since $\text{SAVC} = w/\text{AP}_n$ and $\text{SMC} = w/\text{SMC}$). If input prices fall in the short run, the cost curves shift downward to indicate the lower production costs.

Furthermore, if the medical firm increases the quality of care or adopts a more severe patient case-mix, the cost curves respond by shifting upward. That is because a higher quality of care or a more severe patient case-mix means that a unit of labor is less able to produce as much output in a given amount of time. In terms of our formal analysis above, a higher quality of care or a more severe patient case-mix reduces the average and marginal productivity of the labor input and thereby raises the costs of production. For instance, a nurse can care for many more patients within an hour when these patients are less severely ill and quality of care is of secondary importance. Conversely, a reduction in the quality of care or a less severe patient case-mix is associated with lower cost curves.

Finally, a change in the amount of the fixed inputs can alter the costs of production. For example, it can be shown that excessive amounts of the fixed inputs lead to higher short-run costs (Cowing and Holtmann, 1983). We discuss the specific reasoning underlying the relation between fixed inputs and short-run costs when we examine the long-run costs of production later in this chapter.

In sum, a properly specified short-run total variable cost function for medical services should include the following variables:

**(6–12)** $\text{STVC} = f$(output level, input prices, quality of care, patient case-mix, quantity of the fixed inputs).

We suspect that these factors can explain cost differentials among hospitals. Specifically, output influences short-run variable costs by determining where the hospital operates along the cost curve, whereas the other factors affect the location of the curve. Most likely, high-cost hospitals are associated with either more output, higher wages,

---

[8]The position of the average and total fixed cost curves is influenced by the price of the fixed input. We will see in later chapters that the fixed costs do not affect the typical marginal decision in the short run. Therefore, we do not discuss the factors affecting the position of the fixed cost curves.

# Estimating a Short-Run Cost Function for Hospital Services

Cowing and Holtmann (1983) empirically estimated a short-run total variable cost function for a sample of 138 short-term general care hospitals in New York using 1975 data. Along the lines of equation 6–12, they specified the short-run total variable cost (STVC) function in the following general form:

$$(6\text{–}13) \quad STVC = f(q_1, q_2, q_3, q_4, q_5,$$
$$w_1, w_2, w_3, w_4, w_5, w_6, K, A).$$

Each $q_i$ ($i = 1,5$) represents the quantity of one of five different patient services—emergency room care, medical-surgical care, pediatric care, maternity care, and other inpatient care—measured in total patient days; each $w_j$ ($j = 1,6$) stands for one of six different variable input prices for nursing labor, auxiliary labor, professional labor, administrative labor, general labor, and material and supplies; $K$ is a single measure of the capital stock (measured by the market value of a hospital); and $A$ is the fixed number of admitting physicians in the hospital.[1]

Compared to equation 6–12, Cowing and Holtmann's specification of the cost function is more complex and introduces a greater degree of realism into the empirical analysis. First, the hospital is realistically treated as a multiproduct firm, simultaneously producing and selling five different types of patient services. Second, instead of our single variable input price (i.e., hourly nurse wage), six different variable input prices are specified. Finally, Cowing and Holtmann include the number of admitting physicians in the model because they play such a key role in the hospital services production process (see also Insight 6–3).

The authors assumed a multiproduct translog cost function for equation 6–13. We do not discuss the properties associated with this specific functional form; it suffices to note that this flexible form enables us to assess a large number of real-world characteristics associated with the production process.

First, this functional form allows for an interaction among the various outputs so that economies of scope can be examined. **Economics of scope** result from the joint sharing among related outputs of resources, such as nurses, auxiliary workers, and administrative labor. Scope economies exist if the joint cost of producing two outputs is less than the sum of the costs of producing the two outputs separately. For example, many colleges and universities produce both an undergraduate and a graduate education jointly due to perceived cost savings from economies of scope. The same professors, library personnel, and buildings can be used in producing both educational outputs simultaneously.

Cowing and Holtmann found some very intriguing results. First, their study reveals evidence of **short-run economies of scale,** meaning that an increase in output results in a less than proportionate increase in short-run total variable costs. Evidence of short-run economies indicates that the representative hospital operates to the left of the minimum point on the short-run average variable cost curve and implies that larger hospitals produce at a lower cost than smaller ones in the short run. They point out that this result is consistent with the view that aggregate hospital costs could be reduced by closing some small hospitals and merging the services among the remaining ones.

Second, in contrast to scale economies, Cowing and Holtmann discovered only some very limited evidence for economies of scope with respect to pediatric care and other services. They also found some limited evidence to support diseconomies of scope with respect to emergency services and other services. In fact, they argued that the results for both scope and scale economies indicate that larger but more specialized hospitals may be more effective given the significance of the scale effects and the general lack of any substantial economies of scope.

Third, Cowing and Holtmann also noted that the short-run marginal cost of each output, $\Delta STVC/\Delta q_i$, declined and then became constant over the levels of output observed in their study. For example, the marginal cost of an emergency

*(continued)*

**(continued)**

room visit was found to be approximately $32 for 54,000 visits per year and about $20 for 100,000 visits per year. For medical-surgical care, marginal cost was found to fall from $255 per patient day for 6,000 annual patient days to around $100 for 300,000 annual total patient days. For maternity care, the evidence suggests that the marginal costs of $540 per patient day for hospitals with 1,500 total annual patient days declined to $75 for hospitals with 20,000 total annual patient days.

Finally, Cowing and Holtmann estimated the short-run elasticities of input substitution between all pairs of variable inputs. They reported that the results indicate a substantial degree of substitutability between nursing and professional workers, nursing and general workers, nursing and administrative workers, and professional and administrative labor.

[1]Cowing and Holtmann also specify two dummy variables reflecting for-profit versus nonprofit ownership status and teaching versus nonteaching institution as a way to control for differences in quality and case-mix severity across hospitals. The inadequate control for quality and severity of case-mix is one of the few faults we can find with this paper.

increased quality, more severe patient case-mixes, and/or an excessive quantity of fixed inputs.

## The Cost-Minimizing Input Choice

A medical firm makes choices concerning which variable inputs to employ. Recognizing that there is usually more than one way to produce a specific output, medical firms typically desire to produce with the least-cost or cost-minimizing input mix. For example, suppose hospital administrators desire to produce some given amount of hospital services, $q_0$, at minimum total cost, TC, using two variable inputs: registered nurses, RN, and licensed practical nurses, LPN. (For ease of exposition, we ignore the capital input in this example.) These two inputs are paid hourly wages of $w_R$ and $w_L$, respectively. The hospital wants to minimize

**(6–14)**   $TC(q_0) = w_R \cdot RN + w_L \cdot LPN$

subject to

**(6–15)**   $q_0 = f(RN, LPN)$

by choosing the proper mix of registered nurses and licensed practical nurses.

Taken together, equations 6–14 and 6–15 mean that hospital administrators want to minimize the total cost of producing $q_0$ units of hospital services by choosing the "right," or efficient, mix of RNs and LPNs so that $TC(q_0)$ is as low as possible and sufficient amounts of the two inputs are available to produce $q_0$. The efficient combination depends on the marginal products and relative prices of the two inputs. By using a mathematical technique called *constrained optimization*, we can show that the efficient mix of RNs and LPNs is chosen when the following condition holds:[9]

**(6–16)** $MP_{RN}/w_R = MP_{LPN}/w_L.$

Equation 6–16 means that the marginal product to price ratio is equal for both registered nurses and licensed practical nurses in equilibrium. The equality implies that the last dollar spent on registered nurses generates the same increment to output as the last dollar spent on licensed practical nurses. As a result, a rearranging of expenditures on the two inputs cannot generate any increase in hospital services, since both inputs generate the same output per dollar at the margin.[10]

To more fully appreciate this point, suppose this condition does not hold such that

**(6–17)** $MP_{RN}/w_R < MP_{LPN}/w_L.$

In that case, the last dollar spent on a licensed practical nurse generates more output than the last dollar spent on a registered nurse. A licensed practical nurse is more profitable for the hospital at the margin, because the hospital receives a "bigger bang for the buck." But as the hospital hires more LPNs and fewer RNs, the marginal productivities adjust until the equilibrium condition in equation 6–16 results. Specifically, the marginal productivity of the LPNs decreases, while the marginal productivity of the RNs increases due to diminishing marginal productivity.

For example, suppose a newly hired RN can service six patients per hour and a newly hired LPN can service only four patients per hour. At first blush, with no consideration of the price of each input, the RN might appear to be the "better buy" because productivity is 50 percent higher. But suppose further that the market wage for an RN is $20 per hour, while an LPN requires only $10 per hour to work at the hospital. Given relative input prices, the 50 percent higher productivity of the RN costs the hospital 100 percent more. Obviously, the LPN is the better buy. That is, the last dollar spent on an LPN results in the servicing of .4 additional patients per hour, while a dollar spent on an RN allows the servicing of only .3 more patients per hour.

## Long-Run Costs of Production

Up to now, we have focused on the short-run costs of operation and assumed that one input is fixed. The fixed input leads to diminishing returns in production and to U-shaped average variable and total cost curves. In the long run, however, when the

---

[9]The interested reader can consult Chiang (1984).

[10]The astute reader most likely recognizes that equation 6–16 is similar to the utility-maximizing condition noted in Chapter 4.

## The Shadow Price of an Admitting Physician

Most physicians are not hospital employees and paid an explicit salary; instead they are granted admitting privileges by the hospitals. The granting of admitting privileges comes at a cost to the hospital, however. For example, the hospital incurs costs when it reviews and processes the physician's application, monitors the physician's performance to ensure quality control, and allows the physician to use its resources. Based on their empirical procedure discussed in Insight 6–1, Jensen and Morrisey (1986) were able to estimate the shadow price, or implicit cost, of a physician with admitting privileges at a representative hospital. They imputed the shadow price of a physician by using the condition for optimal input use. Following the format

of equation 6–16, the optimal combination of doctors, doc, and nurses, n, is chosen when

**(6–18)** $\quad MP_{doc}/w_{doc} = MP_n/w_n.$

By substituting in the estimated marginal products for doctors (6.05) and nurses (20.3) from table 1 in Insight 6–1, and the sample average for the annual nurses' salary ($23,526), Jensen and Morrisey solved for the shadow price of a doctor, $w_{doc}$. The resulting figure implies that the typical hospital in the sample incurred implicit costs of approximately $7,012 per year from granting admitting privileges to the marginal physician.

medical firm is planning for future resource requirements, all inputs, including capital, can be changed. Therefore, it is also important to analyze the relation between output and costs when all inputs are changed simultaneously in the long run.

### Long-Run Cost Curves

The long-run average total cost curve can be derived from a series of short-run cost curves, as shown in figure 6–8. The three short-run average total cost curves in the figure reflect different amounts of capital. For instance, each curve might reflect the short-run average total costs of producing units of hospital services with physically larger hospitals of sizes $k_1$, $k_2$, and $k_3$. If hospital decision makers know the relation among different-size hospitals and the short-run average total costs, they can easily choose the SATC or hospital size that minimizes the average cost of producing each level of hospital services in the long run.

For example, over the range 0 to $q_a$, hospital size $k_1$ results in lower costs of production than either hospital size $k_2$ or $k_3$. Specifically, notice that at output level $q_1$, SATC$_2$ exceeds SATC$_1$ by a significant amount. Therefore, the hospital administrators choose hospital size $k_1$ if they desire to produce $q_1$ units of hospital services at least cost in the long run. Similarly, from $q_a$ to $q_b$, hospital size $k_2$, associated with SATC$_2$, results in lower costs than either hospital size $k_1$ or $k_3$. Beyond $q_b$ units of hospital services (say, $q_2$), a hospital size of $k_3$ enables lower costs of production in the long run.

The three short-run cost curves in figure 6–8 paint a simplistic picture, since conceptually each unit of hospital services can be linked to a uniquely sized cost-

FIGURE 6–8

## FIGURE 6–8    THE SHORT-RUN AVERAGE COST CURVES AND THE LONG-RUN PLANNING CURVE

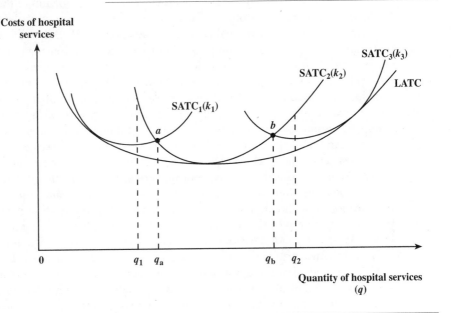

minimizing hospital (assuming capital is divisible). If we assume a large number of possible hospital sizes, we can draw a curve that connects all the cost-minimizing points on the various short-run average total cost curves. Each point indicates the least costly way to produce the corresponding level of hospital services in the long run when all inputs can be altered. Every short-run cost curve is tangent to the connecting or envelope curve, which is referred to as the *long-run average total cost curve* (*LATC*). The curve drawn below the short-run average cost curves in figure 6–8 represents a long-run average total cost curve.

Notice that the U-shaped long-run average cost curve initially declines, reaches a minimum, and eventually increases. Interestingly, both the short-run and long-run average cost curves have the same shape, but for different reasons. The shape of the short-run average total cost curve is based on the law of diminishing productivity setting in at some point. In the long run, however, all inputs are variable, so by definition a fixed input cannot account for the U-shaped long-run average cost curve. Instead, the reason for the U-shaped LATC curve is based on the concepts of *long-run economies* and *diseconomies of scale*.

**Long-run economies of scale** refer to the notion that average costs fall as a medical firm gets physically larger due to specialization of labor and capital. Larger medical firms are able to utilize larger and more specialized equipment and to more fully specialize the various labor tasks involved in the production process. For instance, people generally get very proficient at a specific task when they perform it repeatedly. Therefore, specialization allows larger firms to produce increased amounts of output at lower per-unit costs. The downward-sloping portion of the LATC curve in figure 6–8 reflects economies of scale.

Another way to conceptualize long-run economies of scale is through the direct relation between inputs and output, or returns to scale, rather than output and costs. Consistent with long-run economies of scale is increasing returns to scale. **Increasing returns to scale** result when an increase in all inputs results in a more than proportionate increase in output. For example, a doubling of all inputs that results in three times as much output is a sign of increasing returns to scale. Similarly, if a doubling of output can be achieved without a doubling of all inputs, the production process exhibits long-run increasing returns, or economies of scale.

Most economists believe that economies of scale are exhausted at some point and diseconomies of scale set in. **Diseconomies of scale** result when the medical firm becomes too large. Bureaucratic red tape becomes common, and top-to-bottom communication flows break down. The breakdown in communication flows means management at the top of the hierarchy has lost sight of what is taking place at the floor level. As a result, poor decisions are sometimes made when the firm is too large. Consequently, as the firm gets too large, long-run average costs increase. Diseconomies of scale are reflected in the upward-sloping segment of the LATC curve in figure 6–8.

Diseconomies of scale can also be interpreted as meaning that an increase in all inputs results in a less than proportionate increase in output, or **decreasing returns to scale.** For instance, if the number of patient-hours doubles at a dental office and the decision maker is forced to triple the size of each input (staff, office space, equipment, etc.), the production process at the dental office is characterized by decreasing returns, or diseconomies of scale.

Another possibility, not shown in figure 6–8, is that the production process exhibits constant returns to scale. **Constant returns to scale** occur when, for example, a doubling of inputs results in a doubling of output. In terms of long-run costs, constant returns imply a horizontal LATC curve, in turn implying that long-run average total cost is independent of output.

### Shifts in the Long-Run Average Cost Curve

The position of the long-run average cost curve is determined by a set of long-run circumstances that includes the prices of all inputs (remember, capital is a variable input in the long run), quality (including technological change), and patient case-mix. When these circumstances change on a long-run basis, the long-run average cost curve shifts up or down depending on whether the change involves higher or lower long-run costs of production. For example, an increase in the long-run price of medical inputs leads to an upward shift in the long-run average cost curve. A cost-saving technology tends to shift the long-run average cost curve downward. Conversely, a cost-enhancing technology increases the average costs of production in the long run and shifts the LATC curve upward. Higher quality of care and more severe patient case-mixes also shift the LATC curve upward.

# Hospitals: Mind Your Business

The following article finds an exception to the general argument that higher quality leads to higher costs of production when outcome quality is at issue. It also discusses some similarities between hospital and industrial production.

As industrial executives have learned, high quality does not necessarily mean higher costs. Indeed the opposite is often true. An improved production line and a motivated work force can usually cut costs by reducing parts that have to be scrapped or repaired before shipment. The same seems to be true for hospitals.

A patient who does not receive proper care in the early stages of hospitalization usually needs additional, costly care to recover. For this reason, statistical techniques relating to quality, cost, market share, and profits that were developed by industrial companies are now being applied by hospital managers to locate problem areas and to hone their business strategies. The underlying assumption is that certain activities, like surgical procedures, are the equivalent of product lines, some of which may need to be dropped as unprofitable while others are emphasized to improve earnings. "High rates of surgical complications or nursing errors are indicators of poor quality and are undesirable, primarily because of their effects on the patients, but also because they dramatically increase cost," two researchers wrote in the *Juran Report*, a journal published by the Juran Institute, a quality-consulting firm.

Both the federal government and state agencies now publish data on the results of hospital treatment, including death rates. Using this information, consultants have developed data bases that indicate what could be called "normal" death rates for different types of treatment. A hospital with higher than predicted death rates is assumed to have lower than average quality; one with lower mortality is considered of higher quality.

VHA of New Jersey, an association of 15 hospitals, commissioned such a study by a Chicago firm, Lexecon Health Service Inc., of five types of treatment. Using state-supplied data on deaths, the hospitals were grouped into five categories: average, better than average or much better than average, and worse or much worse than average. The findings supported the argument that poor quality costs more, while high quality produces savings. For example, the hospitals that had the highest quality in surgery on the nervous system had an average cost of $5,742 a case. Those having the worst quality had an average cost of $8,649.

The analysis can go beyond efforts to improve quality, as important as that may be. By studying market share, managers can make strategic business decisions about what services to provide. "In an increasingly competitive environment, hospitals must take a critical look at their product lines," Binns and Early, the authors of the *Juran Report*, argue. "Many institutions must decide between eliminating or investing in unprofitable product lines."

They cited a hospital that had highly profitable, high quality heart surgery with a large market share, but money-losing kidney surgery with a lower quality rating and smaller market share. Treat the heart surgery as a source of income, the authors suggest, and look hard at kidney operations. "Perhaps kidney transplants and other expensive and unprofitable renal procedures are outside the scope of its mission," they wrote.

SOURCE: New York Times News Service, "Hospitals Take Page from Book of Industry," *Worcester Telegram and Gazette*, December 26, 1989. Copyright © 1989 by The New York Times Company. Reprinted by permission.

| FIGURE 6–9 | LONG-RUN DISEQUILIBRIUM OF THE MEDICAL FIRM |

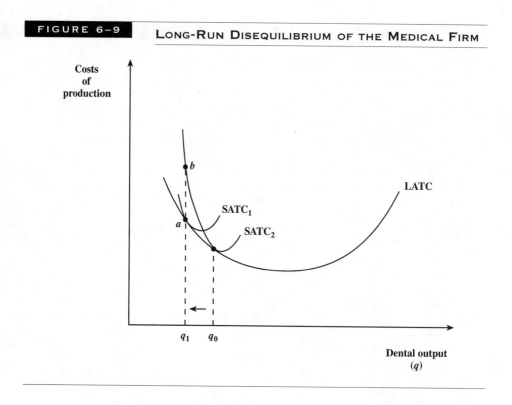

## Long-Run Cost Minimization and the Indivisibility of Fixed Inputs

Long-run cost minimization assumes that all inputs can be costlessly adjusted upward or downward. For an input like an hourly laborer, employment adjustments are fairly simple because hours worked or number of workers can be changed relatively easily. Capital inputs cannot always be as easily changed, however, because they are less divisible. As a result, a medical firm facing a sharp decline in demand may be unable to reduce the physical size of its facility. For example, Salkever (1972) found that hospitals realize less than 10 percent of the desired cost savings per year.[11] Therefore, medical firms may adjust slowly to external changes, not produce in long-run equilibrium, and operate with excess capital relative to a long-run equilibrium point.

Figure 6–9 clarifies this point. Suppose that initially a dental clinic produces $q_0$ amount of output (say, dental patient-hours) with a facility size of 1,200 square feet, as represented by the curve $SATC_2$. This represents a long-run equilibrium point because the efficient plant size is chosen such that $SATC_2$ is tangent to the LATC curve at $q_0$; that is, $q_0$ is produced at the lowest possible long-run cost and 1,200 square feet is the efficiently sized facility. Now suppose output sharply falls to $q_1$ due to a decline in demand. Long-run cost minimization suggests that the dental firm will reduce the size of

---

[11]As cited in Cowing, Holtmann, and Powers (1983, p. 265).

its facility to that represented by $SATC_1$ and operate at point *a* on the LATC curve. It might do this by selling the old facility and moving into a smaller one. Because it may take time to adjust to the decline in demand, the dental clinic may not operate on the long-run curve at $q_1$ (point *a*) but instead continue to operate with the larger facility as represented by point *b* on $SATC_2$. The dental clinic incurs higher costs of production as indicated by the vertical distance between points *b* and *a* in the figure.

Cowing and Holtmann (1983) derived a test to determine whether firms are operating in long-run equilibrium. Using a simplified version of equation 6–12, we can write a long-run total (LTC) cost function as

**(6–19)** $\text{LTC} = \text{STVC}(q, w, k) + r \cdot k,$

where all variables are as defined earlier. According to equation 6–19, long-run total costs equal the sum of (minimum) short-run total variable costs and capital costs. The level of short-run total variable costs is a function of, or depends on, the quantity of output, the wage rate, and the quantity of capital (and other things excluded from the equation for simplification).

According to Cowing and Holtmann, a necessary condition for long-run cost minimization is that $\Delta \text{STVC}/\Delta k = -r$.[12] The equality implies that the variable cost savings realized from substituting one more unit of capital must equal the rental price of capital in long-run equilibrium. That is, the marginal benefits and costs of capital substitution should be equal when the firm is minimizing the long-run costs of production. A nonnegative estimate for $\Delta \text{STVC}/\Delta k$ is a sufficient condition for medical firms to be overemploying capital. A nonnegative estimate implies that the cost of capital substitution outweighs its benefit in terms of short-run variable cost savings.

In their study, Cowing and Holtmann (see Insight 6–2) specified two fixed inputs: capital and the number of admitting physicians. As with capital, hospitals may operate with an excessive number of admitting physicians relative to a long-run equilibrium position. That is because the loss of one admitting physician can mean the loss of many more patients in the future. Cowing and Holtmann estimated the change in short-run total variable costs resulting from a one-unit change in capital and number of admitting physicians. Both estimates were found to be positive rather than negative. Thus, the authors found that the "average" hospital in their New York sample operated with too much capital and too many physicians. Their empirical results suggest that hospitals could reduce their costs by limiting the amount of capital and controlling the number of physicians.

# Neoclassical Cost Theory and the Production of Medical Services

The cost theory introduced in this chapter, typically referred to as *neoclassical cost theory* under conditions of perfect certainty, assumes firms produce as efficiently as

---

[12]This equality can be derived by taking the first derivative of equation 6–19 with respect to *k* and setting the resulting expression equal to zero.

possible and possess perfect information regarding the demands for their services. Based on the underlying theory, the short-run or long-run costs of producing a given level of output can be determined by observing the relevant point on the appropriate cost curve. However, when applied to medical firms, this kind of cost analysis may be misleading for two reasons.

First, some medical firms, such as hospitals or nursing homes, are nonprofit entities or are reimbursed on a cost-plus basis or both. Therefore, they may not face the appropriate incentives to produce as cheaply as possible and, consequently, may operate above rather than on a given cost curve. Second, medical firms may face an uncertain demand for their services. Medical illnesses occur irregularly and unpredictably, and therefore medical firms like hospitals may never truly know the demand for their services until the actual events take place. Accordingly, medical firms may produce with some amount of reserve capacity just in case an unexpected large increase in demand occurs.

Although these two considerations may pose problems when conducting a cost analysis of medical firms, do not be misled into thinking that the material in this chapter is without value. That is clearly not the case. These two considerations are modifications that can and should be incorporated into the cost analysis when possible. Indeed, a strong grounding in neoclassical cost analysis under conditions of perfect certainty is necessary before any sophisticated analyses or model extensions can be properly conducted and understood. In Chapter 10, we discuss how production costs are influenced by nonprofit considerations. Cowing, Holtmann, and Powers (1983, pp. 273–75, and 299) show how uncertainty concerning demand affects production costs and discuss the econometric implications.

## SUMMARY

In this chapter, we focused on characteristics and concepts pertaining to the costs of producing medical services. First, we examined the underlying production behavior of a single medical firm. The short-run production function that resulted from this examination relates productivity to input usage. Among the more important principles we examined was the law of diminishing marginal productivity, the notion that the marginal and average productivities of a variable input first increase but eventually fall with greater input usage because a fixed input places a constraint on production.

Second, we discussed the inverse relation between productivity and costs. Simply stated, increasing marginal and average productivities translate into decreasing marginal and average variable costs. Conversely, declining productivities imply higher per-unit costs of production. As a result, the average variable cost curve is U-shaped, implying that the average variable cost of production first decreases with greater production but at some point begins to increase as output expands. Taking the property of fixed costs into consideration, we also derived a U-shaped short-run average cost curve, which relates average operating costs to the amount of medical services produced.

Finally, we examined some concepts relating to long-run costs of production, including economies and diseconomies of scale. We also discussed the determinants of the optimal input mix.

## Review Questions and Problems

1. Suppose you are to specify a short-run production function for dental services. What inputs might you include in the production function? Which would be the variable inputs and which the fixed inputs?

2. In your own words, explain the law of diminishing marginal productivity. Be sure to mention the reason this law tends to hold in the short run.

3. Explain the difference between technical efficiency and economic efficiency.

4. Discuss the relation between the marginal and average productivity curves and the marginal and average variable cost curves.

5. What does the elasticity of substitution illustrate? How is it expressed mathematically? What two factors affect its magnitude?

6. Explain the difference between the explicit and implicit costs of production. Cite an example of each.

7. Suppose that with 400 patients per year, the SAFC, SATC, and SMC of operating a physician clinic are $10, $35, and $30 per patient, respectively. Furthermore, suppose the physician decides to increase the annual patient load by one more patient. Using short-run cost theory, explain the impact of this additional patient on the SAVC and SATC. Do they increase or decrease? Why?

8. What factors shift the short-run average variable and total cost curves? Explain why these curves would shift up or down in response to changes in these factors.

9. Suppose you are to specify a short-run total variable cost function for a nursing home. Explain the variables you would include in the function. What is the expected relation between a change in each of these variables and short-run total variable costs?

10. What does *economies of scope* mean? Provide an example.

11. Explain the reasoning behind the U shape of the long-run average total cost curve. Why might this cost curve shift upward?

12. You are responsible for hiring one of two hygienists for a dental office. The first dental hygienist has 25 years of experience. Given her record, she is likely to satisfactorily service 16 patients per day. Her hourly wage would be approximately $16 per hour. The other hygienist is new to the industry. He is expected to satisfactorily service 10 patients per day at an hourly wage of $8. Which dental hygienist would be the better hire? Why?

13. Santerre and Bennett (1992) estimated the short-run total variable cost function for a sample of 55 for-profit hospitals in Texas (*t*-statistics are in parentheses below the estimated coefficients).

ln STVC = 1.31 + 0.47ln *q* + 0.80ln *w* + 0.73ln QUALITY
                  (0.69)  (3.31)       (4.42)       (2.58)

+ 0.11ln CASEMIX + 0.29ln *k* + 0.07ln DOC
(1.48)                              (3.16)       (0.88)

+ Other factors

Adj. $R^2$ = .95

$N$ = 55

where STVC = short-run total variable cost, *q* = a measure of output (total inpatient days), *w* = average wage rate or price of labor, QUALITY = a measure of quality (number of accreditations), CASEMIX = an indicator of patient case-mix (number of services), *k* = a measure of capital (beds), and DOC = number of admitting physicians. All variables are expressed as natural logarithms (ln), so the estimated coefficients can be interpreted as elasticities.

*a.* How much of the variation in STVC is explained by the explanatory variables? How do you know that?

*b.* Which of the estimated coefficients are not statistically significant? Explain.

*c.* Does the estimated coefficient on output represent short-run economies or diseconomies of scale? Explain.

*d.* What are the expected signs of the coefficient estimates on *w*, QUALITY, and CASEMIX? Explain.

*e.* Provide an economic interpretation of the magnitude of the estimated coefficient on *w*.

*f.* What do the estimated coefficient on *k* and DOC suggest about the amount of capital and physicians at the representative hospital?

14. Draw a U-shaped LATC curve. Then draw the related long-run marginal cost (LMC) curve, keeping in mind the geometric relation between marginal cost and average cost (see the discussion on short-run cost curves). What is the relation between LATC and LMC when increasing returns to scale are present? Between LATC and LMC when the production process exhibits decreasing returns to scale? What type of returns to scale holds when LMC equals LATC?

15. Describe the two limitations associated with the cost theory provided in this chapter when it is applied to explain the behavior of medical firms.

## References

Anders, George. "Mergers of Hospitals Surge amid Pressures to Cut Costs." *The Wall Street Journal*, December 1, 1993, p. B1.

Chiang, Alpha C. *Fundamental Methods of Mathematical Economics.* New York: McGraw-Hill, 1984.

Cowing, Thomas G., and Alphonse G. Holtmann. "Multiproduct Short-Run Hospital Cost Functions: Empirical Evidence and Policy Implications from Cross-Section Data." *Southern Economics Journal* 49 (January 1983), pp. 637–53.

Cowing, Thomas G., Alphonse G. Holtmann, and S. Powers. "Hospital Cost Analysis: A Survey and Evaluation of Recent Studies." In *Advances in Health Economics and Health Services Research*, Vol. 4, edited by Richard M. Scheffler and Louis F. Rossiter. Greenwich, CT: JAI Press, 1983, pp. 257–303.

Davidson, Joe. "Partial Merger of 2 Hospitals Approved, Allowing for Efficiencies, Competition." *The Wall Street Journal*, June 20, 1994, p. B6.

Jensen, Gail A., and Michael A. Morrisey. "The Role of Physicians in Hospital Production." *Review of Economics and Statistics* 68 (1986), pp. 432–42.

Salkever, David. "A Microeconomic Study of Hospital Cost Inflation." *Journal of Political Economy* 80 (November 1972), pp. 1144–66.

Santerre, Rexford E., and Dana C. Bennett. "Hospital Market Structure and Cost Performance: A Case Study." *Eastern Economic Journal* 18 (spring 1992), pp. 209–19.

Stecklow, Steve. "Two Big New England Doctor Groups, Lahey and Hitchcock, Plan to Merge." *The Wall Street Journal*, September 7, 1994, p. B3.

## CEBS Questions

CEBS Sample Question on Subject Matter from CEBS Course IX Study Manual

1. Explain, in words—not a mathematical formula—the condition that must exist for the most efficient mix of RNs and LPNs. (pages 164–165)

CEBS Sample Exam Questions

1. Economists and accountants treat production costs differently. The difference is that economists consider:
   A. Only the explicit costs
   B. Only verifiable costs
   C. Historical costs
   D. Opportunity costs
   E. Actual costs

2. A medical firm increased all inputs 10 percent and output increased 12 percent. Which of the following statements is (are) correct?
   I. This is an example of an exception to the law of diminishing productivity.
   II. This is an example of increasing returns to scale.
   III. This example must involve the long run, not the short run.
      A. II only
      B. III only
      C. I and III only
      D. II and III only
      E. I, II, and III

3. All the following statements regarding the neoclassical cost theory are correct EXCEPT:
   A. The theory assumes that all firms are operating under conditions of perfect certainty.
   B. The theory assumes that all firms produce as efficiently as possible.
   C. The theory has limited usefulness to medical firms because these organizations usually have short-run cost curves that are not U shaped.
   D. The theory may be difficult to apply to medical firms because some firms may not have the incentive to produce as cheaply as possible.
   E. The theory poses problems for medical firms because the demand for medical services is unpredictable.

*Answer to Sample Question from Study Manual*
The condition that must exist for the most efficient mix of RNs and LPNs is that the last dollar spent on registered nurses (the marginal cost of nurses) must generate the same increment to output as the last dollar spent on licensed practical nurses. In other words, both inputs will generate the same output per dollar at the margin.

*Answers to Sample Exam Questions*
1. D is the correct answer. Economists, unlike accountants, consider both the explicit and implicit costs of production. Implicit costs include opportunity costs. See pages 155–156 of the text.
2. The correct answer is D. Increasing returns to scale involve the long-run when all inputs are increased. Statement I is incorrect because at least one factor must be held constant to apply the concept of diminishing productivity. See pages 147 and 168 of the text.
3. C is the correct answer. The short-run cost curves for medical firms must have a U shape under the assumptions of the theory. See pages 156–162 and 171–172 of the text.

# 7

# Cost-Benefit Analysis

E very day decisions are made in the health care sector concerning the best, or efficient, amount of medical care to provide. At some juncture in the decision-making process, the all-important question becomes: At what point do the added costs of providing more medical care outweigh the benefits in terms of improved health? In practice, the answer to this question is complex because costs and benefits depend on such factors as the availability of medical resources, patient preferences, and the severity of illnesses. Furthermore, because the benefits of medical services (as revealed by demand) are somewhat fuzzy and medical costs are unknown before the episode of care is completed, the efficient amount of medical services can be almost impossible to determine initially. Nevertheless, the true costs and benefits associated with various medical services are important to health care policymakers.

Consider an adult who complains to her physician about chest pains during an annual physical exam. The first thing the physician must do is determine the seriousness of the problem. The pain could simply be the result of stress or could be a sign of more serious trouble, such as an impending heart attack (remember Joe at the beginning of Chapter 1?). When confronted with a patient's chest pains, a physician faces several options. For example, one clinical professor of medicine says,

> To assess chest pain, . . . we can take a history and a physical examination for $100; do an exercise test for $500; perform a nuclear stress test for $1,500; or do coronary angiography for $5,000. Each escalation in diagnostic approach improves the accuracy of diagnosis from 50 percent to 60 to 80 to 100 percent. (Rubenstein, 1994)

Basically, the best medical procedure is chosen by comparing the incremental costs of progressively more expensive medical tests with the benefits of additional medical information provided by greater diagnostic capabilities. Clearly, individual patients, health care providers, and society as a whole face similar cost-benefit analyses on a recurring basis.

This chapter examines how costs and benefits affect medical decisions from the point of view of a health policymaker who is attempting to make informed choices concerning the production or allocation of medical care services. The information provided will make you more knowledgeable about such important concepts as costs, benefits, and efficiency. Specifically, this chapter

- Introduces cost identification analysis.

- Reviews the theory underlying cost-benefit analysis.

- Illustrates how cost-benefit analysis can be used to make health care decisions.

- Explains the concept of discounting to take into account those costs and benefits resulting from health care decisions that occur over time.

- Discusses the monetary value of a life using the human capital and willingness-to-pay approaches.

- Introduces cost effectiveness analysis as an alternative to cost-benefit analysis.

## Cost Identification Analysis

The first type of analysis we will consider is cost identification. Generally speaking, **cost identification** studies measure the total cost of a given medical condition or type of health behavior on the overall economy. The total cost imposed on society by a medical condition or a health behavior is generally one of three major types:

1. Direct medical care costs

2. Direct nonmedical costs

3. Indirect costs

**Direct medical care costs** encompass all costs incurred by medical care providers, such as hospitals, physicians, and nursing homes. They include such costs as the cost of all necessary medical tests and examinations, the cost of administering the medical care, and the cost of any follow-up treatments.

**Direct nonmedical costs** represent all monetary costs imposed on any nonmedical care personnel, including patients. For the patient, direct nonmedical costs include the cost of transportation to and from the medical care provider, in addition to any other costs borne directly by the patient. For example, the patient may require home care or have specific dietary restrictions. Others may also be influenced by the treatment. For instance, the cost of instituting a substance abuse program in the workplace includes not only the direct medical costs of drug and alcohol rehabilitation but also any nonmedical costs the firm incurs while implementing and overseeing the program. Family members may be financially affected as well.

**Indirect costs** primarily consist of the time costs associated with implementation of the treatment. Indirect costs include the opportunity cost of the patient's (or anyone else's) time that the program affects, especially because many health behaviors and medical conditions result in lost productivity due to injury, disability, or loss of life. Consider the substance abuse program discussed above. Costs should reflect the opportunity costs of the time needed to educate workers about the potential dangers of substance abuse. The time cost is borne by the employer and equals the value of forgone production.

By and large, cost identification studies consider the direct and indirect costs associated with medical actions, or adverse medical behavior. For example, Fanslow et al. (1997) estimated the total economic cost of homicides in New Zealand to be slightly more than $53 million in 1992. The total cost for the homicide victims equaled approximately $24 million, which included direct costs of almost $800,000 and a little more than $23 million for lost productivity. The estimated cost for the perpetrators equaled almost $30 million, of which almost 80 percent was direct costs. The remaining $6 million were indirect costs, or lost productivity.

A study by Weiss, Gergen, and Hodgson (1992) provided an economic assessment of a medical condition. The authors estimated that the total annual cost associated with asthma in the United States was over $6.2 billion in 1990. Direct medical costs topped $3.6 billion, while indirect costs exceeded $2.5 billion. The latter included $900 million from lost school days, $800 million from lost work due to illness, and $800 million from lost productivity resulting from premature worker death.

Other cost identification studies provide yearly cost estimates on a per-case basis. For instance, Ernst and Hay (1994) estimated the total costs of Alzheimer's disease to equal $173,932 per case in 1991. Waitzman, Romano, and Scheffler (1994) estimated the per-case cost of 18 different birth defects in the United States for 1988. Among other results, they found that the per-case costs of cerebral palsy and Down's syndrome equaled $445,000 and $410,000, respectively.

Cost identification studies like these are enlightening because they provide us with a sense of the total costs associated with various medical conditions or health behaviors. However, they provide little guidance for decision making. For example, what is the best, or efficient, method to treat Alzheimer's disease? To answer questions like this, we must turn to other types of decision-making techniques, such as cost-benefit and cost effectiveness analysis.

## Cost-Benefit Analysis

In Chapter 1, we introduced the net benefit calculus or decision rule that economic actors utilize when making rational decisions. In a nutshell, it is in the economic agent's best interests to make a particular choice when the decision's expected benefits exceed its expected cost. Recall that the equation looks like the following:

**(7–1)**   $NB^*(X) = B^*(X) - C^*(X),$

where NB* represents the expected net benefits, $X$ equals the individual decision or choice under consideration, B* stands for the expected benefits from that choice, and C* equals the expected costs resulting from that choice.

Formal cost-benefit analysis utilizes the same net benefit calculus to establish the monetary value of all the costs and benefits associated with a given health policy decision. Such information is invaluable to policymakers who are under pressure to utilize scarce resources to generate the most good for society. To illustrate this point, let's suppose that an all-knowing benevolent dictator, called the "surgeon general," is responsible for ensuring the economic happiness of the people in some hypothetical society. The surgeon general realizes that people possess unlimited wants and that numerous goods and services, such as food, clothing, housing, medical care, and automobiles, provide them with satisfaction. The surgeon general also knows that scarcity of resources involves trade-offs; that is, more of one good means less of the others.

The surgeon general's task is to maximize the social utility of the population by choosing the best aggregate mix of goods and services to produce and consume.[1] To accomplish this objective, the surgeon general has the power to allocate land, labor, and capital resources to any and all uses. Consistent with the maximization of the social utility received from all goods and services, we can think of the surgeon general as trying to maximize the **total net social benefit (TNSB)** from each and every good and service produced in the economy. The total net social benefit derived from a good or service is the difference between the total social benefit (TSB) in consumption and the total social cost (TSC) of production. It represents the net benefit, or gain, that the society receives from producing and consuming a particular amount of some good or service. The total social benefit can be treated as the money value of the satisfaction generated from consuming the good or service. The total social cost can be looked at as the money value of all the resources used in producing the good or service.

For example, the total net social benefit from medical services can be written as

**(7–2)**   $TNSB(Q) = TSB(Q) - TSC(Q).$

Equation 7–2 allows for the fact that the levels of benefits, costs, and net social benefit depend on the quantity of medical services, $Q$. The surgeon general maximizes TNSB by choosing the quantity of medical services at which the difference between total social benefit and total social cost reaches its greatest level. Figure 7–1 presents a graphical representation of this maximization process.

---

[1] In the context of the production possibilities curve, the surgeon general is trying to find the specific point that maximizes the collective well-being of the population. The surgeon general is assumed to accept the current distribution of income.

| FIGURE 7–1 | DETERMINATION OF THE EFFICIENT LEVEL OF OUTPUT |
| --- | --- |

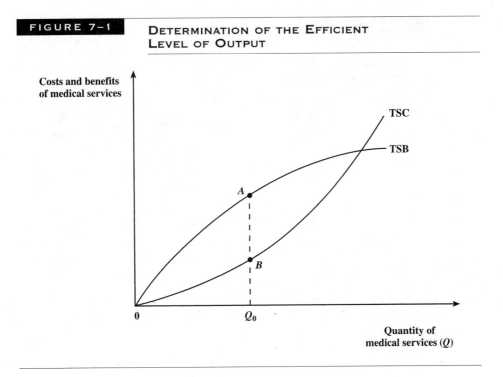

Notice in the figure that total social benefits increase at a decreasing rate with respect to the quantity of medical services. This shape reflects an assumption that people in society experience diminishing marginal benefit (just as an individual consumer does) with respect to medical services and indicates that successive incremental units generate continually lower additions to social satisfaction. Total social costs increase at an increasing rate and reflect the increasing marginal costs of producing medical services.

The slope of the TSB curve can be written as

$$(7\text{–}3) \quad MSB(Q) = \Delta TSB/\Delta Q,$$

where MSB stands for the marginal social benefit from consuming a unit of medical services. Obviously, MSB decreases with quantity since the slope of the TSB curve declines due to diminishing marginal benefit. Similarly, the slope of the TSC curve is

$$(7\text{–}4) \quad MSC(Q) = \Delta TSC/\Delta Q,$$

where MSC represents the marginal social cost of producing a unit of medical services. MSC increases with output as the slope of the TSC curve gets steeper due to increasing marginal cost.

**FIGURE 7-2**     UNDER- AND OVERPROVISION OF MEDICAL SERVICES

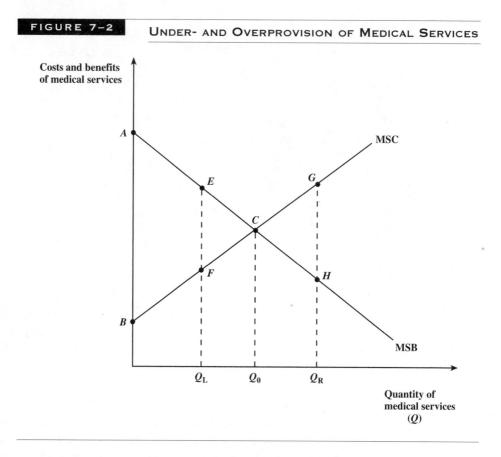

Total net social benefit is maximized where the vertical distance between the two curves is the greatest at distance *AB*. A common principle in geometry is that the distance between two curves is maximized when their slopes are equal. That condition holds at output level $Q_0$ and implies that allocative efficiency, or the best quantity of medical services, results where

**(7-5)**   $\text{MSB}(Q) = \text{MSC}(Q)$.

Thus, the surgeon general chooses output $Q_0$ because it maximizes TNSB.

To illustrate this point in a slightly different manner, figure 7–2 graphs the MSB and MSC curves. Notice that the negatively sloped MSB and the positively sloped MSC reflect diminishing marginal benefit and increasing marginal costs, respectively. The efficient amount of medical services is at $Q_0$ in figure 7–2 because MSB equals MSC. Let us consider why $Q_0$ is the efficient or best level of medical services by examining the figure more closely.

In the figure, units of medical services to the left of $Q_0$ such as $Q_L$ imply that too few medical services are being produced because MSB (point $E$) is greater than MSC (point $F$). At $Q_L$ an additional unit of medical services generates positive additions to TNSB because the marginal net social benefit, the difference between MSB and MSC, is positive. Society is made better off if more medical services are produced. At $Q_0$, where MSB equals MSC, the marginal net social benefit is equal to zero and TNSB is maximized.

In contrast, output levels to the right of $Q_0$ suggest that too many medical services are being produced. For example, at $Q_R$, MSC (point $G$) exceeds MSB (point $H$) and marginal net social benefit is negative, subtracting from maximum total net social benefit. The cost of producing unit $Q_R$ exceeds the benefits at the margin, and society is made better off by not producing this unit. This same argument applies to all units of medical services to the right of $Q_0$.

TNSB is represented by the area below the MSB curve but above the MSC curve in figure 7–2. This is because TNSB is equal to the sum of the marginal net social benefits, or the difference between MSB and MSC for every unit of medical services actually produced. Thus, in figure 7–2, the area $ABC$ represents the maximum TNSB that the society receives if resources are allocated efficiently. (Conceptually, this area is equal to the vertical distance $AB$ in figure 7–1.)

If the surgeon general decides to produce $Q_L$ instead of $Q_0$ units of medical services, society fails to receive the part of the TNSB indicated by area $ECF$. In economics, the lost amount of net social benefits is referred to as a **deadweight loss.** In this example, it measures the cost associated with an underallocation of resources to medical services. Similarly, if the surgeon general chooses to produce $Q_R$ units of medical services, a deadweight loss of area $GCH$ results. Area $GCH$ indicates the net cost to society from producing too many units of medical services and too few units of all other goods and services.

The preceding discussion can be easily couched in terms of the net benefit calculus in equation 7–1. For example, if we solve equation 7–5 for the difference between the marginal social benefit and the marginal social cost, we get

**(7–6)** $\quad \text{NMSB}(Q) = \text{MSB}(Q) - \text{MSC}(Q),$

where NMSB equals the **net marginal social benefit** the society derives from consuming a unit of the good. If NMSB is larger than zero, total net social benefits increases if an additional unit of the good is consumed. Naturally, if NMSB is negative, the society is made worse off if an additional unit of the good is consumed.

### *The Practical Side of Using Cost-Benefit Analysis to Make Health Care Decisions*

Public policymakers concerned with formulating health policies that affect the overall well-being of society, or total net social benefit, must wrestle with the problem of operationalizing equation 7–6. That is no easy task, as it requires that they establish the monetary value of all the costs and benefits associated with a given health policy decision. The problem is complicated by the fact that some of the costs and benefits may be of an indirect nature and therefore difficult to quantify. For instance, suppose you are responsible for estimating the net benefits associated with a rehabilitation program that requires one hour of exercise a day for people who recently had a heart bypass operation. One of the costs you will have to measure is the opportunity cost of the patients' time. Your first inclination may be to base your estimate on the average hourly wage of the people in the program. But what if the people conduct their daily exercise regime on their own time rather than while at work? You now face the problem of determining the opportunity cost of leisure time.[2] As you can see, indirect costs or benefits may be hard to quantify. The benefits, or diverted costs of a medical intervention, fall into four broad categories:

1. The medical costs diverted because an illness is prevented.

2. The monetary value of the loss in production diverted because death is postponed.

3. The monetary value of the potential loss in production saved because good health is restored.

4. The monetary value of the loss in satisfaction or utility averted due to a continuation of life or better health or both.

The first benefit is usually the easiest to calculate and involves estimating the medical costs that would have been incurred had the medical treatment not been implemented. The next two benefits involve projecting the value of an individual's income that would be lost due to illness or death.

The last benefit is the most subjective and therefore the most difficult to quantify, because it involves estimating the monetary value of the pleasure people receive from a longer life and good health. For example, how does one attach a dollar value to the decrease in pain and suffering an individual may experience after hip replacement surgery? Or what is the monetary value of the satisfaction a parent receives from watching a child grow up? Given the difficulty involved in measuring the pleasure of life, many studies simply calculate the other three types of benefits. The resulting figure is considered to reflect a lower bound estimate of total benefits.[3]

## Discounting

The costs and benefits of any medical decision are likely to accrue over time rather than at a single point in time. For example, the benefits of a polio vaccination are felt

---

[2]Although no hard-and-fast rule exists, the opportunity cost of leisure time is most often estimated at some fraction, usually one-half, of the average hourly wage.

[3]In this simple example, we considered the costs and benefits associated with a new medical treatment where one never existed before. As a result, we considered the total costs and benefits experienced by society. In some instances, however, that approach is not appropriate. Consider a new medical treatment that potentially displaces, or complements, an existing one. In this situation, the appropriate practice is to focus on the incremental, or marginal, costs and benefits associated with the new treatment rather than the total costs and benefits. As such, only the added costs and benefits of the new treatment are considered.

primarily in terms of allowing children who might otherwise have been afflicted with polio to lead normal, healthy, active lives. The benefits in this case accrue over many decades. Therefore, an adjustment must be made to account for the fact that a benefit (or a cost) received today has more value than one received at a future date. That is, the net benefit of an activity yielding a stream of future returns must be expressed in **present value** terms before proper comparisons can be made.

In simplest terms, present value means that an individual prefers $100 today rather than a year from now. Even if the individual wants to spend the money a year from now, she or he is still made better off by accepting the money today. For instance, $100 deposited in a savings account offering a 4 percent annual return yields $104 a year later. We say that the present value of $104 to be received a year from now at a 4 percent rate of interest equals $100. In more formal terms, we can state present value, PV, using the following equation:

$$(7\text{--}7) \quad PV = \frac{F}{(1 + r)}$$

where $F$ equals a fixed sum of money and $r$ represents the annual rate of interest, or the rate at which the sum is discounted. In our simple example, $F$ equals $104 and $r$ is 4 percent, or .04, so PV equals $100. Notice that a higher interest rate means the present value of a fixed sum falls. For example, if the rate of interest increases to 5 percent, the present value of $104 decreases to $99.05. Thus, the present value of a fixed sum is inversely related to the rate at which it is discounted.

When referring to sums of money received over a number of periods, the present value formula becomes slightly more complicated. If different sums of money, or net benefits, are to be received for a number of years, $n$, at the close of each period, the formula looks like the following:

$$(7\text{--}8) \quad PV = \frac{F_1}{(1 + r)^1} + \frac{F_2}{(1 + r)^2} + \frac{F_3}{(1 + r)^3} + \ldots + \frac{F_n}{(1 + r)^n}$$

or

$$(7\text{--}9) \quad PV = \sum_i^n F_i/(1 + r)^i,$$

where $F_i$ ($i$ = 1, 2, 3, . . . , $n$) equals the payment, or net benefit, received annually for $n$ years. For simplicity's sake, we normally assume the discount rate is fixed over time. Each annual payment is expressed in today's dollars by dividing it by the discounting factor. The discounting factor equals 1 plus the rate of interest raised to the appropriate power, which is the number of years in the future when the payment is to be received. The sum total, or PV, represents the present value of all annual payments to be received in the future.

In every cost-benefit study in which the effects of a medical treatment or project occur over time, careful consideration must·be given to choosing the discount rate.

That is because the rate at which future payments are deflated can profoundly affect the present value of a project, especially when the costs or benefits do not accrue until far into the future. The earlier polio vaccination example is a case in point. A cost-benefit analysis of a polio vaccination project involves taking the present value of benefits potentially received 70 years into the future (the average American can expect to live about 75 years). Selecting an interest rate that is too high artificially results in the choice of medical interventions that offer short-term net benefits. Conversely, choosing an interest rate that is too low leads to the choice of medical projects that provide long-term net benefits.

Theoretically, the chosen interest rate should equal the rate at which society collectively discounts future consumption, or society's time preference. In an industrial economy, however, there are many interest rates to choose from, including the prime business lending rate, the residential mortgage rate, and the U.S. government bond or T-bill rate. So naturally, the "correct" interest rate is open to interpretation. Most studies choose a discount rate of between 3 and 5 percent or look to private financial markets for guidance. In the latter instance, the interest rate on government bonds is the typical choice. The T-bill interest rate is chosen because it supposedly represents a risk-free rate of return and therefore reflects the rate at which the private sector discounts future streams of income in the absence of risk. Some studies circumvent this problem by presenting a range of estimates based on alternative rates of interest. It is then left to the ultimate decision maker to choose the appropriate rate of discount.

## *The Value of Life*

To properly estimate the total benefits of a medical intervention, we must be able to measure the value of a human life, because many medical interventions extend or improve the quality of life. The most common method used to determine the monetary worth of a life is the human capital approach.[4] The **human capital approach** essentially equates the value of a life to the market value of the output produced by an individual during his or her expected lifetime. The technique involves estimating the discounted value of future earnings resulting from an improvement in or an extension of life. Table 7–1 provides some average estimates of the present value of lifetime earnings by age and gender, discounted at interest rates of 4 and 6 percent. Overall, the numbers in table 7–1 are interesting and deserve discussion. Notice that the discounted value of lifetime earnings initially increases with age and then decreases. The present value figures increase at first because as an individual ages beyond infancy, the value of lifetime earnings that accrue mainly in the middle adult years are discounted over a shorter period of time. Eventually, lifetime earnings decrease with age as productivity and the number of years devoted to work decrease.

The figures in table 7–1 also illustrate the point brought up earlier concerning the importance of choosing the correct discount rate. According to the table, the discounted value of lifetime earnings for a male under one year old equals $421,235 if

---

[4]Economists view expenditures on education and health as personal investments that enhance an individual's ability to command a higher salary in the marketplace; hence the term *human capital*.

| TABLE 7-1 | THE PRESENT VALUE OF LIFETIME EARNINGS BY AGE, GENDER, AND DISCOUNT RATE, 1985 | | | |

| | Males | | Females | |
|---|---|---|---|---|
| Age | 4% | 6% | 4% | 6% |
| Under 1 year | $421,235 | $208,631 | $341,574 | $173,738 |
| 1–4 | 454,561 | 236,117 | 368,388 | 196,515 |
| 5–9 | 519,459 | 293,977 | 420,790 | 244,559 |
| 10–14 | 602,092 | 374,790 | 487,557 | 311,678 |
| 15–19 | 689,576 | 468,782 | 552,141 | 384,026 |
| 20–24 | 745,680 | 541,021 | 578,481 | 425,804 |
| 25–29 | 749,695 | 568,646 | 558,019 | 424,982 |
| 30–34 | 717,630 | 565,043 | 513,796 | 402,176 |
| 35–39 | 653,498 | 532,289 | 454,897 | 364,873 |
| 40–44 | 561,016 | 471,190 | 388,555 | 319,090 |
| 45–49 | 450,452 | 389,462 | 319,279 | 268,529 |
| 50–54 | 311,478 | 294,646 | 249,422 | 214,826 |
| 55–59 | 213,719 | 194,878 | 181,151 | 159,614 |
| 60–64 | 108,880 | 101,085 | 117,333 | 105,272 |
| 65–69 | 42,879 | 39,713 | 67,346 | 61,103 |
| 70–74 | 19,176 | 17,802 | 36,593 | 33,574 |
| 75–79 | 9,383 | 8,789 | 18,847 | 17,531 |
| 80–84 | 4,698 | 4,457 | 9,164 | 8,655 |
| Over 85 | 1,442 | 1,408 | 2,311 | 2,257 |

SOURCE: Dorothy P. Rice, *Cost of Injury in the United States: A Report to Congress, 1989*, Ellen J. Mackenzie and Associates, table C–18.

earnings are discounted at 4 percent and $208,631 if the same earnings are discounted at 6 percent. The larger figure is more than twice the value of the smaller one, and the difference is due solely to a different discount rate. Notice that the relative difference between the two figures diminishes as time increases because earnings are discounted over a shorter time period. As a result, almost no difference exists in the present value of earnings due to the discount rate when we consider a male over age 85.

Data like these can be used to measure the potential benefits of a life-saving medical treatment. For example, suppose a medical treatment saves the life of a 30- to 34-year-old average male. If we assume the male would lead an otherwise normal life, the market value of his life is worth between \$565,043 and \$717,630 depending on whether the 6 or 4 percent discount rate is chosen.

Although the human capital approach is the most widely accepted method for determining the value of a life, the technique is not without shortcomings. One concern is that the approach is unable to control for labor market imperfections. For example, from the figures in table 7–1, it is apparent that the discounted value of lifetime earnings for males is substantially greater than that for females. Gender discrimination in the workplace may account for part of the difference. As a result, women may be penalized and assigned a lower value of life because of their gender. Also, racial discrimination may result in an inappropriate estimate of the value of life when the human capital approach is used.

The human capital approach can also be criticized because it fails to consider any nonmarket returns the individual might receive from other activities, such as leisure. As such, it does not take into account the value of any pain and suffering averted because of a medical treatment, nor does it consider the value an individual receives from the pleasure of life itself. For example, take an extreme view. According to the human capital approach, a chronically unemployed person has a zero or near-zero value of life.

An alternative approach used to measure the value of a life is the willingness-to-pay approach. The **willingness-to-pay approach** is based on how much money people are willing to pay for small reductions in the probability of dying. This kind of information is revealed when, for instance, people install or fail to install smoke detectors in their homes, wear or do not wear automobile seat belts, or smoke or do not smoke cigarettes. For example, assume that people in society choose to spend \$100 per person per year on some device that improves environmental quality and reduces the probability of a person dying by 1 in 10,000. In this case, the imputed value of the average person's life equals \$1 million (\$100 ÷ 1/10,000).

To understand how the willingness-to-pay approach works, consider a person who is deciding whether to purchase a potentially life-saving medical service. The benefit of the life-saving medical service equals the reduced probability of dying, Pr, times the value of the person's life, $V$. Using a cost-benefit approach, the "marginal" person purchases the medical service if the benefit, $\mathrm{Pr} \cdot V$, just compensates for the cost, $C$, or

**(7–10)** $\mathrm{Pr} \cdot V = C,$

although "inframarginal" consumers might perceive greater benefits because they value their lives more highly. Dividing both sides by Pr results in

**(7–11)** $V = C/\mathrm{Pr}.$

Equation 7–11 implies that a lower bound estimate can be calculated for the value of a human life by dividing the cost of a life-saving good or service by the reduced probability of dying.

| TABLE 7-2 | THE IMPLIED VALUE OF A HUMAN LIFE ESTIMATED FROM PEOPLE'S WILLINGNESS TO PAY FOR VARIOUS LIFE-SAVING GOODS OR REGULATIONS (1987 DOLLARS) |
|-----------|--------------------------------------------------------------------|

| Good/Regulation | Estimated Value of a Life |
|-----------------|---------------------------|
| Desire for prompt coronary care | $ 66,000 |
| Automobile air bag purchase | 360,000 |
| Smoke detector purchases | 373,000 |
| EPA requirement for sulfur scrubbers | 500,000 |
| Seat belt usage | 541,000 |
| Wage premiums for dangerous police work | 850,000 |
| EPA regulation of radium content in water | 2,500,000 |
| Wage premiums for dangerous factory jobs | 3,200,000 |
| OSHA rules for workplace safety | 3,500,000 |
| Premium tire usage | 3,600,000 |
| Desire for safer airline travel | 11,800,000 |

SOURCE: Paul M. Barrett, "Price of Pleasure: New Legal Theorists Attach a Dollar Value to the Joys of Living," *The Wall Street Journal*, December 12, 1988, p. A1.

The advantage of the willingness-to-pay approach is that it measures the total value of life and not just the job market value. The imputed value of life generated by the willingness-to-pay approach includes the value of forgone earnings plus the non-market value received from life and good health. As a result, the willingness-to-pay approach generally estimates the value of a life to be higher than that generated by the human capital approach. Miller (1989) reviewed the findings of numerous willingness-to-pay studies and found that the average value of a life equaled $1.95 million in 1985 after-tax dollars. A few years later, Viscusi (1993) found the willingness-to-pay estimates to range between $3 million and $7 million in 1990 dollars. All indications are that the willingness-to-pay estimates are considerably higher than the human capital estimates. Table 7–2 lists various estimates of the value of a human life based on the willingness-to-pay technique.

The major drawback of the willingness-to-pay approach lies in developing reliable data concerning the amount people are willing to pay for incremental reductions in the probability of dying. As table 7–2 shows, the average value of a human life estimated from the willingness-to-pay approach tends to vary considerably. In addition, while the willingness-to-pay may be better than the human capital approach, it is likely to offer only a lower bound estimate for the value of life because it captures only the marginal consumer's valuation process.

### *An Application of Cost-Benefit Analysis—Should College Students Be Vaccinated?*

An increase in the number of reported cases of meningococcal disease in the United States has prompted a discussion as to whether college students should be vaccinated for the disease. Jackson et al. (1995) utilize cost-benefit analysis to determine if such a policy would be an appropriate use of scarce health care resources. That is done by comparing the benefits that would result from a decrease in the number of cases of meningococcal disease to the cost of implementing a vaccination program for all college students.

The cost of this medical intervention equals the cost of the vaccine multiplied by the number of doses needed plus the estimated cost of any side effects occurring because of the vaccine. The total cost of the vaccine was assumed to equal $30 per dose, which accounted for the actual cost of the vaccine plus the cost of administering the vaccine. The authors also assumed that 2.3 million freshmen would enter college every year and that 80 percent of those would receive the vaccine. Regarding side effects, the authors assumed that there would be one severe reaction to the vaccine per 100,000 students vaccinated, which would cost $1,830 per case. Based on these factors, the authors calculate that it would cost $56.2 million a year to administer a vaccination program among college students.

The benefits include the medical costs diverted plus the estimated value of the lives saved because of the vaccine. Treatment costs per case were assumed to equal $8,145, which included seven days of hospitalization and one physician visit per day, and costs for cases occurring in the second, third, and fourth years of college were discounted at a rate of 4 percent. Because there is no way of knowing the rate at which college students contract meningococcal disease, the authors used varying multiples of the baseline rate (the national average for that age group) to calculate the benefits. A total of 58 cases would be prevented at 2 times the baseline rate for a saving of $500,000 in direct medical costs. The cost savings equal $3.1 million at 15 times the baseline rate.

The human capital approach was used to determine the value of lost earnings, and it was assumed that each life saved was worth $1 million. The total benefit from lives saved was $8.8 million for 2 times the baseline rate and $60.7 million for 15 times the baseline rate.

Table 7–3 summarizes the findings for the scenarios where students contract meningococcal disease at 2 times and 15 times the national average. According to the estimates, the net benefit for vaccinating college students is −$46.9 million, assuming a baseline rate of 2 times the national average for that age group. In other words, the estimated costs of this program outweigh the benefits by more than $46 million. Under the assumption that students contract the disease at 15 times the national average, the net benefits equal $60.7 million. In fact, a student rate of 13 times the national average must be employed before the estimated benefits generated by a vaccination

| | TABLE 7-3 | ESTIMATED BENEFITS AND COSTS FOR THE VACCINATION OF COLLEGE STUDENTS AGAINST MENINGOCOCCAL DISEASE (IN MILLIONS OF DOLLARS) | |
|---|---|---|---|

| | Baseline times 2 | Baseline times 15 |
|---|---|---|
| Cost of the vaccination program | $56.2 | $56.2 |
| Total Benefits | 9.3 | 63.8 |
| Direct Medical Benefits | 0.5 | 3.1 |
| Indirect Benefits—Value of Lives Saved | 8.8 | 60.7 |
| Net Benefits—(Benefits-Cost) | −46.9 | 7.6 |

SOURCE: Lisa Jackson et al., "Should College Students Be Vaccinated against Meningococcal Disease? A Cost-Benefit Analysis," *American Journal of Public Health* 85 (June 1995), table 1.

program equal the costs. Using a rate of 2.6 times the national average for that age group, which the authors feel is the maximum possible rate for students, Jackson et al. conclude that the costs of any vaccination program are likely to far outweigh the benefits. Thus, while one cannot ignore the fact that lives would be saved through a vaccination policy, the estimates indicate that such a policy may not be the most efficient way to spend scarce medical care dollars.

## Cost Effectiveness Analysis

The difficulty of measuring benefits is one major drawback of cost-benefit analysis. The problem is even more pronounced in the health care field because the benefits associated with the adoption of a technology or a medical intervention are often in terms of intangible long-term benefits, such as the dollar value of a prolongation of life or an enhancement in the quality of life. As we learned earlier, considerable debate surrounds the most appropriate way to determine the value of a human life. When the health benefits that accrue from a particular policy are clearly defined and deemed desirable, cost effectiveness analysis (CEA) is often employed.

McGuigan and Moyer (1986, pp. 562–63) suggested that the primary difference between cost-benefit and cost effectiveness analysis lies in the basic question being asked: "Cost-benefit analysis asks the question: What is the dollar value of program costs and benefits, and do the benefits exceed the costs by a sufficient amount, given the timing of these outcomes to justify undertaking the program?" In contrast, the question asked in cost effectiveness analysis is: "Given that some prespecified object is

## "Parents, How Much Is Your Young Child Worth?"

Carlin and Sandy (1991) used the willingness-to-pay approach to estimate the value of a young child's life based on the mother's decision to buy and use a child car seat. By purchasing and using a safety seat, the mother revealed how much she was willing to pay for a small reduction in the risk of her child dying in an auto accident. The data in the study came primarily from a 1985 survey conducted in Indiana that gathered information regarding the use of child safety seats by mothers/drivers.

The benefits of using a child car seat were expressed in terms of a decrease in the probability of a child dying in an automobile accident. The authors estimated that during the first four years of life, when a child is supposed to use a safety seat, the average family has a .0958 chance of having an automobile accident. In addition, they estimated that the probability of a child surviving a crash improves by .0043 if the child is harnessed in a safety seat. Therefore, a child who rides in a safety seat faces a .0004119 (.09580 · .0043) reduction in the probability of dying (i.e., roughly 4 in 10,000 chances).

The cost of having a child in a federally approved car seat for four years equals the total cost of the seats needed (estimated to equal approximately $80) plus the opportunity cost of the mother's time spent strapping and unstrapping the child from the car seat over the four years. They estimated that the average mother spends 70 hours over four years on this activity. The 70 hours were multiplied by the mean wage of the mothers/drivers who responded to the survey to determine the opportunity cost of the time involved.

Based on those estimates and other considerations, the authors determined that the imputed value of a young child's life as revealed by the decision to use a safety seat equals $418,597. The authors added to that figure the discounted cost of raising a child to arrive at a total figure of $526,827. The final figure represents the total value of a young child's life as determined by the mother's willingness to purchase and use safety seats and raise her child.

to be attained, what are the costs associated with the various alternative means for reaching that objective?"

With CEA, the analyst estimates the costs associated with a particular technology or treatment in achieving a given health care objective. The objective is normally specified in terms of life-years saved.[5] Other objectives, such as reducing cholesterol levels or blood pressure, may also be specified. Cost effectiveness analysis enables decision makers to make informed choices concerning the use of scarce medical resources by comparing the cost of saving a life-year for different types of medical interventions (e.g., review Insight 1–2 in Chapter 1).

For example, Lindfors and Rosenquist (1995) examined the cost effectiveness of breast cancer screening using mammography. According to their estimates, the cost of breast cancer screening per year of life saved varies between $16,000 and $31,900, with the most cost-effective strategy being a biennial mammogram for women between the ages of 50 and 59. The most costly strategy ($31,900 per life year saved) is an annual screening for high-risk women between the ages of 40 and 49, a biennial screening for low-risk women in the same age bracket, and an annual

---

[5]For a comprehensive review of cost-benefit and cost effectiveness analysis, consult Drummond, Stoddart and Torrance (1987), Mishan (1982), or Warner and Luce (1982).

screening for all women between 50 to 79 years of age. These results are similar to other findings in the literature and are part of an ongoing debate as to whether women in their forties should have a regular mammogram.

Even cost effectiveness analysis is not without its critics. For instance, some argue that life-years saved are not homogeneous. Sometimes a medical intervention is associated with a significant number of life-years saved but a reduced quality of life. Conversely, a medical intervention may result in few life-years saved but an enhanced quality of life. For example, some analysts claim that coronary bypass operations do little to extend the lives of elderly men but do permit them to live out their remaining years much more comfortably.

As a result, another technique, called *utility analysis*, has been used frequently in recent years. **Utility analysis** considers the number of life-years saved from a particular medical intervention along with the quality of life. As such, it adjusts the number of life-years gained by an index (a scale between zero and 1) that reflects health status, or quality of life (Drummond, Stoddart, and Torrance, 1987). For instance, the index may be a weighted average of various health indicators, such as death, pain, or a disability. The difficulty in using utility analysis lies in developing the appropriate index to measure utility.

According to Drummond, Stoddart, and Torrance, two basic methods are used to construct the index. The first method asks people who have the same health condition to assess the quality of their lives. The second describes the condition to a group of people who do not have the condition and asks them to gauge the quality of life, or utility. Those consulted might include a group of individuals who are knowledgeable about the medical outcome, such as physicians and nurses. Once the index has been established, it is multiplied by the number of life-years saved to determine quality-adjusted life-years saved (QALYs). For example, a year of life with an amputed leg may be worth .5 QALYs.

### An Application of Cost Effectiveness Analysis: Autologous Blood Donations—Are They Cost Effective?

Since the rise in the number of cases of acquired immunodeficiency syndrome (AIDS), there has been a growing concern about the safety of the U.S. blood supply. Many are worried that they may receive tainted blood through a transfusion and contract an infectious disease, such as HIV or hepatitis C. This has led to an increase in the number of autologous blood donations.[6] Although more costly than traditional community blood donations, autologous donations are safer because the risk of receiving any contaminated blood is zero. Unfortunately, autologous blood donations are also more costly because they involve more administrative and collection expenses and have higher discarding costs than allogeneic donations. The question now becomes whether the increase in safety brought about by using autologous blood donations is worth the additional costs.

---

[6]An autologous blood donation is one in which the donor and the recipient of the blood are the same person. An allogeneic donation is one in which the donor and the recipient are different people.

| TABLE 7–4 | ESTIMATED COST EFFECTIVENESS OF AUTOLOGOUS BLOOD DONATIONS | | | |
|---|---|---|---|---|
| | Total Hip Replacement | Coronary Artery Bypass Grafting | Abdominal Hysterectomy | Transurethral Prostatectomy |
| Additional cost per unit of autologous blood transfused | $68 | $107 | $594 | $4,783 |
| QALY per unit transfused | 0.00029 | 0.00022 | 0.00044 | 0.00020 |
| Cost effectiveness (row one/row two) | $235,000 | $494,000 | $1,358,000 | $23,643,000 |

SOURCE: Jeff Etchason et al., "The Cost Effectiveness of Preoperative Autologous Blood Donations," *New England Journal of Medicine* 332 (March 16, 1995), Table 4.

Using cost effectiveness analysis, Etchason et al. (1995) estimate the cost per quality-adjusted life-year saved through autologous blood donations for four different surgical procedures: total hip replacement, coronary-artery bypass grafting, abdominal hysterectomy, and transurethral prostatectomy. The added, or marginal, costs of using autologous blood donations are provided in the first row of table 7–4. As you can see, the marginal cost of autologous blood donations varies from $68 to $4,783 per unit. The difference results mostly from the disposed cost of discarded units of blood. The second row of table 7–4 provides the quality-adjusted life-years gained from using autologous donated blood for each of the four procedures. The authors arrived at these figures by first estimating the probabilities of acquiring a number of infections, such as hepatitis C and HIV, through transfusions of allogeneic blood and then estimating the number of disease outcomes that would result from those infections. These figures were used to determine changes in life expectancy for each of the four surgical procedures. Finally, the authors consulted the medical literature and adjusted their life expectancy figures to arrive at estimates for quality-adjusted life-years (QALY). For example, using autologous blood donations for a hip replacement would result in 0.00029 quality-adjusted life-years saved, or approximately 2.5 hours.

The cost effectiveness per unit of autologous blood for each procedure can be arrived at by dividing the marginal cost of using autologous blood by the QALY saved per unit. For instance, according to table 7–4, the costs effectiveness for using autologous blood for a hip replacement equals $235,000 per quality-adjusted life-year, or $68/.00029.

As you can see, the cost effectiveness per unit of autologous blood runs from $235,000 per quality-adjusted life-year saved for a total hip replacement to over $23 million for a transurethral prostatectomy. Although there is no rule concerning what constitutes a cost-effective expenditure for a medical intervention, the estimates generated by Etchason et al. (1995) are high and suggest that the use of autologous blood donations represents a costly way of saving a life.

# The Monetary Value of Improvements in Health from 1970 to 1990: Was It Worth the Cost?

Using a variety of data sources, Cutler and Richardson (1998, 1997) measure the monetary value of improvements in health in the United States from 1970 to 1990. The authors begin by taking a simple years-of-life approach and assume that each added year of life is worth $100,000 with a discount rate of 3 percent. Under this scenario, the authors estimate that the value of health for a newborn between 1970 and 1990 increased by $77,000, while the value of health for a person aged 65 over the same period increased by $159,000. Under a second scenario the authors calculated the improvement in health in terms of quality-adjusted life-years. In this case, they estimate the improvement in health for newborns to

equal $95,000 and that for someone 65 years of age to equal $169,000.

Using cross-sectional data, Cutler and Richardson (1997) also calculate that medical costs increased by $19,000 for infants and $34,000 for a 65-year-old individual from 1970 to 1987 in 1987 dollars. Since the monetary value of the increase in health far outweighs the added cost of medical care, the authors conclude that the rate of return on medical care expenditures from 1970 through 1990 was very high. Thus, while medical care expenditures increased rather dramatically throughout the 1970s and 1980s, they appear to have generated a much greater increase in the value of health capital.

# A Mile a Day Keeps the Heart Surgeon Away

A fitness craze seems to have swept the United States as more and more people are exercising to improve their health. A recent poll indicates that the number of people who follow some type of exercise regime increased from 24 percent in 1961 to 67 percent in 1990. In an attempt to consider the economic cost of exercise, Hatziandrue et al. (1988) used cost effectiveness analysis to estimate the cost of preventing coronary health disease (CHD) events through jogging. A hypothetical group of 1,000 35–year-old men who jogged regularly was followed over 30 years and compared to a similar group who did not exercise to determine the number of CHD events prevented through exercise. In the study, direct costs of jogging included the monetary cost of buying running shoes and other accessories, plus any medical costs due to injury. Indirect costs included the opportunity cost

of people's time while exercising (assumed to be five hours a week) and the costs of any lost wages resulting from an inability to work due to exercise-related injury.

According to the estimates, a total of 78.1 CHD events would be avoided and 1,138.3 QALYs saved through jogging. Each QALY was assumed to equal .8 of a health-year of life saved. The total cost per QALY gained was $11,313. The authors concluded that although exercise is expensive, it is a cost-effective means for lowering the incidence of coronary heart disease. As a means of comparison, the authors pointed out that the cost per QALY for treating mild angina is $40,000, while the cost for treating hypertension is between $25,000 and $65,000 per QALY. The implication is that a healthy lifestyle is a cost-effective way to extend life.

**SUMMARY**

Because resources are limited, allocation decisions must be made based on cost-benefit analysis. If the benefits resulting from a health care decision exceed the costs, it is in the economic agent's best interests to pursue that decision. One problem that frequently arises when utilizing formal cost-benefit analysis is that of determining the monetary worth of a human life. The human capital approach is the most common method used to translate the value of a life into dollars. It involves estimating the discounted value of earnings gained through an extension of life. The willingness-to-pay approach is an alternative method that has been gaining wider acceptance in recent years. With the willingness-to-pay approach, the monetary value of a life is based on the amount people are willing to pay for small reductions in the probability of dying. The advantage of this approach is that it captures the total value of a life rather than simply the market value, as is the case with the human capital approach. Unfortunately, data limitations preclude the widespread use of the willingness-to-pay approach.

Cost effectiveness analysis is another method commonly used to determine the merits of health care policy options. Because the benefits of improved health are difficult to quantify, many analysts elect to use cost effectiveness analysis. The analysis involves estimating the cost of achieving a given health care objective, usually a life-year saved. More sophisticated analyses consider quality-adjusted life-years saved.

The various techniques discussed in this chapter represent a sampling of the tools health care economists have at their disposal for analyzing the economic aspects of resource allocation. These tools provide policymakers with the information they need to make informed decisions concerning the allocation of scarce health care resources across competing ends.

## Review Questions and Problems

1. In previous chapters, we learned that production efficiency is achieved when society is receiving the maximum amount of output from its limited resources. Explain how cost-benefit analysis can be used to achieve that outcome.

2. You have just been hired by your city's department of health. Your first task is to use cost-benefit analysis to evaluate a smoking awareness program that the department has been promoting for two years. Under the smoking awareness program, the department of health sends a team of health care professionals to various private firms free of charge to lecture to employees about the risks of smoking. The lecture takes one hour and is given during the workday. Describe the costs and benefits you should consider in your analysis.

3. In your own words, describe the difference between cost-benefit and cost effectiveness analysis.

4. According to a study by Boyle et al. (1983), it costs $2,900 per life-year gained and $3,200 per quality-adjusted life-year gained to use neonatal intensive care to increase the survival

rates of low-birth-weight infants weighing from 1,000 to 1,499 grams. For newborns weighing between 500 and 999 grams, the figures are $9,300 and $22,400, respectively. Based on these figures, for which group of very-low-birth-weight infants does neonatal intensive care have the most cost effectiveness results? Why?

5. Think of a situation in which cost effectiveness analysis and utility analysis would give you contrary results. Substantiate your answer.

6. As of March 1, 1994, children riding bicycles in New York must wear safety helmets. Assuming the decision to enact this law was based on cost-benefit analysis, what types of costs and benefits do you think were included in the study?

7. The commissioner of health is concerned about the increasing number of reported cases of preventable childhood diseases, such as polio and rubella. It appears that a growing number of young children are not being vaccinated against childhood diseases as they should be. Two proposals to address the problem are sitting on the commissioner's desk. The programs have equal costs, but the commissioner has funding for only one. The first proposal involves providing free vaccinations at clinics around the country. The benefits from a free vaccination program are likely to be experienced immediately in terms of a drop in the number of reported cases of illness. The second program calls for educating young married couples about the benefits of vaccination. The benefits in this instance will not be felt for some years. The commissioner wants to use cost-benefit analysis to determine which proposal should be implemented. Explain to the commissioner the critical role the discount rate plays in determining which program is chosen. In particular, which program is more likely to be chosen if a relatively low discount rate is selected? Why?

8. Distinguish between the human capital and willingness-to-pay approaches for determining the value of a life. Why does the willingness-to-pay approach generally estimate the value of a life to be higher than the human capital approach does?

9. According to Chase (1993), TPA, a heart drug produced by Genentech Inc., costs 10 times more at $2,200 a dose than streptokinase, an alternative heart drug sold by Astra AB and Kabi Farmacia AB of Sweden and by Hoechst AG of Germany. A trial of 41,000 heart attack patients found that the TPA treatment saves 1 more life out of 100 than streptokinase does. Assume a person pays full cost for either drug and chooses TPA over streptokinase. Another otherwise identical person makes the opposite choice. Use the willingness-to-pay approach to calculate the difference in the value of their lives (assume dosage requirements are the same).

10. Read the following passage from an article in *The Wall Street Journal* (October 3, 1995, p. B1) and answer the following questions.

> Diabetic Toby Warbet quit her secretarial job last year because of physical problems, including blurred vision and a general loss of sensation. Such was her desperation that when she heard about an unproven treatment that might help her, she decided to borrow $20,000 from relatives to pay for it. . . . "Even if the chances are one in a million, I was hoping I would be the one," says the Livingston, NJ resident.

*a.* Use the human capital approach to provide a monetary estimate of the value of Toby Warbet's life as of October 3, 1995. Explain.

*b.* Use the willingness-to-pay approach to estimate the value of Toby Warbet's life. Explain.

*c.* Provide a reason for the discrepancy between the two approaches.

## *References*

Barrett, Paul M. "Price of Pleasure: New Legal Theorists Attach a Dollar Value to the Joys of Living." *The Wall Street Journal,* December 12, 1988, p. A1.

Boyle, H. Michael, George W. Torrance, John C. Sinclair, and Sargent P. Horwoord. "Economic Evaluation of Neonatal Intensive Care of Very-Low-Birth-Weight Infants." *New England Journal of Medicine* 308 (June 2, 1983), pp. 1330–37.

Carlin, Paul S., and Robert Sandy. "Estimating the Implicit Value of a Young Child's Life." *Southern Economic Journal* 58 (July 1991), pp. 186–202.

Chase, Marilyn. "Genentech Drug Raises Question of a Life's Value." *The Wall Street Journal,* May 3, 1993, p. B1.

Cutler, David M., and Elizabeth Richardson. "The Value of Health 1970–1990." *American Economic Association Papers and Proceedings* 88 (May 1998), pp. 97–100.

———. "Measuring the Health of the U.S. Population." In *Brookings Papers on Economic Activity: Microeconomics 1997,* edited by Martha Gottron et al. Washington DC: Brookings Institution, 1997.

Drummond, Michael F., Greg L. Stoddart, and George W. Torrance. *Methods for Economic Evaluation of Health Care Programmes.* Oxford: Oxford University Press, 1987.

Ernst, Richard L., and Joel W. Hay. "The U.S. Economic and Social Costs of Alzheimer's Disease Revisited." *American Journal of Public Health* 84 (August 1994), pp. 1261–64.

Etchason, Jeff, et al. "The Cost Effectiveness of Preoperative Autologous Blood Donations." *New England Journal of Medicine* 332 (March 16, 1995), pp. 719–24.

Fanslow, Janet E, et al. "The Economic Cost of Homicide in New Zealand." *Social Science and Medicine* 45 (1997), pp. 973–77.

Hatziandrue, Evridiki I., et al. "A Cost-Effectiveness Analysis of Exercise as a Health Promotion Activity." *American Journal of Public Health* 78 (November 1988), pp. 1417–21.

Jackson, Lisa A., et al. "Should College Students Be Vaccinated against Meningococcal Disease? A Cost-Benefit Analysis." *American Journal of Public Health* 85 (June 1995), pp. 843–46.

Lindfors, Karen K., and John Rosenquist. "The Cost-Effectiveness of Mammographic Screening Strategies." *Journal of the American Medical Association* 24 (September 20, 1995), pp. 881–84.

McGuigan, James R., and R. Charles Moyer. *Managerial Economics,* 4th ed. St. Paul, MN: West, 1986.

Miller, Ted R. *Narrowing the Plausible Range Around the Value of Life.* Washington, DC: Urban Institute, 1989.

Mishan, E. J. *Cost-Benefit Analysis: An Informal Introduction.* 3d ed. London: George Allen and Unwin, 1982.

Rice, Dorothy. *Cost of Injury in the United States: A Report to Congress, 1989.* Ellen J. Mackenzie and Associates, 1989.

Rubenstein, Joel L. "The High Cost of Marginal Benefits." *Boston Globe,* May 12, 1994, p. 70.

Viscusi, W. Kip. "The Value of Risks to Life and Health." *Journal of Economic Literature* 31 (December 1993), pp. 1912–46.

Waitzman, Norman J., Patrick S. Romano, and Richard M. Scheffler. "Estimates of the Economic Costs of Birth Defects." *Inquiry* 31 (summer 1994), pp. 188–205.

Warner, Kenneth, and Bryan R. Luce. *Cost-Benefit and Cost-Effectiveness Analysis in Health Care: Principles, Practice, and Potential.* Ann Arbor, MI: Health Administration Press, 1982.

Weiss, Kevin B., Peter J. Gergen, and Thomas A. Hodgson. "An Economic Evaluation of Asthma in the United States." *New England Journal of Medicine* 326 (March 26, 1992), pp. 862–66.

# II

# Alternative Objectives and Environments Facing Health Care Providers

# 8

# Profit Maximization in Perfectly Competitive Medical Markets

"Genentech's Activase Faces Competition from New Set of Blood-Clot Dissolvers" (*The Wall Street Journal*, November 15, 1994, p. B6).

"Market Forces Are Starting to Produce Significant Cuts in Health-Care Costs" (*The Wall Street Journal*, June 21, 1994, p. A2).

"Price Competition Hits Hospitals" (*Hartford Courant*, May 24, 1994, p. E10).

"Even Before Clinton Reform, Doctors Say They Feel Pinch of Growing Competition" (*The Wall Street Journal*, March 19, 1993, p. B1).

"Yes, the Market Can Curb Health Costs" (*Fortune*, December 28, 1992, pp. 84–88).

The above headlines are just a sampling of the numerous articles in the popular press extolling the virtues of competitive markets for medical services. The strong belief many people hold in the self-correcting tendency of competitive markets should not surprise anybody schooled in economics. According to traditional microeconomic theory, *perfect competition* creates a "survival of the fittest" market mentality and thereby forces firms to satisfy consumer wants and produce with least-cost methods of production. If competition has the power to weave this same magic in medical markets, incentives exist for medical firms to offer high-quality, cost-effective medical products at the lowest possible prices. With health care costs skyrocketing, competitive behavior among medical firms would certainly be a welcome sight in today's health economy.

But are the various features normally associated with perfect competition applicable to medical care industries? That is, do the characteristics necessary for a perfectly competitive framework hold in medical markets? If some particular medical industries do closely resemble the perfectly competitive model, how are the typical firm and the market expected to behave according to economic theory? This chapter answers these questions. Specifically, the chapter

- Discusses the characteristics of perfect competition.

- Analyzes the pricing and output behavior of a perfectly competitive profit-maximizing firm in the goods and services market.

- Derives a supply curve from the model of the competitive firm.

- Develops a supply and demand model of a perfectly competitive market for medical goods and services.

- Explains how price and output are established and why price changes in a perfectly competitive market.

- Uses the resulting supply and demand model to explain rising health care costs in the United States.

- Derives the individual firm's demand for an input.

- Discusses the market demand and supply of a medical input.

- Explains how the price and quantity of a medical input are determined and why changes take place in response to market forces.

## What Is Perfect Competition?

People who have had little exposure to the study of economics tend to have different ideas about what perfect competition entails. To some, perfect competition means that each firm in the marketplace strives to attain the greatest market share by charging low, cutthroat prices. Others believe that perfectly competitive firms compete for customers through advertisements or preferred locations. Perfect competition, however, is an abstract concept—a model—and therefore involves a number of necessary conditions. If any one of these conditions is violated in the real world, firms and markets are unlikely to behave as the perfect competition model predicts. A perfectly competitive market model possesses the following seven characteristics:

1. Consumers pay the full price of the product.

2. All firms maximize economic profits.

3. There is a large number of buyers and sellers, each of which is small relative to the total market.

4. All firms in the same industry produce a homogeneous or standardized product.

5. No barriers to entry or exit exist.

6. All economic agents possess perfect information.

7. All firms face nondecreasing costs of production.

The first characteristic, consumers pay the full price, ensures that consumers are responsive to price differentials among firms. The argument is that consumers are more conscious of and sensitive to price differentials when they bear the full financial burden of their consumption decisions. The second feature guarantees that all firms maximize economic profits and therefore potentially face a financial incentive to satisfy consumer wants and produce at minimum cost. The third and fourth characteristics mean that no one buyer or seller is powerful enough to influence or manipulate the market price of a product. For example, if the third characteristic is not met, a few hospitals may have the power to raise prices by collectively restricting the quantity produced of medical services. The fourth feature of perfect competition implies that the firms in an industry sell products that are easily substitutable in consumption. Easy substitutability makes it difficult for any one firm to establish some degree of market power, because its product is not unique. Taken together, characteristics 3 and 4 imply that each firm faces a considerable amount of *actual competition* from other firms in the industry.

The fifth characteristic suggests that the threat of *potential competition* always exists because nothing prevents new firms from entering the industry. For example, a health insurer may be reluctant to increase premiums for medical insurance if the premium increase will cause new insurance companies to enter the market.

The sixth characteristic of perfect competition implies that all economic agents make informed choices. For example, some economists argue that the American Medical Association (AMA) opposed giving medical care providers, particularly physicians, the right to advertise because doing so would make consumers better informed. Doctors would be less able to act as monopolists if consumers had the ability to gather additional information through advertisements.

Finally, the nondecreasing costs of production characteristic rules out the possibility of a natural monopoly, in which the existence of one firm in the market may be desirable to society because a very large firm can more fully exploit any economies of scale in production.

When applied to medical care industries, many of the characteristics of perfect competition do not hold. Several examples highlight this point. First, consumers are often insulated from the full price of a medical good or service by health insurance coverage. Hence, consumers may be less frugal if they are effectively spending someone else's money. Second, the not-for-profit status of many medical enterprises means that health care providers may fail to maximize economic profits. Third, a single hospital often exists in rural areas and faces little, if any, actual competition from other hospitals or other health care providers. Fourth, large teaching hospitals are often viewed as offering a better product than nonteaching hospitals. The perceived uniqueness of the product may provide a large teaching hospital with some power to influence price. Fifth, physician licensure creates an occupational barrier to entry and may shield highly salaried physicians from new competition. Finally, consumers typically lack perfect information about the prices and technical aspects of medical services. This lack of information places physicians in a strong position to practice opportunistic behavior.

Although the conditions underlying perfect competition are not always met in the strictest sense in the real world, the supply and demand model we will develop in this chapter provides a useful tool for explaining or predicting price and output changes in medical markets. One justification for using the perfectly competitive model is that medical markets are sometimes "reasonably" competitive in the real world. For instance, some health care institutions are organized on a for-profit basis, and hospital price competition is often fierce in major metropolitan areas. Another justification is that the U.S. health economy is currently undergoing considerable structural change, and some of the changes are intensifying price competition among medical care institutions. As a result, the supply and demand model developed in this chapter can often be used as a tool for analyzing economic behavior at the market or aggregate level.

In any case, we will relax the assumptions of perfect competition and examine the likely impact of noncompetitive considerations on the operation of the medical marketplace in later chapters. But before we can comprehend how market imperfections influence economic behavior, we must understand how the market works when it is allowed to function under ideal conditions. The functioning of competitive markets is discussed in the remainder of the chapter. First, we discuss the behavior of a perfectly competitive market for goods and services. Next, a competitive market for medical inputs is examined.

# The Price and Output Behavior of a Competitive Firm in the Short Run

In Chapter 6, we discussed the short-run costs of production with only vague reference to the goal of the medical firm. This section makes one possible objective of the medical firm more explicit. In keeping with our model of perfect competition, we assume that the goal of the medical firm is to maximize economic profits. For-profit medical enterprises (e.g., drug companies and most nursing homes) certainly exist, and we discuss the implications of other goals motivating medical care providers in Chapter 10. For now, we will accept profit maximization as a working assumption for pedagogical and predictive purposes. Even if this assumption does not hold in practice, the profit maximization model provides a valuable benchmark for comparing the behavior of real-world medical firms.

## The Profit Maximization Assumption

According to economists, economic profits represent total revenues less the total explicit and implicit costs of production. If economic profits are greater than zero, they are referred to as *excess profits*. When total revenues equal total costs, a firm is considered to be earning a normal profit because it is receiving sufficient revenues to cover

| FIGURE 8–1 | A GENERAL MODEL OF PROFIT MAXIMIZATION |
|---|---|

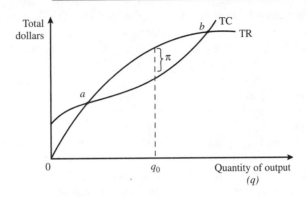

all costs, including a normal return on its physical assets. Finally, if total costs exceed total revenues, a firm is incurring an economic loss.

Economic profits ($\pi$) can be expressed as the difference between total revenues, TR, and total costs, TC, or

**(8–1)**  $\pi(q) = \text{TR}(q) - \text{TC}(q).$

Equation 8–1 takes into consideration the impact output has on both total revenues and total costs. The result is that a firm maximizes economic profits by choosing the appropriate level of output to produce. For example, figure 8–1 depicts total revenue and total cost curves. Notice that the total revenue curve is drawn under the assumption that total revenues increase at a diminishing rate. The total cost curve is taken from figure 6–5 in Chapter 6. Points *a* and *b* in figure 8–1 identify output levels at which the firm breaks even because total revenues equal total costs. At output levels to the left of point *a* and to the right of point *b*, the firm incurs economic losses because total costs exceed total revenues. In the range of output between points *a* and *b*, the firm makes economic profits because total revenues are higher than total costs. Maximum profits are attained at $q_0$ units of output given that the vertical distance is greatest between the total revenue and total cost curves.

A common principle in geometry is that the distance between two curves is maximized when their slopes are equal. Therefore, at $q_0$ the slope of the total revenue curve equals the slope of the total cost curve, or[1]

**(8–2)**  $\Delta \text{TR}/\Delta q = \Delta \text{TC}/\Delta q.$

---

[1]Readers with some background in differential calculus may wish to take the first derivative of equation 8–1 and set it equal to zero to find the level of output at which profits are maximized. Allowing for discrete rather than infinitesimally small changes, the resulting expression implies that profits are maximized when equation 8–2 holds.

These slopes have an economic interpretation. The left-hand side of equation 8–2 represents the additional revenue that is associated with the selling of an additional unit of output and represents marginal revenue (MR). Similarly, the right-hand side of the equation represents the marginal cost of production (MC).

It follows that the profit-maximizing firm produces output up to the point where marginal revenue equals marginal cost (MR = MC). Otherwise, if MR > MC, additional units of medical output generate positive incremental profits, and the firm can realize greater total profits by producing more output. On the other hand, if MC > MR, the last units of medical output generate economic losses, so the firm can increase total profits by producing less output.

An important point about the profit-maximizing condition is worth mentioning at this juncture. The profit-maximizing condition that MR = MC does not necessarily imply that the firm obtains a positive level of economic profits. The profit maximization condition reveals only the level of output at which profits are at their highest level for a given set of circumstances determining the positions of the TR and TC curves. If TC exceeds TR at all levels of output, the highest level of profits coincides with the least amount of negative profits (i.e., economic losses). In this case, the profit-maximizing condition identifies the output level that minimizes economic losses because no level of output generates a positive level of profits. In any event, the firm comes as close as it can to obtaining a positive level of profits.

## Profit Maximization by a Competitive Firm

Figure 8–1 provides a generalized total revenue function facing a firm because the diminishing slope implicitly assumes that price falls as output expands (i.e., the demand curve is downward sloping). A single, small competitive firm, however, can most likely sell additional output without lowering the market price, since it produces only a small fraction of industry output. If so, the firm is considered to be a "price taker," and its total revenues are equal to

$$(8\text{–}3) \quad \text{TR} = P_0 \cdot q$$

where $P_0$ is viewed as being fixed by the marketplace and outside the control of the single firm.

For argument's sake, let's assume generic aspirin is produced and sold in a perfectly competitive market. Figure 8–2 shows that the demand curve facing the individual generic aspirin producer, $d_0$, is horizontal.[2] The horizontal demand curve can be interpreted in two related ways. First, given the individual aspirin manufacturer's small size relative to the industry, the firm can sell any amount of output without affecting the market price. Second, because many substitute suppliers sell the same aspirin product, any one individual supplier faces a perfectly elastic demand.

---

[2]The total revenue curve is a straight line passing through the origin with a slope of $P_0$.

**FIGURE 8–2**     DEMAND AND MARGINAL REVENUE CURVES FOR THE INDIVIDUAL COMPETITIVE FIRM

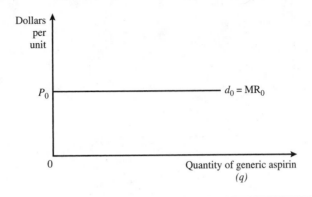

The horizontal demand curve indicates that quantity demanded falls to zero if the aspirin manufacturer raises price above $P_0$. The demand curve also implies that the aspirin manufacturer has no incentive to lower price because it can sell as much output as it wants to at $P_0$. Because price is fixed, the MR associated with an additional unit of output, or $\Delta TR/\Delta q$, is simply $P_0$.[3] This means that the aspirin manufacturer receives the prevailing market price as added revenues for each additional unit of output produced and sold. Because the aspirin manufacturer receives the prevailing market price when selling each additional unit of output, the demand curve also represents the marginal revenue curve; hence, $d_0 = MR_0$.

We can combine the information about the marginal revenue curve with the short-run cost curves to determine the profit-maximizing level of aspirin production. By superimposing figure 6–7 from Chapter 6 and figure 8–2, we can identify the profit-maximizing level of output for the aspirin producer. The resulting graphical model is shown in figure 8–3. Notice that the aspirin manufacturer maximizes profits at the $q_0$ level of output since $MR_0$ equals SMC. Output levels to the left or right of $q_0$ generate incremental profits or losses, and thus profits are not maximized. Because the market price of $P_0$ exceeds the short-run average total costs of $C_0$, the producer realizes a positive economic profit. That is because total revenues represent the rectangular area $P_0aq_00$, while total costs equal the smaller rectangular area $C_0bq_00$. Profits equal the difference between the two areas, or rectangle $P_0abC_0$.

The graph in figure 8–3 is purposely drawn to show an economic profit. As we know, a number of factors affect the positions of the revenue and cost curves. If either the market price declines or average costs increase for some reason, the demand or cost curves shift and the firm's economic profits decline. In that case, the

---

[3]We know that $TR = P_0 \cdot q$ and that $P_0$ is independent of output. Therefore, $\Delta TR = P_0\Delta q$. If we divide both sides of the latter equation by $\Delta q$, we get $MR = P_0$.

FIGURE 8-3    THE PROFIT-MAXIMIZING LEVEL OF OUTPUT FOR
THE INDIVIDUAL COMPETITIVE FIRM

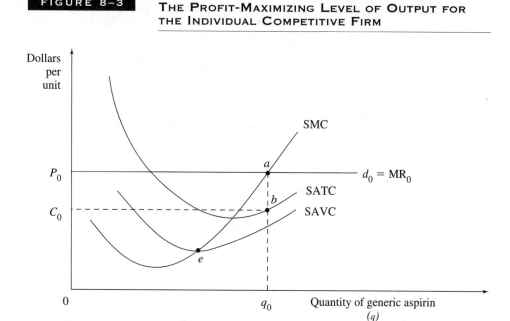

aspirin manufacturer may obtain only a normal profit ($\pi = 0$) or incur economic losses ($\pi < 0$).

### Shutdown Point of the Perfectly Competitive Firm

Experiencing an economic loss, the individual aspirin producer must decide whether to continue production or to shut down. *Shut down* means the firm keeps its assets in the industry but elects not to produce any output. The firm might shut down in the hope that circumstances change in the future such that the market price increases or the average cost of production decreases for some reason (perhaps because input prices fall). In fact, if circumstances do not sufficiently improve, the firm may be forced to exit the industry in the long run.

The short-run theory of the firm explains the point at which a firm, such as the aspirin manufacturer, finds it desirable to shut down rather than continue producing at a loss. The explanation for this behavior lies in the fixed and variable costs of production and the idea that a firm seeks to minimize its short-run losses. For example, let us suppose the aspirin manufacturer's fixed costs of production (e.g., essential administrative salaries, rent, and insurance premiums) equal $5,000 per month. This means that if the aspirin manufacturer shuts down, it incurs out-of-pocket expenses of $5,000 per month. Alternatively, suppose that given the market price, total revenues are high enough to cover the variable costs of production (e.g., labor and material

**FIGURE 8-4** THE INDIVIDUAL COMPETITIVE FIRM'S SUPPLY CURVE

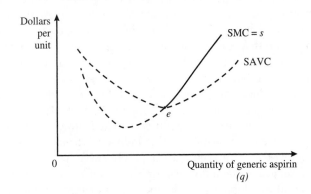

expenses) and some portion, but not all, of the fixed costs. In this case, the aspirin manufacturer can lower its overall losses by continuing to operate. Any operating revenues in excess of the variable costs can be applied toward the $5,000 of fixed costs.

This example illustrates that it is in the firm's best interest to continue production as long as TR > TVC or, alternatively, the market price is greater than SAVC. TR exceeds TVC when the market price equals marginal cost at some point above the SAVC curve in figure 8–3. The firm shuts down if price is less than SAVC because revenues are not sufficient to cover the variable costs and at least some portion of the fixed costs. Finally, if the market price equals SAVC, the firm is indifferent with respect to shutting down versus continuing to operate. Point $e$ in figure 8–3 represents the price at which the firm is indifferent between shutting down and continuing operations. Thus, the shutdown point of the firm occurs where price falls below the minimum point on the SAVC curve.

## Short-Run Supply Theory

The profit maximization rule indicates that the firm produces at the level of output at which $P$ = SMC, while the shutdown rule implies that price must be greater than SAVC. By combining these two rules, we can derive the individual firm's short-run supply curve that identifies the amount of output the firm offers for sale in the market at various prices. As identified in figure 8–4, the individual aspirin manufacturer's supply curve, $s$, is the portion of the SMC curve that lies above the minimum point on the SAVC curve: For any price below point $e$, the firm offers zero units of output for sale in the marketplace, since it can reduce losses by shutting down. For prices above point $e$, the aspirin manufacturer equates price to SMC to determine how much output to offer for sale. Therefore, the portion of the SMC curve above point $e$ represents the individual aspirin producer's short-run supply curve because it identifies the quantity of output that it supplies at various market prices.

Notice that the individual producer's short-run supply curve is positively sloped. A higher price creates an incentive for the firm to increase the quantity supplied of output in the marketplace. The higher price compensates for the increased marginal cost of production that results from diminishing marginal productivity in the short run.

In a manner similar to the derivation of the market demand curve in Chapter 4, we can derive a short-run market supply curve through a horizontal summation of the various individual firms' supply curves. In other words, for a series of market prices, we can add together the quantity supplied by each aspirin manufacturer in the marketplace to obtain the total quantity supplied in the market at each price. Not surprisingly, given the shapes of the individual firms' supply curves, the derivation process reveals a short-run market supply curve for aspirin that is positively sloped. Therefore, just as the individual aspirin producer does, all firms in the aspirin industry respond to a higher price by increasing quantity supplied.[4] This is referred to as the **law of supply.**

## Factors Influencing the Position of the Short-Run Market Supply Curve

In Chapter 6, we saw how the position of the short-run cost curves is conditioned on a set of short-run circumstances that include the prices of the variable inputs, the quantity of the fixed input, the quality of care, and the patient case-mix (if the firm is a service-oriented business). In addition, the cost curves shift when these circumstances change. Because the short-run supply curve of the individual firm is derived from the average variable and marginal cost curves, it follows that the position of the individual firms' supply curves is influenced by this same set of circumstances. Moreover, because the market supply curve represents the horizontal summation of the individual firms' supply curves, its position also depends on the same set of economic circumstances in addition to the number of sellers in the marketplace. Consequently, whenever the prices of inputs, quantity of fixed inputs, quality of care, or patient case-mix changes on a marketwide basis, the position of the market supply curve of medical output is altered. Also, if the number of sellers in the market changes for some reason, the position of the market supply curve is affected.

For example, suppose the original or initial market supply curve is $S_0$ in figure 8–5.[5] Factors that increase quantity supplied shift the market supply curve to the right toward $S_1$. Thus, lower input prices, a cost-saving expansion of capital, reduced quality, less severe case-mixes, and an increased number of sellers cause the supply curve to shift to the right. Equivalently, any change in these factors that leads to higher costs (e.g., higher input prices) reduces supply and shifts the supply curve to the left toward $S_2$.

---

[4]Some adjustments to the market supply curve may have to be made, however. For example, if all firms in the industry expand production simultaneously, wage rates may be driven upward. If input substitutability is limited, the individual firms' cost curves shift upward and the equilibrium level of quantity supplied declines. As a result, the industry supply curve becomes steeper.

[5]Notice that the quantity supplied collectively by all firms in the market is represented by $Q$ rather than $q$, which stands for the individual firm's output.

**FIGURE 8–5**    **CHANGES IN THE MARKET SUPPLY CURVE**

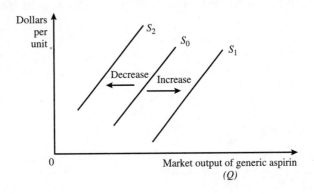

**FIGURE 8–6**    **PRICE ELASTICITY OF SUPPLY**

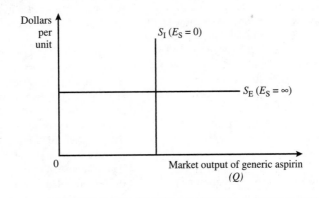

## Price Elasticity of Supply

The *price elasticity of supply* measures the responsiveness of quantity supplied to a change in price. Price elasticity of supply is measured by dividing the percentage change in quantity supplied by the percentage change in price and can be written mathematically as

**(8–4)**   $E_S = \Delta Q_S/Q_S \div \Delta P/P.$

The price elasticity of supply ranges between zero and infinity. The two supply curves in figure 8–6 represent the extreme polar cases for price elasticity of supply.

## Price Elasticity of Supply Estimates for Physician Services in Ontario

Scant empirical evidence exists on the price elasticity of supply for different medical services. One reason is that the necessary data are often unavailable. Another reason is that price changes typically influence both consumer and producer behavior, so empirically it is very difficult to ascribe changes in quantity to the demand or supply side of the medical market. A study by Hurley. Labelle, and Rice (1990), however, was able to provide some estimates of the price elasticity of supply for different physician services in Ontario, Canada. The authors focused on Canada primarily because Canadian consumers face virtually no out-of-pocket charges for medical services and are therefore insensitive to any changes in the actual prices for medical services. As a result, any quantity response to price changes can be attributed solely to the supply side of the market.

In the study, the unit of analysis was an individual physician procedure or service. Quarterly data for total utilization and fees in Ontario, by specialty, were obtained for 28 procedures and services over the period 1975 to 1987. For each procedure, a multiple regression equation was estimated in the following form:

**(8-5)** $U_{i,t} = \beta_0 + \beta_1 FEE_{i,t} + \beta_2 X_{i,t} + e_{i,t}$

where

$U_{i,t}$ = A measure of the utilization of procedure $i$ at time $t$.

$FEE_{i,t}$ = A measure of the fee received for providing procedure $i$ at time $t$.

$X_{i,t}$ = A vector of other independent supply and demand determinants of utilization, such as physicians and nurses per capita, per capita income, and educational attainment.

$e_{i,t}$ = The error term.

$\beta_0, \beta_1, \beta_2$ = The parameters to be estimated.

With estimates of $\beta_1$ and the mean values for $U_i$ and $FEE_i$, Hurley, Labelle, and Rice were able to estimate the price elasticity of supply for each procedure. Table 1 reports their estimates for 23 procedures.

For the first four procedures, the estimated price elasticities of supply were positive and statistically significant. All four estimates were less than 1, implying that quantity supplied was relatively inelastic with respect to price. The supply elasticity for all types of cataract excisions was the most price elastic at .989. The estimate implies that a 10 percent increase in price caused nearly a 10 percent increase in the quantity supplied of this procedure, *ceteris paribus*. The least responsive of the first four procedures with respect to price were consultations for radiation oncology (oncology is the medical science that treats and studies tumors). A 10 percent increase in the fee for this procedure resulted in only a 1.3 percent increase in quantity supplied.

The estimated price elasticities of supply were found to be not statistically different from zero for the next 19 procedures. If correct, the zero price elasticity estimates imply that the supply of these services was perfectly inelastic. According to these results, a price change had no impact on the quantity supplied of these procedures (at least in the range of observed prices).[1] The authors suspect that physicians faced various constraints during this period that prevented them from changing output in response to fee changes. Among the constraints was a limitation on the supply of hospital beds during the period. According to the authors, the number of hospital beds per person fell from 4.83 in 1975 to 3.96 in 1987.

[1]The same study found that the estimated price elasticity of supply was negative for five other procedures. Although this finding conflicts with a competitive supply theory (at least in the short run), a noncompetitive theory developed in Chapter 10 called *supplier-induced demand (SID)* can account for the negative price elasticity estimates. According to the SID theory, a lower price causes physicians to increase quantity supplied to maintain a given level of income.

**INSIGHT 8 – 1**

*(continued)*

**TABLE 1**    PRICE ELASTICITY OF SUPPLY ESTIMATES

| Procedure | Supply Elasticity Estimate |
|---|---|
| **Positive and Statistically Significant** | |
| Consultation—radiation oncology | .126 |
| Cataract excision, all types | .989 |
| Tonsillectomy (SP) | .513 |
| Hysterectomy (SP) | .161 |
| **Not Statistically Different from Zero** | |
| Subsequent hospital visit (GP/FP) | .091 |
| Diagnostic ultrasound (pelvic) | .295 |
| Counseling GP/FP | .153 |
| Family therapy | .170 |
| Individual psychotherapy, psychiatry | .095 |
| Coronary artery bypass | .161 |
| Tonsillectomy (GP/FP) | .051 |
| Herniotomy (SP) | .000 |
| Endoscopy, TURP (SP) | .017 |
| Bronchoscopy | .109 |
| Subsequent hospital visit, orthopedic surgery | −.036 |
| Electrocardiogram, professional component (GP/FP) | −.000 |
| Diagnostic ultrasound (abdominal) | −.019 |
| Individual psychotherapy (GP/FP) | −.052 |
| Annual health exam, age > 14 years | −.033 |
| Carotid endarterectomy | −.122 |
| Appendectomy (SP) | −.143 |
| Hemorrhoidectomy (SP) | −.112 |
| Herniotomy (GP/FP) | −.350 |

SP = specialist

GP = general practitioner

FP = family practitioner

SOURCE: Jeremiah Hurley, Roberta Labelle, and Thomas Rice, "The Relationship between Physician Fees and Utilization of Medical Services in Ontario." In *Advances in Health Economics and Health Services Research*, vol. II, edited by Richard M. Scheffler and Louis F. Rossiter, Greenwich, CT: JAI Press, 1990. table 5.

$S_I$ represents a perfectly inelastic supply curve with respect to price, because quantity supplied is unaffected by a change in the price. In this extreme case, $E_S = 0$ because no change occurs in quantity supplied when price adjusts. $S_E$ indicates a perfectly elastic supply, and $E_S = \infty$. In this instance, a change in quantity supplied has no impact on the price of the output.

Two major factors influence the slope of the short-run market supply curve and the price elasticity of supply. The first factor is the amount of time involved in the production decision. As the time frame lengthens, producers are better able to react to an increase in price. For example, in the very short run, it is often difficult for firms to acquire sufficient resources with which to increase production given a rise in the price of medical products. Therefore, the individual firms' supply curves and the market supply curve are likely to be relatively inelastic the shorter the time period. On the other hand, over a longer time period, firms can locate and employ the necessary additional resources, such as labor and materials, to accommodate an increase in production. Thus, output can more easily expand in response to a rise in the market price. Over a longer time period, quantity supplied in the market is more elastic with respect to price.

The second factor affecting the price elasticity of supply is the degree of substitutability among variable inputs. When inputs are easily substitutable in production, it is less difficult to accommodate an increase in output without incurring higher costs. In essence, substitutability among inputs helps to dampen the usual impact of the law of diminishing marginal productivity on the marginal costs of production. Thus, greater substitutability among variable inputs leads to a greater price elasticity of supply. The firms' individual supply curves and the market supply curve are flatter when variable inputs can be more easily substituted in production.

## Short-Run Equilibrium in a Competitive Market for Medical Services

Now that we learned about demand theory in Chapter 4 and short-run supply theory in this chapter, we are in a position to discuss the mechanics of price determination in a perfectly competitive market; that is, we can examine how prices are determined and the role prices play in a competitive market system through the use of supply and demand analysis. Supply and demand analysis is useful for explaining price and output determination in medical markets where either (1) reasonably well-informed consumers pay the full price for a homogeneous medical product supplied by a large number of sellers or (2) a sufficiently large number of knowledgeable buyer groups (e.g., managed-care organizations) bargain over price with a relatively large number of health care providers. The latter situation is becoming more common as people join various managed-care insurance plans in which the organization negotiates the price for medical products on behalf of its subscribers.

Let us take the first situation and suppose that figure 8–7 depicts the market for generic aspirin. The per-unit price of generic aspirin, $P$, is specified on the vertical axis, and the quantity of generic aspirin, $Q$, is shown on the horizontal axis. The

| FIGURE 8-7 | DETERMINATION OF MARKET PRICE AND QUANTITY |

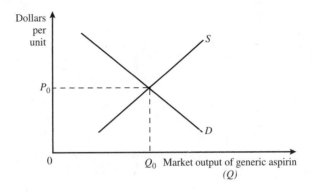

demand curve is downward sloping to reflect diminishing marginal benefit, and the supply curve is upward sloping to indicate that marginal costs increase with respect to the production of aspirin.

The **equilibrium,** or market-clearing, price and output are at the point where the demand and supply curves intersect. Equilibrium occurs when no tendency for further change exists. At the equilibrium price of $P_0$, consumers are willing and able to purchase $Q_0$ units of generic aspirin. In addition, manufacturers of aspirin wish to provide $Q_0$ units on the market at this price. Thus, both consumers and producers are perfectly satisfied with the exchange because both can purchase or sell their desired amounts at a price of $P_0$.

### Surpluses and Shortages

The preceding discussion implies that only one unique equilibrium price can exist in a competitive market given a certain set of circumstances. To see that point, suppose the price of aspirin is above the equilibrium level and equals $P_1$ in figure 8–8. At price $P_1$, consumers are willing to purchase the quantity of aspirin indicated by point *A* on the demand curve. Producers, however, wish to supply the amount indicated by point *B* on the supply curve. The difference between the quantity supplied and the quantity demanded at this price, $P_1$, can be measured by the horizontal distance *AB* and is called a **surplus** or an **excess supply.**

This situation does not represent an equilibrium outcome because price changes in response to the imbalance in the market. Specifically, each individual producer of aspirin faces an incentive to lower the price given a surplus in the market. As price is reduced from $P_1$ to $P_0$, the quantity demanded of aspirin increases and, at the same time, producers offer less aspirin on the market. Due to these market adjustments, price falls to the equilibrium level, where the two curves intersect and the temporary surplus is alleviated.

**FIGURE 8–8**     **SHORTAGES AND SURPLUSES**

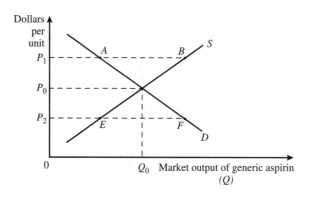

A **shortage** of, or an **excess demand** for, aspirin results when quantity demanded exceeds quantity supplied as indicated by the horizontal distance *EF* in figure 8–8. Notice that the shortage occurs because the price, $P_2$, is below the market-clearing level. In a competitive market, this price is temporary and adjusts upward as consumers bid up the price of the relatively scarce aspirin. As price increases from $P_2$ to $P_0$, some consumers face an incentive to switch to substitutes or postpone their consumption. Moreover, manufacturers face an incentive to offer more aspirin on the market because as the price increases, they are compensated for the higher costs of production. Thus, the price of aspirin is driven upward toward the equilibrium level when a shortage exists, and the temporary imbalance is eliminated.

## Comparative Static Analysis

Although the model of demand and supply is elementary, it is quite powerful and broadens our understanding of health care economics. Most important, it helps us understand how the price and output of medical services are determined in a competitive market setting. In addition, the model has some predictive capabilities; that is, it permits us to predict how the market reacts to an event that influences either the demand for or supply of medical services. Using the model for predictive purposes is sometimes referred to as **comparative static analysis.** Comparative static analysis examines how changes in market conditions influence the positions of the demand and supply curves and therefore the equilibrium levels of price and output. As the demand and supply curves shift, we can trace out price and output effects by comparing the different equilibrium points. Comparative static analysis can be used to explain the effects of market changes in the past or to forecast future market outcomes.

As discussed in Chapter 4, several factors, such as the number of buyers, consumer tastes, income, time costs, and the prices of substitutes and complements,

| FIGURE 8-9 | EFFECTS OF AN INCREASE IN DEMAND |

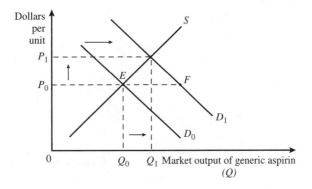

affect the position of the market demand curve for medical services by influencing consumers' willingness and ability to pay. Similarly, various factors, including input prices and technology, determine the position of the supply curve by affecting the costs of production. A change in any one of these factors shifts the corresponding curve and alters the price and output of medical services in the marketplace.

For example, suppose consumer income increases by a significant amount. Assuming aspirin represents a normal good, the higher income causes the demand curve to shift to the right. In figure 8–9, notice that as the demand curve shifts to the right, a temporary shortage of *EF* is created in the market for aspirin if price remains constant. However, price does not remain constant in a competitive market and is eventually bid up from $P_0$ to $P_1$. The higher price creates an incentive for manufacturers to offer more aspirin in the marketplace, and quantity supplied increases from $Q_0$ to $Q_1$. Thus, under normal conditions, supply and demand analysis predicts that a higher price and quantity of aspirin are associated with greater consumer income, *ceteris paribus*.

As another example, suppose manufacturers adopt a cost-saving technology that increases the supply of aspirin. Therefore, the supply of aspirin shifts to the right, as shown in figure 8–10. If the price of aspirin remains at $P_0$, a surplus of *AB* results. In a competitive market, however, the surplus creates an incentive for price to decline from $P_0$ to $P_1$. Consequently, the quantity demanded of aspirin increases from $Q_0$ to $Q_1$ as price declines, and equilibrium is restored. Thus, supply and demand analysis predicts that the adoption of a cost-saving technology causes price to decline and quantity to increase, assuming all else remains constant.[6]

---

[6]When a single market is examined in isolation and spillover effects among markets are ignored, the analysis is referred to as a *partial equilibrium analysis*. Sometimes a change in one market affects price and output in another market, which in turn causes a feedback effect back to the other market. If these feedback effects are significant, a general equilibrium analysis is required to correctly capture the impact of the change. In contrast to partial equilibrium analysis, *general equilibrium analysis* determines the prices and quantities in a number of related markets simultaneously.

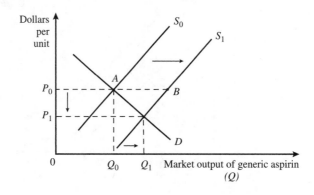

FIGURE 8-10    EFFECTS OF AN INCREASE IN SUPPLY

## Long-Run Entry and Exit in a Perfectly Competitive Market

The entry and exit of firms reflect supply-side adjustments that take place in the long run as the number of sellers changes in the marketplace. In a perfectly competitive market, the number of sellers changes because profits are higher or lower than a normal rate of return. For example, since there are no barriers to entry in a perfectly competitive marketplace, excess profits ($\pi > 0$) create an incentive for firms to enter an industry as they strive to make a higher than normal rate of return. Conversely, economic losses ($\pi < 0$) create an incentive for firms to leave the industry as they try to avoid an unusually low rate of return on investment. Finally, when normal profits ($\pi = 0$) exist in a perfectly competitive industry, the market is in equilibrium and firms have no incentive to either enter or exit the industry.

Long-run entry in response to excess profits can be treated as shifting the short-run market supply curve to the right. Similarly, long-run exit causes the short-run market supply curve to shift to the left. Given a stable demand curve, these adjustments in the short-run supply curve create a change in the price of the good and eventually restore a normal profit situation. In particular, long-run entry lowers price and eliminates excess profits, whereas exit leads to higher prices and eliminates the economic losses of the firms that remain in the industry.

For example, in the mid-1980s, physicians, dentists, and other health care providers became concerned about contracting the AIDS and hepatitis B viruses in the work environment. This concern caused a considerable increase in the demand for form-fitting disposable latex gloves, which are preferred over vinyl gloves because they allow flexibility for detail work and are impermeable to blood and body fluids. From 1986 to 1990, annual sales of latex gloves increased by approximately 58 percent (Borzo, 1991). Initially, as the demand for latex gloves increased, a tremendous shortage of rubber gloves developed. As the shortage gave way to higher prices in the

INSIGHT 8-2

## The Effect of Increased Competition on Dental Prices in New Zealand

Before 1988, only dentists were legally permitted to supply and fit patients with complete or partial dentures in New Zealand. With the passage of the New Zealand Dental Act of 1988, clinical dental technicians (denturists) were also permitted to deal directly with the public and perform comparable denture services. Because the act essentially increased the total dental workforce by around 10 percent, economic theory predicts that the greater supply should have led to a decline in the price of denture services.

Contrary to supply and demand theory, however, Devlin (1994) found that the increased legal supply had no statistically significant impact on the price of denture services. Devlin offers a number of explanations for why denture prices did not decline in response to increased competition. First, many dental technicians illegally supplied denture services before the act. Second, consumers may not have known about the legal availability of dental technicians given that little debate existed over the legislation, and advertising, though legal, is of minor importance in New Zealand dental markets. Third, consumers may believe that dental technicians offer an inferior quality of care relative to dentists. Finally, Devlin notes that "the act itself also imposes some barriers to 'consumer search'; for example, denturists may fit partial dentures only for persons whose oral health is certified by a dentist" (p. 1677).

Although no evidence is offered to show that competition promotes lower prices, this insight is particularly appealing because it shows how the degree of competition is dependent on market conditions, such as consumer information, perceptions of quality, and barriers to exchange.

short run, medical supply manufacturers operated their plants around the clock in an attempt to make higher profits. Consequently, the shortage declined as price increased and created an incentive for increased production.

In the longer run, medical suppliers made plans to construct new manufacturing plants for disposable latex gloves in the hope of making even more profits. According to the popular press, at one point in 1988, 116 permits were pending in Malaysia for the construction of disposable rubber glove factories (Zikos, 1988). These new plants provided for new entry and an increased supply of latex gloves in the long run.

This discussion can be augmented with the help of supply and demand analysis. In figure 8–11, the market for latex gloves and the representative firm in the market are shown in long-run equilibrium before the demand for rubber gloves increases. The equilibrium price and output in the marketplace are $P_0$ and $Q_0$, respectively. The price of $P_0$ also represents the demand curve $d_0$ facing the representative price-taking firm. Given the marginal cost curve MC, the representative firm produces $q_0$ units of latex gloves. Since average total cost, ATC, equals price, the representative firm initially earns a normal profit.

Now, due to the fear of contracting the AIDs virus, the demand for latex gloves increases from $D_0$ to $D_1$ in the marketplace. At the initial price of $P_0$, a shortage of $AB$ is created. Consequently, price begins to rise from $P_0$ toward $P_1$ as physicians and

FIGURE 8-11    THE SHORT-RUN AND LONG-RUN ADJUSTMENTS IN THE MARKET FOR LATEX GLOVES

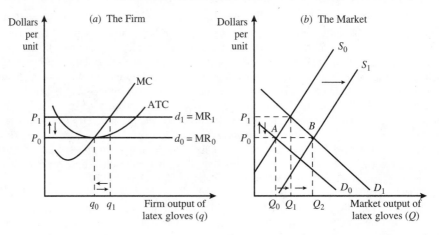

other buyers bid up the price of the scarce latex gloves. As the price increases toward the new short-run equilibrium, the higher price creates an incentive for the medical suppliers in the market to produce more gloves by operating their plants at excess capacity and hiring additional workers.

We can see the strain on capacity more clearly by focusing on the graph of the representative medical supplier. As the market price rises in the short run, the demand curve facing the individual medical supplier increases from $d_0$ to $d_1$, and the individual firm increases output from $q_0$ to $q_1$. Notice that the strain on capacity comes at a higher marginal cost, but producers are adequately compensated for the higher cost by the increased price of $P_1$. Since price exceeds ATC at $q_1$, the representative firm earns short-run excess profits.

In the long run, the excess profits create an incentive to produce a greater supply of latex gloves as new firms enter the market and existing firms build new plants. The entry and construction of new plants increase the market supply curve from $S_0$ to $S_1$, and price falls back from $P_1$ to $P_0$. Output in the market expands further from $Q_1$ to $Q_2$. The representative medical supplier reduces output from $q_1$ back to $q_0$ and once again earns a normal profit.

Thus, the supply and demand model predicts that price and quantity increase in the short run given the increase in demand for latex gloves. In the long run, output expands but price returns to its initial level. We should point out that this particular long-run price adjustment takes place because it is assumed that the individual firm's cost curves remain fixed. If the increased number of suppliers puts upward pressure on the price of an important input such as raw latex or laborers' wages, the marginal and average curves of the representative firm shift upward. As a result, mar-

# Taxes and the Location of For-Profit Hospitals in the United States

As you now know, excess profits create an incentive for firms to enter an industry, whereas economic losses create an incentive for firms to exit an industry. Based upon this long-run supply theory, we can also predict how tax differentials might affect the allocation of economic resources. Taxes indirectly influence the allocation of resources across sectors of an economy by affecting relative after-tax rates of return. If taxes are higher in one sector of an economy than in another, a profit incentive exists for resources to leave the high-tax sector and transfer to the low-tax sector, *ceteris paribus*. As the prices of the goods adjust in response to the reallocation of resources, after-tax rates of return equalize across the high- and low-tax sectors.

Based on a similar argument, studies have examined the factors influencing the mix of not-for-profit and for-profit hospitals in the United States. The mix of these organizations differs significantly across states and regions of the United States. For example, for-profit hospitals control 15 percent or more of all short-term general hospital beds in the South Atlantic, South Central, and Pacific regions, whereas only 1.3 percent of all hospital beds are managed by for-profit hospitals in the New England and East North Central regions. Taking an extreme state-level comparison, investor-owned hospitals manage 32 percent of all short-term general hospitals in Texas, while no for-profit hospitals exist in Connecticut.

Since for-profit hospitals must pay taxes (and nonprofit organizations are exempted from paying most taxes), we would think that for-profit hospitals are more likely to locate in low-tax areas. Therefore, we might expect high-tax states to be associated with a lower market share for investor-owned hospitals and with a higher market share for nonprofit hospitals. With that hypothesis in mind, Gulley and Santerre (1993) examined the factors determining the relative market shares of not-for-profit and for-profit hospitals. Among their results, they estimated the following multiple regression

equation predicting the market share of for-profit hospitals across the 50 states and Washington, D.C., during the period 1967 to 1987 (*t*-statistics are shown in parentheses):

(8–6)

For-profit market share (in beds) = −.014 − .005 state corporate income tax rate
   (.31)  (2.87)
+ .00009 local property tax rate
   (.01)
+ .006 state sales tax rate
   (1.54)
+ All other factors (e.g., income, population, regulatory climate, time trend, state dummy variables)
$R^2 = .88, N = 252.$

Gulley and Santerre provided some empirical support for the theory that taxes influence the location practices of for-profit hospitals. In particular, whereas the local property tax and state sales tax rates were found to have no effect on the for-profit hospital market share, the estimated coefficient on the state corporate income tax rate is negative and statistically significant. The implication is that for-profit hospitals are less likely to locate and expand in states with a high corporate tax rate, all else held constant. Evaluated at the mean, Gulley and Santerre calculated that the for-profit market share elasticity with respect to the corporate tax rate was approximately −.442.[1] As a result, a 10 percent increase in the typical state corporate tax rate tends to reduce the for-profit market share from its sample mean of 6.5 to 6.2 percent.

[1]The relevant elasticity formula is

$$\frac{\Delta MS}{\Delta T} \cdot \frac{T}{MS},$$

where *MS* represents the for-profit market share and *T* represents the tax rate. The left-hand-side quotient is the estimated coefficient on the tax variable in equation 8–6. *T* and *MS* are evaluated at their average values.

ket supply does not shift as far to the right, and therefore market price increases in the long run.

## Using Supply and Demand to Explain Rising Health Care Costs

Although the perfectly competitive model fails to conform to the true features of many medical markets, supply and demand analysis is a useful tool for explaining or predicting medical market behavior (but not necessarily useful for evaluating market performance). Indeed, because most models are imperfect to a degree, some economists believe economic models should be judged by their predictive or explanatory power rather than on the plausibility of their underlying assumptions. In terms of explaining the causes behind rising aggregate health care costs in the United States, the supply and demand model serves as a robust "engine of analysis."

For example, as mentioned earlier, national health care expenditures in the United States as a percentage of gross domestic product increased from 5.1 percent in 1960 to 13.6 percent in 1996. In seeking to explain this phenomenon, economists have focused on various demand-side and supply-side factors that have contributed to the rise in health care costs. Among the demand-side factors, economists have pointed to growing income, an aging population, and greater third-party payments as possible sources of rising health care expenditures.

Specifically, since medical services are a normal good, with an income elasticity slightly greater than 1 in the aggregate (see Chapter 4), increasing income has been cited as one reason why the growing share of the economic pie has been going to medical care. In fact, real disposable personal income per capita (in 1992 dollars) increased from $8,660 in 1960 to $19,158 in 1996. Economic theory also suggests that the demand for medical services increases with age as the depreciation rate of health capital rises. The population age 65 and older grew from 9.2 percent in 1960 to 12.7 percent in 1996. Moreover, economic theory indicates that the market demand for medical services increases in response to a lower consumer coinsurance rate. The out-of-pocket price for health care services fell from 49.2 percent of total health care expenditures in 1960 to only 16.5 percent in 1996.

In terms of the supply and demand model, the changes in these factors created a shift in the demand curve to the right, resulting in a higher price and quantity of medical services over time (see figure 8–9). Because expenditures represent the product of price and quantity, health care expenditures also increased in the United States over the 36–year period due to greater buyer income, an aging population, and a decline in the out-of-pocket price.

On the supply side of the economy, Baumol's cost-disease of the service sector theory provides an interesting explanation for increasing health care costs (Baumol, 1967). The cost-disease argument can be clarified by focusing on the expression for short-run marginal costs. Recall from equation 6–9 in Chapter 6 that MC can be stated as the wage rate, $W$, divided by the marginal productivity of the variable input, $MP_L$ or

INSIGHT 8-4

## A Growing Economy Can Pay Its Health Care Bills

Until recently, many people were alarmed by the rapid growth of health care costs as a percentage of GDP. The overriding concern appears to be that other goods will be less available if more GDP is siphoned off to pay for health care products over time. In a *Wall Street Journal* article, William Baumol pointed out the fallacy behind this line of reasoning. The fallacy deals with the difference between an increase in health care costs at a point in time (a movement along the production possibilities curve) and an increase in health care costs over time (a shifting out of the PPC).

Based on his cost-disease of the service sector theory, Baumol pointed out that productivity stagnation of the service sectors has led to persistent rises in their costs. He notes, however, that increasing productivity in the rest of the economy means that a society can afford more of everything, including more health care services. That is because fewer resources are needed to maintain the same level of output as before in sectors of the economy where productivity is rising. The extra resources can be transferred and used to produce more services, such as health care, in the stagnant sector.

The production possibilities curves in figure 1 can be used to clarify Baumol's view.[1] To simplify things, constant opportunity costs are assumed so that the PPCs are drawn as straight lines. The quantity of all other goods, Z, is shown on the horizontal axis, and units of health care services, H, are given on the vertical axis. Assuming initially that a society operates at point A on the PPC curve labeled MN with $Z_A$ and $H_A$ units of all other goods and health care products, an increase in the quantity of health care services results in a movement upward along the initial PPC at a point in time. The implication is that some amount of all other goods must be given up to receive more units of health care services *at a point in time*.

Now assume productivity growth in the rest of the economy rises but productivity growth remains stagnant in the health care sector over time. The rising productivity in the rest of the economy can be shown by pivoting the PPC at point M and rotating the PPC to the right. Following this procedure, we derive two other PPCs labeled MN' and MN''. Notice that due to the productivity growth in the rest of the economy, health care expenditures can increase over time without causing a decrease in the quantity of all other goods. For example, suppose a society adopts positions B and C on curves MN' and MN'' in the future, implying that the quantities of both health care services and other goods increase over time. That is possible because the rising productivity in the rest of the economy means that some resources can be transferred to the relatively stagnant health care sector. More medical inputs imply more medical output despite a low or zero productivity growth. As Baumol notes, "To achieve greater abundance of everything, society must change the *proportion* of its income that it devotes to the different products but not the *total amount* of labor or products it gives up in exchange."

SOURCE: William J. Baumol, "A Growing Economy Can Pay Its Bills," *The Wall Street Journal*, May 18, 1992, p. A16.

[1]You may want to review Chapter 1 concerning the properties and implications associated with the PPC diagram.

*(continued)*

*(continued)*

(8–7)     $MC = W/MP_1$.

Baumol points out that wages in service industries, such as the health care sector, tend to increase with higher wages in the manufacturing sector. Higher wages in the manufacturing sector result from increases in worker productivity caused by technological

**INSIGHT 8-4**

*(continued)*

**FIGURE 1**     **RISING PRODUCTIVITY GROWTH IN THE REST OF THE ECONOMY AND RISING HEALTH CARE COSTS**

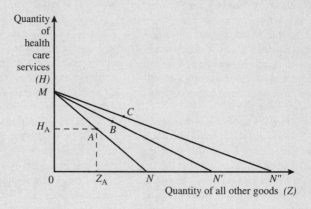

advances. Because the wage rate in the manufacturing sector grew at the same rate as the marginal productivity of the manufacturing workforce, marginal cost in the manufacturing sector remained fairly stable. But because the wage increases in various health care industries are not necessarily matched with commensurate increases in productivity and are tied to the growing manufacturing wage, per-unit costs of medical services are driven upward.

In terms of supply and demand analysis, Baumol's cost-disease theory suggests that the supply curve for health care services shifted to the left over time due to increasing marginal costs of production (e.g., see figure 8–10). As a result, the price of medical services increased. Because the demand for medical services is price-inelastic, the increase in price meant that health care expenditures, the product of price and quantity, also increased.

Cost-enhancing technologies provide another explanation for rising health care costs on both the supply and demand sides of the market. Over the recent past, a number of cost-enhancing technologies, such as computer tomography scans, magnetic resonance imaging, and organ transplant technology, have raised the quality and costs of providing health care services. New technologies tend to supplement rather than supplant old technologies in the medical field. As far as supply and demand analysis is concerned, the widespread adoption of these cost-enhancing (rather than cost-saving) technologies shifted the supply curve to the left, causing health care expenditures to rise given the price-inelastic demand curve. In addition, since these technologies often simultaneously create a demand for new treatments because they can help to extend lives and are less risky, the demand curve also shifted to the right. Consequently, medical care expenditures increased due to the lower supply and greater demand caused by cost-enhancing technology.

In conclusion, rising income, an aging population, a declining out-of-pocket price, and the demand for new treatments have fueled higher health care costs from the demand side of the aggregate medical market. The adoption of new technologies and Baumol's cost-disease theory have contributed to rising medical costs from the supply side. Thus, supply and demand analysis is often useful for explaining market changes even though the assumptions behind the perfectly competitive model do not closely conform to medical market realities.

# The Competitive Market for Medical Inputs

Up to now, we have been discussing how a perfectly competitive market for medical goods and services operates. But the perfectly competitive model of supply and demand can also be used to gain a better understanding of the operation and performance of the markets for medical inputs, such as nurses or human organs. That is, we can use supply and demand to examine why shortages and surpluses of inputs develop and identify the factors that influence the market price of an input. Therefore, in this section we explore the factors that determine the price and employment of medical inputs in competitive markets. We begin with an analysis of the employment decision faced by an individual firm and progress to a market analysis of input price and employment determination.

## The Individual Firm's Demand for an Input

The demand for a medical input by an individual firm can be considered a **derived demand** because it is derived from the demand for the final output of medical services. Take the extreme and suppose there is no demand for medical services. In that case, the demand for a medical input, such as nurses, is nonexistent because no inputs are required for production purposes. Conversely, if the demand for medical services is substantial, a high demand for inputs also exists, because they are vital for production purposes.

More formally, the demand for a medical input by an individual competitive firm is equal to the price of the final product times the marginal productivity of the input, or

**(8–8)**   $d_I = P \cdot MP_I,$

where $d_I$ stands for the demand or willingness to pay for the input, $P$ represents the price of the medical service, and $MP_I$ is the marginal product of the medical input. The right-hand side of equation 8–8 represents the marginal revenue product generated by an

**FIGURE 8-12**   THE INDIVIDUAL COMPETITIVE FIRM'S
DEMAND FOR NURSES

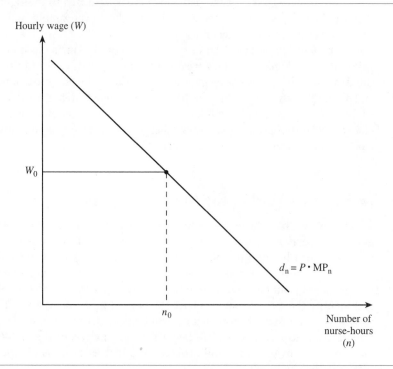

additional input and takes into consideration both the market value of the medical services, $P$, and the productivity of the input. If the medical services command a relatively high price in the marketplace or the input is highly productive (e.g., produces a large amount of output in a short period of time) or both, the demand for the input is high.

As an example, the individual firm's demand for nurse-hours is shown graphically in figure 8–12. The hourly wage of a nurse, $W$, is depicted on the vertical axis, and the quantity demanded of nurses (or-nurse-hours), $n$, is specified on the horizontal axis. Since demand equals $P \cdot MP_n$ the curve is downward sloping with respect to the quantity demanded of nurse-hours. Specifically, as the medical firm employs more nurses, marginal productivity declines given that all other inputs are held constant, as discussed in Chapter 6. Consequently, each additional nurse-hour is of less value to the firm.

At a fixed wage of $W_0$, the individual medical firm demands $n_0$ nurse-hours because the marginal benefit of a nurse-hour in production, $P \cdot MP_n$, equals the marginal cost (i.e., wage rate).[7] Given the downward-sloping demand curve, employers hire more nurses when the wage is lower and fewer nurses when the wage is higher than $W_0$, *ceteris paribus.*

As mentioned above, the firm's demand for an input is determined by the price of the medical services and the marginal productivity of the input. Therefore, whenever the price of the final good or the marginal productivity of the input changes for some exogenous reason, the demand for the input changes. In terms of the graphical model in figure 8–12, the demand curve shifts to the right (left) whenever the demand for the input increases (decreases). Basically three exogenous factors influence the demand for a medical input.

First, a change in the demand for the final product causes a change in the demand for an input. For example, a greater demand for hospital services raises the price of hospital services and thereby increases the revenues associated with each nurse employed. As a result, the demand for hospital nurses increases and the hospital becomes willing to pay a higher wage. Hence, the notion of a derived demand for a factor input. Second, any favorable change in technology or training that raises the marginal productivity of a nurse also increases the demand for nurses. For example, if the productivity of a typical nurse is enhanced by some technological change or training, the hospital is willing to pay a higher wage because the nurse can produce more services within a given period of time.

Third, a change in the price of a related input may cause the demand for another input to change. Two inputs are considered to be complements if they are used together in production, and therefore a higher quantity of one input increases the marginal productivity of the other. Consequently, a lower price for a complementary input often raises the demand for the other input as the firm employs more of the lower-priced complementary input, and this raises the productivity of the other inputs. Thus, assuming that intensive care units (ICUs) and nurses are complementary inputs, a lower price of establishing an ICU leads to an increased demand and willingness to pay for nurses.

Two inputs may be substitutes if one input replaces the other in production to some degree. If this is the case, a lower price for one input causes a decrease in demand for the other. For example, a lower wage for a licensed practical nurse causes a decline in the demand for registered nurses assuming they represent substitute ways of providing nursing services.

## The Market Demand and Supply of a Medical Input

The market demand curve for an input is simply the horizontal summation of the individual demand curves adjusted for any price changes that occur in the output

---

[7] In a competitive labor market, the individual firm/employer is a wage taker and in effect faces a horizontal supply curve for labor. The assumption is that an individual firm (employer) can hire an input without affecting the market wage, since the firm is one of many small buyers in the input market. Contrast this case to the monopsony model described in Chapter 9.

**FIGURE 8-13**     THE MARKET FOR NURSES

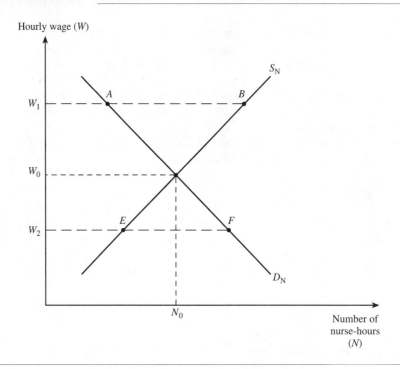

market.[8] Not surprisingly, the market demand for an input is also negatively sloped, as shown in figure 8–13, because it represents the horizontal summation of the individual firms' demand curves. The market demand curve for an input shifts whenever the price of an output, technology or training, or the price of a related input changes on a marketwide basis.

The slope of the market supply curve of an input depends on the net impact of the substitution and income effects associated with a change in the wage rate. The opportunity cost of leisure time and its impact on the labor decision is the basis of the substitution effect. The easiest way to illustrate this point is with an example. Suppose a nurse who typically works 35 hours a week at $25 per hour is offered a raise of $5 per hour. Given that an hour of leisure time is now worth $30 an hour, the nurse may now be willing to work three additional hours per week. In this case, the higher wage provides an incentive to substitute income for leisure. Thus, the substitution effect posits that a direct relation exists between the wage rate and the quantity supplied of an input.

---

[8]For example, as firms in the industry collectively employ more inputs and produce increased output, they may have to lower price to expand sales.

Counteracting the positive impact of the substitution effect is the negative income effect of a wage change on labor supplied. Since leisure time is considered to be a normal good, at some point a higher wage may motivate a labor input to demand more leisure and spend additional time pursuing alternative, nonwork activities. For example, suppose a nurse is paid $50 per hour for a 35–hour workweek and then receives a raise of $5. The nurse can now earn the same weekly pay of $1,750 by working approximately 32 hours per week given the $55–an-hour wage. The three hours less of work time can be spent pursuing leisure activities. For the income effect, there exists an inverse relation between the wage rate and the quantity supplied of an input.

The market supply curve depicts the net impact of the substitution and income effects for all input suppliers collectively. Generally, a market supply curve is drawn on the premise that the substitution effect dominates over the income effect. The implication of the positively-sloped market supply curve in figure 8–13 is that a higher wage motivates a greater quantity supplied of nurse-hours.

Various nonwage determinants of input supply affect the location of the supply curve and create shifts in the supply curve as they change. The wage rate in an alternative job is one important determinant of input supply. For example, suppose the supply curve in figure 8–13 specifically represents the supply of "hospital" nurses. In addition, suppose physicians are offering nurses a higher average wage rate to work in private clinics. If a sufficient wage differential arises between nursing services at hospitals and those at physician clinics, a sizable number of nurses may leave the hospital market in search of suitable employment in the market for physician services. The reduced supply of hospital nurses can be represented by a shift to the left of the supply curve for hospital nurses.

Another factor that affects the input supply curve is the quantity and quality of job amenities. For example, one particular job (or occupation) may provide a better working environment than the other. Job amenities, such as air conditioning, a favorable location, free parking, and tuition reimbursement, normally affect the supply of inputs to a particular job. Holding other things constant, a greater quantity and quality of job amenities leads to a greater supply of inputs (a supply curve that is located farther to the right).

## Equilibrium in the Market for an Input

The demand and supply curves in figure 8–13 illustrate how equilibrium is obtained in an input market. At a wage rate of $W_0$, quantity demanded is equal to quantity supplied and the market for nurses is in equilibrium. If the wage rate is $W_1$, however, a surplus of nurses, or unemployment, exists in the market equal to the horizontal distance $AB$. In a competitive market, an incentive exists for the wage rate to adjust downward toward equilibrium. As the wage rate falls, more nurses are hired and some nurses voluntarily withhold additional services from the market. On the other hand, if the wage rate is temporarily below equilibrium at $W_2$, a shortage of nurses exists and there are job vacancies equal to the horizontal distance $EF$. In a competitive market,

FIGURE 8–14     AN INCREASE IN THE MARKET DEMAND
FOR NURSES

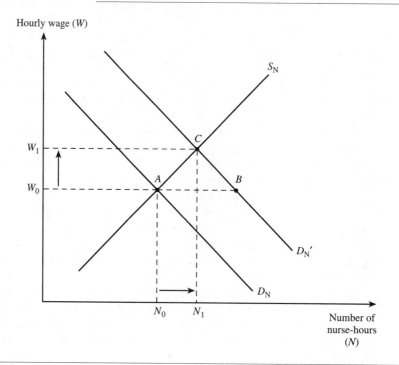

this temporary shortage is eliminated as the wage rate increases toward the equilibrium point and the quantity supplied of nurses increases and employers substitute with less expensive inputs.

### Comparative Static Analysis

As mentioned earlier, various nonwage factors, such as the demand for the final product, technological change, and the price of a related input, influence the demand for an input. In addition, such determinants as the alternative wage and job amenities influence the supply of an input. Consequently, as these demand and supply factors change in the input market, they alter the price or wage of an input and the quantity of the input employed.

For example, figure 8–14 represents a situation where the market for hospital nurses is initially in equilibrium at $A$ with a wage rate of $W_0$ and a level of employment equal to $N_0$. Now suppose the final demand for medical services increases in the marketplace, which causes the price of medical services to rise. Since it represents a

# Economic Incentives and the Supply of Psychiatric Labor Services

Economic theory tells us that a higher wage creates an incentive for medical inputs to offer more labor services in the marketplace assuming the substitution effect dominates over the income effect. Generalizing beyond this labor supply theory, economists believe that performance-based pay may encourage greater worker productivity and motivate employees to work harder. Normally, it is very difficult to empirically observe the relation between pay and productivity because the necessary data are unavailable. A study by Daniel Hunt (1980) overcomes the usual data problem and offers interesting insights into the economic motivation underlying the labor productivity of psychiatric residents.

Specifically, an experiment was conducted at a university hospital outpatient clinic to examine the relation between economic incentives and productivity. A revenue-sharing scheme was implemented that gave professional funds (for journals, books, travel-related expenses to professional conferences, etc.) to 14 psychiatric residents based on their personal productivities and fixed salary. Specifically, when a resident generated clinic revenues equal to 40 percent of his or her base salary, 10 percent of any additional clinic revenues were credited to the resident's professional fund account. After generating clinic revenues equal to 60 percent of salary, 15 percent of revenues was deposited into the professional fund account. Finally, at 80 percent of salary, the resident received 20 percent of any further collections as professional funds. The basic idea of the payment scheme was to present the 14 residents with an economic incentive to generate more clinic revenues by increasing their time spent treating psychiatric patients.

The experiment lasted for 11 months. Data for the number of patient-hours per resident were collected for the period and compared to data for the 11 months immediately preceding the incentive plan period. Amazingly, the incentive plan period was the first year in the clinic's history in which no patient waiting list was required. Even more striking, all but one resident had patient loads above the mean of the preincentive period. On average, patient-hours per resident increased from about

300 in the preincentive period to approximately 420 in the incentive plan period. The average amount deposited in the professional fund was approximately \$364. Clearly, the economic incentive of more monies for professional activities motivated the psychiatric residents to increase the quantity supplied of labor-hours.

Using these figures, we can approximate a wage elasticity of labor supply to examine the sensitivity of the residents' labor time with respect to the increase in the performance-based professional funds. Following the general concept of elasticity, the wage elasticity of labor supply can be written as:

$$(8\text{--}9) \quad E_{LW} = \Delta L/L \div \Delta W/W,$$

where $L$ represents the amount of labor time supplied and $W$ represents the "wage" or professional fund payment. Based on the findings from the experiment, the change in the typical resident's labor-hours, $\Delta L$, is simply 420–300, or an increase of 120 patient hours over the 11–month period. The change in the wage, $\Delta W$, as measured by professional funds, is \$364 since there were no performance-based professional funds in the previous period. Following the customary practice of using the averages of quantities and prices (in our case, patient-hours and professional funds) in the two periods as the base amounts, the wage elasticity of labor supply is estimated to be:

$$(8\text{--}10) \quad E_{LW} = 120/360 \div 364/182 = .165.$$

The resulting wage elasticity of .165 implies that the quantity supplied of residents' labor was inelastic with respect to a change in the amount of professional funds. On average, a 10 percent increase in professional funds raised the psychiatric resident's productivity by approximately 1.65 percent. While this elasticity may seem small, it compares favorably to the labor supply elasticities generally found for other occupations. In any case, the wage elasticity was not zero; therefore, the quantity of labor supplied did respond to economic incentives. The overall implication of this insight is that medical workers are motivated by economic incentives.

## The Regulated Market for Human Organs[1]

In the United States, the sale of human organs for transplantation is prohibited by the National Organ Transplant Act of 1984, and human organs, such as kidneys, hearts, and livers, can only be donated. In effect, the suppliers of human organs receive a zero price for each organ donated. As a result, relatively few human organs are supplied because a market incentive is nonexistent.

Figure 1 provides a graphical illustration of the market for human kidneys. The market demand for human kidneys, $D$, is drawn with its typical downward-sloping shape. Two supply curves are drawn. The inelastic or fixed supply curve, $S$, reflects the fact that human kidneys cannot be sold; thus, price is unimportant and the quantity of kidneys donated depends solely on other, nonprice factors. The positively sloped supply curve, $S'$, allows for the possibility that human organs can be sold and suppliers are responsive to a price incentive.

Notice that $Q_S$ kidneys are donated or supplied at a zero price in this example. At this zero price, however, $Q_D$ kidneys are demanded. Because quantity demanded exceeds quantity supplied at a zero price, a shortage of $Q_S Q_D$ kidneys results. Thus, this analysis suggests that a shortage of human organs will exist as a result of the law banning the sale of human organs for transplantation.

Assuming the recipients pay a zero price under the present law banning the sale of human organs, consumer surplus equals the total area under the demand curve, or area $ACQ_S O$ in figure 1.[2] Kidney donors receive no producer surplus under the present law.

On the other hand, $Q_0$ kidneys are supplied and demanded if human kidneys can be sold at a market-clearing price of $P_0$. The shortage under the present law is eliminated. At the higher price of $P_0$, more individuals are willing to supply human organs due to the profit incentive. Fewer kidneys are demanded as some potential buyers turn to kidney dialysis, a substitute for transplantation, or choose to forgo transplantation. In this case, consumer surplus equals the area $AEP_0$ and producer surplus is represented by area $P_0 EQ_x 0$. A net gain to society of area $CEQ_x$ results from an exchange of human organs for money. (This same area reflects the deadweight loss associated with the current law prohibiting the sale of human organs.)

Of course, society may be opposed to the sale of human organs for ethical reasons. Although many lives could be saved, the idea of reimbursing individuals for giving up parts of their bodies may repulse some people. In addition, legal considerations may impede the efficient and equitable operation of the market. Before the sale of human organs for transplantation is legalized, all the economic, legal, and ethical ramifications must be carefully weighed.

[1]Much of this analysis is borrowed from Barney and Reynolds (1989), Kaserman and Barnett (1991), and Pindyck and Rubinfeld (1995). The interested student should also read Barnett, Blair, and Kaserman (1992).

[2]Pindyck and Rubinfeld (1995) point out that hospitals and intermediaries may capture the consumer surplus if the fixed number of kidneys is rationed based on willingness to pay.

derived demand, the market demand for nurses also increases and the demand curve shifts to the right from $D_N$ to $D'_N$. Notice the consequence of this demand-side change in the figure. Initially the wage rate of $W_0$ may be "sticky" and take some time to adjust. Given that the wage rate is slow to adjust, more nurses are demanded than supplied, and a shortage of nurses represented by distance $AB$ develops. In a competitive market, however, the shortage of nurses causes the wage rate to increase

## INSIGHT 8-6

### (continued)

### FIGURE 1  THE MARKET FOR HUMAN KIDNEYS

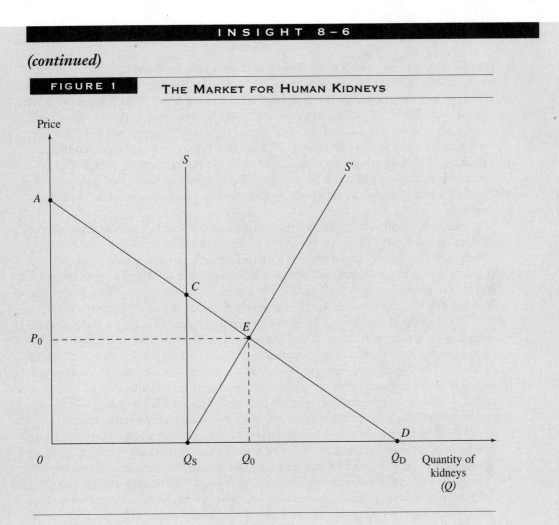

to $W_1$. In the short run, the shortage is alleviated to some degree as presently employed nurses work overtime or some voluntarily unemployed nurses reenter the marketplace. Also, some health care providers may switch to less costly substitutes, if available, to make up for the shortage of nurses. In the long run, the higher wage creates an incentive for more individuals to enter nursing schools to acquire the education necessary to become a career nurse.

## SUMMARY

In this chapter, we saw that price plays a central role in determining the quantity supplied of goods and services in a perfectly competitive market. Based on a profit-maximizing objective, we generated an individual firm's short-run supply curve for medical services from the marginal and average variable cost curves. The supply curve represents the amount of medical services the representative health care provider is willing to offer for sale on the market at various prices. Given that the marginal cost of production rises with output over the relevant range, a higher price is necessary to make it profitable for an individual firm to offer increased output on the market. Consequently, the short-run supply curve is positively sloped for an individual firm.

Next, we constructed the short-run market supply curve by horizontally summing the individual firms' supply curves in the marketplace. The short-run market supply curve is also positively sloped because each individual firm has a positively sloped supply curve. The implication is that a higher price motivates health care providers to increase the quantity supplied of medical services in the marketplace. Thus, supply theory predicts that the quantity supplied of medical services usually increases with price.

We then developed a model illustrating how the forces of supply and demand interact to determine market price and output within a competitive market setting. As such, the discussion built on the theories of demand and costs presented in Chapters 4 and 6. The supply and demand model we developed can be used to explain how changes in market conditions influence the market price and quantity of a medical good or service in a perfectly competitive setting. The model also has predictive capabilities and can be used to explain current or forecasted future market trends.

We used the supply and demand model to explain the causes underlying rising health care costs in the United States. We argued that greater buyer income, an aging population, a declining out-of-pocket price, and demand for new treatments provide a demand-side explanation for higher health care costs. Cost-enhancing technologies and increasing input prices in excess of productivity gains (Baumol's cost-disease theory) offer a supply-side explanation for rising health care costs.

We learned that the supply and demand model can be used to examine input markets, as well. The derived demand for a medical input is downward sloping and reflects the fact that more of the input is demanded at a lower price. The supply of an input is usually upward sloping and indicates that a higher input price leads to a greater quantity supplied of the input. Both demand and supply determine the market price and employment of a medical input. Those inputs in high demand but limited supply are more highly paid in a competitive input market.

Job vacancies (input shortage) and unemployment (input-surplus) normally occur in competitive markets in response to changes in the supply of or demand for inputs. Changes on the demand side of the input market result from fluctuations in the demand for the final output of medical services, technology, the price of a substitute input, or the price of a complementary input. The supply side of the market responds to changes in job amenities or input prices at other jobs. Eventually input prices adjust to restore equilibrium in competitive input markets.

## Review Questions and Problems

1. Suppose the supply curve of medical services is perfectly inelastic. Analyze the impact of an increase in consumer income on the market price and quantity of medical services. Next, assume the demand for medical services is perfectly inelastic while the supply curve is upward sloping. Explain the impact of an increase in input prices on the market price and quantity of medical services.

2. Suppose that in figure 8–11, the price of raw latex increases in the long run as firms enter the market. Trace through the effects of the long-run adjustments by assuming that the individual firm's cost curves shift upward as a result of the increase in the price of raw latex as firms enter the market. Show graphically and explain verbally why the market price of latex gloves increases in the long run.

3. In the country of Drazah Larom (*moral hazard* spelled backwards), health insurance is nonexistent and all medical markets are perfectly competitive. Use supply and demand analysis to explain the impact of the following changes on the price and output of physician services.

    *a.* A decrease in the wage of clinic-based nurses.

    *b.* The adoption of cost-enhancing medical technologies.

    *c.* An aging population and a correspondingly more severe patient case-mix.

    *d.* Declining consumer income.

    *e.* A lower market price for physician services (be careful here!).

4. In the country of Drazah Larom, Tiforp Hospital was initially producing $q_0$ of hospital services at a market price of $P_0$ and receiving a normal profit. Then, for some reason, employee wages at the hospital increased. Trace through the effect of this wage increase on the levels of output and profits at Tiforp Hospital in the short run. What may happen to Tiforp Hospital in the long run? Explain.

5. Assume that the Hcuo Dental Clinic in Drazah Larom is in equilibrium with the following revenue, cost, and output figures:

    $P = 545$

    SAFC $= 515$

    SATC $= 555$

    $q = 200$ units

    Should the Hcuo Dental Clinic operate or shut down? Why? Be specific in your explanation.

6. Determine the impact of a 10 percent increase in price on the quantity supplied of physician services in the market if the price elasticity of supply is:

    *a.* $E_S = 2.25$.

    *b.* $E_S = .50$.

    *c.* $E_S = .25$.

Draw the market supply curves that might reflect these different price elasticities of supply.

7. In the 1980s, a shortage of registered nurses in the United States led to an increase of almost 21 percent in the real average hourly earnings of RNs from 1981 to 1989 (Pope and Menke, 1990). This increase was the highest of any occupational group. Use supply and demand theory to show the shortage and explain why a dramatic rise in the wage rate occurred. Was there still a shortage of registered nurses by 1994?

8. Using supply and demand analysis, show graphically and explain verbally some of the factors that may have led to rising health care costs in the United States from 1960 to 1996.

9. In the mid-1980s, female nurses became increasingly aware that a relatively large number of attractive job opportunities existed outside the medical services industry. In fact, a large number of colleges offered life and transfer credits for nurses so that they could change careers at less cost. Using an equilibrium model of the market for nurses, show what impact this market change had on the wage rate and employment of nurses. Work through the comparative statics and explain whether a temporary shortage or surplus occurred and the various market adjustments that took place as a result of the temporary imbalance.

10. Assume the sale of human organs is legalized and a free market develops. Furthermore, assume the market is in equilibrium. Trace through the price and output effects of

   *a.* An increase in the incomes of potential buyers of human kidneys.

   *b.* A decrease in the price of kidney dialysis.

   *c.* The development of a new drug that leaves the immune system intact while preventing transplant rejection (Waldholz, 1992).

   *d.* A greater willingness by individuals to supply human kidneys.

11. The following passage appeared in *Modern Healthcare* (November 13, 1995, p. 46):

   "Hospitals are price-takers," Miller said. "As long as there's an overcapacity of hospitals, hospitals are going to be price-takers, not pricemakers."

   *a.* Show graphically how economists treat a price-taking firm with respect to demand and marginal revenue.

   *b.* What does a price-taking assumption imply about the price elasticity of demand facing a firm? What are the two reasons given for that particular price elasticity?

   *c.* Are hospitals truly price-takers in the technical economic sense of the phrase? Explain.

12. A June 10, 1996, *Wall Street Journal* article titled "Americans Eat Up Vitamin E Supplies" discusses the shortage that existed for vitamin E at that time. According to the article, the shortage was created by two changes in the marketplace. First, the supply of soybeans, from which vitamin E is extracted, declined sharply. Second, a stream of scientific research from mainstream institutions shows that vitamin E helps to ward off such ailments as heart disease and cancer and some symptoms of aging.

*a.* Using two separate supply and demand graphs, graphically show and verbally explain how a shortage is created by each of the two changes.

*b.* Explain what eventually happens to price because of a shortage in a free market.

*c.* Explain how suppliers and buyers adjust their behavior as the shortage is eliminated in each of the two cases.

*d.* Suppose the government formed a vitamin E commission and the commission set a price ceiling at the initial level. Explain how the price ceiling would affect the market for vitamin E.

## References

Barnett, Andrew H., Roger D. Blair, and David L. Kaserman. "Improving Organ Donation: Compensation versus Markets." *Inquiry* 29 (fall 1992), pp. 372–78.

Barney, Dwayne L. Jr., and R. Larry Reynolds. "An Economic Analysis of Transplant Organs." *Atlantic Economic Journal* 17 (September 1989), pp. 12–20.

Baumol, William J. "A Growing Economy Can Pay Its Bills." *The Wall Street Journal*, May 18, 1992, p. A16.

———. "Macroeconomics of Unbalanced Growth: The Anatomy of Urban Crisis." *American Economic Review* 57 (June 1967), pp. 415–26.

Borzo, Greg. "Glove Shortage Creates Anxiety." *Health Industry Today* 54 (November 1991), p. 1.

Devlin, Nancy Joy. "The Effects of Denturism: New Zealand Dentists' Response to Competition." *American Journal of Public Health* 84 (October 1994), pp. 1675–77.

Gulley, O. David, and Rexford E. Santerre. "The Effect of Tax Exemption on the Market Share of Nonprofit Hospitals." *National Tax Journal* 46 (December 1993), pp. 477–86.

Hunt, D. Daniel. "Effects of Incentives on Economic Behavior and Productivity of Psychiatric Residents." *Journal of Psychiatric Education* 41 (spring 1980), pp. 4–13.

Hurley, Jeremiah, Roberta Labelle, and Thomas Rice. "The Relationship between Physician Fees and the Utilization of Medical Services in Ontario." In *Advances in Health Economics and Health Services Research*, vol. 11, edited by Richard M. Scheffler and Louis F. Rossiter. Greenwich, CT: JAI Press, 1990, pp. 49–78.

Kaserman, David L., and A. H. Barnett. "An Economic Analysis of Transplant Organs: A Comment and Extension." *Atlantic Economic Journal* 19 (June 1991), pp. 57–63.

Pindyck, Robert S., and Daniel L. Rubinfeld. *Microeconomics*. Englewood Cliffs, NJ: Prentice Hall, 1995.

Pope, Gregory C., and Terri Menke. "DataWatch: Hospital Labor Markets in the 1980s." *Health Affairs* 9 (winter 1990), pp. 127–37.

Waldholz, Michael. "New Drug Leaves Immune System Intact While Preventing Transplant Rejection." *The Wall Street Journal*, August 7, 1992, p. B8.

Zikos, Joanna. "It's Tough to Get Grip on Rubber Gloves." *The Worcester Evening Gazette*, August 10, 1988, p. 1.

## CEBS Questions

CEBS Sample Question on Subject Matter from CEBS Course IX Study Manual

1. Study Figure 8–3 in the text and answer the following questions: (page 209)
   a. At the quantity of output that maximizes profits, are average total costs at their minimum? Explain.

b. Identify the rectangles for total revenues, total costs, and total profits.

## CEBS Sample Exam Questions

1. A medical firm projects the following figures for its short-term planning:

   Total Revenue     $1,000,000
   Fixed Costs        400,000
   Variable Costs     800,000

   What should the firm do?
   A. Shut down because the firm will lose $200,000
   B. Shut down but only if the $200,000 is extremely important to the firm
   C. Shut down, the fixed costs seem too high in relation to the variable costs
   D. Continue operations because the fixed costs are much lower than the variable costs
   E. Continue operations because the firm can lower its overall losses by continuing to operate

2. Which of the following is (are) correct statements regarding the equilibrium price in a perfectly competitive market?
   I. The equilibrium price is shown by the intersection of the demand and supply curves.
   II. The equilibrium price is said to be a market-clearing price.
   III. A medical product can have more than one equilibrium price if there is an imbalance in the market.
   A. I only
   B. II only
   C. III only
   D. I and II only
   E. I, II, and III

3. All the following statements regarding the cost and revenue curves of a firm in a perfectly competitive market in the short run are correct EXCEPT:
   A. The marginal cost curve cuts the average total cost curve at its minimum point.
   B. The point of maximum profit is where average total costs are at their minimum.
   C. The demand curve for the firm is a horizontal line.
   D. All the cost curves decrease and then increase.
   E. The demand curve shows the marginal revenue to the firm.

*Answer to Sample Questions from Study Manual*
   a. Average total costs are not at their minimum point where the quantity of output represents maximized profits. Average total costs are at their minimum where the marginal cost curve intersects the average total cost curve, which is a point to the left of maximum profits. The reason is that

profits can be improved as long as the marginal cost curve is below the marginal revenue (= demand) curve. At these levels, greater output means more extra revenues than extra costs.

b. The rectangle for total revenues is $P_oaq_o0$. For total costs: $C_obq_o0$. For total profits: $P_oabC_o$.

*Answers to Sample Exam Questions*

1.  The correct answer is E. By continuing operations, the firm can pay the variable costs and $200,000 of the fixed costs. The loss will be $200,000. If the firm shuts down temporarily it will lose $400,000. A key aspect of this question is that it deals with the short run. See pages 210–211 of the text.

2.  The correct answer is D. The law of supply and demand implies that only one equilibrium price can exist in a competitive market given a certain set of circumstances. See page 217 of the text.

3.  The correct answer is B. The point of maximum profit is where marginal cost equals marginal revenue. See pages 208–209 of the text.

# 9

# Profit Maximization in Imperfect Markets

I n June 1994, Marion Merrell Dow Inc. settled an antitrust lawsuit with the Federal Trade Commission (*The Wall Street Journal*, 1994). In the lawsuit, the FTC claimed that Marion Merrell had created a monopoly in the market for gastrointestinal drugs by acquiring a generic drug maker in October 1993. Before the acquisition, the two companies were the only FDA-approved manufacturers of the gastrointestinal drug dicyclomine hydrochloride. In the settlement, Marion Merrell agreed to restore competition by licensing a new entrant into the market.

On October 6, 1994, Columbia/HCA Healthcare Corporation, the country's largest for-profit hospital chain, announced its merger with Healthtrust, the second largest for-profit hospital chain in the United States. The newly created organization now owns more than 300 hospitals and over 100 outpatient centers in 37 states (Feder, 1994).

On March 28, 1995, Wellpoint Health Networks and Health Systems International, two large health maintenance organizations in California, announced that they planned to merge and form the fifth largest HMO in the country with a stock market value in excess of $4 billion (Freudenheim, 1995).

The mergers and acquisitions just described dramatically illustrate that the defining characteristics of a perfectly competitive market are not always met in some health care markets. Recall that the model of perfect competition assumes a large number of firms with small market shares, no barriers to entry, homogeneous products, and perfect information. Given that most health care markets do not conform to the perfectly competitive ideal in the real world, in this chapter we relax the competitive assumptions and extend our economic analysis to consider the impact of various imperfections on market behavior. Specifically, this chapter

- Discusses the structural characteristics of various market settings and illustrates how they influence a firm's market or monopoly power.

- Introduces the monopoly model.

- Analyzes the implications of price discrimination.

- Examines quasi-competitive markets.

- Discusses the impact of imperfect information on the market outcome.

- Introduces the monopsony model.

- Analyzes the impact of product differentiation.

- Introduces the structure, conduct, and performance paradigm.

Before we begin, some general comments concerning the scope of this chapter are necessary. Throughout the chapter, we retain the assumption of profit maximization. We also continue to assume that consumers pay the full price of the medical good. Clearly, these assumptions are somewhat unrealistic given the present nature of medical markets in the United States. But just as one crawls before walking, we must understand the implications of imperfect markets under the assumption of profit maximization before tackling more complex issues, such as the role of not-for-profit organizations and the presence of third-party payers in noncompetitive markets. We relax the profit maximization assumption in the following chapter and analyze the effect of third-party payments on the market outcome in Chapter 13.

## Market Structure and Market Power

In the competitive model, the firm is a price taker because it lacks the ability to influence the market price. When the structural characteristics of a competitive market are not fulfilled, however, the firm may have some ability to influence price. Economists say that a firm in this position has a certain amount of *monopoly power*. The amount of leverage the firm has over price is a matter of degree and is dictated by the level of competition in the market, or the extent to which the structural characteristics of perfect competition are not met. For example, if there are few firms in the market, the product is highly differentiated, barriers to entry are substantial, and the cost of acquiring knowledge regarding the price and quality of the product is high, the firm is likely to have broad discretion in establishing price. A firm operating in such a noncompetitive market is said to have a significant amount of monopoly power.

Table 9–1 presents the various factors that interact to affect the degree of monopoly power that a firm possesses. Across the top of the table, the degree of monopoly power is measured from zero to 100 percent. A firm with zero monopoly power has no ability to influence price, whereas a firm with 100 percent monopoly power has maximum ability to control price. The next row gives the various market types commonly identified by economists, from the most competitive (perfect competition) to

| TABLE 9-1 | MARKET STRUCTURE AND MONOPOLY POWER | | | |

**Degree of Monopoly Power**

| | 0% | | ... | 100% |
|---|---|---|---|---|
| | **Perfect Competition** | **Monopolistic Competition** | **Oligopoly** | **Pure Monopoly** |
| **Characteristics** | | | | |
| Number of sellers | Many | Many | Few, dominant | One |
| Type of product | Homogeneous | Differentiated | Homogeneous or differentiated | Homogeneous by definition |
| Barriers to entry | None | None | Substantial | Complete |
| Consumer information | Perfect | Slightly imperfect | Perfect or imperfect | Perfect or imperfect |

the least competitive (pure monopoly). Next, the table lists the major characteristics of each type of market structure, including the number of sellers, the type of product produced (homogeneous or differentiated), the existence or absence of barriers to entry, and the level of consumer information. It should be apparent that table 9–1 is patterned after the structural characteristics of a highly competitive market as discussed in Chapter 8.[1] The number of sellers and type of product determine the degree of actual competition, while barriers to entry determine the likelihood of potential competition. The existence of imperfect information on the part of consumers may lead to opportunistic behavior on the part of producers.

Table 9–1 helps to clarify the attributes of the various market types. We already know the characteristics of a perfectly competitive market: It has many sellers, a homogeneous product, no barriers to entry, and perfect consumer information.

*Monopolistic competition* refers to a market that has numerous sellers, a product that is somewhat differentiated across firms, no barriers to entry, and some imperfections concerning consumer information. As you can imagine, a market of that type is reasonably competitive and is likely to lead to minimal or zero economic profits in the long run because barriers to entry are nonexistent. The fact that each firm provides a slightly differentiated product allows for the possibility of profits, particularly in the short run.

A few dominant firms and substantial barriers to entry characterize an *oligopolistic market*. The dominant firms in this setting are likely to earn an economic profit primarily because high barriers to entry prevent potential competitors from penetrating the market. Competition among the few dominant firms, provided collusion does not take place, is likely to dampen profits somewhat.

---

[1]Three of the seven structural characteristics of a perfectly competitive market listed in Chapter 8 (items 1, 2, and 7) are not specifically referred to in the table. We are assuming that consumers pay the full price for the product, firms maximize profits, and each firm faces nondecreasing costs.

Finally, the least competitive market structure is a *pure monopoly*, in which one firm is the sole provider of a product in a well-defined market with complete or perfect barriers to entry. As we will learn shortly, these circumstances offer the greatest potential for earning an economic profit in both the short and long run.

# The Monopoly Model

If a firm has some ability to influence price, the competitive model is an inappropriate tool of analysis and a noncompetitive model should be employed. The difference between the two models comes into play on the revenue side. In a competitive market, the average and marginal revenue curves are horizontal because the firm is a price taker. A firm with some degree of monopoly power, on the other hand, faces a downward-sloping demand curve and marginal revenue curve because it has some ability to influence the market price. To illustrate how a noncompetitive model can be used to examine firm behavior, we will consider a pure monopoly in which there is only one producer of the product in the entire market. This situation is the logical opposite of a perfectly competitive market.

## Demand and Revenue Curves for a Monopolist

In precise terms, a monopolist is the sole provider of a product in a well-defined market with no close substitutes. Because it is the only firm in the market, a monopolist faces the *market* demand curve, which is always downward sloping. Given the downward-sloping demand, the only way the monopolist can increase output demanded, $Q$, is to lower the price of the product. Since total revenue, TR, equals $P \cdot Q$, we know that average revenue, AR, equals $(P \cdot Q)/Q$, or $P$. In other words, the market demand curve for the product represents the AR curve.

More important for determining the profit-maximizing level of output is the marginal revenue curve. As you know from Chapter 8, marginal revenue, MR, equals the change in total revenue, $\Delta$TR, divided by the change in output, $\Delta Q$. It represents the additional revenue brought about by each additional unit of output. In the case of perfect competition, marginal revenue is constant and equals the price of the product. Remember that when a firm operates in a highly competitive market, it can sell all the output it wants without influencing the prevailing market price. That is not the case with a monopoly. Because the firm has to lower its price to sell more output, marginal revenue is not constant. Its value hinges on what happens to the change in total revenue when the firm alters its price.

Specifically, the change in total revenue is influenced by two opposing forces when a monopolist lowers the price of its product. On the one hand, total revenue increases because the firm is selling more output; on the other hand, TR falls because the firm has lowered its price. Figure 9–1 illustrates the relation between price and marginal revenue under the assumption that the firm has lowered its price from $P_0$ to $P_1$. The darkly shaded area, labeled *a*, equals $\Delta P \cdot Q_0$ and represents the loss in revenue that results when $Q_0$ amount of output that was once sold at price $P_0$ is now sold

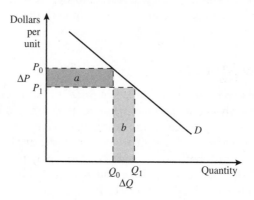

FIGURE 9-1  THE DOWNWARD-SLOPING DEMAND CURVE OF A MONOPOLIST

at price $P_1$. The lightly shaded area, labeled $b$, equals the increase in revenue that results because the firm is selling $\Delta Q$ more output. In more precise terms, $b = \Delta Q \cdot P_1$. Therefore,

**(9–1)**   $\Delta TR = a + b$.

Whether the change in total revenue, and therefore marginal revenue, is positive or negative is dictated by the sum of the areas $a$ and $b$. If the area of $a$ exceeds that of $b$, $\Delta TR$ is negative. Since MR equals the change in total revenue divided by the change in $Q$, the value of MR is also negative. The opposite is true if the area of $b$ is larger than that of $a$. In that case, both $\Delta TR$ and MR are positive.
In general terms,[2]

**(9–2)**   $MR = P + Q \cdot (\Delta P/\Delta Q)$.

Because $\Delta P/\Delta Q$ is always negative (the law of demand) and $Q$ is positive, we can conclude that MR is always less than $P$. In graphical terms, the implication is that the MR

---

[2]The following relation can be derived very easily. From equation 9–1,

**(9–1a)**   $\Delta TR = a + b$,

or   $\Delta TR = \Delta P \cdot Q_0 + \Delta Q \cdot P_1$.

After dividing both sides of the equation by $\Delta Q$, rearranging the terms, and remembering that $MR = \Delta TR/\Delta Q$, we get

**(9–1b)**   $MR = P_1 + Q_0 \cdot (\Delta P/\Delta Q)$.

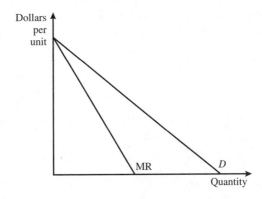

**FIGURE 9–2**   THE DEMAND AND MARGINAL REVENUE CURVES FOR A MONOPOLIST

curve always lies below the demand curve. This is illustrated in figure 9–2 under the assumption that the demand curve is linear. The only exceptions occur if the demand curve is either perfectly elastic or perfectly inelastic. These exceptions are unlikely with a market demand curve.[3]

Marginal revenue can also be expressed in terms of the price of the product and the price elasticity of demand, which is illustrated in the following equation:[4]

$$(9–3) \quad \mathrm{MR} = P \cdot \left(1 - \frac{1}{|E_\mathrm{D}|}\right).$$

[3] In the perfectly elastic case, the demand curve is horizontal and the slope of the demand curve equals zero ($\Delta P/\Delta Q = 0$), so MR = P. In the latter case, the demand curve is vertical and its slope equals negative infinity ($\Delta P/\Delta Q = -\infty$). MR is undefined for all practical purposes.

[4] If we multiply the last term in equation 9–2 by a well-chosen one, ($P/P$), we get

$$(9–2a) \quad \mathrm{MR} = P + Q \cdot \left(\frac{\Delta P/P}{\Delta Q/P}\right)$$

After rearranging the terms, we get

$$(9–2b) \quad \mathrm{MR} = P \cdot \left(1 + \frac{1}{\frac{\Delta Q/Q}{\Delta P/P}}\right).$$

We arrive at equation 9–3 after substituting

$$E_\mathrm{D} = \frac{\Delta Q/P}{\Delta P/Q}$$

in absolute terms into equation 9–2b.

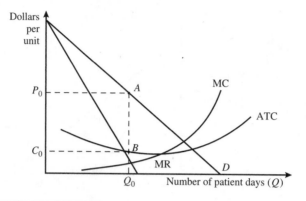

**FIGURE 9-3**

THE MONOPOLY MODEL OF NURSING HOME SERVICES

Equation 9–3 indicates that MR is directly related to the price of the product and inversely related to the elasticity of demand. Note that the absolute value of $E_D$ ranges from zero to positive infinity. It is easy see from equation 9–3 why the MR curve lies below the demand curve. Since the value $|E_D|$ lies between zero and positive infinity, MR is always less than price. Again, the only exceptions occur if the demand for a product is either perfectly elastic or perfectly inelastic.

Equation 9–3 also points out that a monopolist operates only on the elastic portion of the demand curve. It stands to reason that a monopolist will consider producing a unit of output only if doing so will generate some additional revenue, or MR > 0. According to equation 9–3, that occurs when $|E_D|$ is greater than 1, or demand is elastic. If $|E_D|$ equals 1 (unitary price elasticity), MR equals zero. Marginal revenue takes on negative values when demand is price inelastic.

### The Monopolist's Profit-Maximizing Level of Output

Employing the same short-run cost curves developed in Chapter 6, we can determine the profit-maximizing level of output for a privately owned, for-profit nursing home.[5] The cost curves along with the revenue curves appear in figure 9–3. The demand curve is assumed to be linear for simplicity's sake. As you know from Chapter 8, a nursing home maximizes profits by equating marginal revenue and marginal costs. That occurs at $Q_0$, where output is measured in terms of number of patient days. Naturally, the nursing home will charge the highest price it can and still provide $Q_0$ patient days. It determines the price by examining the demand curve and determining how much consumers are willing to pay for $Q_0$ patient days. In this case, the price

---

[5]We also assume that patients lack long-term health insurance. That allows us to focus on the impact monopoly power has on the pricing and production decisions.

equals $P_0$. Profits can also be ascertained from the graph. Price minus average cost equals the average profit per unit sold. If that amount is multiplied by output, total profits can be obtained. The area $P_0ABC_0$ in the figure represents profits.

Figure 9–3 is purposely drawn so that the monopolist earns excess profits. However, a firm is not guaranteed excess profits simply because it has a certain degree of market power or is a monopolist. The amount of profits depends on the demand for and the average cost of producing output. Although the monopolistic firm may be able to influence price, it cannot fix or establish the positions of the demand and average cost curves. The position of the demand curve is determined by external factors, such as income or tastes and preferences. Likewise, the location of the average cost curve is determined by uncontrollable variables, such as the prices of inputs or technology. Therefore, at any point in time, even a monopolist may incur economic losses in the short run.

In the long run, the firm may earn a profit provided it continues to maintain a monopoly position in the market. In fact, it is possible that profits will increase in the long run. The firm may alter its plant size to lower costs. That causes the short-run cost curves to shift downward (see the discussion on long-run costs in Chapter 6). Naturally, the firm will choose that plant size that maximizes profits.[6] However, the precise level of profits in the long run depends largely on the existence of barriers to entry.

### Barriers to Entry

For a firm to maintain its market power in a medical market for an extended period of time, some type of barrier to entry must exist to prevent other firms from entering the industry. By definition, barriers to entry are nonexistent in perfect competition. In the health care field, two of the most common barriers to entry are economies of scale and legal restrictions.

A monopolist that experiences long-run economies of scale over the entire market demand curve has a **natural monopoly.** Remember that when a firm is subject to economies of scale, it is operating on the downward-sloping portion of the long-run average cost curve, LRAC, and the average cost of production decreases as output expands. A firm in that situation has a cost advantage that results from the scale of production. Potential competitors could not effectively compete with the established firm on a cost basis. Thus, economies of scale can serve as a barrier to entry that insulates the firm from potential competitors. Price regulations are often necessary when a firm is considered to be a natural monopoly (e.g., local telephone service and electric utility service).

The empirical evidence suggests that hospitals experience weak economies of scale in the long run. In addition, what economies of scale do exist appear to be exhausted at the 200-to-300-bed range (see Chapter 15). This implies that in most reasonably sized communities, two or more hospitals are likely to be competing with one

---

[6]For a more detailed discussion of the monopoly model, consult Hirshleifer (1988).

another. In contrast, a single hospital in a very small, rural community is likely to have a natural monopoly position. Even in that situation, however, potential competition limits the degree to which the existing rural hospital can raise prices and earn economic profits.

Legal restrictions that prevent an individual or a firm from providing health care services can also serve as a barrier to entry. For example, every state in the United States has a medical board composed of physicians that establishes and maintains the criteria necessary for a license to practice medicine. The criteria include minimum educational requirements, such as a degree from an accredited medical school plus an internship at a recognized institution, along with passing a medical exam. Some analysts argue that the American Medical Association (AMA) has lobbied for these restrictions so that established physicians can maintain monopoly positions and thereby earn economic profits. Others contend that these barriers exist primarily to protect consumers from incompetent doctors. Because consumers lack the information they need to make informed decisions, they must be afforded some means of protection.[7] Regardless of the motives behind these restrictions, licenses constitute a barrier to entry. Occupational licenses restrict supply and prevent a competitive outcome in the physician services market.

Perhaps a more telling example of the use of legal restrictions to restrain competition is the development of health maintenance organizations (HMOs). HMOs initially appeared on the health care scene in the 1940s with the inception of the Health Insurance Plan (HIP) of Greater New York and the Kaiser Foundation Plan. HMOs provide health care services to subscribers on a capitation basis rather than on a fee-for-service basis as most hospitals do; that is, they provide health services to enrollees for a fixed fee. The established medical community, particularly hospitals, immediately realized the competitive threat HMOs posed. Fearing that HMOs would intensify the level of competition by becoming alternative providers of health care services, they began turning to the legal system to restrict the development of HMOs.

Throughout the 1960s and 1970s, state regulators used *certificate of need (CON)* laws and other legal means to deter the growth of HMOs. A CON law requires health care providers to obtain government approval before constructing new buildings or purchasing a specified dollar amount of capital equipment. Havighurst (1982) reported that HMOs were victims of many forms of regulatory discrimination. For example, some HMOs were denied certificates of need to practice in an area, and others suffered endless delays in receiving approvals for expansion projects. In the mid-1970s, the federal government initiated a policy of enhancing the competitiveness of HMOs. It began with the passage of the HMO Act of 1973 and culminated with the 1979 amendments of Public Law 93–641. The latter piece of legislation severely restricted the ability of state regulatory authorities to limit the growth of HMOs. Since that time, the number of individuals enrolled in HMOs has grown from

---

[7]We address this issue in more detail in Chapter 11.

| FIGURE 9-4 | A COMPARISON OF THE MONOPOLY AND COMPETITIVE MODELS |

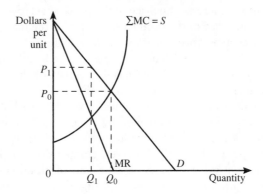

approximately 6 million in 1976 to over 59 million by 1995 (Health Insurance Association of America, 1997/98).[8]

These two examples illustrate the impact legal restrictions have had on the degree of competition in the health care field. In both instances, established health care providers were able to use their political influence to erect legal barriers to entry to secure and protect their monopoly positions.

## A Comparative Look at the Competitive and Monopoly Models

Thus far, we have examined two different models of firm behavior that represent opposite ends of the competitive spectrum. The first is perfect competition, in which each firm faces intense competition from numerous competitors and has little, if any, ability to affect the overall market price of the product. The second is the monopoly model, in which the firm is the only producer of a given product in a particular market. One question to be addressed is how these models compare in terms of the price charged and the amount of output provided. To answer this question, let's consider a competitive market such as the one depicted in figure 9–4, where $D$ is the market demand curve and $S$ is the market supply curve, which equals the horizontal summation of the individual firms' MC curves. The equilibrium price and quantity equal $P_0$ and $Q_0$, respectively.

Now suppose one firm gains control of the entire industry so that there exists a monopolist with multiple plants. Assuming no change in costs or in the number of plants producing output, the market supply curve represents the marginal cost curve of

---

[8]For additional information on this subject, see Havighurst (1982). In particular, Chapter 8 of his book gives an excellent review of the relationship between HMOs and health regulators over the years.

a multiplant monopolist, and profit maximization dictates that the firm produce up to the point where MC = MR. Under those circumstances, the monopolistic firm produces $Q_1$ units of output and charges $P_1$. As Figure 9–4 illustrates, the monopolist restricts output to increase the price of the product relative to the competitive outcome. As a result, the price of the product now exceeds the marginal cost of production.

Recent changes in the market for blood illustrate the impact of competition on prices in medical markets. Currently the market for blood services is divided between the American Red Cross, which has 46 percent of the market, and America's Blood Centers, which controls 47 percent of the market. The remaining 7 percent comprises individual hospital blood banks. According to Hensley (1998), most regional markets are monopolies controlled by either the American Red Cross or America's Blood Centers because federal policy developed during the 1970s sanctioned local blood monopolies. Recently, however, competition has intensified in some markets and has lowered prices. For instance, a unit of blood costs less than $60 in Florida, where competition is very intense, and slightly more than $100 in upstate New York, where competition is minimal (Hensley, 1998, p. 26). These figures provide clear evidence of the impact of market structure on prices. Probably the most telling commentary on market structure comes from Ken Wiebeck, who was interviewed for the Hensley article. Wiebeck states: "Competition can spur you on to better things. If you have a monopoly, it can cause you to get lazy and fail to see opportunities and take them" (p. 28).

## Price Discrimination

Up to now, we have assumed the monopolistic firm practices uniform pricing: All buyers pay the same price for a good or service. In some instances, a monopolist can increase profits by charging customers different prices for the same product. For example, SmithKline, a major pharmaceutical company, once offered price discounts on Tagamet, an antiulcer drug, to patients without health insurance coverage for drugs. The patient presented a coupon, much like a grocery store coupon, to the pharmacist and received a specified dollar rebate off the list price.

A practice of this kind is known as **price discrimination** if the cost of production is the same for different buyers. For price discrimination to take place, three conditions must be satisfied. First, the firm must be able to segment its market into at least two distinct submarkets based on the price elasticity of demand or willingness to pay. Second, the firm must possess some degree of monopoly power. Finally, something must prevent arbitrage from taking place. In other words, consumers cannot be able to buy the product in one market at a low price and sell it in another market at a higher price. Arbitrage cannot take place if a good or service is incapable of being resold (e.g., a tonsillectomy).

For example, a pharmaceutical company may be able to charge consumers who have health insurance a higher price for a particular drug than those without insurance, since the market for pharmaceutical services often meets the three conditions stated above. We know from Chapter 4 that consumers with health insurance have a less elastic demand for health care services than those without insurance. In

## CON Regulations as Barriers to Entry into the Dialysis Industry

Many health economists hypothesize that certificate of need (CON) laws unduly restrict entry into various health care markets. Until recently, however, they have been unable to point to any direct empirical evidence showing an inverse relation between the presence of CON laws and entry of medical firms. Ford and Kaserman (1993) filled the void by analyzing the impact of certificate of need laws on entry of new firms into the dialysis industry.

Specifically, the authors used multiple regression analysis to explain entry into the dialysis industry in the 50 states from 1982 to 1989. As independent variables, they specified a 0/1 dummy variable indicating whether the state possessed CON regulations regarding dialysis clinics in a particular year, along with a number of control variables. The control variables essentially captured the

potential profitability of firms entering the dialysis industry in the 50 states and included various cost and demand-side factors.

The authors found that the presence of CON laws significantly reduced the entry and expansion of dialysis firms. That finding, in conjunction with previous research on the dialysis industry, led Ford and Kaserman to conclude that

> by maintaining unnecessarily high levels of industry concentration and by restricting supply. CON regulation of the dialysis industry has sustained the monopoly power of incumbent clinics and, thereby, provided the wherewithal to increase profits by reducing service quality. Thus, CON regulation has promoted the interests of incumbent suppliers to the detriment of consumers (patients) (p. 790).

addition, individual consumers would most likely find little profit in the buying and selling of prescription drugs given the high cost of finding potential buyers.

Figure 9–5 depicts the situation of a pharmaceutical company that has segmented the market for a particular drug into two submarkets: consumers with health insurance (panel *a*) and consumers without health insurance (panel *b*).[9] Note that the demand for the drug is less elastic in panel *a* than in panel *b*. To keep things simple, we assume the marginal cost is constant so that the MC is horizontal and equal for the two submarkets. A profit-maximizing pharmaceutical company in this situation charges those consumers with health insurance a higher price for the drug ($P_a$) and those without insurance a lower price ($P_b$).

Equation 9–3 can also be used to illustrate the price discrimination model. A drug company facing two distinct submarkets attempts to maximize profits by equating marginal cost with marginal revenue in each market. Given the expression for marginal revenue in equation 9–3, we get

$$\text{(9–4)} \quad \text{MC} = P_a\left(1 - \frac{1}{|E_a|}\right) = P_b\left(1 - \frac{1}{|E_b|}\right),$$

where $P_a$ and $E_a$ equal the price and elasticity of demand, respectively, for consumers with insurance and $P_b$ and $E_b$ equal the same for consumers without insurance.

---

[9]For simplicity, we assume that consumers with medical insurance have a positive copayment.

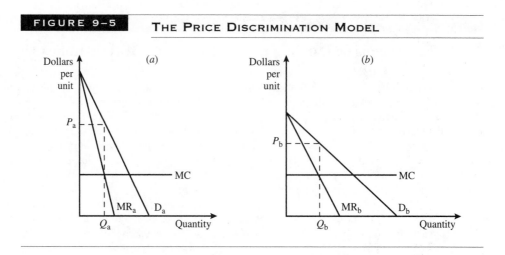

FIGURE 9–5 THE PRICE DISCRIMINATION MODEL

Assuming MC is held constant, along with the elasticity of demand in each market, it is easy to see that the pharmaceutical firm charges a higher price in that market where the demand is less elastic. In other words, $P_a$ exceeds $P_b$ because $E_a$ is less than $E_b$.

For example, assume the marginal cost of producing 100 doses of a given drug is $6 and $E_a$ and $E_b$ equal $-1.10$ and $-1.30$, respectively. If we substitute these numbers into equation 9–4, we find that $P_a$ equals approximately $67 and $P_b$ equals about $26. As before, consumers with insurance are charged a higher price for the drug.

In summary, a monopolist practices price discrimination to take advantage of the fact that some consumers are less sensitive to price than others. In our example, the pharmaceutical company charges those patients with medical insurance a higher price because they have a less elastic demand for medical services.

## A Brief Look at Quasi-Competitive Models

Now that the discussion of perfect competition and monopoly has been concluded we need to turn our attention to the two quasi-competitive models introduced at the beginning of this chapter: **monopolistic competition and oligopoly.**

In a monopolistically competitive market structure, there are many firms and no or minimal barriers to entry. The distinguishing characteristic of monopolistic competition is that firms within the same industry sell a slightly differentiated product. The product differentiation may result from a preferred location, different levels of quality (either real or perceived), or because of advertising and other promotional strategies. Because of product differentiation, each firm faces a downward sloping demand curve that is highly but not perfectly elastic. Since the demand curve is downward sloping rather than horizontal as in the perfectly competitive case, the monopolistically competitive firm has some limited ability to raise price without losing all of its sales. Product differentiation leads to a certain degree of brand loyalty and that is why the individual firm can raise price and continue to sell output. Every thing held equal, a more differentiated product translates into a less elastic demand curve facing the monopolistically competitive firm.

Like the monopolist depicted in figure 9-3, the individual firm can earn an economic profit in the short run if the price charged is greater than average total cost at the level of output where marginal cost equals marginal revenue. However, the absence of any barriers to entry prevents excess profits from continuing in the long run in a monopolistically competitive industry. Over time other firms are attracted to the industry by the possibility of earning economic profits. As more firms enter the market, each firm sees its market share slowly diminish which translates into a decrease in the demand for its product. The demand curve faced by each firm continues to shift to the left until the market price for the product is driven down to point where economic profits are zero, or price equals average total cost. At that point firms are no longer attracted to the industry and the market settles into a long-run equilibrium situation where economic profits are zero[10].

**Oligopoly** is a market structure with a few large or dominant firms and relatively high barriers to entry. The market may involve as few as two firms or as many as a dozen or more firms. The important point is that the number of firms must be sufficiently limited so the behavior of any one firm influences the pricing and output decisions of the others in the market. Mutual interdependence is the critical factor that distinguishes oligopoly from other market structures. Since the nature of the interdependence can vary and depends upon a number of factors, such as the number of firms in the industry, the nature of the product, the strength of the barriers to entry and government policy, economists have been unable to develop a general model of oligopoly behavior. As a result, a number of both formal and informal models have been developed which depict firm behavior under a variety of different scenarios. Since it is beyond the scope of this text to delve into all of these models, we have limited the discussion to three models of firm behavior: a *collusive oligopoly*, the *price leadership model* and the *kinked demand curve model*.

In a *collusive oligopoly* all the firms in the industry work together and jointly maximize profits by collectively acting as if they are a monopolist. To illustrate the point assume that there are only three identical nursing homes in a given market with very similar demand curves and that these firms have decided to collude and jointly maximize profits. Under these circumstances, the firms collectively act like the monopolist depicted in Figure 9-3 and joint profits are maximized at $Q_0$ level of output where the marginal cost curve intersects the marginal revenue curve. In this case, the price per patient day equals $P_0$.

While it appears that firms in an oligopoly have a strong incentive to collude and form a cartel, there are a number of factors which make collusion difficult. First and foremost is the fact that overt collusion is prohibited by the Sherman Antitrust Act. Second, cost differences make it more difficult for firms to work jointly and agree on

---

[10]Naturally, the opposite occurs if the average firm in the industry is experiencing an economic loss. Firms exit the industry and the demand curve faced by each remaining firm shifts to the right as market share improve. The price begins to rise and eventually economic losses are zero. At this point firms no longer have the incentive to leave the industry and the market settles into long-run equilibrium.

**FIGURE 9–6**    THE KINKED DEMAND CURVE

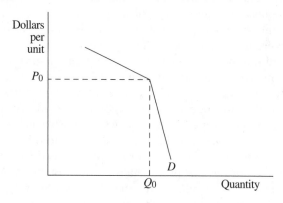

a common price. Third, the ability to collude becomes more difficult as number of firms entering into the agreement increases. It stands to reason that it is much easier for two firms to enter into an agreement than it does a dozen. Finally, each firm continuously faces a profit incentive to cheat on the cartel. For instance, one firm may grant a secret price concession to a large buyer to improve sales. Naturally, when the other firms in the industry learn of this behavior they will abandon the collusive agreement and strike out on their own. For these and other reasons, collusive agreements are much more difficult to negotiate and maintain than most people imagine.

*Price leadership* is an informal model that suggests that the firms in an industry agree that one firm will serve as a price leader. The rest of the firms in the industry simply match the price of the leader. Because explicit price collusion is illegal, this arrangement is likely to be implicit or informal as the industry looks to one firm to establish prices. As you can imagine, this informality can lead to problems because other firms in the industry may have a difficult time interpreting a price change from the industry leader. For example, let's assume that the price leader decreases its price. Other firms in the industry can interpret this either as a simple reaction to an overall decrease in demand or as an aggressive attempt on the part of the price leader to improve market share. In the first case the firms would simply lower prices and go on about their business. In the second case, however, they may aggressively counteract this move by decreasing their prices even farther in an attempt to initiate a price war.

The *kinked demand curve* model highlights the mutual interaction among firms by illustrating how firms react when one firm alters its price. Let's begin by assuming that we have a typical hospital in an oligopoly-type market with no collusion. Further, let's assume that the market price equals $P_0$ per patient-day and that at that price this hospital produces $Q_0$ patient-days. This situation is depicted in figure 9–6.

The question becomes, How are other firms likely to react if this hospital increases or decreases the price of an average patient-day? If this hospital lowers its prices, other hospitals are likely to follow suit for fear of losing market share. The result is going to be a very small increase in quantity demanded because the entire market is forced to lower the price of an average patient-day. In other words, the demand curve facing the hospital is highly inelastic when it lowers the price of medical services as illustrated in figure 9–6. The same is not true if this hospital increases the average price of a patient-day. Under these circumstances, the other hospitals in the market are likely to stand pat in hopes of improving market share by luring customers away with a lower relative price. This hospital is likely to lose a large number of customers as they react strongly to the price increase and seek medical services elsewhere. Figure 9–6 illustrates that the hospital faces a highly elastic demand curve if it increases the price of medical services.

The kinked demand curve shows us that once the price of the product is established, a firm essentially faces two separate demand curves depending upon whether it increases or decreases the price of its services. The demand curve is relatively flat or elastic if the firm increases its price because few if any firms are likely to follow suit. On the other hand, the demand curve is relatively steep or inelastic if the firm lowers its price because competitors will be forced to match the lower price. One implication of this model is that firms have little incentive to alter prices and may elect to compete on a nonprice basis. For example, rather than lower its price to enhance revenues, the hospital depicted in figure 9–6 may decide to institute an advertising campaign that touts its highly trained and caring medical staff, or its new billing process that allows patients to be admitted and discharged from the hospital without all the paperwork.

## Imperfect Consumer Information

Many health economists argue that consumers lack sufficient information about the price and quality of many medical services. Insufficient consumer information exists partly because most medical services are technically sophisticated and health insurance negatively affects the consumer's financial incentive to acquire information. The lack of adequate consumer information can lead to opportunistic behavior on the part of health care providers. Health care providers may raise price above or quality below the competitive level.

Insufficient consumer information is not unique to the medical industry. Indeed, consumers generally lack sufficient information regarding the quality of many nonmedical goods and services that are technically complicated, such as legal services, education, computers, and automobiles. For example, as consumers we often place a lot of faith in our local automobile mechanic to properly fix the "whateveritis" rather than opportunistically replace a number of (expensive) "whadyacallits." Medical services, like automotive repairs, can provide suppliers with an incentive to defraud customers because there is an additional cost of separate diagnosis and repair (Darby and Karni, 1973). For example, despite the abundance of sophisticated diagnostic equipment, the causes of some medical problems remain uncertain until the body is opened for visual inspection. Once the body is opened, it's typically best to have any necessary surgery performed at that time.

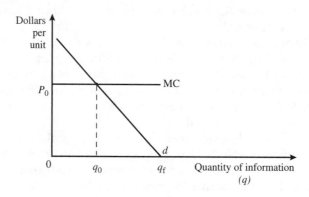

**FIGURE 9-7**   **THE DEMAND FOR INFORMATION**

In the competitive model, economic agents are assumed to be perfectly informed about the prices and quality of all goods and services in the marketplace. The assumption presupposes that information is a free good that can be acquired without expending resources. But acquiring information, just like purchasing any good or service, comes at a cost. For example, a consumer may have to purchase and incur the time costs of reading various magazines, newspapers, and consumer reports to acquire information about the quality and prices of different automobiles. In terms of medical care services, a consumer may have to consult with friends or investigate various clinics to find a physician with the desired characteristics. Because acquiring information has a cost, most people find it efficient to possess less-than-perfect information about goods and services. That is, they choose to be **rationally ignorant.**

### The Demand for Information

Figure 9–7 illustrates the concept of rational ignorance. The dollar cost and benefits of acquiring medical information are shown on the vertical axis, and the quantity of medical information is depicted on the horizontal axis. Following convention, the individual consumer's demand curve for (or marginal private benefit of) medical information, $d$, is downward sloping to reflect that incremental amounts of information yield successively lower benefits. The marginal cost of acquiring information, MC, is assumed to be some constant amount, and therefore the curve is horizontal. If medical information is a free good ($P = 0$), the consumer purchases $q_f$ amount of information where the demand curve hits the horizontal axis. For discussion purposes $q_f$ reflects full or perfect information. Given a nonzero price of acquiring information, however, the consumer finds it optimal to purchase only $q_0$ amount of information where marginal benefit and cost are equal. Therefore, this model predicts that the consumer will choose to be rationally ignorant because the cost of additional information outweighs its benefit.

Of course, consumers are more knowledgeable about the prices and quality of certain goods and services compared to others.[11] This is due to differences in the marginal benefit (demand) for and costs of acquiring information about different products. One of the more important factors affecting the marginal benefit of information is consumer expenditures on a product. In short, the marginal benefit of information is greater for more expensive goods (Stigler, 1961). For example, people are usually more willing to search for price and quality information about a $25,000 automobile than they are for a 50-cent container of salt (i.e., the demand for automobile information is located farther to the right). It follows from this argument that the demand for medical information is higher when consumers pay a greater share of the medical bill (i.e., a higher consumer copayment share) because they have a financial incentive to be better informed.

Similarly, the type of product is an important determinant of the cost of acquiring information. Economists differentiate among products based on the products' search, experience, and credence attributes (Nelson, 1970; Darby and Karni, 1973). Consumers can easily evaluate **search attributes,** such as size, color, and design, before purchase by either visiting the vendors or relying on external sources (e.g., magazines or friends). Nonmedical examples of "search goods" include clothing, food, and audio and video equipment.[12] These products contain attributes that can be inspected before purchase with the five senses of touch, taste, smell, sight, and hearing. Lynch and Schuler (1990) found empirically that waiting areas, patient rooms, food, location, community reputation, and demeanor of staff are examples of search attributes relating to hospital services.

**Experience attributes** can be properly evaluated only after purchase. Nonmedical examples of "experience goods" include restaurant meals, college professors, and haircuts. According to Lynch and Schuler's findings, outpatient testing, emergency care, surgical care, and child birthing are hospital examples of experience goods.

Finally, **credence attributes** are imperfectly evaluated even after repeat purchasing. Most professional medical services and pharmaceutical products are "credence goods." Lynch and Schuler found that the competence of the medical and nursing staffs of hospitals fall within this classification. Since the attributes of experience and credence goods can be known only through purchasing (or repeat purchasing), the marginal cost of acquiring information is higher than for a search good (i.e., the cost curve is higher). The implication is that consumers possess less information about the quality of experience and credence goods relative to search goods, *ceteris paribus.*

## Consumer Information, Product Pricing, and Quality

In the competitive model, all consumers are perfectly informed about prices and all identical products sell at the same lowest possible price. Otherwise, high-priced

---

[11]In addition, some people are better informed than others about the price and quality of various products because of differences in the "taste" for information and the costs of gathering, processing, and storing information.

[12]Although most products contain various amounts of the three types of attributes, search goods, for example, have a high proportion of search attributes.

## Optometrist Advertising, Pricing, and Quality

As mentioned in the text, some economists argue that advertising can enhance competition by providing information and thereby lead to lower prices. Others argue that since consumers are less knowledgeable about quality than about prices, price competition for medical services can result in an undesirable outcome as health care providers react to an increase in quantity demanded by lowering quality. For example, health care providers may treat the increased volume of patients that results from price advertising by spending less time with each individual patient.

Concerned about the potential price-quality trade-off, Kwoka (1984) examined the impact of advertising on the price and quality of optometric services. First, he categorized five types of optometrists based on advertising practice: (1) optometrists for whom advertising was restricted by law, (2) optometrists who did not advertise by choice in nonrestrictive areas (NONE), (3) optometrists who did not advertise in the Yellow Pages or newspapers but instead had storefronts with prominent signs or displays (STORE), (4) optometrists who were small-firm media advertisers (SMED) and advertised in the Yellow Pages and/or

newspapers, and (5) optometrists who were large media advertisers (LMED) and affiliated with large regional or national optical firms.

Kwoka then specified the price and quality of an eye examination as a function of the various optometrist advertising classifications and a number of control variables. To do that, all but the first optometric advertising classification were represented by a series of 0/1 dummy variables that took on the value of 1 when a particular advertising category was applicable for an optometric firm and took on zero otherwise. The expectation was that a lower price and, perhaps, a lower amount of quality for an examination would be associated with optometric firms that relied more heavily on advertising. For a measure of the quality of optometric services, Kwoka used the time spent in the eye examination (TIME). The following regression equations were estimated ($t$-statistics in parentheses):

(9–5)  $\text{PRICE} = 30.63 - 1.40\ \text{NONE}$
$(10.41)\quad (.98)$
$- 6.13\ \text{STORE} - 9.88\ \text{SMED}$
$(2.15)\qquad\qquad (5.90)$

businesses lose sales to low-priced businesses when consumers are perfectly informed. Given the costs of acquiring information in real-world markets, however, firms at different locations may charge dissimilar prices for the same product. Positive information or search costs mean the consumer may find it uneconomical to seek out all available suppliers. As a result, any one individual supplier faces a less than perfectly elastic demand and is able to restrict output and raise price to some degree. Even if a person knows of a lower price at another firm, the transaction costs may outweigh the monetary savings from going to the lower-priced store. As a result of information and transaction costs, the price of a product in the real world is likely to be dispersed and higher, on average, than the competitive ideal (since theoretically prices cannot be lower than the competitive level). The average price and degree of price dispersion depend on the marginal benefits and costs of acquiring price information. Higher benefits and lower costs of acquiring information imply lower and less dispersed prices.

The relation between information and product quality is a little more involved. High-quality goods cost more to produce than low-quality goods. If consumers are perfectly informed, high-quality goods sell at a higher price than goods of lower qual-

**INSIGHT 9-2**

**(continued)**

$$- 11.19 \text{ LMED} + \text{OTHER FACTORS}$$
$$(8.43)$$
$$R^2 = .64$$
$$N = 147$$

and

(9–6)   $$\text{TIME} = 41.23 + 11.71 \text{ NONE}$$
$$(6.48) \quad (2.79)$$
$$- .87 \text{ STORE} - 3.14 \text{ SMED}$$
$$(.18) \qquad\qquad (.80)$$
$$- 4.89 \text{ LMED} + \text{OTHER FACTORS}$$
$$(1.29)$$
$$R^2 = .52$$
$$N = 147$$

Taken together, these two regression equations imply that more extensive advertising leads to lower prices but does not adversely affect the quality of optometric services. In particular, notice in equation 9–5 that the coefficient estimates are larger (in absolute terms) on the various advertising variables from the least amount of advertising, NONE, to the most amount of advertising,

LMED. That means the average price of optometric services was lowest for the optometrists who relied most heavily on advertising. For example, the parameter estimate on LMED in the price equation can be interpreted as meaning that the large-firm advertiser had a price that was $11.19 lower, on average, than that of the typical optometrist who was legally restricted from advertising.

The quality of an optometric examination as measured by TIME, was found to be unaffected by the degree of advertising.[1] In fact, according to the results above, nonadvertisers in advertising markets, NONE, were associated with longer examinations than the restrictive subsample. Based on further empirical work, Kwoka concluded that the removal of advertising restrictions would cause prices for optometric services to decline by 20 percent, on average, without a decline in overall market quality.

[1]Kwoka found some limited evidence suggesting that the quality of optometric services falls with a greater amount of advertising. These two results reflect the overall conclusions reached in the paper, however.

ity in a competitive market. In the real world with imperfect information, however, consumers are not fully knowledgeable about product quality. Consequently, if consumers base their willingness to pay on the average quality in the market and pay the average price, low-quality products drive out high-quality products, and the process continues until no products remain. The implication is that the level of product quality is higher when consumer information is more abundant.

Thus, when the marginal benefit of information is high and marginal cost is low (i.e., consumers are better informed), sellers are likely to either offer the same low prices and high quality or offer a variety of goods along a low to high price/quality spectrum. Based on that argument, some economists claim that advertising serves to promote competition. They argue that advertising helps to lower the cost of acquiring information concerning price and quality (shifts the MC curve downward in figure 9–7) and thereby promotes lower prices and higher quality. In fact, studies by Benham (1972) and Cady (1976) found that the prices of eyeglasses and prescription drugs were higher, on average, where price advertising was prohibited (also see Insight 9–2).

Other economists (e.g., Klein and Leffler, 1981) argue that brand names and trademarks serve a similar purpose for promoting competition. Because the quality of

## The Monopsony Power of Blue Cross Plans in the Late 1970s

According to Feldman and Greenberg (1981), there were 70 Blue Cross plans in the United States in 1977, each selling hospital insurance in a different state or a populous part of a state. The market share of the Blue Cross plans ranged from 6.4 percent of the population in Rockford, Illinois, to 85.4 percent in Providence, Rhode Island. Blue Cross plans functioned as nonprofit organizations, whereas commercial insurance companies, such as Aetna, Prudential, and Travelers, operated on a for-profit basis. Blue Cross plans generally did not compete with one another, so each plan was treated as operating in a separate market and competing with the commercial companies.

Given the relatively high market share of the plans existing in many regions of the United States in the late 1970s and early 1980s, Blue Cross was seen as having monopsony power over the price paid for hospital services, especially relative to the smaller, less powerful for-profit commercial insurance companies. In particular, Blue Cross possessed the market power to disallow some hospital costs and, as a result, received a greater discount on charges than did commercial insurance companies.

Seeking to assess the monopsony power of Blue Cross plans in the market for hospital services, Adamache and Sloan (1983) estimated a system of equations predicting the discount, premiums, and market share of 66 individual Blue Cross plans in 1979. One of their hypotheses was that the hospital discount, $D$, increases with the market share of the Blue Cross plan, $S_B$, *ceteris paribus*. They obtained the following multiple regression results for the discount equation (standard errors in parentheses):

$$(9\text{–}8) \quad D = -.25 + .18\, S_B$$
$$(.11)\,(0.8)$$
$$+ \text{ OTHER FACTORS}$$

Adjusted $R^2 = .15$
$N = 66$

As expected, the estimated coefficient on the market share of the Blue Cross plan, $S_B$, was positive and statistically significant (i.e., the coefficient estimate was more than twice the size of the standard error). The finding implies that the discount increased with the market share or monopsony power of the Blue Cross Plan. Adamache and Sloan reported that the discount elasticity was substantial at 1.8, meaning that a 1 percent increase in market share led to a 1.8 percent higher hospital discount than the average Blue Cross plan could have negotiated.[1]

[1]According to Frech (1988), the Blues used their monopsony power to pursue the promotion of very complete insurance and a large market share rather than a reduction in hospital output.

experience and credence goods cannot be properly evaluated until after purchase (or repeat purchase), brand names and trademarks help to identify, or "signal," businesses that are confident enough in the quality of their products to invest in establishing a reputation. Given the sunk-cost nature of the investment, the argument is that a business will not sacrifice its established reputation by offering shoddy products on the market and take the chance of losing repeat buyers.

A client relationship is also claimed to promote a more optimal allocation of resources when information imperfections exist. According to Darby and Karni (1973), "a client relationship is an implicit understanding that the customer will return for future services as long as he does not detect fraud or low quality services. The client will be better able to judge the quality and costs of services over an extended period of repeated sampling" (p. 80). The repeated sampling helps to increase quality by improving the customer's judgment. Repeat sampling thus gives the firm the opportu-

**FIGURE 9–8**      **A MONOPSONY MODEL**

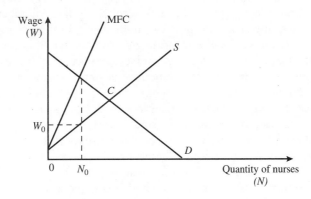

nity and incentive to establish customer "goodwill," which to the firm is part of its organizational capital. An ongoing business does not want to jeopardize its goodwill by offering inferior products.

In sum, the problem of imperfect consumer information is not unique to the medical services industry. Some analysts argue that in free markets with imperfect information, such market institutions as advertising, brand names, trademarks, and client relationships emerge to promote competition by reducing the consumer's marginal cost of acquiring information. The increased amount of consumer information is claimed to lead to lower prices and higher quality, on average. Later in this chapter, we will examine some anticompetitive or negative aspects of advertising, brand names, and trademarks in a discussion of product differentiation.

## Monopsony and the Market for Medical Services

The perfectly competitive assumptions are also violated when there is an influential buyer of medical services or medical inputs. An influential buyer may have some market power to set the price of the medical service or input. If so, the influential buyer is labeled a **monopsonist.** State governments are sometimes argued to wield monopsony power because they are the sole buyers of Medicaid services in their respective states. Blue Cross and Blue Shield plans are also claimed to possess some monopsony power over the pricing of medical services due to their large market share in many states (e.g., see Insight 9–3).

When a monopsony exists in an otherwise competitive marketplace, economic theory suggests that both the price and quantity of the service or input are lower than the competitive level. Figure 9–8 clarifies the logic underlying this point by examining the impact of a monopsonist in the labor market for nurses. The wage and the number of nurses are shown on the vertical and horizontal axes, respectively. The market demand for and supply of nurses are labeled *D* and *S*, respectively (ignore the MFC curve for now).

In a competitive market consisting of a large number of buyers, each individual buyer acts as a wage taker. For example, suppose we view the market for nurses to be a populated metropolitan area with a relatively large number of hospitals. Being a wage taker, any single hospital can individually hire more nurses without affecting their market wage. In effect, the single hospital faces a horizontal individual (rather than the market) supply curve for nurses. To maximize profits and determine the optimal number of nurses, the competitive hospital sets the demand for nurses equal to the prevailing wage. As all the competitive hospitals in the market act in a similar manner, the wage and employment level associated with point $C$ in figure 9–8 results.

In contrast, we can think of a rural hospital as possessing some degree of monopsony power, because alternative employment opportunities can be limited for nurses in rural areas. A rural hospital, being a monopsonist, is not a wage taker and instead faces the market supply curve, which is positively sloped. This implies that the monopsonistic hospital must pay a higher wage to attract more nurses. But to attract more nurses, the monopsonist must not only pay the new nurse(s) a higher wage but must also pay a higher wage to those nurses already employed at the hospital (we assume the hospital is unable to practice wage discrimination). Since the monopsonistic hospital has to raise the wage to both new and existing nurses, the total incremental cost of hiring an additional nurse exceeds the market wage. As a result, the marginal factor cost (MFC) curve lies above the market supply curve, as depicted in figure 9–8.[13]

To determine the profit-maximizing amount of the input, the monopsonistic hospital equates demand to marginal factor cost. In the figure, the profit-maximizing amount of the input occurs at $N_0$ nurses. The wage necessary to attract this number of nurses can be read off the supply curve as $W_0$. Thus, both the wage and the number of nurses hired are lower than the competitive ideal at point C. Note also that the marginal nurse is paid less than his or her monetary worth to the hospital because at $N_0$, $D$ exceeds $W_0$. This condition implies that the monopsonistic hospital pays a nurse less than the value of his or her output generated in production, a situation sometimes referred to as *monopsonistic exploitation*. Monopsonistic exploitation may be one reason hospital employees often unionize to counteract the monopsony power of employers.[14] In fact, a strong union theoretically can raise wage and employment to the

---

[13]The marginal factor cost of hiring an additional nurse is the wage paid to the new nurse, $W$, plus the change in wages, $\Delta W$, paid to those already employed times the number of nurses already employed, $N$, or

**(9–7a)**     $\mathrm{MFC} = W + \Delta W \cdot N.$

Thus, for a monopsonist, the marginal factor cost exceeds the wage by $\Delta W \cdot N$. For a wage taker that faces a horizontal supply curve for an input, $\Delta W$ equals zero, so $\mathrm{MFC} = W$. For example, assume a hospital that employs 20 nurses at $20 per hour decides to employ one more nurse. To attract this additional nurse, the hospital must offer $21 an hour. If all the presently employed nurses also receive a $1 hourly raise, the marginal factor cost of employing the 21st nurse equals $41 per hour.

[14]Booten and Lane (1985) analyzed the market for nurses in Utah and found some evidence supporting a monopsony model. They found that only three firms controlled 26 of the local hospitals in Utah. Even in the largest metropolitan area of Salt Lake City, the largest hospital controlled 51 percent of its market.

competitive level and in effect turn the monopsonist into a wage taker.[15] The exact outcome depends on the relative bargaining strengths of the monopsonistic hospital and the union.[16]

# Product Differentiation

For the most part, we have been assuming that medical firms sell a homogeneous product within any particular industry.[17] All firms within the same industry are viewed as selling a perfectly identical product, so there is no reason other than price for consumers to choose one firm's product over another's. We now relax that assumption and assume that each medical firm within the same industry sells a slightly different product. As an example, Byrns and Stone (1992) cited an enterprising Seattle dentist who "combines a coffee bar, his dental office and a masseuse. Patients sip coffee before an appointment, and then have their feet massaged while their teeth are being filled" (p. 563). By offering these complementary services, the dentist's product becomes differentiated from those of other dentists in the same market.

Many other examples of product differentiation in medical markets can be cited. Not too long ago, a hospital in Chicago announced that the next emergency room visit would be free for anybody who had to wait more than 30 minutes for a visit. In that case, the hospital was attempting to differentiate its product based on waiting time. Within the context of the health services industry, a medical firm might differentiate its product by choosing a particular location, product quality, or promotional activity. In the following discussion, we examine each of these ways of differentiating medical products.

## Spatial Differentiation

**Spatial differentiation** means that firms attempt to differentiate themselves based on a locational advantage. Real estate economists often claim that the three most important determinants of the market value of a property are "location, location, and location." Location also serves an important function in medical markets. For example, medical firms may try to attain a favorable location where they are conveniently located next to potential consumers. A pharmacy may locate next to a medical center, or a physician clinic may locate close to a local hospital. Lynch and Schuler (1990) cite a number of studies showing that location is one of the most important criteria consumers use when selecting general care and emergency care facilities.

---

[15]Within a competitive supply and demand model, a strong union may increase the wage above the competitive level, but the higher wage comes at the cost of reduced employment. In that case, the quantity demanded of nurses declines in response to the higher wage, and a permanent surplus of nurses results. Only in a monopsony model can a union attain both a higher wage and a higher employment level.

[16]In general, when a monopsony buyer faces a monopoly supplier, the situation is referred to as a *bilateral monopoly*.

[17]In the section on imperfect consumer information, we allow for quality differences. We also alluded to product differentiation when monopolistic competition was briefly discussed.

Because some firms are spatially differentiated from their competitors, consumers may be willing to pay a higher than competitive price for medical services if they place a high value on convenience.[18] In fact, more affluent individuals may value convenience given their higher time costs. Other medical firms located farther away can attract consumers by charging a price closer to the competitive level. Their customers most likely place less value on convenience and more on monetary savings.

## Quality Differentiation

Quality is another attribute by which medical firms may differentiate their services. We mentioned in Chapter 4 that quality differentials are reflected in the structure, process, or outcomes of a medical firm. To stress a structural quality difference, a young suburban physician may seek to project the image of an old-fashioned country doctor. The local pediatric dentist may call himself "Bert" to capitalize on the fanciful imaginations of children. A local community hospital may emphasize its well-qualified and caring staff. A health care provider may gain a competitive advantage by providing creative play areas for children in the waiting room or offering the newest and best high-tech medical equipment.

Differences in process quality may show up in the method of treatment. For instance, a hospital may boast of its high percentage of vaginal rather than cesarean section births. Another may emphasize short waiting times and quick appointments. Still another may push the fact that it supplies high outcome quality, perhaps citing high patient satisfaction and a low in-hospital mortality rate.

## Image Differentiation

Medical firms may also differentiate their services through promotional activities. Closely linked to quality differentiation, promotional activities can alter the way consumers perceive a product and change the image of the product in their minds. For this reason, the use of promotional activities is sometimes referred to as **image differentiation.** Specifically, some medical firms may choose to aggressively advertise their products or expend resources on building a brand name. As mentioned earlier, advertising and brand-name recognition can provide a flow of information to consumers about the quality of the product and be "procompetitive." Some economists, however, are concerned that such promotional activities are used to establish brand loyalty, mislead consumers, and thereby cause "habit buying" rather than "informed buying." In this view, promotional activities are "anticompetitive."

There are three basic types of advertising. **Informative advertising** provides information about the availability, price, and attributes of a product or service. For example, a new walk-in clinic may use local newspaper advertising to inform people about the types of medical services it offers and the hours it is open. This type of advertising generally occurs in the initial phase of the product life cycle, when a good or service is new to the market and advertising is used to create a new demand for it.

---

[18]The competitive model implicitly assumes that all medical firms are located at the same point in space.

**Persuasive advertising** attempts to persuade consumers that the attributes of product A are better than those of B. Sometimes the advertising message points out real differences, but often the advertising is used to create imaginary or perceived differences across goods or services. For example, both Bayer and generic brands contain the same aspirin ingredient, yet many people are willing to pay a much higher price for the Bayer product. Some argue that this is because past advertising successfully convinced people that Bayer aspirin is a superior product. Instead of creating a new market demand, persuasive advertising attempts to attract consumers from competitor firms. This type of advertising typically takes place in the middle years of the product life cycle, when the growth of market sales is beginning to slow down.

Finally, **reminder advertising** is used to "reinform" consumers about the availability and attributes of a successful product in the marketplace. Reminder advertising usually takes place in the mature stages of the product life cycle, when the growth of market sales has stabilized and the firm attempts to retain its market share. For example, a local hospital may mail advertising brochures to people in the area to remind them about the various medical services offered and its caring staff in an effort to maintain and preserve goodwill.

### Product Differentiation and Consumer Demand

According to the anticompetitive view, product differentiation is used to manipulate the demand for medical services. For instance, a successful advertising campaign can influence consumer tastes and preferences and thereby affect the position of the demand curve for the product. Advertising may affect the position of the demand curve in two ways. First, the demand curve may shift upward as a result of successful advertising because consumers are now willing to pay a higher price for the firm's product. Second, advertising may cause the demand curve to become less price elastic and, as a result, give the medical firm some ability to reduce output and raise the price of the good or service.[19]

Figure 9–9 highlights the effect of advertising on demand. The price and number of dental visits are shown on the vertical and horizontal axes, respectively. Suppose initially that no advertising takes place, so the competitive dental clinic faces the horizontal demand curve labeled $d_1$. Further, suppose the dental clinic finds it profitable to produce $q_1$ dental visits at a price of $P_1$.[20] Notice that given the horizontal demand curve, a reduction in the quantity of visits cannot affect price.

Now suppose the dental clinic runs an innovative advertising campaign (or differentiates its product by location or quality) and other clinics in the area have insufficient time to react with a similar activity. For example, suppose the dental clinic comes out with a catchy slogan, "We Cater to Cowards."[21] If the advertising program is successful, the demand curve shifts upward and becomes less price elastic as people become less sensitive to price and more sensitive to the perceived

---

[19]According to the procompetitive view of advertising, demand becomes more price elastic because advertising provides more information to consumers.

[20]Of course, the optimal amount depends on marginal cost and revenue. For simplicity, we do not specify those curves.

[21]One of the authors of this text fell prey to this slogan.

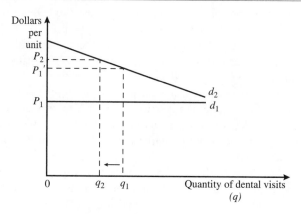

**FIGURE 9–9**    THE EFFECT OF ADVERTISING ON DEMAND

quality difference. For discussion purposes, let us suppose the demand curve $d_2$ results from the advertising campaign. Notice that the dental clinic has the option to charge a higher price of $P_1'$ for output $q_1$ or increase its market share beyond $q_1$ by charging a slightly lower price than $P_1'$. In addition, since the dental clinic faces a downward-sloping rather than horizontal demand curve, it might instead reduce output to $q_2$ and raise price even farther to $P_2$. In all three cases, the dental clinic has some ability to influence price because people perceive that its services are different from those of other clinics and, consequently, become less sensitive to the actual price of the service.

As another example, many public health officials claim that the purpose behind cigarette advertising is to manipulate the demand for cigarettes. Of major concern is advertising aimed at influencing teenager demand for cigarettes. A report by the Centers for Disease Control found that among smokers aged 12 to 18, preferences were greater for Marlboro, Newport, and Camel, three brands that are heavily advertised (Ruffenach, 1992). RJR Nabisco's "Old Joe" advertising campaign for Camel cigarettes was of particular concern to health officials. As George Will (1992) writes:

> A study of children aged 3 to 6 showed that Old Joe was not quite as familiar as the McDonald's and Coca-Cola emblems but was more familiar than the Cheerios' emblem. An astonishing 91 percent of 6–year-olds recognized Old Joe, about as many as recognized Mickey Mouse.

Advertising or other types of product differentiation may also be used by existing firms to create a barrier to entry. If existing firms can control consumers through advertising, new firms have a difficult time entering a market because they are unable to sell a sufficient amount of output to break even financially. It follows that product differentiation directed toward creating artificial wants, habit-buying, or barriers to entry results in a misallocation of society's scarce resources.

One implication of the analysis is that firms face an incentive to misuse society's resources as they attempt to differentiate their products in the marketplace. Resources are misused if they are employed to create illusory rather than real value. However, while some firms may be able to charge a higher than competitive price and misuse society's inputs for manipulative purposes, it is doubtful that all product differentiation causes inefficiencies. In other words, product differentiation provides some benefits. For example, as we discussed earlier in the context of imperfect consumer information, advertising can reduce the cost of acquiring information. Hence, advertising can help to lower the price of the good or service.

Even when price and quality information is not directly provided, a large advertisement in the Yellow Pages or the local newspaper, for example, may signal consumers that the firm is willing to incur an expense because it is confident that it is offering a quality product at a reasonable price. Through repeat buying, the firm hopes to get a sufficient return on its advertising investment. In this case, the mere presence of an expensive advertising message generates information about the quality of the product. Similarly, firm A may use persuasive advertising only if it truly believes it offers a better product than firm B. Otherwise, the advertising is not cost effective in the long run. A brand name serves a similar purpose. Firms that establish a brand name can lose a valuable investment by selling inferior products.[22]

When evaluating the social desirability of product differentiation, it is useful to remember that all products are homogeneous within the abstract model of the competitive industry. However, most people agree that variety is the spice of life. People like diversity and enjoy choosing among a wide assortment of services selling at different money and time prices. People also receive utility when buying goods of different colors, shapes, and sizes. In this vein, the higher than competitive price that is paid for product differentiation may simply reflect the premium consumers place on variety. Nevertheless, economic theory suggests that firms may use product differentiation as a way to increase demand in some situations. If supply creates demand in this manner, some of society's scarce resources may be wasted.

## Structure, Conduct, and Performance Paradigm

When conducting an industry study, economists tend to rely on the structure-conduct-performance paradigm developed in the field of industrial organization. The first element in the industrial organization triad, **market structure,** establishes the overall environment or playing field within which each firm operates. Essential market structure characteristics include the number, type, and size distribution of the sellers and buyers, barriers to entry, the type of product offered for sale, and whether any asymmetry of information exists between buyers and sellers. **Market conduct,** the second element, shows up in pricing, promotion, and product innovation

---

[22]Considering advertising, trademarks, and brand names as quality signals, Robinson (1988) points out that "a signal can be heard as long as it stands out over and against the background level of noise. As each seller amplifies his or her signal, the background noise level rises, necessitating further amplification on the part of individual sellers. This is clearly undesirable from a social perspective because the signaling mechanism imposes costs" (p. 469).

strategies. Whether a firm decides its policies independently or in conjunction with other firms in the market has a crucial impact on the conduct of the industry. The third element, **market performance,** feeds off conduct and is reflected in the degree of production and allocative efficiencies, technological progress, and equity.

Overall, the industrial organization triad predicts that the structure of an industry determines the conduct of the firms, which in turn influences market performance.[23] While significant feedback effects exist among the three elements, the overriding implication of the model is that the structure of the market indirectly affects industrial performance through its impact on market conduct.

Microeconomic theory, as reviewed in Chapter 8 and this chapter provides the link among the three elements in this triad. For example, according to conventional microeconomics, when the firms in a market are numerous, are similarly sized, and sell a homogeneous product, they are likely to behave in a perfectly competitive manner. Competition creates an incentive for firms to produce as cheaply as possible and to satisfy consumer wants. Conversely, when the firms in an industry are few in number and barriers to entry exist, traditional microeconomic theory suggests that firms are likely to behave in a monopolistic manner. Either a single seller or a cartel of a relatively few sellers may restrict output and raise price above the competitive level. The implication is that monopolistic industries often fail to satisfy consumer wants and produce with least-cost methods of production.

When this paradigm is applied to health care industries, however, the analysis becomes muddled for two reasons. First, conventional microeconomic theory is based on a profit maximization assumption, whereas many medical organizations are organized on a not-for-profit basis. As discussed in Chapter 10, a large number of goals other than maximum profits may motivate the decision makers in not-for-profit medical organizations. Second, the industrial organization triad may not be appropriate for a nonmanufacturing environment such as a health care industry where quality usually matters more than price to consumers and government takes a more active role in the production, regulation, and distribution of output. These considerations diminish the role profits and price play in the allocation of health resources and rationing of medical goods and services.

Despite these considerations, the structure-conduct-performance paradigm remains a useful tool for analyzing health care markets. Even the conduct of nonprofit organizations is influenced by market structure to some degree. For instance, market structure places a restraint on the maximum price non-profit firms can charge, and even nonprofit organizations are subject to a financial solvency constraint. Also, remember that for-profit firms are strongly represented in the health care sector. For example, almost 14 percent of all community hospitals, 34 percent of all home health and hospice care agencies, 43 percent of all mental health facilities, and 73 percent of all nursing homes are organized on a for-profit basis.[24] All pharmaceutical and commercial health insurance companies and nearly all physician, dental, and optometric

---

[23]See Scherer and Ross (1990) and Hornbrook and Berki (1985) for a more detailed discussion of the structure-conduct-performance paradigm.

[24]Source: *Statistical Abstract of the United States,* various years.

| FIGURE 9-10 | THE INDUSTRIAL ORGANIZATION TRIAD |

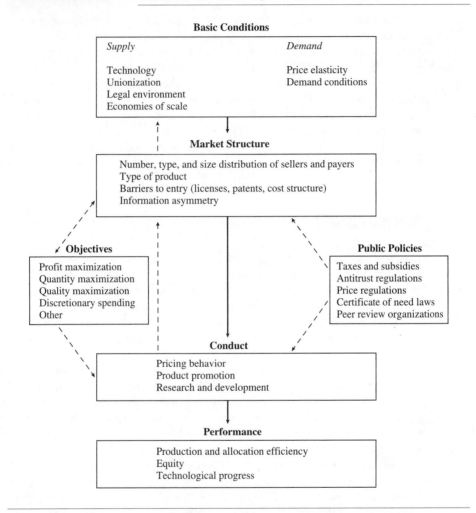

clinics are organized on a for-profit basis.[25] A conservative "back-of-the-envelope guesstimate" suggests that at least 40 percent of all health care output is "produced" in the for-profit health economy. Thus, while the quest for profits may have a smaller impact on the behavior of firms in the health care sector than on that of firms in other industries, profits still play an important role.

All this means is that the investigator should conduct the industry analysis more carefully and be cognizant of the peculiarities of health care industries when drawing

---

[25]Some physicians, dentists, and optometrists are affiliated with HMOs and PPOs, which are organized on a nonprofit basis.

any inferences from the structure-conduct-performance paradigm. With this in mind, figure 9–10 depicts an industrial organization triad that incorporates some of the peculiarities and shows that the conduct of medical firms depends on market structure in conjunction with the specific objectives motivating the firms. Important structural elements include the different reimbursement practices of various types of health care buyers, including HMOs, PPOs, and traditional fee-for-service insurers, and barriers to entry such as professional licensure. In addition, the triad allows for the possibility that various kinds of public policies influence the structure and behavior of medical organizations. For example, CON laws have been claimed to create barriers to entry and monopoly pricing behavior. The investigator should also keep in mind that an important basic condition underlying the structure of most health care industries is a low price elasticity of demand.

## SUMMARY

Many of the conditions for perfect competition are not met in real-world medical markets. This chapter pointed to the implications of noncompetitive factors on the price and quantity sold of medical services. In every situation discussed where the criteria for a competitive market are not met, the allocation of resources changes.

First, if barriers to entry are substantial, medical providers have the ability to restrain output and increase the price of the product for the purpose of increasing profits.

Second, information imperfections may exist in real-world medical markets. The typical consumer/patient chooses to be rationally ignorant due to the high cost of acquiring information. Economic theory suggests that price is higher and quality is lower when information imperfections exist. Some market institutions, such as advertising, trademarks, and brand names, help to overcome the inefficiencies associated with imperfect information.

Third, the market fails to allocate resources in a competitive manner when the buyer side of the market is concentrated. Monopolistic buyers are able to reduce price below the competitive level. This creates an incentive for an underemployment of resources. In fact, labor unions often become involved to offset the negative impact of monopsonistic employers in labor markets.

Fourth, economists continue to disagree over the merits of product differentiation, especially advertising. Some argue that advertising promotes habit buying and results in anticompetitive outcomes. Other economists believe advertising encourages informed buying and is procompetitive.

Finally, the structure, conduct, and performance paradigm provides a useful way of analyzing real-world industries. The industrial organization triad predicts that market structure indirectly affects market performance through its impact or conduct. According to the model, when firms are more numerous, barriers to entry are lower, and products are more homogeneous in a market, consumer wants are more likely to be satisfied at the lowest possible costs. When conducting an investigation of real-world health care industries, however, it is important to consider the peculiarities of health care markets.

## Review Questions and Problems

1. For years, private insurance companies have offered policies that cover the cost of nursing home care for elderly people. How would the pricing behavior of nursing homes with regard to private-pay patients be influenced if these policies were widely purchased?

2. The chapter points out that the extent to which a monopolist earns a profit also depends on demand. Use the monopoly model to illustrate this point. In particular, graph the situation of a monopolist earning zero profits (i.e., a normal profit).

3. According to economic theory, a monopsonist pays a lower wage than does a competitive firm. Use the most recent issue of *Hospital Statistics*, published by the American Hospital Association, to calculate the market share (based on staffed beds) of the four largest short-term general hospitals in one of the largest and one of the smallest cities in your state. Use this same source to calculate an average wage by dividing the total payroll by the number of employees. Do these two observations support the theory? What other variables affecting the supply and demand for inputs should be held constant before any meaningful comparison can be made? (Hint: See the discussion on input markets in Chapter 8.)

4. Explain why economic profits are zero under monopolistic competition in the long run.

5. Utilize a kinked demand curve to illustrate why prices may be rigid in an oligopolistic market.

6. Use the four market structures provided in the chapter to explain the critical role played by barriers to entry in determining the level of competition in any given market.

7. Critically evaluate the following statement: "Advertising is good because it always promotes competition."

8. Use economic theory to explain why consumer apathy may be efficient.

9. Explain the differences among search, experience, and credence attributes. Cite some medical and nonmedical examples in your explanation.

10. What beneficial role do trademarks, brand names, and client relationships serve when information imperfections otherwise exist?

11. Suppose you are the chief executive officer of a large pharmaceutical company that produces a drug for curing the common cold. The marginal cost of producing a dose of the drug is $100. Suppose further that you are able to segment the market for the drug into those patients with and those without health insurance coverage. The price elasticity of demand in the two submarkets is –1.5 and –2.0, respectively. Using the appropriate equation presented in the chapter, calculate the profit-maximizing price you would charge in each submarket. Which submarket pays a higher price? Why?

12. Using the appropriate equation presented in the chapter, prove that marginal revenue is negative when demand is price inelastic.

13. Explain the economic reasoning underlying the following statement: "People often fail to acquire information about the price they pay for medical services because of health insurance."

14. Discuss the two ways product differentiation affects the demand for a product.

15. Explain how lack of information affects the price and quality of a medical good relative to a perfectly competitive situation.

16. Describe what is wrong with the following statement made by an uninformed (hypothetical) politician: "For-profit nursing homes are bad because the owners charge whatever price they want."

17. Explain what may be wrong with the following statement made by the same uninformed (hypothetical) politician: "For-profit nursing homes are bad because the owners charge the highest possible price."

## *References*

Adamache, Killard W., and Frank A. Sloan. "Competition between Non-Profit and For-Profit Health Insurers." *Journal of Health Economics* 2 (1983), pp. 225–43.

Benham, Lee. "The Effect of Advertising on the Price of Eyeglasses." *Journal of Law and Economics* 15 (October 1972), pp. 337–52.

Booten, Lavonne A., and Julia I. Lane. "Hospital Market Structure and the Return to Nursing Education." *Journal of Human Resources* 20 (1985), pp. 184–96.

Byrns, Ralph T., and Gerald W. Stone. *Economics.* New York: HarperCollins, 1992.

Cady, John F. "An Estimate of the Price Effects of Restrictions on Drug Price Advertising." *Economic Inquiry* 14 (December 1976), pp. 493–510.

Darby, Michael R., and Edi Karni. "Free Competition and the Optimal Amount of Fraud." *Journal of Law and Economics* (April 1973), pp. 67–88.

Feder, Barnaby J. "A Hospital Leader Widens the Gap." *New York Times,* October 6, 1994, p. D1.

Feldman, Roger, and Warren Greenberg. "The Relation between the Blue Cross Market Share and the Blue Cross 'Discount' on Hospital Charges." *The Journal of Risk and Insurance* 48 (1981), pp. 235–46.

Ford, Jon M., and David L. Kaserman. "Certificate-of-Need Regulation and Entry: Evidence from the Dialysis Industry." *Southern Economics Journal* 59 (April 1993), pp. 783–91.

Frech, H. E. "Monopoly in Health Insurance: The Economics of Kartell v. Blue Shield of Massachusetts." In *Health Care in America,* edited by H. E. Frech. San Francisco: Pacific Research Institute for Public Policy, 1988, pp. 293–320.

Freudenheim, Milt. "Two Health Care Providers in California Agree to a Merger." *New York Times,* March 28, 1995, p. D1.

Havighurst, Clark C. *Deregulating the Health Care Industry: Planning for Competition.* Cambridge, MA: Harper & Row, 1982.

Health Insurance Association of America. *Sourcebook of Health Insurance Data, 1997/98.* Washington, DC: Health Insurance Association of America, 1995.

Hensely, Scott. "Out for Blood." *Modern Healthcare* June 22, 1998, pp. 26-32.

Hirshleifer, Jack. *Price Theory and Applications.* 4th ed. Englewood Cliffs, NJ: Prentice Hall, 1988.

Hornbrook, Mark C., and Sylvester E. Berki. "Practice Mode and Payment Method." *Medical Care* 23 (May 1985), pp. 484–511.

Klein, Benjamin, and Keith B. Leffler. "The Role of Market Forces in Assuring Contractual Performance." *Journal of Political Economy* 89 (August 1981), pp. 615–41.

Kwoka, John E. "Advertising and the Price and Quality of Optometric Services." *American Economic Review* (March 1984), pp. 211–16.

Leffler, Keith B. "Persuasion or Information? The Economics of Prescription Drug Advertising." *Journal of Law and Economics* (April 1981), pp. 45–74.

Lynch, James, and Drue Schuler. "Consumer Evaluation of the Quality of Hospital Services from an Economics of Information Perspective." *Journal of Health Care Marketing* 10 (June 1990), pp. 16–22.

"Marion Merrell, FTC Settles Charges of Drug Monopoly." *The Wall Street Journal*, June 23, 1994, p. B7.

Nelson, Phillip. "Information and Consumer Behavior." *Journal of Political Economy* (March–April 1970), pp. 311–29.

———. "Advertising as Information." *Journal of Political Economy* 82 (August 1974), pp. 729–54.

Robinson, James C. "Hospital Quality Competition and the Economics of Imperfect Information." *Milbank Memorial Quarterly* 66 (1988), pp. 465–81.

Ruffenach, Glenn. "Study Says Teen-Agers' Smoking Habits Seem to Be Linked to Heavy Advertising." *The Wall Street Journal*, March 13, 1992, p. B8.

Scherer, F. M., and David Ross. *Industrial Market Structure and Economic Performance.* 3rd ed. Boston: Houghton Mifflin, 1990.

Schmalensee, Richard. "A Model of Advertising and Product Quality." *Journal of Political Economy* 86 (June 1978), pp. 485–503.

*Statistical Abstract of the United States, 1994.* 114th ed. Washington, DC: U.S. Department of Commerce, 1994.

Stigler, George. "The Economics of Information." *Journal of Political Economy* (June 1961), pp. 213–25.

Will, George. "Where There's Smoke There's Cancer and Death, Too." *Norwich Bulletin*, February 16, 1992.

## CEBS Questions

CEBS Sample Question on Subject Matter from CEBS Course IX Study Manual

1.  Explain the concept of rational ignorance. (p. 256)

CEBS Sample Exam Questions

1.  A monopolist will maximize profits if it produces an output where:
    A. Average total costs are minimized.
    B. Marginal costs equal marginal revenue
    C. Marginal costs equal demand
    D. Marginal revenue is zero
    E. Marginal revenue exceeds demand

2.  Which of the following is (are) conditions that must be satisfied for price discrimination to take place?
    I. The firm must possess some degree of monopoly power.

II. The demand curve must be price elastic.

III. Arbitrage must take place.
    A. I only
    B. II only
    C. I and II only
    D. I and III only
    E. II and III only

3. All the following are correct statements regarding the types of economic markets EXCEPT:
    A. The major difference between perfect competition and monopolistic competition is that the latter has differentiated products.
    B. A pure monopolist may face a kinked demand curve.
    C. Monopsony is power to influence the market price by a buyer.
    D. Oligopolistic markets often have substantial barriers to entry.
    E. The demand curve for a pure monopolist is downward sloping.

*Answer to Sample Question from Study Manual*

Acquiring information, just like purchasing any good or service, comes at a cost. A consumer may have to expend much effort and time in selecting a physician or a hospital that possesses certain desired characteristics. This is the case not just for medical services but also for nonmedical goods and services that are technically complicated, such as legal services, computers and automobiles. Since becoming an educated consumer entails a cost, most people find it efficient to possess less than perfect information about goods and services. They choose to be rationally ignorant.

*Answers to Sample Exam Questions*

1. The correct answer is B. See page 248 of the text.
2. A is the correct answer. Statement II is incorrect because elasticity is not necessarily involved at all. Statement III is incorrect because arbitrage must not take place. See page 252 of the text.
3. B is the correct answer. A kinked demand curve may exist in oligopoly but not in pure monopoly. The kinked shape results from the fact that an oligopolist may increase prices and other firms may not follow while they will match price decreases. This cannot occur in a pure monopoly because there are no other firms in the industry. See pages 235–236, 254–255, and 260 of the text.

# 10

## Not-for-Profit Objectives

U p to this point, we have assumed that profit maximization is the fundamental force driving the behavior of the typical medical firm. However, not-for-profit health care providers have historically played a major role in the production of health care in the United States. Private nonprofit hospitals control about 70 percent of all hospital beds in the United States. Some health maintenance organizations, nursing homes, and mental health facilities, among other types of medical organizations, are also organized on a not-for-profit basis. Therefore, it may be unrealistic to assume that all medical institutions seek to maximize economic profits. For this reason, we must extend our analysis to account for the likely behavior of not-for-profit organizations. With that goal in mind, this chapter:

- Analyzes the quantity maximization model of firm behavior.

- Introduces a variety of utility maximization models, including the quality maximization, quality and quantity maximization, and managerial expense preference models.

- Discusses the physician-control model.

- Examines the implications of the supplier-induced demand model.

- Provides a theoretical comparison of the behavior of for-profit and not-for-profit organizations.

- Analyzes the ownership conversion issue.

# Alternative Models of Firm Behavior

## Quantity Maximization

Baumol (1967) has argued that rather than pursuing profit maximization, large firms with a substantial amount of monopoly power tend to maximize output subject to a break-even level of profits. Because executive salaries and prestige are more strongly correlated with firm size than with profits, managers try to expand sales at the expense of profits. Figure 10–1 depicts the situation for a hospital where $Q$ stands for the quantity of patient-days. An output- or quantity-maximizing hospital produces output up to the point where the average cost of production equals average revenue, or at $Q_0$ patient-days in figure 10–1. At that point, the hospital is servicing the maximum number of patient-days without incurring an economic loss. If it expanded services beyond $Q_0$, the hospital would operate with an economic loss, since AC exceeds AR. A profit-maximizing hospital with the same cost curves produces up to the point where MR = MC and provides $Q_1$ patient-days and charges $P_1$. In contrast, an output-maximizing hospital produces more output and charges a lower price than a profit-maximizing hospital, *ceteris paribus*.

Davis (1972) points out that most hospitals offer a wide array of services, each with its own price, and it is logical to assume that an output-maximizing hospital follows a pricing strategy that increases the number of patients admitted. The chosen pricing strategy involves a certain degree of *cross-subsidization*. Specifically, the hospital may charge a price below cost on those services for which demand is more elastic to generate more admissions and then make up for the loss by charging a much higher price for those services for which demand is more inelastic. For example, the hospital may charge a price below cost for basic room services to attract more patients and cover the loss by charging a higher price for ancillary services. The net effect is that the hospital breaks even. In the process, however, the hospital services more patients through cross-subsidization.

The long-run implications of the model are interesting (Davis, 1972). In the long run, an output-maximizing hospital may generate some profits to acquire the funds it needs for expansion. It obtains the profits by charging a price that is slightly above the average cost of production. As a result, an output-maximizing hospital should not only provide more output than a profit-maximizing hospital at any point in time but should also have a higher rate of expansion over time.

The quantity maximization model can be used to explain the behavior of a not-for-profit organization. Since such a firm is restricted by law from earning a profit, managers may opt to maximize quantity to increase the firm's market share and enhance its prestige in the community. Economists have pointed out that the assumption of output maximization is consistent with the public's perception concerning how a not-for-profit hospital should operate (Newhouse, 1970). From the public's point of view, hospitals are given nonprofit status because they are expected to provide care to some people in the community who otherwise might not receive care due to profit considerations. If the managers of a not-for-profit hospital maximize quantity, they validate the public's view that their firm plays an important role in the provision of

### FIGURE 10-1    THE OUTPUT MAXIMIZATION MODEL

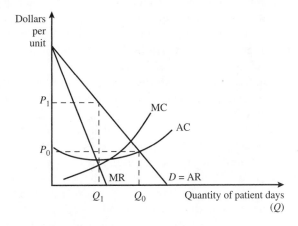

health care to the community at large. That may make it much easier for the hospital to gather community support for such activities as fund-raising.

In the case of a quantity-maximizing not-for-profit hospital, the interests of the managers may also be aligned with the board of trustees, or board of directors, which oversees the general operation of the hospital. Board members, who generally are leading citizens, may also want to maximize quantity to increase their presence in the community. They may wish to be perceived as taking a leading role in the provision of health care to the community.

The quantity maximization model can also explain why in a given community there might be a certain degree of excess capacity in hospital services. A quantity-maximizing hospital may acquire an additional piece of medical equipment even if it does not generate a profit, provided it attracts a sufficient number of additional admittances. Such buying behavior may lead to a duplication of resources and overcapacity as each hospital expands its facility beyond the profit-maximizing point. The quantity maximization model, however, cannot explain why the cost of hospital services has been rising so rapidly over time in recent decades, because it offers only a static rather than a dynamic view of hospital behavior.[1] The other models, discussed next, set quality of services as an attainable goal. Because quality of services is heavily dependent on technology and medical technology has changed dramatically over time, these models may provide a partial explanation for rising health care costs.

---

[1] A static view analyzes behavior or performance at a point in time. Dynamic analysis considers behavior or performance over time.

*Utility Maximization Models*

Over the years, a number of utility maximization models have been developed primarily to explain the behavior of not-for-profit hospitals in an era of rising health care costs. In general, these models argue that because the managers of not-for-profit hospitals are exempt from an ownership constraint and therefore do not have to maximize profits, they are free to pursue their own personal goals rather than profit maximization. Stated in more technical terms, managers are free to address their own personal utility functions. Although some debate exists over what variables belong in the manager's utility function, most analysts agree that if managers are unconstrained they will pursue the five Ps of increased pay, perquisites, power, prestige, and patronage.

Since it is beyond the scope of this section to cover all the utility maximization models of managerial behavior, we discuss three models that best represent this body of literature. The first model hypothesizes that managers maximize the quality of care provided to increase the status or prestige of the institution. The second model builds on the previous two models discussed and suggests that managers jointly choose the optimal quantity and quality of output to provide. The last model is referred to as the managerial expense preference model.

**Quality Maximization**   It has been argued that managers derive utility from the quality of hospital care provided. As you know, quality is immeasurable and is associated with the spectrum of services the hospital offers. Thus, the quality of care is enhanced every time the hospital widens the spectrum of services to patients or retains more specialists on staff. Any increase in the quality of care is also likely to drive up the cost of producing medical services.

Lee's (1971) model of hospital behavior is consistent with the quality maximization argument. The basic premise of the model is that managers of not-for-profit hospitals maximize utility by attempting to enhance the status, or prestige, of their institutions. Since status is defined to be positively related to the "range of services available and the extent to which expensive and highly specialized equipment and personnel (including M.D.'s) are available" (p. 49), the only way managers can achieve their goal is to maximize quality. This quest for status is the force driving the behavior of managers.

According to Lee's theory, the hospital has a desired level of status that it will attempt to achieve. The desired status depends on the mission of the hospital and the hospital's relative standing in the medical community. Because the actual level of status tends to be below the desired level, managers are constantly attempting to improve on status by increasing the quality of care. The hospital must provide that level of quality of care that is consistent with the desired level of status the managers are trying to achieve. For example, a large teaching hospital with a prestigious reputation is obligated to possess the most technologically sophisticated equipment and have a large number of specialists on staff because the managers view their organization as being on the forefront of medical development. In other words, the reputation and status of the hospital demand that it offers the highest-quality care. A small nonteaching hospital, on the other hand, will try to achieve a much more modest status level. The small nonteaching hospital will offer a quality of care below that of a larger hospital but on a par with hospitals of similar status.

Given a relatively inelastic demand for hospital services, managers can pursue a policy of quality maximization with little concern for costs. Any increase in the cost of hospital services associated with an enhancement in quality can be passed on to the payer through a higher price with minimal impact on output. The quest for status through quality maximization may provide one explanation for rising hospital costs in recent years.

Because the physicians on staff at the hospital are also likely to receive utility from any increase in the quality of care, the interests of the managers and medical staff are likely to be aligned in this instance. As the hospital acquires more advanced medical inputs, physicians are given the opportunity to provide more varied and sophisticated medical treatment to their patients. The more sophisticated medical inputs may allow physicians on staff to expand their practices. In addition, the hospital is likely to find it easier to recruit and retain medical personnel if it improves the quality of care. The same argument may apply to the board of trustees. Board members may also receive utility from enhanced hospital status.

The model suggests that new technology is diffused in a tiered fashion. Any new piece of equipment or medical technology is likely to be adopted first by the most status-conscious institutions, such as research and teaching hospitals. Their lofty status requires that research and teaching hospitals be on the cutting edge of medical technology. Hospitals of lesser status acquire the technology only after it has become a more accepted part of medical treatment and some of the hospitals in that status group have begun to acquire it. The implication is that most hospitals acquire new technology not because it is a prudent investment but because managers do not want to jeopardize the institution's status or relative standing in the medical community. Thus, new technology is acquired primarily for defensive purposes. The quality maximization model may explain why there is a tendency in the hospital sector toward duplication of resources and overspecialization. Hospitals are constantly attempting to expand services to enhance their status, not because profit maximization or efficiency calls for the expansion of services.

**Quality and Quantity Maximization**   Feldstein (1971) and Newhouse (1970) extended the quality maximization model by combining it with the quantity maximization model. According to Newhouse, management jointly determines the quantity and quality of output and produces the levels that maximize utility. Since any increase in quality comes at the expense of quantity, and vice versa, managers face an important trade-off and must jointly determine the optimal levels of quality and quantity to produce. Figure 10–2 illustrates this trade-off.

Given that quality can be enhanced only by increasing the cost of production (see Chapter 6), every time a hospital attempts to increase quality, its cost curves shift upward. This situation is depicted in figure 10–2, where initially an output-maximizing hospital produces at point $A$. If management decides to increase quality, that decision causes the average cost curve to shift upward from $AC_0$ to $AC_1$. With no change in demand, the output-maximizing level of output equals $Q_1$ (point $B$), and the increase in

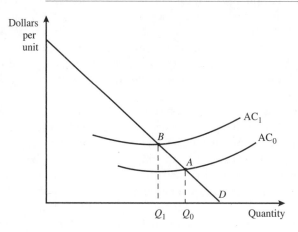

**FIGURE 10-2** THE IMPACT OF CHANGES IN QUALITY ON COSTS

quality is associated with a decrease in output. If quality is adjusted further, a trade-off curve between quality and quantity can be derived.[2] The trade-off curve appears in figure 10–3. Points $A$ and $B$ on the graph correspond to points $A$ and $B$ in figure 10–2. The curve is downward sloping, indicating the trade-off between the quality and quantity of medical care produced.

The quality/quantity maximization model indicates that the managers of not-for-profit hospitals face the dilemma of trying to maximize the level of services provided to the public while at the same time increasing the quality of care to improve the status of the hospital. Because a trade-off exists between the two, managers must choose that mixture of quantity and quality that maximizes their personal utility.

**The Managerial Expense Preference Model** The final model discussed in this section is the managerial expense preference model (Williamson, 1963). The model was developed to explain the behavior of large firms that are not directly managed by major stockholders. The basic tenet of the model is that managers use their authority to divert funds away from profits to serve their own self-interests—that is, to enhance their own utility. Among other things, the funds are used to increase compensation, expand the number of support staff for the purpose of enhancing power and prestige, or offer more perquisites. In a sense, managers absorb profits in the process of increasing their own utility by maximizing the amount of discretionary expenditures.

The ability of managers to provide stockholders with less than the maximum amount of profits stems from the existence of an asymmetry of information between

---

[2]In all likelihood, any increase in quality will lead to an increase in the demand for hospital services. Consumers may be more willing to purchase medical services of higher quality at a higher price. This does not change the analysis, however, provided the increase in demand is relatively small. In terms of figure 10–2, a trade-off between quantity and quality still exists if the AC curve shifts upward by more than the demand curve shifts to the right with any increase in quality.

| FIGURE 10-3 | THE QUALITY/QUANTITY MAXIMIZATION MODEL |

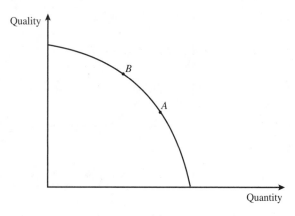

the stockholders and the managers regarding firm performance. Stockholders do not always have the means to fully monitor activities of managers and ensure that they are providing the maximum amount of profits. Managers are afforded a certain amount of freedom to run the firm, provided stockholders receive what they consider an acceptable level of profits.

In the context of the monopoly model we have been working with, managerial expense preference behavior suggests that managers maximize discretionary expenditures by choosing the profit-maximizing level of output and price and then absorbing the profits through discretionary expenditures. Figure 10–4 illustrates this process. For simplicity's sake, assume marginal cost is constant and equals average cost. As such, the marginal and average cost curves are equal and horizontal. The $MC_{true}$ curve equals the true MC and AC cost curves that exhibit production efficiency.

To maximize discretionary expenditures, the difference between revenue and the true cost of production, the firm follows the typical profit maximization rule, producing at the $Q_0$ level of output and charging $P_0$. However, instead of reflecting excess profits, the rectangle $P_0AEC_{EXP}$ represents the amount of profits managers absorb as discretionary expenditures or income. In the process of enhancing their own utility, managers drive up the cost of production in the form of discretionary expenditures. The point $C_{EXP}$ represents the average cost of production after the expense preference behavior of managers has been taken into account. The vertical distance between points $E$ and $C_{EXP}$ (or that between $A$ and $P_0$) represents the inefficiencies brought about by expense preference behavior.[3] The firm reports a normal profit rather than excess profits.

---

[3] In a different context, the inefficiency has been referred to as X-inefficiency. The inefficiency exists because managers of firms with some market power do not have the incentive to employ inputs efficiently. Inputs are either overemployed or are not used to their fullest potential. In addition, managers may pay input prices beyond the necessary amount.

**FIGURE 10–4**     THE MANAGERIAL EXPENSE PREFERENCE MODEL

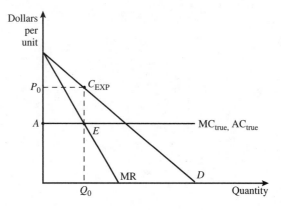

The managerial expense preference model has some interesting implications. The model suggests that managers consciously drive up the cost of production in an attempt to further their own self-interests. The model can also help explain the behavior of not-for-profit firms. Surprisingly, the expense preference model suggests that managers of not-for-profit firms act much like their counterparts working for profit firms; that is, they maximize profits. The difference lies in the extent to which managers absorb profits as discretionary income. Since not-for-profit providers are prohibited by law from earning a profit, all the profits can be diverted by managers. As a result, we should observe not-for-profit firms having higher costs than for-profit firms that are closely controlled by profit-conscious owners, *ceteris paribus.* The cost differential reflects the wider latitude that not-for-profit managers are given to absorb profits. The fact that some of these profits are spent on additional personnel and equipment may help explain the duplication of resources in the health care sector.

In conclusion, utility maximization models have many positive attributes. First, they explain how firm behavior is affected when managers address their own utility functions rather than attempting to maximize profits. Behavior other than profit maximization is especially important to address when we consider that a significant proportion of health care providers function in not-for-profit settings. Second, the models explain why there may be a tendency in the health care sector toward duplication of resources and overspecialization, as in the case of the market for hospital services. Third, utility maximization models help explain why health care costs have increased over the years. Managers who are seeking to advance their personal goals, such as maximizing the quality of output at the expense of profits, are not likely to be overly concerned with the impact any policy change may have on the financial "bottom line." A lack of concern for the bottom line naturally causes the cost of medical care to increase.

These models have their limitations, however. For one thing, they do not explicitly control for the role physicians play in the allocation of medical resources. The role of physician is the focus of the next model of medical firm behavior.

### The Physician Control Model

In many institutional settings, physicians make numerous important resource allocation decisions. As a result, the usual employer–employee nexus does not characterize the relation between a physician and many medical organizations. For example, in most cases, physicians are on staff at a hospital and are not directly employed by the institution (see Insight 6–3 in Chapter 6). To focus on the impact physicians may have on the employment of factor inputs, the physician control model assumes that all production decisions rest in the hands of the doctors on staff.

The resource allocation decisions may be driven by the representative physician's concern for the institution's mission, patients' well-being, or her or his own self-interest. For discussion purposes, we suppose the typical physician attempts to maximize his or her own personal utility. Utility is assumed to depend solely and directly on the physician's income; that is, more income makes the physician better off, so the physician attempts to receive as much as possible.

For simplicity's sake, assume the physician works in a hospital setting and the production of hospital services requires only two inputs: physician time and all other factors. In Chapter 6, we argue that marginal productivity to price ratios are equal between any two inputs when output is efficiently produced. In terms of the present discussion

**(10–1)** $\text{MP}_{\text{Phy}}/W_{\text{Phy}} = \text{MP}_{\text{Oth}}/W_{\text{Oth}},$

where $\text{MP}_{\text{Phy}}$ and $W_{\text{Phy}}$ equal the marginal product and wage of physicians, respectively, and $\text{MP}_{\text{Oth}}$ and $W_{\text{Oth}}$ represent the marginal product and wage of all other inputs, respectively. The equation tells us that resources are efficiently employed if the last dollar spent on physicians and all other inputs generates the same amount of additional output. Since the physician is assumed to maximize personal income, she or he faces an incentive to expand the use of hospital inputs that complement physician services. The objective is to enhance the ability to service patients. For example, physicians may expand the number of beds at the hospital to ensure that none of their patients must wait to be admitted. Or they may push to increase the number of support personnel, such as nurses and technicians. In each instance, the goal is to increase the marginal product of physicians at the expense of other factor inputs. As a result, the equality in equation 10–1 does not hold, and instead

**(10–2)** $\text{MP}_{\text{Phy}}/W_{\text{Phy}} > \text{MP}_{\text{Oth}}/W_{\text{Oth}}.$

The increase in the marginal product gives physicians the ability to attend to more patients in a shorter period of time. This translates into higher income for the physicians and higher costs for hospitals, because other inputs are overemployed. Naturally, for

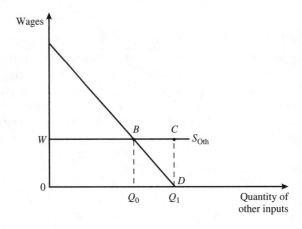

FIGURE 10-5    OVEREMPLOYMENT AND THE PHYSICIAN
CONTROL MODEL

the policy to work, physicians must also be able to restrict the number of doctors on staff at the hospital through some type of affiliation barrier.

Figure 10–5 illustrates the overemployment issue. The curve $S_{Oth}$ represents the market-determined wage of other inputs assuming the hospital faces competitive input markets. An efficiently run hospital would employ a $Q_0$ level of other inputs. Because the physicians essentially face a zero price for other inputs, they force the hospital to employ other inputs up to the point where the marginal product is zero. This occurs at point $Q_1$ in figure 10–5. The area $Q_0BCQ_1$ represents the greater amount of spending on other inputs due to physician control.

The physician control model suggests that physicians distort the allocation of resources to advance their own self-interests. Production efficiency no longer exists because output is not produced with the least-cost combination of inputs. The physician control model may provide another reason for a tendency for duplication of resources in the hospital sector. As physicians pressure hospital administrators to employ other inputs beyond the efficient level, costs are driven up and excess capacity develops.

The physician control model helps to explain the prevalence of not-for-profit firms in the health care field. There are two reasons physicians may prefer to be associated with not-for-profit rather than for-profit hospitals. First, the interests of physicians may be more closely aligned with those of managers in not-for-profit firms than with those of managers in for-profit firms. Managers of not-for-profit firms are more likely to expand hospital services in an attempt to maximize utility. This policy is in the best interests of physicians because it increases their marginal product. Second, the ability of physicians to influence the decision-making process at the hospital may be greater in not-for-profit institutions. In the case of for-profit hospitals,

**FIGURE 10-6**    THE SUPPLIER-INDUCED DEMAND MODEL

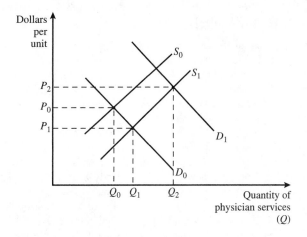

the goal of profit maximization is likely to prevent managers from acquiescing to the pressure exerted by physicians to expand services. Managers of not-for-profit hospitals, on the other hand, may be more susceptible to such pressure. In conclusion, it may be in the best interests of physicians to support not-for-profit rather than for-profit hospitals.

### The Supplier-Induced Demand Theory

The supplier-induced demand theory, or SID thesis, also focuses on the unique role physicians play in the allocation of medical services. Consumers are relatively ill informed concerning the proper amount of medical care to consume because there exists an asymmetry of information regarding the various health care options available. The asymmetry forces consumers to rely heavily on the advice of their physicians for guidance. This implies that physicians are not only the suppliers of physician services but also play a major part in determining the level of demand for those services. For example, physicians advise patients about how frequently they should have office visits, medical tests, and appropriate treatments. This rather unique situation puts physicians in a potentially exploitative situation. It may be possible for physicians to manipulate the demand curves of patients to advance their own economic interests.

For example, assume the market for physician services is initially in equilibrium in figure 10–6, where equilibrium occurs at point $(Q_0, P_0)$ and $Q$ represents the quantity of physician services. Now assume for some reason an increase occurs in the number of practicing physicians. An increased number of physicians causes the supply curve to shift to the right from $S_0$ to $S_1$, which in turn forces the average price of physician services to fall from $P_0$ to $P_1$. Faced with an increase in competition along

## Physician Behavior and the Supplier-Induced Demand Theory: Evidence from Japan and the United States

Some recent international evidence appears to substantiate the supplier-induced demand theory. Japanese consumers spend approximately 40 percent more on prescription drugs than Americans on a per capita basis ("The Strange Ways," 1991). Many reasons may account for the difference, but one explanation is that Japanese physicians prescribe more drugs than American doctors because doing so is financially rewarding. Physicians in Japan not only prescribe drugs, as their American counterparts do, but also sell them to their patients. They purchase the drugs directly from the pharmaceutical companies and sell them to patients at a profit. This unique situation gives Japanese doctors an incentive to prescribe medicine whenever possible. The prescribing behavior may explain the disparity in the level of prescription medicine consumed in the two countries.

In the United States, there is concern that physicians who own diagnostic equipment require that their patients undergo more medical tests to generate additional income. For example, one study revealed that physicians who operate their own imaging equipment are approximately four times more likely to require imaging examinations than physicians without such equipment (Hillman et al., 1990). Those doctors who not do not possess their own imaging equipment must refer patients who need an examination to a radiologist. In addition, physicians who own diagnostic equipment are likely to charge a higher price for each examination. Although it is impossible to determine from the study which group of physicians employs imaging equipment more appropriately from a medical standpoint, the results bring into question whether physicians with an ownership interest use diagnostic equipment more frequently because it generates financial returns.

Both of these articles tend to verify the supplier-induced demand theory. In each case, physicians appear to manipulate the demand for their services to advance their own financial self-interests.

with a loss in income, physicians may exercise their ability to influence patients' behavior by inducing them to demand more services. The increased demand may involve more office visits, additional tests, or even unnecessary surgery. As a result, the demand for physician services increases from $D_0$ to $D_1$. In the end, the price of physician services could actually increase, as shown in figure 10–6, where the new equilibrium price and quantity equal $P_2$ and $Q_2$, respectively.

The SID model can also be described in the context of the principal–agent theory. The principal–agent theory is traditionally used to explain the interaction between the managers of a major corporation, who are the agents, and its stockholders, who are the principals. The fiduciary responsibility of the agent is to manage the firm in the best interest of the principal, and that means maximizing profits. Due to an asymmetry of information between the principal and the agent, the manager is likely to have more information than the stockholders concerning the true operation and performance of the firm. In this situation, the manager has the opportunity to shirk his or her responsibilities to the stockholders by not seeking to maximize profits. Instead, the manager may use company funds to advance her or his self-interests. Advancing self-interests may involve such things as higher pay, a large support staff, or a more luxurious office, as described earlier in the context of the managerial expense preference model.[4]

Concerning the doctor–patient relation, the physician is hired to address the health concerns of the patient, the principal. Specifically, the physician, as agent, is given the responsibility to demand medical services on behalf of the patient, who possesses much less information concerning the appropriateness of medical care. Given that patients are typically covered by health insurance and the physician's personal financial interests are at stake, the physician has the opportunity to exploit the situation by convincing the patient to consume more medical care than is clinically necessary. The increased medical services most likely do no harm, but they do mean increased income for the physician-agent (see Insights 10–1 and 10–2).

In conclusion, the SID model suggests that the potential for a conflict of interest on the part of physicians exists due to an asymmetry of information. The patient lacks the medical background necessary to assess whether the physician is providing the appropriate level of care at minimum cost. The information imperfection allows the physician to abuse his or her advisory role by recommending unnecessary services for which remuneration is forthcoming. The overall cost of health care is therefore driven upward.

# A Theoretical Comparison of the Behavior of For-Profit and Not-for-Profit Health Care Providers

Because not-for-profit institutions are so prevalent in the health care sector, it is important that we examine the behavioral differences between for-profit and not-for-profit firms (see Pauly, 1987; Sloan, 1988; or Weisbrod, 1988). There are five basic institutional differences between these two classes of organizations.

First, when for-profit firms are established, they acquire initial capital by exchanging funds for ownership with the private sector. Ownership gives the private sector a claim on future profits. Not-for-profit firms must rely on donations for their initial capital because they are not privately owned. In a broad sense, they are owned by the community at large. Second, for-profit providers are capable of earning accounting profits and distributing cash dividends to their owners, whereas not-for-profit firms are prohibited from distributing profits. Third, for-profit organizations can easily be sold or liquidated for compensation by their owners, while it is very difficult to sell a not-for-profit organization. Fourth, not-for-profit providers are exempt from certain types of taxes and are eligible to receive subsidies from the government. In fact, it has been argued that the tax exemption and subsidies give not-for-profit firms an unfair advantage over for-profit firms. Finally, not-for-profit providers are restricted by law in the types of goods and services they can provide.

---

[4]In the case of corporate managers, incentive contracts (e.g., bonus pay) might be designed to align the manager's personal interests with the actions desired by stockholders.

### Why Are Not-for-Profit Health Care Providers So Prevalent?

Now that we understand the differences between for-profit and not-for-profit providers, the next item to address is why not-for-profit providers are so prevalent in the health care sector. Weisbrod (1988) discusses the issue in general terms, but his analysis can easily be applied to the health care sector. Not-for-profit firms exist primarily as a result of market failure in the private sector. The market failure results from three factors.

First, the private sector works best when all market participants are perfectly informed. However, given the complexity of medical technology and the difficulty of assessing the appropriateness of medical care, consumers typically possess imperfect information about the health care sector. As a result, many consumers believe they are in a vulnerable situation and can easily be exploited by medical providers for the sake of profits. For that reason, they prefer to deal with not-for-profit providers, which presumably are driven by more altruistic motives.

The second reason for market failure concerns equity. Society as a whole believes each citizen has a right to some minimum level of medical care that would not be provided if health care resources were allocated by the for-profit sector. The profit motive ensures that health care is allocated based on the ability to pay and not on need. As a result, some argue that not-for-profit providers are necessary to meet the needs of those who cannot pay for medical care.

The third reason for market failure involves the presence of externalities. When externalities exist, resources are not efficiently allocated because the for-profit sector does not consider all the costs and benefits associated with production (see the discussion on externalities in Chapter 11).

Thus, for these three reasons, the for-profit sector cannot address the collective need for health care.

The next question that comes to mind is why the public sector does not simply take over the allocation of health care resources in the presence of market failure. The answer, Weisbrod contends, is that consumer needs are heterogeneous. When needs are widely diverse, the government has difficulty developing an appropriate overall policy that meets the desires of all consumers in a cost-effective manner. For example, "one-size-fits-all" medicine most likely would not appeal to everyone. Hence, a multitude of not-for-profit health care providers, such as hospitals and nursing homes, are required to satisfy heterogeneous demands. Each institution can be tailored to fit the individual demands of its constituents. For example, the Shriners run not-for-profit hospitals aimed at treating young cancer victims, while some religious organizations operate nursing homes specifically for elderly members of their own religion.

One last question deserves some discussion. If these market failures are in fact substantial, why is the for-profit sector allowed to operate at all in the health care field? Consumer knowledge and preferences provide the answer to this question. Although some consumers may lack the information they need to make informed decisions, others are much more informed. Informed consumers may "have no institutional preference" and "prefer to deal with any organization, regardless of ownership form, that provides the wanted outputs at the lowest price" (Weisbrod, 1988, p. 124).

## INSIGHT 10–2

# Do Physicians Target Their Income?

Some have argued that physicians have a certain desired, or target, income level they wish to achieve that guides their pricing behavior. This model, commonly referred to in the literature as the target-income hypothesis, contends that physicians will increase the price of medical services when their actual level of income is below a desired level. Like the supplier-induced demand theory, the target income hypothesis assumes the existence of an asymmetry of information, which gives physicians some ability to manipulate prices. The major difference between the two is that with the target-income hypothesis, physicians are trying to achieve a desired level of income rather than simply trying to maximize utility, as is the case with the supplier-induced demand theory.

In an attempt to test the validity of the target-income hypothesis, Rizzo and Blumenthal (1996) examine whether the price of physician services is directly related to the extent to which the target income exceeds actual income for a sample of 871 self-employed primary care physicians. Of primary interest to this discussion is the price equation where the price of physician services was regressed on a series of independent variables, including the predicted target income variable. If the target-income hypothesis is correct, a positive relationship should exist between the predicted target income variable and the price of physician services. Those physicians whose desired incomes deviate farthest from actual income should be charging higher prices for their services.

Utilizing only those physicians who were reimbursed on a fee-for-service basis (499 out of 871 physicians), the authors found evidence to support the target-income hypothesis. In particular, they found that "the predicted value of the income target variable has a positive and significant effect on price, with an elasticity of about 0.3. Thus a 10 percent increase in the ratio of desired to actual income results in a 3 percent increase in the fee for an established patient office visit" (p. 257).

The authors concluded by estimating the model utilizing the remaining 372 physicians who were not reimbursed on a fee-for service basis. Because these physicians were compensated with a salary or other means, they were much less likely to have any discretion over the price of their services. As a result, the authors were not surprised when they found no relationship between price and the predicted target income for this group of physicians. In fact, the authors argue that these results provide further evidence of the validity of the target-income hypothesis. "Target income price occurs only when physicians exercise discretion over pricing and stand to reap the benefit from target income pricing" (p. 260).

Thus, the for-profit sector exists in the health care market primarily to satisfy the demands of these types of consumers.

### *The Economic Implications of Not-for-Profit Firms*

Traditional economic theory suggests that for-profit firms should behave in a more efficient manner than their not-for-profit counterparts. The argument is usually couched within either a property rights or a public choice model. According to Sloan (1988), the property rights theory suggests that for-profit hospitals are more efficient than either not-for-profit or public hospitals. For-profit hospitals are argued to be more efficient because residual claimants in for-profit hospitals put pressure on management to pursue maximum profits that are potentially obtained by producing output with least-cost methods. In contrast, a residual claimant is absent in both the not-for-profit and public hospitals. Thus, the argument is that managers of these two types of institutions pursue goals other than profit maximization. These other goals, including the maximization of quality or discretionary expenditures, may conflict with cost minimization. As a result, not-for-profit firms operate above the cost curves. Although managerial compensation could be tied to hospital performance and provide incentives for efficiency, it is usually assumed that incentive contracts are nonexistent or at least vastly incomplete.

The public choice model (Sloan, 1988) predicts an outcome similar to that of the property rights theory, but is based on bureaucratic behavior. The public choice model probably applies better to the difference between private (both for-profit and not-for-profit) and public hospitals. Public choice theory suggests that unconstrained bureaucrats–politicians, in conjunction with special interest groups, overproduce output (Niskanen, 1991) and produce with some X-inefficiency (Ahlbrandt, 1973) as a way to maximize the size of the budget. The excess spending provides utility directly to public bureaucrats because they are able to obtain more of the five Ps: power, prestige, pay, perquisites, and the ability to award patronage. Excess spending also provides utility to politicians indirectly as they satisfy the rent-seeking proclivities of special interest groups and increase their chances of being reelected (see Chapter 11). The public choice model implies that public hospitals face an incentive to operate with a larger budget for a given level of output than either of the two types of private hospitals.

Others (see Pauly, 1987) take a somewhat different view. According to these analysts, there is little theoretical justification to assert that not-for-profit firms are not cost minimizers. Consider a not-for-profit organization that is maximizing output. Although the managers are not maximizing profits, they still have the incentive to produce output as cheaply as possible. An incentive to minimize costs exists because more output can be produced from a given budget if managers keep per-unit costs to a minimum. Even a quality-maximizing firm faces the incentive to operate on the lowest cost curve associated with a particular level of quality. By operating on the lowest cost curve, managers are able to provide the maximum level of quality from a given budget.

The implication is that not-for-profit firms do not fail to minimize costs but instead operate on a higher cost curve than a for-profit firm for a given level of output due to a different objective, such as quality maximization.[5] Which point of view more accurately portrays the behavior of not-for-profit providers is an empirical question. Logic dictates that both views come into play, at least to some degree. That is, a not-for-profit firm may not only operate on a higher cost curve than a for-profit firm but may also operate at a point slightly above the true cost curve for any given level of output.

---

[5]From an empirical standpoint, it is difficult to determine whether not-for-profit firms overproduce or for-profit firms underproduce quality.

## Technical Efficiency and the Behavior of Not-for-Profit and For-Profit Nursing Homes

Nyman and Bricker (1989) compared the technical efficiency of not-for-profit and for-profit nursing homes to assess whether ownership status influences technical efficiency in the nursing home market. **Technical efficiency** exists when a given amount of output is produced with the fewest inputs. The authors employed a linear programming technique called *data envelopment analysis (DEA)* to determine the factors that influence the technical efficiency of a sample of nursing homes operating in Wisconsin. Briefly, this technique identifies those benchmark firms that produce a fixed level of output with the fewest inputs.[1] The benchmark firms are then used as a "reference set" to calculate an efficiency score for the remaining firms in the sample. The benchmark or most efficient firms are assigned a score of 1, while the less efficient firms are given scores less than 1 depending on their level of technical inefficiency. The efficiency scores in Nyman and Bricker's sample ranged from .226 to 1.

The efficiency scores are then regressed on a series of independent variables to determine the factors that influence the extent to which nursing homes efficiently utilize inputs. In the study, the factors used in the regression equation included a dummy variable controlling for the ownership status of the nursing home. The dummy variable, Profit, equaled 1 if the nursing home was a for-profit firm and zero if it was organized on a not-for-profit basis. The hypothesis was that for-profit homes have higher efficiency scores than not-for-profit homes because their owners force them to utilize inputs in an efficient manner. Following is a synopsis of the findings (*t*-statistics shown in parentheses):

$$(10–3) \quad \text{Efficiency score} = .585 + .044 \text{ Profit}$$
$$(3.95) \quad (2.32)$$
$$+ \text{ All other factors}$$
$$R^2 = .31$$
$$N = 184$$

As you can see, the parameter estimate on the for-profit variable is positive and highly significant, confirming the authors' hypothesis that for-profit homes utilize fewer inputs. The results indicate that for-profit nursing homes employed "4.5 percent fewer inputs per patient day" than otherwise comparable not-for-profit homes (p. 593). Although the result can be attributed to many factors, the authors believe not-for-profit nursing homes are less efficient due to managerial incompetence.[2] Because managers of not-for-profit homes are not disciplined by owners who have a residual claim on profits, they are able to act in an inefficient manner and employ more than the efficient amount of inputs. The authors go on to state that if for-profit managers similarly acted in an inefficient manner, they would be replaced by the owners. The authors' interpretation is not inconsistent with the managerial expense preference model. Because the managers of not-for-profit nursing homes are not pressured by owners to operate in an efficient manner, they increase costs by expanding discretionary expenditures and employing more than the minimum amount of inputs.

If these results reflect managerial behavior in the nursing home industry, ownership status appears to affect firm performance. In the absence of an ownership constraint, managers of not-for-profit nursing homes act in an inefficient manner by overemploying labor inputs and operating at a point above the cost curve of for-profit nursing homes.

[1] The inputs used were total nursing hours, total social service worker hours, total therapist hours, and total all other hours in an average day.

[2] According to the authors, the results did not stem from quality differences between for-profit and not-for-profit nursing homes because quality was controlled for in the regression equation.

It is important to note that regardless of how the inefficiencies are defined, not-for-profit firms are able to operate inefficiently only if they have a certain degree of market power or consumers are insensitive to price increases. Any firm, whether a not-for-profit or for-profit provider, must achieve production efficiency on the lowest cost curve if it is to operate in a highly competitive market (assuming consumers are price conscious). The potential for deviations away from cost minimization exists only if the market is noncompetitive in nature. If the degree of price competition in the medical sector intensifies in the coming years, the behavioral differences between for-profit and not-for-profit providers are likely to diminish.

## The Ownership Conversion of Not-for-Profit to For-Profit Health Care Providers

One of the more controversial trends taking place in health care today is the ownership conversion of hospitals, health insurance plans, and managed care organizations from not-for-profit to for-profit entities. For example, from 1980 to 1990, 110 not-for-profit hospitals converted to for-profit entities (Needleman et al., 1997), and a number of Blue Cross and Blue Shield plans have converted or are in the process of converting to for-profit organizations. A case in point is Blue Cross of California, which completed its conversion to a for-profit firm in May 1996 and, in the process, endowed two charitable trusts with assets of $3 billion.

Advocates for conversion argue that with a greater reliance on for-profit ownership, health care resources will be allocated more efficiently.[6] The upshot will be lower-cost health care. Opponents question the cost savings and are concerned about equity issues. If for-profit hospitals provide fewer community benefits than not-for-profit hospitals, the community at large, and the poor in particular, will be adversely affected if conversions continue to take place. Two issues lie at the center of the conversion controversy. First, are for-profit hospitals more efficient providers of medical care than not-for-profit hospitals? And, if so, do they pass these efficiency gains on to consumers in terms of lower prices? Second, do not-for-profit hospitals provide more community benefits than their for-profit counterparts?

With regard to the efficiency question, numerous studies have investigated the impact of ownership on efficiency and the quality of medical care. Although many of the studies have found that hospital ownership types tend to behave differently (e.g., Hoerger, 1991; Santerre and Bennett, 1992), as Sloan (1988) notes, "Empirical evidence reveals little or no difference in efficiency of ownership type" (p. 138). Although prices are found to be higher in for-profit hospitals, many analysts point out that voluntary hospitals enjoy tax advantages and also receive additional revenues from philanthropy. These factors may hold prices down in not-for-profit hospitals relative to for-profit hospitals. In addition, the small cost differences that are observed are most likely caused by quality or amenity differences, which are difficult to quantify objectively.

---

[6]For discussion purposes, we confine the analysis to the conversion of not-for-profit hospitals.

Despite the fact that not-for-profit hospitals have played a major role in the United States since the mid-nineteenth century, many debate whether they currently merit their tax-exempt status (see Potter and Longest, 1994). This leads to our second issue, whether not-for-profit hospitals provide essential community benefits that would not otherwise be provided by for-profit hospitals. Researchers have been wrestling with this issue for a number of years, primarily because of the difficulty in precisely defining and measuring community benefits.

Clement et al. (1994) offer five different community benefits that need to be considered. The first is uncompensated care, which equals charity care and bad debts. Clearly, a community is better-off when those who cannot afford to purchase necessary medical care receive it without regard to income. Although no one debates the fact that charity care is a community benefit, some dispute whether bad debt should be considered a community benefit. Every business establishment incurs a certain level of bad debt that results when customers refuse to pay their bills despite the fact that they have the financial means to do so. The question becomes what portion of bad debt incurred by not-for-profit hospitals constitutes a community benefit? The failure to include bad debt in uncompensated care understates the level of community benefits, while if all bad debt is included, the level of community benefits will be overstated.

The second community benefit equals the net cost of education and research. It stands to reason that communities gain when hospitals undertake medical research and educational programs. A third community benefit arises when not-for-profit hospitals provide medical services below cost. For example, a not-for-profit hospital may open an outpatient clinic in a less affluent neighborhood knowing full well that the revenues generated will not cover the cost of running the clinic. The fourth community benefit occurs when not-for-profit hospitals provide medical services at a price below that which they would charge if they maximized profits.[7] The final community benefit occurs when the not-for-profit hospital generates some net income and these funds are used to support community benefits in the future. As you might imagine, this is the most difficult community benefit to quantify.

After reviewing the literature, Shactman and Altman (1996), along with Claxton et al. (1997), conclude that not-for-profit hospitals generate significantly more community benefits than for-profit hospitals and that the monetary value of those benefits exceeds the subsidy received through their tax-exempt status. The empirical evidence also indicates that there is a wide dispersion in the level of community benefits provided across not-for-profit hospitals, with large not-for-profits providing the bulk of the community benefits.

The actual conversion of a not-for-profit hospital to a for-profit entity is a complicated matter fraught with controversy. First, there are the problems of determining the fair market value of a community asset and of establishing what to do with the funds once the value of the hospital has been negotiated. In many cases a charitable foundation is established to serve the medical needs of the community. For

---

[7]The quantity maximization model provides an economic explanation for this behavior.

example, the Alliance Healthcare Foundation of San Diego, California, was established with assets of $100 million in 1994 when the Community Care Network, Inc., was sold to Value Health. The foundation funds grants aimed at providing access to medical care to the underserved in San Diego County ("Conversion Foundations," 1997).

The issue of ownership conversion is likely to be with us for a long time as policy analysts wrestle with developing the proper response to this trend. At present, many state and local governments no longer take the view that not-for-profit hospitals are valuable community assets worthy of tax-exempt status. For example, communities in Utah, Pennsylvania, and Vermont have challenged the tax-exempt status of not-for-profit hospitals with varying degrees of success (Potter and Longest, 1994). Given that empirical evidence indicates that not-for-profit hospitals are as efficient as their for-profit counterparts and that they provide more community benefits than their for-profit hospitals, one can question whether this is the proper policy response.

## SUMMARY

This chapter is divided into two major sections. In the first section a series of models of firm behavior are presented as alternatives to the traditional profit maximization model. Despite the alternative goals that are entertained, traditional demand and cost theories are still an integral part of the various models.

The first model introduced is the quantity maximization model, which argues that large firms with a considerable amount of monopoly power may maximize output rather than profits. The next group of models examined are the utility maximization models. According to these models, when managers are free from an ownership constraint, they are in a better position to maximize their own personal utility functions. As a group, these models can be used to explain the duplication of resources and overspecialization that occurs in the health care sector. The section closes with a look at the physician control model and the supplier-induced demand theory. Both models point to the important role physicians play in the allocation of medical resources.

The second major section of the chapter takes a theoretical look at the behavior of for-profit and not-for-profit health care providers. Although economic theory predicts behavioral differences between for-profit and not-for-profit organizations, it does not establish the exact nature of those differences. It may be that a not-for-profit firm simply operates on a higher cost curve than an otherwise identical for-profit firm as a result of increased quality, or that it operates on a point above the true cost curve because of a lack of discipline created by a profit constraint. The chapter closes with a discussion of the controversy surrounding the ownership conversion of health care organizations from not-for-profit to for-profit entities. At the heart of the issue is the inability of economists to accurately predict the long-run efficiency and equity implications of conversions.

## Review Questions and Problems

1. Compare and contrast the various managerial objectives in the quantity maximization, quality maximization, quality/quantity maximization, and managerial expense preference models.

2. In your words, discuss the fundamental difference between the profit maximization and utility maximization models. Also, identify what factors are likely to enter into a manager's utility function.

3. Use the quality maximization model to describe the role not-for-profit hospitals play in the diffusion of new medical technologies.

4. A recent study by Mark (1996) found that not-for-profit psychiatric hospitals were no more efficient than their for-profit counterparts after controlling for quality. At the same time, the study found that not-for-profit psychiatric hospitals provided a higher quality of care as measured by the number of violations and complaints received. Use the quality/quantity maximization model to explain these results.

5. Executives of not-for-profit hospitals have been criticized for being overcompensated (but see Santerre and Thomas, 1993). Use the managerial expense preference model to illustrate the theory behind these accusations.

6. According to Schlesinger et al. (1996), the not-for-profit firm "must engage in activities that generate prestige or otherwise enhance the reputation of those affiliated with the agency" (p. 712). For example, a not-for-profit hospital may conduct medical research in a particular area in order to develop a national reputation and gain what Schlesinger refers to as "prestige from exclusivity" (p. 712). Use the quality maximization model to explain this behavior.

7. Some economists have suggested that the best way to control medical costs is to remove the profit incentive for health care providers, particularly hospitals. This would involve making all hospitals not-for-profit institutions. Use the utility maximization and physician control models to explain the likely impact such a policy would have on the cost of producing hospital services. What would happen if instead a policy were instituted that reduced barriers to entry in the hospital sector and therefore made the market more competitive?

8. According to Lutz (1993), the attorney general of Texas recently challenged the tax-exempt status of the Methodist Hospital of Houston. At the heart of the controversy was a disagreement over the amount of charitable care the hospital had been providing in recent years. The attorney general claimed that the hospital provided only $25.9 million in charity care from 1986 through 1990. Using a much broader definition of charity care that included items that were not reimbursed, such as the costs of community service programs and education, the hospital claimed it had provided $191.9 million of charity care from 1986 through 1990. In addition, the hospital was criticized for adding in 1989 an extravagant, nine-story building called the John S. Dunn Tower that included a spacious, two-story lobby, a health club, and a gourmet restaurant. Use the economic theory

developed in this chapter to put the debate between the attorney general of Texas and Methodist Hospital in a broader context.

9. Use the physician control model to illustrate why a cost-conscious administrator of a not-for-profit hospital may wish to limit the ability of the physicians on staff to influence the overall hiring practices at the hospital.

10. Auto mechanics have been accused of making needless repairs to increase their bills. Use the supplier-induced demand model to explain that behavior. What would happen to the amount of repairs if every car owner took a course in auto repair at a local school?

11. Discuss the ownership conversion issue in the context of theories X and Y introduced in Chapter 1. In particular, which theory is likely to support the conversion of health care providers from not-for-profit to for-profit entities? Why? Also, which theory is likely to oppose any efforts that make it easier for firms to convert? Why?

## *References*

Ahlbrandt, Robert. "Efficiency in the Provision of Fire Services." *Public Choice* (fall 1973), pp. 1–5.

Baumol, William. *Business Behavior, Value and Growth*. Englewood Cliffs, NJ: Prentice Hall, 1967.

Claxton, Gary, Judith Feder, David Shactman, and Stuart Altman. "Public Policy Issues in Nonprofit Conversions: An Overview." *Health Affairs* 16 (March/April 1997), pp. 9–28.

Clement, Jan P., Dean G. Smith, and John R. C. Wheeler. "What Do We Want and What Do We Get from Not-for-Profit Hospitals?" *Hospital and Health Services Administration* 39 (summer 1994), pp. 159–76.

"Conversion Foundations: A Listing." *Health Affairs* 16 (March/April 1997), pp. 238–42.

Davis, Karen. "Economic Theories of Behavior in Nonprofit, Private Hospitals." *Economic and Business Bulletin* (winter 1972), pp. 1–13.

Feldstein, Martin S. "Hospital Cost Inflation: A Study of Nonprofit Price Dynamics." *American Economic Review* 61 (December 1971), pp. 853–72.

Hillman, Bruce J., et al. "Frequency Costs of Diagnostic Imaging in Office Practice—A Comparison of Self-Referring and Radiologist-Referring Physicians." *New England Journal of Medicine* 323 (December 6, 1990), pp. 1604–08.

Hoerger, Thomas J. "Profit Variability in For-Profit and Not-for-Profit Hospitals." *Journal of Health Economics* 10 (October 1991), pp. 259–89.

Jacobs, Philip D. "A Survey of Economics Models of Hospitals." *Inquiry* 11 (June 1974), pp. 83–97.

Lee, Maw Lin. "A Conspicuous Production Theory of Hospital Behavior." *Southern Economic Journal* 38 (July 1971), pp. 48–58.

Lutz, Sandy. "Charity Care and the Law: Case Is Far from Closed." *Modern Healthcare*, March 8, 1993, pp. 26–28.

Mark, Tami L. "Psychiatric Hospital Ownership and Performance." *Journal of Human Resources* 31 (summer 1996), pp. 631–49.

Needleman, Jack, Deborah J. Chollet, and JoAnn Lamphere. "Hospital Conversion Trends." *Health Affairs* 16 (March/April 1997), pp. 187–95.

Newhouse, Joseph. "Toward a Theory of Nonprofit Institutions: An Economic Model of a Hospital." *American Economic Review* 60 (March 1970), pp. 64–74.

Niskanen, William A. *Bureaucracy and Representative Government*. Chicago: Aldine-Atherton, 1971.

Nyman, John A., and Dennis L. Bricker. "Profit Incentives and Technical Efficiency in the Production of Nursing Home Care." *Review of Economics and Statistics* 71 (November 1989), pp. 586–94.

Pauly, Mark V. "Nonprofit Firms in Medical Markets." *American Economic Review Proceedings* 77 (May 1987), pp. 257–62.

Potter, Margaret A., and Beaufort B. Longest, Jr. "The Divergence of Federal and State Policies on the Charitable Tax Exemption of Nonprofit Hospitals." *Journal of Health Politics, Policy and Law* 19 (summer 1994), pp. 393–420.

Rizzo, John A., and David Blumenthal. "Is the Target Income Hypothesis an Economic Heresy?" *Medical Care Research and Review* 53 (September 1996), pp. 243–66.

Santerre, Rexford, and Dana C. Bennett. "Hospital Market Structure and Cost Performance: A Case Study." *Eastern Economic Journal* 18 (spring 1992), pp. 209–19.

Santerre, Rexford E., and Janet M. Thomas. "The Determinants of Hospital CEO Compensation." *Health Care Management Review* 18 (summer 1993), pp. 31–40.

Shactman, David, and Stuart H. Altman. "The Conversion of Hospitals from Not-for-Profit to For-Profit Status." *Council on the Economic Impact of Health System Change*, September 26, 1996.

Scherer, F. M., and David Ross. *Industrial Market Structure and Economic Performance*, Boston: Houghton Mifflin, 1990.

Schlesinger, Mark, Bradford Gary, and Elizabeth Bradley. "Charity and Community: The Role of Nonprofit Ownership in a Managed Care System." *Journal of Health Politics, Policy and Law* 21 (winter 1996): pp. 697–752.

Sloan, Frank A. "Property Rights in the Hospital Industry." In *Health Care in America*, edited by H. E. Frech III. San Francisco: Pacific Research Institute for Public Policy, 1988, pp. 103–41.

"The Strange Ways of Japanese Medicine Makers." *Fortune*, July 29, 1991.

Weisbrod, Burton A. *The Nonprofit Economy*. Cambridge, MA: Harvard University Press, 1988.

Williamson, Oliver E. "Managerial Discretion and Business Behavior." *American Economic Review* 53 (December 1963), pp. 1032–57.

## CEBS Questions

CEBS Sample Question on Subject Matter from CEBS Course IX Study Manual

1. Summarize the physician control model. (pages 285–286)

CEBS Sample Exam Questions

1. Which of the following is directly relevant if a hospital wants to use the cross-subsidization technique?
   A. The concept of utility maximization
   B. The asymmetry of information between hospital staff and managers
   C. The attempt to produce at the lowest average cost
   D. The managerial expense model
   E. The elasticity of demand for various services

2. Conclusions regarding utility maximization models when applied to health care include which of the following?
   I. These models can explain how firm behavior is affected when managers address their own utility functions rather than attempting to maximize profits.

II. These models require a firm to consider accounting profits rather than economic profits.

III. These models can explain why there may be a tendency in the health care sector toward duplication of resources and overspecialization.
    A. I only
    B. II only
    C. III only
    D. I and II only
    E. I and III only

3. All the following are basic institutional differences between for-profit and not-for-profit health care providers EXCEPT:
    A. Initial capital for the for-profits is provided by selling securities, while donations are used for the initial capital for the not-for-profits.
    B. Not-for-profits normally can offer a wider variety of the types of goods and services they can provide.
    C. For-profits can earn and distribute accounting profits, while not-for-profits cannot.
    D. For-profits can be sold or liquidated for compensation to their owners, but it is very difficult to sell a not-for-profit.
    E. Not-for-profits are exempt from some taxes and are eligible to receive government subsidies.

*Answer to Sample Question from Study Manual*
The physician control model assumes all production decisions in institutional settings rest in the hands of the doctors on staff, the physician attempts to maximize his or her own personal utility, and utility is measured by the physician's income. When output is efficiently produced, the marginal productivity to price ratios will be the same for all inputs. The model can be explained by analyzing only two inputs: physician time and all other factors. In this model, physicians will expand the use of hospital inputs that complement his or her services. Because the cost of other inputs is essentially zero to the physician, these inputs will be overemployed in order to maximize the marginal productivity of physicians. Some type of affiliation barrier must exist to restrict the number of doctors on staff.

*Answers to Sample Exam Questions*
1. The correct answer is E. Cross-subsidization is the practice of charging prices that are below costs on services for which the demand is more elastic and charging much more than cost for services that have more inelastic demand. See page 278 of the text.
2. The correct answer is E. Utility maximization models do not require a firm to consider accounting profits instead of economic profits. See page 284 of the text.
3. The correct answer is B. Not-for-profits are restricted by law in the types of goods and services they can provide. See page 289 of the text.

# III

## *Government and Health*

# 11

# Government, Health, and Medical Care

"Lilly's Prozac Is Cleared by FDA to Treat Bulimia" (*The Wall Street Journal*, April 27, 1994, p. B6)

"FTC Acts to Block Hospital Merger; Wide Impact Seen," (*The Wall Street Journal*, February 1, 1994, p. B7).

"Some States Try Taxing Doctors to Cover the High Cost of Health Care for the Poor" (*The Wall Street Journal*, January 14, 1994, p. B1).

"Antitrust Laws Used by U.S. against Doctors" (*The Wall Street Journal*, November 4, 1993, p. B6).

"My War against Medicare's Bureaucracy" (*The Wall Street Journal*, July 28, 1993, p. A14).

U p to this point, we have given little attention to the role and effects of government intervention in the U.S. health care system. Yet, as the above headlines suggest,[1] government plays an important role in the various medical markets and either directly or indirectly influences the health of the population in a number of ways. For example, regulatory and taxing policies affect the production or consumption of certain products (e.g., prescription drugs, narcotics, alcohol, and tobacco) and thereby beneficially or adversely affect the population's health. Regulations also have the potential to alter the price quantity, or quality of medical services and can inhibit or promote efficiency in the allocation of resources. The degree of government intervention varies considerably across the country. Some state governments choose to actively regulate the

---

[1]FDA and FTC stand for the Food and Drug Administration and the Federal Trade Commission, respectively.

production and reimbursement of nursing home, hospital, and psychotherapy services. Other state governments take more of a laissez-faire attitude toward the health care industry.

We have already seen several examples of government intervention in the health care sector. For instance, earlier chapters pointed out that government created legal barriers to entry, such as professional licensure requirements and CON laws, often confer monopoly status on the established health care providers in a market. In addition, we know that the Medicare and Medicaid programs provide public health insurance to elderly persons, people with disabilities, and selected economically disadvantaged groups. These are just a few of an immeasurable number of government policies that affect the conduct and performance of medical care markets and the health status of American consumers.

This chapter provides an overview of the impact of public sector policies on the allocation of medical resources and the distribution of medical output. Although the design, complexity, and nature of health care policies differ across states and federal health care policies are multidimensional in scope, a common body of economic theory is drawn upon to analyze such policies.

This chapter

- Examines the reasons for government intervention in a market-based health care system.

- Discusses the implications of various types of public sector involvement, such as price and quality regulations and antitrust laws.

- Explores the methods used by government to redistribute income in society and the reason for such redistribution.

## Reasons for Government Intervention

Two general alternative views or models describe why government intervenes in a market-based health care system. These are the public interest and special interest group theories of government behavior. According to the **public interest theory**, government serves to promote the general interests of society as a whole and chooses policies that enhance efficiency and equity. Recall from Chapter 7 that an efficient allocation of resources is achieved when, for a given distribution of income, each good and service is produced at the point where marginal social benefit equals marginal social cost. In the presence of market imperfections, such as imperfect consumer information or monopoly, markets fail to allocate resources efficiently. We will see shortly that market failure also occurs when public goods such as national defense or externalities like air pollution are involved, or when distributive justice is a concern.

The public interest is served when government corrects instances where the market fails to allocate resources efficiently or to distribute income equitably. When the market fails, government attempts to restore efficiency and promote equity by encouraging competition, providing consumer information, reducing harmful externalities, or redistributing income in society. Consequently, the public interest model of government behavior predicts that the laws, regulations, and other actions of government enhance efficiency and equity.

According to the **special interest group theory** (Stigler, 1971; Peltzman, 1976; and Becker, 1983), the political forum can be treated like any private market for goods and services; that is, the amounts and types of legislation are determined by the forces of supply and demand. Vote-maximizing politicians represent the suppliers of legislation, while wealth-maximizing special interest groups are the buyers of legislation. In this model, incumbent politicians attempt to increase their probability of being reelected by supplying legislation that promises to redistribute wealth away from the general public and toward various special interest groups. In return, politicians expect votes, political support, and campaign contributions. Professional lobbies representing the special interest groups negotiate with politicians and arrive at the market-clearing prices and quantities of different kinds of legislation. Special interest group legislation changes over time when relative power shifts among different interest groups. Power or political pressure is determined by the amount of resources the group controls, the size of the group, and the efficiency with which the group transforms resources into pressure.

The successful politician stays in office by combining the legislative programs of various special interest groups into an overall fiscal package to be advanced in the political arena. The beneficiaries are the special interest groups, while the costs fall disproportionately on the general public. For example, individual pieces of legislation that provide protection from imported automobiles, milk price supports, and a larger education budget individually benefit those associated with the Automobile Workers Union, the American Dairy Association, and the National Education Association, respectively. The same politician can offer wealth transfers to each of these three groups and in return receive their combined votes, political support, and contributions. Naturally, special interest groups and politicians are made better off by the political exchanges; otherwise, these exchanges would not occur. Politicians retain or acquire elected positions, while the special interest groups receive wealth-enhancing legislation.

The general public, however, is unknowingly made worse off by the political exchanges. Individuals are typically rationally ignorant about the wealth implications of government activities because the personal cost of acquiring information about the true effect of legislation is high, whereas the corresponding private benefit is low. For example, suppose a certain piece of legislation redistributes $250 million a year away from the general public to a special interest group. Although this wealth transfer is a large amount of money in absolute terms, it is insignificant when expressed in per capita terms. In the United States, the cost of this wealth transfer is only about $1 per person. Raising the per capita cost of special interest group legislation to $100 increases the total wealth transfer to $25 billion. Yet even at a potential per-person savings of $100, few people are likely to become involved due to the money and time costs associated with political activity. To challenge special interest group legislation, a group or an individual must organize a legitimate counter political movement, inform others, circulate a petition, and engage in lobbying. All these activities entail sizable personal time and money costs.

Ross Perot's grassroots bid for the presidency in 1992 exemplifies this point on a grandiose scale. Perot attempted to challenge the political establishment by running for president as a third-party candidate. After spending millions of his own money, he garnered a respectable 19 percent of the overall vote, but not enough to win the presidential election. Imagine all the other potential "Perots" who never get involved in the political process at even the local or state level because of the staggering costs involved.

The special interest group model of government behavior implies that the typical individual consumer is "nickeled and dimed" by wealth-transferring legislation. Even worse, the wealth transfer is not simply a dollar-for-dollar transfer from the general public to the special interest groups. The political negotiations leading to the wealth transfer involve scarce resources such as the politicians' time and professional lobbies. As more resources are diverted to political negotiations, fewer are available for productive purposes. Consequently, inefficiencies are normally associated with special interest group legislation.

Therefore, according to the special interest group theory of government behavior, public regulations and laws exist because some special interest group benefits at the expense of the general public. Individuals in a special interest group are collectively powerful because they share a common concentrated interest. Consumers as a group, however, are generally diverse, fragmented, and powerless. Organization costs typically prohibit general consumers from taking action even when wealth transfers are known.

As an example, Ohsfeldt and Gohmann (1992) analyzed whether various state regulations concerning AIDS-related health insurance underwriting practices are influenced by the pressure of special interest groups. They focused on state regulations prohibiting (1) questions during the insurance application process about past HIV testing, (2) insurers from requiring insurance applicants to submit to HIV antibody tests, (3) questions on the application regarding sexual orientation, and (4) the exclusion of any AIDS-related costs from the services covered by the health insurance contract. As of 1988, 23 states had none of the four regulations, 3 had only one, 8 had two, 5 had three, and 4 had all four regulations in place.

The authors argued that the losers from these insurance regulations are private health insurance companies (due to lower profits) and private insurance holders with a low average risk for AIDs (higher premium costs). Individuals who gain include those at high risk for AIDS (lower premium costs) and private providers of health care services (higher profits from more generous private insurance coverage). In general, the empirical findings of their regression analysis support the hypothesis that the presence of state regulations restricting AIDS-related health insurance underwriting practices is related to special interest group pressure. Specifically, Ohsfeldt and Gohmann found that underwriting regulations are more likely in states where the AIDS prevalence rate (as a proxy for the AIDS group) is high and insurance industry strength is low.

The public interest and special interest group models are two contrasting theories regarding the reasons government intervenes in a market-based system. In the real world, government most likely intervenes for both reasons. In some instances, government actions correct for market failure and thereby promote efficiency and equity. In other situations, government policies enhance the well-being of specific groups at an overall cost to society and thereby cause an inefficient allocation of resources and an inequitable distribution of income. Indeed, a careful cost-benefit analysis would have to be conducted before the winners and losers could be identified and the efficiency and equity implications determined for each piece of legislation. It is important to remember that both the government and the marketplace are imperfect institutions and, as a result, both fail to some extent; that is, government failure and market failure can coexist. Our job as policymakers or informed consumers is to determine which institution can accomplish which objective in the more efficient and equitable manner.

# Types of Government Intervention

Government can alter the performance of markets in terms of efficiency and equity by providing public goods, levying taxes, correcting for externalities, imposing regulations, enforcing antitrust laws, operating public enterprises, and sponsoring redistribution programs. As an example of a public good, a government health officer inspects the sanitary conditions at local restaurants to protect the public's health. To correct for an externality, the government taxes the emissions of firms to reduce the level of air or water pollution in an area. A certificate of need (CON) law is essentially a health care regulation that restricts entry into hospital and nursing home markets, whereas the Sherman Antitrust Act of 1890 prohibits independent physicians from discussing their pricing policies to prevent monopolistic practices, such as price fixing. A hospital operated by the Veterans Administration provides an example of a government medical enterprise. Finally, the Medicare and Medicaid programs are examples of public medical care redistribution programs. Each of these government policies either indirectly or directly influences the allocation of medical resources and the distribution of medical output in the U.S. health economy. The following sections discuss the effects of these types of government intervention in more detail.

## Public Goods

One legitimate function of government is to provide public goods. A public good must satisfy two criteria. First, unlike with a private good, more than one individual can simultaneously receive benefits from a public good. That is, a public good exhibits no rivalry in consumption, thus allowing one person to increase his or her consumption of the good without diminishing the quantity available for others. Second, it is costly to exclude nonpaying individuals from receiving the benefits of a public good.

National defense is a good example of a public good. Everyone simultaneously benefits, and it is impossible to exclude nonpayers from receiving the benefits of national defense.

The preservation of water quality in public swimming areas by the local public health department is another example of a public good. A large number of people can simultaneously enjoy the benefits of improved water quality (at least until the beaches become overcrowded). In addition, it is costly to exclude nonpayers from receiving the benefits of improved water quality at the local pond (unless the entire pond can be fenced off).

Because of the high cost of excluding nonpaying individuals, private firms are unwilling to produce and sell public goods; thus, the private sector fails to provide public goods, and government intervention is necessary. Government ensures that public goods are produced in either the private or public sector and collects the necessary funding through taxation.[2]

Some people incorrectly consider medical services to be public goods because they are so essential for life. From a theoretical standpoint, however, the benefits of medical services are almost completely internalized by the individual buyer, and the cost of excluding nonpayers from receiving medical care is very low. Simply put, prospective patients can be required to pay the necessary fee at the door of the medical facility or be denied access to medical services. Thus, medical services are not public goods.[3]

### Externalities

Ordinarily, all costs and benefits are fully internalized by the parties directly involved in a market transaction, and others not involved in the exchange are unaffected. For example, consider an individual who wakes up one morning with a bad toothache and decides to visit the dentist. After some probing, the dentist informs the patient that a wisdom tooth is causing the problem and recommends that the tooth be extracted immediately. The (uninsured) patient consents, the task is expertly performed, and the $100 fee is paid at the desk. In a competitive market, the $100 fee reflects the marginal benefit the individual receives from being relieved of pain and the dentist's marginal cost of providing the service. Notice that in this example, only the individual consumer and dentist internalize the benefits and costs of the market transaction. This transaction is efficient because both parties are made better off; otherwise the transaction would not have taken place.

Sometimes, however, a market transaction affects parties other than the individual consumer and producer. In this situation, an externality occurs. An **externality** is an unpriced byproduct of production or consumption that adversely or beneficially affects another party not directly involved in the market transaction. When an externality occurs, either the individual buyer or the individual producer does not fully

---

[2]The aggregate demand for a public good is derived through a vertical summation of individual demands. See Rosen (1995, Chapter 5).

[3]Closely related to a public good is the notion of a *merit good.* Musgrave and Musgrave (1989) point out that people are often bound by similar historical experiences or cultural traditions. The common bond gives rise to common interests, values, and wants, "wants which individuals feel obliged to support as members of the community" (p. 57). For example, people in the community may believe that everyone needs at least some minimal amount of food, housing, or medical services and therefore may be willing to support the provision of those merit goods through redistribution of income.

## Special Interest Group Antilegislation

The preceding discussion examined how special interest groups purchase legislation offering wealth transfers. Another implication of the model is that a special interest group might pay politicians to refrain from supplying new legislation as a way to maintain the status quo and preserve their profits. The following newspaper article highlights this point and illustrates the competitive nature of the political marketplace and the influence of political action committees (PACs) during the 1992 election year. The interested reader may also see Makinson (1992) for more information about special interest groups' lobbying efforts.

WASHINGTON—Bracing for a fight over national health insurance, political action committees representing the medical and insurance industries have increased their congressional campaign contributions by 22 percent in the most recent election cycle, according to a study released yesterday. The PACs—representing individual companies and trade coalitions— donated a total of about $10 million to candidates during the first fifteen months of the 1992 election cycle. Most of the PACs oppose a "single payer" national health care system that would eliminate the need for the hundreds of insurance companies that now provide coverage.

"Health and insurance PACs are increasing the amount of money they spend on congressional campaigns because they want to blunt and undermine the groundswell of support for a 'single payer' national health care insurance system," said Robert Brandon, political director of Citizen Action, a Washington-based consumer advocacy group, which issued the report. The increase in health PACs' donations far outpaced the contributions of other PACs. Spending by other PACs increased by an average of only 14.5 percent.

PACs targeted members of committees likely to be most involved with health care legislation—the Senate Finance, and House Ways and Means, and the House Energy and Commerce committees. About 45 percent of the money contributed to members of the House went to members of the Ways and Means and Energy and Commerce, according to the study. The insurance industry is most worried about legislation sponsored by Marty Russo, D-Ill., which has attracted 74 co-sponsors in the House. It would create a "single-payer" system.

Brandon said industry opposition to the legislation and increased PAC contributions are "a clear statement that the health care industry and insurance companies are more interested in maintaining their enormous profits at the expense of the nation's economy and the health of the American people."

SOURCE: Justin Blum, "Insurance PACs Increase Giving." *Norwich Bulletin*, July 23, 1992. Copyright 1992. Gannett Company, Inc. Reprinted with permission.

---

internalize all the costs and benefits of the transaction. As a result, external costs or benefits are generated, and the product is usually under- or overproduced from a societal perspective. In the following discussion, we examine the impact and implications of demand-side and supply-side externalities.

**Demand-Side Externalities**   A demand-side externality occurs when the marginal social benefit diverges from the marginal private benefit associated with a good or service. A **positive demand-side externality** means that marginal social benefit is greater than marginal private benefit; a **negative demand-side externality** implies that marginal social benefit is less than marginal private benefit. Cigarette smoking provides a contemporary example of a negative demand-side externality.

According to Manning et al. (1989), external costs are associated with cigarette smoking, meaning smokers impose costs on nonsmokers. The external costs are generated in three ways. First, collectively financed programs, such as health insurance, pensions, sick leave, disability insurance, and group life insurance, are financed by taxes or group premiums and do not differentiate between smokers and nonsmokers. Because smokers have shorter life expectancies, they pay less taxes and premiums into the system. Second, smokers usually also incur higher health care costs than nonsmokers.[4] Third, external costs arise when nonsmokers die prematurely from both passive smoking and smoking-related fires. The implication is that nonsmokers subsidize smokers and incur costs for which they are not compensated in the private marketplace.

Figure 11–1 shows the effect of cigarette smoking on resource allocation. The supply curve, $S$, corresponds to both marginal private and social costs and represents the marginal costs of using various inputs to produce cigarettes. Thus, it is assumed that all resource costs of production are internalized by the individual cigarette producers. On the demand side of the market, we must allow for the fact that the marginal private benefit, MPB, is likely to be greater than the marginal social benefit, MSB, of cigarette consumption. The MPB curve in the figure represents the marginal private benefit received from smoking, or the private demand curve for cigarettes. The MSB curve considers the additional costs inflicted on society and therefore lies to the left of the MPB curve. The external costs underlie the difference between the two benefit curves.

For discussion purposes, we assume external costs per pack are the same at each level of cigarette consumption so that the two benefit curves are parallel to each other. We also assume the marginal social benefit is positive at every level, although it might be negative if the external costs exceed the marginal private benefits of cigarette consumption. Manning et al. (1989) estimated the external costs of cigarette smoking at approximately 15 cents per pack, exclusive of the costs due to passive smoking (2,400 deaths annually) and smoking-related fires (1,600 deaths annually). If we consider the value of lives lost from passive smoking and smoking-related fires, the total external costs increase to approximately 38 cents per pack.[5]

Consumers compare their marginal private benefit only to price (i.e., their internal costs) when deciding how many packs of cigarettes to purchase. Thus, in the process of maximizing personal utilities, consumers purchase $Q_0$ packs of cigarettes. This amount of cigarette consumption is inefficient from a societal perspective because at $Q_0$, the marginal social cost, $MSC_0$, exceeds the marginal social benefit, $MSB_0$, of cigarettes; that is, some nonsmokers are adversely affected by the consumption of cigarettes, and these external costs are not considered by smokers in the private marketplace. Since the individual consumers and producers do not fully internalize all the

---

[4]Since smokers may die earlier and fail to live to the more medically intensive years of life, it is unclear theoretically whether smokers always incur higher overall health costs than nonsmokers.

[5]The authors used a $1.66 million estimate of the willingness to pay for mortality reductions.

---

**FIGURE 11-1**    EXTERNAL COSTS OF CIGARETTE SMOKING

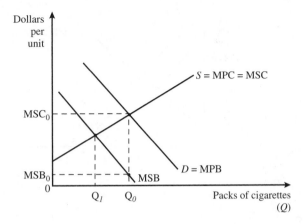

costs and benefits of their actions, the quantity of cigarettes is overproduced and over-consumed. An efficient quantity of cigarettes exists at $Q_1$, where marginal social benefit equals marginal social cost. Because individual consumers and producers are unlikely to voluntarily alter their consumption and production behavior, some type of government intervention, such as a tax on cigarettes, may be necessary to curb this harmful type of consumption activity.[6]

This example represents a negative consumption externality because others not directly involved are made worse off by the exchange. A positive consumption externality can also occur when a consumption activity generates external benefits. A vaccination to prevent an infectious disease, such as rabies, is an example of a positive consumption externality. Figure 11–2 illustrates the logic underlying this example.

In the figure, the number of dogs receiving a rabies vaccine is shown on the horizontal axis. The marginal private benefit curve, MPB, reflects the value dog owners place on the rabies vaccination. The marginal social benefit curve, MSB, reflects the MPB plus all external benefits. The external benefits include the dollar benefit others receive when a dog gets the rabies vaccine and prevents the spread of the infection to humans or other animals. The supply curve, S, reflects the resource cost of providing the rabies vaccine.

In a free market, consumers compare their marginal private benefit to price when deciding whether to get the rabies vaccine for their dogs. As a result, $Q_0$ represents the

---

[6]Manning et al. (1989) point out that the average cigarette tax of 37 cents per pack nearly pays for the 38 cents of external costs from smoking in the United States. Their estimate of the external costs of alcohol, 48 cents per ounce, is well above the current excise and sales tax average of 23 cents per ounce. They conclude that smokers compensate for their external costs, but drinkers do not.

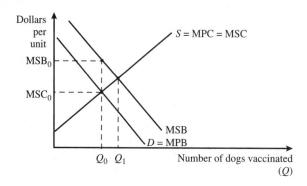

**FIGURE 11–2**    EXTERNAL BENEFITS OF RABIES VACCINES

total number of vaccinations in a free market where demand and supply intersect. But notice that at $Q_0$, the marginal social benefit, $MSB_0$, is greater than the marginal social cost, $MSC_0$, of providing the rabies vaccine. An inefficient outcome occurs because some individuals place very little value on the rabies vaccination (when maximizing personal utility) since they do not consider its external benefits. From a societal perspective, therefore, there are too few rabies vaccinations in a free market. An efficient number of vaccinations occurs at $Q_1$. This implies that government intervention of some kind, such as a mandatory requirement and a fine, may be needed to ensure the efficient number of rabies vaccinations. (For example, many states require a rabies vaccination to obtain a dog license, and failure to get a dog license results in a fine.)

In sum, externalities can arise on the demand side of a market if the social costs and benefits of a consumption activity are not fully internalized by the participants directly involved in the exchange. If the consumption activity generates either external benefits or costs, the good or service is likely to be under- or overproduced from a societal perspective. Consequently, government intervention may be necessary to correct the market's failure to allocate society's resources efficiently.

**Supply-Side Externalities**    As you now know, an externality creates an inefficient allocation of resources when the actions of one market participant affect another and no compensation is forthcoming. As in the case of a demand-side externality, the presence of an externality on the supply side usually distorts the allocation of resources in a market economy. A **negative supply-side externality** exists if a firm inflicts an uncompensated cost on another party in the process of production. In this case, a deviation arises between the marginal social cost and the marginal private cost of production. Because the firm bases its output decision on the private cost of production and not on the social cost, the good is usually overproduced. Figure 11–3 depicts this situation for a competitive market.

**FIGURE 11–3**    NEGATIVE SUPPLY-SIDE EXTERNALITY

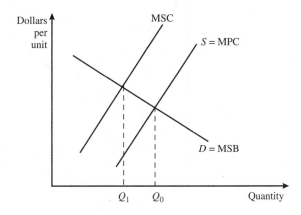

The demand curve, or marginal social benefit curve, is labeled $D = $ MSB; the supply curve, or marginal private cost curve, is labeled $S = $ MPC. The latter curve represents the amount it costs private industry to produce each additional unit of output. The MSC curve stands for the marginal social cost of production, and it lies above the MPC curve because it equals not only the marginal private cost of production but also the additional per-unit cost the firm inflicts on others. The distance between the two cost curves represents the per-unit dollar value of the cost imposed on society. The cost may reflect the greater health hazards from such factors as air pollution and toxic waste or higher time costs resulting from congested highways.

Profit maximization dictates that the good be produced up to point $Q_0$, where the marginal private cost equals the marginal social benefit, or the price. At $Q_0$, however, the marginal social cost of production exceeds the marginal social benefit of the product. From a societal perspective, resources are efficiently allocated if the $Q_1$ level of output is produced because the marginal social cost of production equals the marginal social benefit and the total social surplus is maximized. Because the market fails to assign the total social cost of production to the firm, the good is overproduced and resources are inefficiently allocated.

A classic example of a negative supply-side externality is acid rain. When fossil fuels are burned, they release sulfur and nitrogen oxides into the atmosphere; these substances combine with water to raise the acidic level of the water supply. Acid rain has caused extensive damage to marine and wildlife in certain regions of the country, such as New England. Because sulfur and nitrogen oxides can be carried hundreds of miles by wind currents, it is extremely difficult to assign costs to them. As a result, many of the producers of these emissions do not bear the full cost of production.

In the health care sector, the problem of hazardous waste disposal by hospitals can be analyzed in the context of a negative externality. This became a national issue in the summer of 1988, when vials of blood, used syringes, and other hospital waste

FIGURE 11–4        POSITIVE SUPPLY-SIDE EXTERNALITY

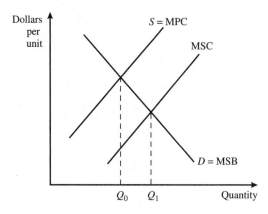

washed up onshore at a public beach in New Jersey (Baker, 1988). When five of the vials of blood tested positive for AIDS antibodies, many people became concerned that hospitals were attempting to pass the high cost of waste disposal on to the public by not properly disposing of infectious waste. From the public's perspective, the cost of inappropriate disposal of medical waste was in terms of an increased risk of accidentally acquiring AIDS.

Rutala, Odette, and Samsa (1989) estimated that U.S. hospitals produce approximately 15 pounds of waste per patient per day and that infectious waste makes up 15 percent of that total. The authors noted that the Environmental Protection Agency (EPA), along with many states, has begun to regulate the hazardous waste disposal of hospitals in an attempt to properly assign costs. In 1986, only 57 percent of the states had regulations regarding hazardous waste disposal; by 1988, this number had increased to 88 percent. Rutala, Odette, and Samsa also stated that if EPA guidelines became regulations, it would cost U.S. hospitals approximately $167 million a year to comply. In addition, they estimated that as of 1988, 40 percent of U.S. hospitals fail to comply with the guidelines concerning waste disposal established by the EPA.

A **positive supply-side externality** occurs if firms in one market (say, A) provide uncompensated benefits for firms in another market (say, B). In that case, the marginal social cost is less than the marginal private cost of production; that is, the MSC curve lies below the MPC curve in market A (see figure 11–4). The distance between the two curves reflects the benefits received by the firms in market B. Since no compensation is paid to the firms in market A, they lack the incentive to produce the efficient amount of output. The profit-maximizing level of output equals $Q_0$, but at this amount the MSB exceeds the MSC. If total social surplus is to be maximized, output should expand to $Q_1$. Since the firms in market A are not financially rewarded for the benefits other firms receive, they do not produce up to the point where total social surplus is maximized.

| FIGURE 11–5 | A TAX AS A CORRECTIVE INSTRUMENT |

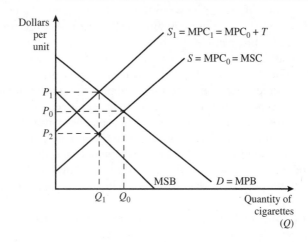

The transfer of medical knowledge across international borders is a good illustration of a positive supply-side externality. For example, assume the research funded by one country leads to a major breakthrough in the treatment of cancer that significantly lowers medical costs. This advance in medical knowledge is likely to be written up in a medical journal and, in the absence of intellectual property rights, quickly adopted by other countries at little or no cost. The firm in the country that developed the treatment and incurred the cost of research is not compensated for the full benefit of the breakthrough. Consequently, private medical researchers in any one country may face an incentive to underproduce medical knowledge in the absence of government subsidies because they would fail to receive a suitable return on their research investment.

In conclusion, economic theory suggests that the presence of an externality on the supply side impedes the market's ability to allocate resources efficiently. This occurs because production decisions are based solely on the private cost of production incurred by the firm rather than on the social cost.

**Taxes and Subsidies as Corrective Instruments**  By using taxes and subsidies, government can alter economic incentives and correct the unconstrained tendency of the market to misallocate society's resources when externalities are present. Specifically, taxes and subsidies can be used to alter the price of a good and discourage either overconsumption or underconsumption. Market participants are forced to consider the true net social benefit of their actions. For example, government can encourage an efficient amount of cigarettes by imposing a per-unit tax, $T$, on cigarette manufacturers equal to the vertical distance between MPB and MSB at $Q_1$ in figure 11–5. The per-unit tax raises the marginal private costs of producing cigarettes by the amount of the tax. As a result, the market price of cigarettes increases to $P_1$ and cigarette consumption falls to the socially efficient level (MSB = MSC). Cigarette producers receive $P_2$, the difference between the market price of $P_1$ and the per-unit tax (or vertical distance between the MPB and MSB) as after-tax revenues per unit.

Notice in this example that both sellers and consumers share the burden from the cigarette tax. The consumers pay the portion $P_1 - P_0$, and the sellers pay the portion $P_0 - P_2$. The sellers' portion of the tax burden typically results in a smaller profit margin or is shifted backward on to input suppliers. In our example, the cigarette tax may force producers to pay lower wages to their employees or lower the prices they pay to tobacco farmers. Whether consumers or producers pay a greater share of the cigarette tax depends on the relative magnitudes of the price elasticities of supply and demand. In general, when the price elasticity of demand exceeds the price elasticity of supply, the producer pays a greater fraction of the tax burden. The consumer incurs a relatively greater portion of the tax burden when the price elasticity of supply exceeds the price elasticity of demand.[7]

Governments face an incentive to tax goods for which demand is price inelastic. That is because the quantity demanded declines by a smaller percentage than the percentage increase in taxes when demand is price inelastic. Thus, the total tax revenue to government, the product of the per-unit tax and quantity, increases when demand is price inelastic. In fact, one reason "sin taxes" on cigarettes and alcohol products are so politically popular is that the demand for these two products is price inelastic, thus providing a fruitful source of revenues for government.

The point is that taxes or a threat of fines can be used to discourage socially harmful activities. In contrast, subsidies can be used to encourage socially beneficial activities that are otherwise undervalued in the marketplace. Recall that underproduction and underconsumption occur when marginal social benefit exceeds marginal private benefit. A subsidy that reduces price creates an incentive for more buyers to engage in a socially beneficial activity.

**A Market Solution for Externalities?**　In the preceding section, we treated an externality as a situation where the market fails to allocate resources efficiently because a portion of the costs and benefits is not internalized by those participating in the exchange. Government is usually needed to tax a harmful activity or subsidize a beneficial one. In some situations, however, the market can automatically correct for any externalities because individuals—those who are harmed and those who benefit from the activity—bargain and come to agree on a mutually satisfying solution. As a result, the presence of an externality does not always require government intervention.

For this to happen, three conditions must hold (Coase, 1960). First, clearly specified property rights must be assigned to either the benefiting party or the harmed party. (Property rights are laws that describe what people can do with their property.) Second, the involved parties must have an equal amount of bargaining power; otherwise, one party in the ensuing negotiation may have an unfair advantage. Third, the

---

[7]The answers to several questions at the end of the chapter provide the logic behind this statement.

---

**FIGURE 11–6**    **A MARKET SOLUTION TO AN EXTERNALITY**

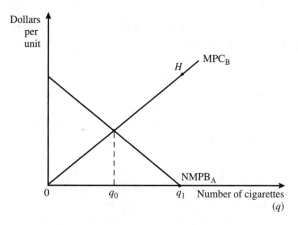

transaction costs of negotiation, or bargaining costs, must be low to ensure that the bargaining actually takes place.

Figure 11–6 represents a situation where the bargaining between parties provides a solution to an externality problem. The horizontal axis measures the quantity of cigarettes, and the vertical axis reflects the associated dollar costs and benefits. The downward-sloping $NMPB_A$ curve shows the net marginal private benefit (MPB less the constant market price or, equivalently, the consumer surplus per cigarette) that person A receives from smoking cigarettes in a two-person dormitory room. $MPC_B$ stands for the marginal private cost, or damages, that cigarette smoke imposes on person B. The curve is upward sloping to reflect the assumption that marginal private costs are likely to increase with a greater amount of cigarette smoking.

Suppose smoking is allowed in the dormitory rooms and person A is totally inconsiderate of person B's welfare. In this situation, person A is essentially granted property rights to the air in the room and faces a zero price for her actions (because the price per cigarette has been subtracted out from MPB). To maximize her utility, she smokes $q_1$ number of cigarettes, where NMPB equals zero. This amount of smoking, however, causes considerable harm to person B as indicated by point H on the $MPC_B$ curve.

Given this scenario, person B faces an incentive to bribe person A into smoking fewer cigarettes in the room, or at least smoke them when B is not around. As long as person A receives a sum of money (or some in-kind compensation of equal monetary value) greater than the NMPB for a given quantity of cigarettes, she is made better off by smoking less in the room and taking the bribe. According to figure 11–6, person B is willing to pay a price, as indicated by the MPC, that is higher than the NMPB for all levels of cigarette smoking greater than $q_0$. For points to the left of $q_0$, NMPB exceeds MPC and person B is not willing to compensate person A enough for further reductions in smoking. As a result, bargaining ceases given the assignment of property rights. At $q_0$, the amount of smoking is optimal for both persons A and B.[8]

Now suppose college policy changes such that smoking is not allowed in the dormitory room unless all roommates consent. The nonsmoker, person B, is essentially assigned the property rights, and the origin in figure 11–6 represents the initial position before bargaining takes place. At zero cigarettes, however, the marginal benefit to person A greatly exceeds the marginal cost to person B. Therefore, person A faces an incentive to bribe or compensate person B to accept some positive amount of smoking in the room. Person B might leave the room while person A smokes or install a smoke-eater mechanism in the room with some of the money received from person A. In any case, bargaining results in $q_0$ cigarettes, where $NMPB_A$ equals $MPC_B$. As Coase pointed out, the final outcome is invariant as to who is assigned the property rights. Both assignments lead to $q_0$ for an efficient outcome. The assignment determines who incurs the externality costs.

The "private market" reaches an efficient outcome in this case due to equal bargaining power. For instance, if person A is physically larger than person B, the threat or actual use of violence might influence the relative bargaining power of the two parties. If so, physical violence rations the scarce air in the room, and the outcome is likely to be unsatisfactory to person B. Also, high transaction costs can prevent the exchange from taking place. If the group affected by the externality is large, free-rider effects will make cooperation on an efficient bribe very difficult to achieve. For example, suppose three smokers and three nonsmokers share a suite of rooms in the dormitory. If the members of each group are heterogeneous, they may disagree on the appropriate payment, and the externality will remain uncorrected. Moreover, some individuals in the group may attempt to free-ride the bribes of others. In fact, some restaurants voluntarily designate smoking and nonsmoking areas due to the high transaction costs of negotiation among restaurant customers, among other reasons. Because the model does not apply to a large-group setting, the Coase theorem is limited in scope.

In any event, one lesson of the Coase theorem is that government is not *always* needed to correct for an externality. The assignment of property rights can produce an efficient outcome to an externality problem as long as bargaining costs are low. Government is needed only to assign and enforce property rights. Note that in the process of assigning property rights, government determines who "should" incur the externality costs.

## Regulations

A government regulation that attempts to control either the price, quantity, or quality of a product or the entry of new firms into the marketplace represents another kind of government intervention. According to the public interest theory, the regulation is

---

[8]If $MPC_B$ exceeds $NMPB_A$ at all levels of cigarette consumption, no smoking takes place in the room.

## Alcohol Commercial Bans and Alcohol Abuse:
## An International Perspective

Some products, like cocaine and marijuana, are banned, whereas the consumption of other medically harmful products, such as cigarettes and alcoholic beverages, is presently legal in the United States (although alcoholic beverages were banned during the Prohibition era from 1920 to 1933). Instead of directly banning legal but potentially harmful products, the government can try to influence adverse consumption practices indirectly through such policies as "sin" taxes, bans on commercial advertising, educational programs, and minimum age requirements. Saffer (1991) examined the effect on alcohol abuse of banning broadcast advertising of alcoholic beverages on television and radio. Given the controversy regarding whether advertising creates a demand for a product by manipulating consumer tastes, this study is especially interesting.

In his empirical investigation, Saffer used a panel data set that included 17 OECD countries for the years 1970 through 1983. Three measures of alcohol abuse—the per capita consumption of pure alcohol from beer, wine, and spirits; liver cirrhosis mortality rate; and motor vehicle mortality rate—were specified as the dependent variables in separate regression equations. Two dummy variables were employed to control for the banning of alcohol advertising broadcasts. One dummy variable took on the value of 1 if the country banned broadcast advertising of all types of alcoholic beverages (i.e., beer, wine, and spirits) and zero otherwise. The other equaled 1 if only spirits advertising was disallowed and zero otherwise. Saffer controlled for other explanatory variables, including the real price of a liter of pure alcohol and real income in each country.

Among the findings, the multiple regression results indicated that countries with a ban only on advertising spirits had about a 16 percent lower alcohol consumption rate than countries with no ban. Countries with bans on the advertising of all types of alcoholic products had about an 11 percent lower alcohol consumption rate than those that banned only spirits advertising. Some persuasive evidence was also found linking alcohol advertising bans to lower motor vehicle and liver cirrhosis mortality rates.

Apparently an advertising ban has the potential to reduce the consumption of alcoholic beverages and, more important, the harmful impact of excessive alcohol consumption on good health. If alcohol advertisements contain little useful information, the benefits of a ban may outweigh the cost. The same argument has been used to continue the ban on cigarette advertisements on radio and television in the United States.

justified because a market imperfection exists that would otherwise cause a misallocation of society's resources. For example, insufficient consumer information often justifies government-imposed quality requirements. As another example, government might grant monopoly status to a firm and regulate its price because one large firm can produce output more cheaply than a large number of small firms (i.e., a natural monopoly, such as an electric utility or a short-distance telephone company). The effect of government regulations in medical markets is hard to predict. Whether government impedes or promotes efficiency and equity depends on a host of factors, such as the competitiveness of the market, the cost structure faced by the individual medical firm, objectives motivating medical decision makers, and whether or not the exclusion principle holds (i.e., externalities, third-party payer, or public good

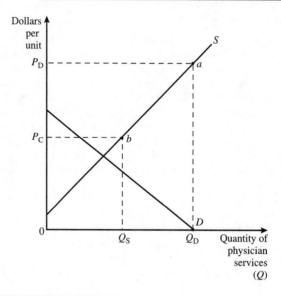

**FIGURE 11-7**  EFFECT OF A FEE-FOR-SERVICE THIRD-PARTY PRICE CEILING IN A SUPPLY AND DEMAND MODEL

considerations). We now examine the effects of several types of government regulations in a number of different settings.

**The Effects of a Fee-for-Service Third-Party Price Ceiling within a Supply and Demand Model**  The price paid for a good or service is one item the government might regulate. Government may regulate the price by establishing a maximum price or reimbursement level. In that case, the government sets a **price ceiling** for a product, and producers are prohibited by law from charging a higher price to consumers covered under the ceiling. Figure 11–7 shows the effect of a price ceiling within a supply and demand model. Suppose the supply and demand curves in the figure represent the market for physician services. To simplify the discussion, we assume consumers have complete rather than partial health insurance coverage for physician services.

Given the demand, consumers wish to purchase $Q_D$ units of physician services, since they pay a zero monetary price because they have full health insurance coverage. According to the model, output $Q_D$ is supplied by the physicians in the market, and total physician expenditures are represented by area $P_D a Q_D 0$ if the market price equals $P_D$. Now suppose that for cost containment reasons, the government sets a physician price ceiling at $P_C$. The lower price creates an incentive for physicians to reduce the quantity supplied to $Q_S$ and for expenditures on physician services to decline to $P_C b Q_S 0$.

# The Cost of Waiting for Hospital Services in Canada

We discussed some of the features associated with the Canadian health care system in Chapter 2. Among those features, consumers pay a zero out-of-pocket price for receiving most types of medical care services, and physicians and hospitals are directly reimbursed by the government. No balance billing is allowed, meaning physicians and hospitals are prohibited from charging patients for services beyond the payments they receive from the government. Given that consumers pay and health care providers receive a different price in Canada, excess demand results if quantity demanded at the zero consumer price exceeds quantity supplied as discussed in the text.

Because price does not perform a rationing function in Canada, the scarce medical services must be rationed by some nonprice method. Queues are the nonprice method used to ration hospital services, and waiting lists are the inevitable outcome. In fact, some articles in the popular press

and professional journals have suggested that the waiting lists are excessive and socially costly. Prolonged pain, anxiety, inconvenience, and loss of productive time are some of the social costs associated with long waiting lists for hospital services.

In an interesting study, Globerman (1991) estimated the cost of waiting for hospital services in British Columbia. Table 1, based on his study, displays the waiting times for hospital admissions in British Columbia as of 1989. Column 1 identifies the specialty, and column 2 shows the percentage of people who are experiencing significant difficulty in performing their work or daily duties because of their medical condition for each specialty. Column 3 identifies the estimated total waiting time in person-weeks for each medical specialty.

To assess the social cost of waiting Globerman first measured the loss of productive time by multiplying total weeks spent waiting (column 3) by the percentage of patients experiencing difficulty

### TABLE 1 — WAITING TIMES FOR HOSPITAL ADMISSIONS IN BRITISH COLUMBIA, 1989

| Specialty | Percentage of Patients Experiencing Difficulty | Total Waiting Time (in person-weeks) |
|---|---|---|
| Plastic surgery | 14.8 | 37,588 |
| Gynecology | 14.4 | 83,812 |
| Ophthalmology | 46.2 | 136,276 |
| Otolaryngology | 16.3 | 100,613 |
| General surgery | 26.9 | 144,595 |
| Neurosurgery | 68.3 | 14,285 |
| Orthopedics | 59.6 | 63,664 |
| Cardiology | 88.0 | 51,860 |
| Urology | 15.7 | 230,963 |
| Internal medicine | 46.2 | 4,752 |

*(continued)*

## *(continued)*

carrying out activities (column 2) for each medical specialty. To measure the cost in monetary terms, Globerman multiplied the loss of productive time for all medical specialties combined by average weekly industrial earnings for British Columbia in 1989. The assumption is that the average industrial wage serves as a suitable measure of the opportunity cost of waiting for hospital services. Of course, some elderly people in the queue may be retired from the workforce so the industrial wage overestimates their opportunity cost.

The cost of waiting was calculated to be approximately 0.2 percent of the provincial gross domestic product in 1989. Although that percent may seem low, two points concerning the magnitude of the waiting costs should be made. First, the costs of pain and anxiety, for example, are not included in the calculation. Second, as Globerman noted, the estimated cost of waiting for hospital services is

comparable to the total forgone wages and salaries associated with strikes and lockouts in British Columbia in 1989. Strike and lockout costs have long been a concern of economic policymakers in Canada. Because excess demand for hospital admissions may impose even greater societal costs than work stoppages, this seemingly low estimate may be cause for much alarm. Consequently, efficiency improvements may be in order.

The reader should be reminded, however, that the figures are purely estimates and the calculations rely on a host of assumptions. More studies are needed before any sweeping generalizations can be made. Nonetheless, Globerman's study focuses on an important policy question in addition to providing a useful application of several economic concepts, including shortages, nonprice rationing, and opportunity costs.

Notice that because the reimbursement price, $P_C$, is set below $P_D$, quantity demanded, $Q_D$, exceeds quantity supplied, $Q_S$, and the price ceiling results in a shortage of physician services. In a price ceiling situation where a shortage ensues and the price mechanism is not employed as a rationing device, some unintended outcomes may occur. For one, physicians may treat patients on a first-come, first-served basis even if some patients require more urgent attention than others. Physicians may also reduce the quality of visits in an attempt to lower costs. The quality reduction may mean a longer waiting time for a visit or shorter time spent with physicians during the actual visit. In addition, some unethical physicians may accept illegal side payments from wealthy people who want to jump to the front of the waiting line.

Political concerns may also dictate how a scarce medical service is rationed when a shortage exists. Perhaps politicians decide that medical services should be rationed on the basis of age, illness, or the amount of campaign contributions the individual donates. For example, in Great Britain, where price has virtually no rationing role, less rationing of medical care occurs for children than for adults. According to Aaron and Schwartz (1984), "Health expenditures per child in Britain are 119 percent of expenditures per prime age adult, whereas in the United States they are only 37 percent as much" (p. 97).

The point is that medical cost containment is typically not a free lunch. According to the above model, cost containment under plausible circumstances can result in shortages, longer waiting lines, nonprice rationing, and reductions in the quality of

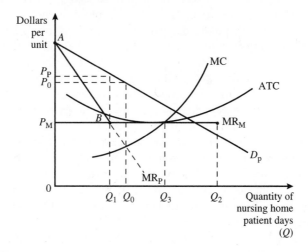

**FIGURE 11–8**    THE IMPACT OF MEDICAID ON THE
NURSING HOME MARKET

care. Society has to seriously consider the likely trade-offs before adopting cost containment strategies.

**The Effects of a Price Ceiling in a Dual Market Profit-Maximizing Monopoly Model: The Case of Medicaid**    The federal government implemented the Medicaid program in 1966 in an attempt to provide health care to poor individuals. Included in the program are elderly people who cannot afford to pay for nursing home care. The monopoly model helps to illustrate the impact of the Medicaid reimbursement policy on the behavior of nursing homes (Scanlon, 1980) when they service the dual markets of private pay and medicaid payments.

Figure 11–8 shows the revenue and cost curves for a profit-maximizing nursing home with private-pay patients. A profit-maximizing firm provides services to $Q_0$ number of patients and charges $P_0$. Under Medicaid, the nursing home receives a flat fee from the government for each patient who qualifies for public assistance. The analysis in the figure shows how the flat reimbursement fee influences the revenue curves of a for-profit nursing home assuming $P_M$ equals the government-established Medicaid fee. The marginal revenue curve, which incorporates the Medicaid fee, is kinked and has two distinct sections; it is represented by the curve $ABMR_M$ in the figure. The portion $AB$ is downward sloping and is derived from the demand curve for private-pay patients, $D_P$. The segment $BMR_M$ is horizontal and reflects the fixed level of compensation the nursing home receives from the government for each public-pay patient. Since the fee is fixed, marginal revenue is constant and the $MR_M$ curve is flat. At the $P_M$ price level, we suppose a maximum of $Q_2$ public-pay patients demand nursing home care.

A profit-maximizing nursing home serves a total number of $Q_3$ patients, because at this level marginal revenue equals marginal costs. Of the total number of patients, $Q_1$ are private-pay patients and the remainder ($Q_1 Q_3$) are public-pay patients. The model indicates that private-pay patients pay a higher price for the same nursing home services than public-pay patients. According to the figure, private patients pay $P_P$, while the nursing home receives $P_M$ for each public patient.

In addition, the figure suggests that at the government-established price of $P_M$ there is an excess demand for nursing home services by public-pay patients amounting to $Q_3 Q_2$ individuals. Naturally, any increase in the fee established by the government reduces the excess demand. As the fee increases, the horizontal segment of the MR curve shifts upward and the nursing home expands its number of public-pay patients. The higher reimbursement rate also increases public outlays for Medicaid.

An interesting policy dilemma concerns what criteria the government should use to establish the flat fee. If the goal is to service all those patients who desire nursing home care but are unable to afford it, the government should set the price high enough to result in zero excess demand. This is likely to be very costly and allow the nursing home to earn an economic profit. On the other hand, if the goal is to force the nursing home to provide services to public-pay patients at the least-cost level, the government should offer a fee of $P_M$ as shown in the figure. At this level, the marginal revenue curve is tangent to the average total cost curve at its minimum point, and long-run efficiency is achieved. This would be the price for nursing home services if the market were perfectly competitive. The major disadvantage in this instance is that many elderly persons would likely be unable to obtain nursing home care at that price.

There is a third alternative, however. The government could pursue a policy that minimizes barriers to entry while at the same time offering to compensate nursing homes at the least-cost rate of $P_M$. Since nursing homes earn a profit from their private-pay patients, more firms would enter the market in the quest for economic profits. As this occurred, the price for nursing home services would drop and there may no longer be an excess demand for public-pay patients. The only drawback of this policy is that as more public-pay patients entered nursing homes, the cost of the Medicaid program would increase. That may not be a desirable outcome, because the federal government and most state governments presently face severe budget constraints. The existing nursing homes would likely resist this policy because it means lower profits.

**The Effects of a Price Ceiling in a Quantity/Quality Maximization Model**   The previous two analyses of a price ceiling assume that firms maximize profits. Recall, however, that other objectives may motivate medical firms since many are non-profit institutions. Another common assumption is that hospital decision makers maximize both the quantity and quality of hospital services, as discussed in the previous chapter. Let's examine the effect of a price ceiling when this objective holds with the use of figure 11–9 (borrowed from figure 10–3). This figure shows the trade-off between the quality and quantity of hospital services in the utility function of the hospital decision makers given a break-even level of profits. Suppose that initially the unregulated hospital decision makers choose point *A* with $QL_A$ level of quality and $QT_A$

**FIGURE 11-9**     EFFECT OF A PRICE CEILING IN A
QUANTITY/QUALITY MAXIMIZATION MODEL

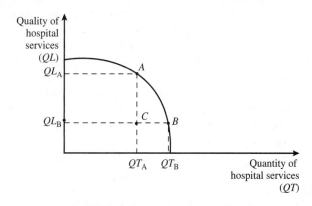

units of hospital services. A price ceiling that reduces the average revenue per unit of hospital services means the hospital must lower costs to break even. It lowers costs by reducing the quality of services. The model predicts that if the hospital lowers quality to $QL_B$ because of the price ceiling, quantity increases to $QT_B$.

Two important caveats are in order at this point. First, if health care providers are not subjected to an "all payer" price regulation, they may react by increasing the price of hospital services to the consumers in the unregulated market to offset the lower, regulated price. This practice is referred to as **cost shifting.** For instance, suppose figure 11–9 represents only the Medicare hospital services submarket. Health care providers might attempt to remain at point *A* and cover the losses on the Medicare submarket, the dollar value of area $QL_AACQL_B$, by increasing the price of hospital services to non-Medicare patients. Indeed, Murray (1993) claims that Medicare reimburses hospitals for only about 90 percent of the cost of servicing Medicare patients, whereas Medicaid reimburses at about 80 percent of costs. Costs are shifted to private-pay patients, who reimburse at about 128 percent of actual costs. The ability to shift costs depends on the price elasticity of demand for private pay hospital services.

Second, the exact behavioral response of the medical firm is more multidimensional than presented thus far and depends largely on the base to which the price ceiling is applied (Cromwell, 1976). Specifically, hospitals may react to a lower charge by adjusting the length of stay, number of patients, or quality of services. For example, if hospitals are paid according to a per diem price ceiling (i.e., average revenue per patient-day), they may respond to a lower per diem charge by increasing the number of patient-days to obtain additional revenues and also by lowering quality. The number of patient-days can be increased by increasing the number of new admissions and/or increasing the average length of stay. By increasing the patient's length of stay, hospitals can use the profits received from the later days to subsidize the more costly, service-intensive earlier days and make greater profits.

As another example, hospitals (or nursing homes) that are reimbursed on a per-case or per-patient basis are likely to respond to a lower per-case charge by admitting more patients to obtain additional revenues and lowering quality and length of stay. In this regard, some observers have argued that harmfully low DRG payments, which are per-case reimbursements, have caused hospitals to release their Medicare patients "quicker and sicker."

In addition, some critics have argued that the DRG per-patient payment has created an incentive for patient dumping by hospitals. **Patient dumping** refers to the practice whereby private hospitals fail to admit severely sick patients and instead dump them on public hospitals. In practice, this may happen because the DRG payment is based on the historical cost of providing services to patients with an average level of sickness and does not necessarily cover the cost of providing hospital services to those patients with severe illnesses.

In sum, the impact of a price ceiling within a quantity/quality maximization model is difficult to predict before the fact. It depends on the base to which the price ceiling is applied and the degree of cost shifting that takes place. The degree of cost shifting, in turn, is a function of the price elasticity of demand in the unregulated market.

**The Effects of Quality Regulations**    Government may also attempt to regulate the quality of medical services when consumers are rationally ignorant. As mentioned earlier, quality differences show up in the structure, process, and outcomes of production. Because procedural and outcome guidelines are more difficult to set and enforce, quality regulations are typically directed at the structure of operation. For example, a public agency may require that medical workers be professionally licensed or may mandate a minimum staff-to-patient ratio. In both cases, the assumption is that a higher level of structural quality promotes increased quality at the process and outcomes stage.

Regulations aimed at the quality of the employees typically mean higher costs of production and thereby reduce the supply of medical services in the medical marketplace. The reduction of supply occurs because the acquisition of a professional license requires a greater human capital investment by the medical employee that raises the cost of providing the medical service. Figure 11–10 shows the implications of a quality regulation, such as professional licensing. The original supply and demand curves for medical employees are $S_0$ and $D_0$ and the corresponding market wage and employment levels are $W_0$ and $N_0$ respectively. Professional licensing, which raises the cost of entering an occupation due to the increased human capital investment, reduces supply to $S_1$ and thereby raises the wage rate to $W_1$. The difference between $W_1$ and $W_0$ captures the **compensating wage differential** necessary to attract the marginal worker with the appropriate professional license to the labor market.

Two questions follow from the analysis. First, is professional licensing truly associated with increased procedural and outcomes quality? If not, the result may not justify the method of controlling quality. Second, was a professional group behind the implementation of the professional licensing requirement? This question follows because

## FIGURE 11-10    EFFECT OF PROFESSIONAL LICENSURE

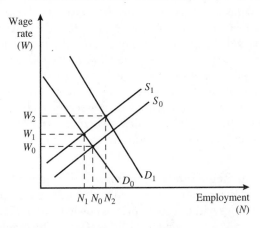

those inframarginal individuals in the labor group (especially those who lack the required license but are grandfathered in) obviously gain from the higher wage rate.

Svorny (1987) provides an interesting way to analyze the second question by comparing a professional license to a trademark or brand name. All three of these devices may signal quality assurance to consumers. Specifically, Svorny argues that the higher wage resulting from the professional license creates a financial incentive for the typical medical worker to perform efficiently, satisfy patient wants, and provide a desirable amount and quality of output. This is because opportunistic behavior, when discovered, results in job termination and causes the medical worker to receive a low or negative return on the original human capital investment. The quality assurance generated by the higher wage, in turn, raises the marginal value of the employee's services to the consumer. The higher quality assurance can be represented by a shift to the right of the demand curve from $D_0$ to $D_1$ in figure 11–10.

Due to the greater demand arising from the increased quality assurance, the wage rate increases further to $W_2$ and employment rises from $N_1$ to $N_2$. Svorny goes on to note that the model provides a useful test of whether professional licensure requirements (and other quality regulations) serve the public interest or some special interest group, such as the entrenched medical employees. If the quality regulation provides benefits (quality assurance) that exceed its cost (human capital investment), the shift of the demand curve to the right should be greater in magnitude than the shift of the supply curve to the left. Thus, employment should increase overall if society is made better off and the public interest is served by the quality regulation (i.e., $N_2$ should exceed $N_0$). However, if the opposite occurs—the supply curve shifts to the left by more than the demand curve shifts to the right—the quality regulation favors special interests.

Svorny used the analysis to test whether basic science certification and citizen requirements for medical licensure made any difference in the number of physicians per capita across the 48 contiguous states of the United States in 1965. She noted that both requirements potentially involve some degree of human capital investment that increases wages and establishes a future return to discourage opportunistic behavior. Using multiple regression analysis, Svorny found an inverse relation between both requirements and the number of physicians. The theory suggests an inverse relation is evidence for the special interest model of the regulatory process.

The implication is that these quality regulations result in lower rather than higher consumption of physician services. A lower consumption of physician services results because the licensure restrictions increased entry costs by more than they increased the consumer benefits from quality assurance. Overall, the study found evidence supporting the special interest group theory of the regulatory process.

**Government Regulations: A Summary**    As should be evident from the preceding discussion, it is very difficult to predict, before the fact, the precise impact of government regulations without some prior knowledge of market structure, cost conditions, and the objectives of the medical firms. Generally, regulations are more likely to inhibit efficiency when markets are competitive and the exclusion principle holds (no externalities or third-party payments) and more likely to promote efficiency when markets are monopolistic and the exclusion principle does not hold. Remember that monopoly power can accrue to medical firms if consumers are price insensitive or uninformed and the marketplace is structured in a noncompetitive manner. Of course, one way to judge the welfare implications of a regulation after the fact is to observe empirically its impact on performance indicators such as the price, quantity, and quality of medical services. In practice, this requires a sound empirical study based on a solid grounding in health economic theory.

## Antitrust Laws

Government also intervenes in a market economy by enacting and enforcing antitrust laws. Antitrust laws are concerned primarily with promoting competition among the firms within an industry and prohibiting firms from engaging in certain types of market practices that may inhibit efficiency. The Sherman Antitrust Act, passed in 1890, is the cornerstone of all antitrust laws. Other antitrust laws, such as the Clayton Act of 1914, the Federal Trade Commission Act of 1914, and the Cellar-Kefauver Amendment of 1950, either clarify, reinforce, or extend the Sherman Act. The Sherman Act stipulates two important provisions:

> **Section 1:** Every contract, combination in the form of trust or otherwise, or conspiracy, in restraint of trade or commerce among the several states or with foreign nations, is hereby declared illegal.

> **Section 2:** Every person who shall monopolize, or conspire with any other person or persons to monopolize any part of the trade or commerce among the several states, or with foreign nations, shall be guilty of a misdemeanor.

The Sherman Antitrust Act has been interpreted as prohibiting anticompetitive business practices, such as price fixing, boycotting, market allocations, and mergers, that promote inefficiencies and inequities in the marketplace. **Price fixing** occurs when business rivals in an industry abide to a collusive agreement, refrain from price competition, and fix the price of a good or service. Essentially, the firms collectively act as a monopolist, maximize joint profits, and, according to monopoly theory, create a higher price and a lower level of output. An agreement among a number of large hospitals to establish the price of various hospital services is an example of price fixing. Physicians who have been denied staff privileges frequently allege that the existing hospital physicians violated Section 1 of the Sherman Act by unlawfully conspiring to exclude them from the hospital (Jacobsen and Wiggins, 1992).[9]

A **boycott** is an agreement among competitors not to deal with a supplier or a customer. For example, suppose that in response to a Blue Shield ban on balance billing, the physicians in an area collectively agree not to offer services to Blue Shield patients.[10] While it is legal for any one physician to unilaterally refrain from dealing with Blue Shield, the combination is in violation of the Sherman Antitrust Act. In this case, the rival physicians are essentially trying to fix the price of medical services charged to Blue Shield subscribers.

**Market allocation** occurs when competitors agree not to compete with one another in specific market areas. This business practice can ultimately produce the same undesirable outcome that price fixing does, since each firm within the area is free to set a monopoly price and restrict output with no concern about competitive entry.

Price fixing, boycotting, and market allocations are *illegal per se;* that is, they are unreasonable by their very nature and therefore illegal. To be found in violation of the Sherman Act, the plaintiff must only prove that those practices took place.

The Sherman Act (in conjunction with Section 7 of the Clayton Act) has also been cited as a basis for preventing horizontal mergers among firms. A **horizontal merger** takes place when two or more firms in the same industry combine together. The economic concern is that a merger may harm consumers by making it easier for the remaining firms in the market to collude, expressly or tacitly (e.g., by following the leader), and thereby force price above the competitive level.

Although a combination of two or more competitor firms can result in higher prices to the consumer, the merger may also benefit the consumer if economies exist with respect to large-scale production. Larger firms may not only produce with economies of scale and organizational economies but also have better access to technological innovations. Any cost or resource savings mean society can produce more output from a given amount of inputs. For example, according to hospital officials, a proposed merger of the 710-bed Iowa Methodist Medical Center and the 319-bed Iowa Lutheran Hospital in Des Moines "could save as much as $12 million annually during the first three years of the merger" (Burda, 1993, p. 24). Similarly, officials at

---

[9]See Felsenthal (1992) for an insightful discussion of how physicians and hospitals have attempted to fend off low-cost competitors, such as nurse-midwives, chiropractors, and optometrists.

[10]A physician boycott of this kind occurred in *Kartell v. Blue Shield of Massachusetts*, 749 F.2d 922 (1984). See Frech (1988) for an economic assessment of this antitrust suit.

**FIGURE 11-11**     WILLIAMSON'S MERGER TRADE-OFF

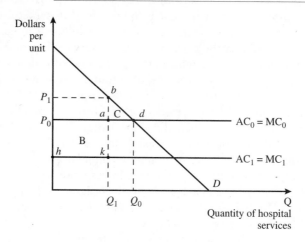

St. Joseph Mercy and North Iowa Medical in Mason City claimed their proposed merger "would reduce their operating expenses by $2 million to $3 million per year." Thus, potential anticompetitive and procompetitive effects must be properly weighed when determining the social desirability of a merger. Assessing the net social benefits of a business practice such as a merger is referred to as the **rule of reason** doctrine.

The Williamson (1969) merger trade-off model in figure 11-11 provides an insightful way to conceptualize the net social benefit of a horizontal merger. Suppose the market in some geographical area is competitive before the merger and the industry is characterized by constant costs. As a result, the market price and quantity of hospital services are $P_0$ and $Q_0$, respectively, where the demand curve intersects the original marginal cost curve, $MC_0$. Now suppose a merger of two hospitals in the area makes it easier for the remaining firms to collude and reduce output to $Q_1$ and raise price to $P_1$. Relative to the original competitive equilibrium, a deadweight loss of area *bad* occurs. The deadweight loss reflects the social cost, C, associated with the merger.

Suppose that due to the horizontal merger and the associated greater production efficiency, the per-unit cost of producing hospital services declines from $AC_0$ to $AC_1$. Cost savings might accrue from economies of scale at the firm level, improved access to capital markets, purchasing discounts, or managerial economies. This reflects some important resource cost savings to society. Resources are saved and can be used for other purposes if a larger firm is more efficient in production. Compared to the costs in a competitive market, the total resource cost savings is measured by area $P_0akh$. The area reflects the social benefit, B, that arises from the merger. The net benefit of the merger is found by subtracting the deadweight loss of area C from the resource cost savings of area B. As drawn, the merger provides positive net benefits to society. Of course, actual mergers may cause net benefits or losses depending on the relative magnitudes of the cost savings and deadweight losses. The bottom line is that a proposed horizontal merger should be given careful scrutiny using cost-benefit analysis.

Although the Sherman Act was enacted in 1890, the health care field escaped its purview until the mid-1970s.[11] Up to that time, it was believed that members of the medical profession, like other professionals, such as lawyers and engineers, were exempted from antitrust laws. In the *Goldfarb v. Virginia State Bar* case of 1975, the Supreme Court unanimously rejected any claim to a professional exemption and stated

> The nature of an occupation, standing alone, does not provide sanctuary from the Sherman Act . . . nor is the public service aspect of professional practice controlling in determining whether section 1 includes professions.

Some early signs appear to indicate that the courts may aggressively enforce antitrust laws in health care markets. For example, in *Arizona v. Maricopa County Medical Society* in 1982, the Supreme Court condemned as price fixing the attempt by a professionally sponsored foundation to set a maximum price on the fees charged to member physicians for services underwritten by insurers that had agreed to abide by the foundation's fee schedule. Typically, when firms collude and pursue their joint interests, they agree to a price floor rather than a price ceiling. The foundation claimed the maximum price was fixed for the benefit of the consumer. In this particular case, the Supreme Court invoked the per se illegality of price fixing, but opened the door to a possible rule of reason ruling in the future. The Court explained that the public service aspect and other features of the medical profession may require that a particular practice that could be properly viewed as a violation of the Sherman Act in another context be treated differently. The Court went on to explain that in *Maricopa*, the price-fixing arrangement was premised on neither public service nor ethical norms nor quality of care considerations.

Two recent merger cases, *Hospital Corporation of America v. FTC* (807 F.2d 1381 [7th Cir. 1986]) and *U.S. v. Rockford Memorial Corporation* (898 F.2d 1278 [7th Cir. 1990]) also demonstrate the Court's willingness to enforce antitrust laws aggressively and disallow horizontal mergers in the hospital services industry if they tend to lessen competition. In the *Rockford* case, for example, the U.S. government brought suit to prevent the horizontal merger of Rockford Memorial Corporation and Swedish American Corporation, both of which are nonprofit institutions. Citing a high postmerger market share and, consequently, the potential for monopoly pricing, the Court ruled against the merger.[12]

However, not all health policy analysts believe antitrust laws should be stringently enforced in the health services industries. Some argue that various institutions, such as third-party payments, nonprofit organizations, and excessive government regulations, mean that antitrust laws are less applicable and necessary in health care markets

---

[11]See Havighurst (1983) and Kopit (1983) for a thorough discussion of the application of antitrust laws to the health care industry.

[12]More discussion of merger policy in the hospital industry is provided in Chapter 15.

than in other markets. With health care costs continually increasing, many analysts claim that the enforcement of antitrust laws could actually worsen the situation as cost-minimizing joint ventures and mergers are discouraged. Indeed, recent legislation in Maine, Minnesota, Ohio, Wisconsin, and Washington allows hospitals to cooperate if the benefits of the proposed venture substantially outweigh the disadvantages of any reduction in competition (Felsenthal 1993). In 1993, the Department of Justice and the Federal Trade Commission issued a joint statement of antitrust enforcement in health care markets, basically echoing the notion that the procompetitive and anticompetitive effects of various business activities, such as mergers, joint ventures, joint purchasing, and provider networks, will be weighed when making an antitrust determination.[13]

In contrast, other analysts believe antitrust laws are necessary for promoting price competition and encouraging cost containment. Antitrust policies are claimed to foster competition and discourage monopolistic practices, thus giving firms an incentive to satisfy consumer wants and to produce and price at minimum costs. For example, HMOs are beginning to wield considerable pricing power, leading some doctors to form a united negotiating front to counteract their power (Anders, 1993). As a result, the Justice Department and the Federal Trade Commission have recently enforced antitrust laws against various groups of doctors, claiming that physicians have engaged in price fixing and the boycotting of certain HMOs. Overall, however, it remains to be seen how stringently and consistently antitrust laws are enforced in the various health care markets.

### Public Enterprise

Instead of indirectly influencing the structure, conduct, or performance of private industry, government may take a more direct role in health care provision by producing and distributing a specific health care service. For example, many local governments are responsible for providing county and city hospital services to local residents. In addition, some nursing homes and mental health facilities are operated by local or state government agencies. Moreover, the federal government runs and operates Veteran Administration and military hospitals. Despite the fact that the government may operate health care facilities, economic analysis is still useful for analyzing the many production decisions that take place. Valuable resources are used in production, and some type of economizing behavior occurs.

The primary difference between public enterprise and private, for-profit enterprise is the lack of a profit motive. Like not-for-profit entities, public health care providers may pursue goals other than profit maximization. The upshot is that public health care providers may not minimize the cost of producing a given quantity of medical care services or attempt to satisfy consumer wants. Of course, even public agencies are subject to least-cost constraints of various kinds. For example, bureaucrats and politicians are either directly or indirectly influenced by the consumer/voters' response

---

[13]See http://www.ftc.gov/reports/hlth35.htm#2.

to excessive taxation. The potential loss of job tenure may create a sufficient incentive for cost minimization even in public facilities.

Many analysts argue that public medical facilities are more likely to provide services to the more severely ill patients. Unlike their for-profit (and even not-for-profit) counterparts, public medical facilities do not have to worry about the profit consequence of servicing high-cost patients. Therefore, public provision of medical services is often argued to be more equitable because all individuals, rich and poor, are provided with equal access to public facilities.

Lindsay (1976) developed a useful model of government enterprise that may explain why public hospitals tend to operate with lower per-unit costs of production than proprietary hospitals. The author assumed that politicians tie managerial compensation to the level of net social income that public organizations generate. Net social income, an analogue to profits in the private sector, is the difference between the social value of the output and the total cost of production. Higher managerial pay results from a higher level of net social income.

To estimate the value of the output provided by the public agency, politicians monitor the levels of various attributes associated with the product. Some attributes are observable and measurable; others are not. Bureau managers, in pursuit of higher pay, face an incentive to divert resources away from the production of attributes that are not easily measurable to those that are to increase the perceived social value of their output. Therefore, a financial incentive exists to make the output of public institutions contain too few "invisible" attributes, such as quality (as reflected in the number of staff visits to a hospital ward, words of encouragement, number of smiles, etc.), and too many visible attributes, such as quantity (e.g., number of patients). Lindsay's model of government enterprise predicts that the average cost of government enterprise—that is, total cost divided by visible output—will be lower than the comparable average cost of proprietary enterprise.[14] The author offers some empirical evidence to support his view of government enterprise.

## The Redistribution Function of Government

In addition to providing public goods, correcting for externalities, enforcing regulations and antitrust laws, and operating public enterprises, another function of government is to redistribute income more equitably because a pure market system cannot guarantee that everyone receives an adequate level of income. Some people own very little labor, capital, and land resources, and hence are often unable to generate a subsistence level of income in the marketplace. Redistribution involves taxing one group and using the resulting tax revenues to provide subsidies to another group. One may question why people in a free democratic society, such as that of the United States, support redistribution and rely on government to administer various programs. One

---

[14]Managers of private organizations are disciplined to a greater degree by the marketplace and forced by consumer demand to provide the desired level of quality. Price fails if private firms fail to satisfy the quality demands of customers, unlike in a public agency, where price is essentially fixed by politicians.

justification for redistribution advanced by economists is the existence of interdependent utility functions such that donors get utility from increasing the welfare of recipients. More formally, when utility functions are interdependent, person A derives utility when person B is made better off. Person B might be made better off by receiving some income or benefits in kind, such as housing or food, from person A.

Consequently, redistribution takes place in a free society because it provides utility to both recipient and donor groups. Government must administer and require people by law to contribute to the redistribution scheme through taxation because some people in the donor group might otherwise attempt to "free-ride" the voluntary contributions of others. For example, person C may also derive utility if person B is made better off, but may attempt to free-ride by relying on the sole contributions of person A to finance the redistribution program. Person A, in turn, may decide not to voluntarily contribute to the redistribution scheme given that others, such as person C, will indirectly benefit but will not share in the overall costs. Given the likelihood of a free-rider problem on a large scale, redistribution tends to be underprovided in a free market. So, in effect, government acts as an intermediary or fiscal agent by legally stipulating and collecting the necessary taxes from the donor group and redistributing the income to the recipient group.

For a redistribution scheme to be considered equitable, the two principles of *vertical* and *horizontal equity* must be satisfied. **Vertical equity** means that "unequals are treated unequally." To determine whether this principle has been satisfied in practice, a standard of comparison must first be selected. In terms of financial equity, the usual standard of comparison is income. As a result, the principle of vertical equity is satisfied when people with higher incomes are treated differently than those with lower incomes. This principle by itself, however, does not establish whether the net taxes (i.e., taxes less subsidies) of higher-income people should be higher or lower than those of people with lower incomes. Therefore, notions of fairness dictate that net taxes be based on "ability to pay"; that is, those with more ability to pay should incur a greater net tax liability.

Even this additional principle is ambiguous, because it is unclear how much more net taxes higher-income people should pay or whether taxes, when assessing burden, should be expressed in absolute terms or as a fraction of income. For example, suppose a household with $10,000 of income pays $2,000 in net taxes and another household with $100,000 pays $4,000 in net taxes. In absolute terms, the richer household pays more taxes. When taxes are expressed as a fraction of income, however, taxes comprise only 4 percent of the rich household's income compared to 20 percent of the poor household's income.

In practice, many consider that vertical equity is achieved when the net tax system is sufficiently progressive. A redistribution scheme is considered to be **progressive** if net taxes as a fraction of income increase with income. Ignoring the subsidy side of the redistribution issue, the federal income tax system comes closest to being a progressive tax scheme. The underlying belief is that higher-income individuals should pay more taxes in both absolute and relative terms.

In a **proportional** redistribution scheme, net taxes as a fraction of income remain constant with respect to income. The Medicare tax is a proportional tax because all payroll income is subject to a fixed percentage rate.

# Why Government Should Subsidize Medical Students' Education

Cutler (1993) argued that the U.S. government should pay for the entire cost of a medical student's education just as governments do in most European countries, Canada, and Japan. Cutler claimed that a subsidy directed toward medical education will promote better access to medical services and help control costs.

It is clear that significant changes are required in the health-care system. There appears to be general agreement that these changes should focus on controlling cost, providing access to adequate care and ensuring that the quality of care remains high. In the debate over how to achieve these goals, comparisons are commonly made between the health-care systems in the United States and countries such as Britain, Germany, Sweden, France, Japan and Canada. These comparisons usually focus on the cost of care and how it is delivered.

Strikingly missing from these discussions is the fact that college and medical education is funded by the national government in these countries. The cost of this subsidy is not included in the reported cost of health care abroad. Acceptance of this financial responsibility gives these countries a degree of control over the system and helps them manage costs, provide access and ensure quality. All of the currently popular approaches to health-care reform have failed to acknowledge or incorporate the funding of medical education as an ingredient in the solution.

While there may be no overall shortage of physicians, the nation does suffer from insufficient numbers of general practitioners. Further, rural and inner-city areas have shortages of virtually all types of physicians. The number of U.S. medical school graduates has fallen 6 percent in the past eight years. Despite the use of about 17,500 foreign medical graduates, several thousand hospital residency positions currently go unfilled.

How will this country develop the number of generalists needed to treat the current patient population and the additional people who will seek care when access is broadened? How will physicians be encouraged to practice in underserved areas? What will induce our best and brightest college graduates to endure the economic and personal sacrifices required to go to medical school and to become health-care practitioners?

Students seeking a career in medicine must commit 11 years and tens of thousands of dollars to their education. According to the Association of American Medical Colleges, "The mean indebtedness for all 1990 (medical) graduates was $46,224 with 31.6 percent having debt in excess of $50,000." As governmental support for tuition grants and scholarships decreases, the indebtedness of medical graduates continues to rise. In 1992, more than 80 percent of medical school graduates had taken on some degree of debt to help pay for their education. To a large extent, debt drives many graduates into the more lucrative medical specialties and away from the fields that offer lower financial return.

The Association of American Medical Colleges has shown that students who graduated in 1990 with a debt of $75,000 needed incomes of $145,000 a year just five years after graduation from medical school to reasonably manage the loan repayments. However, these new physicians spend their first three years after graduation in internships and residencies at salaries in the $30,000–$40,000 range. They will enter medical practice at about 30 years of age, having dedicated many years and more than $100,000 to their education and facing a substantial debt.

Students in the comparison countries go to school for free and do not accumulate debt. They have no education-related financial

*(continued)*

**(continued)**

problems driving them into high-paying specialties. Because these societies accept responsibility for funding health-care education, they retain the right to determine the numbers of students entering each specialty. They can direct, to some extent, where the graduates practice. And they can control the level of reimbursement for service. The degree to which each of these countries exercises these prerogatives varies, but all accept their responsibility to fund education as a prerequisite to controlling the health-care system. Compared with these countries, the United States bears little of the costs of health-care education.

Surprisingly, the annual cost to society to fund the tuition for all students would be remarkably small—about $900 million. This translates into about one-tenth of a cent for every dollar spent on health care or less than one-half of one cent for every dollar spent to administer the health-care system each year. With the acceptance of this responsibility, we would likely encourage more students to enter the healing professions while gaining several rights that can, in the long run, open access and help control costs.

SOURCE: Leslie S. Cutter, "Why Government Should Pay for Medical Students' Education," *Hartford Courant*, January 27, 1993, p. D13. Reprinted by permission of Leslie S. Cutler.

Finally, net taxes as a fraction of income fall with income if the redistribution scheme is **regressive**. A sales tax is generally considered to be a regressive tax because although everyone pays the same tax rate, consumption expenditures as a fraction of income tend to decrease with income.

**Horizontal equity** means that "equals should be treated equally." Using income as the standard of comparison, horizontal equity implies that individuals with the same income should pay the same amount of net taxes. If not, the resulting outcome is not fair according to the principle of horizontal equity.

With these principles of horizontal and vertical equity in mind, let's examine supply-side and demand-side subsidies as different ways to redistribute medical services.

**Supply-Side Subsidies**   A **supply-side subsidy** is essentially a grant of money from a third party that is aimed at reducing the internal costs of producing some consumer-oriented good or service. As an example, the subsidy may be awarded to an institution like a public hospital or used to finance the education of an important labor input, such as a nurse or physician. A supply-side subsidy typically expands the production of a good in the marketplace by lowering the marginal private cost of production. Given a downward-sloping market demand curve, the net price (market price less subsidy) of the good to the consumer declines and quantity demanded increases.

In the absence of any positive externalities, economists generally argue that a supply-side subsidy leads to a misallocation of resources in a market economy. The subsidy distorts market prices and provides a false signal that production is cheaper than it really is. Output in the subsidized sector expands and resources are drawn from nonsubsidized sectors. Hence, too much output is produced in the subsidized sector

## Who Pays for Medical Services in the United States?

As discussed in the text, vertical equity holds when the net tax burden, expressed as a fraction of income, increases with income. With equity analysis in mind, Holahan and Zedlewski (1992) analyzed the distribution of the health care financing burden associated with the current U.S. health care system. Specifically, the authors determined the financing burden on the nonelderly population in 1989 and took into account employer and employee contributions to health insurance premiums, private nongroup insurance premiums, out-of-pocket expenses, tax savings resulting from the exemption on employer-paid health benefits, and the taxes paid to finance Medicaid, Medicare, and the health benefit tax exclusion.

A microsimulation model employing demographic, economic, and health insurance data from the 1990 *Current Population Survey* was used to assign the various types of health care expenses and tax payments to nonelderly families in different income brackets. Data were also used from a variety of other sources that detail health care spending in the United States. For the families in each income decile, the assignment considered the type of insurance (e.g., private versus public and employer-based versus nongroup insurance), the extent of insurance coverage based on premiums, if any, and the amount of income and payroll taxes paid into the system.

The results showed that the distribution of the health care financing burden is regressive. People in the lowest income decile devoted nearly 20 percent of their cash income to finance health care compared with about 8 percent for people in the highest income decile. However, the authors failed to deduct the value of the Medicaid benefits and uncompensated care typically received by the families in each income decile from their financing burden to determine the "net" tax burden. After correcting for the receipt of medical subsidies, the net financial burden of people in the lowest income decile was about −27 percent.[1] As we might expect, people in the lowest income decile were more likely to receive Medicaid benefits and uncompensated care, and the value of the benefits, on average, exceeded the amount paid into the system. The equivalent fraction for people in the highest income decile remained at approximately 8 percent because Medicaid benefits and uncompensated care constituted such a small amount. In addition, the adjusted results imply that the net financial burden initially rose from the first to the fourth income decile (to about 12 percent), remained roughly constant over the fourth to seventh income decile, and declined thereafter. Consequently, the net financial burden of the health care system appears to fall disproportionately on the middle-income classes.

[1]Authors' estimates based on figures provided in the study by John Holahan and Sheila Zedlewski, "Who Pays for Health Care in the United States? Implications for Health System Reform," *Inquiry* 29 (summer 1992), pp. 231–48.

and not enough resources are allocated to the nonsubsidized sectors. Some economists also argue that supply-side subsidies are an inequitable way of redistributing income. Because the subsidies are directed at the supply side of the market, individuals with different levels of income similarly benefit from the lower prices at the subsidized firms. Rich and poor alike end up paying the same price when redistribution takes place with a supply-side subsidy. Therefore, the principle of vertical equity is sometimes compromised with a supply-side subsidy.

**Demand-Side Subsidies** Because a supply-side subsidy is often viewed as inefficient because it distorts resource allocation and as inequitable because it benefits all rather than only poor consumers, many economists favor **demand-side subsidies.** Often (but not always, as in the case of Medicare or the tax exemption on health care benefits) people must qualify for demand-side aid by passing a means test. A means test requires that a household of a certain size has a combined income below some stipulated level to be eligible for the aid. Tying eligibility to household income is one way to satisfy the principles of vertical and horizontal equity. In practice, however, the principle of horizontal equity is violated for Medicaid services because the 50 states specify different guidelines for income eligibility.

One type of demand-side aid is an **in-kind** subsidy that provides needy individuals with specific goods or vouchers for such items as food, housing, medical services, or transportation. The food stamp program, Medicare, and Medicaid are examples of in-kind subsidies. A second type of demand-side aid is a cash subsidy. People are granted a certain amount of income that they can use to purchase various goods and services of their own choice. Aid to Families with Dependent Children (AFDC) and the Supplemental Security Income (SSI) programs provide recipients with cash subsidies. The in-kind subsidy attempts to increase the quantity demanded of a specific good, whereas the cash subsidy is designed to increase the demand for various goods based on the recipient's preferences. Both programs are typically funded by taxes and do not directly affect the prices of the goods and services in the marketplace as long as the subsidized individuals are relatively few in number. A cash subsidy is preferred over in-kind aid if the goal of the donor group is to raise the utility of the recipients to the highest possible level for a given amount of transfer payments. The cash subsidy provides more utility per dollar because recipients are free to choose how they spend the money. If the donor group's goal is to ensure that the recipients consume at least a minimal amount of some specific goods, it can more easily target specific purchases with in-kind aid given the difficulty associated with enforcing spending restrictions on cash subsidies.

### SUMMARY

Government intervention is often necessary to correct situations where the market fails to allocate resources efficiently or distribute income fairly. In this context, government has been assigned the task of providing public goods, correcting externalities, redistributing income, and regulating the marketplace. We should keep in mind, however, that market failure is a necessary but not a sufficient condition for government intervention. Although markets may fail and impose costs on society, the costs of government intervention may be much greater. For example, it may cost the government $10 million in labor and capital costs to correct a problem in the marketplace that is imposing $8 million of damages on society. If so, it is efficient to leave the problem uncorrected. Also, both markets and governments fail in certain circumstances. One objective of economics is to determine which institution can provide which particular services in the most efficient and equitable manner.

## Review Questions and Problems

1. Discuss the two views of government intervention in a market-based health care system. What role does the politician play in both of these views?

2. Health officials have suggested that the spread of AIDS can be partly contained if more males use condoms while engaging in sexual intercourse. Use the concept of a demand-side externality to explain why the number of condoms sold in the United States is likely to be lower than the optimal number. Explain some ways the government might promote a more optimal use of condoms.

3. Draw a perfectly competitive market model for nursing home services. Discuss the effect of an all-payer price ceiling on allocative efficiency, transfer of surplus between producer and consumer, and the quality of nursing home care. Also, examine the effect of an all-payer price ceiling on a profit-maximizing, monopolistic nursing home and a situation where nursing home decision makers maximize the utility derived from the quantity and quality of nursing home services. How might the results change in all three cases if the price ceiling pertained only to some and not all buyers? Explain.

4. The discussion on price ceilings supposed that the medical firm faces increasing marginal costs of production. Suppose a for-profit, monopolistic hospital is experiencing economies of scale (i.e., downward-sloping average and marginal cost curves) in the relevant range. Show graphically and discuss in writing the problems associated with a price ceiling set where the demand curve intersects the marginal cost curve and a price ceiling set where the demand curve intersects the average cost curve. Think in terms of allocative efficiency and financial solvency.

5. A price floor with entry restrictions reduces output and promotes nonprice competition in a perfectly competitive goods market. Similarly, a wage floor in a competitive market causes unemployment (you might work through the graphical proof). Suppose, however, that a hospital in some area is a monopsony buyer in the market for nurses (you might look back at the monopsony model in Chapter 9). Graphically examine and discuss in writing how a government or a union could increase the wage rate (i.e., set a wage floor) and actually raise the employment level of nurses.

6. Allied health professionals (e.g., social workers) are required by law to possess a professional certificate in some states; in others, they are not. Assuming sufficient data exist, discuss how you might test empirically whether this law exists to protect the public interest or to provide benefits to special interests.

7. Minnesota and Tennessee, among other states, have recently begun to tax the sales of health care providers, such as hospitals and physicians. Analyze the incidence of this sales tax for three different scenarios: (*a*) The demand for medical services is completely inelastic, while the supply curve is positively sloped to the right; (*b*) the demand curve is downward sloping and supply is completely inelastic (for this case, it is best to shift the demand curve downward by the amount of the per-unit tax); and (*c*) the demand curve is downward sloping and the supply curve is positively sloped. When does the consumer or the health care provider pay a larger portion of the tax? Why?

8. Do you think subsidies should be provided to lower the cost of a medical education? Why or why not? Use a graphical model in your explanation, if possible.

9. Answer the following questions regarding redistribution.

 *a.* Why must the government perform the redistribution function?

 *b.* What are horizontal and vertical equity?

 *c.* What are the differences among proportional, progressive, and regressive taxation?

 *d.* What are the three ways subsidies can be provided in practice?

 *e.* Comment on the relative efficiency and equity of these three methods.

10. Define *price fixing, boycotting,* and *market allocations.* How have these business practices been viewed by the courts? Explain.

11. Discuss why the courts use a rule of reason when determining whether to allow a horizontal merger.

12. According to Lindsay (1976), why are the average costs of production likely to be lower for a public hospital than for an otherwise identical private hospital?

## *References*

Aaron, Henry J., and William B. Schwartz. *The Painful Prescription: Rationing Hospital Care.* Washington, DC: Brookings Institution, 1984.

Anders, George. "Regulators Aim at Fees Doctors Charge HMOs." *The Wall Street Journal,* May 14, 1993, p. B1.

Baker, James N. "Blood in the Water." *Newsweek,* July 18, 1988, p. 35.

Becker, Gary S. "A Theory of Competition among Pressure Groups for Political Influence." *Quarterly Journal of Economics* 93 (August 1983), pp. 371–400.

Blum, Justin. "Insurance PACs Increase Giving." *Norwich Bulletin,* July 23, 1992.

Burda, David. "Flurry of Merger Plans Has Eyes Focused on Iowa." *Modern Healthcare,* April 12, 1993.

Coase, Ronald. "The Problem of Social Cost." *Journal of Law and Economics* 3 (October 1960), pp. 1–44.

Cromwell, Jerry. "Hospital Productivity Trends in Short-Term General Nonteaching Hospitals." *Inquiry* 11, no. 2 (1976), pp. 181–87.

Cutler, Leslie S. "Why Government Should Pay for Medical Students' Education." *Hartford Courant,* January 27, 1993, p. D13.

Felsenthal, Edward. "New Rules Let Hospitals Start Joint Ventures." *The Wall Street Journal,* May 14, 1993, p. B1.

———. "Antitrust Suits Are on the Rise in Health Field." *The Wall Street Journal,* October 29, 1992, p. B1.

Frech, H. E. "Monopoly in Health Insurance: The Economics of *Kartell v. Blue Shield of Massachusetts.*" In *Health Care in America,* edited by H. F. Frech. San Francisco: Pacific Research Institute for Public Policy, 1988, pp. 293–322.

Globerman, Steven. "A Policy Analysis of Hospital Waiting Lists." *Journal of Policy Analysis and Management* 10 (spring 1991), pp. 247–62.

Havighurst, Clark C. "The Contributions of Antitrust Law to a Procompetitive Health Policy." In *Market Reforms in Health Care,* edited by Jack A. Meyer. Washington, DC: American Enterprise Institute, 1983, pp. 295–322.

Holahan, John, and Sheila Zedlewski. "Who Pays for Health Care in the United States? Implications for Health System Reform." *Inquiry* 29 (summer 1992), pp. 231–48.

Jacobsen, Raymond A. Jr., and Robert B. Wiggins. "Denials of Staff Privileges Face Increased Antitrust Scrutiny." *Health Care Management Review* 17 (fall 1992). pp. 7–15.

Kopit, William G. "Health and Antitrust: The Case for Legislative Relief." In *Market Reforms in Health Care*, edited by Jack A. Meyer. Washington, DC: American Enterprise Institute, 1983, pp. 323–31.

Lindsay, Cotton M. "A Theory of Government Enterprise." *Journal of Political Economy* 84 (October 1976), pp. 1061–77.

Makinson, Larry. "Political Contributions from the Health and Insurance Industries." *Health Affairs* 11 (winter 1992), pp. 119–34.

Manning, Willard G., et al. "The Taxes of Sin: Do Smokers and Drinkers Pay Their Way?" *Journal of the American Medical Association* (March 17, 1989), pp. 1604–09.

Murray, Alan. "Health Care: A Magic Asterisk." *The Wall Street Journal*, January 25, 1993, p. Al.

Musgrave, Richard A., and Peggy B. Musgrave. *Public Finance in Theory and Practice*. New York: McGraw-Hill, 1989.

Ohsfeldt, Robert L., and Stephan F. Gohmann. "The Economics of AIDS-Related Health Insurance Regulations: Interest Group Influence and Ideology." *Public Choice* 74 (July 1992), pp. 105–26.

Peltzman, Sam. "Toward a More General Theory of Regulation." *Journal of Law and Economics* 19 (August 1976), pp. 211–40.

Rosen, Harvey S. *Public Finance*. Homewood, IL: Richard D. Irwin, Inc., 1995.

Rutala, William A., Robert L. Odette, and Gregory P. Samsa. "Management of Infectious Waste by U.S. Hospitals." *Journal of the American Medical Association* 262 (September 22–29, 1989), pp. 1635–40.

Saffer, Henry. "Alcohol Advertising Bans and Alcohol Abuse: An International Perspective." *Journal of Health Economics* 10 (1991), pp. 65–79.

Scanlon, William J. "A Theory of the Nursing Home Market." *Inquiry* 17 (spring 1980), pp. 25–40.

Stigler, George J. "The Theory of Economic Regulation." *Bell Journal of Economics and Management Sciences* 2 (1971), pp. 137–46.

Svorny, Shirley V. "Physician Licensure: A New Approach to Examining the Role of Professional Interests." *Economic Inquiry* 25 (July 1987), pp. 497–509.

Williamson, Oliver E. "Economies as an Antitrust Defense: Reply." *American Economic Review* 59 (December 1969), pp. 954–59.

## CEBS Questions

CEBS Sample Question on Subject Matter from CEBS Course IX Study Manual

1. Using the special interest group theory, identify the likely winners and losers from a favorable tax treatment policy for long-term care premiums. (page 306)

CEBS Sample Exam Questions

1. In a supply and demand model, what is the effect of a fee-for-service third-party price ceiling on physician services? (Assume consumers have full health insurance).

    A. The quantity demanded will exceed the quantity supplied and a shortage of physician services will be created

B. The price of physician services will increase

C. Supply and demand will not apply after the price ceiling is imposed

D. The demand curve for physician services will become kinked

E. Prices for physician services will become more volatile

2. The Sherman Antitrust Act has been interpreted as prohibiting anticompetitive business practices in health care that include which of the following?
I. Boycotting
II. Profit maximization
III. Price fixing
   A. I only
   B. III only
   C. I and II only
   D. I and III only
   E. I, II, and III

3. All the following are reasons for government intervention in a market-based health care system EXCEPT:
   A. Provision of public goods
   B. Correction for externalities
   C. Enforcement of regulations and anti-trust laws
   D. Redistribution of income
   E. Improvement in managerial quality

*Answer to Sample Question from Study Manual*

Owners of nursing homes, providers of services to such facilities, individuals suffering from debilitating diseases such as Alzheimer and strokes and their family members would be the winners. The loss of revenues resulting from such a policy would produce losers in the section of the population that relies heavily on public welfare programs and public funding.

*Answers to Sample Exam Questions*

1. A is the answer. The lower price creates an incentive for physicians to reduce the quantity supplied and for expenditures on physician services to decline. See pages 320 and 322 of the text.

2. D is the answer. Statements I and III are correct. Statement II is false, the Act doesn't prohibit businesses from maximizing profits. See pages 328–329 of the text.

3. E is the answer. The government doesn't exercise its instruments of taxation and subsidies in the market to alter the performance of managers. See page 333 of the text.

# 12

# Government as Health Insurer

E ver-rising medical care costs, coupled with an aging population, have forced the federal government to rethink its vital role as health insurer under the Medicaid and Medicare programs, two public health insurance programs that entail sizable public expenditures. Combined federal and state expenditures on Medicaid and Medicare totaled $350 billion or approximately 34 percent of all national health care spending in 1996 (Levit et al., 1998). Moreover, current population projections suggest that the percent of population 65 years and older will increase significantly from 12.7 percent in 2000 to 18.5 percent in 2025. An older population means that Medicare physician and hospital expenditures along with Medicaid nursing home expenditures should rise substantially in future years. As a result, the graying of American society has the potential of either imposing a lofty tax burden on the working generation in the early 21st century or requiring the elderly to pay greater out-of-pocket costs or both.

Given the importance of the Medicaid and Medicare programs, this chapter

- Describes the structure and operation of the Medicaid and Medicare programs.

- Discusses recent reforms that have taken place in the Medicaid and Medicare programs.

The information presented should be useful to you in your role as a concerned citizen, health care policymaker, or future recipient of Medicare services.

## Why Does the Government Produce Health Insurance?

In the case of the Medicare and Medicaid programs, which are the focus of this chapter, government acts as a *producer* of health insurance for certain segments of U.S.

society (elderly persons, some disadvantaged groups, and people with certain disabilities). As a producer, government collects the tax and/or premium revenues, bears some residual risk, and establishes the reimbursement paid to health care providers.[1] Economists normally argue that government should intervene when a market fails to allocate resources efficiently or distribute income equitably. As we saw in earlier chapters, an inefficient allocation of resources occurs when a small number of powerful sellers dominate the industry, barriers to entry are substantial, consumers lack perfect information, or the exclusion principle does not hold (i.e., externality or public good considerations). An inequitable distribution of income results when some people lack the production characteristics needed to generate a sufficient level of income in the private marketplace.

Usually, when markets fail, government intervenes by either subsidizing the prices of goods and services when inequities are present (e.g., food stamps and housing allowances) or regulating the production of goods and services when inefficiencies otherwise exist in an unregulated environment (e.g., electric utilities). That is, government typically subsidizes or regulates private production instead of directly producing the good or service. Consequently, the current system of public production of health insurance for certain population segments raises the following two related questions:

1. What is the source of market failure in the private health insurance industry that necessitates government intervention?

2. Why does the government act as a producer of health insurance for certain population segments?

Since individual buyers tend to internalize the benefit (i.e., financial security; see Chapter 5) health insurance provides, it appears that externality or public goods considerations can be ruled out. Also, as Chapter 13 confirms, private health insurers are numerous, and each insurer typically possesses a relatively small market share. In addition, barriers to entry are low, so a monopoly market structure cannot substantiate government intervention. Ruling out the exclusion principle and monopoly structure leaves imperfect information as the primary economic rationale for government intervention in the health insurance industry.

In particular, consider that public health insurance presently coexists with private for-profit (e.g., Metropolitan, Prudential, or Travelers) and private non-profit (Blue Cross/Blue Shield, and some freestanding HMOs and PPOs) health insurance in the United States. As we saw in Chapter 10, different forms of ownership may coexist in markets where imperfect information exists and demands for services are heterogeneous. The imperfect information exists because some consumers lack the information they need to understand the technical terms and conditions contained in health insurance policies. Think about it. The description and explanation of health insurance nomenclature, such as deductibles, copayments, benefit coverage, and

---

[1]The government often pays private health insurance companies to "administer" public health insurance. Private health insurers process the claims and pay the stipulated amounts to health care providers.

maximum liability, can be mind-boggling for even the most educated individuals (Garnick et al., 1993).

Individual consumers who are uninformed may feel vulnerable to noncompetitive behavior on the part of for-profit insurers and therefore may prefer to deal with not-for-profit insurance providers that they perceive as being less likely to profit from consumer ignorance. However, not all people are uninformed. Some people are fairly knowledgeable or belong to group policies represented by informed individuals. Informed consumers may be willing to deal with for-profit health insurance providers, especially when offered quality coverage at a low price.

As a result, it is likely that government acts as a producer of health insurance in the United States as a result of informational problems and an associated demand for government-produced health insurance by certain population segments. It should be noted that the Medicare and Medicaid programs were originally structured to provide health insurance to the "medically needy"—elderly, disabled, and poor individuals—a unique group in society. As a producer, the government not only subsidizes the health insurance to promote equity but also helps to avoid the inefficiencies normally associated with information imperfections in the private health insurance market.[2]

In 1964, President Lyndon Johnson declared a "war on poverty" and, as part of the overall package, Congress amended the Social Security Act of 1935 to include Title XVIII, the Medicare program, and Title XIX, the Medicaid program. The passage of these two pieces of legislation was a watershed of sorts because before that point, the federal government played only a minor role in the financing of health care services in the United States. In this section, we look more closely at the purpose and structure of Medicaid and Medicare.

# The Medicaid Program

The Medicaid program is designed to provide medical coverage to certain individuals with low incomes. Federal and state governments jointly share the cost of the program, but states administer the program and have wide latitude in determining eligibility and the medical benefits provided. As a result, it is difficult to describe the program except in the broadest of terms.

Eligibility under the Medicaid program is determined at the state level and varies extensively across states. At a minimum, states must provide medical coverage to most individuals covered under other federal income maintenance programs, such as the Aid to Families with Dependent Children and Supplemental Security Income programs, to receive matching federal funds. Among other additional requirements, states must also provide coverage to children under the age of six and to pregnant women whose family incomes are below 133 percent of the federal poverty level, and to all children born after September 1983 who are under 19 years of age and are in families with incomes at or below the federal poverty level. The federal government also requires that certain basic medical benefits be provided, such as (but not limited

---

[2]Due to imperfect information, adverse selection problems are also associated with the private provision of health insurance. See Chapter 13.

| TABLE 12-1 | TOTAL NUMBER OF MEDICAID RECIPIENTS, TOTAL VENDOR PAYMENTS FOR MEDICAID, AND PERCENT OF MANAGED CARE ENROLLMENT, SELECTED YEARS 1972–1996 |
| --- | --- |

| Year | Total Number of Recipients (millions) | Total Vendor Payments (millions) | Percent of Enrollees in Managed Care[1] |
| --- | --- | --- | --- |
| 1972 | 17.6 | $6,300 | — |
| 1975 | 22.0 | 12,242 | — |
| 1980 | 21.6 | 23,311 | — |
| 1985 | 21.8 | 37,508 | — |
| 1990 | 25.3 | 64,859 | — |
| 1991 | 28.3 | 77,048 | 9.5% |
| 1992 | 30.9 | 90,814 | 11.8 |
| 1993 | 33.4 | 101,709 | 14.4 |
| 1994 | 35.0 | 108,270 | 23.2 |
| 1995 | 36.3 | 120,141 | 29.4 |
| 1996 | 36.1 | 121,685 | 40.1 |

[1]Prior to 1991, managed care enrollment was either zero or negligible.

SOURCE: U.S. Department of Health and Human Services Social Security Administration, *Annual Statistical Supplement, 1996*, tables 8.E1 and 8.E2. The information on managed care was obtained from the Health Care Finance Administration Web page (http://www.hcfa.gov).

to) inpatient and outpatient hospital services, physician services, prenatal care, and vaccines for children.

As you can see from table 12–1, the total number of Medicaid recipients hovered between 21 million and 23 million throughout most of the 1970s and 1980s. At the close of the 1980s, however, things changed dramatically as economic growth stagnated throughout the country and changes in the Medicaid program expanded eligibility. From 1989 to 1993, the number of Medicaid recipients increased by over 40 percent to more than 33 million individuals. A breakdown of the recipients in 1996 shows that the single largest group was dependent children under age 21, accounting for 46 percent of the recipients. The next largest group, with 20 percent of the recipients, was adults with families of dependent children. This was followed by individuals with permanent and total disabilities (17 percent). Individuals 65 years of age and older accounted for 12 percent of the Medicaid enrollees. The remaining 5 percent includes the blind and others.

A look at total vendor payments per group tells a slightly different story. The lion's share of vendor payments went to individuals with permanent and total disabilities (42 percent). The next largest group was elderly persons, with 31 percent of total payments, followed by dependent children with 14 percent. Finally, adults of families with dependent children accounted for 10 percent of the medical payments. The change in order between the two groupings based on total recipients and total costs reflects the high cost of caring for elderly and disabled individuals. For example, in 1996 the average Medicaid payment for elderly and disabled persons was $8,622 and $9,142, respectively. For dependent children the average payment was only $1,048, and for adults it was just $1,722. Much of the difference is explained by the high cost of nursing home care for elderly and disabled Medicaid recipients.

## *The Financing and Cost of Medicaid*

Medicaid is financed jointly by the federal and state governments, with the federal portion varying between a low of 50 percent and a potential high of 83 percent in 1997. Those states with the lowest per capita income receive the largest federal subsidy. In 1997, a total of 11 states and the District of Columbia were reimbursed at the minimum level. Mississippi received the largest subsidy (77.22 percent) followed by Arkansas (73.29 percent). The average share subsidized by the federal government in 1997 was 57 percent.

The cost of the Medicaid program has increased substantially over time. As table 12–1 indicates, the Medicaid program cost a little more than $6 billion in 1972 and that figure ballooned to over $121 billion by 1996. A number of reasons account for this large increase in cost. First and foremost was a significant rise in the number of enrollees, especially between 1988 and 1993 when overall enrollments went from 22.9 million to over 33 million. The increase was primarily due to a number of changes in the Medicaid program that extended coverage to children and pregnant women. For example, federal mandates dictated that by 1990 Medicaid coverage was to be extended to children under the age of six and pregnant women in families with incomes below 133 percent of the federal poverty line. According to Holahan and Liska (1997), the federal mandate and other changes extended coverage to 4.5 million additional children and pregnant women.

Another reason for the increase in cost was a significant increase in medical prices that forced states over the years to increase reimbursement rates to medical care providers. High rates of medical price inflation and technological advances largely account for the increase in medical prices. Also coming into play was an increase in the number of elderly and disabled individuals in need of long-term medical care.

Efforts on the part of states to increase federal funding of Medicaid also contributed to rising Medicaid costs. As you can imagine, these efforts were met with some resistance from the federal government, which has had its own budgetary difficulties. Some of these efforts have been dubbed "Medicaid maximization" and involve shifting state-run health programs into the Medicaid program so that they will qualify for matching federal funds. Mental health and mental retardation services were the most common services shifted into state Medicaid programs (Coughlin et al., 1994).

Finally, **disproportionate share hospital payments** contributed to the rise in Medicaid expenditures. This was a way for states to acquire federal funds and help defer the expenses of hospitals that cared for a disproportionately high number of low-income individuals. Coughlin et al. describe these programs as follows:

# Interstate Differences in Medicaid Fees

Most analysts agree that the fees paid for Medicaid services tend to be notoriously low, especially when compared to the prices paid by other payers (e.g., Medicare and private insurers) for equivalent services. In fact, the Supreme Court recently ruled that health care providers, such as hospitals and nursing homes, may sue state governments to force them to provide adequate reimbursement for Medicaid services (Bacon, 1990). Price differentials are important, as research indicates that health care providers decide whether to participate in the treatment of Medicaid patients partly on the basis of how Medicaid fees compare to non-Medicaid prices. Generally, higher Medicaid fees tend to increase access to physician care for Medicaid enrollees. Thus, unreasonably low Medicaid fees can lead to access problems for Medicaid recipients.

Curious about the precise extent to which Medicaid fees vary across the states and among different payer types, Schwartz, Colby, and Reisinger (1991) reported on a survey concerning Medicaid fees for 23 different physician services in 1989. According to the authors, "Federal statute requires only that state Medicaid programs set physician fees that are sufficiently high to ensure reasonable access to care. Broad state discretion in setting those fees results in wide variations in fee levels" (p. 132).

For example, the results of the survey suggest that the lowest physician fee paid by a state Medicaid program for an established-patient, intermediate office visit was $10 in West Virginia, while the highest physician fee paid was $45 in Alaska. Similarly, the physician fee paid by the state Medicaid program for a routine electrocardiogram ranged from $10 in Florida to $55 in Alaska, while the physician fee paid for a vaginal delivery ranged from $200 in South Dakota to $901 in Georgia. Interstate physician fee differentials for the other services were typically even greater. The authors point out that the interstate physician fee disparity remains even after geographical cost-of-living differentials are considered and note that the variation in physician fees may reflect deliberate state Medicaid policy decisions.

The authors also compared Medicaid physician fees to the fees paid by Medicare and private health insurers for similar physician services in the 50 states. They found that Medicaid physician fees were typically 57 to 67 percent of the usual, customary, and reasonable (UCR) Medicare physician fees paid at that time (see the discussion in the text concerning UCR Medicare fees). In addition, the ratio of Medicaid to Medicare physician fees varied by state. For instance, the Medicaid to Medicare physician fee ratio for an intermediate office visit ranged from 35 percent in New York to 124 percent in Tennessee. For total hysterectomies, the ratio of Medicaid to Medicare fee ranged from 17 percent in New York to 145 percent in Georgia.

Finally, the authors show that the interstate ratio of the Medicaid to private insurer physician fee for a vaginal delivery averaged 53 percent and ranged from 18 percent in New Jersey to 100 percent in Nevada and South Carolina. Schwartz, Colby, and Reisinger concluded by noting that "Medicaid beneficiaries in different states may face different degrees of access to medical care simply because of where they reside" (p. 138). The varying degrees of access across states most likely violates the principle of horizontal equity.

---

Providers, usually hospitals, donated funds or paid a tax to the state. The states would then use the donations or tax revenue to make Medicaid payments and, in the transaction, receive federal matching dollars. Generally the programs operated so that providers were held harmless; that is, providers were refunded their full donations or tax contribution. Most often they received a bonus.

From 1992 through 1996 there was a decided drop in the rate of growth of Medicaid expenditures highlighted by a less than 1 percent increase in expenditures in 1996. Holahan and Liska (1997) note three reasons for this decline. First, there has been a slowdown in enrollment growth (enrollments actually fell in 1996). This slowdown can be attributed to an improved economy, which has caused fewer individuals to require aid; to states' efforts to curb welfare programs; and to a plateauing of new enrollments resulting from the recent expansions in the Medicaid program. Second, recent federal legislation has significantly curbed the disproportionate-share payment schemes mentioned above.

Finally, the rate of increase in payments per enrollee has subsided. In all likelihood the reduction in payments per enrollee is the direct result of the significant increase in Medicaid managed care enrollments. According to table 12–1, Medicaid managed care enrollments have increased fourfold from less than 10 percent in 1991 to over 40 percent in 1996. This trend is likely to continue as recent legislation makes it easier for states to expand Medicaid enrollments.[3] A case in point is the Balanced Budget Act of 1997, which abolishes the need for states to receive federal waivers before requiring Medicaid recipients to enroll in managed care plans. It is worth noting that the percent of Medicaid recipients enrolled in managed care plans varies widely across states. For example, as of June 1997, all Medicaid enrollees in Tennessee were enrolled in managed care plans, while none were enrolled in managed care plans in Wyoming.

Now the question becomes whether the decrease in the rate of growth of Medicaid expenditures is the beginning of a trend or simply a one-shot deal. Holahan and Liska (1997) are of the opinion that the decrease is the beginning of a trend and they base their argument on the fact that both enrollments and payments per beneficiary are likely to grow at modest rates over the next few years.

## The State Children's Health Insurance Program

In 1996 approximately 42 million people in the United States were without health insurance coverage and almost a quarter of that group were children under the age of 18. Feeling the political pressure to address what some felt was a national disgrace, Congress enacted the State Children's Health Insurance Program (CHIP) as part of the Balanced Budget Act of 1997.[4] The ultimate objective of CHIP is to decrease the number of uninsured children by providing federal funds to states that initiate plans to expand insurance coverage to low-income, uninsured children. The federal government has committed approximately $40 billion to the program over a 10-year period from 1998 through 2007. For the fiscal years 1998–2000, state allotments will be based on the percentage of low-income, uninsured children in the state adjusted by a geographic cost factor. After that point a blended rate based on the number of insured and uninsured low-income children in the state will be used.

---

[3]This information was obtained from the Health Care Financing Administration Web site (http://www.hcfa.gov).

[4]The following discussion is based on information obtained from the Health Care Financing Administration Web site (http://www.hcfa.gov).

**INSIGHT 12-2**

## The Cost Effectiveness of Recent Changes in the Medicaid Program

A number of changes have taken place over the years in the Medicaid program to extend coverage to the uninsured, particularly children and pregnant women. For example, in 1990 the federal government established that states must cover pregnant women in families with incomes equal to or less than 133 percent of the poverty level and gave states the option of covering pregnant women with incomes up to 185 percent of the poverty rate. These changes in part explain why Medicaid enrollments increased from 22 million in 1975 to over 36 million in 1996. With this increase in enrollments came a substantial increase in expenditures that is documented in table 12–1. The question now becomes whether these changes in the Medicaid program generated significant improvements in overall health. Research by Currie and Gruber (1996a) focuses on one aspect of this question; namely, has the expansion of Medicaid eligibility for pregnant women from 1979 through 1992 improved health outcomes for children?

The researchers began their work by utilizing a simulation model to estimate the impact of recent changes in Medicaid policy on eligibility. According to their estimates, the percentage of pregnant women eligible for Medicaid insurance coverage increased from 12.4 percent in 1979 to 43.3 percent in 1991. The authors point out that while eligibility significantly increased, there was substantial variation across states. The next step in their research was to establish the degree to which this improvement in eligibility translated into improvements in health. According to their regression results, the increase in eligibility was related to an overall decrease in the infant mortality rate of

8.5 percent and 11.5 percent for those specific groups targeted by the Medicaid changes.

The final step in the analysis was to determine if this improvement in health was achieved in a cost-effective manner. According to their simulation results, each additional eligible woman under the targeted changes generated a $224 increase in Medicaid expenditures. They also found that a 1 percent increase in targeted eligibility caused the infant mortality rate to drop by 0.041 deaths per 1,000 births. "These findings imply that the cost of saving a life through the targeted eligibility changes was $840,000" (p. 1287).

It is worth noting that in a related study, Currie and Gruber (1996b) estimate the impact of expanded Medicaid eligibility on the health outcomes of previously uninsured children. According to their results based on data from 1982 to 1992, expanded eligibility brought about a 5.1 percent decrease in child mortality at a cost of approximately $1.61 million per life saved.

Together these two studies suggest that recent expansions in Medicaid eligibility have generated measurable improvements in health, particularly among the young. The results also indicate that these improvements were brought about at a cost of between $840,000 and $1.6 million per life saved. Although these figures seem to be rather high at first blush, we need to keep in mind that the willingness-to-pay literature, as summarized in Chapter 5, estimates the value of a life to range between $3 million and $4 million. Thus, the expansion of insurance coverage via the Medicaid program appears to provide health benefits in excess of cost.

---

CHIP is designed to give states considerable latitude when addressing the problem of uninsured children. Each state that elects to participate in the program must submit a plan for approval that articulates how it intends to utilize the funds. States have the option of expanding insurance coverage through their existing Medicaid programs, developing separate child health insurance programs, or a combination of the two. As of August 1998, 47 states, including the District of Columbia, had submitted plans, and slightly more than half of those plans are based on Medicaid expansion. The others call for either a separate child health insurance program or are a combination of the two.

According to estimates supplied by the Congressional Budget Office (1998), CHIP will extend health insurance coverage to approximately 2.3 million children by 1999. Despite the fact that some of these children would have been covered by some type of health insurance anyway, the State Children's Insurance Program should play a significant role in extending health insurance coverage to uninsured children.

# The Medicare Program

The primary objective of the Medicare program is to improve access to medical care for elderly people by underwriting a portion of their medical expenditures. Anyone of age 65 or older is eligible for the program.[5] It is made up of two distinct components: Part A, the Hospital Insurance program, which is compulsory, and Part B, the Supplementary Medical Insurance program, which is voluntary. The Hospital Insurance portion of the program primarily covers (1) inpatient hospital services, (2) some types of posthospital care, and (3) hospice care.

The number of people age 65 or older covered under Part A has increased rapidly over the years and reflects the growing elderly population. In 1966, when the program first began, slightly more than 19 million elderly individuals were enrolled, and by 1995 the number had grown to more than 33 million. The Supplementary Medical Insurance program provides benefits for (1) physician services, (2) outpatient medical services, (3) emergency room services, and (4) a variety of other medical services.

Although Part B of Medicare is voluntary and requires a monthly premium to participate, a large number of elderly people have elected to purchase the insurance. During the initial year of the program, slightly more than 17 million elderly people participated, and by 1995 the number had increased to 31 million, almost matching the number of enrollees in the compulsory portion of Medicare. This trend reflects the fact that the federal government heavily subsidizes the cost of the supplementary insurance program.

## The Financing and Cost of Medicare

Since its inception, total expenditures on the Medicare program have increased at a brisk pace. In 1966 the federal government spent $7.7 billion on the Medicare program; by 1980, this figure had increased almost fivefold to $37.8 billion. As of 1996, total expenditures exceeded $203 billion with an annual rate of growth between 1980 and 1990 topping 11 percent. In more recent times the rate of growth has slowed somewhat with an annual growth rate of 10.6 percent in 1995 and 8.1 percent 1996 (Levit et al. 1998). The rise in Medicare expenses is explained by increases in both the number of enrollees and reimbursement per enrollee, with the latter accounting for most of the increase. From 1967 through 1995, the average annual rate of growth in enrollment was 1.9 percent, and the average level of reimbursement per enrollee grew at an average annual rate of 11.2 percent.

---

[5]In addition, the Medicare program covers some individuals younger than 65 who are severely disabled or suffer from kidney disease.

| TABLE 12–2 | RECEIPTS AND EXPENDITURES FOR THE HOSPITAL INSURANCE PROGRAM, SELECTED YEARS 1966–1996 (IN MILLIONS OF DOLLARS) |
|---|---|

| | Total Receipts | | | Total Expenditures | Contributions to Trust Fund |
|---|---|---|---|---|---|
| | **Payroll** | **Other** | **Interest** | **Total Expenditures** | **Contributions to Trust Fund** |
| 1966 | $1,858 | $53 | $32 | $999 | $944 |
| 1970 | 4,881 | 940 | 158 | 5,281 | 698 |
| 1975 | 11,502 | 814 | 664 | 11,581 | 1,399 |
| 1980 | 23,848 | 1,100 | 1,149 | 25,577 | 520 |
| 1985 | 47,567 | 459 | 3,362 | 48,414 | 2,974 |
| 1990 | 72,013 | −91 | 8,451 | 66,997 | 13,376 |
| 1995 | 98,421 | 1,873 | 10,820 | 117,604 | −2,577 |
| 1996 | 110,585 | −274 | 10,222 | 129,929 | −5,326 |

SOURCE: U.S. Department of Health and Human Services Social Security Administration, *Annual Statistical Supplement 1997*, Table 8.A1.

Table 12–2 lists total expenditures and funding sources for the Hospital Insurance program. The main source of funding has been a payroll tax of 2.9 percent, which employees and employers share equally. The payroll tax accounted for over 89 percent of total revenues in 1996. The second largest revenue source has been interest income emanating from the Federal Hospital Insurance Trust Fund, which was established at the inception of the program and has built up over the years. Interest income topped $10 billion in 1996 and accounted for 8.5 percent of total receipts. The column "other" in table 12–2 includes transfers from the railroad retirement account and reimbursements from general revenues for uninsured persons' military credits. This account was negative in 1996 primarily because of a lump-sum general revenue adjustment for military wage credits.

The last column in table 12–2 provides the net contribution to the trust fund, which equals total receipts minus total expenditures. The trust had assets of $124 billion in 1995, down from $132 billion in 1994.

The enrollee is also responsible for a portion of inpatient expenses through a deductible and coinsurance payment. The first three columns of table 12–3 supply deductible and coinsurance information. In 1966 the deductible was $40, increased steadily through the years, and by 1997 was $760. Once the deductible is met, Medicare covers all inpatient hospital expenses for the first 60 days. From the 61st to the 90th day, the enrollee is required to pay a daily coinsurance payment equal to one-quarter of the inpatient hospital deductible. After the 90th day, Medicare no longer covers hospital inpatient expenses. However, each enrollee is provided with an additional 60–day lifetime reserve. The reserve can be used only once and has a daily

| TABLE 12–3 | THE COST SHARING AND PREMIUMS FOR MEDICARE, SELECTED YEARS 1966–1997 |
|---|---|

| | Hospital Insurance | | | Supplementary Medical Insurance | | |
| | Deductible | Daily Coinsurance | | Payment | | |
| | 1–60 days | 61–90 days | After 90 days | Annual Deductible | Coinsurance Rate | Monthly Premium |
|---|---|---|---|---|---|---|
| 1966 | $40 | $10 | — | $50 | 20% | $3.00 |
| 1970 | 52 | 13 | $26 | 50 | 20% | 5.30 |
| 1975 | 92 | 23 | 46 | 60 | 20% | 6.70 |
| 1980 | 180 | 45 | 90 | 60 | 20% | 9.60 |
| 1985 | 400 | 100 | 200 | 75 | 20% | 15.50 |
| 1990 | 592 | 148 | 296 | 75 | 20% | 28.60 |
| 1995 | 716 | 179 | 358 | 100 | 20% | 46.10 |
| 1996 | 736 | 184 | 368 | 100 | 20% | 42.50 |
| 1997 | 760 | 190 | 380 | 100 | 20% | 43.80 |

SOURCE: U.S. Department of Health and Human Services Social Security Administration, *Annual Statistical Supplement 1996*, Table 2.C1.

coinsurance rate of one-half the inpatient hospital deductible, which equaled $380 in 1997.

The Supplementary Medical Insurance program, or Part B of Medicare, is financed partly through premium payments for enrollees. As you can see from table 12–4, premium payments contributed over $18 billion in 1996, or 22 percent of total receipts. The premium payment as a fraction of total receipts was rather stable throughout the preceding decade. The largest source of revenue has been contributions by the government and represents the extent to which the federal government subsidizes premiums. Over the years, the government has consistently provided approximately three-quarters of total revenues. The final source has been interest income from a trust fund, which has provided only a small fraction of revenues over the years. As with the Hospital Insurance trust funds, contributions are made when receipts exceed expenditures. The contributions appear in the last column of table 12–4. By 1996, the fund had assets of $28 billion.

Despite the rapid growth in enrollees over the years, Supplementary Medical Insurance premiums had to be increased to provide the necessary revenues. As noted earlier, this is largely because expenditures per enrollee grew at a much faster pace than the number of new enrollees. According to table 12–3, the monthly premium was $43.80 in 1997, up from $3 a month in 1966. In addition, the enrollee is obligated to pay an annual deductible equal to $100 and a coinsurance rate equal to 20 percent on most charges.

| TABLE 12–4 | RECEIPTS AND EXPENDITURES FOR THE SUPPLEMENTARY MEDICAL INSURANCE PROGRAM, SELECTED YEARS 1966–1996 (IN MILLIONS OF DOLLARS) |
| --- | --- |

| | Total Receipts | | | Total Expenditures | Contributions to Trust Fund |
| --- | --- | --- | --- | --- | --- |
| | **Premiums** | **Government** | **Interest** | | |
| 1966 | $322 | $0 | $2 | $203 | $122 |
| 1970 | 1,096 | 1,093 | 12 | 2,212 | −11 |
| 1975 | 1,918 | 2,648 | 107 | 4,735 | −62 |
| 1980 | 3,011 | 7,455 | 408 | 11,245 | −371 |
| 1985 | 5,613 | 18,250 | 1,243 | 23,880 | 1,226 |
| 1990 | 11,302 | 33,035 | 1,558 | 43,987 | 1,908 |
| 1995 | 19,717 | 39,007 | 1,582 | 66,599 | −6,293 |
| 1996 | 18,763 | 65,035 | 1,811 | 70,408 | 15,201 |

SOURCE: U.S. Department of Health and Human Services Social Security Administration, *Annual Statistical Supplement 1996*, Table 8.A2.

## Recent Medicare Program Reforms

Facing a growing federal deficit and an elderly population frustrated by ever-rising deductibles, copayments, and premiums, Congress was forced to alter the Medicare program over the years. The objective has always been to contain costs while at the same time improving access to medical care for elderly people. Instead of going through the tedious process of examining each policy change, we focus on three of the most significant reforms to the Medicare program. The first major reform took place in 1983, when a new payment system for hospitals was implemented based on diagnosis-related groups (DRGs). The second was the passage of the Omnibus Budget Reconciliation Act of 1989, which significantly altered the method of payment to physicians. Finally, the Balanced Budget Act of 1997 radically expanded plans available to beneficiaries and the rate of managed care.

**Diagnosis Related Groups**   In just five years (1975 to 1980), Medicare expenditures on inpatient hospital services grew by over 120 percent from $8.8 billion to $19.5 billion (U.S. Department of Health and Human Services, 1993). In reaction to the expenditure increase, Congress instituted a prospective payment system (PPS) to compensate hospitals for medical services provided to Medicare patients.

Under the PPS, every Medicare patient is classified based on his or her principal diagnosis into one of approximately 500 or so diagnosis-related groups (DRGs) upon entering a hospital. The prospective payment received by the hospital is a fixed dollar amount per discharge and largely depends upon the DRG classification with

| TABLE 12–5 | FIVE MOST COMMON DRGs IN 1996 | |
|---|---|---|

| DRG # | DRG Description | Total Discharges |
|---|---|---|
| 127 | Heart failure and shock | 709,714 |
| 089 | Simple pneumonia and pleurisy, with age greater than 17 and with complications and/or comorbidities. | 431,389 |
| 014 | Specific cerebrovascular disorders, except transient ischemic attack | 379,967 |
| 088 | Chronic Obstructive Pulmonary Disease | 361,545 |
| 209 | Major joint and limb reattachment procedures of lower extremities | 358,660 |
| Total Top 5 DRGs | | 2,241,275 |
| Total DRGs | | 11,749,394 |

SOURCE: http://www.hcfa.gov/stats/medpar/ss96d&s.txt

adjustments made for factors that contribute to cost differences across hospitals. In particular, each fixed payment is made up of three major components.[6] The first is a base payment for the average cost of a Medicare case adjusted for differences in input prices across metropolitan statistical areas or statewide rural areas. The next component is the relative weight attached to the DRG that reflects the relative cost of the individual case. Finally, additional payments may be made to the hospital for outliers, which are patients who require a longer than average length of stay or increased medical attention. Adjustments are also made if the hospital is a teaching facility or has a disproportionate share of low-income patients. In 1996 the average Medicare payment per case was $6,709.

The DRG weight is an index number based on total medical charges that reflects the relative costs across all hospitals of providing care to the average patient in a particular DRG. The higher the DRG weight, the higher the prospective payment. In 1998, the relative weight ranged from a low of .208 for DRG 448 (an allergic reaction for someone under age 18) to a high of 16.8723 for DRG 103 (heart transplant). The five most common DRGs, accounting for 19 percent of all short-term hospital stay discharges in 1996, are shown in table 12–5.

Prior to 1983, hospitals were paid on a retrospective basis for the actual medical services provided. As discussed in Chapter 2, under a retrospective payment system, health care providers bill for actual costs incurred. Economists have long argued that a retrospective payment system has the potential to drive up medical costs for two reasons. First, a retrospective system provides little incentive for cost efficiency, because hospitals are not penalized for any excess costs of production; higher costs can simply

---

[6]The following discussion can be found in Chapter 5 of the *Report to the Congress: Medicare Payment Policy, 1998.*

be passed on to the third-party payer. Second, when payment is based on the type and quantity of medical services actually provided, an incentive likely exists for hospitals to provide unnecessary medical services. For instance, a patient may stay an additional day in the hospital to recuperate from surgery even if it is not medically necessary. The hospital earns additional profits due to the longer stay.

With a prospective system, fees are set in advance on a per-case basis. Hospitals essentially become price takers and face a perfectly elastic demand curve for Medicare patients. Referring to figure 8–11 in Chapter 8, we see that long-run equilibrium is achieved in a competitive market when the MR and MC curves intersect at the minimum point of the AC curve. A Medicare fee set near the long-run competitive price achieves essentially the same outcome. Inefficient behavior is no longer tolerated because hospitals are unable to pass higher costs on to the third payer, which in this case is the government. Under the PPS, hospitals that provide medical care at a cost below the preset fee retain the difference, whereas hospitals that incur costs in excess of the preset fee must sustain the loss. Naturally, inefficient hospitals have a difficult time operating in such an environment.

Finally, since compensation is now on a per-case basis, rather than a per-item basis, hospitals have the incentive to provide only necessary medical services. Any hospital that elects to provide additional medical services, such as allowing the patient to stay an additional day to recuperate after surgery, receives no additional compensation and thus has no economic incentive to provide those services (see the discussion surrounding figure 2–2).

Medicare's PPS appears to have successfully diminished the overall rate of growth in hospital expenditures. Over the eight years prior to the inception of the PPS (1977 to 1984), expenditures for the hospital insurance program grew at an average annual rate of over 15 percent. The rate dropped to 8.75 percent over the eight years immediately after the program was put in place (1985 to 1992). However, most of the decrease in the rate of growth took place when the program was first introduced. In particular, the average annual rate of growth in expenditures was only 5.1 percent from 1985 through 1988. The relative increase in Medicare hospital spending after 1988 may indicate that the ability of the PPS to control the costs may have waned over time as hospitals began to learn how to game the system (e.g., see Insight 12–3.)

Much has been written concerning the impact of the DRG program on the market for hospital services.[7] Foremost on the minds of many researchers is whether the Medicare prospective payment system has had a deleterious effect on the health status of Medicare patients. They fear that hospitals may react to the Medicare price controls by providing a lower quality of medical care (see the discussion surrounding figure 11–9). After reviewing the literature on the subject, however, Feinglass and Holloway (1991) concluded that there "is little direct, generalizable evidence that PPS has reduced the quality of care of Medicare patients" (p. 107).

---

[7]For a review of the literature, consult Coulan and Gaumer (1991), Feinglass and Holloway (1991), or Chapter 15 in this text.

# The Economics of DRG Creep

The DRG weight is an important factor in determining the prospective payment. In fact, Steinwald and Dummit (1989) note that a "DRG with a weight of two is paid twice as much as a DRG with a weight of one, and so on. The array of patients across DRGs in a hospital is the hospital's case-mix, and the average DRG weight for these patients is the hospital's case-mix index" (p. 36).

Steinwald and Dummit further point out that under the PPS, hospital case-mix is the most important factor determining payment variations across hospitals and that a small amount of change in DRG case-mix indexes can have large impacts on aggregate payments to hospitals. Consequently, hospitals may face a financial incentive under the PPS to artificially place their patients into higher-weighted DRGs and raise their case-mix index to increase reimbursement. Artificial increases in the case-mix under the PPS are referred to as *DRG creep*. For example, the average hospital case-mix index increased by nearly 7 percent from 1984 to 1987 at U.S. hospitals (Steinwald and Dummit, 1989).

It is not clear, however, whether hospitals have attempted to game the PPS by purposely placing patients in more lucrative DRGs to raise reimbursement or whether real changes have caused the higher case-mix indexes. Researchers point to three possible reasons for real changes in the case-mix indexes. First, hospital records, the main source of information for DRG assignments, may have been incomplete and inaccurate when the PPS first began. The PPS may have provided hospitals with a financial incentive to improve the accuracy and completeness of their medical record documentation and coding. The improved record-keeping may have shown up in higher case-mix indexes. Second, the increasing availability over time of more aggressive treatments and new technologies may have shifted patients into higher-weighted DRGs and thus increased the average case-mix index. Third, due to the PPS, patients in lower-weighted DRGs may have been moved from the hospital to an outpatient setting, causing the frequency of lower-weighted DRGs to decline relative to high-weighted DRGs. The average case-mix may have increased as a result of the shift to outpatient settings.

The upshot is that the average hospital case-mix may have increased due to both real changes in patient needs and financial manipulation of DRG assignments. As Steinwald and Dummit argue, "evidence on DRG case-mix change in the years since the beginning of PPS clearly indicates the strong influence of financial incentives on documentation and coding practices. It is not possible to distinguish this type of change from real case-mix change with much precision" (p. 45).

Closely related to the issue of quality is the impact of the DRG system on admissions and length of stay. Economic theory suggests that hospitals may react to the fixed PPS price by attempting to increase admissions as a way to raise revenues (again, see the discussion concerning figure 11–9). In fact, just the opposite occurred after the PPS was implemented. The number of admissions under Medicare actually dropped by 11 percent during the first eight years of the PPS, and a large portion of the decrease took place within the first two years (Hodgkin and McGuire, 1994). The reason for the drop in admissions is difficult to explain. Feinglass and Holloway (1991) attribute the decline to the implementation of utilization review programs that screen the use of inpatient medical services and to the switch to outpatient facilities as a result of the PPS. The switch to outpatient treatment is substantiated by the fact that hospital outpatient surgery for Medicare patients doubled between 1983 and 1985 (Feinglass and Holloway, 1991). The new payment system also shortened the average length of stay for inpatient hospital visits. Estimates indicate that the average length of stay fell by 14.6 percent from 1982 to 1985 (Feinglass and Holloway, 1991).

The decline in admissions, coupled with the decrease in average length of stay, caused the overall number of inpatient days for Medicare clients to decrease by 20.7 percent from 1982 to 1988 (Schwartz and Mendelson, 1991). The decline in inpatient days during the mid-1980s largely explains the decrease in the overall rate of growth in Medicare hospital expenditures discussed earlier. The more recent increases in the overall rate of growth in Medicare expenditures may also indicate that the cost savings resulting from fewer inpatient days have largely been exhausted. The unsustained reduction of Medicare expenditures led Muller (1993) to report that the "effectiveness of the reforms began to diminish by 1986" (p. 298).

The prospective payment system has also had a significant negative impact on the overall financial condition of hospitals. Financial impacts are to be expected, since hospitals are no longer able to bill Medicare for medical services on essentially a cost-plus basis. Fisher (1992) examined the financial performance of over 4,600 hospitals that were continuously involved with the PPS from 1985 through 1990. Overall, the proportion of hospitals that reported profits dropped marginally from 77.2 percent in 1985 to 72.4 percent in 1990. However, the proportion of hospitals that reported Medicare profits dropped more dramatically over the same period, from 84.5 percent in 1985 to 40.7 percent in 1990. Fisher also found a positive correlation between overall profitability and Medicare PPS inpatient net profits.

**The Omnibus Budget Reconciliation Act of 1989**   As the cost of Part B escalated over the years, Congress responded with various changes, including freezes on physician payments and annual limits on increases in fees. Despite these cost containment measures, Medicare expenditures for physician services continued to rise, placing an even greater financial burden on both the federal government and the elderly population. Forced into action, Congress passed the Omnibus Budget Reconciliation Act of 1989, or OBRA 1989, which was directed at restructuring the physician payment system. The act contained four major provisions:

1. A new payment system that bases compensation primarily on resources utilized was to be implemented.

2. A procedure was established for Congress to monitor the rate of growth in physician fees over time.

3. Limits were put on charges physicians may assess patients that are beyond the amount paid by Medicare.

4. The Agency for Health Policy Research was established to develop outcomes research and provide guidelines.

Each of these changes is discussed in turn next.

***Resource-Based Relative Value Scale System***   At the core of OBRA 1989 is a new fee schedule that was introduced in 1992. Prior to OBRA 1989, physicians were compensated based on the usual-customary-reasonable (UCR) or the customary-prevailing-and-reasonable (CPR) method. Under this method, physicians were paid the lowest of the bill submitted, the customary charge of the physician, or the prevailing rate in the area for services provided. The general consensus was that the UCR-CPR method of payment contributed to the increase in physician expenditures over the years. According to Yett, Der, Ernst, and Hay (1985), the UCR-CPR method of payment creates an incentive for physicians to increase their fees over time to raise what constitutes the reasonable rate in the future. The inflationary bias is especially acute when the overall rate of inflation is high.

In addition, the UCR-CPR method was criticized for creating distortions in relative prices of various types of physician services. Fees for technical procedures were overvalued, whereas fees for evaluations and management services were undervalued. As a result, primary care physicians, who generally provide more evaluation-type services such as physical exams, were being compensated less than specialists, who provide more technical services such as surgery. The price differential tended to distort physicians' income and potentially had an impact on the composition of physician services provided (Oliver, 1993).

The *resource-based relative value scale (RBRVS)* system of fees considers the time and effort of physician work, or physician resources, necessary to produce physician services. The relative work values are based on the research of William Hsiao and colleagues at Harvard University (Hsiao et al. 1988) and make up approximately half of the total value of physician services under the new fee schedule. The other half is accounted for by practice and malpractice expenses. A conversion factor that translates the scale into a fee schedule has also been developed. Yearly adjustments are made in the conversion factor to account for inflation and any other changes that take place.

Since the RBRVS fees are now based on relative work effort, the new fee schedule no longer provides a historical momentum for future fee increases. That is because past fee increases no longer provide the basis for future increases by inflating the "reasonable" rate. Also, a resource-based fee schedule no longer provides physicians with an incentive to supply more technical medical procedures, such as surgery, than evaluation and management services, such as office visits with established patients, which are more time consuming. As a result, physicians who provide primary care should see Medicare revenues increase, whereas those who provide more specialty types of care should see revenues decrease. This view is substantiated by the fact that in 1992, family practitioners saw fees increase by 10 percent while specialty surgeons endured an 8 percent decrease (Physician Payment Review Commission, 1993). Such changes are likely to have a major impact on the types and volume of physician services provided at the margin and the relative incomes of physicians in various specialties.

The RBRVS fee schedule is not without its critics, however. According to Hadley (1991), the entire approach is inconsistent with the theory of cost. A resource-based method determines the value of a service primarily by physician work effort and fails to consider input prices. Thus, contrary to the theory of costs presented earlier, input prices play no role in determining the marginal and average costs of production or the supply and prices of physician services. An example similar to the one developed by Hadley proves this point. In 1993, slightly more than 38,000 general surgeons were practicing in the United States. What would have happened had this number doubled by 1994, *ceteris paribus?* Supply and demand theory suggests that the average fee for surgical services would have dropped as the supply of general surgeons increased, or the supply curve would have shifted to the right. With a resource-based payment scheme, however, lower surgical fees do not result from a greater supply of surgeons because fees are based on work effort. Input prices play no role in determining market price.

Also, one might criticize the resource-based fee schedule on the grounds that it constitutes a price control. If relative fee schedules are set incorrectly, shortages or surpluses of different physician services may result. For example, more generous relative fees for primary care services may encourage an oversupply of those services and an undersupply of specialist services in the future. Consequently, considerable care must be taken when establishing the appropriate fees for the different services.

Despite these criticisms, the RBRVS method of physician payment has been adopted by other third-party payers, both public and private. As of early 1994, 12 state Medicaid programs had adopted RBRVS and another 8 programs intended to adopt it shortly. In addition, one-third of more than 300 third-party payers recently surveyed stated that they utilize RBRVS in some capacity, while another 40 percent are considering its use (Physician Payment Review Commission, 1994).

*Medicare Volume Performance Standards*    In an attempt to gain more control over the growth of Medicare expenditures, Congress adopted a Medicare volume performance standards (VPS) system that establishes expenditure limits. Each year Congress establishes a target rate of growth for physician expenditures under Medicare, or a VPS. The target considers such items as inflation, the number and ages of enrollees, barriers to access, the level of inappropriate care given, changes in technology, and any legislated changes in the program. Whether or not the target was met in a given year is used as a basis for determining the extent to which fees are updated the following year through the conversion factor. In other words, if the actual rate of growth in physician expenditures exceeds the VPS in a given year, the increase in physician fees for the following year may be set lower than planned through updates in the conversion factor. If, on the other hand, the actual rate of increase is below the target, the increase in fees may move upward (Physician Payment Review Commission, 1993).

The benefits from a VPS system are twofold. First, the VPS gives Congress a mechanism with which to control the rate of growth of physician expenditures. Second, the VPS gives physicians, as a group, the incentive to provide appropriate care. If excessive amounts of inappropriate care are provided, overall expenditures are driven upward, and this dampens the extent to which fees are increased in the future. Critics, however, point out that the system provides inappropriate incentives to physicians because it fails to take physician practice style into account. Given the wide variation in practice styles, a uniform payment system provides inequitable payments for medical services. In addition, a free-rider problem may exist because such a large number of physicians participate in the system. No one physician has the incentive to eliminate inappropriate care because there is no direct relationship between individual physician behavior and future fees increases (Holahan and Zuckerman, 1993;

Miller and Welch, 1993). Ginsburg (1993) responds to the latter criticism by pointing out that the intent was to directly influence the behavior of physician organizations rather than that of individual physicians. The general idea is that the VPS will put pressure on physician organizations to monitor and control individual physician behavior.

***Limits on Balance Billing and the Assignment Issue***   Faced with the prospect that the new RBRVS fee schedule, along with the expenditures caps, could inhibit access to medical care by forcing up out-of-pocket payments for Medicare recipients, Congress put specific limits on the amount physicians can charge patients above the Medicare rate. When Part B was initially implemented, physicians were allowed to balance-bill patients for charges in excess of the established Medicare fee on a case-by-case basis. When this occurred, the physician was responsible for collecting the entire fee from the patient, and the patient received directly from Medicare a reimbursement check equal to the allowable fee less the 20 percent copayment. Under those circumstances, the physician bore the total risk of nonpayment.

To minimize the level of balance billing and therefore improve access to medical care, Medicare gave physicians the option to accept the assignment of benefits. Physicians who accept **assignment** give up the right to balance-bill, but in return receive a "guaranteed" payment directly from Medicare equal to the preset fee minus any deductibles or copayments. The remainder of the bill had to be collected directly from the patient. The decision to accept assignment presents physicians with a classic risk-return trade-off. Physician who opt to balance-bill and not accept assignment receive higher fees but take on the added risk of nonpayment by patients.

The assignment rate, as measured by the percentage of total claims submitted that were assigned, hovered around 60 percent during the earlier years of the Medicare program. As table 12–6 shows, however, the rate fell thereafter and bottomed out at around 50 percent in the late 1970s. In response to the lower assignment rate, Congress passed the Medicare Participating Physicians program in 1984, which altered the method of assignment. Now physicians had to elect to either participate or not participate. Physicians who elected to participate had to accept assignment for all patients covered under Part B. Those who opted not to participate were still free to accept assignment on a case-by-case basis. To encourage participation, Congress provided a variety of incentives. For example, nonparticipating physicians had their fee schedule frozen under Medicare, while participating physicians saw a modest increase. These changes brought about the desired outcome, as the assignment rate increased from 53.9 percent in 1983 to 59 percent in 1984 and 68 percent in 1985. Later Congress made further changes in favor of participation. For example, the Omnibus Budget Reconciliation Act of 1986 placed maximum limits on the amount nonparticipating physicians could charge Medicare patients. As a result, the assignment rate reached 81 percent in 1990.

Fearing that the new fee schedule, along with voluntary performance standards, would cause the assignment rate to fall as physicians felt the pinch of more stringent price controls, OBRA 89 placed even further constraints on the ability of physicians to practice balance billing. By 1991, physicians could not bill patients in excess of

| TABLE 12-6 | ASSIGNMENT RATES FOR MEDICARE CLAIMS, 1969–1996 | |
| --- | --- | --- |
| | **Total Number of Claims** | **Assignment Rate**[1] |
| 1969 | 37,542 | 61.5% |
| 1970 | 42,148 | 60.8 |
| 1975 | 79,980 | 51.8 |
| 1980 | 150,048 | 51.5 |
| 1985 | 279,559 | 68.5 |
| 1990 | 474,226 | 81.1 |
| 1995 | 647,855 | 94.7 |
| 1996 | 678,030 | 95.9 |

[1]The assignment rate is the percent of claims received that is considered assigned.

SOURCE: U.S. Department of Health and Human Services Social Security Administration, *Annual Statistical Supplement 1996*, Table 8.B10.2.

125 percent of the Medicare rate. This rate fell to 120 percent in 1992 and to 115 percent in 1993 for most services. It should be noted that in 1993, the actual balance-billing rate was only 109.25 percent because nonparticipating physicians received only 95 percent of the Medicare fee for participating physicians (115 percent times 95 percent). As a result, the assignment rate increased to about 96 percent by 1996.

***Health Outcomes Research***  Finally, OBRA 89 calls for the government to take a much more active role in outcomes research for the purpose of developing practice guidelines. The long-run objective is to contain the growth of physician and hospital expenditures in the future by minimizing the uncertainty surrounding alternative medical treatments. Outcomes research "involves not only the investigations of the link between medical care and outcomes, but also activities aimed at establishing which providers or systems of health care deliver a better quality of care than others" (Guadagnoli and McNeil, 1994, p. 14).

Payers are pressing for outcomes research so that medical guidelines can be developed to contain costs by eliminating ineffective medical care. Whether this will happen is open to question. For one thing, there is some debate concerning the level of inappropriate care. Some recent studies suggest that it is much lower than previously thought. For another, Guadagnoli and McNeil (1994) contend that outcomes research may force up costs because it may uncover some costly medical procedures that currently are underutilized. Physicians desire medical guidelines because

| TABLE 12–7 | AVERAGE ANNUAL GROWTH RATES IN MEDICARE EXPENDITURES, 1991–1995 |
|---|---|
| **Medical Service** | **Average Annual Rate of Growth, from 1991–1995** |
| **Part A** | |
| Inpatient services | 9.2% |
| Skilled nursing facility | 37.7 |
| Home health care | 30.6 |
| Hospice | 37.4 |
| **Part B** | |
| Physician services | 6.0 |
| Outpatient services | 12.0 |
| Home health care | 29.4 |
| Laboratory services | 5.8 |

SOURCE: Physician Payment Review Commission, *Annual Report*, 1997, Table 1–1.

they will aid them in treatment decisions and potentially diminish the possibility of malpractice suits. Another issue is whether guidelines can be effectively developed and implemented given the complexity of developing appropriate data sets and the difficulty in transferring this information into specific recommendations (Guadagnoli and McNeil, 1994). Many illnesses are patient specific, and consequently appropriate treatment cannot be standardized.

**Balanced Budget Act of 1997**   Despite the many changes in the Medicare program, many felt that rising Medicare costs throughout the 1990s could have jeopardized the financial viability of the program. One estimate indicated that if nothing were done, the trust fund for Part A of Medicare would be exhausted by 2001 (PPRC, 1997). A glance at table 12–7 indicates that the growth in expenditures has been rather uneven in recent years. For example, while expenditures for inpatient and physician services grew at annual rates of 9.2 and 6.0 percent from 1991 through 1995, expenditures for skilled nursing facilities, home health care, and hospice grew at annual rates in excess of 30 percent. Realizing that something needed to be done, Congress enacted the Balanced Budget Act of 1997 (BBA). According to MedPAC, BBA changes are expected to save $115 billion in Medicare expenditures from 1998 through 2002. While some will debate these figures, all agree that this piece of legislation profoundly changed the Medicare program.

The centerpiece of the legislation is the **Medicare + Choice** program, which significantly increases the types of insurance plans available to participants and alters the way in which Medicare pays for those plans. The Medicare + Choice program changes Medicare in four important ways (Christensen, 1998):

- The number of capitation plans available to beneficiaries is greatly expanded.

- The conditions that participating plans must fulfill have been relaxed.

- The method of calculated payment rates to plans has been adjusted.

- The enrollment process for beneficiaries has been changed.

To extend the range of options available to beneficiaries, the BBA allows a number of alternative types of risk-based health insurance plans to participate in the program.[8] Previous to this, only health maintenance organizations were allowed to offer risk-based insurance plans to Medicare participants. Now PPOs, PSOs, FFS plans, and MSAs will be allowed to participate, greatly expanding the range of options available to consumers.[9] To participate, plans must be licensed under state law and at a minimum cover the same medical services currently covered under the traditional Medicare fee-for-service plan. In an attempt to make it easier for plans to participate, the BBA made two changes. First, it dropped the fifty-fifty rule that required that at least half of the plan's enrollment come from the private sector. Second, it lowered the minimum enrollment requirements for PPOs to participate in the program (Christensen, 1998).

The BBA also significantly changes the method for calculating the monthly capitation payment received by private health plans who enter into risk contracts with Medicare. HMOs who contracted with Medicare prior to 1998 receive a monthly capitation payment equal to 95 percent of the average expected costs of similar beneficiaries who were enrolled in the traditional Medicare plan (calculated at the county level).[10] In addition, capitated payments are further adjusted based on a number of factors, including age, gender, and Medicaid enrollment status.

There are a number of methodological problems with this payment method. First and foremost is the fact that the capitation payment does not consider the health status of the enrollees. The available research indicates those individuals who enrolled in Medicare HMOs, as opposed to the traditional Medicare plan, were healthier and therefore had substantially lower medical costs. As a result, Medicare pays more to insure those individuals than it would have if these individuals had remained in the fee-for-service plan, despite the 5 percent reduction in payment to the HMO. According to a recent report by MedPAC (1998), new enrollees in Medicare managed care plans had health care costs that were 35 percent less than those of their counterparts in the

---

[8]Under a risk-based Medicare contract, the insurance plan agrees to accept a predetermined capitation fee for each Medicare beneficiary enrolled in the plan. In return the insurance plan accepts full risk for all covered medical expenses.

[9]PPO stands for Preferred Provider Organization, while PSO stands for Provider-Sponsored Organizations, FFS stands for fee-for-service, and MSA for Medical Savings Accounts.

[10]The logic is that health maintenance organizations have a cost advantage over traditional fee-for-service organizations. Since they should be able to provide medical services at a reduced cost, Medicare reduces the payment by 5 percent.

traditional Medicare plan. At the same time, those individuals who disenrolled from the Medicare managed care plans had medical costs 60 percent higher than the Medicare fee-for-service average in the first six months after disenrollment. To rectify this problem, the BBA requires that Medicare capitation payments be risk-adjusted beginning in the year 2000 (MedPAC, 1998).[11]

It will be interesting to see the extent to which this policy accomplishes its intended goal given the disappointing record the private insurance industry has had in predicting individual health care expenditures. According to Luft (1995), risk assessment models can predict only about 10 percent of the variance in health care expenditures for individuals even after health status and prior use are factored into the analysis. A highly skewed distribution of medical expenditures coupled with the inherent unpredictability of medical expenditures are the two main reasons offered by Luft as to why individual medical expenditures are so difficult to estimate. About the only thing we know for certain is that while improved risk assessment and risk adjustment payment mechanisms on the part of the federal government will reduce the level of risk selection, the problem will never completely go away. The ultimate objective from Medicare's point of view is to create an incentive for private insurance plans to provide high-quality care at the lowest possible price to the elderly, especially those who are chronically ill.

Aside from the risk selection problem, the old method for setting the capitation payment had the problem of establishing payment rates that were highly variable from year to year within any given county. That variability tended to discourage companies from participating in the program because it was simply too difficult to project enrollment and profitability. To decrease the level of uncertainty and, therefore, encourage more plans to participate, the BBA mandates a new payment method. Under the new method, the "payment rate for each county is calculated as the highest of a blend of the local and national rate, a minimum payment amount (or floor) or a minimum increase from the previous year's county rate" (MedPAC, 1998).

The BBA also changes new-enrollment procedures. Each year an annual coordinated election period is established similar to an open enrollment period whereby individuals receive information on the available plans and make their selections. In addition, limits are placed on the ability of enrollees to switch plans. Under the old system enrollees could change plans at any time on a monthly basis (Christensen, 1998). These changes are likely to attract insurers to the Medicare program by enhancing their ability to predict enrollments.

Success with the price controls on inpatient hospital and physician services (see table 12–7) also prompted Congress to call for prospective payment schedules for skilled nursing facilities, hospital outpatient facilities, home health agencies, and rehabilitation facilities in the BBA legislation. These payment schedules are to be

---

[11]**Risk assessment** involves modeling and calculating the expected medical costs for a person or group of individuals, while **risk adjustment** "is the process of setting capitation rates that reflect health status, paying plans more to care for ill beneficiaries and less to care for healthy ones" (MedPAC, 1998, p. 27). **Risk selection** occurs in a health insurance plan when a disproportionate share of individuals with either high or low medical costs enroll in a given plan, or when a disproportionate share of high or low medical care users selects the same plan (Gauthier et al., 1995, p. 15). Obviously, when the capitation payment is fixed, private plans have the incentive to enroll healthier individuals with lower medical costs.

developed and put in place over the next few years with the last ready to go in October 2000 for rehabilitation facilities.

The BBA also addresses some issues with regard to Part B of the Medicare program. As we discussed previously, OBRA 1989 mandated a resource-based relative value scale system of payment for physician services. Practice and malpractice expenses are still based on historical charges. The BBA requires that a resource-based method of payment be extended to practice expenses starting in 1999 and malpractice expenses in 2000.

In addition, the BBA replaces the volume performance standard with a new system that ties conversion factor updates to a sustainable growth target. This target is tied to the rate of medical inflation, changes in fee-for-service enrollment, growth in the overall economy and any changes in spending resulting from any modifications in government policy. The old way of basing updates in the conversion factor on the volume performance standard system had come under criticism in recent years for a number of reasons. First, under the volume performance standard system, separate conversion factors were used for primary services, surgical services and nonsurgical services, thus distorting relative payments across physician services over time. To remedy this problem a single conversion factor has been established (MedPAC 1998).

Most important, however, was the fact that the volume performance standards were generating spending targets that were much too low. Previously, the target was based on the growth in the volume and intensity of physician services minus any legislated deduction to slow the rate of growth in spending. In recent years the growth in volume and intensity slowed down while at the same time the legislated deduction was increased. "As a result, performance standards, which originally were well above the gross domestic product growth are now projected to drop well below" (PPCS 1997, p. 252). Beginning in 1999 the updates in the conversion factor will be determined by a sustainable growth rate system that will be tied more closely to the overall economy. The idea is to link spending for physician services under Medicare more closely to what the economy can afford to finance over time.

## Medicare and Managed Care

There is no doubt that many of the recent changes in the Medicare program have encouraged beneficiaries to join managed-care insurance plans. While only a small percentage of Medicare recipients are currently enrolled in managed-care plans, that number has increased in recent years. In 1990 only 3.3 percent of all Medicare enrollees were taking part in risk-contracting plans and that number expanded to 14 percent in 1997. All indications are that this percentage will grow in the future, especially with the passage of the Balanced Budget Act of 1997.

The major question that needs to be addressed is whether managed-care Medicare has the potential for offering quality medicine at a reduced price. According to Oberlander (1997), four benefits can potentially be derived from expanding the role of managed care in Medicare. First, it has been argued that managed care can provide medical care at a much lower cost than fee-for-service (see Chapter 5 for a more detailed review of this issue). Second, it has been suggested that managed care plans can offer a wider array of medical benefits than traditional fee-for-service plans. Next, proponents of managed care have argued that managed care plans can offer a higher quality of care than the traditional fee-for-service Medicare plan.

Finally, proponents point out that since MCOs have an administrative structure all ready in place which monitors the behavior of medical care providers, establishes the level of necessary treatment, and negotiates reduced prices from medical providers, they are in a position to assist the government in managing the Medicare program. In other words, with managed care a portion of the government's regulatory responsibilities can be shouldered by the insurers. As an added advantage, MCOs are much closer to the providers than the federal government, and thus are in a much better position to prevent medical care providers from "gaming" the system.

Oberlander (1997) points out that critics of managed care have two concerns. First, they argue that MCOs provide an inferior quality of care. What concerns the critics the most is that in the quest to control costs MCOs have imposed policies that are especially burdensome to the elderly. This is particularly true for those elderly who are chronically ill. Two examples of policies that weigh heavy on the chronically ill elderly are shorter hospital stays and restricted access to specialists.

Second, critics argue that with a capitation payment system, MCOs are likely to retain most of the savings that may develop. This argument goes back to the risk selection issue discussed in the previous section. Despite the use of risk adjustment as mandated by the BBA, some have argued that MCOs will still be able to attract beneficiaries that are healthier than the capitation payment will reflect, thus allowing them to continue to capture most of the savings that come from managed cost. The government is left with paying more for healthier beneficiaries because of inflated capitation payments while at the same time insuring the less healthy and more costly Medicare beneficiaries under the traditional fee-for-service plan.

Oberlander (1997) closes the article by reviewing the available empirical evidence on the performance of MCOs in Medicare in terms of cost savings, benefit coverage, and the quality of medical care provided. Since the available evidence is still somewhat scanty, the author focuses primarily on HMOs because these organizations have had the longest involvement with Medicare. The author cautions the reader not to overextend the analysis because it is too early to tell whether other types of MCOs behave differently without more empirical evidence. Despite these limitations there is still something to be learned from examining the behavior of HMOs in Medicare.

The evidence regarding cost savings is similar to that reviewed in Chapter 5. Medicare HMOs appear to generate a cost savings of about 11 percent with most of that due to shorter hospital stays. The ability of Medicare to reap these savings, however, has been compromised by the risk adjustment problem discussed earlier. It remains to be seen how far the BBA will go toward alleviating that problem and thus allow the government to reap the additional savings from managed care.

With regard to benefit coverage, HMOs appear to include more items than the basic coverage established by the traditional Medicare plan. The most common additional benefit appears to be an annual physical, which was covered by 95 percent of

## Advertising of MCOs—Information or Persuasion?

While everyone agrees that advertising is a fact of life in today's business environment, economists have long debated whether advertising enhances or diminishes society's overall well-being. As we learned in Chapter 9, proponents state that advertising provides consumers with additional information that can be used to make an informed decision, the result being a more efficient allocation of resources brought about through enhanced competition. Critics contend that advertising results in anticompetitive outcomes by creating artificial wants, habit buying, and barriers to entry. A recent study by Neuman et al. (1998) may rekindle that debate. Neuman et al. analyze newspaper and television ads placed by HMOs. They also review the presentations at marketing seminars to gain an understanding of the marketing strategies employed by HMOs to attract Medicare-eligible customers.

According to their findings, HMOs convey the message that they can provide more benefits at a lower cost than traditional Medicare plans. More importantly, the authors conclude that HMOs have developed and implemented marketing strategies based on attracting healthy seniors. To support their conclusion they cite the fact that "nearly half

of all television ads include images of physically active seniors, in the midst of strenuous activities such as mountain biking, swimming and jogging up stairs" (p. 135). In addition, "none of the newspaper and television ad images includes beneficiaries in hospital beds or wheelchairs or with walkers, canes, or obvious handicaps or illnesses" (p. 135). They also report that in almost all cases the font size used in the fine print that appeared in TV and newspaper ads was smaller than the smallest print recommended for individuals 65 years old and older. What is even more astonishing is that one out of three seminars to prospective enrollees were held in facilities that were not wheelchair accessible.

Overall, the evidence supports the proposition that HMOs have been making a concerted effort to enroll healthy seniors and to avoid those with greater potential medical needs. Although it is difficult to determine the extent to which these advertising campaigns are impacting the decisions made by the elderly when choosing an insurance plan, there is no doubt that their intent is to play on the risk selection problem in order to improve the bottom line.

the risk plans in 1995. Other additional benefits include eye exams, offered by 88 percent of the plans, and immunizations, covered by 86 percent of the plans (Oberlander, 1997). As far as quality, Medicare HMOs appear to equal or even exceed the quality of medical care provided in the traditional fee-for-service setting. However, there is some evidence to suggest that the chronically ill elderly may receive inferior care in a managed care environment.

Overall, Oberlander (1997) concludes that managed care has not lived up to its expectations and that significant reforms may be needed. In the future, with increasing Medicare enrollments in managed care plans, special attention must to be paid to ensure that MCOs provide high-quality care at an appropriate price.

### SUMMARY

This chapter focused on Medicaid and Medicare, two public health insurance programs that account for a high and rising share of total health care costs in the United

States. Many states are beginning to turn to managed care as a way to contain Medicaid expenditures. Whether managed care offers the solution to Medicaid cost containment will most likely be a lively source of debate in the future.

In the Medicare program, both the Hospital Insurance and Supplementary Medical Insurance programs have been revised, particularly in terms of method of payment for medical services, due to cost containment pressures. The diagnosis-related group (DRG) and resource-based payment programs have extended government control over medical fees under Medicare. In addition, the government has altered the method of paying for Medicare plans and expanded the role of Medicare Managed Care.

## Review Questions and Problems

1. Using economic theory, justify the need for the Medicaid and Medicare programs.

2. Discuss the methods states use to contain Medicaid costs. What are the supply, demand, and quantity implications of each containment method?

3. In 1983, Congress adopted the prospective payment system (PPS) to compensate hospitals for medical services. Prior to that point, hospitals were paid on a retrospective basis. Provide the economic justification for such a move.

4. What is DRG creep? Why is it a problem?

5. Explain some of the advantages and disadvantages of the resource-based method of payment for physician services under Medicare.

6. The muffler on your car suddenly needs repair, and there are only two automobile repair shops in town. You drive to the first shop, and the mechanic tells you to leave the car and he will repair it. Payment will be due when you pick it up. A mechanic at the second shop looks at your car and guarantees that she will charge you only $99.95 to repair the muffler, as advertised. Which repair shop is likely to provide costly needless repairs to your car, and why? Which one may underprovide quality? In your answers, discuss the concepts of prospective and retrospective payment for services.

7. What is the assignment problem? How have recent changes in the Medicare program addressed the problem?

8. Discuss how health outcomes research is supposed to contain rising medical costs.

9. Explain how the Medicare + Choice program alters the role of private insurance in the Medicare program.

10. What does the government hope to achieve by expanding the role of managed care in Medicare programs?

11. What is the risk selection program and how does it contribute to higher Medicare expenditures? How might the problem be contained?

*References*

Bacon, Kenneth A. "Hospitals Now Can Sue States over Medicaid." *The Wall Street Journal*, June 15, 1990, p. B1.

Christensen, Sandra. "Medicare+Choice Provisions in the Balanced Budget Act of 1997." *Health Affairs* 17 (July/August 1998), pp. 224–31.

Coughlin, Teresa A., et al. "State Responses to the Medicaid Spending Crisis: 1988 to 1992." *Journal of Health Politics, Policy and Law* 19 (winter 1994), pp. 837–64.

Coulan, R. F., and G. L. Gaumer. "Medicare's Prospective Payment System: A Critical Appraisal." *Health Care Financing Review* (Annual Supplement, 1991). pp. 45–77.

Currie, Janet, and Jonathan Gruber. "Saving Babies: The Efficacy and Cost of Recent Changes in the Medicaid Eligibility of Pregnant Women." *Journal of Political Economy* 104 (December 1996a), pp. 1263–96.

———. "Health Insurance Eligibility, Utilization of Medical Care and Child Health." *Quarterly Journal of Economics* 111 (May 1996b), pp. 431–66.

"Expanding Health Insurance Coverage for Children under Title XXI of the Social Security Act." *Congressional Budget Office*. http://www.cbo.gov. (February, 1998).

Feinglass, Joe, and James J. Holloway. "The Initial Impact of the Medicare Prospective Payment System on U.S. Health Care: A Review of the Literature." *Medical Care Review* 48 (spring 1991), pp. 91–115.

Fisher, Charles R. "Hospital and Medicare Financial Performance under PPS, 1985–1990." *Health Care Financing Review* 14 (fall 1992), pp. 171–83.

Garnick, Deborah W., et al. "How Well Do Americans Understand Their Health Coverage?" *Health Affairs* 12 (fall 1993), pp. 204–12.

Gauthier, Anne K., et al. "Risk Selection in the Health Care Market: A Workshop Overview." *Inquiry* 32 (spring 1995), pp. 14–22.

Ginsburg, Paul B. "Refining Medicare Volume Performance Standards: Commentary." *Inquiry* 30 (fall 1993), pp. 260–64.

Guadagnoli, Edward, and Barbara J. McNeil. "Outcomes Research: Hope for the Future the Latest Rage?" *Inquiry* 31 (spring 1994), pp. 14–24.

Hadley, Jack. "Theoretical and Empirical Foundations of the Resource-Based Relative Value Scale." In *Regulating Doctors' Fees: Competition, Benefits and Control under Medicare*, edited by H. E. Frech III. Washington, DC: AEI Press, 1991.

Health Care Financing Administration. http://www.hgfa.gov.

Helbing, Charles. "Hospital Insurance Short Stay Hospital Benefits." *Health Care Financing Review* (Annual Supplement, 1992), pp. 55–96.

Hodgkin, Dominic, and Thomas G. McGuire. "Payment Levels and Hospital Response to Prospective Payment." *Journal of Health Economics* 13 (1994), pp. 1–29.

Holahan, John, and David Liska. "The Slowdown in Medicaid Spending Growth." *Health Affairs* 16 (March/April 1997), pp. 157–63.

Holahan, John, and Stephen Zuckerman. "The Future of Medicare Volume Performance Standards." *Inquiry* 30 (fall 1993), pp. 235–48.

Health Insurance Association of America. *Source Book of Health Insurance Data*. Washington, DC: HIAA, 1995.

Hsiao, William C., et al. "Results and Policy Implications of the Resource-Based Relative-Value Scale." *New England Journal of Medicine* 319 (September 29, 1988), pp. 881–88.

Langwell, Kathryn, and James P. Hadley. "Insight from the Medicare HMO Demonstrations." *Health Affairs* 9 (spring 1990), pp. 74–84.

Levit, Katharine R., et al. "National Health Spending Trends in 1996." *Health Affairs* 17 (January/February 1998), pp. 35–51.

Luft, Harold S. "Potential Methods to Reduce Risk Selection and Its Effects." *Inquiry* 32 (spring 1995), pp. 23–32.

Medicare Payment Advisory Commission. *Report to the Congress: Medicare Payment Policy*. Vols. I and II. Washington, DC: March 1998.

Miller, Mark E., and W. Pete Welch. "Growth in Medicare Inpatient Physician Charges per Admission, 1986–1989." *Inquiry* 30 (fall 1993), pp. 249–59.

Muller, Andreas. "Medicare Prospective Payment Reforms and Hospital Utilization." *Medical Care* 31 (1993), pp. 296–308.

Neuman, Patricia, et al. "Marketing HMOs to Medicare Beneficiaries." *Health Affairs* 17 (July/August 1998), pp. 132–39.

Oberlander, Jonathan B. "Managed Care and Medicare Reform." *Journal of Health Politics, Policy and Law* 22 (April 1997), pp. 595–632.

Oliver Thomas R. "Analysis, Advice, and Congressional Leadership: The Physician Payment Review Commission and the Politics of Medicare." *Journal of Health Politics, Policy and Law* 18 (spring 1993), pp. 113–74.

Physician Payment Review Commission. *Annual Report to Congress.* Washington, DC: 1997.

Physician Payment Review Commission. *Annual Report to Congress.* Washington, DC: PPRC, 1994.

Physician Payment Review Commission. *Annual Report to Congress.* Washington, DC: PPRC, 1993.

Schwartz, Anne, David C. Colby, and Anne Lenhard Reisinger. "Variation in Medicaid Physician Fees." *Health Affairs* 10 (spring 1991), pp. 131–39.

Schwartz, William B., and Daniel N. Mendelson. "Hospital Cost Containment in the 1980's." *New England Journal of Medicine* 324 (April 11, 1991), pp. 1037–42.

"States Turning More to Managed Care for Medicaid." *The Nation's Health*, March 1995, p. 11.

Steinwald, Bruce, and Laura A. Dummit. "Hospital Case-Mix Changes: Sicker Patients or DRG Creep?" *Health Affairs* (summer 1989), pp. 35–47.

U.S. Department of Health and Human Services, Social Security Administration. *Annual Statistical Supplement; 1997.* Washington, DC: 1997.

U.S. Department of Health and Human Services, Social Security Administration. *Annual Statistical Supplement, 1993.* Washington, DC: 1993.

Wilensky, Gail R., and Louis F. Rossiter. "Coordinated Care and Public Programs." *Health Affairs* 10 (winter 1991), pp. 62–77.

Yett, Donald E., William Der, Richard L. Ernst, and Joel W. Hay. "Fee-for-Service Reimbursement and Physician Inflation." Journal of Human Resources 20 (spring 1985), pp. 278–91.

## CEBS Questions

CEBS Sample Question on Subject Matter from CEBS Course IX Study Manual

1. What are ways in which Congress over the years has encouraged physician participation in the Medicare program? (pages 361–362)

CEBS Sample Exam Questions

1. Not counting the 60 day lifetime reserve, Medicare covers hospital inpatient expenses for a maximum of:
   A. 30 days
   B. 60 days
   C. 90 days
   D. 120 days
   E. 360 days

2. The Balanced Budget Act of 1997 contained which of the following major changes in the Medicare program?
    I. The Act limited reimbursement of Medicare expenditures to two-thirds the cost of comparable services in 1995, the base year of cost measurement
    II. The Act expanded the number of alternative types of risk-based health insurance plans eligible to participate in the plan.
    III. The Act changed the method of calculating the monthly capitation payment received by private health insurance plans that enter into risk contracts with Medicare.
    A. II only
    B. III only
    C. I and II only
    D. II and III only
    E. I, II, and III

3. All the following statements regarding the financing and cost of Medicaid are correct EXCEPT:
    A. The cost is financed jointly by the federal and state governments
    B. In the years 1992 through 1996 the rate of growth in Medicare expenditures has increased dramatically
    C. Federal mandates, such as required coverage of children and pregnant women, have increased Medicaid expenditures
    D. The percent of Medicaid recipients enrolled in managed care plans varies widely across states
    E. Disproportionate share hospital payments have contributed to the rise in Medicaid expenditures

*Answer to Sample Question from Study Manual*
The ways in which Congress has encouraged physician participation has been by guaranteeing reimbursement minus any deductibles or copayments directly from Medicare, by placing limits on the amount nonparticipating physicians could charge Medicare patients, and by placing constraints on balance billing.

*Answers to Sample Exam Questions*
1. C is the answer. Except for the 60-day lifetime reserve, after the 90th day Medicare stops paying hospital inpatient expenses. See page 352 of the text.
2. D is the answer. The first statement is false but the other two are true. The **Medicare + Choice** program introduced by the Act increased the types of insurance available to the Medicare participants and required that Medicare capitation payments be made on a risk adjusted basis beginning in the year 2000. See pages 363–364 of the text.
3. B is the answer. In the years 1992 through the 1996 the rate of growth in expenditures dropped. All other statements are correct. See page 349 of the text.

# IV

# *Health Industry Studies*

# 13

# The Private Health Insurance Industry

O ur pal Joe was sort of lucky. Sure he suffered a heart attack. That, in itself, can be a medically frightening and painful experience. But as a federal employee, Joe and his family were covered by a sound and generous health insurance policy so at least they did not have to bear the sharp psychological sting of the financial insecurity that can result from an unexpected medical occurrence.[1]

However, Leo, Joe's brother, was not so fortunate. You see Leo worked as a machinist in a specialty parts fabrication shop that employs five workers. Given the competitive nature of the market for specialty machined goods, Leo's employer was financially unable to sponsor any health insurance for the workers. But Leo and his wife, Sarah, really didn't care about the lack of health insurance anyway. They are both in their early fifties, which is relatively young by today's standards, and seemed to be in great health. They had built up a small nest egg of $50,000 and planned on using the money to support an early semi-retirement where Leo would quit his job and open a machine shop in his garage. At 65 years of age both Leo and Sarah would be eligible for Medicare and then they were all set—or so they thought.

Then all hell broke loose. Sarah found a lump on her breast! A visit to a local doctor confirmed her most feared suspicion. She was diagnosed with a cancerous tumor. Since Sarah had not received annual physicals due to what she considered an unnecessary out-of-pocket expense, the cancer was at an advanced stage. Too late for a simple lumpectomy or chemotherapy, a radical mastectomy was deemed the necessary treatment. Not only were Leo and Sarah distraught over Sarah's physical and mental well-being, but also saddened that their hard-earned life savings would be completely wiped out.

---

[1]Federal employees, including those who work in the legislative and executive branches, are covered by the Federal Employee Health Benefits (FEHB) program. The FEHB program gives the subscriber a choice of over 400 different health insurance plans (see Moffitt, 1992).

This story helps to raise a number of important questions:

1. Who exactly are the uninsured? That is, are specific groups or individuals, like employees of small businesses, at a greater risk of being uninsured than others?

2. Suppose that Leo had participated in a group health insurance policy with his employer but decided to change jobs. Would he and Sarah be immediately eligible for health insurance with the new employer, especially with Sarah's condition already diagnosed?

3. If Leo had a group health insurance policy with his employer, could the employer legally raise his health insurance premiums or exclude Sarah from the policy?

This chapter deals with these questions, among others, and raises a host of other problems and issues pertaining to the private health insurance industry. The examination is couched in terms of the structure conduct and performance paradigm discussed in Chapter 9. Specifically, this chapter:

- Provides a brief history of the private health insurance industry.

- Analyzes the structure of the private health insurance industry in terms of the number and types of sellers, buyer characteristics, barriers to entry, and other factors.

- Describes the conduct of firms in the private health insurance industry with respect to pricing methods, managed care effects, and risk selection.

- Assesses the performance of the private health insurance industry with regard to the number of insured and uninsured, pricing, moral hazard, and innovativeness.

## A Brief History of the Private Health Insurance Industry

The modern private health insurance industry started around 1929 when Baylor University in Dallas began accepting insurance premiums from local schoolteachers to cover any medical services provided at the university hospital (Temin, 1988).[2] The idea quickly spread during the Great Depression of the 1930s as a number of hospitals adopted similar financing methods. Shortly thereafter, the American Hospital Association created and organized several insurance plans, named Blue Cross, which allowed subscribers free choice among the hospitals within a given city. Corresponding to the alleged public service nature of Blue Cross plans, premiums were determined

---

[2]According to Sapolsky (1991), a few paternalistic employers, including General Motors and Procter & Gamble, established welfare programs with medical benefits for their employees prior to 1926.

by community rating.[3] The Blue Cross plans enjoyed a virtual monopoly position in the hospital insurance market throughout the 1930s.

The hospital insurance market expanded and the level of competition intensified during World War II, when the federal government imposed wage and price controls. Because wage increases were restricted, the only way employers could attract additional laborers was to offer fringe benefits, such as private health insurance. Initially, employers did not report the value of the fringe benefits to the Internal Revenue Service, but eventually regulations were passed requiring employers to include the value of medical care as part of reported wage income. By that time, however, workers had become accustomed to the tax-exempt status of medical insurance and expressed considerable alarm. Congress responded, and health insurance has remained tax exempt ever since (Friedman, 1992).

Commercial insurance companies were slow to branch off into the health insurance market because they were uncertain about its profitability (Sapolsky, 1991) and doubted whether medical care was an insurable risk due to the difficulty in predicting losses accurately (Iglehart, 1992). The Blue Cross experience demonstrated the viability of health insurance to commercial insurers. By the time the commercials entered the industry in the late 1940s, Blue Cross plans were viewed as pro-union, having established a strong union allegiance. As employers looked to alternative sources for private health insurance, commercial plans searched for clients. The commercial insurance segment later grew as the rate of union membership declined among workers and experience rating became more common among employer groups. According to Temin (1988), "Blue Cross accounted for only two-thirds of hospital insurance by the war's close, and it had less than half of the market in the 1950s and 1960s" (p. 89).

Today the private health insurance industry is the source of funds for 33 percent of all health care expenditures, providing coverage to roughly 70 percent of the population. The modern health insurance industry is very pluralistic, composed of many different types of health plan providers that include health maintenance organizations, preferred provider organizations, self-insurers, third-party administrators, and traditional insurers with and without utilization review. Some of these insurers are nonprofit entities, whereas others are for-profit organizations. Moreover, many of them rely on different methods of reimbursing health care providers for medical services rendered to their subscribers. The rest of this chapter examines the structure, conduct, and performance of the private health insurance industry.

# The Structure of the Private Health Insurance Industry

As noted in Chapter 9, structure is an important feature of an industry because it influences the conduct and performance of the member firms. The private health

---

[3]Community rating determines premiums based on a broadly defined group; thus, personal health risk matters very little as a determinant of the price an individual pays for insurance. On the other hand, experience rating determines premiums based on a much narrower definition of the group; hence, individuals pay a price closer to their expected medical costs. The two rating schemes are described and compared more fully shortly.

insurance industry, or at least the group health insurance industry, is probably best described as conforming closely to the characteristics of perfect competition. According to Gabel and Jensen (1992),

> Group health insurance shares many of the characteristics of an atomistic competitive market. More than a million buyers (employers) purchase their product from over a thousand insurers, health maintenance organizations, and third party administrators. Exit and entry into the market is relatively free. One insurer's product can easily substitute for a competitor's. This is particularly true for indemnity products without utilization management (p. 250).

In the following discussion, we take a closer look at some of the structural characteristics associated with the private health insurance industry.

## Number, Types, and Size Distribution of Health Insurers

Table 13–1 reveals that about 185 million people had some type of private health insurance as of 1995. Of these, about 77 million people were enrolled in commercial plans, nearly 66 million subscribed to Blue Cross/Blue Shield plans, 61 million belonged to self-insured plans, and 59 million subscribed to health maintenance organizations. (In the table, people who belong to other managed care organizations like PPOs sponsored by commercial insurers or the Blues are included in the membership figures for the two insurers.)

As mentioned at the beginning of the chapter, many analysts consider the private health insurance industry to be structurally competitive. The exact number of commercial health insurers is unknown (largely because insurance companies provide many different insurance products, such as automotive, casualty, life, and health insurance product lines, and can easily switch among them), but estimates range from 500 to 1,250 companies. National Underwriters lists 748 commercial health insurers in *Profiles of 1992 Health Insurers*. Most of the listed health insurance companies are national, or at least regional, in scope since they are usually licensed in a large number of states. Whereas the top companies like Prudential and Aetna are large in an absolute sense, the private for-profit segment of the industry appears to be relatively unconcentrated since the top four commercial health insurers account for only about 22 percent of premiums: the top eight have a 35 percent share. Economists often consider four-firm concentration ratios of around 40 percent as reflecting mild oligopoly.[4]

There are 55 independent Blue Cross and Blue Shield plans across the United States, each usually operating in a different geographical area.[5] Unlike the commercial companies, which sell all types of health insurance, Blue Cross plans normally specialize

---

[4]The four-firm concentration ratio represents the percentage of industry output produced by the largest four firms. As the ratio increases in value, the four firms produce a greater concentrated share of industry output. The implication is that the firms possess greater market power as the four-firm concentration ratio increases in magnitude.

[5]Data taken from http://www.bluecares.com

| TABLE 13-1 | TYPES OF PRIVATE HEALTH INSURERS AND NUMBER OF ENROLLEES. 1995 (MILLIONS) |
|---|---|

| | |
|---|---|
| Total private insurance | 185.3 |
| Insurance companies | 76.6 |
|    Group policies | 83.3 |
|       Fully insured | 37.1 |
|       ASO | 39.9 |
|       MPP | 6.3 |
|    Individual | 7.0 |
| Blue Cross/Blue Shield | 65.6 |
| Self-insured | 61.0 |
| HMO | 59.1 |
|    Blue Cross/Blue Shield | 8.8 |
|    Insurance Companies | 8.5 |
|    Independent | 41.8 |

Source: *Source Book of Health Insurance Data 1997/98*, Washington, DC: Health Insurance Association of America, Table 2–11.

in hospital insurance and Blue Shield specializes in medical-surgical insurance. The Blues, being primarily organized on a nonprofit basis, typically do not compete among themselves except in a few places like Ohio and the Maryland–Washington, DC area (Frech, 1993), but they do compete with commercial insurers and plans in the "other" category. As mostly nonprofit entities, the Blues are often exempt from state taxes, such as property taxes, and state premium taxes tend to be lower for the Blues than for commercial insurers. Collectively, the Blue plans represent the nation's largest provider of managed care, involving more than 41.3 million people. The 72 Blue PPOs collectively covered 22.5 million people while the 84 Blue HMO and 66 POS plans covered 12.4 and 6.4 million, respectively, in 1996. The market shares of the Blue plans vary considerably across the states, with the Northeast having the greatest market share.

The market share of the self-insured plans has been growing most rapidly over the last three decades, from 49.7 million members in 1990 to 61.0 million in 1995. The growth occurred largely because self-insured plans expanded as they are exempt from premium taxes, which can run as high as 2 percent, and are subject to the Employee Retirement Income Security Act (ERISA) of 1974, which exempts self-insured plans from providing state-mandated benefits. According to Iglehart (1992), "there are now 900 such mandates nationwide, the most frequent among them being those for alcohol treatment (required in 42 states), mammography screening (41 states), mental health care (32 states), and drug abuse treatment (31 states)" (p. 1719).

As noted in Chapter 2, large employers with self-insured plans assume the risk, although third-party administrators (TPAs) may administer the plan. In 1992 for example, administrative services only (ASO) arrangements accounted for 45 percent of total commercial health insurance business and minimum premium payment (MPP) arrangements accounted for another 15 percent (Health Insurance Association of America, 1995). Under an ASO arrangement, a corporation or other organization (e.g., a labor union or a fraternal society) establishes a self-funded health plan and pays a fee to an insurance carrier for processing claims. Under MPP arrangements, employers self-fund their plans but purchase stop-loss insurance for excessive claims.[6]

Due to medical cost control concerns, many employers have turned to MCOs for their health insurance coverage. Presently over 500 HMOs operate in the United States enrolling about 59 million people or slightly over 20 percent of the population, with 10 states having more than 25 percent of their population enrolled in HMOs. The regional market share of HMOs is lowest in the southern states and highest in the New England and Pacific states. Maryland has the highest HMO enrollment at about 41 percent of the population (Health Insurance Association of America, 1997/98). The top four and eight HMOs accounted for approximately 31 and 45 percent, respectively, of all HMO members in the nation as of 1995.

Finally, about 117 million people are enrolled in 2,687 PPOs (Health Insurance Association of America, 1997/98). Texas contains the most PPO networks with 88, followed by 85 PPOs in Florida. Data on the size distribution of PPOs in the United States are unavailable.

These figures on the number and size distribution of the various insurers portray a very pluralistic health insurance industry composed of a large number of competing commercial, Blue Cross and Blue Shield, self-insured, and independent HMO plans. Let us now turn to the structure of the buyer side of the private health insurance industry.

## Buyer Characteristics

Characteristics of the buyer also play a significant role in health insurance markets. Particularly important in health insurance markets is whether the health insurance policy is purchased individually or through a group. Group premiums are lower partly because of the discount obtainable through monopsony buying power. In addition, agents for the group policies, such as employers or union representatives, generally possess the requisite knowledge to make more informed choices than an individual buyer of health insurance. It is probably for these reasons that "state regulation of commercial premiums tends to focus on the adequacy of benefit to premium ratios of policies sold to individuals; commercial group insurance premiums tend to be unregulated" (Adamache and Sloan, 1983, p. 226).[7] The Clinton administration's proposal to encourage

---

[6]Stop-loss insurance is protection purchased by self-funded buyers against the risk of large losses or severe adverse claims experience.

[7]Adamache and Sloan also note that "state regulation of the Blues' rates tends to be on the total premium, not to the benefit-to-premium ratio, and applies to group as well as individual insurance" (p. 226).

purchasing alliances through the proposed National Health Security Act of 1993 reflected the belief that price discounts are obtainable through group buying. As table 13–1 shows, an overwhelming majority of commercial health insurance is purchased through a group rather than individually. While the data are unavailable, a majority of Blue and "other" plan policies are most certainly purchased through groups rather than by individuals or families.

### Barriers to Entry

When high enough, barriers deter the entry of new firms. In the private health insurance industry, scale economies in administering health insurance may serve as a barrier to entry. Scale economies enable existing firms with large volumes of output to underprice new, low-volume competitors and discourage their entry. Pricing to deter entry is referred to as **limit pricing.** Blair, Jackson, and Vogel (1975) examined the existence of economies of scale by using multiple regression analysis to investigate the relationship between administration expenses and the size of insurance output for a sample of 307 insurance companies in 1968. If per-unit administrative costs declined with output, that would be evidence that scale economies exist in the administration of health insurance.

As a measure of average administrative costs, the authors used total operating costs divided by health premiums. As a measure of the size of health insurance output, they selected the dollar value of premiums written. While premiums written captured both insurance output and price differences across firms, the use of premiums was legitimate if output was homogeneous and competitive pressure forced firms to charge the same price. Blair, Jackson, and Vogel found that per-unit administrative costs were inversely related to output, as measured by premiums, suggesting that long-run economies of scale exist in the administration of health insurance. The policy implication of the empirical findings is that the administration of health insurance should be centralized among a few insurance companies if the goal is to minimize administrative costs.

In a follow-up study, Blair and Vogel (1978) used survivor analysis (Stigler, 1958) to examine the existence of economies of scale in the provision of health insurance. **Survivor theory** supposes that firm-size classes with expanding populations are more efficient than those with shrinking populations over time. Firms in expanding size classes have obviously met and survived the market test. The survivor test, unlike the econometric test discussed earlier, reflects overall economies in the provision of health insurance, not just scale economies associated with the administrative function. To conduct the survivor test, Blair and Vogel constructed seven firm-size classes for commercial health insurers based on real premium volume. They then analyzed the percentage of commercial health insurers falling into the various size classes over the period 1958 to 1973.

The authors found that the percentage of firms and total premium volume fell in the smallest firm-size category over time. The other six firm-size classes either grew or remained relatively constant as a percentage of either total premium volume or total firms. Thus, the results of their survivor test suggest that the optimal size extends over quite a large range of output, except for the smallest size category, providing support for constant returns to scale. According to Blair and Vogel (p. 528), the econometric and survivor tests, taken together, indicate that the administrative scale economies "must have been swamped by diseconomies elsewhere" in some other function(s), such as risk bearing, marketing, and so on.

Finally, state price and quality regulations also exist and may deter entry of new insurance firms. But these barriers to entry do not appear to be overly restrictive, because well over 100 insurance companies typically operate within a state. All in all, barriers to entry are of minor importance in the health insurance industry.

## Consumer Information

One of the likely noncompetitive features of the private health insurance industry concerns consumer knowledge. Recall that when individuals possess imperfect information they may pay higher prices and/or receive lower quality when compared to a situation with perfect information. For those people belonging to a group plan, this problem may not be as severe since specialists, like human resource managers or union representatives, often provide individuals with the information to make more educated choices. However, those people purchasing individual plans may lack the technical information needed to accurately assess the true value of a health insurance policy. For instance, an individual may be confronted with numerous plans, each offering slightly different benefits, exclusions, and out-of-pocket payments.

Prior to the Omnibus Budget Reconciliation Act (OBRA) of 1990, the market for medigap insurance provided a good example of the importance of consumer information when purchasing insurance. As mentioned earlier, medigap policies are purchased by individuals to cover any medical payments not reimbursed by Medicare, such as the monthly premium under Part B. Prior to the act, insurers were allowed to offer any number of medigap policies. Reinhardt (1992) pointed out that these policies have been so difficult to comprehend that "many of the elderly have been induced to buy multiple, duplicate policies—probably an intended byproduct of an intended confusion" (p. A5). Reinhardt goes on to note the low payout rate (percent of premiums paid out as benefits) and therefore higher price among commercial insurers for medigap policies (66 percent on average compared to 93.4 percent for traditional Blue Cross/Blue Shield policies) and on small business insurance plans (as low as 77 percent for firms with fewer than 20 employees).

Included as part of the Omnibus Budget Reconciliation Act of 1990 was a provision to reform the medigap market. The legislation attempted to provide more informed consumer choice and thereby promote competition in the medigap market. The law stipulated that after July 1992 only 10 standard insurance policies, based on increasing levels of comprehensiveness, could be sold as Medicare supplements to individuals. The basic belief was that 10 policies represented sufficient choice and that standardization would facilitate comparisons and promote informed buying of medigap policies.

According to McCormack, Fox, Rice, and Graham (1996), the legislation had the intended impact. After the law when into effect, consumer complaints declined considerably in various states because shopping for a policy became easier and more straightforward. Many of those interviewed believed that consumer confusion declined as a result of standardization and because consumers were able to make more informed decisions. In addition, the researchers found that the price of medigap insurance declined, as theory suggests when consumers make more informed decisions. Specifically, the price of an individual medigap policy fell from an average of $1.29 per benefit dollar during the period 1990–1992 to an average of $1.27 for the period 1993–1994.

However, other individual health insurance policies are not as standardized as medigap policies are now. Those not covered by Medicare and who purchase individual plans often face a choice among multitude plans with varying benefits, clauses, and exclusions. Although diversity of choices often provides utility, diversity can also be costly when it leads to confused choice. Consequently, informational imperfections may result in some noncompetitive behavior in the individual policy segment of the private health insurance industry.

# The Conduct of the Private Health Insurance Industry

The structure of the private health insurance industry appears to be highly competitive. Numerous insurance providers, low barriers to entry, and relatively homogeneous products all point to that conclusion. Now we examine how a competitive market structure affects the conduct of private health insurers as the structure, conduct, and performance paradigm suggests it should. Among the behavioral aspects discussed are pricing, managed care effects, cherry picking behavior, and adverse selection.

## Price Competition among Health Insurers

Health insurers determine premiums by using community or experience rating. When an insurance company uses **community rating,** the premium is based on the risk characteristics of its entire membership. However, pure community rates may differ by geographical location due to cost-of-living considerations, type of contract (individual or family), and benefit design (level of copayments, deductibles, and benefit coverage). Rates paid by individuals in the plan do not differ according to health history or status if premiums are community rated (Chollet and Paul, 1994). As a result, some cross-subsidization among subscribers takes place as low-risk individuals subsidize high-risk individuals. That is, low-risk people pay more than their expected medical costs, and high-risk people pay less when the plan is community rated. For example, elderly and nonelderly subscribers pay the same community-rated premium even though elderly people use medical services more intensively.

In contrast, when premiums are determined using **experience rating,** insurers place individuals, or a group of individuals, into different risk categories based on various identifiable personal characteristics, such as age, gender, industrial occupation, and prior illnesses. Premiums are then based on geographical location, type of contract, and benefit design but also on the relation between risk category and expected health care costs as determined by using historical data. Under experience rating, individuals or groups of individuals pay a price closer to their expected medical costs.

In either case, a private health insurance company sets the premium equal to the expected benefits to be paid out (E[BEN]), plus any marketing and administrative expenses (ADMIN), federal, state, and local taxes (TAX), and profits (PROFIT), or

**(13–1)** Premium = E(BEN) + ADMIN + TAX + PROFIT.

The dollar benefits the insurance company expects to pay out are equal to the actual benefits, BEN, plus some forecast error, $e$; that is,

**(13–2)** E(BEN) = BEN + $e$.

Since people can expect to receive some of their premiums back in the form of reimbursed medical expenditures, health economists sometimes measure the price of insurance, or loading fee, using the ratio of premiums to actual benefits paid out, or Premium/BEN. The ratio can be obtained by substituting equation 13–2 into equation 13–1 and dividing by the actual dollar benefits paid out, or

**(13–3)**
$$\text{Price} = 1 + \frac{\text{ADMIN} + \text{TAX} + \text{PROFIT} + e}{\text{BEN}}.$$

The price of health insurance reveals the average amount that must be spent in premiums to receive one dollar in benefits. For example, a price of $1.25 means the representative individual pays $1.25 to receive $1 in benefits, on average. The remaining 25 cents is the loading fee. The magnitude of the loading fee depends on a host of factors, including the administrative technology, tax laws, any forecast errors, and the competitive nature of the market for private health insurance (Sindelar, 1988).

In a competitive market, the loading fee is driven to a normal level, that is, a level that is sufficient to pay for necessary administrative and marketing costs, taxes, and a normal profit rate (if a commercial insurer). Given that the health insurance industry is structurally competitive, at least in the group health insurance market, incentives most likely exist for price competition among health insurers.

However, many health insurers have begun to compete not only on the basis of price (loading fee) but also on the ability to control health care costs—the actual health benefits paid out. Prior to the 1980s, the nonprofit Blue Cross plans dominated many markets and were controlled by hospital interests. Lacking incentives, Blue Cross plans pursued a policy of encouraging complete health insurance coverage. The policy led to high hospital prices and medical costs and elevated health insurance premiums (Hay and Leahy, 1987).[8] Now that health care benefits have grown to such a large fraction of total compensation (see Insight 5–1), private health insurance sponsors, including employers, unions, and governments, have become more cost conscious and have

---

[8]The **moral hazard** problem associated with complete insurance coverage is discussed in the section on performance.

## Tracing the Profitability Cycle of Health Insurance

Over the past several decades, private health insurers have generally experienced three consecutive years of underwriting gains, followed by three consecutive years of underwriting losses, in the group health insurance market. This phenomenon is referred to as the **underwriting or profitability cycle.** The profitability cycle holds for both commercial insurers and nonprofit Blue Cross and Blue Shield plans. Health insurance premium increases are shown to follow the profitability cycle with a lag of about two years (Gabel, Formisano, Lohr, and Di Carlo, 1991).

In seeking to explain the root cause of the cycle, Gabel, Formisano, Lohr, and Di Carlo (1991) point to three broad causes: supply and demand forces, industry pricing actions, and external factors. According to the authors, supply and demand forces can affect the profitability of health insurers in two ways.

First, because of free entry in health insurance markets, firms enter the market in times of excess profits. As a result, price falls and some firms experience losses and exit the market. Exit reduces supply, price increases, and profits return. The cycle begins once again.

Second, the "cobweb" model may explain the cycle. When the price of health insurance is relatively high in the present period, insurers act on the information by deciding to sell more insurance policies in the next period. The greater supply, in turn, leads to lower prices in the next period, especially because the demand for group health insurance is relatively price inelastic and modest supply changes lead to dramatic price changes. Hence, current prices affect future supply decisions, and this results in a continual cycling of prices and profits.

Industry pricing actions consider that insurers may reduce prices to increase market share and raise them later to compensate for past losses. In addition, actuarial pricing techniques often extrapolate the recent past to the future from recent claims experience. If decision makers form "adaptive expectations," they will systematically overestimate true premiums in periods of falling claims and underestimate true premiums in periods of rising claims. According to Gabel, Formisano, Lohr, and Di Carlo, this type of pricing behavior, although irrational, has been shown to result in a cyclical profitability pattern.

Another industry pricing explanation supposes that all insurers tacitly collude at first and follow the pricing pattern of the leader firm(s). At some point, however, individual firms are tempted to reduce prices to gain greater market share, and the informal cartel breaks down. Eventually, the pattern repeats itself.

Finally, external factors, including underlying claims events and general economic conditions, may cause the profitability cycle. That is, medical care costs and general factors ranging from the budget deficit, national unemployment, and interest rates may follow a business cycle pattern and generate the insurance profitability cycle.

No studies to date have tested the alternative explanations for the profitability cycle. A lack of suitable data most likely accounts for the void in the literature. In a more recent study, Gabel and Jensen (1992) point to industry pricing policies as the primary culprit behind the profitability cycle. Specifically, they write,

> Because insurers forecast a continuation of the experience of the recent past in the future, they systematically understate and overstate trends. As sellers of a substitutable product in a competitive market, and based on erroneous projections of future costs, when earning underwriting profits, insurers attempt to increase market share by underpricing their competitors, only to face financial losses subsequently. This sets up the next phase of catch-up pricing, where premiums increase by excessive double digit amounts (p. 260).

*(continued)*

*(continued)*

One of the most important lessons of this insight is that premium increases must be properly interpreted in the context of the profitability cycle. To say that premium increases are low this year does not mean some trend of low premium increases has set in. Rather, the low premium increases of today may mean tomorrow's premium increases will be larger if the profitability cycle continues to hold.

demanded health care cost containment from private insurers. In response, most of the large commercial insurers, such as Aetna, Prudential, and Metropolitan, and Blue Cross plans have added managed-care policies to their traditional insurance product lines. As discussed next, managed-care policies are designed to control health care costs. Thus, competition has created an incentive for health insurers to hold down both the loading fee and actual medical benefits paid out.

In trying to contain both the loading fee and benefits paid, health insurers now face an interesting trade-off. Managed care contains health care costs (or benefits paid out) most effectively through various administrative functions such as utilization review. However, more spending on administrative functions leads to a higher loading fee (see equation 13–3). Economic principles suggest that an insurer chooses the optimal amount of an input by equating its marginal benefit and marginal cost. Hence, the optimal amount of administrative services occurs when the marginal medical cost savings (marginal benefit) equals the price (marginal cost) of an additional administrative input. Cost containment means that managed-care activities will continue to increase in scope and, consequently, larger loading fees are likely to result. The magnitude of the premium level, the sum of benefits paid out, and the loading fee, will reflect the overall success or failure of managed-care activities. With that idea in mind, the following section discusses the role and effects of managed-care organizations.

### Managed-Care Organizations and Insurance Premiums

Managed-care organizations (MCOs), which include HMOs and PPOs, integrate the delivery of health care with the insurance function. Advocates have claimed that MCOs are capable of reducing the level and growth of health insurance premiums. The reduction of health insurance premiums comes about in two ways. First, because MCOs are prepaid, they face a profit incentive to contain medical costs by adopting utilization controls and by negotiating discounted medical prices. In response to competition, MCOs lower health insurance premiums in line with the actual costs of servicing their own subscribers. Second, the competition from MCOs motivates traditional insurers to make similar improvements in utilization and costs and to reduce their premiums or face the prospect of losing business.

As discussed in Chapter 5, a host of studies (e.g., Manning et al., 1984; Rapoport, 1992; Miller and Luft, 1994) have found that MCOs, especially HMOs, attain medical cost savings of about 15 to 20 percent through a reduced hospital-intensive practice style.[9] The question is whether lower medical costs translate into reduced premiums for MCOs compared to conventional fee-for-service insurance. Simple averages of monthly premiums by plan type suggest that premium levels are lower in MCOs. For example, in 1997 the average monthly premium for a family was $503 if covered by a conventional insurer but only $430, $444, and $464 if insured by an HMO, a PPO, or a POS plan, respectively (Health Insurance Association of America, 1997/98). The simple averages are misleading, however, because the scope and level of benefits and patient cost sharing may differ across plan types.

Some economists argue that the reduced medical costs associated with MCOs may not result in lower premiums. One reason premiums may not be lower in MCOs is that the greater administrative costs (loading fee) associated with MCOs swamp any medical cost savings (benefits paid out) as pointed out above.

As another explanation, Feldman, Dowd, and Gifford (1993) note that "many companies accuse HMOs of 'shadow-pricing,' that is, setting their premiums just below those of commercial carriers. HMOs can profit from shadow pricing if they tend to enroll a disproportionate share of young, healthy workers in the firm" (p. 781). The authors compared the weighted average HMO and fee-for-service (FFS) premiums in firms that offer both HMOs and FFS plans to the premium of FFS-only firms. They found that offering an HMO plan raises rather than lowers the average premium of an insurance policy for family and single coverage. Insurance premiums might rise if HMOs skim the healthiest patients and thereby drive up FFS costs and premiums (Baker and Corts, 1995).

McLaughlin (1988) argues that the health insurance market has responded to managed care insurance with cost-increasing rivalry, not price competition. That is, both FFS insurers and managed-care insurers have chosen to compete on service offerings rather than on price.

While the verdict on the relation between MCOs and the level and growth of economywide insurance premiums is still out, a couple of studies have examined the effects of managed care competition on the growth of indemnity insurance premiums and on the level of HMO premiums in specific markets. Wickizer and Feldstein (1995) provide some empirical evidence that MCOs may have led to lower health indemnity insurance premiums over time. Specifically, the researchers use multiple regression analysis to isolate and examine the impact of the HMO market penetration rate on the growth of indemnity insurance premiums for 95 insured groups over the period from 1985 to 1992. They find empirically that the HMO penetration rate had an inverse impact on the growth of indemnity insurance premiums. As an illustration, they estimate that the real rate of growth in premiums would be approximately 5.9 percent instead of 7 percent for an average group located in a market where the HMO penetration rate increased by 25 percent. The authors conclude by noting that their results "indicate that competitive strategies, relying on managed care, have significant potential to reduce health insurance premium growth rates, thereby resulting in substantial cost savings over time (p. 250)."

---

[9]See the various health care industry studies in the following chapters for detailed information about the relation between managed care and medical cost savings.

In addition, Wholey, Feldman, and Christianson (1995) use multiple regression analysis to examine the impact of HMO competition on the level of HMO premiums across various metropolitan areas in the U.S. for the years 1988 to 1991. The authors find that more competition, as measured by the number of HMOs in the market area, reduces the size of HMO premiums. Their study, however, is unable to determine the impact of managed care competition on indemnity insurance premiums or the impact of indemnity insurance competition on managed care premiums, so much remains to be determined empirically.

In sum, MCOs have achieved sizable medical cost savings from various utilization and cost control techniques. To date, little systematic evidence suggests that the cost savings have led to lower health insurance premiums on an economywide basis. High administrative costs, a lack of consumer price consciousness, and an absence of price competition in health insurance markets may be some of the reasons lower health insurance premiums have not materialized on a broad scale.

## Cherry-Picking Behavior and Benefit Denial

Many health care experts believe that competition among insurers in conjunction with experience rating provides an incentive for insurers, as a group, to offer health insurance to healthy individuals but deny coverage to people with poor health. The best cherries (the healthy) are picked off the tree, while the worst are left dangling. The reasoning behind the cherry-picking behavior is rather straightforward. Facing increased market competition, insurers are forced to lower premiums. One way to lower premiums is to insure only low-risk individuals. The end result is that health insurance companies tend to compete for low-risk individuals, that is, healthy people. Those in poor health are either denied access to health insurance or charged prohibitively high prices.

Individuals who belong to large, employment-based group policies, which are the predominant form of private health insurance in the United States, are relatively insulated from this problem. While premiums for experience-rated group policies are adjusted annually based on the actual claims experience of the group and changes in medical care prices, the total cost is distributed equally among all group members, thus minimizing the burden for any one individual.

In contrast, people who lack access to large-group coverage have difficulty obtaining health insurance at comparable premiums (Beauregard, 1991). People who apply for insurance, either individually, as a family, or through small businesses, are usually subject to stringent insurance underwriting procedures because providing insurance to these individuals is much riskier. A health status questionnaire or physical exam is normally required. Depending on the resulting risk status of the individual(s), insurance companies usually offer health insurance at an increased premium and/or exclude coverage for any preexisting conditions for a period of one year or more. Preexisting conditions are serious illnesses that were diagnosed before the policy took effect and might include cancer, heart disease, AIDS, or care for low-birthweight babies. Conditions that trigger higher rates vary widely across insurance companies but routinely include such common conditions as hypertension, allergies, arthritis, and asthma. Thus, for individual purchasers of health insurance, especially those with chronic health problems or high-risk conditions, high premiums may be an obstacle to obtaining coverage (Beauregard, 1991).

While this view of cherry-picking behavior and access denial is generally accepted at face value, empirical studies on this topic have been relatively lacking. The only study to date, by Beauregard (1991), used data from the 1987 National Medical Expenditure Survey to estimate the number of uninsured people who were denied private health insurance or could purchase only limited coverage because of poor health.

Beauregard's study found that benefit denial is not as widespread as typically believed. In particular, only a very small proportion of the uninsured population, less than 1 percent, was found to have ever been denied private health insurance due to poor health. However, the author cautions that the figure does not include currently insured individuals whose policies exclude coverage for preexisting conditions. In 1995, about 60 percent of group health insurance plans excluded coverage for preexisting conditions. Moreover, 10 months was the average waiting period before a new employee receives coverage for a preexisting condition (Jensen et al., 1997). Finally, Beauregard's findings do not consider the number of individuals who do not apply for private health insurance because they fear denial.

## Adverse Selection and Community versus Experience Rating

**Adverse selection** is a situation where an information asymmetry can lead to undesirable results in insurance markets. Adverse selection occurs when high-risk consumers who know more about their own health status than insurers do, subscribe to an insured group composed of lower-risk individuals. To secure low premiums, the high-risk consumers withhold information concerning their true health status. Once insured, the insurer has no alternative but to increase premiums on all plan subscribers in the next period due to the higher-utilization rates of high-risk consumers. As low-risk subscribers leave the high-priced plans, "musical insurance plans" result as high-risk individuals follow low-risk individuals in pursuit of lower premiums. In addition, some insurers may find it difficult to earn a normal profit. Alternatively, some low-risk individuals may eventually find it cheaper to self-insure. If so, high-risk individuals will end up in homogeneous pools paying high premiums or being excluded from health insurance coverage.

An unstable environment of this kind is undesirable because it imposes substantial adjustment costs on society as people continually change insurers and insurers adjust employment levels to meet demand. In fact, the unstable environment may be one reason health insurers have been reluctant to pay for preventative types of care such as annual physical exams. Why should the insurer pay for the yearly exam when in all likelihood, the benefits of reduced future medical costs cannot be appropriated because individuals have changed plans?

Insurers can prevent adverse selection to some degree by limiting people's ability to change plans or through prior screening and experience rating. However, experience rating, which charges different premiums to individuals based on risk status, is often viewed as being unfair and costly. Proponents of community rating argue that experience rating is inequitable because some people are charged a higher price for insurance simply because of their poor health status. The inequity of experience rating

## Adoption of Community Rating in New York State

As of April 1, 1993, the state of New York requires that health insurers adopt community rating for all individual and small-group policies. Insurers must accept all applicants and charge all policyholders the same premium regardless of health status, gender, occupation, or age (State Health Watch, 1994). The law intends to prevent insurance companies from taking all the good risks and leaving the bad ones, thereby providing individuals with greater access to health insurance. One concern was that community rating would lead to a reduction in the number of individuals covered because low-risk individuals would choose not to purchase health insurance. Another concern was that premiums would increase as insurers and low-risk individuals left the market because of community rating.

Chollet and Paul (1994) write that as of December 1994, "New York State's experience with insurance market reform has not confirmed the fears of those opposing such reforms" (p. 21). The authors report that insurance premiums increased across the entire small-group market by only 4.6 percent during the first year, compared to a 19 percent rate increase requested by commercial insurers one year earlier. According to the study, the community rating system decreased premiums for 34 percent of policyholders in the small groups.

However, premiums increased for 48 percent of policyholders by as much as 40 percent. Eighteen percent of policyholders faced premium increases of more than 40 percent. Thus, a greater percentage of policyholders saw premium increases rather than decreases.

McCaughey (1994) reports that most of the premium increases reflect one-time adjustments for younger people. For example, the average premium for a 30–year-old man rose by 81 percent. In addition, group rates for small businesses with young workers shot up by an average of 113 percent. Consequently, the law has made health insurance less affordable for young people but more affordable for elderly individuals.

The report by Chollet and Paul also found that only four insurers left the insurance market in New York State. The withdrawing insurers had insignificant market shares in the small-group market, so their exit had no major impact. Still to be determined is whether the community rating law has resulted in an increased or a decreased number of insured in New York State. The available evidence suggests that only a very small reduction occurred in the number of small-group and individual policies in effect from March 31, 1993, to January 1, 1994 (−1.2 percent).

is particularly acute when the poor health status is uncontrollable rather than a function of a chosen adverse lifestyle. Advocates of community rating claim that experience rating also encourages cherry-picking behavior and causes higher administrative expenses as insurers laboriously sift through applicants to find low-risk individuals. According to opponents of experience rating, if insurers community-rated and accepted all applicants for coverage, they would be more interested in creating systemwide medical cost savings rather than choosing among individual low-risk subscribers.

Not surprisingly, proponents of experience rating point to the inefficiency and inequity of community rating. Under a community rating scheme, low-risk individuals are discouraged from purchasing insurance because the premium is set higher than their expected medical costs. Consequently, low-risk individuals are made worse off by community rating. Also, proponents claim that experience rating creates an incentive for people to adopt favorable lifestyles. That is, if people are required to pay more for health insurance because they smoke cigarettes or drink excessively, they will be more inclined to practice good health behaviors. Advocates of experience rating also claim there is no good reason why high-risk people are likely to be less wealthy than low-risk people, and thus a community rating system can end up redistributing income from the poor to the rich. For example, young low-income individuals may subsidize wealthy elderly individuals under a community rating system.

# The Performance of the Private Health Insurance Industry

The structural characteristics of the private health insurance industry imply that individual insurers should behave competitively. Both the sellers and the buyers of private health insurance are numerous and relatively small, and insurance firms typically sell a homogeneous product. Barriers to entry into the private insurance industry are low. Competition means the price and output of private health insurance should approach an efficient level.

According to some of the topics covered in the section on conduct, however, unfettered competition in the private health insurance industry may not be totally desirable. One reason is that price competition encourages cherry-picking behavior and denial of coverage for preexisting conditions by health insurers. Such behavior limits the ability of the private health insurance industry to provide universal health insurance coverage, which is a primary goal of many health policymakers. In addition, critics have claimed that the private health insurance industry has failed to contain health care costs.

In this section, we examine evidence on the performance of the private health insurance industry more thoroughly. We will consider measures capturing the price and output of health insurance and the factors influencing the supply and demand of health care cost containment innovations.

## Output of Private Health Insurers

**Private Health Insurance Coverage** One measure of the performance of an industry is the amount of output provided. Incentives should exist so suppliers produce the optimal amount of a product—neither too much nor too little. In the case of the private health insurance industry, optimal provision implies that the right number of people are covered by private health insurance and each person is neither overinsured nor underinsured. Theoretically, the right number of insured individuals occurs at the level where the marginal social benefit and marginal social cost of health insurance coverage are equal. Those pushing strongly for universal health insurance coverage in the United States apparently believe that marginal social benefit exceeds costs at all levels of the population.

Table 13–2 sheds some light on the first aspect of optimal insurance coverage. From 1950 to 1995, the number of people insured by private health insurance skyrocketed from 76.6 million to 185.3 million, or from 50.3 percent to 70.5 percent of the population. Notice that the percentage of people covered by private health insurance reached a peak of over 80 percent in 1980 but declined thereafter. There are a

| TABLE 13-2 | PERSONS WITH PRIVATE HEALTH INSURANCE COVERAGE, SELECTED YEARS, 1950–1995 | |
|---|---|---|
| **Year** | **Number (millions)** | **Percentage of Population** |
| 1950 | 76.6 | 50.3% |
| 1960 | 122.5 | 67.8 |
| 1970 | 158.8 | 77.4 |
| 1980 | 187.4 | 82.3 |
| 1990 | 181.7 | 72.7 |
| 1991 | 181.0 | 71.7 |
| 1992 | 180.7 | 70.5 |
| 1993 | 180.9 | 70.1 |
| 1994 | 182.2 | 69.9 |
| 1995 | 185.3 | 70.5 |

SOURCE: *Source Book of Health Insurance Data 1997–1998*, Washington, DC: Health Insurance Association of America, Table 2.5.

number of reasons for the relative decline in private health insurance coverage from 1980 to the present date.

One simple reason for the relative decline in private health insurance coverage is the increasing percentage of people 65 years of age and older who are eligible for Medicare coverage because of their age. In fact, those individuals 65 years of age and older increased from 11.3 percent to 12.8 percent of the population from 1980 to 1995 (*Statistical Abstract of the United States*). Rising health insurance premiums provide the second and probably most significant reason for the decline in private health insurance coverage. Specifically, health insurance premiums rose rapidly from the mid-1980s to early 1994, causing many employers, mostly small businesses, to either raise employee contributions or drop their health insurance coverage altogether (Acs, 1995).

A third explanation for declining coverage deals with occupational shifts from traditionally higher coverage manufacturing sector jobs to lower coverage service sectors jobs. However, Long and Rodgers (1995) find employment shifts explain only about 15 percent of the decline in employer provided private health insurance coverage. The final reason for declining coverage is the growing fraction of people covered by Medicaid. For example, almost 22 million people were covered by Medicaid in 1980. This same figure mushroomed to over 33 million people by 1996 (*Statistical Abstract of the United States*). While many people became eligible for Medicaid coverage because they lost private health insurance coverage due to the reasons above, a study by Cutler and Gruber (1995) found that liberalized government programs caused some families to drop their private health insurance coverage in favor of Medicaid. Hence, public coverage crowded out private coverage.

**Who Are the Uninsured?**    Although the long-term growth of private health insurance coverage has been fairly impressive, about 41.7 million people, or 15.6 percent of the population, were uninsured at a point in time in 1996, even after allowing for public health insurance coverage. As we will mention later, the uninsured are particularly disadvantaged both physically and psychologically, because they lack health insurance coverage. Policymakers generally wish to know which groups and individuals are more at risk so that policies might be properly designed to reduce the number of people who are uninsured. Let us examine which groups and individuals are more likely to be uninsured.

A survey by Bennefield (1997) reached a number of conclusions regarding who represent the uninsured in the United States. First, almost 31 percent of the poor had no health insurance of any kind during 1996 despite the existence of such programs as Medicaid and Medicare. Second, almost 30 percent of the individuals in the age group 19 to 24 were found to be uninsured. Typically, young adults who are not full-time students and who are excluded from parental insurance have jobs that offer no health insurance coverage.

Third, larger percentages of blacks and Hispanics than whites were uninsured. About 22 percent of blacks and 34 percent of Hispanics were uninsured in 1996, compared to 12 percent of whites not of Hispanic origin. Fourth, among adults, the likelihood of being uninsured declined with educational attainment. For example, 25 percent of the individuals without a high school diploma were uninsured whereas only 7.6 percent of those with a bachelor's degree or higher lacked health insurance coverage. (Curiously, among the poor, educational attainment had no impact on health insurance coverage.)

Fifth, part-time workers and those without a job were more likely to be uninsured compared to those who worked full-time during the year. Specifically, about 22 percent of part-time workers and 25 percent of the unemployed lack health insurance coverage compared to a figure of 16 percent for full-time workers. Sixth, noncoverage rates fall as household income rises. For instance, slightly over 24 percent of households, with annual incomes of $25,000 or less, lacked health insurance coverage. The comparable figure for households with annual incomes of $75,000 or more was only 7.6 percent. Finally, health insurance coverage was found to rise with firm size. Only 28 percent of the workers in firms hiring less than 25 workers had health insurance coverage in 1996 compared to an overall average of 53 percent for all firms and a rate of 67 percent in firms hiring 1,000 or more persons.

**Problems with Measuring the Uninsured**    Some critics argue that the reported statistic for the uninsured is deceptive because it masks some other underlying problems. Some believe the true percentage is much higher because the reported rate fails to count underinsured people and ignores **job lock,** the idea that nonportable employer-provided health insurance limits job mobility. The 1990 report of the Pepper Commission defines **underinsurance** as health insurance that leaves the person covered at risk of spending more than 10 percent of income on health care in the event of a costly illness. An estimated 13 percent of the under-65 population were underinsured by this definition in 1981—about 20 million people in 1982. (Bodenheimer, 1992)

The nonportability of employer-sponsored health insurance means workers and their dependents face the possibility of being without health insurance while the former are between jobs. Long waiting periods, preexisting health conditions, and the potential for less extensive health insurance coverage at the new job all increase the financial risk associated with costly, unanticipated medical events. In addition, the resulting job lock disrupts the proper functioning of a macroeconomy because workers are discouraged from switching to more efficient jobs. The resulting immobility of labor resources leads to a lower level of labor productivity and national income. Whether job lock truly inhibits job mobility is a concern for many health care policymakers.

Cooper and Monheit (1993) used data from the 1987 National Medical Expenditure Survey to examine the severity of job lock. They empirically studied the factors influencing job mobility, including workers' insurance status at the initial job and the prospects of obtaining coverage at a new job, initial wages and expected wage offers at new employment, other fringe benefits, and workers' and dependents' health status. The authors found that those individuals most likely to change jobs are young workers with little experience, part-time workers, people with limited education, and workers earning low hourly wages.

More important for our concerns, Cooper and Monheit found that married men who expect to lose health insurance coverage are 23 percent less likely to change jobs. Madrian (1994) concurs with Cooper and Monheit's findings and estimates that job lock reduces the voluntary employment turnover rate of married men with employer-provided health insurance by 25 percent, from 16 percent to 12 percent per year.[10]

As a result, some people argue that the reported statistic underestimates the true extent of uninsured individuals due to underinsurance and job lock concerns. Others believe the reported uninsured rate provides an overestimate. As mentioned earlier, a large percentage of young individuals lack health insurance. Most of them are healthy and are without coverage only briefly. Because young, single adults may view the price of health insurance as too high and the risk of uninsurance as low, they may choose to be uninsured.

Another issue concerns how long individuals remain in an uninsured state. The reported rate measures the number of uninsured only at a point in time, not the duration of the uninsured spell. Swartz (1994) explains that the median spell without health insurance is about six months. A median uninsured spell of six months means 50 percent of all spells without insurance are rather short and end before six months. However, another 50 percent of spells last longer than six months. At least 28 percent

---

[10]But compare these two studies to Kapur (1998).

of uninsured spells last more than one year, and 15 to 18 percent last more than two years. Swartz estimates that about 58 million people were without health insurance for at least one month and 21 million Americans were uninsured for at least a year in 1992. Being uninsured, as Swartz notes,

> frequently means receiving fewer services than insured patients and running a higher risk of dying when hospitalized. Even with fewer services, being hospitalized without health insurance is expensive. At a minimum, we can speculate that the nearly 3.5 million people hospitalized during an uninsured spell in 1992 had $7 billion worth of hospital expenses. For the 58 million people who had at least 1 month without insurance during 1992, the fear of being unlucky and drawing the "go to a hospital" card with its chancy care and high bills is real. (p. 65)

Some of the spells without private health insurance reflect the fact that people are between jobs. Seventy-three percent of employees covered by health insurance work for companies that require a waiting period averaging three months before extending medical insurance benefits to a new employee (Steinmetz, 1993). Swartz, Marcotte, and McBride (1993) found that monthly family income, educational attainment, and industry of employment in the month prior to losing health insurance are the characteristics that have the greatest impact on the duration of a spell without health insurance.

**Health Insurance Portability and Accountability Act of 1996**    Concern over the nonportability of health insurance, lengthy waiting periods for preexisting conditions, and insurance benefit denial led to the passage of the Health Insurance Portability and Accountability Act (HIPAA) in 1996. The basic idea behind HIPAA was to make it more difficult for health insurers to segment insurance risk pools and deny or revoke access to specific individuals or groups on the basis of health status. Considered by many as the most significant federal health care reform legislation since the passage of the Medicare and Medicaid programs in 1965, HIPAA created the first national standards for the availability and portability of group and individual health insurance coverage.

Prior to HIPAA (or Kassebaum/Kennedy Act) uniform standards were lacking in the health insurance industry for two reasons. First, states had been granted authority over health insurers within their jurisdictions by the McCarran-Ferguson Act of 1945 (Nichols and Blumberg, 1998). Some states chose to aggressively regulate and set standards in the health insurance industry, others did not. Second, the federal government has full responsibility for self-insured plans under the Employee Retirement Income Security Act (ERISA) of 1974. States are therefore unable to regulate the health insurance of a large percentage of U.S. workers. Furthermore, no federal regulations existed regarding the availability and portability of health insurance for self-insured plans.

HIPAA has wide-sweeping implications as the law generally applies to all health plans, including large and small group plans, state regulated plans, self-funded ERISA plans, indemnity and HMO plans, and individual plans. The major provisions as they relate to the health insurance industry are:[11]

### Guaranteed Access and Renewability

1. With certain exceptions, insurers participating in the small group market (2 through 50 employees) cannot exclude a small employer or any of the employer's eligible employees from coverage on the basis of health status.

2. Eligibility or continued eligibility of any individual to enroll in a group plan, regardless of size, cannot be conditioned on the following health-related factors: health status, medical condition (physical or mental), claims experience, receipt of health care, medical history, genetic information, or evidence of insurability or disability.

3. Individuals within a group plan cannot be charged a higher premium based on their health status. This requirement does not restrict the amount an employer may be charged for coverage under a group plan.

4. Except for certain specific exceptions (e.g., fraud, nonpayment, discontinuance of market coverage), all group coverage in both the small and large group markets and individual coverage must be renewed.

5. Generally, individual insurers must provide coverage to individuals coming off of group insurance if the individual had previous coverage for 18 months, was not eligible for other group coverage, was not terminated from the previous plan due to nonpayment, and was not eligible or had exhausted COBRA-type coverage.[12]

6. Individual insurers must guarantee to provide at least two policies. These two policies may be the insurer's most popular plans, based on premium volume, or a package of lower-level and higher-level coverage plans based on actuarial averages. The latter plans must be covered under a risk-spreading mechanism. States may elect to institute an approved alternate mechanism to provide group to individual coverage.

### Portability

1. Employees moving from one employer to another (and individuals coming off group coverage to individual coverage) are protected against a newly imposed preexisting condition limitation. In general, a plan may not impose

---

[11]There are other provisions regarding such things as medical savings accounts, tax deductibility of health insurance costs for the self-employed, long-term care insurance, and life insurance.

[12]The Consolidated Omnibus Reconciliation Act of 1985 (COBRA) requires employers to offer their former employees an option to purchase health insurance for a maximum of 18 months after termination of employment. The employee must pay the full premium plus a 2 percent administration fee.

# Who Pays for Employer-Mandated Health Insurance?

To reduce the number of uninsured, various policymakers over the years have pushed for an employer-mandated health insurance program in the United States. For example, Clinton's ill-fated National Health Security Act of 1993 required that employers provide health insurance to their full-time employees and finance at least 80 percent of the premiums (see Chapter 17). As a result, many believed, at the time, that employees would pay the remaining 20 percent of the mandated health insurance costs.

Economic principles suggest, however, that the actual economic incidence of a mandate (or tax) may differ from its statutory or legal incidence. For example, in the case of employer-mandated health insurance, it might be the case that employers simply pass on the legal share of the mandate to the employee in the form of lower wages. If so, the employee could actually pay the entire cost of the mandate.

Lee (1996) provides a conceptual model that can be used to examine who pays for an employer-mandated health insurance program. The model is presented graphically in figure 1. The figure depicts a competitive labor market in equilibrium where $W$ stands for the annual money wage and $L$ represents the number of full-time workers. Assuming no health insurance benefits are initially provided, equilibrium is at point $W_0, L_0,$ where the supply and demand curves intersect. We will now compare this initial equilibrium to one with a mandated health insurance program.

According to Lee's analysis, the mandate shifts both the supply and demand curves. The demand curve shifts to the left by the amount of the per employee cost of the insurance program, M. The shift of the demand curve to the left from $D_0$ to $D_1$ reflects that the maximum willingness to pay is determined by the value of the marginal revenue product, as discussed in Chapter 8, and that any insurance costs must be potentially offset by wage reductions. The interesting question than becomes: What happens to the supply of labor?

Just as the shift in demand reflects the per employee cost of the health insurance, the shift in the supply curve captures the benefit of the mandated insurance to the typical employee. Recall from Chapter 8 that one factor that shifts supply is the value of job amenities. If the supply curve shifts to the right by the dollar amount of the mandated benefit, it means that the typical employee values the health insurance by exactly the same amount that it costs. That is, the employee is willing to give up wage income equal to the cost of the mandated health insurance. A supply curve that shifts to the right by less than the mandated cost suggests that the value of the health insurance is less than its cost.

For discussion purposes, let us suppose that the supply curve shifts to the right by more than demand from $S_0$ to $S_1.$ That would mean that the new equilibrium wage becomes $W_1$ and that the employee pays more than the full cost of the mandated benefit. The implication is that the mandated health insurance is efficient since its benefit exceeds its cost. That is, the mandate makes employees better off, and it shows in the form of a much lower wage.

If, on the other hand, the supply curve shifts to the right by less than the mandated insurance costs, wages decline but by less than the mandated cost, reflecting that wage income is more important than health insurance at the margin. (You may want to work through this exercise.) Workers would be made worse off by the mandated benefit in this case. Consequently, the economic incidence is determined by the degree to which employees gain from the mandate. When they benefit more, employees pay a greater amount for mandated benefits in the form of lower wages.

*(continued)*

## (continued)

FIGURE 1   THE IMPACT OF AN EMPLOYER MANDATE ON A LABOR MARKET

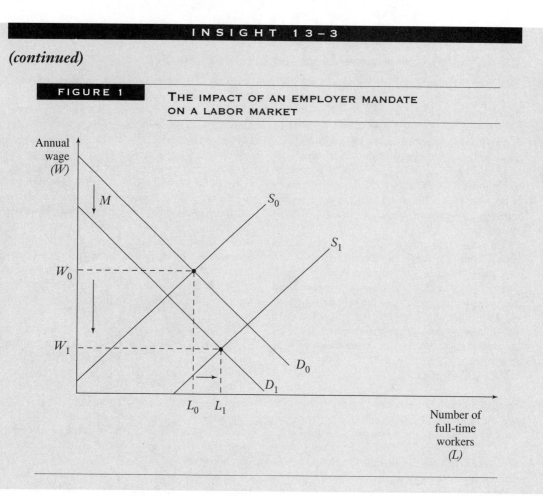

a new preexisting condition if no more than 63 days have passed between covered jobs, not including any applicable employer waiting period for new hires. The plan must also give credit for the portion of the preexisting condition satisfied under a prior plan, which can include individual coverage, dependent coverage, etc.

2.  There is a maximum exclusion period for preexisting conditions. The period is no more than 12 months, or 18 months for a late enrollee. The look-back period to determine a preexisting condition is no more than six months prior to the person's enrollment date.

3.  Preexisting condition exclusions may not apply in the case of pregnancies, or for newborns and adopted children who are covered by insurance 30 days from the date of birth or adoption.

By setting national standards, proponents hope that HIPAA will encourage health insurers to compete more on the basis of efficiency and quality rather than risk selection. Moreover, by setting national standards for availability and portability, it is hoped that there will be greater opportunities for risk-pooling. Opponents fear that the reforms will raise the price of health insurance to individuals and thereby reduce the number of insured individuals. It should be pointed out that HIPAA does not change how health care is delivered or how it is financed. Moreover, HIPAA does not increase access to health insurance for the uninsured or regulate the rates that health plans can charge (Atchinson and Fox, 1997). While HIPAA represents a major step, advocates of health care reform believe there is much more work to be done in health insurance markets.

**Overinsurance, or the Moral Hazard Problem**   Consumers normally pay the full cost of acquiring goods and services and internalize the full resource cost of their actions. Paying the full price creates a financial incentive for people to economize and use societal resources efficiently. **Moral hazard** refers to a situation where individuals, once they are covered by health insurance, change their behavior because they are no longer liable for the full cost of their actions. In particular, people may choose to pursue activities that increase the probability and/or magnitude of the loss covered by health insurance. For example, some individuals may choose to overconsume medical services (e.g., visit the doctor more often than medically necessary), pay higher than necessary prices for medical care, or fail to produce a sufficient amount of home health care services (e.g., diet and exercise). All these activities increase either the magnitude of the medical expenses or the probability of an illness occurring. The moral hazard problem manifests itself because insurers are unable to monitor the actions of the insured and an asymmetry of information results. If sufficient information existed about the true behavior of the insured, insurers could simply charge a higher premium to discourage such individuals from pursuing costly medical activities.

To the individual consumer, the current health insurance premium represents a sunk cost and is unaffected by his or her spending on medical care services.[13] In addition, any one individual is likely to believe that his or her own medical spending in isolation does not affect the future premiums of the insured group. However, if a sufficient number of people act in a similar fashion and increase their spending on medical services due to the moral hazard situation, future insurance premiums increase to reflect the greater benefits paid out.

Seidman (1982) likens the moral hazard problem to restaurant bill splitting. If two people have lunch together and decide to split the bill, each person may realize that he or she is paying only one-half of the cost of an additional dollar spent on the meal. Therefore, each individual might purchase the higher-priced imported beer rather than the lower-priced domestic beer or order the restaurant specialty rather than the less expensive special of the day. Of course, if both people behave similarly and overspend, the

---

[13]Sunk costs are irretrievable costs and therefore have no bearing on future events.

| FIGURE 13-1 | THE EFFECT OF MORAL HAZARD ON MEDICAL SERVICES UTILIZATION |

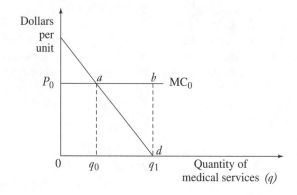

restaurant bill is higher than it would be if they paid separately for their own meals. Also, each person's share of the bill falls as the size of the sharing group increases (say, from two to six). As a result, the incentive to overspend increases with the size of the group, *ceteris paribus*, when the bill is split.

In terms of the market for medical services, moral hazard results from five different types of actions.[14] First, at any point in time when an insured event takes place, the quantity demanded of medical services may exceed the amount the consumer would buy if he or she paid the full cost. Quantity demanded may be greater because the insured consumer faces a price that lies below the marginal cost of the medical service. Figure 13–1 helps to explain the reasoning behind this moral hazard effect. The curve $MC_0$ represents the true marginal cost or market price, $P_0$, of producing units of medical services, $q$. The individual's willingness-to-pay or uninsured demand curve for medical services is represented by curve $d$. If the consumer has to pay the full cost, she or he consumes $q_0$ units of medical services. Medical expenditures equal the area $P_0aq_00$.

If the consumer pays a zero coinsurance with no deductible, however, $q_1$ units of medical services are demanded. At this quantity, medical expenditures increase to area $P_0bq_10$. The implication is that insurance lowers the consumer's out-of-pocket price and creates an incentive to overconsume medical services. For example, the consumer may visit the local physician more often than is medically necessary. The degree to which insurance leads to overconsumption depends on the price elasticity of demand for medical services. Less overconsumption results when the uninsured demand is more price inelastic. For instance, if the uninsured demand curve in figure 13–1 is perfectly inelastic (completely vertical), no overconsumption results from a lower price because of insurance coverage.

---

[14]Coyle (1990) is credited with categorizing the first two and the fourth moral hazard effects.

Second, the moral hazard problem may show up over time as consumers have less incentive to guard against the insured event. Reductions in preventative activities such as exercise or dieting may raise the probability of an illness occurring. As consumers compensate for a poorer health status with more medical services, the demand curve in figure 13–1 effectively shifts to the right and a higher quantity demanded is associated with a zero price. The greater demand leads to increased medical expenditures.

Moral hazard may arise from a third type of behavior that deals with technological advances in medical care. Third-party payments may encourage the development and adoption of new technologies offering low-benefit, high-cost care (Weisbrod, 1991). The adoption and diffusion of these high-priced technologies, in turn, cause the demand for health insurance and the range of services covered by health insurance to increase. A vicious cycle encompassing health insurance, technology, and rising medical costs is set in place. In terms of figure 13–1, the rapidly developing technologies offering high-cost, low-benefit medicine are responsible for shifting the demand curve to the right and thereby raising medical expenditures.

Moral hazard results in a fourth behavioral change as insurance lowers the consumer's incentive to monitor the behavior of health care providers. Less monitoring gives the health care provider the incentive to prescribe unnecessary tests or surgery. Since the consumer's out-of-pocket costs are largely unaffected by the unnecessary services, the consumer has little incentive to seek a second opinion. As a result, the supplier-induced demand curve in figure 13–1 shifts to the right and results in greater medical expenditures.[15]

Finally, a moral hazard effect occurs when insurance lowers the consumer's incentive to shop around and find the lowest price for medical services. In terms of figure 13–1 less comparison shopping means the price and the marginal cost curve are at an artificially higher level than $MC_0$; thus, medical expenditures increase.

Insurers can reduce the extent of the moral hazard problem by increasing the coinsurance and making the consumer pay a larger share of the full cost. The higher coinsurance creates an incentive for the consumer to purchase fewer medical services, shop around and pay the lowest possible price, produce medical services in the home when doing so is cost effective, and acquire more medical information to prevent opportunistic behavior by health care providers. Of course, the higher coinsurance also increases the consumer's financial insecurity, because a greater proportion of his or her income is subject to uncertainty. The optimal coinsurance considers risk and balances the cost of the moral hazard problem with the benefit of financial security (less financial risk). Therefore, it is very likely that the optimal coinsurance is not zero except for purely catastrophic medical events.

Since health insurance enables the consumer to avoid risk, the net social costs of excess insurance are found by subtracting the social benefit of risk avoidance from the social cost due to excess medical spending. Feldstein (1973) showed that the net social costs of overinsurance depend on values for the following parameters: the price elasticity of demand for medical services, the gross price change resulting from insurance

---

[15]The reader may want to review the supplier-induced demand theory in Chapter 10.

coverage, the change in quality induced by insurance coverage, and the degree of risk aversion. Specifically, net social costs increase with a greater price elasticity of demand, a lower degree of risk aversion, and a higher gross price change or quality resulting from increased insurance coverage.

Feldman and Dowd (1991) provide the most up-to-date estimate of the net social costs of excess health insurance. Based on plausible values for the above parameters, they estimated that in 1984 the welfare loss ranged from $33.4 billion to $109.3 billion, or from .9 to 2.9 percent of GNP. The policy implication is that sizable welfare gains are possible with an increase in the average copayment rate for medical services covered by health insurance.

## The Price of Private Health Insurance

Another measure of the performance of an industry is the price of the product relative to cost. A high price/cost margin normally denotes the presence of some monopoly power. As noted earlier, the price of health insurance is the loading fee, which covers administrative costs, marketing expenses, profits, and taxes. Recall that economists often express the price of health insurance as the premium to benefit ratio. A premium to benefit ratio greater than 1 reflects the loading fee. In a competitive market, administrative cost, marketing expenses, and profits will be kept to a normal level such that the price of insurance, net of taxes, reflects a reasonable or normal amount.

Table 13–3 shows the price of health insurance for commercial insurance companies, combined self-insured companies and HMOs, and Blue Cross/Blue Shield plans for selected years from 1950 to 1995. Over the entire 45-year span, the prices for the commercial plans fell substantially. For instance, the individual commercial insurance price declined from $2.01 to $1.46 per benefit dollar over the period. The price for Blue Cross/Blue Shield plans also decreased over the entire period, but by only 4 cents per benefit dollar. Notice that the 1995 price of a group commercial insurance plan was appreciably lower than the price of the individual commercial plan—27 cents lower per benefit dollar. The higher risk of individual plans and the individual consumer's higher costs of acquiring price and quality information most likely account for the observed price differential.

Also note that the combined self-insured and HMO price in 1995 was about 11 cents per benefit dollar lower than the group commercial health insurance price of $1.19 and 5 cents lower than the Blue Cross/Blue Shield price of $1.13 per benefit dollar. The price of health insurance was $1.14 in 1995 compared to about $1.54 in 1950 for the industry as a whole (not shown).

Some health policy analysts (e.g., Woolhandler and Himmelstein, 1991) argue that the 14 cents per benefit dollar for administrative costs, marketing expenses, profits, and taxes is much too high compared to either the publicly provided health insurance in the United States (about 3 cents) or the provincial health plans in Canada (almost 1 cent) and reflects the wastefulness of a private health insurance program. However, Danzon (1992) points out that in a world of imperfect information and costly transactions, the overhead expenditures of private insurers do not represent pure waste. The overhead provides benefits by helping to avoid even larger costs to

| TABLE 13–3 | PRICE OF PRIVATE INSURANCE IN THE UNITED STATES, SELECTED YEARS, 1950–1995 |

| | Insurance Companies | | | Self-Insured and HMOs | Blue Cross and Blue Shield |
|---|---|---|---|---|---|
| Year | Total | Group | Individual | | |
| 1950 | $1.62 | $1.44 | $2.01 | — | $1.17 |
| 1960 | 1.57 | 1.23 | 2.47 | — | 1.08 |
| 1970 | 1.26 | 1.09 | 2.11 | — | 1.04 |
| 1980 | 1.18 | 1.12 | 1.73 | $1.07 | 1.03 |
| 1990 | 1.22 | 1.19 | 1.55 | 1.11 | 1.12 |
| 1991 | 1.19 | 1.16 | 1.51 | 1.10 | 1.12 |
| 1992 | 1.19 | 1.16 | 1.52 | 1.09 | 1.12 |
| 1993 | 1.20 | 1.17 | 1.56 | 1.09 | 1.15 |
| 1994 | 1.22 | 1.19 | 1.46 | 1.09 | 1.14 |
| 1995 | 1.22 | 1.19 | 1.46 | 1.08 | 1.13 |

Note: Price is measured by dividing premium income by medical benefits paid out.

Source: Health Insurance Association of America, *Source Book of Health Insurance Data*, various editions.

policyholders. Benefits accrue from controlling incentives to overuse medical care due to the moral hazard problem.

According to Danzon, "private insurers compete by devising ways to control moral hazard more cost effectively, including structured copayments, utilization review, case management, selective contracting with preferred providers, and provider-targeted financial incentives such as capitation and other risk-sharing forms of prospective reimbursement. The costs of implementing these strategies appear as claims administration costs to insurers, providers and patients" (p. 26). She goes on to note that the total overhead costs from society's perspective are measured by overhead plus the net social loss associated with moral hazard. In the absence of the tax subsidy on employer-provided health benefits, competition creates incentives for insurers to minimize the total overhead costs.

Danzon also comments that the 1980s was a time of intense innovation in strategies to control moral hazard. Indeed, some signs of the competition to control moral hazard are apparent in table 13–3. Notice that the prices of the various plans, other than the individual commercial insurance plans, have tended to increase from 1980 to 1990 but leveled off thereafter. For example, the price of commercial group insurance increased from $1.12 to $1.19 and the price of the Blues plans rose from $1.03 to $1.13 during the period 1980 to 1995. Even the price of the combined self-insured and HMO plans increased slightly since 1980. The higher price per benefit dollar reflects the greater administrative costs necessary to control the moral hazard problem.

### *The Private Health Insurance Industry and Health Care Cost Containment Innovations*

Societal welfare is enhanced when the firms in an industry create and introduce new product or process innovations. In the private health insurance industry, innovations involve new ways to control health care costs and counter the effects of moral hazard. Cost containment innovations presently in use include consumer cost sharing, HMOs, PPOs, and utilization review programs. Although these innovations have been around for some time, Havighurst (1988) asks why commercial health insurers took so long to develop and adopt them. The question is whether monopolisticlike commercial insurers purposely restricted these socially desired innovations or external market and legal forces precluded their development and adoption.

For possible explanations, Havighurst looked to the demand and supply sides of the private health insurance market and first questioned whether a demand for health care cost containment had existed initially. Specifically, the tax exemption on employer-sponsored health insurance premiums may have reduced consumers' demand for cost containment innovations. Since the government essentially picks up 50 percent of the additional dollar spent on health insurance, consumers face an incentive to purchase overly generous plans offering first-dollar fee-for-service medicine.[16] Tax-induced consumption habits of this kind imply that little consumer demand exists for cost containment innovations.

As another factor on the demand side, Havighurst pointed out that employers "rely upon their health benefits plan as a principal symbol of their beneficence toward their employees" (p. 293). Moreover, union representatives typically point to the "health plan as proof of the good things that they have been able to accomplish for the rank and file." Given these attitudes, employers and union representatives may also have had little demand for cost containment innovations.

Seeking an explanation from the supply side of the market for the lack of cost-saving innovations, the author questioned whether commercial health insurers had been (1) too small, (2) unable to capture the benefits of cost containment innovations, (3) constrained by laws and regulations, (4) engaged in collusive agreements, or (5) restrained by either the medical profession or competition from the Blues. Havighurst believes that the relatively small local market share of most insurers, while a disadvantage, had not imposed a complete obstacle to obtaining medical price discounts from health care providers. He claims that "hospitals are very sensitive to occupancy rates and any insurer with the ability to move even a small percentage of patients to another facility would have no trouble getting the attention of a hospital administrator" (p. 237).

Regarding the second supply-side reason, Havighurst agrees that the lack of intellectual property rights may have reduced the incentive for private insurers to introduce new cost-saving innovations because any innovation could be quickly imitated by a competitor. However, the author explains that "there are many strategies that an insurer could adopt with only minimal spillover benefits for its competitors" (p. 239). Havighurst also believes that legal restrictions did not seriously prevent commercial

---

[16]The 50 percent figure reflects the combined federal income tax, Social Security tax, and state income tax rates.

insurers from adopting cost containment innovations. In fact, he questioned why, unlike the Blues, commercial insurers failed to challenge many laws unfavorable to the introduction of cost containment innovations. The author concludes that private insurers "have been content to live with legal constraints on their own competitive behavior except where those constraints did not bind their competitors as well" (p. 242).

Havighurst wonders whether private insurers collectively agreed to refrain from adopting cost containment innovations. By not adopting cost containment practices, commercial insurers could preserve their comfortable, traditional, and profitable ways of doing business. Given the structurally competitive nature of the private health insurance industry (as described earlier in this chapter), Havighurst notes that "collusion would not be a successful policy in any event" (p. 244). In terms of medical profession restraints, Havighurst contends that there had been ample evidence of professional resistance to cost containment, but because of antitrust enforcement in the 1970s, insurers "can no longer claim fear of professional retaliation as an excuse for refraining from aggressive cost containment" (pp. 246–48). Finally, the author notes that Blue Cross, with its large discounts, health care provider sponsorship, and tax-exempt status, may have been able to cut prices for health insurance whenever a commercial insurer attempted to introduce cost containment practices.

The upshot is that a number of factors may have inhibited commercial insurers from adopting cost containment innovations. According to Havighurst, most of the factors "absolve commercial insurers from blame for neglecting cost containment. There are, however, several points at which industry members might have opted to compete but chose instead to adhere to traditional patterns" (p. 254). It is interesting to note that five of the largest commercial insurers—Aetna, CIGNA, Travelers, Metropolitan, and Prudential—left the Health Insurance Association of America (HIAA), a national trade group, to form their own organization, the Alliance for Managed Competition, in the early 1990s. They left HIAA partly because it had been slow to endorse and encourage managed-care insurance. Now, according to Scism (1994), smaller health insurers are beginning to follow the big firms into managed care and are forming partnerships with them to gain access to managed-care networks.

One implication of Havighurst's analysis is that the government may want to place a limit on the tax subsidy for health insurance. With a tax exemption limit, commercial insurers should face a greater incentive from the demand side of the market to develop and adopt more cost containment innovations in the future.

## SUMMARY

Many analysts consider the health insurance industry to be structurally competitive. Most states have well over one 100 insurance companies that sell private health insurance. Health insurance is fairly homogeneous, at least within a particular product line, such as traditional or managed-care health insurance. While state regulations and administrative economies exist, barriers to entry do not appear to be very binding on the entry of new health insurance companies, perhaps because existing insurance companies can easily switch among alternative insurance product lines (health, casualty, life, etc.).

Individual buyers may possess imperfect information regarding the quality of health insurance. However, the information problem is much less severe in the group insurance submarket. Thus, overall the market for private health insurance appears to be highly competitive. While the market demand for health insurance is found to be inelastic, an individual insurer is likely to face a highly elastic demand curve given the relatively large number of competing insurers.

Competitive insurance markets in conjunction with experience rating can give rise to cherry-picking behavior, the notion that only healthy individuals are offered adequate health insurance coverage. Less healthy people are denied access to health insurance, are not covered for preexisting conditions, or are charged prohibitively high prices. This problem is also more pronounced in the individual health insurance market.

In terms of performance, the price of private health insurance (premium to benefits) has tended to decline over the long run. In the recent short run, the price has increased moderately in response to cost containment efforts. Some output problems continue to prevail in the market for private health insurance. First, moral hazard results as overinsured individuals change their behavior and increase the probability and magnitude of a health loss. Indeed, many health economists have pointed to the moral hazard problem as the prime reason underlying rising medical care expenditures in the United States. Second, adverse selection, which occurs when high-risk individuals join a low-risk group, can impose substantial adjustment costs on society as high-risk people pursue low-risk individuals from plan to plan. Appropriate pricing and utilization review can reduce the extent of the moral hazard and adverse selection problems.

Third, a significant percentage of Americans lack health insurance coverage. Some argue that this figure is biased downward because it fails to consider underinsurance and job lock. Others believe it is biased upward because many uninsured people choose to be without health insurance and because the spell without insurance coverage is relatively short.

## Review Questions and Problems

1. Many economists point to moral hazard as the primary reason underlying rising health care costs in the United States.

   *a.* Explain the general argument behind moral hazard.

   *b.* Explain the five ways by which moral hazard takes place (explain with a graph when possible).

   *c.* How does price elasticity of demand influence the moral hazard problem?

   *d.* Explain how an insurer could reduce the scope of the moral hazard problem by introducing a consumer copayment.

   *e.* What two considerations determine the optimal copayment rate?

2. Many economists argue that the group health insurance industry is highly competitive. Based on various determinants of industry structure, explain the reasoning underlying this view.

3. Fully explain the two reasons the individual health insurance market may be less competitive than the group health insurance market.

4. Blair, Jackson, and Vogel found that substantial economies of scale exist in the administration of health insurance, yet survivor analysis finds no scale economies in the provision of health insurance. How can this inconsistency be explained?

5. Explain why someone may make the following seemingly contradictory statement: "High administrative costs are good because they sometimes lead to lower costs of providing health insurance."

6. Private insurers tend to experience three consecutive years of profits followed by three consecutive years of losses. What are the various explanations offered for this profit cycle?

7. Managed-care plans tend to lower health care costs, yet the level and growth of managed-care premiums are similar to those of traditional fee-for-service insurance plans. How can that be explained?

8. What does *cherry-picking behavior* mean? What does the evidence suggest about this type of behavior? Why is it less troublesome in the group health insurance market?

9. What does *adverse selection* mean? How does this type of behavior impose costs on society?

10. Explain why experience rating may be more efficient and equitable than community rating. Explain why community rating may be more efficient and equitable than experience rating.

11. Why is it so difficult to measure the number of people who lack health insurance? Explain fully.

12. How can overinsurance coexist with underinsurance and uninsurance?

13. How is the price of health insurance measured? What happened to the price of health insurance in the United States from 1950 to 1980? What has happened since 1980? Why?

14. Explain some of the reasons commercial insurers may have been reluctant to introduce and adopt cost containment innovations.

15. Would a theory X'er favor community or experience rating? Why?

16. Provide a description of the typical uninsured person.

17. What were the main reasons behind the Health Insurance Portability and Accountability Act? What are the main features of the act?

18. Suppose the government imposes an employer-mandated pet insurance program. All employers must sponsor and finance an insurance policy for the pets (dogs and cats) of their employees. Use the appropriate graphical model of a labor market to illustrate and explain who will pay for the mandate.

*References*

Acs, Gregory. "Explaining Trends in Health Insurance Coverage between 1988 and 1991." *Inquiry* 32 (spring 1995), pp. 102–10.

Adamache, Killard W., and Frank A. Sloan. "Competition Between Non-Profit and For-Profit Health Insurers." *Journal of Health Economics* 2 (December 1983). pp. 225–43.

Atchinson, Brian K., and Daniel M. Fox. "From the Field: The Politics of the Health Insurance Portability and Accountability Act." *Health Affairs* 16 (May/June 1997), pp. 146–50.

Baker, Laurence C., and Kenneth S. Corts. "The Effects of HMOs on Conventional Insurance Premiums: Theory and Evidence." National Bureau of Economic Research Working Paper: 5356, November 1995, pp. 1–33.

Beauregard, Karen M. *Persons Denied Private Health Insurance Due to Poor Health.* AHCPR Pub. No. 92–0016. 1991.

Bennefield, Robert L. "Health Insurance Coverage: 1996." *Current Population Reports,* P60–199, U.S. Department of Commerce, Washington, DC, September 1997.

Blair, Roger D., and Ronald J. Vogel. "A Survivor Analysis of Commercial Health Insurers." *Journal of Business* 51 (July 1978), pp. 521–29.

Blair, Roger D., Jerry R. Jackson, and Ronald J. Vogel. "Economies of Scale in the Administration of Health Insurance." *Review of Economics and Statistics* 57 (May 1975), pp. 185–89.

Bodenheimer, Thomas. "Underinsurance in America." *New England Journal of Medicine* (July 23, 1992), pp. 274–78.

Chollet, Deborah J., and Rebecca R. Paul. *Community Rating: Issues and Experience,* Technical report, Washington, D.C.: Alpha Center, December 1994.

Cooper, Philip F., and Alan C. Monheit. "Does Employment-Related Health Insurance Inhibit Job Mobility?" *Inquiry* 30 (winter 1993), pp. 400–16.

Coyte, Peter C. "Canada." In *Advances in Health Economics and Health Services Research, Comparative Health, Systems,* edited by Richard M. Scheffler and Louis F. Rossiter. Greenwich, CT.: JAI Press, 1990, pp. 103–43.

Cutler, David M., and Jonathan Gruber. "Does Public Insurance Crowd Out Private Insurance?" National Bureau of Economic Research, Working Paper no. 5082 (Cambridge, MA: 1995).

Danzon, Patricia M. "Hidden Overhead Costs: Is Canada's System Really Less Expensive?" *Health Affairs* 11 (spring 1992), pp. 21–43.

Feldman, Roger, and Bryan Dowd. "A New Estimate of the Welfare Loss of Excess Health Insurance." *American Economic Review* 81 (March 1991), pp. 729–301.

Feldman, Roger, Bryan Dowd, and Gregory Gifford. "The Effect of HMOs on Premiums in Employment-Based Health Plans." *Health Services Research* 27 (February 1993), pp. 779–811.

Feldstein, Martin S. "The Welfare Loss of Excess Health Insurance." *Journal of Political Economy* (March–April 1973), pp. 251–80.

Frech, H. E. III. "Health Insurance: Designing Products to Reduce Costs." In *Industry Studies,* edited by Larry L. Duetsch. Englewood Cliffs. NJ: Prentice Hall, 1993, pp. 307–23.

———— "Monopoly in Health Insurance: The Economics of Kartell v. Blue Shield of Massachusetts." In *Health Care in America,* edited by H. E. Frech III. San Francisco: Pacific Research Institute for Public Policy, 1988, pp. 293–330.

Friedman, Milton. "The Folly of Buying Health Care at the Company Store." *The Wall Street Journal,* February 3, 1992, p. A14.

Gabel, Jon R., and Jensen, Gail A. "Can a Universal Coverage System Temper the Underwriting Cycle?" *Inquiry* (summer 1992), pp. 249–62.

Gabel, Jon, Roger Formisano, Barbara Cohr, and Steven Di Carlo. "Tracing the Cycle of Health Insurance." *Health Affairs* (winter 1991), pp. 49–61.

Havighurst, Clark C. "The Questionable Cost-Containment Record of Commercial Health Insurers." In *Health Care in America*, edited by H. E. Frech III. San Francisco: Pacific Research Institute for Public Policy, 1988, pp. 221–58.

Hay, Joel W., and Michael J. Leahy. "Competition among Health Plans: Some Preliminary Evidence." *Southern Economic Journal* 50 (January 1987), pp. 831–46.

Health Insurance Association of America, *Source Book of Health Insurance Data 1994*. Washington, D.C.: Health Insurance Association of America, 1995.

Health Insurance Association of America, *Source Book of Health Insurance Data 1997/98*. Washington, DC: Health Insurance Association of America, 1998.

Iglehart, John K. "The American Health Care System—Private Insurance." *New England Journal of Medicine* 326 (June 18, 1992), pp. 1715–20.

Jensen, Gail A, Michael A. Morrisey, Shannon Gaffney, and Derek K. Liston. "The New Dominance of Managed Care: Insurance Trends in the 1990s." *Health Affairs* 16 (January/February 1997), pp. 125–36.

Kapur, Kanika. "The Impact of Health on Job Mobility: A Measure of Job Lock." *Industrial and Labor Relations Review* 51 (January 1998), pp. 282–98.

Lee, Dwight. "Why Workers Should Want Mandated Benefits to Lower Their Wages." *Economic Inquiry* 34 (April 1996), pp. 401–7.

Long, Stephen H., and Jack Rodgers. "Do Shifts Toward Service Industries, Part-time Work, and Self-Employment Explain the Rising Uninsured Rate?" *Inquiry* 32 (spring 1995), pp. 111–6.

Madrian, Brigitte. "Employment-Based Health Insurance and Job Mobility: Is There Evidence of Job-Lock?" *Quarterly Journal of Economics* (February 1994), pp. 27–54.

Manning, Willard, et al. "A Controlled Trial of the Effect of a Prepaid Group Practice on Use of Services." *New England Journal of Medicine*, 310 (June 7, 1984), pp. 1505–10.

McCaughey, Elizabeth. "Health Insurance for All." *The Wall Street Journal*, April 28, 1994, p. A12.

McCormack, Lauren A., Peter D. Fox, Thomas Rice, and Marcia L. Graham. "Medigap Reform Legislation of 1990: Have the Objectives Been Met?" *Health Care Financing Review* 18 (fall 1996), pp. 157–74.

McLaughlin, Catherine G. "Market Responses to HMOs. Price Competition or Rivalry?" *Inquiry* (summer 1988), pp. 207–18.

Miller, Robert H. and Harold S. Luft. "Managed Care Plan Performance since 1980." *Journal of the American Medical Association* 271 (May 18, 1994), pp. 1512–19.

Moffitt, Robert E. "Surprise! A Government Health Plan That Works." *The Wall Street Journal*. April 22, 1992, p. A14.

National Underwriters. *Profiles of 1992 Health Insurers* (Cincinnati: The National Underwriting Company 1992).

Nichols, Len M., and Linda Blumberg. "A Different Kind of 'New Federalism'? The Health Insurance Portability and Accountability Act of 1996." *Health Affairs* 17 (May/June 1998), pp. 25–42.

Pauly, Mark V. "Taxation, Health Insurance, and Market Failure in the Medical Economy." *Journal of Economic Literature* 24 (June 1986), pp. 629–75.

Rapoport, John, et al. "Resource Utilization among Intensive Care Patients." *Archives of Internal Medicine* 152 (November 1992), pp. 2207–12.

Reinhardt, Uwe. "The Market Won't Make Health Insurers Efficient," *Norwich Bulletin*, April 12, 1992, p. A5.

Sapolsky, Harvey M. "Empire and the Business of Health Insurance." *Journal of Health Politics, Policy and Law* 16 (winter 1991), pp. 747–60.

Scism, Leslie. "Managed Care Thrives as Smaller Insurers Rent HMOs." *The Wall Street Journal*, April 28, 1994, p. B4.

Seidman, Laurence S. "Health Care: Getting the Right Amount at the Right Price." *Business Review*, March-April 1982.

Sindelar, Jody L. "The Declining Price of Health Insurance." In *Health Care in America*, edited by H. E. Frech III. San Francisco: Pacific Institute for Public Policy, 1988, pp. 259–91.

State Health Watch. "Community Rating Law Hikes Premiums in NY" (January 1994), p. 2.

Steinmetz, Greg. "Number of Uninsured Stirs Much Confusion in Health-Care Debate." *The Wall Street Journal*, June 9, 1993, p. A1.

Stigler, George J. "The Economies of Scale." *Journal of Law and Economics* 1 (October 1958), pp. 54–71.

Swartz, Katherine. "Dynamics of People without Health Insurance." *Journal of the American Medical Association* 271 (January 5, 1994), pp. 64–66.

Swartz, Katherine, John Marcotte, and Timothy D. McBride. "Personal Characteristics and Spells without Health Insurance." *Inquiry* 30 (spring 1993), pp. 64–76.

Temin, Peter. "An Economic History of American Hospitals." In *Health Care in America*, edited by H. E. Frech III. San Francisco: Pacific Research Institute for Public Policy, pp. 75–102.

Weisbrod, Burton A. "The Health Care Quadrilemma: An Essay on Technological Change, Insurance, Quality of Care, and Cost Containment." *Journal of Economic Literature* 29 (June 1991), pp. 523–52.

Wholey, Douglas, Roger Feldman, and Jon B. Christianson. "The Effect of Market Structure on HMO Premiums." 14 (1995), pp. 81–105.

Wickizer, Thomas M., and Paul J. Feldstein. "The Impact of HMO Competition on Private Health Insurance Premiums." *Inquiry* 32 (fall 1995), pp. 241–51.

Woolhandler, Steffie, and David U. Himmelstein. "The Deteriorating Administrative Efficiency of the U.S. Health Care System." *New England Journal of Medicine* 324 (May 2, 1991), pp. 1253–58.

# CEBS Questions

CEBS Sample Question on Subject Matter from CEBS Course IX Study Manual

1.  Describe how the Omnibus Budget Reconciliation Act (OBRA) of 1990 addressed the problem of Medicare consumers lacking the necessary technical information to purchase medigap insurance policies. (page 382)

CEBS Sample Exam Questions

1.  When the price of health insurance is expressed as the premium to benefit ratio, which of the following statements is correct?
    A. The cost of insurance companies, self-insured and HMOs, and Blue Cross-Blue Shield plans has increased over the last 40 years
    B. Self-insured and Health Maintenance Organizations (HMOs) have a lower cost than insurance companies
    C. The cost of Blue Cross-Blue Shield is lower than the cost for insurance companies
    D. Individual insurance costs less than group insurance
    E. The ratio is about .80 for most insurance companies

2.  Which of the following is (are) correct statements regarding barriers to entry to the health insurance industry?

    I. Scale economies in administering health insurance may serve as a barrier to entry

    II. Lack of managerial expertise has been shown to be a significant barrier to entry

    III. Barriers to entry are of minor importance in the health insurance industry

      A. I only

      B. III only

      C. I and II only

      D. I and III only

      E. I, II, and III

3. The Health Insurance Portability and Accountability Act of 1996 contains all the following features EXCEPT:

    A. Health insurers that meet specified quality and quantity standards qualify for partial reimbursement of increased costs created by the new legislation

    B. Insurers in the small group market cannot exclude any of the employer's eligible employees from coverage on the basis of health status

    C. Individuals with a group plan cannot be charged a higher premium based on their health

    D. With some exceptions, all group coverage must be renewable

    E. There is a maximum exclusion period for preexisting conditions

*Answer to Sample Question from Study Manual*

Prior to OBRA of 1990, Medicare beneficiaries who wanted to purchase medigap insurance found it difficult to differentiate among the provisions and limitations of a myriad of policies being sold. It was not unusual for individuals to purchase policies that duplicated other policies or, worse, that failed to provide supplemental Medicare coverage. OBRA of 1990 reformed the medigap market. It mandated that only 10 standard policies based on increasing levels of coverage could be sold. The standardization enabled the consumer to assess the value and incremental cost of each of the ten policies.

*Answer to Sample Question from Study Manual*

1. B is the answer. Table 13–3 on page 403 shows that the price of self-insured & HMO plans has been consistently lower than that of other types of insurance.

2. D is the answer. Statements I and III are correct. Scale economies enable existing insurers to underprice new, low-volume competitors and discourage new entrants. However, despite the scale economies barrier, there appears to be no overly restrictive barriers that deter new entrants. See pages 381–382 of the text.

3. A is the answer. All statements are true except A. The Act makes no provisions for subsidizing high-performing insurers. See pages 396 and 398 of the text.

# 14

## The Physician Services Industry

T hroughout the 19th century, the physician services industry was largely unregulated. Many physicians were practicing without proper medical training, primarily because the country was dotted with numerous medical schools of questionable quality. In reaction to this state of affairs, the American Medical Association (AMA) was founded in 1847. At its inception, the organization adopted the improvement of medical education in the United States as its major goal. Although improvements were made over the years, significant changes did not take place until the turn of the 20th century. The impetus for change was the Flexner Report published in 1910 by the Carnegie Foundation.

Concerned that not enough was being done to improve medical education, the Carnegie Foundation, with the blessing of the AMA, asked Abraham Flexner to conduct a study of the medical schools in Canada and the United States. The final report, commonly referred to as the Flexner Report, was highly critical of the medical training provided by an overwhelming majority of the schools in North America. The report was so controversial that Flexner received threats on his life. As a result of the report, many low-quality medical schools were forced to improve or close their doors. In addition, states began to take the role of licensing physicians more seriously (Raffel and Raffel, 1989). Thus, the formation of the AMA, coupled with the Flexner Report, ushered in the modern regulated physician services industry, which requires an individual to fulfill strict educational and licensing requirements before being allowed to practice medicine.

Over the past quarter-century, the scope and complexity of physician services have increased dramatically, and this has had a profound impact on the structure and performance of the industry. Increases in demand for medical services and the introduction of many new, costly technologies have increased expenditures on physician services almost fortyfold since 1960. Nearly gone are the days when an appointment with the doctor meant a visit to a self-employed male physician who owned a solo fee-for-service practice. Today, more than one out of six physicians is a female and only about one-quarter of all physicians are self-employed and operate a solo practice. Multiphysician practices are the norm, and physicians who wish to survive are now forced to negotiate with MCOs for additional patients, adjust to many new and different fee schedules, and subject themselves to utilization reviews.

In keeping with the methodology laid out in the previous chapter, this chapter uses the structure-conduct-performance paradigm to analyze the ever-changing physician services industry. The first part of the chapter describes the current structure of the industry. In particular, it

- Looks at the number and specialty distribution of physicians.

- Examines the mode of practice.

- Analyzes methods of payment for physician services.

- Reviews the reimbursement practices of managed-care buyers.

- Discusses the production and cost of physician services.

The conduct section of the chapter

- Discusses the impact of compensation schemes on physician behavior.

- Examines geographic variations in the use of physician services.

- Looks at the supplier-induced demand hypothesis.

- Reviews the physician practice hypothesis.

- Analyzes the impact of managed care on physician behavior.

Finally, the performance section

- Looks at expenditures on physician services over time.

- Reviews the utilization of physician services.

- Discusses the growth of physician income over time.

## The Structure of the Physician Services Industry

Because the conduct of buyers and sellers depends directly on the structure of the market, we begin with an analysis of the structure of the physician services market. Among the structural elements, we look at the number and specialty distribution of physicians, along with the organizational arrangements adopted by physicians to produce medical services. Next, we review the sources of physician revenues and examine

| TABLE 14-1 | TOTAL NUMBER OF PHYSICIANS BY MAJOR CATEGORIES AND PER 100,000 TOTAL CIVILIAN POPULATION FOR SELECTED YEARS | | | |
|---|---|---|---|---|
| | **1970** | **1980** | **1990** | **1996** |
| Total number of physicians | 334,028 | 467,679 | 615,421 | 737,764 |
|   Patient care | 83.4% | 80.5% | 81.9% | 81.2% |
|   Nonpatient care | 9.7% | 8.2% | 7.1% | 6.1% |
|   Other* | 6.9% | 11.3% | 11.1% | 12.7% |
| Total number of nonfederal physicians per 100,000 civilian population | 148 | 195 | 237 | 271 |
| Total number of nonfederal physicians in patient care per 100,000 civilian population | 125 | 159 | 195 | 220 |

*Complete data for the "other" category were not available in 1972. As a result, the percentages may not add up to 100 percent.

SOURCE: *Physician Characteristics and Distribution in the U.S. 1997/1998* (Chicago: American Medical Association, 1998), Tables A-1 and A-17.

the impact of managed care on the physician services market. Finally, we analyze barriers to entry and the production of physician services.

## The Number of Physicians in the United States

It seems only logical to begin our analysis of the market for physician services with a look at the supply of physician labor, the primary input in the production of physician services.[1] According to table 14–1, the United States experienced a substantial increase in the number of physicians from 1970 to 1996. In 1970, a total of 334,028 physicians were practicing in the United States; by 1996, this number had increased by just over 120 percent to 737,764.

To get a clearer picture of the impact of this increase in physician labor on the delivery of patient care, we need to look at a breakdown of physicians by major professional activities. This information appears in the next three rows in table 14–1. The "patient care" category represents the percentage of physicians involved in direct patient care, while the "nonpatient care" category reflects the percentage of physicians engaged in other professional activities, such as medical teaching and administration. The final category includes the percentage of physicians who were not classified, were inactive, or had an unknown address.

The proportion of physicians in each category remained remarkably stable over time, indicating that the number of physicians in each category grew at roughly the

---

[1] As we will see later in the chapter, physician services are produced with a combination of various inputs, including physician labor, nurse labor, clerical staff, physician assistants, lab technicians, and so on.

same rate. The only major change took place between 1970 and 1980, when the proportion of physicians in "patient" and "nonpatient" care fell relative to the "other" category. In all likelihood, this change reflects improved data collection on the part of the AMA.[2] Since 1980, the proportion of physicians engaged in patient care has hovered around 81 percent. These data indicate that over 80 percent of the increase in physician labor from 1970 to 1996 occurred in direct patient care. By 1996, a total of 598,924 physicians were involved in some aspect of direct patient care.

Although the absolute supply of physicians increased in the United States in recent years, it is impossible to make inferences regarding the relative supply of physicians without comparing the increase in physician labor to the overall increase in population. One crude measure of the relative supply of physician labor is the physician-to-population ratio. Table 14–1 provides the ratios of total nonfederal physicians and total nonfederal patient care physicians per 100,000 civilian population from 1970 to 1996. In both cases, the ratio increased by more than 75 percent, indicating a greater relative availability of physician labor over time. The ratio of total physicians to population increased from 148 in 1970 to 271 in 1996, while the ratio of total patient care physicians to population expanded from 125 to 220.

It is apparent that the United States experienced a significant increase in physician labor over the last two decades. The increase outpaced the overall increase in the population and has led to a greater relative supply of physician labor, as measured by the physician-to-population ratio.

## Specialty Distribution of Physicians in the United States

Table 14–2 provides additional data on the number and distribution of physicians by major specialties from 1970 to 1996. The most dramatic change was the substantial drop in the number of physicians in general practice. Between 1970 and 1996, the number of general practitioners dropped by approximately 70 percent, from 57,948 to 16,895. According to the AMA (1993), this drop was partly the result of the development of the "family practice" category in 1975.[3] By 1996, over 60,000 physicians were in family practice and comprised the second largest category with over 8 percent of the total number of physicians.

By far the single largest category has been internal medicine, with 122,125 physicians in 1996, or 16.6 percent of the total. The number of physicians specializing in internal medicine is almost twice the number of family practitioners. From 1970 to 1996, approximately 80,000 physicians entered internal medicine. The data also suggest that diagnostic radiology experienced the largest percentage increase over the 16–year period aside from family practice, which did not exist in 1970. This specialty grew in excess of 900 percent over two decades.

---

[2]For example, between 1970 and 1975, the AMA established a subcategory of "not classified" that included over 26,000 physicians in 1975. This large increase explains the significant rise in the proportion of physicians classified as "other."

[3]Others suggest that the drop reflects a trend away from primary care medicine and toward specialty care. This issue is addressed later in the chapter.

| TABLE 14–2 | NUMBER AND DISTRIBUTION OF PHYSICIANS BY ELEVEN MAJOR SPECIALTIES FOR SELECTED YEARS* | | | |
|---|---|---|---|---|
| | **1970** | **1980** | **1990** | **1996** |
| Anesthesiology | 10,860 | 15,958 | 25,981 | 33,318 |
| | 3.3% | 3.4% | 4.2% | 4.5% |
| Diagnostic radiology | 1,968 | 7,048 | 15,412 | 20,043 |
| | 0.6% | 1.5% | 2.5% | 2.7% |
| Emergency | 0 | 5,699 | 14,243 | 20,030 |
| | 0 | 1.2% | 2.3% | 2.7% |
| Family practice | 0 | 27,530 | 47,639 | 62,301 |
| | 0 | 5.9% | 7.7% | 8.4% |
| General practice | 57,948 | 32,519 | 22,841 | 16,895 |
| | 17.3% | 7.0% | 3.7% | 2.3% |
| General surgery | 29,761 | 34,034 | 38,376 | 37,943 |
| | 8.9% | 7.3% | 6.2% | 5.1% |
| Internal medicine | 41,872 | 71,531 | 98,349 | 122,125 |
| | 12.5% | 15.3% | 16.0% | 16.6% |
| Obstetrics/gynecology | 18,876 | 26,305 | 33,697 | 38,424 |
| | 5.7% | 5.6% | 5.5% | 5.2% |
| Orthopedic surgery | 9,620 | 13,996 | 19,138 | 22,521 |
| | 2.9% | 3.0% | 3.1% | 3.1% |
| Pediatrics | 18,332 | 28,803 | 40,893 | 53,369 |
| | 5.5% | 6.2% | 6.6% | 7.2% |
| Psychiatry | 21,146 | 27,481 | 35,163 | 38,417 |
| | 6.3% | 5.9% | 5.7% | 5.2% |
| Primary care physicians | 134,354 | 170,705 | 213,514 | 250,589 |
| | 40.2% | 36.5% | 34.7% | 34.0% |

*Data for family practice were not available before 1975, while data for emergency medicine were not available prior to 1980. Primary care includes the general specialties of family practice, general practice, internal medicine, obstetrics/gynecology, and pediatrics and excludes any subspecialties associated with these general specialties.

SOURCE: *Physician Characteristics and Distribution in the U.S. 1997/1998* (Chicago: American Medical Association, 1998), Tables 1, A-2, and A-3.

The last row in table 14–2 indicates the percentage of physicians providing primary care, defined by the AMA as including family practice, general practice, internal medicine, obstetrics/gynecology, and pediatrics. Since 1970, the proportion of primary care physicians has dropped from approximately 40 percent in 1970 to 34 percent in 1996.[4]

---

[4]Not everyone agrees with the AMA's definition of primary care medicine. The Health Professions Education Assistance Act of 1976 (P.L. 94–484) defines primary care as including only family practice, general internal medicine, and general pediatrics.

Many analysts believe the United States has too many specialists and too few primary care physicians and that the problem has worsened over time. According to Schroeder (1992), the growth in the number of specialists relative to primary care physicians is one reason health costs are so high in the United States. Specialists are more prone to overutilize costly new, high-technology medical procedures that drive up medical costs. Higher surgery rates and a greater availability of medical technology in the United States relative to other industrialized nations are used as evidence to support this hypothesis. To prove his point, Schroeder (1984, 1992) compared the proportion of specialists in the United States to that of various Western European countries in 1980. He found the proportion of specialists in Belgium, Germany, the Netherlands, and the United Kingdom to lie between 25 and 50 percent. In the United States, the proportion of specialists was slightly more than 60 percent, substantially higher than in most other developed nations.

A more recent study (Government Accounting Office, 1994) found basically the same thing for 1990. For example, the report found that 58 percent of the doctors in the United Kingdom are in primary care. It is interesting to note that one developed nation has a lower percentage of primary care physicians than the United States. According to the GAO report, only 18 percent of the physicians in Sweden are considered primary care doctors.

Whether the United States has more or less than the efficient level of primary care physicians is difficult to determine objectively. One way researchers have attempted to answer this question is by first establishing the medical *need* for primary care physicians—that is, how many primary care physicians are needed to deliver adequate care to the population. However, from an economic perspective, demand rather than need is really at issue. Next, the most cost-effective way to deliver physician services must be determined. Only after this has been established can one determine the total number of primary and nonprimary care physicians clinically needed to provide medical services to the entire population. These estimates must then be compared to the actual number of primary and nonprimary care physicians practicing in the United States to determine whether a surplus or a shortage of specialists exists. Obviously, the process of calculating the optimal number of many specialists is complicated and laced with value judgments.

Politzer et al. (1996) look to the future to estimate whether the United States will have an adequate supply of physicians in the year 2020. To establish need, the authors conducted a statistical technique called meta-analysis on five alternative projection methods already developed in the literature. Meta-analysis allows them to establish bands of physician requirements for primary and specialty care physicians. Physician supply projections were based on a number of factors, including the number of first-year residency positions likely to exist in the future. The authors conclude that the "future physician supply does not appear well-matched with requirements" (p. 181). For example, assuming a 30/70 ratio of generalists to specialists and an increase in U.S. medical graduates equal to 110 percent of their 1998 levels, the authors project a shortage of approximately 33,000 primary care physicians by the year 2020. The same set of assumptions also generates a surplus of specialists.

Another study with many of the same authors (Gamliel et al., 1995) reaches the same conclusion. According to the results from this study, in all likelihood there will

INSIGHT 14–1

## An Economic Analysis of Specialty Choice

As mentioned in the text, numerous policymakers have voiced concern that the United States has an insufficient number of primary care providers and that the shortage may become more severe in the future. Continuing with this thought, some health policy analysts have argued that the government should adopt policies that encourage a greater number of primary care providers. Policies may be designed with financial incentives to alter the choice between primary and specialty medicine. The effectiveness of various incentive schemes depends on the factors influencing choice of practice. Especially important are economic determinants that affect the relative costs and benefits of becoming a primary or specialist care giver. With that in mind, this insight examines the literature on the economic determinants of specialty choice.

McKay (1990) estimated the impact of various economic factors, such as relative expected earnings, relative expected hours worked, and relative length of training period, on the distribution of medical residents across specialties. The results suggest that the proportion of residents in a given specialty is more responsive to expected hours worked than to expected income. McKay also found that the elasticity of the percentage of residents in a particular specialty with respect to expected earnings varies between .30 and .60,[1] while the elasticity of the percentage of residents in a given specialty to expected hours worked averages between −1.2 and −2.0. Moreover, specialty choice was found to be independent of the length of the residency requirement.

Others examined the impact of student indebtedness on specialty choice. Students who are forced to incur significant amounts of debt to finance their education may be more inclined to choose more lucrative specialties than primary care medicine to generate the financial resources they need to repay their debt. The evidence is mixed, but appears to suggest that indebtedness has little impact on specialty choice. Geertsma and Romano (1986) found that total indebtedness, but not academic indebtedness, is directly related to specialty choice, whereas Bazzoli (1985) and Fox (1993) discovered that indebtedness has only a small marginal impact on specialty choice. Others, such as Rogers, Fincher, and Lewis (1990), uncovered no association between the level of debt and specialty choice.

The studies by Rogers, Fincher, and Lewis (1990) and Kassler, Wartment, and Silliman (1991) also reveal that students entering nonprimary care specialties are motivated not only by higher expected income but also by the prestige associated with specialization, the opportunity for research, and more regular working hours. Students who choose primary care medicine, on the other hand, are more concerned with working directly with patients and providing continuity of care to their patients.

[1]Hurley (1991) finds that the earnings elasticity of specialty choice is higher at 1.05.

be an overall surplus of physicians of between 56,000 and 71,000 doctors by the year 2020, which will be due primarily to an oversupply of specialists. The problem of an oversupply of physicians is further complicated by the fact that the authors forecast a shortage of primary care physicians in the future.

This mismatch between the supply of and the need for physicians raises some interesting policy questions. For instance, what role should the government play in correcting any imbalances that may exist in our health workforce given the fact that it has traditionally subsidized the education of many health professionals, including physicians? Also, what is the role of the market in correcting any labor market imbalances that may develop?

| TABLE 14-3 | DISTRIBUTION OF PHYSICIANS BY EMPLOYMENT STATUS AND MODE OF PRACTICE, 1989 AND 1997 | |
| --- | --- | --- |
| | **1989** | **1997** |
| Employment Status | | |
| Self-employed | 70.1% | 56.6% |
| Employees | 23.9 | 38.8 |
| Independent contractors | 6.0 | 4.7 |
| Size of Practice* | | |
| Solo practice | 53.3 | 45.8 |
| Two-person practice | 12.5 | 10.3 |
| Three-person practice | 9.0 | 8.6 |
| Four-to-eight-person practice | 14.9 | 19.3 |
| Over eight-person practice | 10.2 | 16.0 |

*The sample includes self-employed physicians only.

SOURCE: *Physician Marketplace Statistics*, 1997/98 and 1990 editions (Chicago: American Medical Association). Adapted from Tables 111 and 115 (1997/98) and Tables 51 and 52 (1990).

## Mode of Practice

Economists view the provision of physician services as a production process that involves a multitude of inputs aside from physician labor. It includes other labor inputs, such as nurses, nurse practitioners, physician assistants, medical technicians, and receptionists, along with various nonlabor inputs, such as office space, medical supplies, and diagnostic equipment. In light of this view, it is extremely important to distinguish between physician labor as a strategic input in the production of medical services and the firm, or production arrangement, adopted by physicians to produce medical care. Self-employed profit-maximizing physicians act as entrepreneurs when they combine various inputs, including their own labor, to produce medical care for their patients.

Table 14–3 provides a glimpse of the modes of practice utilized by physicians from 1989 to 1997. The data indicate that the majority of physicians are self-employed. In 1989 slightly more than 70 percent of all physicians were self-employed, and by 1997 this number had dropped to just under 57 percent. This drop appears to have resulted primarily from a decrease in the proportion of physicians operating solo practices. By 1997, fewer than 46 percent of all self-employed physicians were engaged in a solo practice. There was also a decrease in the percentage of self-employed physicians involved in practices with two or three physicians. The only exceptions were practices with between four and eight physicians and those with more than eight physicians.

| TABLE 14–4 | DISTRIBUTION OF PHYSICIAN REVENUES BY SOURCE OF PAYER, 1997 |
|---|---|

| Source | Percentage |
|---|---|
| Government | 41.4% |
|   Medicare | 29.2 |
|   Medicaid | 12.2 |
| Private | 58.6 |
|   Private insurance plans | 44.0 |
|   Out-of-pocket payments | 14.6 |

SOURCE: *Physician Market Place Statistics*, 1997/98 (Chicago: American Medical Association, 1998), Tables 96, 97, 98, 99.

Based on this information there appears to be a trend away from smaller practices toward larger, multidoctor modes of production. This trend might reflect the economies of scope offered by large multidoctor, multispecialty practices or economies of scale in the production of physician services. We review some empirical evidence concerning economies of scale later in the chapter.

By far the greatest change in recent years has been an increase in the proportion of physicians who are not self-employed but are paid on a salary basis. By 1997, 38.8 percent of all physicians were paid on a salary basis, an increase of almost 15 percentage points from 1989. This indicates a growing provision of ambulatory care by hospitals and HMOs.

## Buyers of Physician Services and Methods of Remuneration

A review of the methods of remuneration provides insight into the number and types of buyers of physician services and the extent to which any one buyer, or group of buyers, may exhibit some degree of monopsony power. In 1997 (see table 14–4), 41.4 percent of all physician revenues emanated from the government sector, with Medicare making up over 70 percent of that total. This is in sharp contrast to the market for hospital services, where the government sector accounted for nearly 62 percent of total revenues (see Chapter 15). This suggests that although the government sector is clearly a major player in the physician services market, its ability to exercise monopsony power may not be as great as in the market for hospital services.

Rising health care costs have forced politicians to reevaluate the Medicare and Medicaid programs. For example, after much debate Congress passed the Omnibus Budget Reconciliation Act (OBRA) in 1989, which, among other things, called for major changes in Part B of the Medicare payment system, which provides compensation to physicians for medical services rendered to elderly patients. As of 1992, physicians are now compensated based on resources utilized rather than on the "usual customary and reasonable" rate. This Medicare reimbursement scheme for physician services, referred to as the *resource-based relative value scale* system, is reviewed in Chapter 12. OBRA 1989 was followed by the Balanced Budget Act of 1997, which extended the resource-based method of payment to include practice and malpractice expenses.

The private sector accounted for about 59 percent of physician revenues in 1997, with 44 percent coming from private insurance companies. The remaining 14.6 percent was the result of out-of-pocket payments. This is somewhat different from the hospital services market, where out-of-pocket payments accounted for only 2.6 percent of total revenues. The relatively higher out-of-pocket expenses for physician services are not too surprising, because insurance theory suggests that coverage is lower for more predictable and lower-magnitude losses.

Overall, the private sector accounts for a much greater share of revenues in the physician services market than it does in the hospital services market. This is largely because out-of-pocket payments are a much more important source of funds for physicians than for hospitals. This is not to say, however, that the government plays only a minor role in the physician services market. On the contrary, the recent Medicare reforms indicate that the federal government intends to play a more active role in this market for years to come.

## Reimbursement Practices of Managed-Care Buyers of Physician Services

Managed care, which embodies a very broad set of policies designed by third-party payers to control the utilization and cost of medical care, has had a profound impact on the physician services market. Through the use of alternative compensation schemes, utilization reviews, quality controls, and the like, MCOs hope to modify the behavior of physicians to contain costs. These control mechanisms diminish the autonomy physicians traditionally enjoyed in practicing medicine, and, as a result, many physicians have resisted the movement toward managed care. Despite these reservations, managed care presently has a major impact on the allocation of resources in the physician services market.

The strong presence of managed care in the physician services market is reflected in the fact that 92 percent of all physicians practicing medicine in 1997 had at least one managed-care contract. A more detailed look at the data confirms the significant role of managed care in the physician services market. The proportion of physicians with a minimum of one managed-care contract varied little across regions of the country, practice size, or specialty in 1997. For example, the rate of contract involvement for physicians ranged from a high of 95 percent in New England to a low of 91 percent in the Middle Atlantic region. In relation to practice arrangement, there appears to be a weak but positive connection between practice size and managed-care involvement. Almost 88 percent of those physicians in a solo practice had at least one managed-care contract, while 96 percent of all physicians in a practice with 8 or more doctors had at least one contract. Finally, for almost all specialties the percent of physicians with one or more managed-care contracts topped 90 percent. The lowest was psychiatry with slightly more than 80 percent having signed at least one contract (American Medical Association, 1998).

Managed care also appears to account for a significant proportion of revenue generated by physicians. In 1997, 44 cents out of every dollar generated by practicing physicians was the result of some type of contractual arrangement with an MCO.

## Barriers to Entry

It is generally accepted that substantial barriers to entry in the market for physician services impede competition primarily by legally limiting the supply of physicians. Before being allowed to practice medicine, a person must meet a minimum educational requirement (usually a degree from an accredited medical school), participate in an internship or a residency program at a recognized institution, and pass a medical exam. These various requirements entail substantial time and money costs and raise the opportunity cost of becoming a medical doctor. Advocates for these legal restrictions base their argument on the public interest theory. Market failure brought about by an asymmetry of information between patient and physician concerning the appropriateness and quality of medical care justifies the need for government intervention. Because consumers generally have imperfect information concerning the medical care received given its technical sophistication, they are sometimes unsure about the appropriateness and quality of physician services. As a result, the market cannot be relied on to weed out incompetent doctors or those who would take advantage of their position and prescribe needless and costly medical care.

The necessity of government intervention has also been justified based on the possibility that a negative supply-side externality will occur if incompetent physicians are allowed to practice medicine. For example, if an incompetent physician misdiagnoses a patient infected with the AIDS virus due to a faulty test, others may contract the virus. As a result, government intervention is necessary to ensure that consumers will not become innocent victims of medical malfeasance (Friedman, 1962).

Over the years, proponents of the special interest theory, including Kessel (1958), Moore (1961), Friedman (1962, 1980), and Leffler (1978), have argued that barriers exist primarily to protect the economic interests of physicians. By restricting supply through the creation of educational and training barriers to entry, physicians have succeeded in generating economic profits. As evidence, these analysts point to high physician salaries. Control of medical licensure is the primary mechanism physicians use to restrict their numbers. In the United States, the licensure of physicians is under the control of the states, and most states have medical boards composed of physicians that establish, review, and maintain the criteria for obtaining a license to practice medicine. The fact that these requirements control the process of becoming a physician rather than encourage the maintenance of medical knowledge has been used as evidence to support the special interest interpretation of these restrictions.[5]

Control over medical licensure is not the only method physicians use to maintain their monopoly power. Physicians as a group also play a critical role in the accreditation of medical schools. For example, the Liaison Committee on Medical Education, the main accrediting body of medical schools, is composed of 17 people, 6 of whom are representatives of the American Medical Association (Wilson and Neuhauser,

1985). By maintaining control over the number of medical schools, physicians are in a position to indirectly restrain the supply of their services.

The establishment of limits on the use of physician extenders is yet another method physicians employ to protect their economic interests. Physician extenders, such as physician assistants and nurse practitioners, have the medical training necessary to perform a number of medical tasks traditionally carried out by the physician.[6] Production theory indicates that when more than one variable input is utilized in the production of physician services, a cost-conscious firm combines these inputs to produce in the most cost-efficient manner. For example, let's suppose a staff-model HMO faces an increase in wages for physicians. To counteract this increase, the HMO may attempt to substitute physician extenders for physicians in the production of certain medical services. To limit the possibility of this occurrence, physicians may flex their political muscle to legally limit the duties of physician extenders. The goal would be to legally constrain the marginal rate of technical substitution between physicians and physician extenders to near zero.

Given many of the recent changes in medical care, Svorny (1992) questions the need for medical licensure in the physician market. She believes market incentives can now be relied on to ensure an efficient level of quality. In particular, Svorny points to changes in medical liability, the rapid growth in for-profit medical care providers, the increased use of brand names, and the growth in employed rather than self-employed physicians as lessening the need for the licensure of physicians.

For instance, recent legal decisions have shifted some of the liability for medical malpractice away from physicians and toward institutions, such as hospitals and HMOs. As a result, hospitals and HMOs now have a much greater incentive to monitor the behavior of physicians who practice medicine on their premises by assessing the quality of care provided. Institutional liability decreases the need for licensing because it is now in the self-interests of hospitals to weed out incompetent physicians.

The growth in for-profit medical care providers may have the same effect. Because at least one owner has a financial stake in a for-profit medical institution, there may be a greater incentive to oversee the performance of physicians than in a not-for-profit institution, which is run by a board of directors who have no financial commitment to the institution. The expanded use of brand names by hospitals, group practices, and HMOs also increases the incentive for these institutions to more closely monitor the performance of physicians. An incompetent physician can financially hurt the institution by damaging its reputation and tarnishing its image, which took a substantial amount of time and money to establish. Much goodwill is at stake, and hence there is an increased incentive to dismiss incompetent physicians.

---

[5]The same argument can be made for lawyers and certified public accountants, who are required to pass the bar exam and CPA exam, respectively.

[6]A physician assistant must study for two years in an accredited physician assistant program and pass a certification exam before being allowed to practice. A nurse practitioner is a licensed registered nurse who has received an additional one or two years' training and passed a certification exam. In terms of duties, the difference between the two labor inputs is one of emphasis. Physician assistants concern themselves primarily with the direct application of medical care, whereas nurse practitioners deal mostly in education and wellness.

## Should I Join the AMA?

The AMA, recognized as one of the most powerful professional associations in the United States, provides a variety of services to physicians. First and foremost, the organization serves as a political watchdog, guarding against the passage of any legislation that may jeopardize physicians' monopoly power or self-interest. In addition, the AMA plays a critical role in the establishment and maintenance of standards for licensing and professional conduct. Because these "public" benefits are received by all physicians and not just those who are members of the AMA, the potential for a "free-rider" problem exists. In other words, why should an individual physician join the AMA and pay the dues when the same public benefits will be forthcoming if a sufficient number of other physicians join?

Ohsfeldt (1988) points out that the AMA provides specific benefits exclusively to its membership to negate the free-rider problem. First, the AMA makes it easier for its members to establish networks and obtain referrals from other members. Second, the AMA provides services to its members that enhance their professional knowledge and reputation; for example, members can purchase AMA publications at a reduced rate. Finally, AMA membership confers a degree of prestige that may enhance a member's professional standing and raise his or her earnings potential.

To test this latter hypothesis, Ohsfeldt developed an economic model to estimate the impact of AMA membership on physician earnings. Since income may increase the likelihood that a physician will join the AMA, the author developed a two-equation model that simultaneously considers the impact of AMA membership on earnings and the effect of earnings on the probability of membership. The model consists of a membership equation that predicts the probability that a physician will become a member of the AMA and an earnings equation that estimates the impact of membership on physician earnings.

The dependent variable in the membership equation is a dummy variable that equals 1 if the physician is a member of the AMA and zero if not.[1] The independent variables include an instrumental variable representing earnings, years of practice experience, a set of variables to control for specialty, and a host of other variables. As expected, the author found that earnings positively affect the probability of becoming a member in the AMA, signifying that AMA membership is a normal good. In particular, a $1,000 increase in annual earnings increased the probability of membership by .003; that is, a physician who earns $10,000 more than an otherwise comparable colleague is 3 percent more likely to join the AMA. Practice experience was also found to positively affect membership. The probability of membership increased by .031 percentage points when years of practice experience increased from 15 to 30. The author also found that self-employed physicians and physicians who had a fee-for-service practice were more likely to join the AMA, whereas female physicians were less likely to join.

Regarding the effect of AMA membership on physician earnings, a consolidated version of the estimated earnings equations is found to look like the following:

**(14–1)**  $LogIn = 2.71^* + .023^* \text{Member} + .03^* \text{Yrs} + -.043^* (\text{Yrs}^2/100) + .162^* \text{Self}$
  (6.67)    (1.85)              (5.21)        (−4.11)                (2.17)

  $-.221^* \text{Female} + \text{Specialty dummies} + \text{Other variables}$
  (−2.86)

  $N = 2,708$

## (continued)

where

LogIn = The natural logarithm of income

Member = An instrumental variable that equals 1 if the physician is a member of the AMA and zero if not

Yrs = The number of years the physician has been practicing medicine

Self = A dummy variable that equals 1 if the physician is self-employed and zero if not

Female = A dummy variable that equals 1 if the physician is a female and zero if not

Specialty dummies = Nine dummy variables, each of which takes on the value of 1 if the physician has a particular specialty and zero if not

As always, the *t*-statistics are in parentheses and the asterisk (*) means the coefficient is significant to at least the 10 percent level. The linear and squared years of experience terms capture the typical inverted-U relation between experience and earnings. The positive and negative estimated coefficients on the Yrs and Yrs²/100 variables, respectively, indicate that experience positively affects earnings up to some point, after which it has a negative effect. The parameter estimates on the Self and Female variables indicate that self-employed physicians earn more than non-self-employed physicians while female physicians earn less than males, all else held constant. The estimated coefficients on all the specialty dummies (not reported), with the exception of pediatrics, are positive and significant to at least the 5 percent level, indicating that most specialists earn more than general/family practitioners.

Most important, the estimated coefficient for the membership variable is positive and significant at the 10 percent level. The results indicate that members of the AMA earn approximately 2.7 percent more than nonmembers, *ceteris paribus*. This amount, although statistically significant, is considerably less than the total earnings differentials of 22 percent observed between members and nonmembers in 1982. In any case, this study illustrates how economic theory, along with empirical estimation techniques, can be used to gain a much better understanding of how economic variables influence physician behavior.

[1]Since the dependent variable was not continuous, traditional regression analysis could not be employed. The author utilized a technique called *probit analysis* that predicts the probability of AMA membership for physicians with different characteristics.

The growing use of employed as opposed to self-employed physicians also provides medical institutions with an increased incentive to monitor the activities of physicians. Naturally, it is in the interests of these institutions to eliminate those physicians providing low-quality or unnecessary medical care. In addition, because the physician is a salaried employee, the incentive to provide unnecessary care has been diminished. According to Svorny, all these changes have lessened the need for the licensure of physicians because market forces can now be relied on to force doctors to provide quality medical care at least cost.

These institutional and structural changes imply a weakening of barriers to entry into the physician services market. If this is indeed the case, the level of competition should have intensified over time. To test for this phenomenon, Noether (1986) developed a system of stock and income equations to depict behavior in the physician services market. According to her results, competition in the physician services markets has increased since 1965, and this increase has caused the supply of physician labor to increase by 6 to 20 percent and physician incomes to fall by 19 to 45 percent. All this indicates that the degree of monopoly power in the hands of physicians may have waned in recent years.

## Production, Costs, and Economies of Scale

Thus far, we have focused primarily on the supply of physicians. In this section, the perspective changes from the physician as an input in the production of medical services to the physician as an entrepreneur: one who makes allocation decisions concerning the most cost-effective way to produce medical services. Unfortunately, the literature on the production and cost of physician services is rather thin compared to the multitude of studies on the hospital services market.

The most comprehensive studies on the production of physician services were carried out by Reinhardt (1972, 1973, 1975). In these studies, the author estimated a production function for physician services using data from a survey of doctors in 1965 and 1967. Given the controversy surrounding the most appropriate means to measure output in the physician services market, the author employed three measures of physician output: total weekly patient visits at the office, home, or hospital; weekly office visits; and annual gross billings to patients. Inputs included physician labor, as measured by total practice hours per week; number of auxiliary personnel; medical supplies; and capital equipment. In addition, a host of control variables were included in the estimate equations.

The regression results with total patient visits as a measure of output are particularly interesting. To no one's surprise, Reinhardt found physician labor to be highly correlated with output, with an elasticity of output to physician time equal to .70.[7] Capital inputs appeared to have a far smaller impact on output. The capital elasticity of output was estimated at .05. The effect of auxiliary personnel appeared to be somewhat greater than that of capital, with an elasticity of approximately .32. Finally, Reinhardt found that physicians in group practices were about 5 percent more productive in terms of patient visits than physicians in a solo practice.

In a more contemporary study, Brown (1988) also examined the factors that influence physician output. He found, among other things, that group practice physicians were 22 percent more productive than their counterparts in solo practices. These estimates are substantially greater than Reinhardt's and justify the organizational movement in the physician services market away from solo practices that we discussed earlier in the chapter. Solo practices face some difficulty in competing with group practices with such a significant productivity disadvantage.[8]

---

[7]This output elasticity means the output of physician services increased by 7 percent for each 10 percent increase in physician hours, assuming all other factors remain constant.

[8]The cost differential may reflect the value, or utility, that a proprietor/physician places on working independently and being his or her own boss. Otherwise, why would the proprietor/physician remain in the less profitable solo practice?

| TABLE 14–5 | ESTIMATES FOR THE MARGINAL PRODUCTS OF VARIOUS INPUTS UTILIZED IN THE PRODUCTION OF PHYSICIAN SERVICES |

|  | Marginal Product | Marginal Product<br>Input Price |
| --- | --- | --- |
| Physician hours per week | 2.967 | .114 |
| Registered nurse hours per week | .585 | .104 |
| Practical nurse hours per week | .542 | .129 |
| Physician assistant hours per week | .231 | .040 |
| Technician hours per week | .320 | .067 |
| Secretary hours per week | .192 | .043 |

SOURCE: Douglas M. Brown, "Do Physicians Underutilize Aides?" *Journal of Human Resources* 23 (1988), pp. 342–55.

Brown's study also uncovers some interesting results concerning the efficient use of auxiliary personnel. The marginal products of various labor inputs, presented in table 14–5, clearly show that physicians, registered nurses, and practical nurses are the most productive inputs, whereas secretaries, technicians, and physician assistants are the least productive inputs in the production of physician services. To determine whether physicians are utilizing inputs efficiently, we must compare the marginal product per dollar spent on each input. Recall from Chapter 6 that the firm is optimally utilizing all inputs if the marginal product of the last dollar spent on each input is equal across all inputs. These data appear in the last column in table 14–5. Since the marginal product per dollar spent for physicians' time equals .114 and is higher than the marginal product to price ratio for all other inputs, we can conclude that physicians overutilize auxiliary personnel. The only exception is practical nurses; in this case, the evidence suggests that they are underutilized, with a marginal product per dollar spent of .129.

The literature also suggests that moderate economies of scale exist in the production of physician services. A recent study by Pope and Burge (1996), which estimated the gross revenue production function for self-employed physicians, found the lowest-cost practice size to be 5.2 physicians. The lowest cost practice size is somewhat higher than the average practice size of 2.4 physicians in their sample. The authors also found that group physicians have the ability to handle 17 percent more office visits than physicians in a solo practice.

The literature on survivor analysis also indicates the existence of economies of scale in the production of physician services. As it pertains to the market for physician services, survivor analysis examines the distribution of practice sizes over time to determine which practice size produces medical services most efficiently. Studies by Frech and Ginsburg (1974) and Marder and Zuckerman (1985) indicate that solo and two-physician practices are inefficient at the margin relative to group practices. Relying on more recent data, Marder and Zuckerman also found medium-sized groups to be less efficient than large practices (100 or more physicians). Taken together, these studies suggest that multiphysician practices have a cost advantage over solo practices and that economies of scale exist in the production of physician services at least up to the three-to-seven practice size. Marder and Zuckerman's results go one step further and suggest that economies of scale may exist for practices as large as 100 physicians. Referring to our earlier discussion on the mode of practice (see table 14–3), these results explain why the proportion of solo and two- and three-person practices decreased from 1989 to 1997 relative to physician practices with four-to-eight and over-eight persons.

## Summary of the Structure of the Market for Physician Services

Whether the physician services market is measured based on real expenditures or the number of physicians practicing medicine, it increased dramatically in size over the past two decades. Since 1970, the number of physicians and real expenditures on physician services in the United States have more than doubled. The increase has outpaced the overall growth in the economy and the general population, as illustrated by the significant increase in the physician-to-population ratio from 148 in 1970 to 271 in 1996 per 100,000 total population. This tremendous growth in the physician services market was not unique to the United States. Overall, the physician-to-population ratio for the 22 high-income members of the OECD increased from 142 to 238 over the period 1970 to 1990.[9]

The increase in physician labor in the United States has not been without controversy. Some people believe the United States has too many specialists and too few generalists. This issue is likely to play an integral role in the health care reform debate over the coming years.

The mode of practice in the physician services market has also changed significantly in recent years. There appears to be a movement away from single- and two-physician practices and toward multiphysician practices with four or more physicians. In addition, significant growth appears to be occurring in the number of employed physicians. In all probability, this trend reflects changing economic conditions in the health care field. For instance, productivity studies and survivor analysis studies indicate the existence of economies of scale that confer a distinct cost advantage on large multiphysician practices.

MCOs also appear to play a key role in the physician services market. Over 90 percent of all physicians have at least one contract with an MCO. The growing presence of MCOs in the physician services market may also partly explain the growth of multiphysician practices relative to smaller ones. Since larger practices have a cost advantage over smaller practices, they are in a better position to negotiate price discounts with MCOs.

---

[9]Among those countries are the United Kingdom, Australia, Italy, Belgium, Germany, the United States, and Japan.

Despite the presence of barriers to entry, such as medical licensure, the physician services market has become even more competitive over time as large, institutional buyers challenge the authority of independent physicians. This has caused some policymakers to call for the elimination of these barriers. As the market for physician services becomes more competitive, perhaps market forces can be relied on more heavily to dispose of incompetent or unprofessional doctors.

# The Conduct of the Physician Services Industry

Now that we have established the market determinants of behavior, or the structure of the physician services industry, we are in a position to discuss the conduct of that market. As you know, market structure interacts with economic objectives to establish conduct. We will look at the effects of various compensation schemes on physician behavior, the supplier-induced demand hypothesis, geographical variations in the utilization of physician's services, and the impact of managed-care practices.

## *The Impact of Alternative Compensation Schemes on Physician Behavior*

Concern for growing health care costs has caused third-party payers, both private and public, to seek new ways to reimburse physicians. The traditional fee-for-service method of payment has fallen out of favor because it creates an incentive for overutilization of medical care. The problem becomes particularly acute when the fee-for-service method of reimbursement is combined with a nominal, or zero, consumer copayment, because under these circumstances consumers have little incentive to monitor the behavior of their physicians. To rectify this problem, many managed-care providers and private insurance companies have adopted alternative physician reimbursement schemes.

Based on a survey of over 100 managed care plans in 1994, Gold et al. (1995) uncovered some interesting information concerning the methods presently used to recruit and compensate physicians. Over 70 percent of the managed care plans in the sample said they utilized a careful selection process when recruiting new physicians. Over 60 percent of all plans took into consideration qualitative information, such as professional reputation or patterns of care, during the selection process. However, only 37 percent of the plans reviewed any quantitative data from indemnity claims and/or hospital-discharge data when selecting a new doctor.

As we might expect, staff-model HMOs rely more heavily on a salary-based method of payment, whereas IPA HMOs tend to rely on other methods of payment. According to the sample, 28 percent of staff-HMOs use a salary-based method, while only 2 percent of the IPA HMOs use this method of compensation. Fee-for-service was the main form of compensation for PPOs, with 90 percent of the PPOs in the sample stating that it was the predominant form of payment for physician services.

Sixty percent of all plans in the survey used some type of risk-sharing mechanism when compensating physicians, which included some form of capitation payment, or withholdings or bonuses. Withholdings generally involve more sophisticated reimbursement schemes in an attempt to control costs. According to Hillman (1987), MCOs may direct premiums into a series of special-purpose funds after deducting administrative costs. These funds pay for such items as physician services, hospital services, and outpatient laboratory tests. Sometimes, a specific portion of the payment directed to physicians is withheld until the end of the fiscal year, when it can be established whether there is a surplus or a deficit in the remaining funds. If a surplus exists, the MCO generally returns the withheld portion to the physicians. If a deficit exists, the MCO applies all or part of the withheld funds against the loss. By establishing such a compensation system, the MCO creates a direct financial relationship between its own economic viability and the clinical behavior of its physicians. Those physicians who overutilize medical resources and drive up costs receive less compensation.

With a system of bonuses, the plan gives a portion of any surplus remaining at the end of the year to physicians to elicit cost-effective behavior. Hellinger (1996) states that some MCOs also set up special-purpose referral accounts to pay for the cost of specialists. Primary care physicians may receive some portion of any unused funds in these accounts at the end of the accounting period. The objective is to control the high cost of specialty care by providing primary care physicians with a financial incentive to limit referrals.

Gold et al. (1995) also found that MCOs use a variety of alternative performance-based measures to control costs. For example, 57 percent of the MCOs base pay on utilization or cost measures while almost half of the MCOs consider patient complaints and quality measures when establishing compensation. To a lesser extent, consumer surveys, provider productivity, and enrollee turnover rates are used in the creation of performance-based incentives.

Hillman, Pauly, and Kerstein (1989) used samples of over 300 MCOs to examine the impact of alternative physician compensation schemes on the utilization of medical services and firm profitability. The authors regressed a host of explanatory variables on three measures of MCO performance: the rate of hospitalization, visits per enrollee, and the break-even status of the MCO. The first two variables gauged the utilization of medical resources, and the last measured profitability. The independent variables fell into three categories: physician compensation variables, MCO descriptors, and market characteristics. A total of 11 variables controlled for the various types of compensation schemes used.

Overall, the results indicate that financial incentives affect the medical decisions of physicians and therefore the utilization of medical resources. In terms of utilization of medical services, hospitalization rates were found to be inversely related to whether physicians are paid on a salary or capitation basis. MCOs that used a salary-based method of compensation had 13.1 percent fewer hospitalization days per 1,000 enrollees per year than those using the more traditional fee-for-service methods. Likewise, the capitation method of payment was associated with 7.5 percent fewer hospitalization days. Visits per enrollee were also found to be inversely related to the use of financial penalties. For example, MCOs that established a referral fund whereby the individual physicians were at risk for any deficits had 10.5 percent fewer visits per enrollee, on average. The relationship between type of compensation scheme and profitability, as measured by the break-even status of the HMO, was far from clear. Hillman, Pauly, and Kerstein attributed these findings to the fact that profitability depends on many factors other than the utilization of medical resources. Be that as it may, this work is important because it establishes that clinical decisions are based at least in part on the financial incentives physicians face. This is not to suggest that physicians necessarily jeopardize the welfare of their patients; rather, in some circumstances, physicians consider their own self-interests when making marginal clinical decisions.

## The Supplier-Induced Demand Hypothesis

Without a doubt, one of the most controversial issues in health care economics today is whether the **supplier-induced demand (SID) hypothesis** can be used to explain physician behavior. The basic premise of the SID hypothesis is that physicians abuse their role as medical advisers to advance their own economic self-interests. This involves prescribing medical care beyond what is clinically necessary and can include such items as additional follow-up visits, an excessive number of medical tests, or even unnecessary surgery. Recall that the simplified model of supplier-induced demand, as presented in figure 10–6, hypothesizes that physicians possess the ability to increase the demand for their services *provided an asymmetry of information exists regarding the appropriateness of medical care provided.* In that example, physicians react to an increase in supply by inducing the demand for their services. The purpose is to prevent any loss in revenue that would result if the price of physician services were allowed to fall to a new equilibrium level.[10]

Gaynor and Polachek (1994) found empirically that an asymmetry of information does exist between provider and consumer in the physician services market. Incomplete consumer information was found to exceed incomplete physician information by a factor of approximately 1.5. As economic theory suggests, the authors determined that consumer information is more incomplete for smaller-ticket items, infrequent purchases, more heavily insured goods, and treatments for severe illnesses. They also found more incomplete consumer information to be the case when search costs are higher.

Much has been written about the basic SID model, and it has been criticized on both theoretical and empirical grounds. The major theoretical criticism deals with the fact that the SID model is inconsistent with the competitive framework (Stano, 1985). If the market for physician services is competitive, each physician is a price taker who can sell an unlimited amount of output at the going market price. The constraining factor is an increasing marginal cost, and each physician produces up to the point where the marginal cost of production equals marginal revenue, or price. Given this scenario and assuming there is a cost associated with inducement, physicians lack the incentive to increase the quantity of services.[11] From an individual physician's perspective, any

---

[10]Given that the demand for physician services is relatively inelastic, any drop in price resulting from an increase in supply causes total revenue to decline.

[11]The cost of inducement equals the dollar value of the psychic costs physicians must bear knowing that they are prescribing medical care beyond what is associated with standard medical practice. In addition, there are the costs associated with the possibility that patients will become aware that inducement is taking place and therefore take their business elsewhere.

attempt to provide further services causes the marginal cost of production to rise without an increase in (market) price. Thus, it is not in the physician's self-interest to artificially increase the quantity of services.

The SID model has also been criticized for neglecting to explain what prohibits physicians from continually inducing the demand for their services. Obviously there has to be a limiting factor; otherwise, physicians would be free to position the demand curve for their services anywhere they please. In an attempt to address these and other criticisms, several researchers, beginning with Evans (1974), extended the model to account for the fact that physicians have a certain degree of monopoly power—that is, they face a downward-sloping demand curve for their services. Evans assumed that every physician is a utility maximizer who faces the following utility function:

(14–2)  $U = f(Y, W, D)$,

where $U$ equals utility, $Y$ stands for income earned from the practice of medicine, $W$ represents workload, and $D$ equals the discretionary influence the physician holds over the demand for medical services.

It is assumed that the marginal utility of each additional dollar of income is positive, while the marginal utility of an increased workload and the exertion of discretionary influence are both negative. The latter variable yields negative marginal utility due to the ethical or moral costs associated with the abuse of discretionary influence. Because the physician faces a downward-sloping demand curve, any exertion of discretionary influence increases both the price and the quantity of medical services consumed. This action translates into additional income but also greater workload and abuser costs. Given these constraints, the physician induces demand up to the point where the marginal utility of additional income equals the marginal disutility associated with a greater workload and exertion of discretionary influence.

Evans' model, identified by equation 14–2, advances the literature on SID theory in two important ways. First, it recognizes that each physician possesses a certain degree of monopoly power. The monopoly power, or the ability to influence price, may result from a locational advantage given the importance of convenience or spatial proximity when purchasing physician services. Second, the model maintains that physicians face a cost when they exercise their ability to induce demand. This cost establishes a limit on the extent to which physicians induce demand.[12]

The debate over the relevance of the supplier-induced demand hypothesis has also taken place on empirical grounds. The simplest way to test the validity of the SID hypothesis is to specify a demand equation for physician services similar to equation 4–5 and include an additional explanatory variable, such as the physician-to-population ratio, to control for the availability of physician services. If the parameter estimate on the physician-to-population variable turns out to be positive and

---

[12]Others have developed even more sophisticated models. For example, Stano (1987) developed a model of physician inducement based on the standard theory of the firm with monopoly power. The model is beyond the scope of this book; suffice it to say that Stano theoretically shows that the ability of the physician to induce demand is directly related to the elasticity of demand. As a result, when a physician operates in a competitive setting and the demand curve is perfectly elastic, the ability to induce demand is nonexistent.

statistically significant, it can be inferred that physicians have the ability to induce demand.[13] Auster and Oaxaca (1981) have criticized this method of estimation because the demand equation in this instance is not identified and therefore cannot be estimated properly. An equation is identified if each parameter estimate has a unique value.[14]

The task of reviewing the empirical evidence on the SID hypothesis is daunting given the extensive work on the subject. In one of the earlier studies, Fuchs (1978) uncovered substantial support for the supplier-induced demand hypothesis. In particular, he estimated that a 10 percent increase in the supply of surgeons, as measured by the surgeon-to-population ratio, leads to a 3 percent increase in the per capita surgery rate. Cromwell and Mitchell (1986) also found evidence that surgeons induce demand. However, their estimates were substantially smaller than Fuchs's. They estimated that a 10 percent increase in surgeon density leads to only a .9 percent increase in surgeries and a 1.3 percent increase in elective surgeries per capita. Rossiter and Wilensky (1984) and McCarthy (1985) also uncovered evidence that substantiates the inducement hypothesis, although the magnitude of the inducement was estimated to be marginal. Looking at the issue of physician ownership of ancillary services, Mitchell and Sass (1995) also found evidence of induced demand. According to their findings, physical therapy clinics in Florida owned by physicians required 50 percent more visits from patients than those clinics that received no referrals from owners, with no discernible difference in the quality of care across ownership structures. A partial list of additional studies that corroborate the inducement hypothesis includes

---

[13]In this case, whether the increase in the demand for physician services is the result of induced demand or simply a response to an increase in the supply of physician services is open to considerable debate.

[14]To illustrate this point, we follow the lead of Auster and Oaxaca (1981) and specify a set of linear equations that describe equilibrium in a competitive setting:

**(14–3)** $\quad Q^D = a_0 + a_1 P + a_2 X^D$

**(14–4)** $\quad Q^S = b_0 + b_1 P + b_2 X^S$

**(14–5)** $\quad Q^D = Q^S,$

where $Q^D$ and $Q^S$ represent the quantity demanded and supplied, respectively; $P$ equals price; and $X^D$ and $X^S$ stand for an exogenous demand- and supply-side variable, respectively. The third equation represents the equilibrium condition, which states that the market clears when quantity demanded equals quantity supplied.

Now let's alter the model to consider supplier-induced demand. This necessitates that we include $Q^S$ as a right-hand-side variable in the demand equation. Thus, the demand equation looks like the following:

**(14–6)** $\quad Q^D = a_0 + a_1 P + a_2 X^D + a_3 Q^S$

The parameter $a_3$ is assumed to be larger than zero because any increase in supply should generate a corresponding increase in demand. If we employ the equilibrium condition as specified in equation 14–5 and solve equation 14–6 for $Q^D$, we get

**(14–7)** $\quad Q^D = \dfrac{a_0}{(1 - a_3)} + \dfrac{a_1}{(1 - a_3)} P + \dfrac{a_2}{(1 - a_3)} X^D.$

This equation is indistinguishable from equation 14–3 from an empirical perspective. In other words, if we were to estimate equations 14–3 and 14–7, there would be no difference in the parameter estimates. Since the estimates are not unique, the equation is not identified.

Grytten and Holst (1990), Hemenway and Fallon (1985), Tussing (1983), and Tussing and Wojtowyzc (1986).

A number of studies do not support the supplier-induced hypothesis. For example, based on an analysis of individual physician practices, Stano (1985) found no evidence of inducement. These results were later substantiated by Ferguson and Crawford (1989). In a more recent study, Escarce (1992) employed Medicare enrollment and physician claims data to test the inducement hypothesis. The results indicate that increases in the supply of surgeons are associated with increases in the demand for initial contacts with surgeons but have no impact on the demand for services among surgery patients in terms of intensity of use. Thus, the author attributes the greater demand for surgeries to improvements in access, lower time costs, or better quality. These conclusions do not support the inducement hypothesis.

A study by Pauly and Satterthwaite (1981) deserves particular attention because of its theoretical and empirical contributions to the subject. The authors suggest that the degree of monopoly power physicians possess is inversely related to consumer information. If consumers are informed regarding the reputation of each physician in a given community, the ability of doctors to behave as monopolists is limited. This proposition is consistent with the characteristics of a competitive market outlined in Chapter 8.

At this point, Pauly and Satterthwaite depart from traditional theory and hypothesize that the monopoly power any one physician holds is positively related to the number of physicians within a given community.[15] They base this premise on the notion that as the number of physicians increases, consumers find it more difficult to gather information on each physician. This decrease in consumer information causes the demand curve to become more inelastic and confers a degree of monopoly power on doctors.

If these authors are correct, we should observe the price of physician services to be positively related to the number of physicians practicing in a given area, holding market size constant. This is precisely what the authors found. The price index for routine office visits to primary care physicians was found to be positively related to measures of consumer information, including the number of physicians per square mile. The implication is that if consumers are informed and the asymmetry of information is held to a minimum, physicians have limited monopoly power.

It is obvious from this overview of the literature that the issue of whether physicians possess the ability to induce demand is unlikely to be resolved in the near future.[16] Overall, the evidence suggests that although physicians may possess the ability to induce demand, the extent to which they can do so is much less than initially thought. The only exception may be the market for surgical services, where surgeons possess a greater ability to manipulate demand.

---

[15]Normally, it is assumed that the intensity of competition increases as the number of providers rises.

[16]Review articles by Folland and Stano (1990) and Rice and Labelle (1989) illustrate the liveliness of the debate and the extent of the literature on the subject. The controversy also has an international flavor. For example, Grytten and Holst (1990) examined the utilization of dental services in Norway, while Ferguson and Crawford (1989) looked at the phenomenon of supplier-induced demand in Canada. Finally Grytten, Carlsen, and Sorenson (1995) examined whether supplier-induced demand is a problem for primary care physician services in Norway.

## Geographical Variations in the Utilization of Physician Services

The phenomenon of **small area variations** in the delivery and consumption of physician services across geographic regions has been documented by an almost limitless number of studies worldwide. For example, wide physician utilization variations exist in countries such as Norway, England, and Canada, where government plays a major role in the delivery or financing of health care services (Phelps, 1992). Physician utilization variations also occur among the counties within a single state and among states. For example, Miller and Holahan (1995) found substantial variation in the utilization of physician services across states, with Florida utilizing physician services at a rate 38 percent above the U.S. mean while Montana was 29 percent below the mean. They also found significant variation among urban and rural areas.

In addition, an extensive body of literature has suggested that selected medical services are overutilized. The estimates regarding the proportion of inappropriate medical care given range from 15 to 30 percent, with a number of more recent studies putting it at about 4 percent[17] As a result, the public has become fond of blaming high medical costs on physicians who prescribe needless medical tests or perform unnecessary surgery.

The **physician practice hypothesis** has been used to explain variations in utilization rates across regions. This hypothesis, which is most closely associated with the work of Wennberg (1984, 1985), contends that per capita variations in the use of medical care, particularly surgery, reflect systematic differences in clinical opinions regarding the appropriate amount and type of medical care.

These subjective differences are collectively referred to as "practice style" and exist primarily because of the uncertainty surrounding the practice of medicine. As Eddy (1984) so aptly wrote, "Uncertainty creeps into medical practice through every pore. Whether a physician is defining a disease, making a diagnosis, selecting a procedure, observing outcomes, assessing probabilities, assigning preferences or putting it all together, he is walking on very slippery terrain" (p. 75). Physician uncertainty is likely to be greatest when the diagnosis is rather complicated and the medical procedure is relatively new. As Phelps (1992) writes,

> When the disease is very easy to diagnose, the consequences of not intervening are well understood, and few alternative interventions exist to treat the disease, then observed variability is quite low. . . . Hernia repair and removal of an inflamed appendix (appendectomy) provide two good examples. Alternatively, when the "indications" for surgery are less clear, or when alternative treatments exist (such as surgery or bed rest plus therapy for low back injuries) variations increase. (p. 25)

The rate at which medical technology and knowledge are diffused plays a critical role in determining the level of physician uncertainty and degree of practice variations.

---

[17]Greenspan et al. (1988) estimated that 20 percent of the permanent pacemakers implanted in Philadelphia County in 1983 were unwarranted, while Chassin et al. (1987) notes that 17 percent of coronary angiographies for elderly patients had been unnecessary. However, a more recent group of studies found the level of unnecessary care to be much lower. Leape et al. (1993) found that 2 percent of coronary artery bypass surgeries were inappropriate, while Hilborne et al. (1993) found that 4 percent of percutaneous transluminal coronary angioplasties were inappropriate.

Other factors also come into play, such as the background and set of beliefs of the individual physician.

Phelps (1992) believes different local "schools of thought" evolve regarding appropriate practice style. The schools of thought develop as a physician invents a new medical treatment strategy and other doctors in the immediate local community learn and adopt the practice style. Since no property rights are assigned to treatment strategies, the individual physician faces little financial incentive to test and market the new idea on a broader basis. Consequently, the treatment strategy or practice style remains confined to the local area. Phelps (1992) claims that "allowing doctors to patent treatment strategies offers a tantalizing step into a market economy where 'professionalism' has previously remained. This would be a two-edged sword, however; doctors who produced and patented a strategy for treatment would reap potential profits, but they would also incur liability for subsequent use of that strategy throughout the country" (p. 41).

Addressing the issue of geographic variations from a slightly different but related angle, Chassin (1993) offers the enthusiasm hypothesis. According to him, geographic differences result primarily because certain physicians, for one reason or another, become "enthusiastic" about a particular medical procedure and therefore use it more frequently than other procedures. When the number of enthusiasts in an area becomes sufficiently large, geographic variations occur. Why the number of enthusiasts differs from area to area is open to conjecture. One explanation offered by the author is that a noteworthy teacher from, say, a teaching hospital in an area becomes enamored with a medical technique and persuades residents and other local practicing physicians of its merits. If she or he convinces enough physicians in the immediate area, geographic variations occur. This is especially true because, as Phelps notes, the new idea is not patentable.

The most interesting element of the enthusiasm hypothesis is the manner in which it differs from the more conventional physician practice hypothesis. Recall that under the physician practice hypothesis, the uncertainty surrounding the efficacy of a particular medical procedure is a primary reason for geographic variations. This is not the case with the enthusiasm hypothesis. Enthusiasts are anything but uncertain because they are thoroughly convinced of the benefits their patients receive from their medical procedure.

Despite the large number of studies on the physician practice hypothesis, it is difficult to determine the extent to which physician practice style explains geographic variations in the utilization of medical services. This is largely because it is very difficult to quantify practice style. One way to get around this problem is to look at those studies that use regression analysis to analyze the consumption of medical care and assume the unexplained variation, or residual, is partly the result of practice style. Because not all the residual can be explained by any one factor, we can assume the unexplained variation represents an upper bound estimate of the impact of practice style on the consumption of medical services.

Utilizing the residual approach, Folland and Stano (1990) and Stano (1991) reviewed numerous studies and concluded that a significant portion of the variation in the consumption of medical services can be explained by traditional supply and demand factors. Although the authors do not dismiss the role of physician practice style, they suggest it may not play a very large role in explaining differences in the aggregate consumption of medical care across geographic regions.

Other studies have attempted to test directly the impact of practice style on the quantity and type of medical care consumed on a micro level. For example, Roos (1989) developed an index that measures physician hospitalization practice style and tested whether it affected the probability that elderly patients would be hospitalized. The results indicate that practice style cannot be ignored when examining the decision to hospitalize elderly patients.

Because physician practice style is so difficult to measure, especially at the aggregate level, its impact on the amount and type of medical care consumed is difficult to judge. There is no doubt, however, that the presence of uncertainty means individual physicians will follow different courses of action when treating patients. Insofar as clinical decisions are based on subjective factors, physician practice style is likely to influence medical care.

The well-documented existence of geographic variations in the utilization of medical services has captured a tremendous amount of public attention in recent years and is likely to have a major impact on public policy for years to come. The controversy surrounding physician self-referral laws is a case in point. Recall that Hillman et al. (1990) found that those physicians who own their own imaging equipment are four times more likely to require imaging examinations than those who do not own the equipment (see Insight 10–1). To prevent this form of inducement, then Governor Cuomo of New York signed an antireferral law into effect in 1992. This law prohibits health care providers from referring patients to other providers with whom they have financial interests (DeLany, 1993).

In addition, the Federal Trade Commission (FTC) has recently begun to address the problem of self-referrals by utilizing antitrust laws to prevent joint ventures between physicians and medical companies. One case involves two medical companies from the San Francisco Bay area. According to the FTC, a high percentage of the lung specialists in the area steer patients who need home oxygen and other related services to the two medical companies that they own. This financial arrangement inhibits competition because other companies have little incentive to enter the market and compete with the physician-owned companies. At the time of action by the FTC, 60 percent of the lung specialists in the San Francisco area had a financial interest in the two medical companies. To prevent self-referrals and enhance competition, the FTC ruled, and the companies accepted, that no more than one-fourth of the lung specialists in the area may have a financial interest in the two companies in question (Davidson, 1993).

## The Impact of MCOs on the Physician Services Market

Various programs under the heading of managed care have been implemented in recent years to contain the costs of medical care. Most of these programs are directed at altering physician behavior primarily because physicians make most of the clinical decisions. As noted in Chapter 13, utilization review (UR) is one of the most frequently used methods to contain costs. Programs such as prospective, concurrent, and retrospective

---

**INSIGHT 14-3**

## Does It Pay Physicians to Advertise?

Since the early 1980s, when the last restrictions on physician advertising were lifted, more and more physicians have advertised their services. A case in point is television station KESQ-TV of Palm Springs, California, which developed an advertising segment called the *Health Minute*, featuring local doctors who answer medical questions concerning their specialty practices. To appear on a segment that airs at least three times a week, doctors pay approximately $1,500 (Cooper, 1993). All indications are that the number of advertisements is likely to grow in the future, leading economists to wonder about the market implications. Theory tells us that advertising can either enhance or impede competition (what else did you expect?).

The procompetitive camp argues that advertising leads to a more competitive outcome because it decreases information costs regarding the price and quality of physician services. With more information regarding physician behavior at their disposal, consumers are in a better position to do some comparison shopping. This should cause the market for physician services to approach the competitive outcome in terms of price and quality. The anticompetitive camp argues just the opposite: Since product differentiation is so extensive in the physician services market, advertising arms physicians with the means to enhance their monopoly power. Through advertising, physicians attempt to differentiate themselves from others, thereby causing the demand for their services to not only increase but also become less elastic.

Using data from a sample of over 1,600 self-employed primary care physicians, Rizzo and Zeckhauser (1992) assessed the impact of advertising on the elasticity of demand for physician services. If advertising was found to cause the demand for primary care physician services to become more price elastic, it could be inferred that advertising enhances competition. Naturally, the opposite would be true if advertising were found to cause the demand for primary care services to become less price elastic. The authors found that advertising positively affects price and negatively affects output. From this finding, they inferred that advertising impedes competition by causing the demand for primary care services to become less price elastic. However, they also found a strong positive relation between advertising and quality as measured by the average time spent per office visit or with patients in all practice settings. It appears that those physicians who advertised charged a higher price for their services but also spent more time with each patient. In fact, advertising tended to increase quality (about 78 percent) by a greater percentage than price (about 42 percent). Thus, Rizzo and Zeckhauser showed that advertising lowers the *quality-adjusted* price for physician services and reduces the total quantity of physician services (about 61 percent). The overall impact of advertising on the level of competition is unclear from their analysis.

reviews evaluate the medical decisions of hospitals and physicians in an attempt to minimize medical costs by eliminating unnecessary medical care and educating patients and physicians concerning proper medical treatments.

Overall, the cost savings from UR programs have been modest in recent years. For example, Feldstein, Wickizer, and Wheeler (1988) found that UR programs decreased hospital inpatient days by 8.0 percent and total medical expenditures by 8.3 percent, while Scheffler, Sullivan, and Ko (1991) discovered that Blue Cross and Blue Shield utilization review programs decreased hospital patient days by 4.8 percent and inpatient payments by 4.2 percent. Equally important, Feldstein, Wickizer, and Wheeler (1988) found that UR programs have a one-time effect on decreasing utilization and costs. The implication is that UR programs may not significantly decrease the growth of medical expenditures over time. In fact, one can argue that any cost savings from UR programs may erode over time as physicians learn to practice in this new environment. Put another way, as physicians eventually learn to "game the system" and present their diagnoses and treatment plans in a manner that will make them more likely to be approved, UR programs may become increasingly unable to control costs by influencing physician behavior over time.

The tremendous growth in UR programs has led some to question who is reviewing the reviewers. Since the clinical bases for medical appropriateness and level of claim reviewers' skills vary widely across the insurance industry, there is some concern that consumers may be receiving inferior medical treatment. For example, an insurer may reject legitimate medical claims because the clinical information is dated or because the reviewer misinterpreted a diagnosis. In addition, physicians argue that they are forced to spend too much time trying to understand the nuances of each review process. This involves determining the basis for medical decisions and understanding the appeal process for protesting the rejection of a medical claim. Hence, it has been argued that the government needs to take a more active role in regulating UR programs to ensure consistent application of acceptable medical standards (Field and Gray, 1989).

Second surgical opinion programs comprise another type of UR aimed directly at altering the behavior of physicians, particularly surgeons. These programs, which can be either voluntary or mandatory in nature, have two major objectives. The first is to increase patient knowledge and thereby reduce the asymmetry of information problem. The second is to establish a procedure whereby physicians' decisions are routinely scrutinized by their peers. The ultimate goal is to reduce the number of unnecessary or avoidable operations and thereby reduce medical costs.

Empirical evidence suggests that second opinion programs have failed to significantly reduce medical costs. For one thing, studies have found that voluntary programs have little or no impact on medical cost savings. The evidence on mandatory programs is not much better. For example, Scheffler, Sullivan, and Ko (1991) found that mandatory second opinions have no impact on hospital utilization or payments. After reviewing the literature on the subject, Lindsey and Newhouse (1990) concluded that because of design flaws, studies fail to provide any conclusive evidence of cost savings from second opinions. The implication is that cost savings from second surgery opinions are likely to be small.

Several studies have examined the impact of prepaid health plans on the utilization of physician services. The question is whether prepaid health plans lead to fewer or more physician office visits than fee-for-service practices. According to the exhaustive review made by Miller and Luft (1994), "Most recent data showed either higher rates or little difference in HMO plan office visits per enrollee" compared to fee-for-service plans (p. 1514). Not enough studies were available to enable Miller and Luft to draw a definitive conclusion about the relation between PPOs and the utilization of physician services, however.

Other efforts to control medical costs have involved the development of clinical practice guidelines for physicians. Numerous medical societies and the Agency for Health Care Policy and Research (AHCPR) are in the process of developing and disseminating guidelines that provide physicians and patients with the preferred methods of treating different types of medical conditions. The hope is that guidelines will improve the quality of medical care and at the same time lower costs by providing timely information to physicians concerning the efficacy of various medical procedures. Rice (1993) argues that practice guidelines may backfire and result in higher medical costs. Any cost savings reaped by preventing a few physicians from using an unacceptable medical procedure may be offset by an increase in costs brought about by the adoption of a new, accepted medical procedure by many physicians. Despite the fact that some medical care providers have begun to implement medical guidelines, it is too early to ascertain their overall effect.

## Defensive Medicine and Medical Malpractice Reform

Medical malpractice reform has been one of the most contentious health care issues over the past decade. Critics claim that reform is needed because the high costs of medical malpractice insurance, coupled with the costs of defensive medicine, have contributed significantly to rising health care costs. Although the evidence suggests that the concern over malpractice costs is somewhat exaggerated, the malpractice system in the United States is in need of reform. For example, physician malpractice premiums account for only 1 percent of total health care spending (Carlstrom, 1993), while defensive medicine is estimated to add another $4 billion to $25 billion to the nation's health care bill (Stout, 1993).

According to Kinney (1995), malpractice reform in the United States has fallen into two generations. The first generation took place throughout the 1970s and early 1980s and was directed primarily toward tort and insurance reform. The primary goal was to decrease the number and magnitude of claims. For example, caps on awards aimed to limit the monetary size of settlements, while pretrial screening panels and limits on attorney's fees attempted to limit the number of suits. Other reform measures aimed at making it more difficult for claimants to win by establishing expert witness requirements. Reforms of the insurance industry centered around making it easier and less expensive for physicians to acquire malpractice insurance. Based on her research, Kinney (1995) concluded that these reforms have had very little impact even though almost every state adopted one or more of them.

As a result, a second generation of reforms has been evolving since the late 1980s. These reforms aim at streamlining "the adjudication and compensating system from the perspective of the claimants and providers" (Kinney, 1995, p. 99). One major element has been the development and use of practice guidelines to define a standard of care. Such guidelines make it easier to establish in a court of law whether or not a physician has provided inappropriate care to a patient. Another major component of the second-generation reforms is the establishment of a schedule for damages. A preset schedule of damages for various injuries makes compensation "more predictable and fair" (p. 105).

Enterprise liability, which involves shifting the legal liability away from physicians and onto the hospital or HMO of the affiliated physician, is another reform.[18] With enterprise liability, physicians are relieved from medical liability and therefore are less likely to practice costly defensive medicine. Additional cost savings result due to a reduction in the number of claimants. Instead of having to sue their doctors, the hospitals, and anyone else involved in the case, patients need only sue the health care organization under enterprise liability (Carlstrom, 1993). The number of overall claims also decreases because health care organizations, such as hospitals and insurance companies, have a much greater financial incentive to monitor the behavior of physicians and weed out those who are incompetent. Other changes involve the mandatory use of alternative dispute resolution mechanisms, such as arbitration instead of a trial.

Utilizing Medicare data for serious heart disease patients for 1984, 1987, and 1990, Kessler and McClellan (1996) estimate whether recent malpractice reforms have reduced medical costs. In their paper, they divide recent malpractice reforms into two groups: direct reforms that control the value of awards, and indirect reforms that do not directly impact rewards. Examples of direct reforms are caps on damages and the abolition of punitive damages. Examples of indirect reforms include caps on contingency fees and mandatory periodic payments. They found that direct reforms reduced hospital expenditures from between 5 to 9 percent without any detrimental impact on the quality of care as measured by mortality or medical complications. Kessler and McClellan also found that indirect reforms had no measurable impact on costs.

# The Performance of the Physician Services Industry

Now that we have reviewed structure and conduct, we are in a position to examine the overall performance of the physician services market. Although the physician services industry appears to be structurally competitive in terms of the actual number of physicians, some evidence concerning practice variations and supplier-induced demand suggests that behaviorally physicians may act with some monopoly power. An analysis of performance in this industry sheds some light on the net effect of these two contradictory perspectives. This section examines measures of physician price, output, and income over time in the United States.

### Expenditures on Physician Services

Expenditures on physician services increased dramatically over the previous two decades. According to table 14–6, expenditures on physician services equaled $45.2 billion in 1980 and by 1996 grew to $202.1 billion. This represents an overall increase of almost 350 percent. The annual rate of growth consistently topped 10 percent throughout the 1970s and 1980s. It was not until the early 1990s that the rate of

---

[18]Another alternative is to transfer the liability to the patient's insurance company.

| TABLE 14–6 | TOTAL EXPENDITURES ON PHYSICIAN SERVICES FOR SELECTED YEARS (IN BILLIONS OF DOLLARS) | | |
|---|---|---|---|

| Year | Total Expenditures | Annual Rate of Increase* | Total Real Expenditures** |
|---|---|---|---|
| 1980 | 45.2 | 12.8% | 56.5 |
| 1990 | 146.3 | 12.5 | 88.1 |
| 1993 | 183.6 | 7.8 | 94.0 |
| 1994 | 190.4 | 3.7 | 93.4 |
| 1995 | 196.4 | 3.1 | 92.2 |
| 1996 | 202.1 | 2.9 | 92.1 |

*This is the average annual increase from the previous period. For 1980 it equals the average annual increase from 1970.
**Physician expenditures are deflated by the physician services index of the CPI, where 1982–1984 is the base year.

SOURCE: Katherine R. Levit et al., "National Health Spending Trends in 1996," *Health Affairs* (January/February 1998), Exhibit 2.

increase in physician expenditures began to slow down. In 1993 the annual rate of growth equaled 7.8 percent and it fell again in 1994 to 3.7 percent. In fact, since 1994, the rate of growth in physician expenditures has not exceeded 4 percent, keeping more in line with the rate of growth of the overall economy.

## The Physician Services Price Inflation Rate

The most commonly used instrument to measure movements in the average price of physician services is the consumer price index for physician services, which is provided for selected years from 1980 to 1997 in table 14–7. The data reveal that the average price of physician services increased at an annual rate higher than the general rate of inflation. From 1990 to 1997, the average annual increase in the price of physician services equaled almost 4.9 percent, where the average rate of inflation over the same period was only 3.2 percent.

Because the CPI includes medical services, a more telling comparison can be made with the CPI less medical care services. This comparison reveals an ever-greater disparity between the rate of increase in the price of physician services and that of all nonmedical goods. Between 1990 and 1997, the CPI less medical care grew at an average annual rate of just under 3 percent, almost two percentage points less than the average annual increase in the price of physician services.

Another way to gauge the rate of increase in the price of physician services is to examine data collected by the AMA concerning the average fee for an office visit with established and new patients. Table 14–8 presents these data from 1986 to 1997. In 1986, the average fee for a physician office visit equaled $30.10 for an established patient and $55.57 for a new patient, and these rates increased to $60.63 and $102.46,

| TABLE 14-7 | | | | | | |
|---|---|---|---|---|---|---|

**THE CONSUMER PRICE INDEX AND PHYSICIAN SERVICES FOR ALL URBAN CONSUMERS, SELECTED YEARS***

| Year | CPI for All Items | Annual Rate of Growth | CPI for ALL Items less Medical Care | Annual Rate of Growth | CPI for Physician Services | Annual Rate of Growth |
|---|---|---|---|---|---|---|
| 1980 | 86.4 | 12.4% | 86.8 | 12.4% | 80.0 | — |
| 1985 | 109.5 | 3.8 | 109.2 | 3.9 | 117.1 | 6.9% |
| 1990 | 134.3 | 6.3 | 132.0 | 6.0 | 166.0 | 7.5 |
| 1995 | 154.1 | 2.6 | 149.9 | 2.5 | 213.0 | 4.5 |
| 1996 | 159.2 | 3.3 | 154.9 | 3.3 | 219.4 | 3.0 |
| 1997 | 161.9 | 1.7 | 157.4 | 1.6 | 225.5 | 2.8 |

*All indexes are for December, and the base period is 1982–1984. Rates of growth are from the previous year.

SOURCE: Bureau of Labor Statistics http://stats.bls.gov

| TABLE 14-8 | | | | | | | | | | |
|---|---|---|---|---|---|---|---|---|---|---|

**THE MEAN FEE FOR AN OFFICE VISIT FOR AN ESTABLISHED AND A NEW PATIENT, 1986–1997***

| | 1986 | 1987 | 1990 | 1991 | 1992 | 1993 | 1994 | 1995 | 1996 | 1997 |
|---|---|---|---|---|---|---|---|---|---|---|
| Established patient | 30.10 | 31.82 | 39.87 | 42.08 | 46.43 | 52.89 | 56.24 | 59.39 | 58.57 | 60.63 |
| Annual rate of increase | 7.3% | 5.7% | 7.5% | 5.5% | 10.4% | 13.9% | 6.3% | 5.6% | −1.4% | 3.5% |
| New patient | 55.57 | 59.69 | 74.84 | 83.04 | 88.17 | 91.77 | 97.16 | 102.75 | 97.32 | 102.46 |
| Annual rate of increase | 7.5% | 7.4% | 9.2% | 11.0% | 6.2% | 4.1% | 5.9% | 5.8% | −5.3% | 5.3% |

*The sample includes active nonfederal patient care physicians, excluding residents.

SOURCE: *Socioeconomic Characteristics of Medical Practice 1997/98* (Chicago: American Medical Association, 1998), Tables 24 and 26.

respectively, by 1997. The average rate of increase from 1990 to 1997 was 6.4 percent for regular patients and 5.3 percent for new patients. It is interesting to note that according to table 14–8, the mean fee for both established and new patients actually fell in 1996 by 1.4 percent and 5.3 percent, respectively.

The CPI and AMA data both indicate that although the rate of growth in the average fee for physician services decreased in the 1990s, it still exceeded the general

| TABLE 14–9 | REVENUE PER SELF-EMPLOYED PHYSICIAN, 1986–1996 (IN THOUSANDS OF DOLLARS) | | | | | | | | |
|---|---|---|---|---|---|---|---|---|---|
| | **1986** | **1987** | **1990** | **1991** | **1992** | **1993** | **1994** | **1995** | **1996** |
| Practice expenses per physician | 118.4 | 123.7 | 150.0 | 168.4 | 183.4 | 182.2 | 183.1 | 201.6 | 217.6 |
| Before-tax income | 131.1 | 146.2 | 185.6 | 191.0 | 208.3 | 218.0 | 210.2 | 230.8 | 231.6 |
| | 249.5 | 269.9 | 335.6 | 359.4 | 391.7 | 400.2 | 393.3 | 432.4 | 449.2 |

Source: *Socioeconomic Characteristics of Medical Practice 1997/98* (Chicago: American Medical Association, 1998), Tables 30 and 46.

rate of inflation. During the 1990s, physician fees grew at an annual rate of between 4.9 and 6 percent, whereas the overall price level, excluding medical care, grew in the neighborhood of 2 to 3 percent. These figures overstate the inflation of physician fees for two reasons. First, the fees reported may not adequately reflect any discounts given to patients because they are covered by Medicare or belong to an HMO. Given the expanding role of MCOs, it is safe to assume the volume and extent of discounts negotiated with physicians increased over time. This means that there may be a significant disparity between the fee reported and the transaction fee. Second, the figures fail to consider any improvements in the quality of physician services that have taken place over time.

The next item to establish is the causes underlying the rapid increase in physician service prices. Was the rise fueled by higher practice expenses or by physicians seeking increased monopoly prices? In the latter case, higher prices translate into increased income for physicians. In the former case, the rise could result from the adoption of costly new technologies, improvements in quality, or simply higher input costs.

One way to determine the cause of price increase for physician services is to examine the growth in average cost per self-employed physician over time as measured by expenses plus total income before taxes per physician. If output per worker remains fairly constant, the rate of growth in the price of physician services should approximate the rate of growth in revenues per physician over time. All indications are that the output per physician as measured by patient visits has remained fairly stable over time. For example, total patient visits per physician, one crude measure of output per physician, remained fairly constant from 1987 through 1997, decreasing marginally from 117.7 to 110.6.[19] Table 14–9 implies that higher practice expenses accounted for 50 percent of the increase in average revenue per physician between 1986 and 1996. The remaining 50 percent can be attributed to increases in average physician income.

---

[19]The explanation is relatively straightforward. Total revenue per physician equals price times output per physician. Consequently, the rate of change in total revenues per physician can be found by summing the rates of change for price and output per physician. If output per physician remains constant over time, revenue growth per physician equals the percentage change in price. Visits per physician, a measure of output per physician, remained fairly constant from 1984 to 1992, decreasing marginally from 118.1 to 114.8.

| INSIGHT 14–4 |

# The Economics of Hospital Admitting Privileges

Traditionally, physicians must be granted admitting privileges at a hospital before being allowed to admit patients and utilize the hospital's medical facilities. In return for these privileges, a physician accepts certain duties and responsibilities, which can vary substantially across hospitals. For example, a small hospital may require only that the physician serve on a committee or two at the hospital, while a larger teaching hospital may require the physician to hold a staff appointment and share in some of the teaching responsibilities.

Regardless of the duties specified, it is clear that admitting privileges place the hospital and physician in a symbiotic relationship. From the physician's perspective, admitting privileges positively impact earnings by enhancing productivity. Among other things, admitting privileges give the physician the opportunity to provide a broader scope of medical services along with having access to more expensive inpatient services (Rizzo and Goddeeris, 1998).

To gain a better understanding of the relationship between hospitals and physicians, Rizzo and Goddeeris (1998) estimated the effects of hospital admitting privileges on physician earnings for a sample of self-employed physicians in 1992. In particular, they utilized regression analysis to estimate the effect on earnings of an exogenous change in admitting privileges after holding constant a host of control variables. For primary care physicians they found that admitting privileges

have no impact on earnings. The authors argue that these findings were not surprising given that primary care physicians derive a relatively small portion of their income in a hospital setting.

The same cannot be said for specialists, however. The authors found a strong positive relation between earnings and the number of admitting privileges held by a specialist. As economic theory would suggest, the authors also found the relation to be nonlinear. According to table 1, the marginal impact on earnings for a specialist having admitting privileges at one hospital is over $65,000 and increases to over $103,000 when a specialist acquires admitting privileges at a second hospital. At three hospitals, the marginal impact reaches its peak at over $106,000 and from that point begins to decrease. The marginal impact on earnings actually becomes negative when the representative specialist acquires admitting privileges at a fifth hospital.

Overall, the evidence indicates that most specialists cannot generate enough patients from one hospital and that it is in their financial interests to have admitting privileges at more than one hospital. Maximum income appears to be reached when a specialist has admitting privileges at four different hospitals. Beyond that point, however, the added time costs of having admitting privileges at one more hospital appear to outweigh any additional revenue that might be generated.

*(continued)*

Since 1993, however, practice expenses have accounted for a much greater share of the increase in revenue per physician. Almost 72 percent of the increase in revenue per physician resulted from increased practice expenses.

Overall, the evidence indicates that the growth in total revenue per physician was the result of increases in both practice costs and physician income. Slightly more than half of the increase in average revenue per physician can be attributed to higher practice costs, while the remaining portion was garnered by physicians in terms of higher income. In more recent years, however, increases in practice expenses have accounted for slightly more than 70 percent of the increase in revenue per physician, as average

**(continued)**

| TABLE 1 | ECONOMIC IMPACT OF HOSPITAL ADMITTING PRIVILEGES FOR SPECIALISTS | |
| --- | --- | --- |

| Number of Admitting Privileges | Estimated Earnings | Marginal Earnings |
| :---: | :---: | :---: |
| 0 | $42,845 | — |
| 1 | 108,700 | $65,855 |
| 2 | 212,214 | 103,514 |
| 3 | 318,809 | 106,595 |
| 4 | 368,556 | 49,747 |
| 5 | 327,862 | –40,694 |
| 6 | 224,436 | –103,426 |

SOURCE: John A. Rizzo and John H. Goddeeris, "The Economic Returns to Hospital Admitting Privileges," *Journal of Health Politics, Policy and Law* 23 (June 1998), Table 7.

physician income appears to have stagnated. What cannot be determined is *why* practice costs increased. In all likelihood, the increase results from a combination of higher input prices and quality improvements in the delivery of medical care.

## The Utilization of Physician Services

Expenditures on physician services increased significantly in the past two decades, with most of that increase occurring during the 1980s. From 1980 to 1996, physician expenditures increased by roughly 9.5 percent per year. Over the same period, the CPI for physician services increased by slightly more than 6 percent. Combined, these figures suggest that almost two-thirds of the average annual increase in physician expenditures was the result of price increases, while the remaining one-third was due to increased utilization. Regarding the increase in price, we know that approximately one-half of the increase was due to higher practice costs and the other half to higher physician income. Taken together, these estimates indicate that approximately one-third of the increase in expenditures on physician services financed increased utilization, while another one-third occurred as a result of increased practice costs. The remaining one-third resulted in higher physician incomes.

More recently, however, a significant slowdown has occurred in the growth of expenditures on physician services resulting primarily from a decrease in the rate of increase in real physician expenditures and physician income. From 1993 to 1997, the

| TABLE 14-10 | REAL MEAN PHYSICIAN INCOME AFTER EXPENSES AND BEFORE TAXES, 1986–1996 (IN THOUSANDS OF DOLLARS) | | | | | | | | |
|---|---|---|---|---|---|---|---|---|---|
| | **1986** | **1987** | **1990** | **1991** | **1992** | **1993** | **1994** | **1995** | **1996** |
| All physicians* | 107.9 | 114.3 | 122.3 | 123.4 | 127.6 | 129.3 | 121.4 | 126.9 | 125.0 |
| Annual rate of growth | 5.3% | 5.9% | −.08 | 0.9% | 3.4% | 1.3% | −6.1% | 4.5% | −1.5% |
| Ratio of physician to college faculty compensation** | 2.5 | 2.6 | 2.7 | 2.7 | 2.8 | 2.8 | 2.6 | 2.7 | 2.7 |

*The sample includes all nonfederal patient care physicians, excluding residents. All figures were deflated using the December CPI for all urban consumers where 1982–84 = 100.
**The sample includes the full-time faculty from doctoral-level schools.

SOURCES: *Socioeconomic Characteristics of Medical Practice 1997/98* (Chicago: American Medical Association, 1998), Table 46; *Academe*, various issues of the March–April issue.

average rate of growth in nominal expenditures on physician services fell to approximately 4.4 percent per year. Over the same period, the CPI for physician services increased by 4.25 percent per year, indicating almost no growth in real physician expenditures. Figures on total revenue per physician from 1993 to 1996 suggest that only one-quarter of the increase in price can be attributed to increases in physician income. The remaining three-quarters of the price increase resulted from increases in practice expenses.

*Physician Income*

The last item we need to consider is whether the increase in physician income was substantial enough to allow an improvement in physicians' real purchasing power, or real income. Data for real physician income (i.e., total physician income deflated by the CPI) from 1986 to 1996 appear in table 14–10. Over the period, physicians experienced a total increase in real income of 16 percent, with the largest annual increases occurring in 1986 and 1987. Real income appeared to reach its peak of $129,300 per year in 1993 and since that time has decreased modestly in real terms. By 1996 annual real income equaled $125,000. Simon and Born (1996) argue that much of this decline in real income can be attributed to the growth in managed care.

To gauge the relative standing of physician income, we need to compare real compensation to the growth in real income sustained by other professionals with extensive graduate training. In particular, consider the ratio of total physician income to total compensation of college faculty at doctoral granting institutions (see table 14–10). The ratio remained rather stable throughout the 1980s and into the early 1990s. In 1986, the average physician earned 2.5 times the earnings of the average college professor, and by 1992 the ratio increased to 2.8. Since that time, the ratio has remained relatively stable at between 2.8 and 2.7. These relative income figures suggest that although physicians experienced significant real gains in purchasing power in recent years, the gains were similar to those of other professionals with graduate training.

This conclusion is substantiated by a study that looked at the relative income of physicians from an investment perspective (Weeks, Wallace, Wallace, and Welch, 1994). If expenditures on higher education are treated as an investment in human capital and the increment to earnings received in the job market as a return on that investment, the rate of return received on investments in higher education can be calculated. Utilizing that approach, Weeks, Wallace, Wallace, and Welch compared the rates of return on educational investments for various professionals, including physicians. According to their results, primary care physicians receive an annual rate of return of 15.9 percent on educational investments over a working life, while specialists receive a 20.9 percent return. As a point of comparison, the authors found that businesspeople and attorneys receive a 29.0 and 25.4 percent rate of return, respectively. These findings imply that physicians receive a rate of return on investments in educational expenditures that is comparable to, if not less than, that of other professionals.

## SUMMARY

The physician services market has experienced profound changes in recent years, with both the size and scope of the market increasing substantially. Since 1970 the size of the market has approximately doubled, whether measured on the basis of real physician expenditures or the number of practicing physicians. The mode of production has also changed considerably, with economies of scale forcing physicians into large-group practices as opposed to small-group or solo practices. All these changes, coupled with an erosion of barriers to entry, have intensified the level of structural competition in the physician services market. Most of the monopoly power physicians currently possess appears to result primarily from the asymmetry of information that exists between doctor and patient. Although the level of competition varies across regions, overall the market can be classified as monopolistically competitive. The physician services industry contains a large number of sellers, moderate barriers to entry, a certain amount of product differentiation, and some information imperfections.

The well-publicized geographic variations in physician utilization rates have been the source of much concern for policy analysts and politicians alike. The evidence indicates that much of this concern is uncalled for, since most of the variation can be explained by traditional supply and demand factors.

Without a doubt, the single greatest change in the physician services market has been the growing presence of managed care. Over 90 percent of all physicians are involved with at least one MCO. All indications suggest that these numbers will increase in the future. Managed care has ushered in an entirely new set of compensation schemes, along with a host of utilization review programs. The evidence on compensation schemes suggests that clinical decisions are sensitive to the method of payment.

For example, the utilization of medical resources is inversely related to whether the physician is compensated on a salary or capitation basis rather than the more traditional fee-for-service system. Findings concerning the impact of utilization review programs on utilization and costs have been mixed, however. For instance, second opinion programs appear to have little impact on the level of medical care. There does appear to be a movement toward the development and use of clinical guidelines for physicians. It remains to be seen whether such efforts will affect the amount and cost of physician care.

## Review Questions and Problems

1. Physician assistants have long argued that they have the ability to provide as much as 70 percent of the medical services provided by primary care physicians at a much lower cost. Yet government regulations limit their ability to work independently of physicians. Explain what would happen to the level of competition in the physician services market if all the statutes limiting the activities of physician assistants were eliminated.

2. Many have argued that the United States has too many specialists and too few primary care physicians. Assuming this to be true, utilize the studies on the economics of specialty choice to develop some policies aimed at persuading medical students to choose primary care medicine.

3. Discuss how enhanced competition in the physician services market has affected the ability of physicians to induce the demand for medical services.

4. Analyze the alternative compensation schemes discussed in this chapter that private insurers use to pay physicians. Think in terms of the incentive to provide an excessive amount of medical services. Use figure 2–2 as your basis for discussion.

5. As you know, various medical groups are in the process of developing medical guidelines. Assuming guidelines are developed and widely adopted by physicians, how will this affect the physician services market?

6. Some argue that practice variations exist because information on practice style is disseminated slowly. Charles Phelps (1992) argues that physicians should be allowed to patent and sell their practice strategies. Explain how this policy might affect practice variations.

7. Discuss the theoretical and empirical issues surrounding the supplier-induced demand theory.

8. Discuss the factors that have contributed to the increase in expenditures on physician services over the past decade.

9. Explain the many institutional and structural changes that might make physician licensing obsolete.

10. Why may the physician inflation rate be exaggerated?

*References*

American Medical Association. *Physician Characteristics and Distribution in the U.S., 1997/98.* Chicago: AMA Center for Health Policy Research, 1998a.

———. *Physician Marketplace Statistics, 1997/98.* Chicago: AMA Center for Health Policy Research, 1998b.

———. *Socioeconomic Characteristics of Medical Practice, 1997/98.* Chicago: AMA Center for Health Policy Research, 1998c.

Auster, Richard D., and Ronald L. Oaxaca. "Identification of Supplier-Induced Demand in the Health Care Sector." *Journal of Human Resources* 16 (summer 1981), pp. 327–42.

Bazzoli, Gloria J. "Does Educational Indebtedness Affect Physician Specialty Choice?" *Journal of Health Economics* 4 (1985), pp. 1–19.

Brown, Douglas M. "Do Physicians Underutilize Aides?" *Journal of Human Resources* 23 (summer 1988), pp. 342–55.

Bureau of Labor Statistics. http://stats.bls.gov.

Carlstrom, Charles T. "Enterprise Liability: A Prescription for Health Care Reform." *Economic Commentary, Federal Reserve Bank of Cleveland*, July 1, 1993.

Chassin, Mark R. "Explaining Geographic Variations: The Enthusiasm Hypothesis." *Medical Care* 31 (supplement 1993), pp. YS37–YS44.

Chassin, Mark R., et al. "Variations in the Use of Medical and Surgical Services by the Medicare Population." *New England Journal of Medicine* 314 (January 30, 1986), pp. 285–90.

Cooper, Jim. "Doctors Try Dose of TV." *Broadcasting and Cable*, October 25, 1993, p. 47.

Cromwell, Jerry, and Janet B. Mitchell. "Physician-Induced Demand for Surgery." *Journal of Health Economics* 5 (1986), pp. 293–313.

Davidson, Joe. "Antitrust Laws Used by U.S. Against Doctors." *The Wall Street Journal*, November 4, 1993, p. B6.

DeLany, John. "New York's Anti-Referral Laws and Doctors Shall Not Be Entrepreneurs." *Hospital News* 4 (April 1993), p. 14.

Eddy, David M. "Variations in Physician Practice: The Role of Uncertainty." *Health Affairs* 3 (summer 1984), pp. 74–89.

Escarce, Jose J. "Explaining the Association between Surgeon Supply and Utilization." *Inquiry* 29 (winter 1992), pp. 403–15.

Evans, Robert G. "Supplier-Induced Demand: Some Empirical Evidence and Implications." In *The Economics of Health and Medical Care*, edited by M. Perlman. London: Macmillan, 1974.

Feldstein, Paul J., Thomas M. Wickizer, and John R. C. Wheeler, "Private Cost Containment: The Effects of Utilization Review Programs on Health Care Use and Expenditures." *New England Journal of Medicine* 318 (May 19, 1988), pp. 1310–14.

Ferguson, Brian S., and Allan Crawford. "Supplier-Induced Demand: A Disequilibrium Test." *Applied Economics* 21 (May 1989), pp. 597–609.

Field, Marilyn J., and Bradford H. Gray. "Should We Regulate Utilization Management?" *Health Affairs* 8 (winter 1989), pp. 103–12.

Folland, Sherman T., and Miron Stano. "Small Area Variations: A Critical Review of Propositions, Methods and Evidence." *Medical Care Review* 47 (winter 1990), pp. 419–65.

Fox, Marc. "Medical School Indebtedness and Choice of Specialization." *Inquiry* 30 (spring 1993), pp. 84–94.

Frech, H. E., and Paul B. Ginsburg. "Optimal Scale in Medical Practice: A Survivor Analysis." *Journal of Business* 47 (1974), pp. 23–36.

Friedman, Milton. *Capitalism and Freedom.* Chicago: University of Chicago Press, 1962.

———. *Free to Choose.* New York: Harcourt Brace Jovanovich, 1980.

Fuchs, Victor R. "The Supply of Surgeons and the Demand for Operations." *Journal of Human Resources* 13 (supplement, 1978), pp. 35–56.

Gamliel, Sandy, et al. "Will Physicians Meet the Managed Care Challenge?" *Health Affairs* 14 (summer 1995), pp. 131–42.

Gaynor, Martin, and Solomon W. Polachek. "Measuring Information in the Market: An Application to Physician Services." *Southern Economic Journal* 60 (April 1994), pp. 815–31.

Geertsma, Robert H., and John Romano. "Relationship between Expected Indebtedness and Career Choice of Medical Students." *Journal of Medical Education* 62 (July 1986), pp. 555–59.

Gold et al. "A National Survey of the Arrangements Managed-Care Plans Make with Physicians." *New England Journal of Medicine* 333 (December 21, 1995), pp. 1678–83.

Government Accounting Office. *Primary Care Physicians Managing Supply in Canada, Germany, Sweden, and the United Kingdom.* Washington, DC (May 1994).

Greenspan, Allan M., et al. "Incidence of Unwarranted Implantation of Permanent Cardiac Pacemakers in a Large Medical Population." *New England Journal of Medicine* 318 (January 21, 1988), pp. 158–63.

Grytten, Jostein, Fredrik Carlsen, and Rune Sorenson. "Supplier Inducement in a Public Health Care System." *Journal of Health Economics* 14 (1995), pp. 207–29.

Grytten, Jostein, and Dorthe Holst. "Supplier Inducement: Its Effect on Dental Services in Norway." *Journal of Health Economics* 9 (1990), pp. 483–91.

Hellinger, Fred J. "The Impact of Financial Incentives on Physician Behavior in Managed Care Plans: A Review of the Evidence." *Medical Care Research and Review* 53 (September 1996), pp. 294–314.

Hemenway, David, and Deborah Fallon. "Testing for Physician-Induced Demand with Hypothetical Cases." *Medical Care* 23 (April 1985), pp. 344–49.

Hilborne, Lee H., et al. "The Appropriateness of the Use of Percutaneous Transluminal Coronary Angioplasty in New York State." *Journal of American Medicine* 269 (February 10, 1993), pp. 761–65.

Hillman, Alan L. "Financial Incentives for Physicians in HMOs." *New England Journal of Medicine* 317 (December 31, 1987), pp. 1743–48.

Hillman, Alan L., Mark V. Pauly, and Joseph J. Kerstein. "How Do Financial Incentives Affect Physicians' Clinical Decisions and the Financial Performance of Health Maintenance Organizations?" *New England Journal of Medicine* 321 (July 13, 1989), pp. 86–92.

Hillman, Bruce J., et al. "Frequency and Costs of Diagnostic Imaging in Office Practice—A Comparison of Self-Referring and Radiologist-Referring Physicians." *New England Journal of Medicine* 323 (December 6, 1990), pp. 1604–08.

Hurley, Jeremiah E. "Physicians' Choices of Specialty, Location and Mode." *Journal of Human Resources* 26 (winter 1991), pp. 47–71.

Kassler, William J., Steven A. Wartment, and Rebecca A. Silliman. "Why Medical Students Choose Primary Care Careers." *Academic Medicine* 66 (January 1991), pp. 41–43.

Kessel, Reuben. "Price Discrimination in Medicine." *Journal of Law and Economics* 1 (1958), pp. 20–53.

Kessler, Daniel, and Mark McClellan. "Do Doctors Practice Defensive Medicine?" *Quarterly Journal of Economics* 111 (May 1996), pp. 353–90.

Kinney, Eleanor D. "Malpractice Reform in the 1990s: Past Disappointments, Future Success?" *Journal of Health Politics, Policy and Law* 20 (spring 1995), pp. 90–135.

Leape, Lucian L., et al. "The Appropriateness of Use of Coronary Artery Bypass Graft Surgery in New York State." *Journal of the American Medical Association* 269 (February 10, 1993), pp. 753–60.

Leffler, Keith B. "Physician Licensure: Competition and Monopoly in American Medicine." *Journal of Law and Economics* 21 (1978), pp. 165–86.

Levit Katharine R. et al. "National Health Spending Trends in 1996." *Health Affairs* 17 (January/February, 1998): pp. 35–51.

Lindsey, Phoebe A., and Joseph P. Newhouse. "The Cost and Value of Second Surgical Opinion Programs: A Critical Review of the Literature." *Journal of Health Policy, Politics and Law* 15 (fall 1990), pp. 543–70.

Marder, William D., and Stephen Zuckerman. "Competition and Medical Groups." *Journal of Health Economics* 4 (1985), pp. 167–76.

McCarthy, Thomas R. "The Competitive Nature of the Primary-Care Physician Services Market." *Journal of Health Economics* 4 (1985), pp. 93–117.

McKay, Niccie L. "The Economic Determinants of Specialty Choice by Medical Residents." *Journal of Health Economics* 9 (1990), pp. 335–57.

Miller, Mark E., and John Holahan. "Geographic Variations in Physician Utilization." *Medical Care Research and Review* 52 (June 1995), pp. 252–78.

Miller, Robert H., and Harold S. Luft. "Managed Care Plan Performance Since 1980." *Journal of the American Medical Association* 271 (May 18, 1994), pp. 1512–19.

Mitchell, Jean M., and Tim R. Sass. "Physician Ownership of Ancillary Services: Indirect Demand Inducement or Quality Assurance." *Journal of Health Economics* 14 (1995), pp. 263–89.

Moore, Thomas. "The Purpose of Licensing." *Journal of Law and Economics* 4 (1961), pp. 93–117.

Noether, Monica. "The Growing Supply of Physicians: Has the Market Become More Competitive?" *Journal of Labor Economics* 4 (1986), pp. 503–37.

Ohsfeldt, Robert L. "The Effect of AMA Membership on Physicians' Earnings." *Industrial and Labor Relations Review* 42 (October 1988), pp. 20–33.

Pauly, Mark V., and Mark A. Satterthwaite. "The Pricing of Primary Care Physicians' Services: A Test of the Role of Consumer Information." *Bell Journal of Economics* 12 (autumn 1981), pp. 488–506.

Phelps, Charles E. "Diffusion of Information in Medical Care." *Journal of Economic Perspectives* 6 (summer 1992), pp. 23–42.

Politzer, Robert M., et al. "Matching Physician Supply and Requirements: Testing Policy Recommendations." *Inquiry* 33 (summer 1996), pp. 181–94.

Pope, Gregory C., and Russel T. Burge. "Economies of Scale in Physician Practice." *Medical Care Research and Review* 53 (December 1996), pp. 417–40.

Raffel, Marshall W., and Norma K. Raffel. *The U.S. Health System: Origins and Functions.* 3rd ed. New York: John Wiley and Sons, 1989.

Reinhardt, Uwe E. "A Production Function for Physician Services." *Review of Economics and Statistics* 54 (February 1972), pp. 55–66.

———. "Manpower Substitution and Productivity in Medical Practices: Review of Research." *Health Services Research* 8 (1973), pp. 200–27.

———. *Physician Productivity and Demand for Health Manpower.* Cambridge, MA: Ballinger Publishing Company, 1975.

Rice, Thomas H. "An Evaluation of Alternative Policies for Controlling Health Care Costs." In *Building Blocks for Change: How Health Care Reform Affects Our Future*, edited by Jack A. Meyer and Sharon Silow-Carrol. Washington, DC: The Economic and Social Research Institute, 1993.

Rice, Thomas H., and Roberta J. Labelle. "Do Physicians Induce Demand for Medical Services?" *Journal of Health Politics, Policy and Law* 14 (fall 1989), pp. 587–600.

Rizzo, John A., and John H. Goddeeris. "The Economic Returns to Hospital Admitting Privileges." *Journal of Health Politics, Policy and Law* 23 (June 1998), pp. 483–515.

Rizzo, John A., and Richard J. Zeckhauser. "Advertising and the Price, Quantity, and Quality of Primary Care Physician Services." *Journal of Human Resources* 27 (summer 1992), pp. 381–421.

Rogers, Lauran Q., Ruth-Marie E. Fincher, and Lloyd A. Lewis. "Factors Influencing Medical Students to Choose Primary Care or Non-Primary Care Specialties." *Academic Medicine* 65 (September supplement, 1990), pp. S47–S48.

Roos, Noralou P. "Predicting Hospital Utilization by the Elderly: The Importance of Patient, Physician, and Hospital Characteristics." *Medical Care* 27 (October 1989), pp. 905–17.

Rossiter, Louis F., and Gail R. Wilensky. "Identification of Physician Induced Demand." *Journal of Human Resources* 19 (spring 1984), pp. 232–44.

Scheffler, Richard M., Sean D. Sullivan, and Timothy Hoachung Ko. "The Impact of Blue Cross and Blue Shield Plan Utilization Management Programs, 1980–88." *Inquiry* 28 (fall 1991), pp. 263–75.

Schroeder, Steven A. "Western European Responses to Physician Oversupply." *Journal of the American Medical Association* 252 (July 20, 1984), pp. 373–84.

———. "Physician Supply and the U.S. Medical Marketplace." *Health Affairs* 11 (spring 1992), pp. 235–54.

Simon, Carol J., and Patricia H. Born. "Physician Earnings in a Changing Managed Care Environment." *Health Affairs* 15 (fall 1996), pp. 124–33.

Stano, Miron. "An Analysis of the Evidence on Competition in the Physician Services Markets." *Journal of Health Economics* 4 (1985), pp. 197–211.

———. "A Further Analysis of the Physician Inducement Hypothesis." *Journal of Health Economics* 6 (1987), pp. 227–238.

———. "Further Issues in Small Area Variations Analysis." *Journal of Health Politics, Policy and Law* 16 (fall 1991), pp. 573–88.

Stout, Hilary. "Clinton Mulls Barring Lawsuits against Doctors." *The Wall Street Journal*, April 29, 1993, p. A2.

Svorny, Shirley. "Should We Reconsider Licensing Physicians?" *Contemporary Policy Issues* 10 (January 1992), pp. 31–38.

Tussing, A. Dale. "Physician-Induced Demand for Medical Care: Irish General Practitioners." *Economic and Social Review* 14 (1983), pp. 225–47.

Tussing, A. Dale, and Martha Wojtowyzc. "Physician-Induced Demand by Irish GPs." *Social Science and Medicine* 23 (1986), pp. 851–60.

Weeks, William B., Amy E. Wallace, Myron M. Wallace, and H. Gilbert Welch. "A Comparison of the Educational Costs and Incomes of Physicians and Other Professionals." *New England Journal of Medicine* 330 (May 5, 1994), pp. 1280–86.

Wennberg, John E. "Dealing with Medical Practice Variations: A Proposal for Action." *Health Affairs* 3 (summer 1984), pp. 6–32.

———. "On Patient Need, Equity, Supplier-Induced Demand, and the Need to Assess the Outcome of Common Medical Practices." *Medical Care* 23 (May 1985), pp. 512–20.

Wilson, Florence A., and Duncan Neuhauser. *Health Services in the United States.* 2nd ed. Cambridge, MA: Ballinger Publishing Company, 1982.

# CEBS Questions

CEBS Sample Question on Subject Matter from CEBS Course IX Study Manual

1. Advocates for the elimination of medical licensure requirements point to which recent changes to advance their position? (pages 423 and 425)

CEBS Sample Exam Questions

1. Which statement describes average physician income in recent years?
   A. Gains have been far greater than those of other professionals
   B. Gains in income have been similar to those of other professionals with graduate training
   C. Decreases have been substantial
   D. Specialty physicians have experienced substantial increases while general practitioners have experienced substantial decreases
   E. Only research physicians have experienced an increase in real income

2. Which of the following statements regarding the supplier-induced demand (SID) hypothesis regarding physician behavior is (are) correct?

I. An important element of the hypothesis is the asymmetry of information that exists regarding the appropriateness of medical care provided

II. The SID hypothesis suggests that physicians are not motivated by increases in personal income

III. The SID model has been criticized both on theoretical and practical grounds

    A. III only

    B. I and II only

    C. II and III only

    D. I and III only

    E. I, II, and III

3. All the following statements regarding the structure of the market for physician services are correct EXCEPT:

    A. There has been a significant increase in the physician-to-population ratio in the past two decades

    B. Over 90 percent of all physicians have at least one contract with a managed care organization

    C. Many experts believe there are too many general practitioners and not enough specialists

    D. The physician services market has become more competitive over time

    E. There appears to a movement away from single and two-physician practices toward multi-physician practices

*Answer to Sample Question from Study Manual*

Proponents question the need for medical licensure given: 1) the recent shifts in medical liability from physicians to institution; 2) the growth in for-profit medical care providers; and 3) the growing use of employed rather than self-employed physicians. The growth in for-profit providers and employed physicians has created a greater incentive for institutions to monitor the performance of physicians and, if necessary, to terminate incompetent physicians.

*Answers to Sample Exam Questions*

1. B is the answer. See Table 14–10 and text on page 447.

2. D is the answer. The basic premise of the SID hypothesis is that physicians abuse their role as health care providers to augment their personal income. Therefore, Statement II is false. Statements I and III are correct. See pages 431–434 of the text.

3. C is the answer. It is believed that there are too many specialists in the United States and not enough primary care physicians. The other statements are all true. See page 428 of the text.

# 15

# The Hospital Services Industry

J ust about everyone, either as a patient, a visitor, or an employee, has had some experience at a hospital. Some people conceive of hospitals as cold, lifeless facilities that spell gloom and doom. Others imagine hospitals as wondrous places where miraculous life-saving feats, such as human organ transplants, are performed. Regardless of one's view, it is safe to say that the hospital of today bears little resemblance to its early-19th-century predecessor. According to Peter Temin (1988), a noted economic historian,

> Hospitals were primarily nonmedical institutions throughout most of the nineteenth century. They existed for the care of marginal members of society, whether old, poor, or medically or psychologically deviant. Medicine was practiced outside the hospital, and the medical staffs of hospitals were small. Hospitals were charitable institutions, and they looked for moral rather than physical improvement in their patients. . . . In short, the nineteenth century hospital was closer to an almshouse than to a modern hospital. (pp. 78–80)

With the development of the germ theory of disease, the advent of new technologies, and increased urbanization, the "modern" hospital replaced the old-style version in the years following 1880. Hospitals have subsequently evolved into vibrant centers of medical and business activities.

Today's hospital is a technological marvel. The once simple hospital bed can now cost up to $10,000 when it includes customized accessories, such as automatically inflating air mattresses for patients with bed sores, voice-activated adjustments for paraplegics, and in-bed weight scales for bedridden patients (Anders, 1993a). Aided by advances in computer and pharmaceutical technologies, the modern hospital has proven capable of offering numerous therapeutic and diagnostic services that extend and improve the quantity and quality of lives. Indeed, one may point to the success of modern medicine as the culprit behind the ever-rising cost of delivering hospital services. Accounting for expenditures of $358.5 billion and 40 percent of all personal health care expenditures in 1996, the hospital services industry is the largest of the medical care industries.

This chapter explores the structure, conduct, and performance of the hospital services industry. Specifically, the chapter

- Describes the number, types, and size distribution of U.S. hospitals.

- Defines the relevant product and geographical markets for hospitals.

- Examines sources of barriers to entry in the hospital services industry.

- Discusses the relation between managed care and hospital structure and behavior.

- Focuses on hospital competition, regulation, and pricing behavior.

- Assesses the output and pricing performance of the hospital services industry.

# The Structure of the Hospital Services Industry

According to the industrial organization triad, as discussed in Chapter 9, the structural competitiveness of an industry can be evaluated to some extent by focusing on a number of characteristics affecting the degree of actual and potential competition. *Actual competition* refers to the intensity of the competition that currently coexists among the firms in an industry. Among the more important factors influencing the degree of actual competition are the number and size distribution of the existing firms, the type of product offered for sale, and the amount of information consumers possess. *Potential competition* depends on how easy it is for new firms to enter an industry. The degree of potential competition can be measured by the magnitude of any barriers to entry resulting from economies of scale or legal impediments, such as patents and government restrictions. These and other structural characteristics of the hospital industry are discussed in more detail below.

## Number, Types, and Size Distribution of U.S. Hospitals

Table 15–1 provides information on the number and types of U.S. hospitals. Hospitals are classified by type of service and ownership for three selected years. The first half of the table shows the number of hospitals, and the second half identifies the number of beds associated with each type of hospital. The data identify a trend toward fewer hospitals and hospital beds in the United States since 1980. Specifically, the

| TABLE 15–1 | NUMBER AND TYPES OF HOSPITALS IN THE UNITED STATES, SELECTED YEARS 1980–1996 | | |
|---|---|---|---|
| | **1980** | **1990** | **1996** |
| **Number** | | | |
| All hospitals | 6,965 | 6,649 | 6,201 |
| Nonfederal | 6,606 | 6,312 | 5,911 |
|   Community hospitals | 5,830 | 5,384 | 5,134 |
|     Nonprofit | 3,322 | 3,191 | 3,045 |
|     For-profit | 730 | 749 | 759 |
|     State and local | 1,778 | 1,444 | 1,330 |
|   Long-term general and special | 157 | 131 | 112 |
|   Psychiatric | 534 | 757 | 636 |
|   Tuberculosis | 11 | 4 | 3 |
| Federal | 359 | 337 | 290 |
| **Beds (1,000)** | | | |
| All hospitals | 1,365 | 1,213 | 1,062 |
| Nonfederal | 1,248 | 1,115 | 989 |
|   Community hospitals | 988 | 927 | 862 |
|     Nonprofit | 692 | 657 | 598 |
|     For-profit | 87 | 101 | 109 |
|     State and local | 209 | 169 | 155 |
|   Long-term general and special | 39 | 25 | 19 |
|   Psychiatric | 215 | 160 | 106 |
|   Tuberculosis | 2 | .5 | .2 |
| Federal | 117 | 98 | 73 |

SOURCE: American Hospital Association, *Hospital Statistics*, various years, Table 2.

total number of hospitals and hospital beds declined by 11 and nearly 22 percent, respectively, resulting in a total of 6,201 hospitals operating with approximately 1.1 million beds as of 1996.

Hospitals can be separated into those operated by the federal government and those that are nonfederal hospitals. Federal hospitals are usually based at military institutions or run by the Veterans Administration. Based on service offerings and average length of stay, nonfederal hospitals can be grouped into community, long-term

| TABLE 15-2 | SIZE DISTRIBUTION OF ALL COMMUNITY HOSPITALS, 1996 | | | |
|---|---|---|---|---|
| | Percentage of Hospitals in Each Bed Size Category | | | |
| Bed Size Category | All Hospitals | Nonprofit Hospitals | For-Profit Hospitals | Public Hospitals |
| 6–24 | 5.1% | 3.5% | 1.4% | 10.9% |
| 25–49 | 17.6 | 13.1 | 10.9 | 31.8 |
| 50–99 | 22.0 | 19.5 | 27.0 | 24.7 |
| 100–199 | 26.1 | 26.9 | 38.7 | 17.0 |
| 200–299 | 13.5 | 16.3 | 14.2 | 6.7 |
| 300–399 | 7.0 | 9.4 | 4.1 | 3.3 |
| 400–499 | 3.8 | 5.2 | 1.3 | 2.0 |
| 500 and over | 4.9 | 6.1 | 2.2 | 3.6 |

SOURCE: American Hospital Association, *Hospital Statistics*, 1998, Table 4.

general and special, psychiatric, and tuberculosis hospitals. Community hospitals, the largest category, provide general medical and surgical services and specialty services, such as ear, nose, and throat care, obstetrics and gynecology, or orthopedic services, and offer short-term stays (i.e., an average length of stay of less than 30 days). The other three nonfederal hospital classifications are based on either a long-term stay or a specialized medical service.

Community hospitals can be further differentiated based on type of ownership.[1] The dominant ownership type is the nonprofit hospital, representing about 59 percent of the community hospitals and controlling nearly 69 percent of all community hospital beds as of 1996. The nonprofit market share in terms of total beds remained fairly stable over the 16–year period. For-profit hospitals currently account for almost 15 percent of all community hospitals. The market share (in beds) of for-profit hospitals rose from 9 percent in 1980 to 13 percent in 1996, with the increase corresponding to a decline in the state and local government market share from 21 to 18 percent.

Table 15–2 depicts the size distribution of all community hospitals and by ownership type for 1996. Approximately 26 percent of the community hospitals fall into the size category between 100 and 199 beds. In addition, nearly 50 percent of all community hospitals fall within the 50 to 199 bed size category. The same size pattern holds individually for both nonprofit and for-profit hospitals, except that for-profit hospitals are smaller than nonprofit hospitals, on average. In particular, a much greater percentage of nonprofit hospitals (37 percent) than for-profit hospitals

---

[1]The other three types of nonfederal hospitals can also be classified according to ownership type.

(22 percent) operate with more than 199 beds. Using figures for the number of hospitals and beds in table 15–1, we can see that the average nonprofit hospital with 196 beds is larger than the typical for-profit hospital containing 144 beds.

Table 15–2 also shows that public hospitals are much smaller, on average, than either the typical nonprofit or for-profit hospital. Figures from table 15–1 suggest that the average public hospital functions with almost 117 beds. The small size is probably due to the fact that a large fraction of public hospitals provide county hospital services in sparsely populated rural areas.

Although tables 15–1 and 15–2 provide some insight into the ownership structure and size distribution of the different types of hospitals, they offer little information about the market power held by individual hospitals in the United States. The geographical market for hospital services is primarily local in scope, whereas the data in the tables are summarized at the national level. In addition, although hospitals compete among themselves, they might also be viewed as competing against other types of health care providers, such as freestanding surgical centers. Before we can draw any behavioral or performance implications from market structure statistics, we must properly define the product and geographical markets.

## Defining the Relevant Product and Geographical Markets for Hospital Services

Although some hospitals produce specialized services, such as psychiatric or nose, throat, and eye care services, most hospitals can be treated as multiproduct firms that simultaneously offer a multitude of diagnostic and therapeutic services. The large number and variety of services make it very difficult in practice to define and measure the relevant product market (RPM). Some health economists, such as Wilder and Jacobs (1987), have proposed that the RPM should be based on specific diagnoses, such as obstetrics, nervous system, tonsillectomy, or hernia repair services. However, Frech (1987) notes that hospitals are potential suppliers of most medical services even if they do not presently produce them, since they are capable of shifting resources from producing one service to producing another. Furthermore, some hospital services, such as X rays, blood tests, and surgery, are complements to one another, reflecting the joint nature of the hospital production process. The implication is that the hospital RPM should be treated as a cluster of hospital services. As Frech (1987) notes, "The hundreds or thousands of individual procedures or services should not be viewed as individual markets" (p. 266).

One problem associated with a cluster of hospital services approach to defining the relevant product market is that some hospital facilities provide different levels of care in terms of the degree of technical sophistication and quality of services rendered or the seriousness and complexity of illnesses treated. Thus, some hospitals may not be in the same relevant product market because the level of care differs. Professionals in the hospital industry generally distinguish among four types of care.

*Primary* care services involve the prevention, early detection, and treatment of disease. Services of this nature include obstetrics, gynecology, internal medicine, and general surgery. A hospital that limits itself to providing primary care typically has some diagnostic equipment to perform X ray and laboratory analysis. *Secondary* care involves more sophisticated treatment and may include cardiology, respiratory care, and physical therapy. Equipment and laboratory capabilities are more sophisticated in secondary care hospitals. *Tertiary* care is designed to arrest disease in process, including heart surgery and such cancer treatments as chemotherapy, and requires still more sophisticated equipment than do primary or secondary services. Community hospitals normally provide both primary and secondary care, and some offer tertiary care. Research hospitals associated with university medical schools are argued to provide state-of-the-art *quaternary*-level care.[2]

Another potential problem with the cluster of services approach is that hospital and nonhospital providers offering partial product lines are excluded from the relevant product market. Those excluded include specialized hospitals, physician clinics, and freestanding outpatient surgery centers. The cluster of services approach to the RPM typically excludes outpatient services when determining a hospital's relevant product market, largely because it is so difficult or costly to account for the relatively numerous and small market shares of providers delivering outpatient services. In effect, the cluster of hospital services approach treats hospital outpatient services as belonging to a separate market: the market for outpatient or ambulatory care services. Consequently, the size of the hospital market is measured in inpatient terms by either beds, admissions, or inpatient days.

Once the RPM is defined as a **cluster of inpatient hospital services,** the next step is to determine the relevant geographical market (RGM). The proper geographical area reflects both the travel costs involved and the ability of the patients to switch to alternative suppliers when price is raised or quality is reduced by a nontrivial amount. Due to data availability and practical concerns, many researchers have based the RGM on geopolitical boundaries, such as counties, metropolitan areas, or cities. Some have used health service areas to define the RGM; others, such as Luft et al. (1986), have used a fixed 5- or 15-mile radius around each hospital as the appropriate RGM. The problem with RGM definitions of these kinds, however, is that they are based on convenience rather than on sound economic principles.

According to Elzinga and Hogarty (1978), patient flow data should be analyzed when determining the RGM. Patient flow data reflect both the consumer's willingness to travel and the ability to substitute among hospital providers. An appropriately defined RGM has small percentages of patients flowing into and out of it. This means geographic markets are defined such that only a small percentage of people leave to purchase hospital services elsewhere and a small fraction of individuals enter from outside the area to buy hospital services. Based on such a definition of the RGM, geographical market areas tend to be small or local in nature. For example, in *U.S.* v. *Rockford Memorial,* the court ruled that Rockford, Illinois, and the immediate hinterland was the RGM because 87 percent of Rockford Memorial's patients came from the area immediately surrounding Rockford and 90 percent of Rockford residents were

---

[2] See *U.S.* v. *Carilion,* 707 F. Supp. 840 (W.D. Va. 1989); 843.

## Determining the Number of Equally Sized Hospitals a Market Area Can Support Efficiently

Public health planners often want to know how many hospitals are required in a certain area. This insight points out some of the factors that influence the optimal number of hospitals. Suppose we are interested in calculating the number of hospitals, $N$, that is sufficient to service a market area of a given population size at the lowest possible cost. We can calculate the number of hospitals by dividing the total number of beds per day demanded in a market area, B, by the minimum efficient bed size of a hospital, MES, or

$$(15–1) \quad N = B/MES.$$

The **minimum efficient size** of a hospital reflects the initial point at which any economies of scale are completely exhausted. In our example, the minimum efficient size point is measured in terms of number of hospital beds. For instance, if 300 beds are typically demanded on a daily basis and the minimum efficient size of a hospital is 150 beds, the market area could support two equally sized efficient hospitals.

Definitionally, the number of beds demanded per day equals the average daily inpatient census, which is found by dividing the total annual number of inpatient days (TIPD), by 365 days. Total inpatient days, in turn, equals the product of the admission to population ratio (APR), population (POP), and average length of stay (ALOS) in the market area, or

$$(15–2) \quad TIPD = APR \cdot POP \cdot ALOS.$$

Since equation 15–2 when divided by 365 days equals B, equation 15–1 can be rewritten as

$$(15–3) \quad N = [(APR \cdot POP \cdot ALOS)/365]/MES.$$

Finally, allowing for some desired excess capacity, EC, expressed as a fraction of total beds demanded, the number of equally sized efficient hospitals can be stated as

$$(15–4) \quad N = [(1 + EC)(APR \cdot POP \cdot ALOS)/365]/MES.$$

For example, suppose the desired excess capacity is 15 percent, or .15, the admission to population ratio equals .13, the population in the market area is 100,000, the average length of stay is 8 days, and the minimum efficient scale is 150 beds. Plugging these numbers into equation 15–4 establishes that 2.18 equally sized hospitals are sufficient to satisfy the demand for inpatient hospital care in the market area at least cost. The optimal number of hospitals increases with desired excess capacity, the admission to population ratio, the population in the market area, and average length of stay. The number decreases with a larger minimum efficient scale. An analysis such as this can be used as a planning tool for hospitals and governments alike (e.g., see problem 3 at the end of the chapter).

hospitalized in Rockford itself. A relatively small geographical market area for hospital services should not be surprising. As Judge Posner noted in this antitrust case, "For highly exotic or highly elective hospital treatment, patients will sometimes travel long distances, of course. But for the most part hospital services are local. People want to be hospitalized near their families and homes, in hospitals in which their own— local—doctors have hospital privileges."[3]

---

[3] *U.S. v. Rockford Memorial*, 898 F.2d 1278; 1284 (1990).

## *Measuring the Structural Competitiveness of the Market*

After the relevant product and geographical markets are defined, market share data are used to gauge the degree of structural competition or concentration within a market area.[4] The Herfindahl-Hirschman index (HHI) is the most commonly used method of measuring the degree of concentration in the market. The HHI is derived by summing the squared market shares, expressed as percentages, of all the hospitals in the relevant market, or

$$(15\text{--}5) \quad \text{HHI} = \sum_{i=1}^{N} S_i^2,$$

where $0 < \text{HHI} \leq 10,000$ and $S_i$ stands for the percentage market share or percentage of industry output produced by the $i$th hospital. For the hospital services industry, market share can be calculated by using the number of inpatient days, beds, admissions, or net inpatient revenues (gross revenues less charity care, bad debt, and contractual allowances or discounts), which serve as measures of output.

When a market area is dominated by one hospital (a monopolist), the HHI takes on the maximum value of 10,000. The HHI takes on a value closer to zero when a greater number of hospitals, $N$, exists in the market area and/or when a given number of hospitals are more similarly sized. As the value of the HHI approaches zero, an industry is considered to be less structurally concentrated (or more competitive).

For example, suppose there are five hospitals within a geographical area with market shares of 35, 30, 20, 10, and 5 percent. Applying equation 15–5, the HHI is computed as 2,650. Now suppose the two smallest hospitals merge. The postmerger HHI is now ($35^2 + 30^2 + 20^2 + 15^2$), or 2,750. Notice that a smaller number of hospitals leads to a higher value for the HHI and reflects the greater concentration of output among a smaller number of hospitals in the marketplace. Finally, suppose the market shares of the four remaining hospitals become equal over time. If so, the HHI becomes 2,500. Hence, the HHI has a lower value and the market is structurally more competitive when a larger number of equally sized hospitals exist.

Although microeconomic theory predicts that firms are more likely to form a cartel and behave in a monopolistic manner by restricting output and raising price (and reducing quality) when firms are fewer in number, it is unable to predict the precise value of the HHI at which collusion among firms takes place. The HHI reflects only the structural competitiveness of the market; it reveals nothing explicit about the behavioral intensity of competition among the hospitals. Consequently, economic theory is unable to identify a specific competition—monopoly cutoff level for the HHI.

However, by consulting the Department of Justice (DOJ) Merger Guidelines, we can get a rough approximation of what HHI value constitutes a near monopoly (at

---

[4]See Baker (1988) for a thorough discussion of the many assumptions and difficulties associated with defining the RGM and RPM.

least according to DOJ policymakers). The DOJ generally challenges a merger when the postmerger HHI would be above 1,800 and the merger would increase the premerger HHI by more than 50 points, or a merger that would lead to a postmerger HHI above 1,000 and raise the premerger HHI by more than 100 points. A merger that has a postmerger HHI of less than 1,000 is seldom challenged by the DOJ. Obviously, DOJ officials believe monopolylike market conditions arise when the HHI is at least above 1,000.

Schramm and Renn (1984) point out that many hospital markets already exceed the threshold concentration figure set by the Justice Department. For instance, according to Insight 15–1, only two hospitals of equal size are necessary in a market area with a population of 100,000 based on plausible figures for excess capacity, the admission to population ratio, average length of stay, and the minimum efficient scale. Two hospitals of equal size result in an HHI of 5,000, well above the DOJ threshold of 1,800. When assessing the competitiveness of a market, however, the DOJ also considers the degree of potential competition as reflected by any barriers to entry into the market.[5] Barriers to entry into the hospital services market are the topic of the next section.

## Barriers to Entry

According to Schramm and Renn (1984), "an entry barrier is a condition that imposes higher long-run costs of production on a new entrant than those borne by firms already in the market" (p. 880). Entry barriers make it difficult for new firms to enter markets and, during periods of excess demand, allow existing firms to make supranormal economic profits. State certificate of need (CON) laws are often cited as a type of entry barrier into the hospital services industry, as we saw in Chapter 9. Schramm and Renn take issue with this view of CON laws, however. They point out that the hospital industry is usually characterized by excess capacity rather than excess demand. According to them, it would be irrational for new hospitals to enter in the presence of excess capacity because hospitals already in the industry can satisfy any expansion in demand. Therefore, according to their view, excess capacity rather than CON laws deters entry into the industry.

Noether (1987), however, found that hospital prices were 4.0 to 4.9 percent higher, on average, in areas where CON laws exist. Furthermore, she noted, "In at least two states, a surge in notices of intent to build has been noted since abolition of the entry review program" (p. 37). Both of these findings suggest that CON laws deter entry and allow entrenched firms to raise prices. Thus, it is not surprising that, in 1987, the federal government ended its policy, which began in 1975, of encouraging the development of CON programs. According to Baker (1988), nearly one-quarter of the states abolished their CON laws by the end of 1987.[6]

---

[5]The DOJ Merger Guidelines also allow for "efficiency" and "failing firm" defenses. See Scherer and Ross (1990, p. 186) or http://www.ftc.gov/bc/docs/horizmer.htm, which contains the 1992 Horizontal Merger Guidelines.

[6]For a comprehensive review of the empirical literature on the CON program and some additional empirical findings, see Conover and Sloan (1998).

Baker (1988) argues that even in the absence of CON laws, entry into the hospital industry may be difficult. The technological specifications for modern hospital buildings, including wide corridors and doorways, large elevators, strongly supported flooring, and extensive plumbing, require about four to nine years of planning and construction time. Combined with minimum efficient scale requirements and learning curve considerations, new hospitals may be unwilling to enter even if an independent hospital or colluding hospitals raise price above the competitive level.

In the following paragraphs, we discuss cost structure considerations involving minimum efficient scale, learning curve effects, and multiplant economies as possible sources of barriers to entry.

**Cost Structure**   The cost structure faced by the firms in an industry may serve as another deterrent to potential competition. In particular, economies of scale, learning curve effects, and multiplant economies can all make it costlier for new firms to enter markets. Specifically, long-run economies of scale provide high-volume entrenched firms with a relative cost advantage over new firms entering the market with low volumes of output. Facing economies of scale, the entrenched firms can discourage new entry by pricing the product just below the break-even price of potential entrants. This **limit-pricing** strategy keeps out potential competitors and allows the entrenched firms to make excess economic profits.

The econometric evidence in support of economies of scale in the hospital services industry is mixed, however. For instance, hospital cost studies in the 1960s, which simply related hospital costs to measures of output and capacity, generally concluded that "there was evidence of significant economies of scale, at least up to moderately sized hospitals of around 500 beds" (Cowing, Holtmann, and Powers, 1983, p. 264). However, post-1970 hospital cost studies, controlling for other determinants of hospital costs, including case-mix, input prices, and the number of admitting physicians, reveal that "economies of scale may exist for small hospitals but . . . moderate- and large-size hospitals can generally be characterized by constant returns to scale" (Cowing, Holtmann, and Powers, 1983, p. 276). Unfortunately, the econometric evidence for the post-1970 studies is suspect because the cost functions employed are generally not well grounded in neoclassical cost theory, as presented in Chapter 6. In addition, like the hospital cost studies of the 1960s, the 1970 research fails to treat hospitals as multiproduct firms and assumes rather than tests for long-run cost minimization (see Chapter 6).

To overcome the limitations associated with the hospital cost studies of the 1960s and 1970s, econometric analyses by Cowing and Holtmann (1983), Grannemann, Brown, and Pauly (1986), Eakin and Kniesner (1988), Vita (1990), and Fournier and Mitchell (1992) rely to a much greater degree on neoclassical cost theory and treat hospitals as multiproduct firms. Yet even for these studies, we cannot draw definitive conclusions about the existence and extent of *long-run* economies of scale. This is because most of the studies found that hospitals fail to operate in long-run equilibrium, largely due to the indivisibility of capital; therefore, they estimate short-run economies of scale.

| TABLE 15-3 | A COMPARISON OF THE SIZE DISTRIBUTION OF COMMUNITY HOSPITALS, SELECTED YEARS 1970–1996 |
|---|---|

| | Percentage of Hospitals in Each Bed Size Category | | | |
|---|---|---|---|---|
| Bed Size Category | 1970 | 1980 | 1990 | 1996 |
| 0–24 | 6.8% | 4.4% | 4.2% | 5.1% |
| 25–49 | 22.6 | 17.7 | 17.4 | 17.6 |
| 50–99 | 25.4 | 25.1 | 23.5 | 22.0 |
| 100–199 | 21.8 | 23.5 | 24.3 | 26.1 |
| 200–299 | 10.1 | 12.3 | 13.7 | 13.5 |
| 300–399 | 6.1 | 7.1 | 7.6 | 7.0 |
| 400–499 | 3.2 | 4.6 | 4.1 | 3.8 |
| 500 and over | 4.0 | 5.4 | 5.3 | 4.9 |

SOURCE: American Hospital Association, *Hospital Statistics*, various years, Table 4.A.

Econometric problems aside, the literature fails to provide any strong and consistent econometric evidence for the presence of long-run economies of scale in the production of inpatient services. In fact, the limited evidence from recent studies suggests that the production process for inpatient hospital services exhibits long-run diseconomies of scale, at least for the average-size firm in the various studies (in particular, see Vita [1992], Eakin and Kniesner [1988], and Grannemann, Brown, and Pauly [1986]). The implication of the recent econometric studies is that long-run economies of scale are not a serious deterrent to potential entrants.

Given the problems associated with econometric studies, some researchers have relied on the **survivor test** developed by Stigler (1958) to determine whether economies of scale exist (Bays, 1986). According to the survivor technique, firm or plant sizes that account for an increasing fraction of industry output over time are considered to be efficient because they have apparently met and survived the market test. Correspondingly, those that provide a declining share are viewed as inefficient. The survivor test provides a broad measure of efficiency, capturing the ability of firms to both produce with least-cost methods and satisfy consumer wants in the long run.

Table 15–3 shows the percentage of community hospitals in each bed size category for 1970, 1980, 1990, and 1996. According to the figures, the percentage of hospitals in the first three bed size categories fell over the 26–year period (although there has been a slight increase in the first two quite recently), implying that hospitals of those sizes operate with diseconomies of scale. In contrast, the percentage of hospitals in the next three bed size categories, ranging from 100 to 399 beds, increased over the period, suggesting that economies of scale exist. The size category of 100 to 199 beds registered the largest percentage point increase from 1970 to 1996, indicating that hospitals in that size category may be the most efficient, at least from a survivor perspective. Finally, the percentage of hospitals in the last two bed size categories, 400 to 499 and 500 and more beds, increased from 1970 to 1980 and declined thereafter. The relative decline of hospitals in these two bed size categories might reflect the inefficiency of large hospitals, particularly in the price-conscious period after 1980.

Considering both the econometric evidence and the survivor test, a best guesstimate is that the long-run average cost of a short-term community hospital reaches its lowest point at a plant size of around 200 beds, give or take 100 beds. The long-run average cost curve is probably shallow, with costs rising only modestly to the left and right of the minimum point(s). It is important to remember, however, that economies of scale are limited by the size of the market; that is, demand conditions and transportation costs limit the economies of scale that can be realized. Thus, hospitals in rural areas operate with fewer beds than the number dictated by economies of scale considerations simply because the market is smaller. Also, some small hospitals may satisfy niche or specialized demands and continue to operate profitably despite their relative size. All in all, it does not appear that economies of scale are a significant deterrent to potential entrants into the hospital services industry.

**Learning-by-doing** is another characteristic associated with the cost structure the individual hospital faces. Learning-by-doing results when a hospital produces more cumulative output over time and gains greater experience. The greater cumulative output and experience translates into lower average costs of production for a given level of quality or a higher level of quality for a given level of costs. Studies focusing on learning economies in the hospital industry usually investigate the latter of the two relations: how the volume of output affects the quality of patient outcomes.

For example, Farley and Ozminkowski (1992) analyzed whether patient outcomes improve in hospitals as the volume of admissions increases for specific diagnoses and procedures. They found that over time, greater volume at a hospital leads to significantly lower risk-adjusted inhospital mortality rates for three types of admissions: acute myocardial infarction, hernia repair, and respiratory distress syndrome in neonates. Providing further evidence for learning economies in hospital care, Stone, Seage, Hertz, and Epstein (1992) found that the relative risk of death for AIDS patients is more than twice as great in low-experience hospitals. Their results further indicate that the better outcome at high-AIDS-experienced hospitals is not associated with greater use of medical services. For example, AIDS patients in low-experience hospitals are more likely to be placed in an ICU, have longer ICU stays, and tend to have longer overall lengths of stay and higher costs.[7]

If "practice makes perfect," as the studies suggest, hospitals with greater volume may tend to attract an even larger market share over time. The learning economies, combined with limit-pricing techniques, may discourage new firms from entering the industry. Thus, most evidence suggests that learning-by-doing may act as a barrier to

---

[7]However, unlike Farley and Ozminkowski (1992), Stone, Seage, Hertz, and Epstein (1992) did not correct for the likelihood of reverse causation—the so-called selective referral bias. It is entirely possible that AIDS patients flock to those hospitals that provide higher-quality care; that is, higher quality leads to higher admissions rather than the reverse.

entry into hospital markets and provide existing firms with some market power to raise price.

Membership in a **multihospital system** or chain may also provide an existing hospital with a cost advantage relative to a potential freestanding hospital that is contemplating whether to enter the market. The American Hospital Association (AHA) defines a multihospital system as two or more hospitals that are owned, leased, sponsored, or managed by a single corporate entity. According to data from the AHA (1998), 2,909 hospitals, or approximately 47 percent of all hospitals, belonged to a multihospital chain in 1996. Approximately 75 percent of for-profit hospitals were part of a chain in 1990 compared to 41 percent of nonprofit hospitals and 8 percent of public hospitals (Menke, 1997).

According to Morrisey and Alexander (1987), a member of a multihospital system may possess four general advantages over an independent hospital, which may result in lower average costs at any given level of output:

(1) *economic benefits* such as economies of scale and access to capital;
(2) *improved personnel and management benefits* such as ability to recruit, train and retain high-quality medical and administrative staffs, expand patient referral networks, and provide access to specialists to assist in coping with increasingly complex environments;
(3) *organizational benefits* due to expansion of the service area, increased market penetration, and organizational survival through reduced financial deficits, manpower shortages, and facilities problems; and
(4) *community benefits* such as improved access and quality of care through enhanced resources, lower costs, and improved regional planning. (p. 61)

With these four potential advantages in mind, several empirical studies have examined whether system affiliation actually confers any significant performance differential. While some minor differences have been found, statistical studies have generally established that system affiliation does not lead to lower costs of production. For example, the 18 studies reviewed by Ermann and Gabel (1984) reveal contradictory evidence regarding cost differences between multihospital and independent hospitals. In addition, Renn, Schramm, Watt, and Derzon (1985) found no significant differences in costs between investor-owned chains and freestanding for-profit hospitals or between system-affiliated and freestanding nonprofit hospitals. Finally, Santerre and Bennett (1992) found that system affiliation leads to higher rather than lower costs for nonprofit and public hospitals and has no impact on the costs of for-profit hospitals. Thus, available studies suggest empirically that system affiliation offers no major cost advantage to established hospitals.[8]

In sum, learning-by-doing appears to be the only significant cost structure basis for barriers to entry. Evidence suggests that more experience is associated with lower

---

[8]But compare Menke (1997) who uses more recent data for 1990 and finds that system-affiliated hospitals have lower costs.

| **TABLE 15-4** | SOURCES OF HOSPITAL FUNDS, 1996 | |
| --- | :---: | :---: |
| | **Dollars (billions)** | **Percent** |
| Total hospital care expenses | 358.5 | 100.0% |
| All private funds | 137.9 | 38.5 |
| Out-of-pocket | 9.2 | 2.6 |
| Private insurance | 113.4 | 31.6 |
| Other | 15.3 | 4.3 |
| Government | 220.6 | 61.5 |
| Federal | 181.6 | 50.7 |
| State and local | 39.1 | 10.9 |

SOURCE: Katherine R. Levit et al., "National Health Expenditures, 1996," *Health Care Financing Review* 19 (fall 1997), table 11.

costs and higher quality, implying that potential entrants may be deterred from entering markets when the existing hospitals possess considerable expertise. Thus, learning economies may give existing firms the potential to raise price above the competitive level and earn excess economic profits. In contrast, economies of scale and multiplant economies seem to have very little impact on the relative long-run costs of existing and new hospitals.

### *Number, Types, and Size Distribution of the Buyers of Hospital Services*

Another important dimension of the market structure of an industry is the number, types, and size distribution of the buyers. According to the monopsony model developed in Chapter 9, a single buyer (monopsonist) or a few large buyers (oligopsonists) may have the ability to negotiate significant price discounts. Table 15-4 shows the main sources of hospital funds in 1996. Of the $358.5 billion spent on hospital services, governments at all levels are collectively responsible for slightly over 61 percent, with the federal government being the main purchaser at nearly 51 percent. The relatively high percentage implies that the federal government may wield considerable monopsony power in the pricing of Medicare services due to its large share in both national and local markets. Similarly, some state governments may be able to achieve significant price discounts for Medicaid services in local markets, where they purchase a large fraction of all hospital services.

Nearly 39 percent of hospital care spending originates in the private sector. Individual consumers, accounting for only 2.6 percent of all hospital payments, are most often price insensitive and therefore have very little impact on the market price of hospital services. The private insurance category, representing commercial insurance companies, Blue Cross plans, HMOs, and PPOs, directly accounts for 32 percent of all spending on hospital services. Whether these buyers face an economic incentive to bargain successfully for low hospital prices depends on a host of considerations, including their individual goals (i.e., profit or nonprofit objectives), the competitiveness of the insurance market, and the buyers' market penetration rates. In general, these private payers are better able to negotiate hospital price discounts when they individually represent a relatively large market share of subscribers in local hospital markets and thereby acquire some monopsony power. For example, some researchers have found that a greater Blue Cross market share resulted in lower hospital prices during the 1970s (see Insight 9–3).

However, a high market penetration rate, if associated with some monopoly power in health insurance markets, may negatively affect the willingness of insurers to secure low hospital prices. That is, insurers that are insulated from competitive pressure in the "health insurance market" may face a smaller financial incentive to negotiate low prices in the "hospital services market," especially when maximum profits are not the sole objective. Another complicating factor when assessing the relative willingness and ability of insurers to contain costs is the type of hospital reimbursement practice. As we will see, third-party payers reimburse for hospital services in a wide variety of ways. With those considerations in mind, let us discuss hospital reimbursement policies in the context of managed-care organizations (MCOs), which have continued to become increasingly influential buyers of hospital services.

**Managed Care and Hospital Market Structure**   Some health policy analysts believe managed care is an integral part of any legitimate solution to cost containment problems in the U.S. health economy. According to them, the financial incentives normally associated with MCOs, such as HMOs and PPOs, directly motivate health care providers to use medical resources more efficiently. Furthermore, in a price-sensitive environment, the resulting lower costs and premiums at MCOs force conventional health plans to adopt similar improvements in health care delivery and costs or face the undesirable prospect of a reduced market share.

For cost savings to accrue, MCOs must employ the proper reimbursement methods so that health care providers have a financial incentive to adopt cost-effective practices. MCOs contracting with hospital providers choose among a variety of hospital reimbursement plans, including usual and customary charges, discounted usual and customary charges, per diem payments, DRG payments, and capitation payments. Some of these reimbursement schemes shift a greater amount of financial risk onto hospital care providers. For instance, DRG payments and capitation fees shift much more risk onto hospital care providers than do usual and customary charges. "At-risk" charges generally create more incentives for cost-effective practices because the health care providers are responsible for absorbing any cost overruns. According to Hoy, Curtis, and Rice (1991), the choice of reimbursement strategy "depends on the organizational structure of the managed care plan, the market characteristics of the geographic area, the utilization management techniques associated with the plan, and the insurer's philosophy of provider risk sharing" (p. 26).

| TABLE 15–5 | HOSPITAL REIMBURSEMENT METHODS OF THE HMO AND PPO PLANS OF COMMERCIAL INSURANCE COMPANIES | |

| | Percentage of Insurers Weighted by Total Premium | |
| Method | HMO Plans | PPO Plans |
| --- | --- | --- |
| Usual and customary charges | 12.4% | 17.5% |
| Discounted usual and customary charges | 70.8 | 35.3 |
| Per diem payment | 5.3 | 24.9 |
| DRG payment | 4.7 | 21.5 |
| Capitation | 6.8 | 0.0 |

SOURCE: Elizabeth W. Hoy, Richard E. Curtis, and Thomas Rice, "Change and Growth in Managed Care," *Health Affairs* 10 (winter 1991), Exhibit 6.

Comparative data are unavailable for the different hospital reimbursement practices adopted by the various types of MCOs. Hoy et al., however, provide some information regarding the hospital reimbursement practices of HMO and PPO plans sponsored by commercial insurance companies, such as Aetna, Prudential, Metropolitan, and Travelers. Recall that MCOs are also owned by Blue Cross/Blue Shield plans and independent companies, such as Kaiser Foundation Health Plans and Health Insurance Plan of Greater New York. Although the data on hospital reimbursement methods are limited to the managed-care plans owned by commercial insurers, they are nonetheless interesting, fairly representative, and deserving of discussion. The data are shown in table 15–5.[9]

Several implications of the data should be noted. First, notice that fewer than 20 percent of the PPOs and HMOs owned by commercial insurers reimburse hospital providers on the basis of usual and customary charges, with the most popular reimbursement method being the discounted charge. Second, according to the data, PPO plans are much more likely to use per diem payments than HMOs. Specifically, nearly 25 percent of insurer-owned PPOs reimburse by per diem payments, whereas the comparable figure for insurer-owned HMOs is only 5.3 percent. Recall that per diem payments provide incentives to reduce the quantity of hospital services but not length of stay.

Third, the reimbursement schemes of insurer-owned HMOs are generally less oriented toward hospital risk sharing than are those of PPOs. Notice that almost 22 percent of the insurer-owned PPOs reimburse hospitals with either DRG or

[9]In 1990, commercial insurers owned or managed 43 percent of all HMOs and enrolled 27 percent of all HMO enrollees (Gold, 1991). Comparable data on the sponsorship of PPOs are unavailable.

capitation payments, whereas only 11.5 percent of insurer-owned HMOs reimburse with these at-risk charges. Hoy, Curtis, and Rice (1991) provide a rationale for this finding by noting that physician gatekeepers and the strong orientation toward avoiding hospitalization make hospital risk sharing less critical to HMOs.

Due to the large variety of reimbursement practices suggested by the data, it is evident that not all HMOs or PPOs should be treated or expected to behave similarly with respect to the buying of hospital services. Indeed, Feldman et al. (1990) found that IPA/HMOs are less likely than the more tightly organized staff-network (S/N) HMOs to switch hospitals and concentrate patients at specific hospitals on the basis of price. They argue that a strong and ongoing physician affiliation is more important to IPA physicians than is price. This view is substantiated by the fact that the elasticity of demand for hospital admissions was found to be more elastic for S/N HMOs (−3.044) than IPAs (−1.024). Moreover, Feldman, Kralewski, Shapiro, and Chan (1990) show that S/N HMOs secure larger discounts for inpatient services than IPAs. They found that the average discount is 26 percent for general medical and surgery care services at S/N HMOs but only 4 percent at IPAs. The authors also determined that S/N HMOs are more likely to use per diem charges than IPAs, which tend to employ discounted charges.

In sum, the number, size distribution, and types of buyers are important structural features of local hospital markets. Government is responsible for a majority of all hospital purchases and, with the associated monopsony power, has some ability to influence hospital prices and costs through the Medicare and Medicaid programs at the national or state level. The private sector, composed of a large number of different types of insurer/buyers, may be able to influence hospital prices at the local level. The ultimate success of private insurers in negotiating low prices and controlling costs in local hospital markets depends on a host of factors, including the chosen hospital reimbursement strategy, the competitiveness of the hospital and insurance markets, and the goals of the insurer.

### Type of Product

Whether the hospitals in a market offer a differentiated or standardized product is another determinant of market structure. According to the anticompetitive view, product differentiation causes the demand curve to become less price elastic and enables the firm to restrict output below and raise price above the competitive level. As discussed in Chapter 9, there are three dimensions to product differences: spatial, quality, and image. Hospital choice studies have confirmed that these kinds of product differences matter in the hospital services industry. For example, from their review of the literature, Lane and Lindquist (1988) cited seven categories of factors—care, staff, physical facilities, clientele, experience, convenience, and institutional—that strongly affect the choice of hospital. Of these factors, quality of care and staff, equipment and technology, and convenient location were found to be among the more important determinants of choice of hospital. Cost or price appears to play a secondary role in hospital choice, most likely due to the patient's low out-of-pocket price for hospital services.

**INSIGHT 15-2**

## Informed Choices and Financial Incentives

Informed choices are crucial for competition to work in health care markets. Buyers must be informed about prices and quality so that they can make efficient choices. As a result, the U.S. Health Care Financing Administration and a number of state organizations have begun to chart hospital performance by collecting and assessing hospital-specific data on the charges, utilization, and outcomes of various medical procedures. Similar to the way *Consumer Reports* rates refrigerators, cars, and stereo equipment, these organizations assess hospitals according to several criteria. For example, the Pennsylvania Health Care Cost Containment Council released 1988 data comparing 33 Pittsburgh-area hospitals on 55 common hospital procedures. The number of patients, average length of stay, average charge, and risk-adjusted mortality rates and complication rates were compared (Winslow, 1990). The risk-adjusted outcome figures attempted to adjust for the severity of patients' illnesses so that results would be standardized across hospitals.

Similarly, four major Cincinnati employers and the Cleveland Health Quality Choice Initiative recently tried to reduce health care costs with new systems for rating hospitals on the basis of cost and quality of care (Winslow, 1993a, 1993b). If collected properly, the data should help employers, insurers, and consumers make informed choices and exert pressure on hospitals to improve services. High-quality, low-cost hospitals will be rewarded, while low-quality, high-cost hospitals will be disciplined by the informed buying. The inefficient hospitals will be forced to change their practice patterns and adopt more cost-effective ways to treat patients. Some observers expect the process

to promote hospital mergers and cause unprofitable product lines to be cut as hospitals pursue cost-saving strategies.

Many employers are beginning to use financial incentives to induce employees to comparison shop for medical services just as they do for housing, cars, and refrigerators. For example, at International Paper Company (IP), employees are provided with information about the prices and quality of many different medical services offered by various health care providers in the local area (Ruffenach, 1993). In addition, the ceiling on out-of-pocket costs was increased to $6,500 a year so that employee/consumers will be more price conscious. An employee in Greenville, South Carolina, facing gallbladder surgery can use IP's database to find out that the company pays maximums of $1,219 to the surgeon, $257 a day for a semiprivate hospital room, and $178 a day for nursing care. The employee is responsible for any balance billing. IP also provides a listing identifying the numbers, backgrounds, and prices of surgeons in the area.

At the NCR Corporation division of AT&T, employees are given information about the prices the company pays for 11,000 different procedures. These prices provide a benchmark for employees when discussing terms with health care providers. Employees who do not use the company's managed-care network are responsible for paying a higher percentage of some medical bills. This acts as an incentive for employees to stay within the network.

Some companies, such as Quaker Oats Company, provide profiles of local hospitals, including average charges, average length of stay, and how often a given hospital handles a particular surgery.

Marketing and advertising also play important roles in the hospital services industry. The typical hospital spends nearly $500,000 annually on marketing (Japsen, 1997), amounting to approximately .8 percent of sales. While that percentage figure pales in comparison to the advertising-to-sales ratios of 10 percent or more observed in the pharmaceutical, cosmetics, soft drink, cereal, and other industries, Gray (1986) notes that hospitals devote as much as 5 percent of gross sales to advertising in some highly competitive areas of the country. Gray notes, "Hospitals plug such things as Saturday surgery (a convenience for patients), referral services, gourmet food, depression clinics—even free transportation" (p. 183).

Of the total marketing budget at hospitals, about one-half is spent on advertising. About 43 percent of the advertising budget is devoted to print advertisements in newspapers and magazines. The rest of the advertising budget is directed to radio (14 percent), direct mail (12 percent), yellow pages (11 percent), television (11 percent), bus/billboards (4 percent), and other media (5 percent).

Reflecting the significance of advertising competition in the hospital services industry, five of the six hospitals in Des Moines, Iowa, were accused of agreeing to limit their advertising, an action in violation of antitrust laws. The hospitals involved in the suit eventually settled with the Justice Department (Burda, 1993).

## Consumer (Mis)Information

The final factor affecting the market structure of the hospital services industry is the amount of information consumers possess. Due to low out-of-pocket costs, one suspects that consumers are rationally ignorant about the prices of most hospital services. For instance, when asked to estimate the cost of open-heart surgery, consumer estimates ranged from $10 to $99,000 (Ruffenach, 1993). The average figure of $12,804 was almost twice the actual cost of $7,280. Similarly, consumer estimates for a normal delivery of a baby ranged from $45 to $80,000. The average estimate of $2,595 was much closer to the actual cost of $1,999 in this case, but still over 25 percent too high.

In a traditional fee-for-service environment with first-dollar health insurance coverage, consumers most likely do too little comparison shopping. Lacking adequate information, consumers are at a serious disadvantage when purchasing hospital services, and this places hospital decision makers in the enviable position of being able to practice opportunistic behavior. One reason for the growing popularity of MCOs is that these third-party payers, acting essentially as information brokers, perform the comparison shopping task for the consumer/patient. Unlike the general consumer, decision makers in managed-care systems are sufficiently informed about hospital prices and quality, helping to overcome the usual asymmetry of information existing directly between the patient and hospital services provider. In addition, the financial success of MCOs partly hinges on the ability to either employ or contract with high-quality providers at reasonable prices. In the conduct section of this chapter, we examine whether managed-care programs have succeeded in containing hospital care costs.

## Summary of the Structure of the Hospital Services Industry

For all practical purposes, the market for hospital services is best defined as those hospitals offering a similar cluster of inpatient services within the same geographical area. The geographical market area of most primary and secondary care hospitals tends to be local in nature, whereas the market area of tertiary care hospitals may be regional or national in scope. In fact, it is becoming common for large employers and health insurers to negotiate price discounts with hospitals outside local markets for major types of tertiary care services, including organ transplants and major heart surgery.

The structural competitiveness of the hospital services market is determined by the number, types, and size distribution of hospitals; number, types, and size distribution of buyers/insurers; barriers to entry; type of product; and the extent of any asymmetry of information between patients and hospitals. In terms of the supply side, most local hospital markets are characterized by a relatively few competing hospitals except in major metropolitan areas, where hospitals are more numerous. For instance, cities with populations of 100,000 can generally support only two or three hospitals. In addition to the degree of actual competition, the behavior of hospitals depends on the ease of potential entry or the magnitude of any barriers to entry. Learning-by-doing rather than long-run economies of scale or multihospital systems appears to be the major reason for barriers to entry into the hospital services industry. More experienced hospitals tend to have lower costs and higher quality than newer ones. Hence, based on the number of competitors and barriers to entry in most areas, the supply side of the hospital services industry can be characterized as oligopolistic.

Another important structural factor affecting hospital behavior from the demand side of the market is buyer concentration. Simply put, buyer concentration has the ability to negate seller concentration. The federal government, state governments, and some private insurers may possess the appropriate size on the demand side of the market necessary to influence hospital pricing and output behavior. Also, reimbursement policies that place hospitals at risk for high costs have the potential to promote cost-effective medicine.

Finally, hospitals currently compete for patients through nonprice means. For instance, many hospitals rely on advertising and hospital amenities to attract patients. Because patients are typically uninformed about and unresponsive to prices, hospitals may be able to raise price or lower quality below the competitive level. Financial incentives and public information are beginning to take on a much greater role in raising consumer consciousness with regard to hospital prices and quality of hospital services.

# The Conduct of the Hospital Services Industry

The industrial organization triad predicts that market structure influences the conduct of the hospitals within a given market area. According to traditional microeconomic theory, a large number of sellers and low barriers to entry promote competition. More intense competition usually shows up in increased output, higher quality, and lower prices. The general conduct of real-world hospitals is difficult to predict on a market or an aggregate basis, however. Hospitals pursue different objectives, operate in various market settings, face alternative types of reimbursement methods from such diverse payers as HMOs, PPOs, and traditional insurers, and are subject to a variety of government regulations. Ideally, from a societal point of view, we hope that incentives exist such that hospitals act independently and strive to minimize costs and satisfy consumer wants. However, some structural features of the hospital services industry, such as barriers to entry, product complexity, and asymmetry of information, suggest that such incentives may be lacking in many local markets across the nation. Also, a substantial body of empirical evidence indicates that hospitals compete on the basis of cost-enhancing quality instead of price in many markets (contemporary California being a possible exception). In this section, we discuss what is known empirically about the relation between hospital market structure and various measures of conduct, such as price, costs, and quality. We also examine the effects of ownership structure, managed care, and government regulations on the conduct of hospitals. The section closes with a discussion of integrated delivery systems.

## Market Structure and Hospital Behavior

Table 15–6 provides a capsule description of the various empirical studies examining the relation between market structure as measured by the degree of structural competition (e.g., a Herfindahl index of market concentration) and hospital behavior in terms of price, quality, and costs. Most of these studies analyze the impact of hospital competition on costs rather than price or quality because of data availability rather than research intent. Quality is almost impossible to measure, and although hospital-specific cost data are readily available from the American Hospital Association, similar data for total revenues or price are not normally released for confidentiality reasons. Nevertheless, we can draw several worthwhile conclusions from these studies.

First, most of the empirical studies using data prior to 1983 found that *more* competition among hospitals led to *higher* rather than lower production costs. This relation is referred to as the *medical arms race (MAR)*. The argument is that in more competitive areas, hospitals provide physicians with a higher level of hospital quality in the form of advanced medical technologies, excess bed capacity, and amenities in return for admitting their patients. In support of the MAR hypothesis, several of the studies listed in table 15–6 found that increased competition was associated with lower levels of technical efficiency (Wilson and Jadlow 1982), excess bed capacity (Joskow, 1980; Farley, 1985), and a larger number of duplicate specialized services in local markets (Dranove, Shanley, and Simon, 1992; Farley, 1985). However, empirical studies offer little evidence *directly* linking the degree of structural competition to either a greater diffusion of cost-enhancing medical technologies or to a lesser diffusion of cost-reducing medical technologies (e.g., see Romeo, Wagner, and Lee, 1984; Sloan, Valvona, and Perrin, 1986; and Duffy, 1992). The lack of evidence may reflect that the MAR effects of increased hospital competition translate into excess hospital inputs, more amenities, and duplicate services rather than a greater diffusion of medical technologies.

Second, Noether (1988), the only study analyzing both price and cost implications, found that increased hospital competition resulted in higher production costs, presumably through higher quality, but had no impact on hospital prices. Thus, she concluded that even before 1983, after which payer price sensitivity heightened, intense hospital competition was associated with lower quality-adjusted prices. As many

| TABLE 15-6 | EFFECT OF MARKET STRUCTURE ON HOSPITAL BEHAVIOR | | |
|---|---|---|---|
| **Study** | **Sample of Hospitals** | **Year(s) of Data** | **Effect of Increased Hospital Competition** |
| Hersch (1984) | Urban national | 1972 | Increased hospital costs |
| Robinson and Luft (1985) | National | 1972 | Increased hospital costs |
| Wilson and Jadlow (1982) | National | 1973 | Lowered the technical efficiency of producing nuclear medicine services |
| Joskow (1980) | National nonprofits | 1976 | Created excess bed capacity |
| Farley (1985) | National | 1970–77 | Caused higher hospital costs, excess bed capacity, duplicate facilities and services, and increased labor and capital per patient |
| Noether (1988) | National | 1977–78 | Had no effect on hospital prices and increased hospital costs |
| Thorpe (1988) | National | 1980 | Increased hospital costs |
| White (1987) | Florida | 1983 | Increased hospital costs |
| Dranove, Shanley, and Simon (1992) | California | 1983 | Increased the number of specialized services in local markets |
| Zwanziger and Melnick (1988) | California | 1980–85 | Increased hospital costs in 1980, 1982, and 1983 but had no impact on hospital costs in 1984 or 1985 |
| Fournier and Mitchell (1992) | Florida | 1984–86 | Increased the costs of producing most hospital services |
| Robinson and Phibbs (1990) | California | 1982–86 | Increased hospital costs in 1982 and 1986; hospital inflation rate was lower in more competitive markets |
| Santerre and Bennett (1992) | Texas | 1987–88 | Increased costs of nonprofit hospitals; costs of public and for-profit hospitals were unaffected |
| Melnick, Zwanziger, Bamezai, and Pattison (1992) | California | 1987 | Led to a lower Blue Cross PPO–negotiated price for hospital services |

health economists point out, it is the *quality-adjusted* price that matters when drawing inferences about the effects of competition on the economic well-being of consumers. Although Noether's study suggests that greater hospital competition leads to lower quality-adjusted prices and thereby benefits consumers, the lack of substantiating studies makes it difficult to generalize beyond her results.

Third, studies using data after 1983 generally found that increased competition was beginning to constrain hospital prices and costs. The year 1983 serves as a benchmark in the hospital services industry because after that year, prospective payment systems began to replace cost-based systems (e.g., DRG systems), the market share of for-profit hospitals increased significantly, and the practices of MCOs became more commonplace. In simple terms, health care payers became more price conscious, and hospital competition changed from being patient driven to being payer driven (Dranove, Shanley, and White, 1993).

Santerre and Bennett (1992) found that while greater hospital competition increases the costs of nonprofit hospitals, the costs of for-profit and public hospitals are not affected by competition during more recent times of greater payer price consciousness.[10] Even more convincing, Zwanziger and Melnick (1988) established that more intense competition was associated with higher hospital costs from 1980 to 1983 but had no impact on hospital costs in 1984 or 1985. Robinson and Phibbs (1990) corroborate their results and show that the hospital inflation rate was lower in more competitive markets after 1983. Finally, Melnick, Zwanziger, Bamezai, and Pattison (1992) found that more hospital competition led to a lower Blue Cross PPO–negotiated price for hospital services. Taken together, these four studies provide strong support for the premise that market competition can contain health care costs when the demand side of the market is sensitive to prices. Nonetheless, most of the more recent studies were based on California data and may simply reflect the atypical nature of that state, where HMOs and PPOs flourish in large numbers and the state government employs selective contracting for Medicaid services. On the other hand, the California experience may reflect the oncoming wave of the future.

## Hospital Ownership and Hospital Behavior

Another dimension influencing firm conduct is the objective of the hospital as reflected in different ownership structures. As noted previously, nonprofit, public, and for-profit hospitals may be motivated by different goals. It has been argued that the alternative goals of the different hospital ownership structures result in pricing and cost differences or affect the relative willingness to provide charitable care to indigent persons. The argument is usually couched within either a property rights or public choice framework.

Recall from Chapter 10 that the property rights and public choice models, taken together, suggest that for-profit hospitals may be more efficient than nonprofit hospitals, which, in turn, operate more efficiently than public hospitals. Unlike for-profit hospitals, nonprofit and public hospitals lack owners or residual claimants who face a strong, direct financial incentive to monitor their activities and who are able to discipline management when deviations from cost-minimization occur. Public hospitals lack a further incentive to minimize the cost of production. Unlike private hospitals, public hospitals can rely to some extent on direct funding from government in addition to patient-driven revenues. Thus, public hospitals are not at the complete

---

[10]Woolley (1989) found some complementary evidence that competition no longer increases the prices of for-profit hospitals. He found that a merger of two hospitals causes higher profits for competitors because, as he argues, the merger makes it easier for the remaining hospitals to collude and maximize joint profits by restricting output and raising price.

mercy of the marketplace to minimize costs, unlike nonprofit and especially for-profit hospitals.

While studies find empirically that ownership matters, they are unable to reveal any systematically large efficiency differences across ownership types. The cost differences that are sometimes observed can often be explained by unmeasurable variations in quality. Although for-profit hospitals do tend to charge higher prices, the price differences can be easily explained by the fact that not-for-profit hospitals do not pay most taxes, borrow at lower interest rates because interest on their bonds is tax exempt, and receive donations from outside parties.

Sloan (1988) also points out that the cost similarity among hospitals with different ownership structures may suggest that doctors on the medical staff may act as residual claimants in not-for-profit hospitals and thus "have a financial stake in keeping such hospitals efficient. Inefficient hospitals are candidates for acquisition by for-profit hospitals" (p. 138). Hospitals with different ownership arrangements may behave even more similarly in the future with respect to cost and pricing practices, given the ever growing price consciousness among employers, insurers, and consumers.

Most studies have found, however, that public hospitals are much more likely to provide greater amounts of uncompensated care. Uncompensated care is usually defined as bad debts and charity and is measured as a percent of total hospital expenses. As evidence, Mann, Melnick, Bamezai, and Zwanziger (1997) estimate that uncompensated care as a percentage of expenses was 15.4 and 6.3 percent for urban public and rural public hospitals, respectively, in 1994. The comparable figures for nonprofit and for-profit were 5.0 and 4.2 percent, respectively. Not surprisingly, public hospitals have been dubbed the "hospital provider of last resort" because of their charitable nature. In fact, one study found that private hospitals provide less uncompensated care when a public general hospital exists in the area (Thorpe and Brecher, 1987).

These figures on uncompensated care help to motivate two other interesting questions. First, why do for-profit hospitals provide any uncompensated care? Supposedly, the business of for-profit hospitals is business and therefore the maximization of profits or stockholder wealth. Providing care to the indigent subtracts from maximum profits and reduces the return to owners. However, Hertzlinger and Krasker (1987) point out that for-profit hospitals may not deny poor individuals access to care because "hospital costs are mostly fixed and the marginal costs of an additional patient day, generally low. Even an indigent patient contributes somewhat to covering the hospital's fixed costs" (p. 103).

The second question deals with nonprofit hospitals. One reason nonprofit hospitals are granted tax-exempt status is they are supposed to apply any unused revenues (or profits) toward the express purpose for which they were formed. Nonprofit hospitals are formed to provide medical care to the sick and needy and are responsible to the community at large. Therefore, nonprofit hospitals are expected to provide charitable care. The fact that their uncompensated care is only 5 percent of expenses and quite close to that of for-profit hospitals raises the question whether the tax-exempt status of nonprofit hospitals should be revoked. In fact, state and local governments in Texas, Pennsylvania, and Utah, among other states, have introduced legislation intended to pressure nonprofit hospitals into providing more charity care. Nonprofit hospitals would be required to prove that they benefit their areas or lose their tax exemption (Lutz, 1993). Morrisey, Wedig, and Hassan (1996) demonstrate that the concern about the tax-exempt status of nonprofit hospitals may be warranted. Using 1988 and 1991 data for 189 nonprofit hospitals in California, they compare the amount of uncompensated care to the estimated tax subsidy that each nonprofit hospital receives. While not as widespread as commonly believed, the researchers find that nearly 20 percent of all nonprofit hospitals do not provide community benefits sufficient to compensate for the tax subsidies they receive.

## Managed-Care Buyers and Hospital Behavior

Another interesting aspect of hospital conduct is the relation between managed-care institutions, such as HMOs, PPOs, and utilization review organizations, and hospital behavior. The question is whether managed care provides the proper incentives for efficiency without seriously sacrificing quality. Most of the research on the relation between MCOs and hospital behavior has examined the effect of HMOs on hospital costs, utilization rates, or the quality of health outcomes. In general, studies suggest that HMO hospitalization rates are about 15 to 20 percent lower than those of fee-for-service insurance plans after controlling for a host of health-related factors, including ages of the patients, case-mix, severity of illnesses, and hospital-specific influences (Luft, 1981; Manning et al., 1985; Dowd, Feldman, Cassou, and Finch, 1991; Miller and Luft, 1994). Moreover, studies imply that the lower hospitalization rates tend to hold for both staff and IPA/HMOs (Dowd, Feldman, Cassou, and Finch, 1991; Bradbury, Golec, and Stearns, 1991). Even among intensive care patients, a setting that appears to allow very little room for discretion in treatment decisions, some evidence indicates that managed care results in cost savings when compared to traditional insurance (Rapoport, Gehlbach, Lemeshow, and Teres, 1992).

Research has also indicated that inpatient outcomes are not systematically worse (Retchin et al., 1992; Retchin and Brown, 1991; Carlisle et al., 1992; Miller and Luft, 1997) for HMOs compared to fee-for-service medicine, although some disagreement remains about the care of low-income patients in HMOs (compare Ware et al. [1986] and Greenwald and Henke [1992]). The comparable level of quality has surprised some critics of HMOs because they suspected that the prepaid nature of these institutions creates an incentive for an underproduction of care. Consumers, however, are normally sensitive to quality issues, especially in the long run. Quality sensitivity most likely places a constraint on the level of care provided by managed-care institutions. Even MCOs are dependent on repeat buying, and low quality can tarnish a company's image and reduce market share.

It is interesting to note that despite the lower hospitalization utilization rates, McLaughlin (1987) found that the growth of HMOs has not led to a commensurate reduction in total hospital costs per capita at the market level.[11] The relatively low

---

[11]Her results, however, have been criticized on econometric grounds by Zellner and Wolfe (1989).

HMO market share in most areas, a lack of consumer price consciousness, and quality/amenity competition may account for the failure of HMOs to induce price competition at the market level (McLaughlin, 1988).

In contrast to HMOs, there have been only a few published assessments of PPO effects on hospital utilization rates and expenditures. The few existing studies fail to reach a consensus on the *overall* cost containment effectiveness of PPOs. While Zwanziger and Auerbach (1991) report that PPOs lead to a reduction in inpatient expenditures, the increased expenditures stemming from expansions in outpatient benefits tend to swamp these cost savings (Hester, Wouters, and Wright, 1987; Garnick et al., 1990; Diehr et al., 1990).[12] According to Fielding and Rice (1993), PPOs are ineffective in controlling overall costs because the typical participating physician has only 11 enrollees from a particular PPO. Consequently, an individual PPO has limited ability to exert any monopsony power over the prices and utilization practices of physicians.

Another aspect of managed care is **utilization review (UR)**.[13] According to Ermann (1988), UR "programs seek to determine whether specific services are medically necessary and whether they are delivered at an appropriate level of intensity and cost" (p. 683). Utilization management began in 1972 in the public sector when the federal government established professional standards review organizations (PSROs) to provide UR services for Medicare and Medicaid patients as a result of the concern over unnecessary and low-quality care. However, the PSROs proved to be ineffective. For instance, the Congressional Budget Office (1981) reported that "for every dollar spent on PSRO review of Medicare patients, only $.40 in resources were recouped, for a net loss of $.60" (p. xiii). As a result, PSROs were terminated in 1982 and, in the following year, replaced by peer review organizations (PROs). PROs are regionally based organizations that compete for government contracts and are responsible for ensuring the quality of services and eliminating unnecessary care through UR.

The first privately sponsored UR programs began in the mid-1960s and focused on hospital utilization. Private UR programs covered very few employees until the middle to late 1980s, but over the last 10 years the UR industry has developed rapidly, covering about 90 percent of individuals with private medical insurance. In addition to the large national commercial health insurers, such as Metropolitan Life, Aetna, and Travelers, and HMO companies that provide a full spectrum of managed-care services, about 200 companies offer only UR services. Some of these companies are national in scope, but most are regionally or locally based. These companies usually specialize in one area of UR (e.g., medical and surgical or psychiatric and substance abuse); thus, it is not unusual for an employer to contract simultaneously with several UR companies.

There are three types of UR services, based on time of review. **Prospective** UR addresses the necessity of hospital care while it is still being planned and consequently has the capacity to change or avert planned treatments. Prior authorization and

---

[12]But see Smith (1997/98) who finds recently that, on average, PPOs were associated with cost savings of 12 percent per covered life as compared to traditional plans with utilization review. The cost savings were primarily through lower rates of physician visits and hospital admissions.

[13]The following discussion borrows heavily from Bailit and Sennett (1991).

## Drive-Through Deliveries

Managed care organizations developed, in large part, to curb the rising tide of health care costs that arose from traditional fee-for-service insurance. They were initially championed as the providers of cost-effective, high-quality medicine. Times have changed. Critics of managed care now contend that MCOs have gone overboard in their pursuit of cost-savings by unnecessarily denying medical care to patients. As evidence, critics have pointed to the unduly short hospital stays of new moms and babies enrolled in managed-care plans. Indeed, numerous articles have appeared in the popular press citing the drive-through maternity care practices of MCOs. As concern over drive-through deliveries escalated, many state governments and the federal government legislated "motherhood mandates," which established minimum postdelivery hospital stays for new moms and their babies (usually 48 hours following a vaginal birth and 96 hours following a cesarean section).

But is it true that hospital stays are significantly shorter for mothers and newborns enrolled in managed-care plans? Also, is it true that patient well-being is compromised by short hospital stays? Gazmararian and Koplan (1996) attempt to answer these questions.

Specifically, the authors examine national data from the Prudential Healthcare claims system on 13,945 enrollees who had normal vaginal deliveries

in 1994. Of those, 4,547 were enrolled in HMOs, 5,342 belonged to point-of-service plans, and 4,056 were members of indemnity plans. The authors obtained data on hospital length of stay and readmission rates for the mothers and newborns by type of plan, among other variables. Readmission rates were used to determine the quality of care during the initial stay.

The authors found that the length of stay for both new mothers and newborns differed across health plan types. For example, 81.7 percent of the mothers enrolled in HMOs were discharged within one day. The comparable figures for point-of-service and indemnity enrollees were only 61.4 and 48.1 percent, respectively. Only in the Northeast was there no significant difference in the length of stay by type of plan.

No difference was found for newborn readmission rates by plan type. However, among women discharged within one day, those enrolled in HMOs had a readmission rate more than 50 percent higher (0.56) than that of women enrolled in either point-of-service (0.27) or indemnity (0.20) plans. Because most of the maternal readmissions occurred more than three days after delivery, however, the authors note that an additional day in the hospital after delivery would most likely not have prevented most readmissions.

second opinions are examples of prospective UR. **Concurrent** review programs focus on the necessity of continual care for patients and thus intervenes to change planned treatments. For hospitalized patients, review organizations monitor by telephone or through onsite nurses to determine whether patients need certain types of hospital-level care. Finally, **retrospective** programs review care after the fact from records and claims that have little potential to directly affect care provided to patients, except by altering the practice patterns of providers that face retrospective denial of reimbursement.

Although studies on the effectiveness of private UR services in containing hospital costs are relatively limited, the available literature indicates that hospital admissions and length-of-stay prospective review programs have led to a significant reduction in beds per 1,000 employees. In addition, a few studies of hospital review programs report net total health care savings of 4.5 to 8 percent at the individual plan level (e.g., Feldstein, Wickizer, and Wheeler, 1988). Likewise, at the system level, Schwartz and Mendelson (1991) claim that UR programs were associated with a significant reduction in the rate of hospital costs during the 1980s. No evidence yet exists on the relation between UR services and the quality of patient care.

In sum, research has shown that HMOs, PPOs, and UR can contain inpatient hospital costs to some degree. Research further indicates that HMOs contain inpatient care costs without seriously sacrificing health care outcomes. Evidence on the quality implications of PPOs and UR programs is unavailable. The ability of PPOs to contain *overall* health care costs appears to be limited due to the small number of PPO patients assigned to the typical physician.

## Price Regulations and Hospital Behavior[14]

Public policies may also affect the conduct of hospitals. In 1972, Congress passed Section 222 of the Social Security Amendments giving states the authority to establish rate-setting programs. By the late 1970s, more than 30 states had adopted some form of hospital rate-setting program (Coelen and Sullivan, 1981). However, only three of the states had a mandatory "all-payer" program that controls rates for all patient groups, including private payers, commercially insured patients, patients with public insurance, and Blue Cross plans. By 1996 only one state, Maryland, still had an all-payer rate-setting program.

Proponents of rate-setting programs have argued that these programs can contain health care costs with no concomitant reduction in the quality of care because they view hospitals as operating with organizational slack. The organizational slack, taking form in such factors as higher than necessary hospital salaries, duplication of facilities, and unnecessary hospital amenities, results from imperfect markets or hospital objectives other than cost minimization. When slack is present, price regulations or ceilings may promote lower expenditures without an associated reduction in patient care.

Empirical studies have almost unanimously supported the view that state regulation of hospital fees can lower health care costs. For example, Lanning, Morrisey, and Ohsfeldt (1991), whose study correctly controlled for the endogenous nature of state programs, found that states with mature rate-setting programs have 14.6 percent lower per capita health care expenditures than otherwise comparable states without such policies.[15] The reduction in medical costs includes both hospital and nonhospital expenditures, which tends to refute the hypothesis of Morrisey et al. (1984) that rate setting results in an unbundling of services. *Unbundling* refers to the practice whereby decision makers shift the production of services from the regulated (hospital) to the unregulated (physician) sector in response to rate setting.

---

[14]The following discussion is based largely on Anderson (1991).

[15]But see Antel, Ohsfeldt, and Becker (1995). Earlier studies that did not control for the endogeneity of rate setting suggest that the percentage effect is much smaller, at about 2.0 to 4.1 percentage points (see Morrisey, Conrad, Shortell, and Cook, 1984). Some empirical evidence (e.g., Romeo, Wagner, and Lee, 1984) has also linked states' prospective payment systems to a slower diffusion of new medical technologies, although the results are too limited to generalize.

The findings of empirical studies focusing on the relation between rate setting and quality of care have been mixed, however. For example, Shortell and Hughes (1988) found a strong association between the stringency of state rate review programs and higher mortality rates among inpatients after holding other determinants of health status constant. Gaumer et al. (1989) report a small adverse impact of rate-setting policies on mortality at the aggregate level but inconsistent effects at the individual state level and no effect of program stringency on mortality. Conversely, a study by Smith, McFall, and Pine (1993) indicates that regulated states had lower mortality rates among Medicare beneficiaries than unregulated states. Finally, a Rand study (e.g., Kahn et al., 1990; Draper et al., 1990) concluded that the Medicare PPS, which can be considered a federal rate-setting program, has contained hospital costs without generally lowering the quality of care for Medicare patients. However, a comparable study by Fitzgerald, Moore, and Dittus (1988) found that the overall care for Medicare patients with hip fracture worsened since the implementation of PPS. Clearly, more studies are needed before we can make any generalizations about the relation between government rate-setting programs and the quality of care.

## Integrated Delivery Systems

As mentioned in Chapter 14, the autonomous, solo-physician clinic, once the mainstay organization in the physician industry, is being gradually replaced by the multi-physician group practice. Interestingly, the hospital industry is undergoing a similar transformation as many formerly independent hospitals are now becoming part of multihospital chains or systems, as discussed earlier in this chapter. These horizontal mergers among individual physician practices and among individual hospitals take place largely because increased market power is sought after or because of economies of scale, economies of scope, and the other cost advantages associated with health care systems, as previously discussed.

Another organizational transformation currently taking place in the health care sector that involves both the hospital and physician industries is the integration of physician practices with hospitals. According to Robinson (1997, p. 6), "The **integrated delivery system (IDS)** combines physicians and hospitals into a vertically integrated organization with a single ownership and structure, a single chain of authority, and a single bottom line." There are basically four types of IDSs: the physician-hospital organization, the management service organization, the foundation model, and the integrated health organization, although other hybrid organizational forms also exist. These alternative physician-hospital arrangements differ in the degree to which risk, governance, revenue and capital, planning, and management are shared (Burns and Thorpe, 1993). An IDS may include nursing homes, home health care units, and an insurance component in addition to physicians and hospitals.

IDSs have developed in large part due to the financial pressure from MCOs, which in recent years exercised their growing monopsony power to control costs. A movement by the government toward fixed payment systems, such as the prospective payment system for hospitals and the resource-based relative value scale system for physicians, also served as an impetus for change (Burns and Thorpe, 1993; Morrisey, Alexander, Burns, and Johnson, 1996).

Why vertically integrated systems are formed is a question that interests economists, among others. Economists generally analyze organizational arrangements through the "conceptual lens" of agency theory and transaction cost economics (Robinson, 1997; Shortell, 1997). **Agency theory** considers the contractual relationships among firms. According to agency theory, the principal, or owner(s), of the firm enters into a multitude of contracts, either implicitly or formally, with other firms or agents who are the suppliers of inputs. Each contract stipulates the input or product that will be provided, the price that will be paid, and other terms of the agreement, such as product quality and time of delivery. Consequently, agency theory regards the firm as a nexus of many contracts. Within the agency model, the firm essentially serves as a facilitator and coordinator of the many contracts and is responsible for transforming the resulting inputs into an output or multiple outputs. The contractual relationships provide the firm with considerable flexibility to switch among input suppliers when better terms of exchange, such as a lower price or better product quality, become available.

But if agency theory perfectly describes the firm, why do we observe some firms producing inputs internally rather than contracting out for them? For example, why do some hospitals possess their own maintenance staffs, MRI facilities, or nursing home units while others contract out for these same services?

**Transaction costs economics** provides a reason why firms choose to produce inputs or services internally rather than contracting out. Transaction costs refer to the costs associated with the negotiating, writing, and enforcing of contracts and includes the costs of searching out the best price and quality. Transaction cost theory considers that many contracts are incomplete because not all possible contingencies can be written into a contract. **Bounded rationality,** especially in the face of uncertainty, is one reason for incomplete contracts. Bounded rationality refers to the limited capacity of the human mind to formulate and solve problems (Williamson, 1985). When contracts are incomplete, some stipulations will require renegotiation. During the renegotiation process, one of the parties may have an advantage and the advantage can lead to **opportunistic behavior.** Opportunistic behavior involves self-interest seeking with guile and allows for strategic behavior or deception. The potential for opportunistic behavior increases the cost of contractual relationships.

As an example, suppose a hospital contracts with a company to repair the masonry around the bricks on the exterior of its buildings for $17,000. The company rents and installs the necessary scaffolding and begins the repairs. Upon closer inspection, however, the repair crew realizes that a good proportion of the repair is unnecessary and informs the hospital administrator. Naturally, the hospital administrator asks how much of the $17,000 will be returned. The contractor relates that the scaffolding must be rented for a minimum of one month. The contractor also mentions that transporting, installing, and disassembling the scaffolding is very costly. As you can see, the contractor is in a good position to practice opportunistic behavior by inflating the cost figures. Who would have thought to stipulate a contingency of that kind in the contract?

Transaction cost theory suggests that firms may sometimes find internal production more efficient than outsourcing due to the relatively high cost of contracting. The theory by itself, however, suggests that firms should continually find it optimal to vertically integrate through greater internal production or by merging with suppliers. Obviously there must be some limiting factors; otherwise, most firms would be immense.

The same agency relationship discussed above places a limiting factor on the size of firms. Like outside contractors, employees and management are bound to the firm through implicit or formal contracts. For instance, employees are expected to show up for work on time and perform well; otherwise, their jobs may be in jeopardy. While ownership of the nonhuman assets gives the firm more control over internal negotiations than external ones (Hart, 1995), greater firm size may lead to higher production costs at some point. As a firm grows physically larger, it becomes increasingly more complex and costly for the owners to monitor the behavior of management and employees. Inefficient behavior may arise as a result of the high monitoring costs.

For example, consider the large corporation where the principal is represented by the stockholders, and the chief executive officer (CEO) serves as the primary agent. Stockholders, wishing high dividends and stock value appreciation, want the CEO to maximize profits. The CEO, however, may attempt to pursue goals other than maximum profits, especially when he or she is paid a fixed salary. For instance, the CEO may use some of the firm's profit to pay for plush office accommodations, a limousine, or various other expensive perquisites. Alternatively, the CEO may be more interested in empire building and, therefore, may acquire several other unprofitable companies rather than maximize profits. As a result, the corporation may perform poorly because of the CEO's actions. The CEO, however, may blame general economic conditions, and, therefore, the unknowing stockholders may not punish the CEO for the unprofitable behavior.[16]

As another example, salaried employees, particularly when they work as a team, may shirk their responsibilities, engage in on-the-job leisure time, and free-ride on the productive efforts of others. If a sufficient number of those on the team behave similarly, team output suffers and profits decline. The larger the organization, the greater the cost of monitoring the efforts of management and employees because of the proportionately greater interactions among workers (Carlton and Perloff, 1994).

To prevent internal agents, such as CEOs or employees, from operating in an unproductive manner, agency theory suggests that compensation might be tied to performance or profits so as to align the interests of the principal and agents. For instance, the CEO's pay may be linked to the profits or stock value of the company. CEOs often receive bonus pay and stock options as part of their total compensation for that reason. The contracts help to align the interests of the principal and agents so the interests of the principal are better served. It is important to note, however, that

---

[16]This possibility was alluded to in Chapter 10 when we discussed the implications of the utility maximization models. When the ownership constraint is weak, managers may maximize their own personal utilities, which are partly derived from the five Ps of increased pay, perquisites, power, prestige, and patronage.

employment contracts are not always complete, so inefficient behavior may result as the firm continues to produce increasingly more services internally rather than purchasing them in the marketplace. Organizational independence, in contrast to internal production, preserves the risk and rewards for efficient performance (Robinson, 1997).

As another limit on firm size, managerial diseconomies may set in as the firm gets too large because of bounded rationality. Managers at the top may lose sight of the production process taking place at the floor level. Communication flows from top to bottom may break down. Bureaucratic inertia may also set in as regimentation replaces innovation and risk-taking is not properly rewarded. The loss of control, breakdowns in communication, and loss of innovativeness may all place limits on the size of the firm.

As long as decision makers act rationally, each firm can be expected to choose that size where marginal benefit equals marginal cost. A greater amount of internal production creates benefits because of reduced transaction costs but also may come at a cost as larger firms become more costly and complex to monitor and innovation suffers. The costs of contracting and monitoring differ from firm to firm and from industry to industry. Some firms find market exchange more efficient than internal production at the margin. Transaction costs depend on various factors, such as the degree of market uncertainty, the number of suppliers in the market, and how often the service or input must be obtained. In general, when market conditions are more uncertain, the number of suppliers is fewer and frequency of use is greater, transaction costs are greater, and internal production becomes more efficient.

You are probably asking yourself how the discussion on agency theory and transaction cost economics relates to physician-hospital integration. Hospitals and physician practices vertically integrate or fail to vertically integrate for the same reasons as other organizations do. Vertical integration leads to lower transaction costs but can impose incentive problems in large organizations. Robinson (1997) expands upon this theme by noting that a contractual relationship between a hospital and physicians can be thought of as **virtual integration.** The term *virtual integration* is just a convenient way of stating that a combination of two or more organizations takes place through contractual relationships rather than through unified ownership. Robinson goes on to compare the relative advantages of vertical and virtual integration with regard to coordination, governance, and clinical innovation, three key activities in a hospital-physician relationship. Shortell (1997) condenses Robinson's analysis into a convenient diagram, which is presented in figure 15–1.

*Coordination* deals with how the individual parts are woven into an overall productive unit. For example, are the various services that combine to form medical care, such as lab tests, imaging, physician care and inpatient hospital services, all coordinated through one large, unified structure or through two or perhaps more contractual relationships? At the extreme, authority and induced loyalty and commitment might be used to coordinate care in a unified model, while negotiation may be relied upon in a purely contractual network (Robinson, 1997; Shortell, 1997). For instance, a hospital may offer to process the bills of a physician or purchase and then rent a medical facility to a physician as a way of achieving better coordination

| FIGURE 15–1 | CONTINUUM OF ORGANIZATIONAL ARRANGEMENTS |

| Key Activity | Vertical | | Virtual |
| --- | --- | --- | --- |
| Coordination | Unified ownership | ←——→ | Contracts |
| Governance | Centralized nonprofit boards | ←——→ | Decentralized for-profit boards |
| Clinical innovation | Hospitals and physicians joined in salary and equity models | ←——→ | Arms-length relationship with IPAs and physician organizations |

SOURCE: Stephen M. Shortell, "Physician-Hospital Integration and the Economic Theory of the Firm: Comment," *Medical Care Research and Review* 54 (March 1997), p. 27. Reprinted with the permission of Sage Publishers.

through contracting. As another example, hospital and physician services might be better coordinated by allowing more physicians to serve on the hospital's board of trustees.

*Governance* considers who controls the firm's policies and how much flexibility the firm has to adapt and modify its policies when confronted with changing external events. An important aspect of governance is whether the decision-making process is centralized or decentralized and whether it is dependent on for-profit or not-for-profit objectives. Decentralized governance tends to provide more flexibility, but vertical arrangements between decentralized for-profit and not-for-profit organizations may not last because of a clash of missions (e.g., the virtual integration of a Catholic hospital with a physician practice providing abortion services).

*Clinical innovation* is a function of the entrepreneurial, risk-taking spirit. At the one extreme, virtual integration involves arm's length agreements with little sharing of financial risks. At the other extreme, vertical integration, hospitals and physician groups might jointly share in the financial risks of the organization through an ownership stake. One issue here is how the resulting organizational arrangement affects the incentive of the firm to minimize costs and undertake innovative activities. For example, Robinson (1997) notes when "physicians sell their practices and merge into larger systems, they risk losing the entrepreneurial, risk-taking spirit and developing the civil service mentality of the hospital employee" (p. 17). The incentive attenuation might be overcome, however, by providing the physician with an ownership stake in the larger system or by paying performance-based compensation.

Shortell (1997) points out that vertical and virtual arrangements can be thought of as a continuum with respect to the essential activities of coordination, governance, and clinical innovation. Not very often in the real world is integration truly at either extreme but somewhere along the virtual-vertical continuum. Along the coordination continuum, for instance, a corporate joint venture falls somewhere in the middle of contracts and unified ownership. Under a joint venture, a hospital and physician group might remain legally separated but agree to jointly coordinate some single type of patient care, for example. A joint task force or committee represents an intermediate governance structure. A Physician Hospital Organization, where a hospital and physicians jointly own and operate ambulatory care projects or jointly act as an agent for managed-care contracts, provides an example of an organizational structure that falls halfway along the clinical innovation continuum.

Shortell further notes that organizations position themselves along the various continuums depending on the demands of the local marketplace for a coordinated health care system, the organization's own capabilities, and the historical context of the organization. For example, if the local market demands a perfectly seamless, coordinated health care system, the unified ownership of vertical integration will be favored over the contractual relationship.

Many analysts anticipate that IDSs will lead to improved financial performance for hospitals as well as encourage greater quality of care through coordinated delivery systems. Much attention has been directed toward IDSs in the popular press and professional journals. As a result it is surprising to learn that only about 23 percent of all hospitals participated in some kind of physician-hospital arrangement in 1993 (Morrisey, Alexander, Burns, and Johnson, 1996). It is also surprising to learn that studies have failed to find any systematic evidence linking IDSs with greater financial performance (Goes and Zhan, 1995). Perhaps, as managed care continues to evolve, more physicians and hospitals will be pressured into forming vertically integrated systems. As integrated relationships concerning governance, clinical innovation, and coordination develop and mature, the strongest links should survive. We may then observe better financial performance in IDSs.

### Summary of the Conduct of the Hospital Services Market

A number of structural and related factors simultaneously influence the conduct of hospitals in the marketplace. The degree of actual competition, barriers to entry, reimbursement practices of third-party payers, and hospital objectives jointly affect how an individual hospital behaves, and therefore only carefully conceived studies can sort out how any one individual factor in isolation influences hospital conduct. Most empirical studies using data prior to 1983 have found that hospitals competed on the basis of quality rather than price, but recent evidence suggests that the growing price consciousness among health care payers may be causing increased price competition among hospitals.

Empirical evidence also suggests that efficiency differences are quite small among nonprofit, public, and for-profit hospitals after controlling for quality and case-mix differences. The reason cited for the similarity is that physicians act as residual claimants in not-for-profit hospitals and thus ensure that the hospitals behave as efficiently as possible. The provision of indigent care has been found to be considerably higher in public hospitals than in otherwise identical nonprofit and for-profit hospitals. In addition, the amount of indigent care has been found to be quite similar in voluntary and for-profit hospitals, raising doubt about the desirability of the tax-exempt status generally conferred on nonprofit hospitals.

MCOs appear to offer modest hospital cost savings without reducing the quality of patient outcomes compared to traditional fee-for-service medicine. HMOs and UR appear to provide more consistent cost savings than PPOs, however. As consumers become more price conscious and the hospital market becomes more competitive, increased cost savings may result from a managed-care environment. State rate review programs have also proven effective in containing hospital care costs. However, studies investigating the effect of state rate review policies on the quality of hospital outcomes have failed to reach a definitive conclusion.

Finally, MCOs and fixed reimbursement methods have motivated some hospitals and physician practices to form integrated delivery systems. IDSs involve either vertical or virtual (contractual) integration. Vertical integration may offer cost-savings by reducing the transaction costs associated with external market exchanges. Vertical integration can lead to higher operating costs as monitoring costs rise, communication flows break down, or innovation suffers in large corporations. To date, empirical studies have uncovered mixed results regarding improved financial performance in IDSs.

# The Performance of the Hospital Services Industry

This final section focuses on the overall performance of the hospital services industry by assessing the growth of hospital expenditures, the hospital inflation rate, and hospital input utilization in the aggregate. While it might be best to analyze the performance of the hospital industry in each state or, perhaps, in each metropolitan area in the United States given the structural diversity of hospital markets, the analysis would be unwieldy and the necessary data are less widely available at a disaggregated level. As a result, we examine and discuss various hospital pricing and utilization trends over time to get some idea about the overall or aggregate performance of the hospital services industry in the United States.

## The Growth in Hospital Expenditures

Hospital expenditures equal the sum of expenditures on inpatient and outpatient services. As table 15–7 reveals, hospital expenditures were $9.3 billion in 1960, increasing by well over 3,000 percent in nominal terms to $358.5 billion in 1996. On an annual basis, hospital expenditures grew in excess of 10 percent from 1960 to 1991. As a percentage of gross domestic product, hospital spending increased from 1.8 percent in 1960 to 4.8 percent in 1991. These figures imply that a continually rising share of the nation's income has been siphoned off to pay for hospital care in the United States and that hospital spending has grown considerably in both absolute and relative terms.

The encouraging news is that hospital expenditure growth has slowed in more recent times and hospital spending has stabilized as a percentage of gross domestic

| TABLE 15-7 | HOSPITAL EXPENDITURES IN THE UNITED STATES, SELECTED YEARS, 1960–1996 | | |
|---|---|---|---|
| Year | Total Hospital Expenditures (billions of dollars) | Average Annual Change from Previous Period | Spending as a Percentage of Gross Domestic Product |
| 1960 | $9.3 | — | 1.8% |
| 1970 | 28.0 | 11.7% | 2.7 |
| 1980 | 102.7 | 13.9 | 3.7 |
| 1990 | 256.4 | 9.6 | 4.4 |
| 1991 | 282.3 | 10.1 | 4.8 |
| 1992 | 305.3 | 8.1 | 4.9 |
| 1993 | 323.0 | 8.0 | 4.9 |
| 1994 | 335.7 | 3.4 | 4.8 |
| 1995 | 346.7 | 3.3 | 4.8 |
| 1996 | 358.5 | 3.4 | 4.7 |

SOURCE: Katherine R. Levit et al., "National Health Expenditures, 1996," *Health Care Financing Review* 19 (fall 1997), Tables 9 and 13.

product. Specifically, hospital expenditure growth has slowed since 1991, falling to under 4 percent per year in 1994, 1995, and 1996. In addition, hospital expenditures as a percentage of gross domestic product have stabilized at about 4.8 percent since 1991. Many analysts cite the increased enrollment in MCOs as the reason behind the slower growth of hospital expenditures. If so, the interesting question is whether hospital expenditures will continue to grow slowly or, at some point, begin to rise rapidly, as the one-time impact of managed care tapers off.

Hospital expenditures equal the product of the price and quantity of hospital services. As yet, we do not know whether the change in hospital expenditures over time is attributable to higher price changes, an increased quantity of services, or a combination of the two factors. This is an important consideration because, first, a greater quantity of hospital services makes people better off, whereas price increases have the opposite effect of reducing real incomes and consumer welfare. Second, as mentioned earlier, various structural elements of health care markets, such as extensive third-party coverage, may give rise to the overproduction of hospital services at the expense of all other goods and services and thereby result in allocative inefficiency. Thus, to get a better understanding of hospital expenditure growth, we next examine trends in various measures of hospital price and output.

| TABLE 15-8 | HOSPITAL PRICE INFLATION TREND IN THE UNITED STATES, 1980–1997 | |

| Year | General Inflation Rate (urban consumers) | Hospital Services Inflation Rate (urban consumers) |
|---|---|---|
| 1980 | 12.4% | 14.5% |
| 1981 | 8.9 | 14.8 |
| 1982 | 3.8 | 12.6 |
| 1983 | 3.8 | 10.4 |
| 1984 | 4.0 | 7.6 |
| 1985 | 3.8 | 5.0 |
| 1986 | 1.2 | 7.3 |
| 1987 | 4.4 | 7.0 |
| 1988 | 4.4 | 11.0 |
| 1989 | 4.6 | 11.3 |
| 1990 | 6.3 | 11.4 |
| 1991 | 3.0 | 8.9 |
| 1992 | 3.0 | 8.8 |
| 1993 | 2.8 | 7.6 |
| 1994 | 2.6 | 5.5 |
| 1995 | 2.6 | 4.5 |
| 1996 | 3.3 | 4.1 |
| 1997 | 1.7 | 3.2 |

SOURCE: U.S. Department of Labor, Bureau of Labor Statistics, *CPI Detailed Report* (various issues) or http://stats.bls.gov.

## The Hospital Services Price Inflation Rate

The intangible nature of hospital services makes it very difficult to decompose hospital expenditures into price and quantity components. The Bureau of Labor Statistics (BLS) collects data from hospitals to construct a hospital and related services price index. Effective January 1997, the BLS regards the entire hospital visit as the relevant output of hospitals and therefore includes all the individual components, such as the number of days in a hospital room, inpatient treatment, and outpatient procedures, that make up a hospital visit. BLS also now uses the reimbursed or transaction price rather than the list price when calculating the hospital and related services price index.

Table 15–8 lists the economywide inflation rate as measured by the percentage change in the urban consumer price index and the hospital services inflation rate over the period 1980 to 1997. The data have several implications. First, the data suggest that the hospital services inflation rate exceeded the general price inflation rate in every year over the 18-year span. Second, the hospital sector experienced double-digit inflation rates seven times throughout the 18-year period, unlike the entire economy, which faced double-digit inflation only once. The recession of the early 1980s helped to bring inflationary pressures down in both the health sector and the macroeconomy. Third, despite the introduction of the Medicare PPS system and other public and private cost containment practices after 1983, hospital prices continued to rise more quickly than the prices of other goods. While there was a small dip in the hospital services inflation rate to an annual average of 6.7 percent from 1984 through 1987, the average annual rate jumped to 7.6 percent during the period 1988 through 1997, returning to a double-digit level in 1988, 1989, and 1990. Thus, rising hospital prices do not reflect well on the success of cost containment measures in the hospital sector. Finally, the hospital services inflation rate of 3.2 percent in 1997, while at the lowest level since 1980, was still almost double the economywide inflation rate of 1.7 percent.

One problem with the hospital price data is that they are based on list rather than actual charges, although the BLS has made some adjustments recently. Dranove, Shanley, and White (1991) point out that a growing number of patients have been enrolling in various types of MCOs over time. The MCOs negotiate discounts from list prices, and, with rising membership, the size of the discounts has been increasing, widening the gap between list and transaction prices. In fact, these authors and Fisher (1992) found that list price inflation has greatly exceeded actual inflation, by a factor of 2, over recent years. The findings may have broad implications for evaluating not only inflation but also the impact of cost containment strategies.

Measurement errors aside, the time-series data for the hospital services inflation rate suggest that hospital prices have risen more quickly than most other prices in the U.S. economy over the last decade. Unfortunately, the data cannot identify the source of the relative price increase in the hospital sector. Lack of a profit motive, fee-for-service medicine, first-dollar insurance coverage, quality competition, and unbridled hospital pricing power could all conceivably contribute to the relatively high and rising hospital inflation rate in the United States.

However, the normal functioning of a market economy can also provide an explanation for rising hospital prices. That is, relative prices normally rise for goods and services that become more highly valued or more costly to produce than others. Information on marginal social benefit and cost is needed before one can determine whether or not hospital services are efficiently produced. Unfortunately, the marginal benefit and cost of hospital services are difficult to estimate. Therefore, we must resort to analyzing information about input usage and hospital utilization to indirectly identify trends in the output performance of hospitals. We do so in the next section.

## Hospital Input Usage and Utilization

Table 15–9 depicts the hospital staffing ratio (number of full-time equivalent personnel per weighted sum of outpatients and inpatients), occupancy rate (average daily

| TABLE 15-9 | COMMUNITY HOSPITAL INPUTS AND UTILIZATION TRENDS IN THE UNITED STATES, SELECTED YEARS, 1975–1996 |
| --- | --- |

| Year | Hospital Staffing Ratio | Occupancy Rate (%) | Admission Rate (per 100 population) | Average Length of Stay (days) | Outpatient Visits (per 100 population) |
| --- | --- | --- | --- | --- | --- |
| 1975 | 2.98 | 74.9% | 15.5 | 7.7 | 88.3 |
| 1980 | 3.34 | 75.6 | 15.9 | 7.6 | 88.8 |
| 1981 | 3.47 | 76.1 | 15.8 | 7.6 | 88.2 |
| 1982 | 3.53 | 75.3 | 15.7 | 7.6 | 106.9 |
| 1983 | 3.57 | 73.6 | 15.4 | 7.6 | 89.6 |
| 1984 | 3.67 | 69.0 | 14.9 | 7.3 | 89.7 |
| 1985 | 3.85 | 64.9 | 14.0 | 7.1 | 91.7 |
| 1986 | 3.92 | 64.3 | 13.5 | 7.1 | 96.4 |
| 1987 | 4.00 | 64.9 | 13.0 | 7.2 | 101.1 |
| 1988 | 4.04 | 65.5 | 12.8 | 7.2 | 109.8 |
| 1989 | 4.11 | 66.2 | 12.6 | 7.2 | 115.5 |
| 1990 | 4.17 | 66.8 | 12.5 | 7.2 | 120.6 |
| 1991 | 4.27 | 66.1 | 12.3 | 7.2 | 127.5 |
| 1992 | 4.36 | 65.6 | 12.1 | 7.1 | 136.4 |
| 1993 | 4.41 | 64.4 | 11.9 | 7.0 | 142.1 |
| 1994 | 4.54 | 62.9 | 11.8 | 6.8 | 147.9 |
| 1995 | 4.58 | 62.8 | 11.8 | 6.5 | 158.2 |
| 1996 | 4.66 | 61.5 | 11.7 | 6.2 | 166.2 |

SOURCE: American Hospital Association, *Hospital Statistics* (Chicago: AHA, 1998), Table 1.

inpatients per bed), admission rate per 100 population, average length of stay (average days per patient), and outpatient visits per 100 population in acute inpatient care institutions in the United States over the period 1975 to 1996. The first two indicators are intended to represent input usage, and the last three are proxy measures for the quantity or utilization of hospital output.

The data show a number of systematic trends. For one, the hospital staffing ratio increased throughout the period 1975 to 1996, rising from approximately 3 to nearly 5 full-time equivalent employees per patient. The higher staffing ratio may reflect the more severely ill patients resulting from the Medicare PPS, since less-sickly patients are now unlikely to be admitted into hospitals. On the other hand, the greater staffing ratio may represent the expense preferences of hospital administrators. Alternatively, the higher staffing ratio may signify the continuing ability of hospitals to generate revenues to support their nonprofit, human service orientation toward providing more services to patients (Pope and Menke, 1990).

Figures for the hospital occupancy rate point to a similar conclusion regarding rising input usage. While fluctuating around 75 percent in the late 1970s and early 1980s, the average occupancy rate at U.S. hospitals declined from its highest level of around 76 percent in 1981 to about 62 percent in 1996. The decline in the occupancy rate began one year before the Medicare PPS in 1983. The implication is one of excess beds at the typical American hospital. According to Anders (1993b), these beds are not cheap; each costs about $30,000 to $40,000 a year in maintenance, staffing, and depreciation charges.[17] With about 200,000 unnecessary beds in the nation, the aggregate cost of excess bed capacity runs about $6 billion to $8 billion a year.

Data for the hospital admission rate show an interesting trend. The hospital admission rate hovered near 16 per 100 population from 1975 to 1982. Thereafter the rate fell and equaled 11.7 admissions per 100 population in 1996. The decline in the admission rate has surprised some health policy analysts who expected an increase in the admission rate with the advent of the Medicare PPS because reimbursement under this system is based on a per-case charge. Others argue that the reduced hospital admission rate was inevitable as health care providers substituted for inpatient care with less regulated outpatient and nursing home care.

Figures for the average length of stay (ALOS) show a pattern similar to that for the admission rate, roughly constant at 7.6 days in the years preceding the Medicare PPS. After that point, the ALOS fell precipitously to 7.1 days in 1985 and then leveled off through 1990. From 1991 to 1996, the ALOS fell further from 7.2 to 6.2 days. The reduction in length of stay was predicted as hospitals responded to the per-case charge of the Medicare PPS. A portion of the reduction in the hospital admission rate and length of stay shows up in the higher outpatient visit rate over time in the United States. The outpatient visit rate continually increased since 1983 from nearly 90 to 166 outpatient visits per 100 population in 1996, a growth of more than 6 percent per year.

In sum, table 15–9 indicates that each year since 1983, a smaller percentage of people have been admitted into hospitals, and those admitted typically stay for a shorter duration. Also, hospital occupancy rates have fallen but staffing ratios continue to climb, in part to provide more services to more severely ill inpatients and to provide increased outpatient services. Health policy analysts have questioned whether the increased services provided to inpatients and outpatients are inappropriately supplied. Let us examine that question in more detail.

**Do Hospitals Provide Inappropriate Care?** The supplier-induced demand theory, as discussed in Chapter 10, predicts that health care providers may unnecessarily

---

[17]However, see Friedman and Pauly (1981), who estimated that the excess bed cost is about one-tenth of those figures. Gaynor and Anderson (1995) find evidence supporting the figures above, whereas Keeler and Ying (1996) indicate that the cost of excess bed capacity is much greater, at about $25 billion in 1993.

provide various diagnostic and therapeutic services to patients due to the associated financial gain. With this theory and rising health care costs in mind, a number of studies have attempted to determine whether various types of medical services are inappropriately provided to patients. One of the first studies, by Chassin et al. (1987), measured how appropriately physicians performed coronary angiography, carotid endarterectomy, and upper gastrointestinal (GI) tract endoscopy for the Medicare population in 1981 in several areas of the United States.[18] A panel of physicians was selected to rate a number of indications or clinical settings, each consisting of a unique combination of clinical information and other factors considered in recommending treatment, with respect to the appropriateness of each procedure.[19] *Appropriateness* was defined to mean that the expected health benefits (prolonged life, relief of pain, and cure of disease) of a procedure exceed its expected negative consequences (operative mortality, complications, pain, and anxiety) by a sufficiently wide margin. Only medical appropriateness was considered; the monetary costs of the procedure were ignored.

The authors found significant levels of inappropriate use: 17 percent of the cases for coronary angiography, 32 percent for carotid endarterectomy, and 17 percent for upper GI tract endoscopy. Uncertain use rates for these three services were 9, 32, and 11 percent, respectively. Similarly, Winslow et al. (1988), using data for 1979, 1980, and 1982, found an inappropriate rate of 14 percent and an uncertain rate of 30 percent for coronary artery bypass graft surgery. These two studies have been widely cited as offering concrete evidence that a large number of medical services are provided unnecessarily in U.S. hospitals.

Three studies using data for 1990 have raised serious doubt about whether medical services are inappropriately provided. Specifically, Leape et al. (1993), Hilborne et al. (1993), and Bernstein et al. (1993) found very low inappropriate rates for coronary bypass graft surgery (2.4 percent), coronary angioplasty (4 percent), and coronary angiography (4 percent) in a sample of New York hospitals. While the uncertain rate was also low for coronary artery bypass surgery (7 percent), the authors expressed some concern that the uncertain rates for coronary angioplasty and angiography were quite high at 38 and 20 percent, respectively. The authors of these three studies point to changing practice patterns and the regulatory environment in New York as possible reasons for the large differences in the two sets of studies.

**The Concentration of Health Care Expenditures**  Related to the concern over the provision of unnecessary medical care is the concentration of health care spending among a small minority of the U.S. population. Table 15–10 identifies the manner in which health care expenditures are concentrated among the top users of medical care services. According to the figures, 1 percent of the U.S. population

---

[18]The areas studied were Arkansas, Colorado, Iowa, Massachusetts, Montana, Pennsylvania, South Carolina, and northern California. Coronary angiography is an X-ray study of the inside of the heart. Carotid endarterectomy is the removal of the core of the carotid artery, a blood vessel beginning at the large artery of the heart (aorta) and running straight up through the neck, that has become thickened by fatty deposits. Upper gastrointestinal tract endoscopy is an examination of the inside of the body from the mouth to the stomach with a lighting device.

[19]An *indication* is a reason to prescribe a medication or perform a treatment.

| TABLE 15-10 | CONCENTRATION OF HEALTH EXPENDITURES BY THE U.S. POPULATION, SELECTED YEARS, 1970–1987 | | | |
|---|---|---|---|---|
| **Percentage of U.S. Population Ranked by Expenditures** | **1970** | **1977** | **1980** | **1987** |
| Top 1% | 26% | 27% | 29% | 30% |
| Top 2% | 35 | 38 | 39 | 41 |
| Top 5% | 50 | 55 | 55 | 58 |
| Top 10% | 66 | 70 | 70 | 72 |
| Top 30% | 88 | 90 | 90 | 91 |
| Top 50% | 96 | 97 | 96 | 97 |
| Bottom 50% | 4 | 3 | 4 | 3 |

SOURCE: Marc L. Berk and Alan C. Monheit, "The Concentration of Health Expenditures: An Update." *Health Affairs* 11 (winter 1992), Exhibit 1.

accounted for 26 percent of all health care spending in 1970. The top 5 percent was responsible for one-half of all health care spending in the United States in the same year. By 1987, the distribution had become even more concentrated, with the top 5 percent accounting for 58 percent of all health care spending and the top 1 percent accounting for 30 percent. The fact that the distribution of health care expenditures is concentrated among a small fraction of people should not be surprising given that the major users of health care services are severely ill patients receiving high-cost critical care in hospitals. In fact, it has been estimated that one in every seven health care dollars is spent during the last six months of someone's life (Clark, 1992). Data also suggest that 18.8 percent of Medicare patients accounted for 81 percent of all Medicare expenditures in 1991 (Iglehart, 1992). The dilemma, as Aaron (1991) notes, is that successful cost containment may "require rationing of services to the very ill"[20] (p. 53).

---

[20]However, Emanuel and Emanuel (1994) estimate that greater use of advanced directives (e.g., living wills), hospice care, and less aggressive interventions at the end of life will save only 3.3 percent of health care costs. Among the reasons they cite, even less aggressive humane care at the end of life is labor intensive and costly to produce.

## The Relative Performance of Hospitals in the United States and Canada

Because per capita health care expenditures were about 45 percent less in Canada than in the United States in 1990, a number of studies have examined whether variations in hospital performance account for some of the cost differential between the two countries. Using data from 1987, Redelmeier and Fuchs (1993) discovered that costs per hospital admission were 39 percent higher in the United States than in Canada. Moreover, when hospitals in California and Ontario were compared, costs were found to be 63 percent higher in the state than in the province.

These investigators then examined the factors responsible for the higher costs per hospital admission in the United States. While the United States had proportionately fewer hospital beds, fewer admissions, and a shorter mean length of stay than Canada, higher hospital costs were explained partly by a more complex case-mix and slightly higher input prices. However, the real reason for the cost disparity appeared to be a greater amount of resources used per hospital admission in the United States. Higher administrative costs (Woolhandler and Himmelstein, 1991) and the greater decentralization of equipment and personnel in the United States account for the greater use of hospital resources. Specifically, Redelmeier and Fuchs note that U.S. care is scattered among many small community hospitals that often operate far below capacity, unlike in Canada, where care is centralized at large, heavily used hospitals. For example, they point out that the lithotripsy machine at Canada's Wellesley hospital is used nearly 50 times per week, whereas the average use of a similar lithotripsy machine is less than one-tenth that amount at the Stanford University Medical Center.[1]

Interestingly, the greater use of resources in American hospitals does not appear to lead to more favorable health outcomes. For example, Rouleau et al. (1993) found that patients' mortality rates and likelihood of a second heart attack were virtually identical in the two countries, even though U.S. doctors are twice as likely to do heart bypasses and angioplasties as their Canadian counterparts. Echoing these findings, Roos et al. (1992) determined that postsurgical mortality was lower in Manitoba, Canada, than in New England for most of the medical procedures they studied. Consequently, the various studies, taken together, tend to provide convincing evidence that some valuable resource savings might accrue if the United States were to adopt a more centralized hospital system, such as Canada's, without a serious sacrifice of health outcomes.

[1]Haber et al. (1992) reached a similar conclusion that the quantity of inputs and nature of output account for the relatively higher hospital costs in the United States.

## SUMMARY

Hospital expenditures represent the largest component of health care spending, accounting for over 5 percent of U.S. gross domestic product. Without a doubt, any realistic cost containment policies must be directed at the hospital sector of the health economy. The hospital services industry is best characterized as oligopolistic in nature. In most markets there are a few competing hospitals, with existing hospitals generally having a cost advantage over new ones due to learning curve economies. Combined with sophisticated product offerings and patient price inelasticity, hospitals have some ability to raise price above the competitive level and produce with inefficient methods.

Countervailing the ability of hospitals to raise price is the dominance of some third-party payers in the market for hospital services. Government and large insurers, along with managed-care organizations, are beginning to flex their market clout to negotiate price discounts and influence production practices with utilization review and various "at-risk" reimbursement methods. By and large, studies have found that both managed care and government price regulations are able to contain hospital costs at the micro level. In addition, recent studies have found evidence suggesting a decline in the inappropriate use of hospital services.

Despite these changes, hospital care prices and costs continue to rise in the aggregate. Whether the aggregate hospital price and expenditure increase is due to imperfect hospital markets or normal market forces remains to be determined. We must keep in mind, however, that a noncompetitive market structure predicts only higher prices and not continual increases in prices. The only way inflation can be associated with market structure is if the market were to become increasingly monopolistic over time, but that does not appear to be the case (Baumol, 1988). Some health policy analysts want the federal government to encourage increased competition in the entire health sector so that macro-level cost savings are realizable. Others look to government to adopt blanket regulations, such as an "all-payer" Medicare PPS, as a way to contain aggregate hospital care costs. The merits of market-based and government-based solutions continue to be debated.

## Review Questions and Problems

1. Answer the following questions on the number, size distribution, and ownership of American community hospitals.

   *a.* What has happened to the number of community hospitals and beds since the 1980s? Using the demand theory developed in Chapter 4, what reasons can you think of for that change?

   *b.* Which is the dominant form of hospital ownership? What percentage of community beds were owned by for-profit, nonprofit, and public hospitals in 1996? Rank the average for-profit, nonprofit, and public hospital in terms of bed size.

   *c.* Within which particular bed size category do most hospitals operate?

2. Explain how the relevant product market is typically defined for community hospitals. Why? How is the relevant geographical market defined? Why?

3. Suppose desired excess capacity is 15 percent, population equals 1 million, the average length of stay equals eight days, the admission to population ratio is .15, and the minimum efficient scale is 200 beds. Calculate the optimal number of hospitals. Now suppose that, due to a growing elderly population, the admission to population ratio increases to .20 and the average length of stay increases to 10 days. Recalculate the optimal number of hospitals.

4. Assume there are 10 equally sized hospitals in a market area. Calculate the Herfindahl-Hirschman index. Two hospitals in the market area inform the Department of Justice that they wish to merge. According to the current DOJ Merger Guidelines, will the merger be contested? Explain.

5. What are some possible sources of barriers to entry into the hospital industry? What has the literature concluded about the severity of these barriers?

6. Compare and contrast the technique and results associated with the econometric and survivor techniques of determining long-run economies of scale in the hospital services industry.

7. Answer the following questions on the buyers of hospital services.

    *a.* Who is the largest buyer of hospital services?

    *b.* What percentage of hospital costs are paid directly by the consumer?

    *c.* What factors affect the willingness of private third-party payers to negotiate for low hospital prices?

8. What are some of the different ways third-party payers have reimbursed hospitals? Which methods are considered to constitute "at-risk" payments?

9. Studies using data prior to 1983 found that increased hospital competition led to higher hospital prices. How do researchers explain that result? What have more recent studies concluded about the relation between competition and prices in the hospital industry? Why has this change occurred?

10. Explain the property rights and public choice theories concerning how differences in ownership affect the costs of producing hospital services. Why do empirical studies tend to find few cost differences among the various hospital ownership types?

11. According to empirical studies, what effect do managed-care programs have on the costs of producing hospital services? How has managed care affected the quality of care according to studies?

12. According to empirical studies, what effect do state rate review regulations have on the costs of producing hospital services? How have state rate review regulations affected the quality of care?

13. Why may vertically integrated delivery systems lead to lower production costs? Why may these systems lead to higher costs? Use agency theory and transaction cost economics in your explanations.

14. Answer the following questions on the aggregate performance of the hospital sector by filling in the blanks.

    *a.* Hospital expenditures as a fraction of GDP were _____ in 1960 and increased to _____ by 1996.

    *b.* Since 1980, the hospital inflation rate has _____ the general inflation rate in every year.

    *c.* The hospital price inflation rate may be overstated because it is determined by list prices rather than _____ prices and growing _____ in _____ has created a widening wedge between the two.

    *d.* Since 1982, the hospital occupancy rate, admission rate, and average length of stay have tended to_____. The hospital staffing ratio has tended to _____. (Why?)

15. Discuss the general conclusions researchers have reached concerning the provision of inappropriate hospital services.

16. Explain what studies have found concerning the concentration of health care expenditures. What may that finding mean in terms of serious cost containment efforts?

## References

Aaron, Henry J. *Serious and Unstable Condition: Financing America's Health Care.* Washington, DC: The Brookings Institution, 1991.

American Hospital Association. *Hospital Statistics.* Chicago: AHA, 1998.

Anders, George. "Medical Luxury: Hospital Beds Go High-Tech, and Some Cost As Much As a Car." *The Wall Street Journal,* May 6, 1993a, p. A1.

———. "As Outpatient Care Gains, Communities Need to Trim Their Excess Hospital Beds." *The Wall Street Journal,* February 22, 1993b, p. B1.

Anderson, Gerard F. "All-Payer Ratesetting: Down but Not Out." *Health Care Financing Review* (annual supplement, 1991), pp. 35–41.

Antel, John J., Robert L. Ohsfeldt, and Edmund R. Becker. "State Regulation and Hospital Costs." *Review of Economics and Statistics* 77 (August 1995), pp. 416–22.

Bailit, Howard L., and Cary Sennett. "Utilization Management as a Cost-Containment Strategy." *Health Care Financing Review* (annual supplement, 1991), pp. 87–93.

Baker, Jonathan B. "The Antitrust Analysis of Hospital Mergers and the Transformation of the Hospital Industry." *Law and Contemporary Problems* 51 (spring 1988), pp. 93–164.

Baumol, William J. "Containing Medical Costs: Why Price Controls Won't Work." *Public Interest* 93 (fall 1988), pp. 37–53.

Bays, Carson W. "The Determinants of Hospital Size: A Survivor Analysis." *Applied Economics* 18 (1986), pp. 359–77.

Berk, Marc L., and Alan C. Monheit. "The Concentration of Health Expenditures: An Update." *Health Affairs* 11 (winter 1992), pp. 145–49.

Bernstein, Steven J., et al. "The Appropriateness of Use of Coronary Angiography in New York State." *Journal of the American Medical Association* 269 (February 10, 1993), pp. 766–69.

Bradbury, R. C., Joseph H. Golec, and Frank E. Stearns. "Comparing Hospital Length of Stay in Independent Practice Association HMOs and Traditional Insurance Programs." *Inquiry* 28 (spring 1991), pp. 87–93.

Burda, David. "Flurry of Merger Plans Has Eyes Focused on Iowa." *Modern Healthcare* (April 12, 1993), p. 24.

Burns, Lawton R., and Darrell P. Thorpe. "Trends and Models in Physician-Hospital Organization." *Health Care Management Review* 18 (fall 1993), pp. 7–20.

Carlisle, David M., et al. "HMO vs. Fee-for-Service Care of Older Persons with Acute Myocardial Infarction." *American Journal of Public Health* 82 (December 1992), pp. 1626–30.

Carlton, Dennis W., and Jeffrey M. Perloff. *Modern Industrial Organization.* Addison-Wesley, 1994.

Chassin, Mark R., et al. "Does Inappropriate Use Explain Geographic Variations in the Use of Health Care Services?" *Journal of the American Medical Association* 258 (November 13, 1987), pp. 2533–37.

Clark, Nicola. "The High Costs of Dying." *The Wall Street Journal,* February 22, 1992, p. A16.

Coelen, C., and D. Sullivan. "An Analysis of the Effects of Prospective Reimbursement Programs on Hospital Expenditures." *Health Care Financing Review* 2, no. 3 (1981), pp. 1–40.

Congressional Budget Office. *Impact of PSROs on Health-Care Costs: Update of CBO's 1979 Evaluation.* Washington, DC: U.S. Government Printing Office, 1981.

Conover, Christopher J., and Frank A. Sloan. "Does Removing Certificate of Need Regulations Lead to a Surge in Health Care Spending?" *Journal of Health Politics, Policy, and Law* 23 (June 1998), pp. 456–81.

Cowing, Thomas G., Alphonse G. Holtmann, and S. Powers. "Hospital Cost Analysis: A Survey and Evaluation of Recent Studies." In *Advances in Health Economics and Health Services Research,* vol. 4, edited by Richard M. Scheffler and Louis F. Rossiter, Greenwich, CT: JAI Press, 1983, pp. 257–303.

Cowing, Thomas G., and Alphonse G. Holtmann. "Multiproduct Short-Run Hospital Cost Functions: Empirical Evidence and Policy Implications from Cross-Section Data." *Southern Economic Journal* (January 1983), pp. 637–53.

Diehr, Paula, et al. "Use of a Preferred Provider Plan by Employees of the City of Seattle." *Medical Care* 28 (November 1990), pp. 1073–88.

Dowd, B. R., Roger Feldman, Stephen Cassou, and Michael Finch. "Health Plan Choice and the Utilization of Health Care Services." *Review of Economics and Statistics* 73 (February 1991), pp. 85–93.

Dranove, David, Mark Shanley, and Carol Simon. "Is Hospital Competition Wasteful?" *Rand Journal of Economics* 23 (summer 1992), pp. 247–62.

Dranove, David, Mark Shanley, and William D. White. "Price and Concentration in Hospital Markets: The Switch from Patient-Driven to Payer-Driven Competition." *Journal of Law and Economics* 36 (April 1993), pp. 179–204.

———. "How Fast Are Hospital Prices Really Rising?" *Medical Care* 29 (August 1991), pp. 690–96.

Draper, D., et al. "Studying the Effects of the DRG-based Prospective Payment System on the Quality of Care: Design, Sampling, and Fieldwork." *Journal of the American Medical Association* 264 (October 17, 1990), pp. 1956–61.

Duffy, Sarah Q. "Do Competitive Hospitals Really Adopt Technology Faster? An Analysis of the Influence of Alternative Relevant Market Definitions." *Eastern Economic Journal* 18 (spring 1992), pp. 187–208.

Eakin, B. Kelly, and Thomas J. Kniesner. "Estimating a Non-minimum Cost Function for Hospitals." *Southern Economic Journal* (January 1988), pp. 583–97.

Elzinga, K. G., and T. F. Hogarty. "The Problem of Geographic Market Definition Revisited: The Case of Coal." *Antitrust Bulletin* 23 (1978), pp. 1–18.

Emanuel, Ezekiel J., and Linda L. Emanuel. "The Economics of Dying: The Illusion of Cost Savings at the End of Life." *New England Journal of Medicine* 330 (February 24, 1994), pp. 540–44.

Ermann, Dan. "Hospital Utilization Review: Past Experience, Future Directions." *Journal of Health Politics, Policy and Law* 13 (winter 1988), pp. 683–704.

Ermann, Dan, and Jon Gabel. "Multihospital Systems: Issues and Empirical Findings." *Health Affairs* 3 (spring 1984), pp. 50–64.

Farley, Dean E. *Competition among Hospitals: Market Structure and Its Relation to Utilization, Costs and Financial Position.* Research note 7, Hospital Studies Program, National Center for Health Services Research and Health Care Technology Assessment, 1985.

Farley, Dean E., and Ronald J. Ozminkowski. "Volume-Outcome Relationships and Inhospital Mortality: The Effect of Changes in Volume over Time." *Medical Care* 30 (January 1992), pp. 77–94.

Feldman, R., et al. "Effects of HMOs on the Creation of Competitive Markets for Hospital Services." *Journal of Health Economics* 9 (September 1990), pp. 207–22.

Feldman, Roger, John Kralewski, Janet Shapiro, and Hung-Ching Chan. "Contracts between Hospitals and Health Maintenance Organizations." *Health Care Management Review* 15, no. 1 (winter 1990), pp. 47–60.

Feldstein, Paul J., T. M. Wickizer, and J. R. Wheeler. "Private Cost Containment: The Effects of Utilization Review Programs on Health Care Use and Expenditures." *New England Journal of Medicine* 318 (May 19, 1988), pp. 1310–14.

Fielding, Jonathan E., and Thomas Rice. "Can Managed Competition Solve the Problems of Market Failure?" *Health Affairs* 12 (supplement, 1993), pp. 216–28.

Fisher, Charles R. "Trends in Total Hospital Financial Performance under the Prospective Payment System." *Health Care Financing Review* 13 (spring 1992), pp. 1–16.

Fitzgerald, John F., Patricia S. Moore, and Robert S. Dittus. "The Care of Elderly Patients with Hip Fracture: Changes Since Implementation of the Prospective Payment System." *New England Journal of Medicine* (November 24, 1988), pp. 1392–97.

Fournier, Gary M., and Jean M. Mitchell. "Hospital Costs and Competition for Services: A Multiproduct Analysis." *Review of Economics and Statistics* (November 1992), pp. 627–34.

Frech, H. E., III. "Comments on Antitrust Issues." In *Advances in Health Economics and Health Services Research*, vol. 7, edited by Richard M. Scheffler and Louis F. Rossiter. Greenwich, CT: JAI Press, 1987, pp. 263–67.

Friedman, Bernard, and Mark Pauly. "Cost Functions for a Service Firm with Variable Quality and Stochastic Demand: The Case of Hospitals." *Review of Economics and Statistics* 63 (November 1981), pp. 620–24.

Garnick, Deborah W., et al. "Services and Charges by PPO Physicians for PPO and Indemnity Patients: An Episode of Care Comparison." *Medical Care* 28 (October 1990), pp. 894–906.

Gaumer, Gary L., et al. "Effects of State Prospective Reimbursement Programs on Hospital Mortality." *Medical Care* 27 (July 1989), pp. 724–36.

Gaynor, Martin, and Gerard F. Anderson. "Uncertain Demand, the Structure of Hospital Costs, and the Cost of Empty Hospital Beds." *Journal of Health Economics* 14 (1995), pp. 291–317.

Gazmararian, Julie A., and Jeffrey P. Koplan. "Length of Stay After Delivery: Managed Care versus Fee-for-Service." *Health Affairs* 15 (winter 1996), pp. 74–80.

General Accounting Office. *Hospital Costs: Cost Control Efforts at 17 Texas Hospitals.* GAO/AIMD-95–21. Washington, DC, December 1994.

Goes, James B., and Chun Liu Zhan. "The Effects of Hospital-Physician Integration Strategies on Hospital Financial Performance." *Health Services Research* 30 (October 1995), pp. 507–30.

Gold, Marsha R. "HMOs and Managed Care." *Health Affairs* 10 (winter 1991), pp. 189–206.

Grannemann, Thomas W., Randall S. Brown, and Mark V. Pauly. "Estimating Hospital Costs: A Multiple-Output Analysis." *Journal of Health Economics* 5 (1986), pp. 107–27.

Gray, James. "The Selling of Medicine, 1986." *Medical Economics* (January 20, 1986), pp. 180–94.

Greenwald, Howard P., and Curtis J. Henke. "HMO Membership, Treatment, and Mortality Risk among Prostatic Cancer Patients." *American Journal of Public Health* 82 (August 1992), pp. 1099–1104.

Haber, Susan G., et al. "Hospital Expenditures in the United States and Canada: Do Hospital Worker Wages Explain the Difference?" *Journal of Health Economics* 11 (December 1992), pp. 453–65.

Hart, Oliver. *Firms, Contracts, and Financial Structure.* Oxford: Clarendon Press, 1995.

Hersch, Philip L. "Competition and the Performance of Hospital Markets." *Review of Industrial Organization* 1 (winter 1984), pp. 324–40.

Herzlinger, Regina E., and William S. Krasker. "Who Profits from Nonprofits?" *Harvard Business Review* (January-February 1987), pp. 93–106.

Hester, James A., AnneMarie Wouters, and Norman Wright. "Evaluation of a Preferred Provider Organization." *The Milbank Quarterly* 65 (1987), pp. 575–613.

Hilborne, Lee H., et al. "The Appropriateness of Use of Percutaneous Transluminal Coronary Angioplasty in New York State." *Journal of the American Medical Association* 269 (February 10, 1993), pp. 761–65.

Hoy, Elizabeth W., Richard E. Curtis, and Thomas Rice. "Change and Growth in Managed Care." *Health Affairs* 10 (winter 1991), pp. 18–36.

Iglehart, John. "The American Health Care System—Medicare Program." *New England Journal of Medicine* 327 (November 12, 1992), pp. 1467–72.

Japsen, Bruce. "Ad Budget Drop." *Modern Healthcare* 27 (February 17, 1997), pp. 70–71.

Joskow, Paul L. "The Effects of Competition and Regulation on Hospital Bed Supply and the Reservation Quality of Hospitals." *Bell Journal of Economics* (autumn 1980), pp. 421–47.

Kahn, K. L., et al. "Comparing Outcomes of Care Before and After Implementation of the DRG-based Prospective Payment System." *Journal of the American Medical Association* 264 (October 17, 1990), pp. 1984–88.

Keeler, Theodore E., and John S. Ying. "Hospital Costs and Excess Bed Capacity: A Statistical Analysis." *Review of Economics and Statistics* 78 (August 1996), pp. 470–81.

Lane, Paul M., and Jay D. Lindquist. "Hospital Choice: A Summary of the Key Empirical and Hypothetical Findings of the 1980s." *Journal of Health Care Marketing* 8 (December 1988), pp. 5–20.

Lanning, Joyce A., Michael A. Morrisey, and Robert L. Ohsfeldt. "Endogenous Hospital Regulation and Its Effects on Hospital and Non-hospital Expenditures." *Journal of Regulatory Economics* 3 (1991), pp. 137–54.

Leape, Lucian L., et al. "The Appropriateness of Use of Coronary Artery Bypass Graft Surgery in New York State." *Journal of the American Medical Association* 269 (February 10, 1993), pp. 753–60.

Levit, Katherine R., et al. "National Health Expenditures, 1996." *Health Care Financing Review* 19 (fall 1997), pp. 161–200.

Luft, Harold S. *Health Maintenance Organizations: Dimensions of Performance.* New York: Wiley-Interscience, 1981.

Luft, Harold S., et al. "The Role of Specialized Clinical Services in Competition among Hospitals." *Inquiry* 23 (spring 1986), pp. 83–94.

Lutz, Sandy. "Charity Care and the Law: Case Is Far from Closed." *Modern Healthcare* (March 8, 1993), pp. 26–28.

Mann, Joyce M., Glenn A. Melnick, Anil Bamezai, and Jack Zwanziger. "A Profile of Uncompensated Hospital Care, 1983–1995." *Health Affairs* 16 (July/August 1997), pp. 223–32.

Manning, Willard G., et al. "A Controlled Trial of the Effect of a Prepaid Group Practice on Use of Services." *New England Journal of Medicine* 310 (June 7, 1984), pp. 1505–10.

McLaughlin, Catherine G. "Market Responses to HMOs: Price Competition or Rivalry." *Inquiry* 25 (summer 1998), pp. 207–18.

McLaughlin, Catherine G. "HMO Growth and Hospital Expenses and Use: A Simultaneous Equations Model." *Health Services Research* 22 (June 1987), pp. 183–205.

Melnick, Glenn A., Jack Zwanziger, Anil Bamezai, and Robert Pattison. "The Effects of Market Structure and Bargaining Position on Hospital Prices." *Journal of Health Economics* 11 (1992), pp. 217–33.

Menke, Terri J. "The Effect of Chain Membership on Hospital Costs." *Health Services Research* 32 (June 1997), pp. 177–96.

Miller, Robert H., and Harold S. Luft. "Managed Care Performance Since 1980: A Literature Analysis." *Journal of the American Medical Association* 271 (May 18, 1994), pp. 1512–19.

Morrisey, Michael A., and Jeffrey A. Alexander. "Hospital Participation in Multihospital Systems." In *Advances in Health Economics and Health Services Research*, vol. 7, edited by Richard M. Scheffler and Louis F. Rossiter. Greenwich, CT: JAI Press, 1987, pp. 59–82.

Morrisey, Michael A., Jeffrey Alexander, Lawton R. Burns, and Victoria Johnson. "Managed Care and Physician/Hospital Integration." *Health Affairs* 15 (winter 1996), pp. 62–73.

Morrisey, Michael A., Douglas A. Conrad, Stephen M. Shortell, and Karen S. Cook. "Hospital Rate Review: A Theory and an Empirical Review." *Journal of Health Economics* 3 (September 1984), pp. 25–47.

Morrisey, Michael A., Gerald J. Wedig, and Mahmud Hassan. "Do Nonprofit Hospitals Pay Their Way?" *Health Affairs* 15 (winter 1996), pp. 132–44.

Noether, Monica. "Competition among Hospitals." *Journal of Health Economics* 7 (1988), pp. 259–84.

———. *Competition among Hospitals*. Washington, DC: Federal Trade Commission, 1987.

Pope, Gregory C., and Terri Menke. "Hospital Labor Markets in the 1980s." *Health Affairs* 9 (winter 1990), pp. 127–37.

Rapoport, John, Stephen Gehlbach, Stanley Lemeshow, and Daniel Teres. "Resource Utilization among Intensive Care Patients: Managed Care vs. Traditional Insurance." *Archives of Internal Medicine* 152 (November 1992), pp. 2207–12.

Redelmeier, Donald A., and Victor R. Fuchs. "Hospital Expenditures in the United States and Canada." *New England Journal of Medicine* 328 (March 18, 1993), pp. 772–78.

Renn, Steven C., Carl J. Schramm, J. Michael Watt, and Robert A. Derzon. "The Effects of Ownership and System Affiliation on the Economic Performance of Hospitals." *Inquiry* 22 (fall 1985), pp. 219–36.

Retchin, Sheldon M., and Barbara Brown. "Elderly Patients with Congestive Heart Failure under Prepaid Care." *American Journal of Medicine* 90 (February 1991), pp. 236–42.

Retchin, Sheldon M., et al. "How the Elderly Fare in HMOs: Outcomes from the Medicare Competition Demonstrations." *Health Services Research* 27 (December 1992), pp. 651–69.

Robinson, James C. "Physician-Hospital Integration and the Economic Theory of the Firm." *Medical Care Research and Review* 54 (March 1997), pp. 3–24.

Robinson, James C., and Harold S. Luft. "The Impact of Hospital Market Structure on Patient Volume, Average Length of Stay, and the Cost of Care." *Journal of Health Economics* 4 (December 1985), pp. 333–56.

Robinson, James C., and Ciaran S. Phibbs. "An Evaluation of Medicaid Selective Contracting in California." *Journal of Health Economics* 8 (February 1990), pp. 437–55.

Romeo, Anthony A., Judith L. Wagner, and Robert H. Lee. "Prospective Reimbursement and the Diffusion of New Technologies in Hospitals." *Journal of Health Economics* 3 (1984), pp. 1–24.

Roos, Leslie L., et al. "Health and Surgical Outcomes in Canada and the U.S." *Health Affairs* 11 (summer 1992), pp. 56–72.

Rouleau, J. L., et al. "A Comparison of Management Patterns after Acute Myocardial Infarction in Canada and the United States." *New England Journal of Medicine* 328 (March 18, 1993), pp. 779–84.

Ruffenach, Glenn. "Firms Use Financial Incentives to Make Employees Seek Lower Health-Care Fees." *The Wall Street Journal*, February 9, 1993, p. B1.

Santerre, Rexford E., and Dana C. Bennett. "Hospital Market Structure and Cost Performance: A Case Study." *Eastern Economic Journal* 18 (spring 1992), pp. 209–19.

Scherer, F. M., and David Ross. *Industrial Market Structure and Economic Performance*. Boston: Houghton Mifflin, 1990.

Schramm, Carl J., and Steven C. Renn. "Hospital Mergers, Market Concentration and the Herfindahl-Hirschman Index." *Emory Law Journal* 33 (fall 1984), pp. 869–88.

Schwartz, William B., and D. N. Mendelson. "Hospital Cost Containment in the 1980s—Hard Lessons Learned and Prospects for the 1990s." *New England Journal of Medicine* 324 (April 11, 1991), pp. 1037–41.

Shortell, Stephen M. "Physician-Hospital Integration and the Economic Theory of the Firm: Comment." *Medical Care Research and Review* 54 (March 1997), pp. 25–31.

Shortell, Stephen M., and Edward F. X. Hughes. "The Effects of Regulation, Competition, and Ownership on Mortality Rates among Hospital Inpatients." *New England Journal of Medicine* 318 (April 28, 1988), pp. 1100–07.

Sloan, Frank A. "Property Rights in the Hospital Industry." In *Health Care in America*, edited by H. E. Frech III, San Francisco: Pacific Research Institute for Public Policy, 1988, pp. 103–41.

Sloan, Frank A., Joseph Valvona, and J. M. Perrin. "Diffusion of Surgical Technology: An Exploratory Study." *Journal of Health Economics* (March 1986), pp. 31–61.

Smith, David W., Stephanie L. McFall, and Michael B. Pine. "State Rate Regulation and Inpatient Mortality Rates." *Inquiry* 30 (spring 1993), pp. 23–33.

Smith, Dean. "The Effects of Preferred Provider Organizations on Health Care Use and Costs." *Inquiry* 34 (winter 1997/98), pp. 278–87.

Stigler, George J. "The Economies of Scale." *Journal of Law and Economics* 1 (October 1958), pp. 54–71.

Stone, Valerie E., George R. Seage, Thomas Hertz, and Arnold M. Epstein. "The Relation between Hospital Experience and Mortality for Patients with AIDS." *Journal of the American Medical Association* 268 (November 18, 1992), pp. 2655–61.

Temin, Peter. "An Economic History of American Hospitals." In *Health Care in America*, edited by H. E. Frech III. San Francisco: Pacific Research Institute for Public Policy, 1988, pp. 75–102.

Thorpe, Kenneth E. "Why Are Urban Hospital Costs So High? The Relative Importance of Patient Source of Admission, Teaching, Competition, and Case Mix." *Health Services Research* 22 (February 1988), pp. 821–36.

Thorpe, Kenneth E., and Charles E. Brecher. "Improved Access for the Uninsured Poor in Large Cities: Do Public Hospitals Make a Difference?" *Journal of Health Politics, Policy and Law* (summer 1987), pp. 313–24.

Vita, Michael G. "Exploring Hospital Production Relationships with Flexible Functional Forms." *Journal of Health Economics* 9 (June 1990), pp. 1–21.

Ware, John E., et al. "Comparison of Health Outcomes at a Health Maintenance Organization with Those of Fee-for-Service Care." *The Lancet* (May 3, 1986), pp. 1017–22.

White, Stephen L. "The Effects of Competition on Hospital Costs in Florida." *Policy Studies Journal* 15 (March 1987), pp. 375–93.

Wilder, R. P., and P. Jacobs. "Antitrust Considerations for Hospital Mergers: Market Definition and Market Concentration." In *Advances in Health Economics and Health Services Research*, edited by Richard M. Scheffler and Louis F. Rossiter, Greenwich, CT: JAI Press, 1987, pp. 245–62.

Williamson, Oliver E. *The Economic Institutions of Capitalism.* New York: Free Press, 1985.

Wilson, George W., and Joseph M. Jadlow. "Competition, Profit Incentives, and Technical Efficiency in the Provision of Nuclear Medicine Services." *Bell Journal of Economics* (autumn 1982), pp. 472–82.

Winslow, Constance Monroe, et al. "The Appropriateness of Performing Coronary Artery Bypass Surgery." *Journal of the American Medical Association* 260 (July 22–29, 1988), pp. 505–09.

Winslow, Ron. "Data Spur Debate on Hospital Quality." *The Wall Street Journal*, May 24, 1990, p. B1.

———. "Cincinnati Firms Cutting Costs with Hospital-Ranking System." *The Wall Street Journal*, April 2, 1993a, p. B1.

———. "Pioneer Project Publishes First Rankings of Cleveland Hospitals." *The Wall Street Journal*, April 29, 1993b, p. B6.

Woolhandler, Steffie, and David U. Himmelstein. "The Deteriorating Administrative Efficiency of the U.S. Health Care System." *New England Journal of Medicine* 324 (May 2, 1991), pp. 1253–58.

Woolley, J. Michael. "The Competitive Effects of Horizontal Mergers in the Hospital Industry." *Journal of Health Economics* 8 (1989), pp. 271–91.

Zellner, B. Bruce, and Barbara L. Wolfe. "HMO Growth and Hospital Expenses: A Correction." *Health Services Research* 24 (August 1989), pp. 409–13.

Zwanziger, Jack, and Rebecca R. Auerbach. "Evaluating PPO Performance Using Prior Expenditure Data." *Medical Care* 29 (February 1991), pp. 142–51.

Zwanziger, Jack, and Glenn A. Melnick. "The Effects of Hospital Competition and the Medicare PPS Program on Hospital Cost Behavior in California." *Journal of Health Economics* 7 (1988), pp. 301–20.

## CEBS Questions

CEBS Sample Question on Subject Matter from CEBS Course IX Study Manual

1. Discuss the amount of charitable care provided by for-profit and nonprofit hospitals. (pages 478–479)

CEBS Sample Exam Questions

1. The supply side of the hospital services industry can be characterized as:
   A. Perfect competition
   B. Oligopoly
   C. Monopolistic competition
   D. Static dynamism
   E. Pure monopoly

2. The Herfindahl-Hirschman index (HHI)
   I. Is a measure of the degree of concentration (monopoly power) in a market
   II. Is used by the Department of Justice in the evaluation of mergers
   III. Has a maximum value of 100 percent
      A. I only
      B. II only
      C. I and II only
      D. II and III only
      E. I, II, and III

3. All the following statements regarding the utilization of hospital services in recent years are correct EXCEPT:
   A. A smaller percentage of the population has been admitted to hospitals
   B. Hospital admissions typically are for a shorter duration
   C. Hospital occupancy rates have fallen
   D. Outpatient visits (per 100 population) have decreased
   E. Staffing ratios in hospitals have increased

*Answer to Sample Question from Study Manual*
Studies show that for-profit and nonprofit hospitals provide close to the same amount of uncompensated care (4.2% and 5.0% percent of expenses, respectively). The fact that hospital costs are fixed and the marginal cost of an additional patient

day is generally low is believed to be the reasons for the for-profit hospitals providing charitable care. The relative low charitable care provided by nonprofit hospitals indicates that the tax-exempt status of these hospitals may be inappropriate. Communities in which the nonprofit hospitals operate may not be receiving sufficient benefits to compensate for their loss of tax revenues.

*Answers to Sample Exam Questions*
1.  B is the answer. Oligopoly is the market term that best describes the hospital services industry. See page 474 of the text.
2.  C is the answer. Both Statements I and II are correct; however, the HHI index has a maximum value of 10,000, which is a market area dominated by one organization See pages 462–463 of the text.
3.  D is the answer. With the decrease in inpatient admissions and shorter length of hospital stays, outpatient visits have increased. See Table 15–9 and text on pages 493–494.

# 16

# The Pharmaceutical Industry

P harmaceutical products provide enormous benefits. Drugs improve quality of life by relieving pain and have significantly reduced deaths from many diseases, including tuberculosis, kidney infection, and hypertension. Pharmaceutical innovations have virtually eliminated such diseases as whooping cough and polio. In addition, drugs often reduce the cost of treating diseases. For instance, the use of tranquilizers has substantially reduced the hospitalization of mental patients (Peltzman, 1974). Weidenbaum (1993) notes that "the cost of treating ulcers with H-2 antagonist drug therapy runs about $900 a year. The cost of ulcer surgery, by contrast, averages $28,900" (p. 87). Clearly pharmaceutical products have played a major role in the advancement of medical treatment.

The research-based pharmaceutical industry as it is known today began with the development of sulfanilamide in the mid-1930s and penicillin in 1938.[1] With World War II came an increased demand for sulfa drugs and penicillin to protect soldiers from infection. The pharmaceutical industry quickly responded by replacing handicraft methods of preparing drugs, traditionally required for individual prescriptions, with mass production techniques (Egan, Higinbotham, and Weston, 1982). Chemical firms, such as Lederle and Merck, found ways to produce drugs in bulk form, which were then transformed into dosage form (e.g., powders and tablets) by drug companies, such as Upjohn. Pfizer developed a fermentation process to allow penicillin to be produced in large quantities. Penicillin was soon followed by other antibiotics, and research was stimulated in other therapeutic fields as well (Statman, 1983).

Following the war, high potential profits generated further innovation and drew other companies into the pharmaceutical industry. Many drug firms

---

[1]Statman (1983) points out that the drug trade is very old. The Ebers Papyrus lists 811 prescriptions used in Egypt in 550 BC.

expanded and acquired sales forces to market their drugs in finished form. Research and development efforts in the pharmaceutical industry continually expanded during the postwar period.

This chapter provides a contemporary analysis of the pharmaceutical industry. Although the pharmaceutical industry of today closely resembles its postwar antecedent in terms of many supply-side characteristics, we will see that several institutional changes on the demand side of the market have had wide-sweeping effects on the conduct of the industry. The chapter studies the structure, conduct, and performance of the pharmaceutical industry. Specifically, it

- Discusses seller concentration, buyer concentration, barriers to entry, and product differentiation to see whether existing drug firms are endowed with some monopoly power.

- Examines some topics pertaining to the conduct of the pharmaceutical industry, including price competition, promotional strategies, and product innovation. The important question concerns the actual degree of price and product competition that presently takes place in this industry.

- Assesses the performance of the contemporary pharmaceutical industry in terms of aggregate prices, output, and profits. The main query here is whether firms in the pharmaceutical industry have tended to charge high prices and earn excess profits.

## The Structure of the Pharmaceutical Industry

### Number and Size Distribution of Sellers

When one thinks of the pharmaceutical industry, only a few large firms, such as Merck, Pfizer, and Upjohn, normally come to mind because they are research-based firms known for producing and selling brand-name pharmaceutical products. Interacting with these and other brand-name pharmaceutical companies, however, are a multitude of lesser known, smaller firms that primarily manufacture and retail generic drugs and place little, if any, emphasis on new-drug research and discovery. Based on the overall number and relative sizes of drug firms, the pharmaceutical industry appears to be highly competitive. Table 16–1 displays some information on the number and size distribution of pharmaceutical companies in 1992. To put the pharmaceutical industry in proper perspective, it also gives comparative information on some other industries. Based on the four-digit Standard Industrial Classification (SIC) code of 2834 for pharmaceutical preparations, 583 firms exist in the U.S. pharmaceutical industry. The largest four firms account for 26 percent of industry output, and the largest eight are responsible for 42 percent. The Herfindahl-Hirschman index of market concentration (HHI) is very low at 341, implying that the pharmaceutical industry contains a considerable number of equally sized firms, especially when compared to many of the other industries in the table.

| TABLE 16–1 | CONCENTRATION RATIOS FOR SELECTED INDUSTRIES, 1992 | | | |

| SIC Code | Industry Description | Four-Firm Ratio | Eight-Firm Ratio | Number of Firms | HHI Index |
|---|---|---|---|---|---|
| 2834 | Pharmaceutical Preparations | 26 | 42 | 583 | 341 |
| 2026 | Fluid Milk | 22 | 30 | 525 | 181 |
| 2043 | Cereal Breakfast Foods | 85 | 98 | 42 | 2253 |
| 2711 | Newspapers | 25 | 37 | 6761 | 241 |
| 2841 | Soap and Detergents | 63 | 77 | 635 | 1584 |
| 2911 | Petroleum Refining | 30 | 49 | 131 | 414 |
| 3011 | Tires and Inner Tubes | 69 | 87 | 114 | 1897 |
| 3221 | Glass Containers | 78 | 89 | 35 | 2126 |
| 3273 | Ready-Mixed Concrete | 6 | 11 | 3249 | 25 |
| 3334 | Primary Aluminum | 59 | 82 | 30 | 1456 |
| 3411 | Metal Cans | 54 | 70 | 161 | 1076 |
| 3552 | Textile Machinery | 21 | 33 | 480 | 197 |
| 3721 | Aircraft | 79 | 93 | 151 | 2717 |

SOURCE: U.S. Bureau of the Census, "Concentration Ratios in Manufacturing," *1992 Census of Manufacturers*, MC92–S–2, table 4.

Data from the *Census of Manufacturers* also suggest that the degree of overall seller concentration in the pharmaceutical industry has remained fairly stable over time. For instance, the four-firm concentration ratio was approximately 28 percent in 1947, 22 percent in 1963, and still only 22 percent by 1987. Compare those figures to the pharmaceutical four-firm concentration ratio of 26 percent that we observe for 1992. Since 1992, the aggregate level of seller concentration may have increased to some degree because of the 19 or more mergers involving relatively large drug companies. Hoffmann-La Roche and Boehringer Mannheim, Glaxo and Burroughs Wellcome, and American Home and American Cyanamid are three recent examples of mergers and acquisitions among major pharmaceutical companies (PhRMA, 1998). Pollard (1990) argues that economies of scale exist in research and marketing. If so, the recent merger wave makes sense as firms attempt to spread their research and marketing costs over a bigger revenue base. In the conduct section of this chapter, we review the empirical evidence concerning firm size and pharmaceutical innovation to see whether research and marketing economies justify the recent mergers.

Pharmaceutical market analysts claim that the four-digit SIC pharmaceutical industry is defined much too broadly for one to draw meaningful conclusions about the level of competition from the concentration ratio or HHI. The four-digit SIC

| TABLE 16–2 | CONCENTRATION RATIOS FOR THERAPEUTIC MARKETS, 1972 |
|---|---|

| Therapeutic Market | Four-Firm Ratio |
|---|---|
| Analgesics | 60% |
| Antacids | 86 |
| Antibacterials | 80 |
| Antibiotics (broad- and medium-spectrum) | 60 |
| Antihistamines | 59 |
| Antiobesity products | 83 |
| Antispasmodics | 57 |
| Ataraxics and tranquilizers | 76 |
| Cardiovasculars | 54 |
| Diabetic therapy | 76 |
| Diuretics | 74 |
| Muscle relaxants | 50 |
| Oral contraceptives | 86 |
| Psychostimulants | 85 |
| Sedatives | 46 |
| Sulfonamides | 81 |

SOURCE: Meir Statman, *Competition in the Pharmaceutical Industry: The Declining Profitability of Drug Innovation.* (Washington, DC: American Enterprise Institute, 1983), table 20.

industry classification contains all drug products despite their intended use. Most drugs, however, are not substitutes in consumption because they treat different illnesses and therefore do not belong in the same relevant product market. For example, a physician looking to relieve a patient's ulcer condition does not choose among various brands of antidepressants and antiulcer drugs. So instead, many point to therapeutic markets as a better way to narrowly define the relevant product market for pharmaceutical goods. Therapeutic markets are designed to include only those drugs that treat common diseases or illnesses. In our example, all antiulcer drugs, such as Tagamet, Zantac, and Pepcid, are included in the same therapeutic or relevant product market.

For example, four-firm concentration ratios for 16 different therapeutic markets in 1972 (the most recent year for which systematic data are available) are shown in table 16–2. According to the data, the lowest four-firm concentration ratio was 46 percent in the sedatives therapeutic market, whereas the highest was 86 percent for

| TABLE 16-3 | TOP THREE DRUGS AS A PERCENTAGE OF TOTAL PRESCRIPTION DRUG SALES, 1992 |
|---|---|

| Company | Percentage |
|---|---|
| Glaxo Inc. | 75% |
| Pfizer | 60 |
| Upjohn | 58 |
| Eli Lilly | 56 |
| SmithKline Beecham | 53 |
| Merck & Co. | 52 |
| Marion Merrell Dow | 50 |
| American Home Products | 32 |
| Johnson & Johnson | 30 |
| Bristol-Myers Squibb | 28 |

SOURCE: Boston Consulting Group, *The Changing Environment for U.S. Pharmaceuticals* (Boston: Boston Consulting Group, 1993), Figure 2–25.

antacids and oral contraceptives. Some more recent data for 1995 suggest that the four-firm concentration ratios were 55 percent and 66 percent for the analgesics (pain-killers) and antacid markets, respectively (Welsch, 1995; Tanouye, 1995). These therapeutic market concentration ratios are much higher than those observed above for the aggregate pharmaceutical market. This implies that only a few major drugs normally compete within a typical therapeutic market. Thus, seller concentration ratios based on therapeutic markets paint a more monopolistic view of the pharmaceutical industry.

One reason for the high seller concentration ratios in therapeutic markets is that firms tend to make most of their profits from one or a few key drugs. These key drugs are often protected from competition by legal patents or trademarked brand names, as we will see. Table 16–3 lists the percentage of total drug sales accounted for by the three best-selling drugs at 10 of the largest U.S. pharmaceutical companies in 1992. The figures show that 75 percent of Glaxo's sales came from three drugs. Glaxo's antiulcer drug, Zantac, with sales of $3.5 billion in fiscal year 1993, represented nearly half the company's sales (Bishop, 1994). Similarly, Pfizer received 60 percent of its sales from its top three drugs. Seven of these 10 large pharmaceutical companies derived at least 50 percent of sales from their three best-selling products.

## The Buyer Side of the Pharmaceutical Market

In contrast to the concentrated nature of the seller side of many therapeutic markets, the buyer side is very fragmented. To see why this is so, consider table 16–4, which

| TABLE 16-4 | BUYERS OF PHARMACEUTICAL PRODUCTS, 1996 | |
|---|---|---|
| **Source** | **Expenditures (billions of dollars)** | **Percentage of Total** |
| Total | $91.4 | 100.0% |
| All private | 78.1 | 85.4 |
| Out-of-pocket | 50.3 | 55.0 |
| Private insurance | 27.8 | 30.4 |
| All government | 13.3 | 14.5 |
| Federal | 7.5 | 8.2 |
| State | 5.8 | 6.3 |

Note: Includes spending on drugs and other medical nondurables. Percentages do not sum to 100 percent due to rounding.

SOURCE: Katherine R. Levit et al., "National Health Expenditures, 1996," *Health Care Financing Review* 19 (fall 1997), Table 11.

lists the main purchasers of pharmaceutical products in 1996. Unlike spending on hospital and physician services, a large percentage of drug expenditures is paid directly by consumers. Out-of-pocket expenses amount to $50.3 billion and represent over one-half of all pharmaceutical (and other nondurable medical) expenditures. Private insurance is the next largest buyer of ethical drugs, accounting for roughly 30 percent of all pharmaceutical spending. Government purchases explain the remaining 14.5 percent of the $91 billion spent on pharmaceutical products in 1996. It is worth noting that pharmaceutical expenditures represented 8.8 percent of all health care spending and 1.2 percent of GDP in 1996.

**The Realized Demand for Pharmaceutical Products**   Although consumers are responsible for footing most of the drug bill, they generally are not responsible for making the choice concerning which specific drug to buy. Since the passage of the Federal Food, Drug and Cosmetic Act of 1938, consumer access to powerful drugs has been severely restricted (Temin, 1992). The 1938 act gave drug manufacturers the responsibility to assign new drugs to either of two classes: over-the-counter (OTC) or prescription (Rx).[2] Directions for use on the label make a drug available for self-medication. A prescription-only warning makes a drug available only by a physician's prescription. The Food and Drug Administration has to approve the manufacturer's proposed label.

---

[2]According to the *Henry Holt Encyclopedia of Word and Phrase Origins*, "Rx. The Latin 'recipere,' 'take this,' provides the R in the symbol Rx used by pharmacists for centuries, while the slant across the R's leg is a sign of the Roman god Jupiter, patron of medicine. The symbol looks like Rx and is pronounced that way."

**INSIGHT 16–1**

## Orphan Drugs and the Salami-Slicing Problem

In 1983, Congress passed the Orphan Drug Act to stimulate the development of "orphan drugs." Orphan drugs treat rare diseases, and pharmaceutical companies have little incentive to produce them because development costs are too high and/or potential markets are too small to make such ventures profitable.

If the Food and Drug Administration (FDA) determines that a particular drug should be considered an orphan, the company that holds the patent receives two major incentives from the government. First, the company may be awarded tax credits for up to 50 percent of the drug development costs. Second, the firm is awarded the exclusive right to market the drug for seven years. The intent is to stimulate the development of drugs necessary to treat rare diseases. According to PhRMA (1998), 140 orphan drugs have been approved under the Orphan Drug Act as of 1996.

The orphan drug policy has come under criticism because some believe pharmaceutical companies are undermining the program by earning excess profits. For example, in the mid-1980s, the FDA designated AZT (azidothymedine) an orphan drug. AZT is used in the treatment of AIDS (acquired immunodeficiency syndrome), and Burroughs Wellcome, a British pharmaceutical company, holds the exclusive patent on it in the United States. In 1986, patients were paying approximately $10,000 a year for the drug and Burroughs was earning a substantial economic profit. The firm came under fire from various activist groups and the U.S. government for taking advantage of its monopoly position and charging too much for AZT. This pressure led Burroughs to reduce the price of AZT to $6,400 in 1989.

Others claim that drug companies misuse the program by misrepresenting their data so that a drug is granted orphan status by the FDA. To be designated as an orphan, a drug must be used to treat a rare disease that afflicts fewer than 200,000 people. Many drugs treating more than 200,000 people in total, however, have been granted orphan status. By presenting evidence to the FDA regarding only one of the many possible uses for a particular drug, a company can set its target market for that particular "use" of a drug at fewer than 200,000 people. In fact, an imaginative company could simultaneously develop several orphan-type uses for a given drug. Thus, a designated orphan drug may treat a number of diseases with a total combined market well in excess of 200,000 people. This practice is commonly referred to as "salami slicing." Instead of presenting the whole salami, the drug company presents only a small slice at a time to receive the incentives provided under the orphan drug program.

Tregarthen (1992) claims that Biogen Incorporated has been very successful at salami slicing. The company received orphan status for a drug called f-IFN-beta to treat metastatic renal cell carcinoma. Two months later, the same drug was granted orphan designation in the treatment of cutaneous malignant melanoma. Approximately two weeks after that, the drug was again given orphan status for the treatment of cutaneous T-cell lymphoma. Still later, this drug was given orphan status for the treatment of two more rare diseases.[1] As you might imagine, the total number of prospective patients for this drug exceeds the 200,000 maximum limit set by the FDA.

Congress is currently looking into this problem and hopes to pass legislation to curb the abuses. The objective is to stimulate the discovery of drugs for rare diseases but at the same time limit the monopoly power firms receive from orphan protection for those drugs that turn out to be big money makers.

SOURCE: Based on Suzanne Tregarthen, "Prescription to Stop Drug Companies' Profiteering," *The Wall Street Journal*, March 5, 1992, p. A15.

[1]According to the *Mosby Medical Encyclopedia* (1992), a carcinoma is a cancerous tumor that starts with the cells covering inner and outer body surfaces. Melanoma is skin cancer of which there are various types. Lymphoma is a tumor of the lymphoid tissue. Lymphoid tissue is netlike and holds lymphocytes, a type of white blood cell, in its spaces

Because prescription drugs remain the dominant type sold today, the "realized demands for pharmaceuticals depend not only on ultimate consumer tastes but also on the behavior of physicians who prescribe these drugs and the retail and hospital pharmacists who dispense the prescriptions" (Caves, Whinston, and Hurwitz, 1991, p. 4). Physicians are not always in a position to serve the best financial interests of consumers, primarily because they are unaffected financially by the choice of prescription and often lack suitable information about the price, effectiveness, and risk of substitute drug products (Temin, 1980). Moreover, customary prescribing behavior minimizes effort and also provides a legal defense if a malpractice suit arises. Custom tends to favor high-priced, brand-name pharmaceutical products, especially because the "trademarked *brandname* attached to a pioneering product by the innovator is short, and easier to remember than its *generic name*, which in turn is a shorter, simpler version of the *chemical name* that describes the molecular structure of the active chemical entity to scientists" (Caves, Whinston, and Hurwitz, 1991, p. 5).

The point is that physicians are responsible for prescribing medicines, yet lack a financial incentive to make cost-effective choices. The result is often the selection of a high-priced, brand-name drug when an equally effective lower-priced generic is available. Back in the 1950s, cost-effective buying was even less common than it is today because states had enacted antisubstitution laws that prevented pharmacists from substituting lower-priced but therapeutically equivalent generics for brand-name drugs. Antisubstitution laws required pharmacists to fill prescriptions as written, precluding the dispensing of a lower-priced substitute when the physician had specified a brand-name product.

By 1984, the last of the antisubstitution laws was repealed (Caves, Whinston, and Hurwitz, 1991). Pharmacists are now permitted to substitute generic products on prescriptions written for brand-name drugs. According to Carroll and Wolfgang (1991), "while consumers and prescribers have the legal right to request or deny substitution, for the great majority of prescriptions they leave choice to the pharmacists. Thus, for the most part, pharmacists determine the extent to which generic substitution will occur" (p. 110). Grabowski and Vernon (1986) point out that generic products generally provide higher profit margins to pharmacists, suggesting that pharmacists face a financial incentive to substitute bioequivalent generic drugs for brand-name drugs. According to Caves, Whinston, and Hurwitz (1991), generic substitution increased remarkably from 5 to 29 percent of brand-written, multisource prescriptions over the period 1980 to 1989.[3] Estimates indicate that the generics' share of the U.S. pharmaceutical market is now about 44 percent (PhRMA, 1998). Temin reports that when explicitly choosing between brand names and generics, pharmacists divide their choices 60 to 40 in favor of brand-name drugs (Caves, Whinston, and Hurwitz, 1991). Some of the reasons for pharmacists' slanted preferences toward brand-name products become apparent in Insight 16–2.

**Third-Party Influences on the Demand for Pharmaceutical Products** Many third-party payers have turned to formularies, drug utilization review, and required

---

[3] A **single-source drug** is normally covered by a patent. A **multisource drug** is available from a number of suppliers.

**INSIGHT 16-2**

## What Factors Influence the Drug Substitution Practices of Pharmacists?

Obviously consumers pay lower prescription prices when pharmacists dispense low-priced generic drugs instead of high-priced brand-name drugs. Economic theory suggests that the substitution practices of pharmacists depend on relative costs and benefits. As we saw in Chapter 1, an activity, X, takes place when its expected benefit, $B^*(X)$, exceeds its expected cost, $C^*(X)$. Expected benefit (cost) takes into account both the probability of occurrence and the magnitude of the gain (loss).

Carroll and Wolfgang (1991) point out that the dispensing of generic drugs may provide pharmacists with time, financial, psychological, and social benefits. In terms of time benefits, the lower prices associated with generic drugs may mean less time spent dealing with consumer complaints about prescription prices. Pharmacists might derive financial benefits from substituting generic drugs, since they yield larger profit margins. Additional financial benefits may arise if lower generic prices promote greater consumer loyalty. Psychological benefits reflect the satisfaction pharmacists may receive when saving customers money. Finally, the dispensing of a product other than the one prescribed by the physician may provide pharmacists with the social benefit of an enhanced professional status.

Pharmacists may also incur certain costs when they dispense generic substitutes. In particular, Carroll and Wolfgang note that there exists the potential for financial, time, psychological, performance, and social costs associated with the dispensing of generic drugs. The financial costs reflect the likelihood that a lawsuit will result from substituting a generic drug. Time costs arise if generic drugs involve more time spent communicating with the patient. Psychological costs accrue from any worries about generic drug quality, while performance costs emanate from the increased use of generic drugs that are not bioequivalent. Social costs reflect the possibility of a diminished role for pharmacists if they continually dispense generic

substitutes and physicians react by specifying "dispense as written" more frequently.

To assess the relative importance of these various costs and benefits associated with generic substitution, Carroll and Wolfgang collected data via a mail questionnaire from 401 pharmacists. The questionnaire contained a list of 24 multiple-source, frequently prescribed brand-name drugs. Pharmacists were asked about their willingness to substitute with generic drugs, including items to assess the probability and importance (or magnitude) of the various types of costs and benefits associated with generic substitution.

The authors found that pharmacists' perceptions of costs and benefits of generic substitution significantly influenced their substitution decisions. Pharmacists perceived that the greatest benefit of generic substitution comes from dimensions relating to cost savings (financial and psychological benefits). Pharmacists expected highly probable and important benefits from increased profits and from feeling good about saving customers money. Pharmacists who faced greater expected benefits were more likely to engage in generic substitution.

Pharmacists anticipated the most losses from dimensions relating to product quality (performance and psychological costs). Those pharmacists who expected higher costs were less likely to substitute. Pharmacists believed that financial losses from legal liability were important but improbable. Social losses were also considered unlikely.

Carroll and Wolfgang concluded that efforts to increase the incidence of generic substitution should focus on the quality and monetary savings of generic drugs, since these two factors tend to influence pharmacists' willingness to substitute. The authors argued that better information about the comparability of generic drugs, higher dispensing fees for generic products, and elimination of laws requiring pharmacists to pass on cost savings to consumers should all create a greater incentive for generic substitution.

generic substitution as ways to control the decisions of prescription-writing physicians or pharmacists and rein in pharmaceutical costs. A **formulary** is a list of selected pharmaceutical products that physicians are required to prescribe. The listed drugs are thought to be medically effective and reasonably priced. Virtually all hospitals use formularies. A majority of HMOs and a large percentage of PPOs also use formularies to restrict choice and control costs of pharmaceuticals (Boston Consulting Group, 1993). In 1990, about 20 states had formularies that either restrict drugs from Medicaid reimbursement or require a physician to obtain approval before prescribing certain medications (Moore and Newman, 1993).

Like hospital utilization review, **drug utilization review** is designed to monitor the actions of physicians. By monitoring, third-party payers can ensure that physicians follow the formulary and can single out physicians who inappropriately prescribe medicines. More than 80 percent of all HMOs employ mandatory utilization review (PhRMA, 1998). Third-party payers also sometimes require that pharmacists substitute lower-priced generic products for higher-priced brand-name products whenever medically possible. Seventy percent of HMOs mandate that their pharmacists substitute generics for branded prescriptions whenever possible (PhRMA, 1998).

The federal Maximum Allowable Cost (MAC) program, which began in 1974, also mandates drug substitution in government health programs, such as Medicare and Medicaid. The MAC program limits reimbursement for multiple-source drugs to the lowest cost at which chemically equivalent drugs are generally available, plus a reasonable fee for dispensing a drug (Schwartzman, 1976). If a doctor prescribes a specified drug whose price exceeds the MAC price, the pharmacist can obtain reimbursement only for the MAC price unless the doctor certifies in writing that the drug is medically necessary. Such certification entitles the pharmacist to full reimbursement. Otherwise, the pharmacist must bill the patient for the difference between the price of the drug and MAC reimbursement (Schwartzman, 1976).

Two laws enacted during the 1990s by the federal government effectively impose price controls on drugs sold to Medicaid patients and federal agencies (Price Waterhouse, 1993). First, under the Omnibus Budget Reconciliation Act of 1990, federal matching subsidies are granted to state Medicaid programs only for drugs covered by a manufacturer rebate agreement. The rebate agreement normally contains both a basic and an additional component. The basic rebate per unit dispensed is the difference between the average manufacturer price and the "best price" for a drug, the latter being the lowest price charged to any other private or government buyer. There is also a minimum basic rebate equaling about 15 percent of the average manufacturer price. The additional rebate per unit dispensed equals the excess of the increase in the average manufacturer price over the increase in the urban consumer price index since September 1990.

The second federal law affecting pharmaceutical prices is the Veterans Health Care Act of 1992, which influences the price federal agencies, such as the Veterans Administration and the Department of Defense, pay for pharmaceutical goods. The act mandates that drug manufacturers enter into pricing agreements with the Federal Supply Schedule, the Veterans Administration depot, and the Department of Defense depot as a condition for conducting business with the federal government. The price of a branded drug purchased under these agreements must be no higher than 76 percent of the nonfederal average manufacturer's price during the most recent year. In addition, any increase in the price of a prescription drug is limited to the increase in the urban consumer price index.

The intent behind both the Medicaid rebate scheme and the Veterans Health Care Act is to reduce the prices the federal government pays for pharmaceutical goods as a way to control drug costs. One unintended consequence of these laws is that drug manufacturers may be forced to raise their prices to nonfederal buyers to maintain profits. If so, the federal government is merely shifting the drug cost burden to other buyers.

In sum, consumers pay high out-of-pocket costs for pharmaceutical products, yet exert only a very small influence over the choice and prices of prescription products. Physicians, pharmacists, and third-party payers have more control over the ultimate choice and price paid. Recent changes, such as required substitution, formulary restrictions, and drug utilization review, suggest that the buyer side of the market has become more cost conscious for those drugs paid by a third-party payer. Changes such as these most likely increase the elasticity of demand for any one company's pharmaceutical product and make the seller side of the market more price competitive, especially as more and more individuals enroll in MCOs.

### Barriers to Entry

Economic theory suggests that barriers to entry prevent potential competition and confer monopoly status on pharmaceutical companies. Three types of barriers to entry into the pharmaceutical industry are typically cited. The first and most effective source is a *government patent* that gives the innovating firm the right to be the sole producer of a drug product for a legal maximum of 20 years.[4] The argument is that a patent is necessary to protect the economic profits of the innovating firm over some time period. Otherwise, easy imitation, lower prices, and smaller profits reduce the financial incentive for firms to undertake risky and costly, but socially valuable, research and development activities. The economic rationale underlying the patent system is that even though the patent confers monopoly power on the innovator, the monopoly restriction of output is better than having no product at all. That is, the new drug might not be introduced on the market if not for the patent protection; thus, some of the drug is better than none.

Patent protection does not guarantee that the company will remain perfectly insulated from competition. Lu and Comanor (1994) observe that a pharmaceutical patent is granted for a new drug's *chemical composition*, not its *therapeutic novelty*. This means a new drug may receive patent protection because of a different chemical composition even though it treats the same disease that an established, already patented drug does. For example, SmithKline held a patent on its antiulcer drug, Tagamet,

---

[4] The legal patient period was changed from 17 to 20 years in 1996.

until May 1994. Prior to patent expiration, SmithKline faced competition from Glaxo's Zantac and Merck's Pepcid, which are also antiulcer drugs but have different chemical compositions. In fact, while Tagamet was first to market and was the world's biggest-selling drug at one point, Glaxo's Zantac took over as drug leader for more than six years. While Zantac was considered less of a scientific breakthrough, it was marketed more aggressively (Moore, 1993). Thus, a legal patent does not guarantee a monopoly position. The entry of new brand-name drugs expands the choices of physicians and provides competition for an established drug with a similar indication.[5]

Another point concerning a legal patent is that its effective duration is often less than 20 years because the FDA takes a number of years to approve a product for commercial introduction. With the passage of the Drug Price Competition and Patent Term Restoration Act of 1984 (Waxman-Hatch Act), the effective life of a new drug patent is extended by a maximum of 5 years, but not beyond 14 years of effective life, if it can be shown that the FDA delayed its introduction into the market by at least that amount of time.

The Waxman-Hatch Act not only increased the effective patent life of new drugs but also quickened the approval process for generic drugs. No longer must producers of generic drugs prove safety and effectiveness; they need only show that the generic is bioequivalent to a brand-name drug (i.e., contains the same active ingredient[s]). Consequently, the act has made it easier for generics to enter pharmaceutical product markets once the patent period expires. Partly in response to this act and to third-party pressure for drug cost control, the generic share of prescriptions increased sharply from 19 percent in 1984 to over 44 percent by 1997 (PhRMA, 1998). Overall, the impact of the Waxman-Hatch Act is interesting. On the one hand, it increased the monopoly power of the drug innovator by extending the effective patent life. On the other hand, the Act enhanced postpatent competition by reducing the cost of generic entry.

The second type of barrier to entry into the pharmaceutical industry is a **first-mover** or **brand loyalty advantage** (Schmalensee, 1982). A drug innovator can usually acquire and maintain a first-mover advantage because the quality of a substitute generic product is generally unknown and requires one to experience it. Generic drugs can be considered experience goods because consumers normally lack the knowledge they need to judge or experience the drugs' quality. Physicians have little time or financial incentive to seek out information about the efficacy and risk of new generic products. Furthermore, the cost of a bad consumption experience can be particularly harmful in terms of a prolonged illness, adverse side effect, or malpractice suit when switching from a known brand name to an unknown generic drug (Scherer and Ross, 1990). Therefore, unless a generic drug offers different and important therapeutic advantages or a very large discount, physicians and consumers, when faced

---

[5]According to the *Mosby Medical Encyclopedia* (1992), "an indication is a reason to prescribe a medication or perform a treatment, as a bacterial infection may be an indication for prescribing a specific antibiotic or as appendicitis is an indication for appendectomy" (p. 411).

with the choice, are reluctant to choose generic over brand-name drugs after the patents expire.

Many industrial organization economists believe that a first-mover advantage confers monopoly power on the innovator of a new product. A first-mover advantage allows pioneer firms to charge high prices and maintain a dominant market share even after the expiration of a patent. McRae and Tapon (1985) write,

> Being first on the market with a new product or process enhances a firm's image; in many industries, this enhanced image may be further exploited after patent expiry through the continued promotion of brand names. To the extent that consumer preference schemes give a market advantage to pioneering brands, it appears that the trademark protection of brand names effectively replaces patent protection after 17 years. *De facto*, the combination of patent and trademark protection may produce a composite entry barrier which extends indefinitely into the future (p. 44).

It is because of a first-mover advantage that McRae and Tapon found that compulsory licensing of patented pharmaceuticals was not sufficient to induce more competition in the Canadian pharmaceutical industry. **Compulsory licensing** means that a firm is given legal permission to import or manufacture a patented drug if it pays a stipulated royalty rate (of 4 percent in Canada) to the patent holder. Despite the effective elimination of the patent barrier through the compulsory licensing program, the market power of first entrants, in terms of high prices and market shares, declined only modestly over a six-year period in Quebec. The authors attribute that finding to the high postpatent barrier associated with first-mover brand loyalty.

Finally, *control over a key input*, such as a specific chemical or active ingredient, can also make it difficult for new firms to enter a drug market (Ballance, Pogany, and Forstner, 1992). New competitors require access to the input, and the originating firm may sell it to the new entrants only if it is profitable to do so. If it is not, and replication is difficult or costly, new firms may find it unprofitable to enter the industry.

In sum, significant barriers to entry exist in the pharmaceutical industry. Legal patents and brand names may give entrenched firms an advantage over potential entrants. Theoretically, the advantage translates into monopoly power and the ability to maintain market share despite high prices. FDA approval lags reduce the effective patent life, but brand-name recognition typically increases the effective monopoly period for a drug product.[6]

---

[6]Schwartzman (1976) also examined economies of scale in pharmaceutical manufacturing, promotion, and research and development as barriers to entry. While Schwartzman found no evidence supporting manufacturing economies, he noted that larger firms tend to be associated with promotion and R&D economies. These two economies make it harder for small potential competitors, but not large ones, to compete with entrenched pharmaceutical companies. This and other studies on research economies are taken up in the conduct section.

## Consumer Information and the Role of the FDA

As with most medical goods and services, a substantial amount of technical knowledge is necessary to judge a pharmaceutical product. Because pharmaceutical products are experience goods, or in some cases credence goods, they are difficult to evaluate on an a priori basis. Consumers therefore face some risk when directly purchasing pharmaceutical products. Temin (1980) points to three types of risk. First, there is the risk associated with overpaying or receiving a pharmaceutical product of inferior quality. Second, an adverse reaction to a drug may lead to sickness or death. Third, a consumer may purchase the wrong drug or take the wrong dosage and therefore fail to recover from an illness or injury.

In the early 1930s, before prescription-only pharmaceuticals became the norm, drug products were less complex and were limited mainly to anti-infection drugs. Thus, self-medication was more feasible during that time period. Today, however, many substitute drugs are available to treat any given disease, and some are associated with adverse side effects for certain patients. Others cannot be used in conjunction with other drugs or alcoholic beverages. It is not surprising that physicians, as experts, are assigned the role of prescribing most medicines to consumers as a way to reduce consumer risks.

The FDA also plays an important role in protecting consumers from the risks associated with drug purchases. In addition to determining whether drugs should be assigned over-the-counter or prescription status, the FDA must approve a new drug before it can be sold in the marketplace. Government approval is necessary, it is argued, because drug firms may otherwise perform insufficient testing in an attempt to gain a first-mover advantage or to avoid high costs. The elixir sulfanilamide and thalidomide tragedies in the 1930s and 1960s are two examples where people have either died or become harmed by unsafe drug products.[7]

Because the market may fail in the absence of government intervention and provide either unsafe or ineffective drugs, the FDA has been assigned the role of approving new drugs. Many critics (e.g., Grabowski and Vernon, 1983) argue that the stringent regulations of the FDA since 1962 have led to higher R&D costs and a lower number of new chemical entities introduced into the marketplace. We explicitly address this notion later in the chapter. Grabowski and Vernon point out that the FDA tends to err on the side of conservatism, resulting in long FDA approval times and a slower rate of pharmaceutical innovations. The economic argument goes like the following.

Suppose the safety and effectiveness of a new drug submitted to the FDA for approval are associated with some uncertainty. An all-knowing FDA approves the drug application when the therapeutic benefits of the drug outweigh its risk. Thus, a correct decision means the FDA approves a safe and effective product or rejects an

---

[7]The elixir sulfanilamide disaster occurred when Massengill Company used diethylene glycol as a solvent to formulate a liquid form of sulfanilamide without testing it for toxicity. More than 100 children died from the poisonous chemical. The other tragedy happened in Germany and other European countries when thalidomide, a sleeping pill, caused babies to be born without hands or feet (phocomelia).

**FIGURE 16-1**     FDA DECISION MAKING ON NEW DRUG APPLICATIONS

State of the World

|                    |         | New Drug Is Safe and Effective | New Drug Is Not Safe and Effective |
|--------------------|---------|--------------------------------|------------------------------------|
| FDA Decision       | Accept  | Correct decision               | Type 2 error                       |
|                    | Reject  | Type 1 error                   | Correct decision                   |

SOURCE: Henry G. Grabowski and John M. Vernon, *The Regulation of Pharmaceuticals: Balancing the Benefits and Risks* (Washington, DC: American Enterprise Institute, 1983), Figure 1.

unsafe or ineffective one. Due to uncertainty, however, the FDA may make two types of errors, as shown in figure 16–1.

The first error, called *type 1* error, occurs when the FDA rejects the application for a new drug that is truly safe and effective. In contrast, a type 2 error occurs when the FDA approves a drug that is unsafe or ineffective. As Grabowski and Vernon (1983) write, "Both types of error influence patients' health and well-being since consuming a 'bad' drug or not having access to a 'good' drug can have deleterious effects on health" (p. 10). One would think either type of error is random and therefore equally likely to occur in an uncertain world. However, that is not the case. An FDA member who unknowingly commits a type 2 error faces personal losses: job loss and political indignation. Moreover, the outcome of a type 2 error is eventually known and highly visible.

The cost associated with a type 1 error, on the other hand, is borne by a third party (the drug manufacturer or a sick patient) rather than by an FDA member and therefore is less visible. The rejection of a good drug may never be known. Thus, according to this view, the FDA faces an incentive to reject rather than accept, or at least delay the approval of, a drug more often than is necessary in a perfect world.

Interestingly, an unconstrained market faces incentives to accept "bad" drugs and commit a type 2 error. Profit-seeking drug firms wishing to be the first to market with a new drug may skimp on necessary testing. The FDA faces an incentive to reject or delay "good" drugs and commit a type 1 error. Longer approval periods translate into further testing, higher R&D costs, lower expected profitability, and fewer drug innovations. Thus, both the market and the government potentially make mistakes. The gnawing question is which institution, the market or the government, makes fewer and less costly ones.

# The Switch from Rx to OTC

Due to high medical care costs, the FDA adopted a policy in the mid-1970s, which continues today, of switching selected drugs from Rx to OTC status if pharmaceutical companies can prove that any misuse of the drugs will not endanger a consumer's health. Since consumers can self-medicate and avoid a visit to a physician, they often gain from the switch.[1]

Pharmaceutical companies value the switch from Rx to OTC because they can avoid the intense generic and brand-name competition that results after their patents expire, especially given that big brand-name drugs generally gain three years' exclusivity after receiving OTC status. The exclusivity, which resulted from the Waxman-Hatch Act of 1984, means no other companies can make a similar OTC version until the three-year period expires (Tanouye and Burton, 1993). In addition, drug companies value the switch because Rx drugs are more heavily regulated by the government than OTC drugs. Well-known examples of recent switches include Advil, a pain killer; Monistat 7, a vaginal yeast infection treatment; and Benadryl, an allergy medication.

To get a sense of the magnitude of the net benefit of switching drugs from Rx to OTC status, Temin (1992) focused on the benefits and costs associated with the OTC switch of cough and cold medicines. The benefit of switching to OTC cough and cold medicines is the consumer surplus associated with a lower price and the medical savings, in terms of both time and money, resulting from fewer physician visits. The cost includes any resource costs the FDA incurs for reviewing the switch and the expected costs of any adverse reactions from misusing the drugs.

First, Temin measured the consumer surplus from OTC cough and cold medicines. Consumer surplus is the triangle below the demand curve and

above the actual market price (assuming a linear demand curve). Since the area of a triangle equals one-half the base times the height, consumer surplus equals one-half of the quantity sold times the price differential between the maximum willingness to pay for the first unit and the actual price paid.

To estimate the maximum willingness to pay for the first unit, Temin estimated a demand for cough and cold medicines. As economic theory suggests, the demand for cough and cold medicines was found to be negatively related to price, with an own-price elasticity of about −.5 to −.74. Demand was also found to be positively related to advertising expenditures on cough and cold medicines. Using the estimated demand equation, Temin solved for the maximum willingness to pay for the first unit and determined the price differential. Multiplying the price differential by one-half of the annual sales revealed that the consumer surplus from switching cough and cold medicines amounted to $700 million in 1989.

Adding the consumer surplus to the resource saving from the reduced use of medical services (monetary and time costs of visiting a physician) gave a total gain of $770 million. Temin notes that there was virtually no cost to the cough and cold medicine switch because the FDA devoted very few resources to it and because cough and cold medicines present no dangerous adverse side effects. Thus, the implication is that consumers are clearly better off with the switch to OTC cough and cold medicines to the tune of $770 million per year. However, Temin cautions that the costs of some switches may be greater than their benefits and thus should be given careful scrutiny.

---

[1]Insurance policies, however, frequently cover the cost of prescription drugs but not OTC drugs.

### *The Structure of the Pharmaceutical Industry: A Summary*

From an aggregate market perspective, the seller side of the pharmaceutical industry appears to be highly competitive with a large number of equal-size companies. Closer examination, however, reveals that a small number of drugs generally compete within a given therapeutic market. Legal patents and brand loyalty can make it difficult for new firms to enter various therapeutic markets by establishing a barrier to entry.

On the buyer side of the market, consumers are found to pay high out-of-pocket costs for pharmaceutical goods. This by itself suggests that the demand for pharmaceutical goods may be elastic with respect to price. However, physicians have historically been the decision makers responsible for choosing among prescription drugs. One suspects that, given no financial incentives, physicians are not very sensitive to drug price differentials, especially if patients have medical insurance.

The demand for pharmaceutical products covered by third-party payments may have become more sensitive to price differentials. Third-party payers have shown signs of price responsiveness, as evidenced by drug formularies, mandated generic substitution, and drug utilization review programs. Managed-care institutions, such as HMOs and PPOs, are increasingly relying on these kinds of drug programs. Finally, the government plays a major role in the pharmaceutical industry, from approving new drugs for commercial introduction and the switch from Rx to OTC and the direct financing of 14 percent of pharmaceutical expenditures.

## The Conduct of the Pharmaceutical Industry

In this section, we analyze evidence regarding the behavior of pharmaceutical companies in recent years. Three practices of drug firms are examined: pricing, promotion, and product innovation. The basic question is whether evidence exists for competitive or monopoly behavior in the pharmaceutical industry. For example, we ask the following four questions, among others:

1. Are drug prices lower when drug firms face more intense competition?

2. Are newcomers more likely to enter pharmaceutical markets when existing firms' profits are high during the postpatent period, or do postpatent barriers prevent entry?

3. Is drug promotion informative or persuasive? Do the promotion expenditures of established firms impede the entry of new firms?

4. Is a large firm size necessary for product innovation in the pharmaceutical industry?

### *Pricing Behavior*

The relatively high concentration of sales among a few firms and substantial barriers to entry in many therapeutic markets imply that pharmaceutical companies possess the ability to price their drug products above the marginal costs of production and generate economic profits. In addition, first-mover advantages may mean that leading firms have the power to maintain brand-name prices above costs and still dominate the market over generic companies even after patent expiration. Promotion expenditures by the leading pharmaceutical firms may help to reinforce the habit-buying practices of many buyers, especially physicians.

The potential for monopoly pricing has motivated several researchers to examine the pricing practices of pharmaceutical companies. One of the first studies on pharmaceutical competition, by Hurwitz and Caves (1988), analyzed how generic competition affected the postpatent pricing practices of 56 leading brand-name pharmaceuticals during 1978 and 1983. In particular, they developed a sample of 56 observations by drawing from a list of drug products that had eventually become available as generics but were originally subject to patents held by the pharmaceutical firms that developed them.

Next, the authors estimated a multiple regression equation relating the leading firm's market share (in terms of pills sold) during 1978 and 1983 to the relative drug prices of the leader and follower firms, sales promotion spending by the leader and follower firms, and several variables reflecting the degree of brand loyalty to the leading firm's product. The relative difference in the prices of drugs offered by the leading firm and follower firms was calculated as $(P_L - P_F)/P_F$ where $P_L$ and $P_F$ reflect the weighted average drug prices of the leading firm and those of the follower firms, respectively. The expectation was that the relative drug price ratio inversely affects the market share of the leading firm, as the law of demand suggests.

The logarithm of the leading firm's and follower firms' sales promotion expenditures were also specified to capture own- and cross-promotion effects. Sales promotion outlays were calculated to include spending on detailing (i.e., personal promotion by pharmaceutical salespersons), medical journal advertising, and direct-mail advertising. The expectation was that own-promotion causes the market share of the leading firm to increase, whereas cross-promotion causes the leader's market share to decline.

Several variables were also included to capture the brand loyalty built up by the leader during the patent period. One such variable was the number of years the leader's brand was marketed exclusively under a patent (i.e., the effective patent life). The market share of the leading firm was expected to increase with the effective patent life given the greater opportunity to establish goodwill and entrench buying habits. However, because goodwill and buying habits might also erode as health professionals gain some experience with generic substitutes, Hurwitz and Caves also specified the number of years since the entry of the first generic competitor and the total number of generic suppliers. The hypothesis was that the market share of the leading firm decreases with respect to both of these variables as health professionals and consumers gain more information about the availability of generic brands.

Hurwitz and Caves obtained some interesting results and were able to explain about 66 percent of the variation in the leading firm's market share. The results generally supported the various hypotheses. First, as expected, a higher positive price differential between the leader and follower firms was associated with a reduction in the leading firm's market share, *ceteris paribus*. Specifically, the authors calculated that a

10 percent increase in the average leader's price differential resulted in a market share loss of less than one-half of 1 percent. This result suggests that the leader's market share declined by very little when price was raised above the followers' average prices—not too surprising, the authors argue, when one considers that the average price differential was 127 percent, yet the average leader commanded a 63.4 percent market share.

The regression results associated with the other variables proved interesting, as well. First, the own- and cross-promotion effects were found to positively and inversely affect the leader's share, as expected. Thus, one implication of the analysis is that producers of generic brands are able to penetrate the leader's market share through their promotional outlays and pricing policies. Second, the results indicated that a longer "monopoly" marketing period helps to build brand loyalty and to prevent generic entry from chipping away at the leader's share. Third, the regression analysis showed that the leader's market share falls with a greater number of generic firms as health care professionals become more experienced with generic brands. The arrival of an additional supplier was estimated to reduce the leader's market share by about 1.25 percentage points, on average.

In sum, Hurwitz and Caves found that price differentials affect the choice between brand-name and generic products, but buyers are relatively insensitive to relative price changes. Goodwill established during the patent period extends the effective patent life of a pharmaceutical product as buyers continue to pay a substantial premium after the patent has expired. Finally, promotion by the leader firms helps to protect market share from eroding, but promotion by followers tends to reduce the leader's market share.

In another study, Caves, Whinston, and Hurwitz (1991) examined the effect of generic entry on both brand-name and generic pricing practices. The study covered the postpatent competition between 30 brand-name and a number of generic drugs over the period 1976 to 1987 and reached a number of interesting conclusions. First, the authors found that the innovator's (the leading brand-name firm's) price initially rises after patent expiration up until the point where a generic competitor enters the market. That finding implies that leading pharmaceutical firms do not engage in **limit pricing** because they would otherwise set a low price to discourage or limit entry.[8] Second, the authors discovered that the innovator's price declines with a greater number of generic entrants, but by only 4.5 percent, on average. Third, they found some evidence indicating that innovators' prices were more sensitive to entry during the 1980s compared to past periods, most likely reflecting the growing price consciousness of pharmaceutical buyers. Fourth, Caves, Whinston, and Hurwitz found that generic producers enter markets offering prices much lower than the brand-name price. Generic prices also fall with further generic competitor entry, potentially declining to 17 percent of the brand-name producer's preentry price. Despite the huge discount, generic producers were found to gain a relatively small market share.

---

[8]Limit pricing occurs when the dominant or innovator firm prices its product just below the break-even price of a potential entrant as a way to discourage entry. The price of a dominant firm tends to decline over time if limit pricing is practiced.

Grabowski and Vernon (1992) examined the pricing patterns associated with 17 major pharmaceutical products that were first exposed to generic competition from 1983 to 1987. The 1980s are a particularly interesting period, because barriers to entry by generic companies had been lowered by the Waxman-Hatch Act. Among their results, Grabowski and Vernon found that a 10 percent increase in the brand-name profit margin at time of entry resulted in a 6 percent increase in the number of entrants by the end of the first year. Thus, the entry of new generic products is sensitive to expected profits in the product market, as economic theory suggests, when barriers to entry are low.

In addition, the authors found that price accounts for most of the variation in a generic company's market share but noted that other factors, such as first- (or second-) mover advantages and perceptions of quality differences among generic suppliers, may also be important in specific circumstances. As far as pricing patterns are concerned, their evidence, like that of Caves, Whinston, and Hurwitz (1991) suggests that generics offer significant discounts and that their prices decline substantially over time.

One seemingly inconsistent finding of Grabowski and Vernon's study was that branded drugs' prices increase in nominal terms by 11 percent after two years of entry. One suspects that innovator firms react to competition by lowering price. But Grabowski and Vernon note that the higher branded drug price occurs in response to the dynamics of a segmented market. That is, as generics enter the market and satisfy price-sensitive buyers with lower prices, brand-name firms are left with buyers who are relatively price insensitive. As a result, brand-name companies are able to raise price, at least in the short run, because they now effectively face a less elastic demand for their pharmaceutical products. Although the innovator's price increases, the average market price of a drug is found to decline to 79 percent of the preentry price after two years as generics attain a greater share of the market. On average, brand-name drugs lose one-half of the market to generics after two years, according to Grabowski and Vernon.

A study by Lu and Comanor (1994) is particularly interesting because it examined price competition among the brand-name producers of 148 new molecular entities between 1978 and 1987. Prior studies have not examined price competition among rival patented products.

Lu and Comanor argue that an innovator's pricing decision is influenced by several factors, including the drug's therapeutic properties, physician brand loyalty, adoption rate by demanders, and the reactions of rivals. As a result, their empirical model links a measure reflecting a drug's relative price to its FDA rating as an indicator of therapeutic novelty, a dummy variable indicating whether the drug treats an acute or a chronic illness as a measure of frequency of buying, and the number of branded substitute suppliers as an indicator of rivalry. According to the authors, therapeutic novelty should lead to a higher relative price, while the number of substitute suppliers should result in a lower relative price.

Lu and Comanor discovered that a greater number of substitute branded products results in lower prices, as expected. In addition, they found that the therapeutic novelty of a drug influences pricing strategy over time. In particular, the authors noted that therapeutically innovative drugs are generally introduced under a modified price-skimming strategy. A modified price-skimming strategy means that therapeutically innovative drug prices are initially set high and then held relatively constant over time. Imitative drugs, on the other hand, are introduced under a market penetration strategy. The prices of imitative drugs are low at first to enlarge market share, but are then increased over time as information about their availability spreads.

Finally, Wiggins and Maness (1994) examined price competition among 98 anti-infective products (e.g., penicillins, tetracyclines, erythromycins, and cephalosporins) over the 1984 to 1990 period. Their analysis provides two major conclusions. First, in contrast to the studies cited above, they found that prices fall sharply with initial entry. Second, they found that subsequent entry continued to reduce prices although at a much smaller rate even when there were a relatively large number of competitors. The authors argue that the increased price sensitivity may result from the easier entry of generics brought on by the Waxman-Hatch Act of 1984 and/or because anti-infectives may be more price sensitive than other segments of the pharmaceutical industry.

Taken together, these five studies suggest that both prepatent and post-patent price competition often exist in pharmaceutical markets. The prices of both brand-name and generic products are found to be lower when a greater number of substitute products are available. Pioneer firms sometimes raise the prices of their branded products upon entry in response to a less elastic demand. The goodwill established during the patent period plays an important role, allowing established firms to maintain a large market share despite the huge discounts offered by generic companies.

## Promotion of Pharmaceutical Products

Medicines are cited as one of the first products advertised in printed form (Leffler 1981). Timely product information is especially valuable in the pharmaceutical industry due to the continual introduction of new life-saving drugs. With about 22,000 different drugs on the market, doctors have a great deal to learn and remember (Schwartzman, 1976). Before prescribing, doctors must know the appropriate drug, the correct dosage, and the properties of the drug for different patients, classified by various characteristics, such as age, weight, and general health status. Thus, it is not surprising that promotion expenditures can run as high as 20 to 30 percent of sales for many research-based pharmaceutical companies. Nearly 70 percent of the promotional budget is spent on personal promotion by detailers (pharmaceutical salespersons), and another 27 percent is spent on journal advertising. Direct-mail advertising accounts for the rest of the promotional budget (Hurwitz and Caves, 1988).

It is unclear to economists whether pharmaceutical promotion strategies enhance or reduce societal welfare. As we saw in Chapter 9, advertising may promote or impede competition depending on whether informed or habit-buying behavior results. Studies on this topic by Leffler (1981), Hurwitz and Caves (1988), and Caves, Whinston, and Hurwitz (1991) found evidence supporting both the informational and persuasion effects of pharmaceutical promotion.

# Can Physician Drug Recommendations Be Bought?

According to the text discussion, it is theoretically unclear whether the promotion practices of drug companies encourage or impede competition. Essentially it depends on whether drug promotion practices encourage informed or habit buying. Because the effect of drug promotion is uncertain, many managed-care organizations and hospitals have turned to drug formularies as a way to control physician prescribing behavior. The intent is to include only effective and reasonably priced drugs on the formulary as a means of controlling overall drug costs.

A study by Chren and Landefeld (1994), however, found that the prescription drug recommendations of physicians are influenced by the marketing practices of drug companies even in the face of managed-care drug controls, such as drug formularies. Specifically, the authors compared the interactions with drug companies of 40 physicians who had recommended that certain drugs be added to a hospital's formulary with 80 other physicians who had not made such requests.

Chren and Landefeld discovered that those physicians who recommended drug adoptions were more likely to have received monetary support from drug companies for travel, lodging, speaking, engagements, or research expenses. Yet the two groups of physicians had not differed in the frequency of their exposure to drug companies' other promotional activities, such as visits from detailers. According to the study, all but 6 of the 52 requested drugs were added to the hospital formulary, including 20 drugs classified as having little or no advantage over drugs already on the formulary. Another 13 drugs added to the formulary were classified as having only a modest advantage over existing drugs.

The study raises some doubt about whether managed care can restrain drug costs through formulary restrictions, unless, of course, tighter scrutiny is placed on the formulary approval process. The authors contend that stricter guidelines may be necessary to minimize or eliminate physician relationships with pharmaceutical companies.

Specifically, Leffler found that advertising intensity is greater for newer and more important pharmaceutical products, which, he argues, reflects the informational content of the promotion message. Leffler, as well as Hurwitz and Caves, found that the new entrants' promotion expenditures helped them to expand their market shares. Caves, Whinston, and Hurwitz concluded that increased generic competition results in less advertising by the innovator, which, they argue, must reflect the informational rather than persuasive content of the innovator's pharmaceutical advertising during the preentry period.

The evidence for persuasive advertising is equally strong. In particular, Leffler found that less detailing of younger physicians occurs for older products. That is, advertisers tend to direct their advertisements to the physician age group that was in medical school when the drug product was originally introduced. Thus, the creation of brand loyalty and reinforcement of habit buying must be the real purpose behind advertising. Hurwitz and Caves found that the leading firms' promotion expenditures preserved their market share from new generic entrants. Finally, the study by Caves, Whinston, and Hurwitz notes that generic firms gain relatively small shares despite their huge discounts, perhaps reflecting the goodwill built up by the innovator's promotion expenditures during the patent period.

## Product Innovation

The most important contribution associated with the pharmaceutical industry is the timely introduction of new drug products that can extend or improve lives. New drug discoveries require research and development activities. In this section, we look at several issues relating to the R&D process, including the various stages of the R&D process, determinants of R&D, and the relation between firm size and innovative activity.

**Stages of the R&D Process**   Product innovation in the pharmaceutical industry is both very risky and time consuming. The research and development (R&D) process for new chemical entities is normally spread over many years, and only a small fraction of new drug discoveries are eventually approved for marketing. Research and development costs constitute a sizable proportion of sales revenues. For example, table 16–5 shows that R&D expenditures for research-based pharmaceutical companies ranged from a low of 10.9 in 1974 and 1978 to a high of 20.4 percent of sales in 1994.

Due to the high cost and risk associated with R&D, the decision-making process underlying new-drug development tends to unfold sequentially. At several points in the R&D process, a company reviews the development status of a drug and makes a decision about whether to continue or abandon the project. The decision rests on the expected net profitability of the proposed drug and thus takes both expected revenues and costs into consideration. Expected revenues depend in part on the therapeutic properties of the drug, the size of the target market, and the number of substitute drugs. Anticipated costs depend on the frequency and severity of adverse reactions to the drug and the projected additional development, marketing, distribution, and production costs (DiMasi, Hansen, Grabowski, and Lasagna, 1991).

Researchers generally identify eight stages in the R&D process; these stages are summarized in table 16–6, including the duration of each stage, in months. DiMasi, Hansen, Grabowski, and Lasagna (1991) estimate that the preclinical period of discovery, animal testing, and IND filing lasts about 42.6 months. Almost 58 percent of the (uncapitalized) expected costs per marketed new chemical entity (NCE) are incurred during this period, most likely reflecting the huge number of misses before a pharmaceutical company discovers a drug that warrants further testing at the clinical stage.

DiMasi, Hansen, Grabowski, and Lasagna estimated that the clinical period from the initiation of Phase I testing to drug approval lasts about 98.9 months, with the FDA approval process taking about $2\frac{1}{2}$ years, on average. The average time needed to complete the entire process from synthesis to marketing approval is estimated at 12 years.[9] About 75 percent of the NCEs in Phase I testing enter Phase II testing, and about 36 percent eventually enter Phase III testing. Only 18.3 percent of the drugs that entered clinical trials during 1980–1984 are now marketed (DiMasi, 1995).

---

[9] Some overlap occurs across the various stages.

| TABLE 16–5 | R&D AS A PERCENTAGE OF U.S. SALES, ETHICAL PHARMACEUTICAL, RESEARCH-BASED PHARMACEUTICAL COMPANIES, 1970–1996 |
| --- | --- |

| Year | Company-Financed Domestic U.S. R&D (millions of dollars) | R&D as a Percentage of Sales and Exports |
| --- | --- | --- |
| 1970 | $ 558.6 | 11.4% |
| 1971 | 619.6 | 11.2 |
| 1972 | 648.0 | 11.6 |
| 1973 | 697.5 | 11.2 |
| 1974 | 784.5 | 10.9 |
| 1975 | 894.5 | 11.3 |
| 1976 | 973.6 | 11.0 |
| 1977 | 1,053.0 | 11.1 |
| 1978 | 1,159.1 | 10.9 |
| 1979 | 1,319.8 | 11.2 |
| 1980 | 1,544.1 | 11.9 |
| 1981 | 1,866.2 | 13.3 |
| 1982 | 2,265.6 | 14.0 |
| 1983 | 2,663.1 | 14.7 |
| 1984 | 2,976.4 | 14.6 |
| 1985 | 3,370.7 | 15.1 |
| 1986 | 3,870.9 | 15.1 |
| 1987 | 4,503.2 | 16.1 |
| 1988 | 5,228.7 | 16.7 |
| 1989 | 6,019.3 | 16.8 |
| 1990 | 6,800.1 | 16.2 |
| 1991 | 7,923.6 | 16.6 |
| 1992 | 9,309.1 | 17.9 |
| 1993 | 10,473.0 | 19.9 |
| 1994 | 11,100.8 | 20.4 |
| 1995 | 11,833.9 | 19.4 |
| 1996 | 13,576.4 | 19.8 |

SOURCE: PhRMA, *Industry Profile* (Washington, DC, July 1998), Table 2.

**TABLE 16-6**    STAGES OF THE DRUG DEVELOPMENT PROCESS

1. *Discovery stage.* Basic research synthesis of new chemicals and early studies of chemical properties. Identification of a specific new chemical entity worthy of further testing.

2. *Preclinical animal testing.* Short-term animal toxicity testing for evidence of safety in the short run in preparation for human testing.

3. *IND filing.* A request is made for authorization to begin human testing by filing a notice of claimed investigational exemption for new drug (IND). If there is no hold on the application, the firm begins clinical testing 30 days after filing. (42.6 months for the first three stages)

4. *Phase I of clinical testing.* Dosage administered to a small number of healthy volunteers for information on toxicity and safe dose ranges in humans. Data are gathered on the drug's absorption and distribution in the body, its metabolic effects, and the rate and manner in which the drug is eliminated from the body. (15.5 months)

5. *Phase II of clinical testing.* Drug is used on a larger number of people whom the drug is intended to benefit. Evidence of therapeutic effectiveness and additional safety data are obtained. (24.3 months)

6. *Phase III of clinical testing.* Large-scale tests on humans over a longer period to uncover unanticipated side effects and additional evidence of effectiveness. (36.0 months)

7. *Long-term animal studies.* The effects of prolonged exposures and the effects on subsequent generations are determined. Such studies are typically conducted concurrently with other studies. (33.6 months)

8. *New-drug approval.* Application for commercial marketing of the new drug. Review of evidence by the FDA. Marketing for approved uses may begin upon notification by the FDA. (30.3 months)

SOURCES: Adapted from Joseph A. DiMasi, Ronald W. Hansen, Henry G. Grabowski, and Louis Lasagna, "Cost of Innovation in the Pharmaceutical Industry," *Journal of Health Economics* 10, (1991), pp. 107–42, and John R. Virts and J. Fred Weston, "Expectations and the Allocation of Research and Development Resources," in *Drugs and Health,* ed. Robert Helms (Washington, DC: American Enterprise Institute, 1981), pp. 21–45.

**Determinants of R&D Spending**[10]    As with any investment, the optimal amount of R&D spending depends on the expected future streams of revenues less costs or economic profits. Expected marginal revenues, MR, decline with respect to R&D expenditures due to the law of diminishing marginal productivity.[11] The marginal or opportunity cost, MC, is likely to rise or remain constant with respect to R&D spending. The expected net profits from R&D are maximized when MR is set equal to MC. In mathematical terms, the firm finds the optimal amount of R&D spending, $R^*$, by solving the following equation:

**(16–1)**  $MR(R, X) = MC(R, Z),$

---

[10]This section is based on Grabowski and Vernon (1981).

[11]R&D can be considered as an input in the discovery of new drugs. Thus, the marginal revenue—or, more correctly, the marginal revenue product of R&D—is equal to the market price of the resulting new drug, *P,* times the marginal productivity of R&D, MP, in the innovation process. See Chapter 8 for further details.

where $R$ equals investment expenditures on R&D, $X$ stands for a vector of exogenous factors influencing the rate of return from new-drug R&D, and $Z$ represents a vector of exogenous variables influencing the marginal cost associated with new-drug R&D.

Solving equation 16–1 for $R$ yields a reduced-form equation for the optimal level of R&D spending in terms of $X$ and $Z$:

**(16–2)**  $R^* = f(X, Z)$.

Variables that increase the rate of return, $X$, lead to increased spending on R&D. Similarly, variables that raise the opportunity cost, $Z$, lead to lower R&D expenditures.

Grabowski and Vernon (1981) were among the first to estimate an R&D regression equation based on equation 16–2 for a pooled sample of 10 pharmaceutical companies taken over the entire 14-year period from 1962 to 1975. For a factor influencing the firm's expected rate of return in each time period, they used an indicator of past R&D success, measured by the number of NCEs per dollar of R&D spending in the previous five years. The expectation was that R&D spending increases with greater past success. They also specified an index of firm diversification as a revenue-influencing factor. The argument was that a more diversified firm is better able to exploit R&D spending on a number of different drugs and thus is more inclined to undertake R&D.

To control for factors influencing the opportunity cost of R&D, $Z$, the authors specified a variable measuring each firm's cash flow margin in each year. The opportunity cost of internal funds is less than that of external funds, so R&D spending was expected to increase with the cash flow margin.[12] Following convention, R&D spending was deflated by sales to get a measure of R&D intensity.

Their regression results provide important insights. As expected, R&D investment spending was found to be influenced by variables affecting marginal benefit and cost. In particular, R&D spending was observed to increase with a greater degree of R&D success and, more importantly, with a larger cash flow margin. This is a critical finding, because, as we will learn later, the decline in R&D spending during the 1970s was due in large part to falling real drug prices and the associated reduction in cash flows. Conversely, the upturn in R&D spending since 1980 (see table 16–5) was due to the reversal in the real drug price trend.

**Firm Size and Innovation**   Another important issue regarding the conduct of pharmaceutical firms is the relation between firm size and innovative activities. The question is whether large pharmaceutical firms are more likely than small firms to engage in successful innovative ventures. Given the importance of product innovation in this industry, antitrust laws concerning mergers may not be enforced so strictly if larger firms are found to be more innovative than smaller ones.

---

[12]Due to transaction costs, the cost of borrowing external funds (i.e., loans from banks or sales of stocks and bonds), is generally higher than that of internal funds.

Economic theory by itself offers only limited insight on the relation between firm size and innovation. Schumpeter (1950) is among the first economists to propose that larger firms may be more successful at innovation than smaller firms because they have the resources necessary to engage in modern large-scale R&D activities. Modern and commercially successful innovations are very expensive to undertake, and therefore small firms may lack the necessary physical and financial resources. In addition, larger firms diversify their R&D efforts among various projects and thus can better absorb the risks associated with innovative activities. Finally, many analysts believe that economies of scale exist in research such that per-unit costs fall with a greater production of R&D activities because more efficient, specialized research inputs are used.

These three factors—resource capability, risk absorption, and research economies—suggest that larger firms tend to face a greater incentive to undertake R&D activities than smaller firms. Opposing this tendency, however, is the argument that greater bureaucratic red tape in larger organizations stifles creativity. Since important decisions are normally made at a centralized level in a large, bureaucratic firm, communication flows ultimately break down and decisions take longer to execute. The resulting time lags delay or discourage new product ideas from being pursued or continued.

Because theory cannot offer a definitive answer, a number of researchers have empirically questioned whether larger drug firms are more innovative than smaller ones. Schwartzman (1976) summarizes the pre-1960s empirical research on firm size and innovation as follows:

> According to Edwin Mansfield and Henry Grabowski, large drug companies do not spend proportionately more money on research than smaller ones. W. S. Comanor observes diseconomies of scale in research. Jerome Schnee concludes that leading companies do not produce proportionately more innovations than other firms[13] (p. 83).

Thus, the pre-1960s research suggests that larger drug firms are not more innovative than smaller ones. Close examination of these studies by Schwartzman, however, revealed poor data for the measurement of firm size or faulty analysis of the data.

Schwartzman's own empirical work, using data for the late 1960s, reached three separate conclusions supporting the premise that large firm size encourages greater innovation in the pharmaceutical industry. First, he found that research effort, as measured by laboratory employment, increases more than proportionately with the size of the drug firm. Second, his study reveals that research output, as measured by either the number of new chemical entities or the number of patents, increases more than proportionately with research effort, indicating economies of scale in research. Third, Schwartzman shows that larger firms discover relatively more new drugs than do smaller firms.

---

[13] See Mansfield (1968), Grabowski (1968), Comanor (1965), and Schnee (1971).

The general conclusions reached by Schwartzman have recently come under attack. Using more recent data for 1982, Acs and Audretsch (1988) analyzed the innovative contributions of small and large firms, defined as firms having fewer or more than 500 employees, respectively. The Small Business Administration constructed the innovation database by examining over 100 technology, engineering, and trade journals covering a number of different manufacturing industries for evidence of new-product innovations. For the pharmaceutical industry, the authors found that larger firms had 9.23 times the innovations of smaller firms in 1982. However, larger pharmaceutical firms also had 19.41 times the employment of smaller drug firms. Together these results indicate that larger firms generate only half the number of pharmaceutical innovations that smaller firms do on a per-employee basis. Thus, according to their empirical results, large firm size may not be necessary for pharmaceutical innovation. Taking all the manufacturing industries in their entire sample into consideration, Acs and Audretsch concluded that small firms are about 43 percent more innovative than their larger counterparts.

In a related study, Acs and Audretsch (1987) analyzed the specific characteristics affecting the differential innovation rates of large and small firms across different industries. The authors determined that large firms tend to have an innovative advantage in industries that are capital intensive, advertising intensive, and relatively concentrated at the aggregate level. In contrast, small firms are more innovative in industries in which total innovation and the use of skilled labor play a large role and some, but not many, large firms exist.

We mentioned earlier that the pharmaceutical industry is characterized by high advertising intensity. This industry characteristic tends to favor the innovation of large pharmaceutical firms. However, most of the characteristics described above suggest that small pharmaceutical companies may be more innovative. First, total innovation plays a very important role in the pharmaceutical industry. In fact, Acs and Audretsch (1988) cite the pharmaceutical industry as the fourth most innovative out of 247 four-digit SIC industries in 1982. Second, the skilled labor of pharmacologists, biochemists, and immunologists, among others, is necessary in the drug industry given the high technical sophistication of pharmaceutical R&D. Third, casual empiricism suggests that the pharmaceutical industry contains an appreciable number of large, highly visible firms. Fourth, Schwartzman (1976) notes that capital requirements for manufacturing are relatively low in the pharmaceutical industry. Finally, we saw that the pharmaceutical industry is characterized by low overall seller concentration.

Thus, the safest conclusion to draw is that a mixture of firm sizes is most favorable for fostering pharmaceutical innovation.[14] While smaller drug firms seem to hold a decisive advantage, the preceding results suggest that the innovativeness of smaller firms is greatest when large firms dominate in an industry. Encouraging innovation

---

[14]Like studies in the past, recent empirical analyses uncover mixed evidence concerning the relation between firm size and innovation. On the one hand, studies by DiMasi, Grabowski, and Vernon (1995) and Henderson and Cockburn (1996) find that research efforts are proportionately more productive in larger firms. Langowitz and Graves (1992), on the other hand, find that research output is subject to diminishing returns with respect to both R&D expenditures and firm size.

through a diversity of firm sizes should not be too surprising. Many researchers note that new ideas are relatively cheap to conceive, but the commercial development and successful marketing of new products are costly and risky. Small firms might have the edge at the discovery stage, but large firms possess development and marketing advantages. Greer (1992) contrasts the innovativeness of large and small firms as follows:

> The foot-dragging behavior of leading firms is so common that theorists have dubbed it "the fast-second strategy." Briefly the idea is that, for a large firm, *innovation* is often costlier, riskier, and less profitable than *imitation*. A large firm can lie back, let others gamble, then respond quickly with a "fast second" if anything started by their smaller rivals catches fire (p. 669).

Greer notes that Genentech, an infant firm in the late 1970s, founded biotechnology. Larger pharmaceutical firms, such as Eli Lilly, followed Genentech's lead into biotechnology in the mid-1980s.

### The Conduct of the Pharmaceutical Industry: A Summary

The studies discussed in this section show that a considerable amount of competition takes place in the pharmaceutical industry. Drug firms sometimes face price competition during the patent period from other branded products, and prices are lower when more branded competition exists. Branded drugs also compete with generics on the basis of price during the postpatent period. Generics offer huge discounts relative to branded products. Also, product competition is particularly important in the pharmaceutical industry. Incentives for new-product development exist because a new drug product, especially a therapeutically important one, can easily supplant others in the market.

However, the degree of competition in the pharmaceutical industry is not perfect. Firms offering single-source drugs are able to raise price above the marginal cost of production because substitutes are unavailable. Furthermore, evidence shows that pharmaceutical marketing is used partly to reinforce the habit-buying practices of physicians. Hence, some drug buyers still remain price insensitive due to brand loyalty.

## The Performance of the Pharmaceutical Industry

In this section, we appraise the performance of the contemporary pharmaceutical industry. Competitive market impediments, such as patents, trademarks, and high promotion expenditures, characterize the pharmaceutical industry and suggest that entrenched companies may possess sufficient monopoly power to raise price, restrict output, and earn excessive profits. Direct aggregate measures of pharmaceutical prices and output are unavailable, but some suitable proxy indicators exist.

First, we compare the prescription drug price inflation rate to the general inflation rate in the United States and identify trends and measurement problems. Second, since product innovation is the true output of the pharmaceutical industry, we examine and evaluate historical data on the number of new chemical entities. Finally, we look at some comparative data on the aggregate profitability of pharmaceutical companies.

## The Relative Price Inflation Rate of Pharmaceutical Products

Table 16–7 shows the prescription drug price and general price inflation rates in the United States for the period 1970 to 1997. Throughout most of the 1970s, the general inflation rate exceeded the pharmaceutical price inflation rate. Specifically, general prices increased at an annual average rate of 7.4 percent, almost twice the rate of 3.9 percent at which drug prices grew. Thus, real or relative drug prices declined throughout most of the 1970s.

From 1981 to 1994, there was a reversal in the relative price trend. Real drug prices continuously surged as the drug price inflation rate outstripped the general price inflation rate. In particular, the average drug price inflation rate of 9.6 percent was 88 percent higher than the mean overall inflation rate of 5.1 percent during the 1980s. It should be pointed out that drug price increases have moderated somewhat in the 1990s with an average annual rate of 4.9 percent, just slightly above the general price inflation rate of 3.2 percent.

In the past, criticism had been raised concerning the method of determining the pharmaceutical price index that is used for computing the drug price inflation rate. Several flaws in the method tended to overestimate the true pharmaceutical price inflation rate, it was claimed (Berndt, Griliches, and Rosett, 1993; Clark, 1993). First, the Bureau of Labor Statistics (BLS), when determining the pharmaceutical price index, undersamples new drug products, which are generally subject to smaller price increases than older products. Berndt, Griliches, and Rosett (1993) estimated that the undersampling of new drugs overstates the true prescription drug price inflation rate by 41 percent.

Second, BLS used to treat generic products entering the market after patent expiration of branded products as new drugs rather than as lower-priced substitutes. Scherer (1993) estimated that if generics were treated as lower-priced substitutes, the prescription drug price inflation rate would have been at least 1.2 percentage points lower during the 1980s.

Third, BLS normally used list prices instead of transaction prices to compute the drug price inflation rate. Some analysts argue, however, that buyer discounts have driven an ever-increasing wedge between list and transaction prices over time, causing the pharmaceutical price inflation rate to be severely overstated. For instance, data show that Sinemet, a drug used for treating Parkinson's disease, and Percocet, a painkiller, had wholesale price increases of 15.1 percent and 10.3 percent, respectively, in 1992. But company officials at Du Pont Merck, a joint venture among Du Pont Company and Merck, and the producers of these drugs, claim that the corresponding actual price changes had been only 4 percent and −6.6 percent after considering rebates and discounts (Tanouye and Waldholz, 1993). The magnitude of the wedge between list and transaction prices is unknown in the aggregate.

| TABLE 16-7 | URBAN CONSUMER PRICE INFLATION RATES, ALL ITEMS AND PRESCRIPTION DRUGS, 1970–1997 | |
|---|---|---|
| **Year** | **All Items** | **Prescription Drugs** |
| 1970 | 5.6 | .2 |
| 1971 | 3.3 | 1.3 |
| 1972 | 3.4 | −1.3 |
| 1973 | 8.9 | .2 |
| 1974 | 12.1 | 5.1 |
| 1975 | 7.1 | 5.8 |
| 1976 | 5.0 | 5.1 |
| 1977 | 6.7 | 7.1 |
| 1978 | 9.0 | 8.3 |
| 1979 | 13.3 | 7.5 |
| 1980 | 12.4 | 9.7 |
| 1981 | 8.9 | 12.5 |
| 1982 | 3.8 | 12.1 |
| 1983 | 3.8 | 9.6 |
| 1984 | 4.0 | 9.9 |
| 1985 | 3.8 | 8.2 |
| 1986 | 1.2 | 9.0 |
| 1987 | 4.4 | 8.1 |
| 1988 | 4.4 | 7.9 |
| 1989 | 4.6 | 9.5 |
| 1990 | 6.3 | 10.0 |
| 1991 | 3.0 | 9.3 |
| 1992 | 3.0 | 5.7 |
| 1993 | 2.8 | 3.3 |
| 1994 | 2.6 | 3.3 |
| 1995 | 2.6 | 2.0 |
| 1996 | 3.3 | 3.2 |
| 1997 | 1.7 | 2.5 |

SOURCE: U.S. Department of Labor, Bureau of Labor Statistics, *CPI Detailed Report* (various issues); http://stats.bls.gov.

# Pharmaceutical Price Differences in the United States and Canada

The relatively rapid growth of drug prices during the 1980s and early 1990s has led many analysts to wonder whether individual drug prices are higher in the United States than in Canada. This concern prompted the General Accounting Office (GAO) to examine the factory price differential associated with 121 drugs matched in the two countries by brand name, manufacturer, dosage strength, and dosage form. The 121 matched drugs included 39 of the 50 most commonly prescribed drugs in U.S. drugstores in 1990. The prices reflected, as closely as possible, what wholesalers and retailers would pay if they purchased the drugs directly from manufacturers on May 1, 1991. Table 1 shows some price differences for selected top-selling drugs.

| TABLE 1 | DIFFERENCES IN DRUG PRICES IN THE UNITED STATES AND CANADA (WHOLESALE PRICE FOR 100 TABLETS IN 1991 U.S. DOLLARS) | | | |
| --- | --- | --- | --- | --- |
| **Drug** | **Use** | **Company** | **United States** | **Canada** |
| Amoxil | Antibiotic | Beecham | $ 17.27 | $ 16.46 |
| Premarin | Postmenopause | Ayerst | 26.47 | 10.10 |
| Ceclor | Antibiotic | Lily | 134.18 | 84.14 |
| Naprosyn | Arthritis | Syntex | 72.36 | 42.64 |
| Tagamet | Antiulcer | SmithKline | 57.16 | 34.27 |
| Pepcid | Antiulcer | Merck | 103.74 | 76.72 |
| Prozac | Depression | Dista | 139.85 | 129.12 |
| Lopressor | Hypertension | Geigy | 35.71 | 15.80 |
| Dilantin | Epilepsy | Parke-Davis | 15.03 | 4.67 |
| Halcion | Tranquilizer | Upjohn | 47.69 | 16.09 |
| Valium | Tranquilizer | Roche | 40.41 | 7.57 |
| Feldene | Arthritis | Pfizer | 167.54 | 123.61 |
| Ativan | Tranquilizer | Wyeth | 49.43 | 6.16 |
| Coumadin | Heart disease | Du Pont | 36.70 | 19.59 |

SOURCE: General Accounting Office, *Prescription Drugs: Companies Charge More in the United States than in Canada*, GAO/HRD-92-110 (Washington, DC: U.S. Government Printing Office, 1992), Appendix II.

The GAO (1992) study found that factory price differentials ranged from 44 percent lower to 967 percent higher in the United States than in Canada. The median price per package (of a common dosage size in the United States) was found to be 43 percent higher in the United States than in Canada. Of the 121 drugs studied, 98 were priced higher and 23 priced lower in the United States.

*(continued)*

**INSIGHT 16–5**

*(continued)*

Nearly half of the drugs were priced 50 percent or above higher in the United States than in Canada.

The study reveals that regulatory forces are the main reason drug prices tend to be lower in Canada than in the United States. In Canada, introductory prices for new patented drugs and price increases on existing drugs are reviewed and controlled by the Patented Medicine Prices Review Board, a quasijudicial price-monitoring board. In addition, provincial drug benefit plans in Canada possess a significant amount of purchasing power and are able to negotiate substantial price discounts. Formularies that list approved drugs and maximum prices are also used to control drug costs in Canadian provinces. Finally, the Canadian patent law has traditionally promoted the sale of

relatively low-cost generic alternatives through the compulsory licensing of patented drugs.

The GAO study concludes by noting that the same regulatory forces, if adopted in the United States, may produce less desirable results. That is primarily because unlike in the United States, which has a large innovative drug industry, most of the innovative prescription drugs sold in Canada are supplied by foreign manufacturers. Foreign manufacturers perform little R&D in Canada, and Canadian-owned drug manufacturers generally produce generic products that require little investment in R&D. Despite the fact that pharmaceutical prices and profits may diminish if Canada's regulatory policies were adopted in the United States, fewer resources may be devoted to new-drug R&D by United States firms.

Finally, BLS does not explicitly adjust the prices of new drugs to reflect changes in quality. Yet, as Scherer (1993) noted, "some new drugs, by improving the quality of life or making expensive surgery unnecessary, plainly yield enormous increments of consumer surplus" (p. 103). Because new pharmaceutical products are introduced at such a rapid rate, quality-adjusted price inflation rates may be lower than the BLS reported rates. If pharmaceutical manufacturers raise drug prices to compensate for the higher quality, however, this factor does not account for any overstating of the drug price inflation rate.

In sum, the reported data suggest that real drug prices declined throughout most of the 1970s and rose over the period 1981 to 1994. Since the end of that period, real drug price growth has appeared to have slowed down, according to reported data. However, reported data may not capture the true difference between the general price inflation rate and the drug price inflation rate because there is ample reason to believe the drug price inflation rate has been overstated in the past. Since the beginning of 1995, BLS has taken steps toward treating new generic versions as substitutes for branded drugs when calculating the drug price index.[15] In addition, BLS now attempts to gather information on actual transaction prices rather than list prices. In the future, any remaining discrepancy in the drug price index is therefore more likely to occur because of the undersampling of new drugs and the difficulty of controlling for drug quality changes over time.

---

[15]See http://stats.bls.gov/cpifact4.htm.

## Output of New Pharmaceutical Products

Another measure of an industry's performance is output. According to theory, societal welfare is enhanced when goods are produced up to the point where marginal social benefit equals marginal social cost (see Chapter 7). Empirically, costs and benefits are hard to measure, so we must often rely on information regarding industrial structure and conduct, as well as sound judgment, to determine whether the right incentives exist for efficient output levels. Because of some monopolistic structural conditions (i.e., patents, trademarks, promotion) existing in the pharmaceutical industry, one might expect some restrictions on output. The question is whether evidence supports this expectation.

The most important measure of pharmaceutical output is the number of new chemical entities (NCEs) introduced into the market. As you know, new drug products extend and/or improve the quality of life and often substitute for expensive types of invasive surgery. Data on the number of NCEs introduced into the United States appear in table 16–8. Until 1960, new drug introductions showed a clear pattern. According to Statman (1983).

> Sixty-seven new drugs were introduced into the U.S. market during the first half of the 1940s. The drug innovation rate doubled during the second half of the 1940s. It increased to 125 during the late 1940s, then nearly doubled again to 205 in the first half of the 1950s. It increased further to 248 during the second half of the 1950s. (p. 6)

However, the 1960s witnessed a decline in the number of NCEs. Although 453 drugs were introduced in the 1950s, only 236 new drugs were introduced during the 1960s. The 1970s saw no reversal in the downward trend since the 1960s, with only 158 NCEs introduced in the marketplace by pharmaceutical companies.

Two reasons have been cited for the decline in drug innovations after the early 1960s. First, the decline may have been caused by a "depletion of research opportunities," as early evidence suggests that the innovation slowdown continued worldwide in the 1970s and 1980s (Grabowski, 1989). Second, the decline may have been the result of the 1962 amendment to the Food, Drug and Cosmetic Act, which significantly increased the costs of pharmaceutical innovations due to safety and efficacy concerns. The so-called Kefauver-Harris Act prompted the FDA to adopt more stringent rules concerning new-drug testing and approval. The greater amount of testing and approval time raised drug manufacturers' costs and reduced the effective patent life of a new drug, thereby discouraging new drug discoveries.

Regardless of the reason, there have been some encouraging signs concerning the innovative activities of pharmaceutical companies since the early 1980s. First, as table 16–8 reveals, the number of NCEs increased from 158 in the 1970s to 202 in the 1980s and then increased even farther to 247 during the first seven years of the 1990s. Second, table 16–5 shows that while R&D intensity shows no clear pattern over the 1970s, an upward trend in R&D intensity emerged during the 1980s and continued through the 1990s. Several explanations for the improvement in innovative activities have been offered.

| TABLE 16–8 | | ANNUAL NUMBER OF NEW DRUG ENTITIES IN THE UNITED STATES, 1940–1997 | |

| Year | New Drugs | Year | New Drugs |
|------|-----------|------|-----------|
| 1940 | 14 | 1970 | 16 |
| 1941 | 17 | 1971 | 14 |
| 1942 | 13 | 1972 | 10 |
| 1943 | 10 | 1973 | 17 |
| 1944 | 13 | 1974 | 18 |
| 1945 | 13 | 1975 | 15 |
| 1946 | 19 | 1976 | 14 |
| 1947 | 26 | 1977 | 16 |
| 1948 | 29 | 1978 | 23 |
| 1949 | 38 | 1979 | 15 |
| 1950 | 32 | 1980 | 13 |
| 1951 | 38 | 1981 | 19 |
| 1952 | 40 | 1982 | 26 |
| 1953 | 53 | 1983 | 22 |
| 1954 | 42 | 1984 | 15 |
| 1955 | 36 | 1985 | 20 |
| 1956 | 48 | 1986 | 24 |
| 1957 | 52 | 1987 | 20 |
| 1958 | 47 | 1988 | 19 |
| 1959 | 65 | 1989 | 24 |
| 1960 | 50 | 1990 | 24 |
| 1961 | 45 | 1991 | 30 |
| 1962 | 24 | 1992 | 26 |
| 1963 | 16 | 1993 | 25 |
| 1964 | 17 | 1994 | 22 |
| 1965 | 25 | 1995 | 28 |
| 1966 | 13 | 1996 | 53 |
| 1967 | 25 | 1997 | 39 |
| 1968 | 12 | | |
| 1969 | 9 | | |

SOURCE: *Statistical Fact Book.* (Washington DC: Pharmaceutical Manufacturers Association, various years), as cited by William S. Comanor and Stuart O. Schweitzer, "Pharmaceuticals," in *The Structure of American Industry*, ed. Walter Adams and James Brock (Englewood Cliffs, NJ: Prentice Hall, 1993), Table 7–2. Since 1990 the figures represent approvals rather than introductions and are from PhRMA, *Industry Profit* (Washington, DC: July 1998), Figure 3.2.

First, the Waxman-Hatch Act of 1984 was designed in part to correct for the regulatory lag created by the 1962 act. As mentioned previously, the life of a new-drug patent can be extended for up to five years (but no more than 14 years in total) to compensate for any approval delay by the FDA. The longer expected effective patent life for new drugs creates a better opportunity for profits and encourages more innovation.

Second, the faster pace of new drug discoveries has been attributed to the recent revolution in methods of drug discovery and development. Previously, pharmaceutical R&D largely involved **molecule manipulation,** the trial-and-error examination of the therapeutic properties of a large number of chemical entities, especially closely related derivatives of known entities (Duetsch, 1993). Today, technologies, such as genetic engineering, monoclonal antibodies, cellular biology, and immunology—all contributing to the creation of biotechnology—enable researchers to better understand the sources of diseases and how the human body potentially reacts to drug treatment. This more scientific approach to R&D is referred to as **discovery by design.** According to the Boston Consulting Group (1993),

> With knowledge about the relation between the structure and function of the molecule targeted for the drug action, small molecules can be designed that interact very specifically with the target. The target molecule is commonly a receptor on a cell surface—for example, the $H_2$ receptors that help to regulate acid production in the stomach. Rational drug design promises to supplement the traditional random search for activity and to provide specific guidance to researchers seeking useful drugs for diseases that have largely resisted treatment in the past (p. 31).

In fact, as a result of genetic engineering, scientists have recently discovered the gene responsible for Huntington's disease, among others (Boston Consulting Group, 1993).

Third, unlike the 1970s, during which real drug prices were declining, real drugs prices were high during the 1980s and for most of the 1990s (review table 16–7). The high real drug prices and the resulting sizable cash flow margins helped to fund R&D expenditures, a necessary ingredient for innovation. Recall that Grabowski and Vernon (1981) found empirically that cash flow is a major determinant of R&D expenditures. Thus, the large number of NCEs in both the 1980s and 1990s may be an indirect function of the relatively high drug prices observed during those periods.

## Profits in the Pharmaceutical Industry

Most complaints aimed at the pharmaceutical industry have concerned excessive profits. Patents, brand loyalty, and an inelastic demand for drugs written by physicians are cited as the causes of high pharmaceutical profits. Some comparative data for the after-tax return on equity (ROE) and return on assets (ROA) are shown in table 16–9 for all manufacturing firms and (SIC 283) drug firms for selected years

## Has the United States Remained the World Leader in Pharmaceutical Innovation?

Competition in the pharmaceutical industry largely involves the development and commercial introduction of new drug products. Market positions in the pharmaceutical industry can shift dramatically and swiftly when companies develop new breakthrough drugs. Until the mid-1970s, the United States was acknowledged as the world leader in pharmaceutical innovation. Evidence after that point initially suggested that the U.S. share of world pharmaceutical R&D spending fell from 60 percent in the 1950s to less than 30 percent by the end of the 1970s. The main explanation was that the declining U.S. position was a natural consequence of the depleted conditions in Europe and Japan after World War II. That is, the United States had an advantage immediately after the war that eroded as the European countries and Japan eventually recovered (Grabowski, 1989).

Some new empirical evidence for the 1980s suggests, however, that the United States may not have lost its leadership position in the world pharmaceutical industry. Specifically, Grabowski (1989) points out that the R&D expenditures of U.S. drug firms grew at an annual rate of 14.3 percent over the period 1980 to 1985, which far surpassed the rate of 1.1 percent from 1973 to 1979. Moreover, the R&D spending of U.S. firms grew at a much faster rate than those of British (8.7 percent), West German (9.8 percent), and Japanese (11.5 percent) drug firms in the first half of the 1980s. One reason Grabowski gives for the greater growth in U.S. R&D spending is the rising optimism concerning technological opportunities that originated from important new drug therapies (e.g., Tagamet) utilizing the discovery-by-design approach. The other explanation is that rising cash flows resulted from pharmaceutical prices growing more quickly than R&D spending during the 1980s. Recall that Grabowski and Vernon (1981)

found that cash flow is a primary determinant of R&D spending.

Further evidence presented by Grabowski indicates that NCEs originating in the United States have been more commercially important than those originating from other countries. According to the evidence, U.S. drug firms accounted for 41.7 percent of the 170 consensus NCEs introduced from 1970 to 1983. (Consensus NCEs are defined as new drugs introduced in at least 6 of 11 major markets during a particular period.) Switzerland, the next largest provider, accounted for a comparatively small 12.9 percent of all consensus NCEs during the period. Because Japanese drug firms concentrated on imitative rather than innovative research, they were responsible for only 4.1 percent of all consensus drugs.

Additional evidence suggests that U.S. firms continue to develop new drugs on a much larger scale than their foreign competitors. According to Ballance, Pogany, and Forstner (1992), U.S. firms accounted for 40 percent of all self-originating drugs under development in 1989. Japanese drug firms, the closest rivals to U.S. companies in this innovation category, were responsible for 20.9 percent of the self-originating drugs under development in the same year.

All the evidence suggests that the United States has not lost its position as the world leader in pharmaceutical research, at least through the 1980s. Grabowski cautions that some early evidence indicates that Japanese drug firms are now adopting an innovative rather than imitative strategy. In addition, he notes that increased generic competition and pending stringent price regulations in the United States could adversely affect the cash flows of branded pharmaceutical companies and result in a less favorable environment for new-product development.

| TABLE 16–9 | RETURN ON ASSETS AND STOCKHOLDER EQUITY FOR DRUG AND ALL MANUFACTURING COMPANIES, VARIOUS YEARS |

| | After-Tax Return on Equity | | | | |
| --- | --- | --- | --- | --- | --- |
| | **1986** | **1989** | **1992** | **1995** | **1997** |
| All manufacturing | 9.6% | 13.5% | 2.6% | 16.2% | 16.6% |
| Drugs (SIC 283) | 24.1 | 25.3 | 22.3 | 27.0 | 23.2 |
| | After-Tax Return on Assets | | | | |
| | **1986** | **1989** | **1992** | **1995** | **1997** |
| All manufacturing | 4.2% | 5.5% | 0.9% | 6.2% | 6.6% |
| Drugs (SIC 283) | 11.8 | 12.5 | 10.5 | 10.4 | 9.5 |

SOURCE: U.S. Bureau of the Census, *Quarterly Financial Report* (various issues).

from 1986 to 1997. ROE and ROA are determined by dividing net income (net sales less operating costs and expenses) after taxes by the value of stockholder equity and the firm's assets, respectively. The data clearly show that the profitability of drug firms, as measured by either ROE or ROA, was consistently much higher than that of the manufacturing industry average. Specifically, the ROE and ROA for drug firms, on average, were more than twice the manufacturing industry average for the five periods.

Researchers point out that pharmaceutical accounting rates of return may be biased upward due to unusually high R&D and marketing outlays (e.g., see Scherer, 1993). Expenditures on these "intangible assets" are expensed, but should be capitalized and then depreciated over an appropriate time period because they ordinarily yield a long-term flow of benefits to drug manufacturers. Studies have found that pharmaceutical returns are 20 to 25 percent lower when R&D and marketing outlays are treated as intangible assets (Office of Technology Assessment, 1993).

Even after accounting biases have been eliminated, pharmaceutical returns generally remain higher than the manufacturing average (Comanor, 1986). Pharmaceutical industry spokespersons point out that research and development is a risky venture. High R&D risks translate into high pharmaceutical returns, because otherwise risk-averse individuals would be unwilling to invest in drug firms. They note that the successful introduction of a pharmaceutical product costs about $200 million or more because a drug firm encounters a large number of misses before finding a commercial hit (DiMasi, Hansen, Grabowski, and Lasagna, 1991).

So is it true that pharmaceutical R&D is a risky undertaking? According to the evidence provided in table 16–9, rates of return in the pharmaceutical industry seem to be more stable than the average return in the manufacturing sector, at least for the five years reported.

INSIGHT 16-7

## An International Comparison of Pharmaceutical Profits

It should be apparent by now that it is very difficult to determine empirically whether or not the accounting profits of U.S. drug companies are excessive. When combined, expenditures on R&D and promotion can account for up to nearly half of the typical brand-name pharmaceutical company's annual budget. Simple interindustry accounting profit rate comparisons fail to account accurately for the intangible asset nature of R&D and promotion outlays. Studies that estimate and evaluate the returns and costs associated with R&D investments depend on a host of assumptions, each tending to reduce the reliability of the results.

An international comparison of pharmaceutical profit rates is another way to evaluate the excessiveness of returns in the U.S. pharmaceutical industry. Because pharmaceutical companies in different countries are more likely to incur similar R&D and promotion investments, the comparison of accounting profit rates should be less problematic. With that in mind, table 1 provides a comparison of the average profit margin on sales for the major pharmaceutical companies in 10 countries. Information on the restrictiveness of pharmaceutical price controls in each country is also listed.

According to the table, the profit rate of pharmaceutical companies in the 10 countries varied widely, averaging 13.1 percent in 1984, 1987, and 1988. Only a very few countries reported a

| TABLE 1 | AVERAGE PROFIT MARGIN TO SALES FOR MAJOR PHARMACEUTICAL COMPANIES IN SELECTED INDUSTRIALIZED COUNTRIES, 1984, 1987, AND 1988 | |
| --- | --- | --- |
| **Country (number of firms)** | **Average Profit Margin on Sales** | **Price Controls** |
| Belgium (1) | 8.0% | Substantial |
| France (4) | 11.8 | Substantial |
| Germany (1) | 2.4 | Limited |
| Hungary (1) | 29.5 | Substantial |
| Italy (3) | 10.4 | Substantial |
| Japan (27) | 5.3 | Limited |
| Netherlands (3) | 8.5 | Limited |
| Sweden (2) | 9.0 | Substantial |
| United Kingdom (4) | 24.7 | Limited |
| United States (26) | 21.7 | Limited |
| Average | 13.1 | |

SOURCE: Robert Ballance, Jano Pogany, and Helmut Forstner, *The World's Pharmaceutical Industries* (Brookfield, VT: Edward Elgar, 1992), Tables 6.1 and 6.2.

**(continued)**

sufficient number of observations to allow us to draw meaningful conclusions. We can conclude that the profit rate of U.S. drug firms (21.7 percent), although well above the average for the entire sample, was lower than the reported profit rate for drug firms in the United Kingdom (24.7 percent). In addition, the relatively high profit rate of U.S. and U.K. drug firms did not appear to be a function of limited price controls. Drug firms in Japan and the Netherlands, which also faced limited price controls, had profit rates far below the sample average. Ballance, Pogany, and Forstner (1992) believe that "differences in profit margins

may well be due to variations in product mix and specialization rather than differences in pricing regulations" (p. 155). These international data fail to support the claim that the profits of U.S. drug firms are uniquely high and suggest that limited price controls do not necessarily account for the relatively high profits of U.S. drug firms.[1]

[1]In addition, a study by the GAO (1994) found that inflation-adjusted pharmaceutical spending growth from 1985 to 1990 was very comparable in the United Kingdom (3.5 percent), Germany (3.9 percent), Sweden (4.5 percent), France (4.7 percent), and the United States (4.7 percent), even though drug prices have tended to rise more quickly in the United States.

Perhaps focusing on aggregate industry returns masks the variability of returns at the individual firm level. Indeed, that seems to be the case. A study by Grabowski and Vernon (1990), which analyzed the returns associated with 100 new-drug introductions during the 1970s, uncovered evidence indicating that pharmaceutical R&D is very risky and costly. Based on a number of assumptions concerning product duration, cash flow margins, R&D costs, and worldwide sales, the authors found that the variation in returns for new-drug introductions is highly skewed, with only the top 30 drugs covering average R&D costs. Moreover, the authors discovered that the present value of the cash flow associated with the 10 least profitable of the top 30 drugs just barely covered the present value of their R&D costs.

One implication of Grabowski and Vernon's study is that a successful drug company must have an occasional "blockbuster" to cover the large fixed costs that characterize the R&D process. Another implication is that the real drug price increases of the 1980s, as evidenced by table 16–7, may have been necessary for the average new-drug innovation to recover its R&D costs. Overall, their study implies that the high rate of profit observed in the pharmaceutical industry may be justified by the significant risk and cost of new-product innovations. The authors found that the average return to R&D equaled the 9 percent industry cost of capital, implying a normal rate of return on pharmaceutical R&D investment.

However, another study on the returns to R&D by the Office of Technology Assessment (OTA, 1993) shows that Grabowski and Vernon's results do not hold for drugs introduced from 1981 to 1983. The OTA study found that each NCE, on average, can be expected to return a net present value of at least $36 million more than necessary to bring forth the investment in R&D. The implication is that drug prices could be reduced across the board by at least 4.3 percent without reducing returns below the amount necessary to repay R&D investors. One reason the OTA's results differ from those of Grabowski and Vernon is that the increasing real drug prices and associated greater pharmaceutical revenues during the 1980s were more than adequate to cover R&D costs. The OTA study claims,

> Together, the findings on returns on pharmaceutical R&D and to the industry as a whole explain why R&D expenditures have risen so dramatically in real terms throughout the 1980s. Investors have followed the promise of high returns on future innovations. Ultimately investment in research is determined by expected revenues. The dramatic increase in real revenues to new drugs throughout the 1980s has sent signals to the industry that more investment will be rewarded handsomely. The industry has responded as expected, by increasing its commitment to investment, including investment in R&D (p. 104).

## *The Performance of the Pharmaceutical Industry: A Summary*

In this section, we reviewed data concerning the prescription drug price inflation rate and profits as measures of industry performance. Drug prices were shown to have increased more rapidly than general prices for all but two years since 1981. The average profit rate in the pharmaceutical industry was also shown to be higher than the average profit rate in the manufacturing sector during the 1980s and 1990s. By themselves, these two performance measures suggest that society's scarce resources may be misallocated in the pharmaceutical industry.

Data regarding the introduction of NCEs paint a somewhat different picture of the pharmaceutical industry. After slowing during the 1960s and 1970s, the number of new chemical entities by U.S. drug firms actually increased during the 1980s and 1990s. The R&D spending of U.S. drug firms also increased during the 1980s, and this trend has continued into the 1990s. Two reasons for the greater innovation of U.S. drug firms in recent years are rising real drug prices and consistent profits. As Grabowski and Vernon (1981) show, a major determinant of pharmaceutical innovation is cash flow.

There may be a lesson to learn here. Perhaps high pharmaceutical prices and profits should be viewed not as indicators of "static" inefficiency but as determinants of "dynamic" efficiency. Static efficiency refers to the efficiency of firms at a point in time and reflects how successfully firms employ a given technology or produce a given product. In contrast, dynamic efficiency relates to the efficiency of firms over time and captures how successful they are at developing new product and process innovations. Most analysts agree that the major contribution of the pharmaceutical industry is the development of new drugs over time. New drugs potentially save and increase the quality of lives. Because a greater cash flow is necessary for new-product development, rising pharmaceutical prices and profits may be reason to smile rather than frown.

## SUMMARY

This chapter assessed the structure, conduct, and performance of the U.S. pharmaceutical industry. Based on a four-digit SIC classification, the pharmaceutical industry was shown to contain a relatively large number of equally sized firms, but disaggregation of the pharmaceutical industry into therapeutic markets showed that only a few major drugs typically compete with one another. Legal patents and brand loyalty built up during the patent period are argued to cause substantial barriers to entry into therapeutic markets. Generic drug companies offering huge discounts are particularly ineffective in influencing the loyalty attached to brand-name drugs because physicians are often responsible for selecting drugs. Physicians are not normally price sensitive since they are effectively spending someone else's money.

Evidence shows that price competition takes place among multisource drugs. Price competition sometimes occurs among branded drugs during the patent period and between generic and brand-name drugs during the postpatent period. Drug prices are usually lower when there are more substitute products. Studies show that generic competition causes the brand-name firm's market share to fall by an average of 50 percent two years after entry. The innovator firm's advertising helps to preserve its market share, while the follower firms' advertising helps them to gain market share.

New-product innovation, the major benefit of the pharmaceutical industry, tends to be a risky endeavor and was shown to depend on past R&D success and cash flow. Debate still continues over the relation between firm size and innovation. The safest conclusion to draw from recent studies is that a mixture of firm sizes in the pharmaceutical industry best favors innovation.

Recent data suggest that real drug prices have risen and pharmaceutical firms have experienced relatively high rates of return since the beginning of the 1980s. The resulting cash flow has financed the increase in R&D spending as a percentage of sales and the resulting greater number of new chemical entity introductions during the 1980 and 1990s. All in all, the pharmaceutical industry seems to best fit the model of a "mild oligopoly." That is, there is some evidence of a few competitors in therapeutic markets, substantial but not perfect barriers to entry based on patents and trademarks, evidence of price and product rivalry rather than cooperation, and evidence of relatively high profits.

The future should witness a continual evolution in the pharmaceutical industry. The demand side of the market will most likely adopt further cost-saving methods, such as formularies, drug review utilization, and generic substitution. Government may be prone to impose price controls if drug prices continue to soar. Seller concentration in many therapeutic markets should diminish as many drug patents soon expire and generic competition increases. It will be interesting to follow the effects of these demand- and supply-side changes on new-drug innovation.

*Review Questions and Problems*

1. Describe three benefits associated with pharmaceutical products. Cite one example of each.

2. How do the four-digit SIC classification and the therapeutic market definition of the pharmaceutical industry differ in terms of seller concentration? Which is the better measure? Why? Think in terms of actual and potential competition.

3. Explain some of the methods adopted by third-party payers to control drug prices.

4. Cite three reasons unconstrained physicians tend to purchase brand-name instead of generic products.

5. What benefits and costs do pharmacists face when dispensing generic drugs?

6. What is the economic rationale behind a patent? Why may the effective patent life of a drug be shorter than the legal life? Why may the effective patent life be longer than the legal life?

7. What two effects did the Waxman-Hatch Act of 1984 have on the supply side of the pharmaceutical market?

8. Why might the FDA tend to delay the drug approval process? Explain in terms of type 1 and type 2 errors.

9. What general conclusions have studies reached concerning drug price competition?

10. What general conclusion have studies reached concerning the promotion of pharmaceutical products? Cite some evidence.

11. What are the two main determinants of R&D spending according to Grabowski and Vernon? What is the relation between firm size and pharmaceutical innovation? Briefly summarize the theoretical considerations and empirical findings.

12. How has the pharmaceutical producer price index compared to the general producer price index since the 1970s?

13. Cite four reasons why the pharmaceutical price inflation rate may have been biased upward in the past.

14. Explain the trend in the number of NCE introductions from after WWII until 1990. What factors account for any changes?

15. What three reasons are claimed to account for the high reported profits of pharmaceutical companies? Do you think drug companies earn excessive profits? Why or why not?

## References

Acs, Zoltan J., and David B. Audretsch. "Innovation in Large and Small Firms: An Empirical Analysis." *American Economic Review* 78 (September 1988), pp. 678–90.
———. "Innovation, Market Structure, and Firm Size." *Review of Economics and Statistics* 69 (November 1987), pp. 567–74.
Ballance, Robert, Jano Pogany, and Helmut Forstner. *The World's Pharmaceutical Industries.* Brookfield, VT: Edward Elgar, 1992.

Berndt, Ernst R., Zvi Griliches, and Joshua G. Rosett. "Auditing the Producer Price Index: Micro Evidence from Prescription Pharmaceutical Preparations." *Journal of Business and Economic Statistics* (July 1993), pp. 251–64.

Bishop, Jerry E. "Bacterium Causes Most Peptic Ulcers." *The Wall Street Journal*, February 10, 1994, p. B6.

Boston Consulting Group. *The Changing Environment for U.S. Pharmaceuticals.* Boston: Boston Consulting Group, 1993.

Carroll, Norman V., and Alan P. Wolfgang. "Risks, Benefits, and Generic Substitution." *Journal of Consumer Affairs* 25 (summer 1991), pp. 110–21.

Caves, Richard E., Michael D. Whinston, and Mark A. Hurwitz. "Patent Expiration, Entry, and Competition in the U.S. Pharmaceutical Industry." *Brookings Papers: Microeconomics 1991*, 1991, pp. 1–66.

Chren, Mary-Margaret, and C. Seth Landefeld. "Physician Behavior and Their Interactions with Drug Companies." *Journal of the American Medical Association* 271 (March 2, 1994), pp. 684–89.

Clark, Lindley H. "Drug Price Rise May Be Exaggerated." *The Wall Street Journal*, October 8, 1993, p. A14.

Comanor, William S. "Research and Technical Change in the Pharmaceutical Industry." *Review of Economics and Statistics* (May 1965), pp. 182–90.

———. "The Political Economy of the Pharmaceutical Industry." *Journal of Economic Literature* (September 1986), pp. 1178–1217.

Comanor, William S., and Stuart O. Schweitzer. "Pharmaceuticals." In *The Structure of American Industry*, edited by Walter Adams and James Brock. Englewood Cliffs, NJ: Prentice Hall, 1995, pp. 177–96.

DiMasi, Joseph A. "Success Rates for New Drugs Entering Clinical Testing in the United States." *Clinical and Pharmacology Therapeutics* 58 (July 1995), pp. 1–14.

DiMasi, Joseph A., Henry G. Grabowski, and John Vernon. "R&D Costs, Innovative Output and Firm Size in the Pharmaceutical Industry." *International Journal of the Economics of Business* 2 (1995), pp. 201–19.

DiMasi, Joseph A., Ronald W. Hansen, Henry G. Grabowski, and Louis Lasagna. "Cost of Innovation in the Pharmaceutical Industry." *Journal of Health Economics* 10 (1991), pp. 107–42.

Duetsch, Larry L. "Pharmaceuticals: The Critical Role of Innovation." In *Industry Studies*, edited by Larry L. Duetsch. Englewood Cliffs, NJ: Prentice Hall, 1993.

Egan, John W., Harlow N. Higinbotham, and J. Fred Weston. *Economics of the Pharmaceutical Industry.* New York: Praeger Publishers, 1982.

General Accounting Office. "Prescription Drugs: Spending Controls in Four European Countries." GAO/HEHS-94-30. Washington, DC: U.S. Government Printing Office, 1994.

———. "Prescription Drugs: Companies Charge More in the United States than in Canada." GAO/HRD-92-110. Washington, DC: U.S. Government Printing Office, 1992.

Grabowski, Henry G. "An Analysis of U.S. International Competitiveness in Pharmaceuticals." *Managerial and Decision Economics* 10 (March 1989), pp. 27–33.

———. "The Determinants of Industrial Research and Development: A Study of the Chemical, Drug and Petroleum Industries." *Journal of Political Economy* (March-April 1968), pp. 292–305.

Grabowski, Henry G., and John M. Vernon. "Brand Loyalty, Entry, and Price Competition in Pharmaceuticals after the 1984 Drug Act." *Journal of Law and Economics* 35 (October 1992), pp. 331–50.

———. "A New Look at the Returns and Risks to Pharmaceutical R&D." *Management Science* 36 (July 1990), pp. 804–21.

———. "Longer Patents for Lower Imitation Barriers: The 1984 Drug Act." *American Economic Review Papers and Proceedings* 76 (May 1986), pp. 195–98.

———. *The Regulation of Pharmaceuticals: Balancing the Benefits and Risks.* Washington, DC: American Enterprise Institute, 1983.

————. "The Determinants of Research and Development Expenditures in the Pharmaceutical Industry." In *Drugs and Health*, edited by Robert Helms. Washington, DC: American Enterprise Institute, 1981, pp. 3–20.

Greer, Douglas F. *Industrial Organization and Public Policy.* New York: Macmillan, 1992.

Henderson, Rebecca, and Ian Cockburn. "Scale, Scope and Spillovers: The Determinants of Research Productivity in Drug Discovery." *Rand Journal* 27 (spring 1996), pp. 32–59.

Hurwitz, Mark A., and Richard E. Caves. "Persuasion or Information? Promotion and the Shares of Brand Name and Generic Pharmaceuticals." *Journal of Law and Economics* 31 (October 1988), pp. 299–320.

Langowitz, Nan S., and Samuel B. Graves. "Innovative Productivity in Pharmaceutical Firms." *Research Technology Management* 35 (March-April 1992), pp. 39–41.

Leffler, Keith B. "Persuasion or Information? The Economics of Prescription Drug Advertising." *Journal of Law and Economics* 24 (April 1981), pp. 45–74.

Levit, Katherine R. et al. "National Expenditures, 1996" *Health Care Financing Review* 19 (fall 1997), pp. 161–200.

Lu, Z. John, and William S. Comanor. "Strategic Pricing and New Pharmaceuticals." Mimeo, University of California at Santa Barbara, 1994.

Mansfield, Edwin. *Industrial Research and Technological Innovation.* New York: W. W. Norton, 1968.

McRae, James J., and Francis Tapon. "Some Empirical Evidence on Post-Patent Barriers to Entry in the Canadian Pharmaceutical Industry." *Journal of Health Economics* 4 (1985), pp. 43–61.

Moore, Stephen D. "Glaxo, SmithKline Renew Their Rivalry in Medicines Used to Prevent Vomiting." *The Wall Street Journal,* November 19, 1993, p. B4D.

Moore, William J., and Robert J. Newman. "Drug Formulary Restrictions as a Cost-Containment Policy in Medicaid Programs." *Journal of Law and Economics* 36 (April 1993), pp. 71–97.

*Mosby Medical Encyclopedia.* New York City: C. V. Mosby, 1992.

Office of Technology Assessment. *Pharmaceutical R and D: Costs, Risks and Rewards.* OTA-H-522. Washington, DC: U.S. Government Printing Office, February 1993.

Peltzman, Sam. *Regulation of Pharmaceutical Innovation: The 1962 Amendments.* Washington, DC: American Enterprise Institute, 1974.

Pharmaceutical Research and Manufacturers of America (PhRMA). *Industry Profile.* Washington, DC (July 1998).

Pollard, Michael R. "Managed Care and a Changing Pharmaceutical Industry." *Health Affairs* 9 (fall 1990), pp. 55–65.

Price Waterhouse. *Financial Trends in the Pharmaceutical Industry and Projected Effects of Recent Federal Legislation.* Report prepared for the Pharmaceutical Manufacturers Association, October 21, 1993.

Scherer, F. M. "Pricing, Profits, and Technological Progress in the Pharmaceutical Industry." *Journal of Economic Perspectives* 7 (summer 1993), pp. 97–115.

Scherer, F. M., and David Ross. *Industrial Market Structure and Economic Performance.* Boston: Houghton Mifflin, 1990.

Schmalensee, Richard. "Product Differentiation Advantages of Pioneering Brands." *American Economic Review* 72 (June 1982), pp. 349–65.

Schnee, Jerome. "Innovation and Discovery in the Ethical Pharmaceutical Industry." Chapter 8 in *Research and Innovation in the Modern Corporation*, edited by Edwin Mansfield, John Rapaport, Jerome Schnee, Samuel Wagner, and Michael Hamburger. New York: W. W. Norton, 1971.

Schumpeter, Joseph. *Capitalism, Socialism and Democracy.* New York: Harper, 1950.

Schwartzman, David. *Innovation in the Pharmaceutical Industry.* Baltimore: Johns Hopkins University Press, 1976.

Statman, Meir. *Competition in the Pharmaceutical Industry: The Declining Profitability of Drug Innovation.* Washington, DC: American Enterprise Institute, 1983.

Tanouye, Elyse. "Heartburn Drug Makers Feel Judge's Heat." *The Wall Street Journal* (October 16, 1995), p. B8.

Tanouye, Elyse, and Thomas M. Burton. "More Firms 'Switch' Prescription Drugs to Give Them Over-the-Counter Status." *The Wall Street Journal*, July 29, 1993, p. B1.

Tanouye, Elyse, and Michael Waldholz. "Senate Study of Drug Prices Could Prove a Bitter Pill for Pharmaceutical Makers." *The Wall Street Journal*, February 3, 1993, p. B1.

Temin, Peter. "Realized Benefits from Switching Drugs." *Journal of Law and Economics* 35 (October 1992), pp. 351–69.

———. *Taking Your Medicine: Drug Regulation in the United States.* Cambridge, MA: Harvard University Press, 1980.

Tregarthen, Suzanne. "Prescription to Stop Drug Companies' Profiteering." *The Wall Street Journal*, March 5, 1992, p. A15.

Virts, John R., and J. Fred Weston. "Expectations and the Allocation of Research and Development Resources." In *Drugs and Health*, edited by Robert Helms. Washington, DC: American Enterprise Institute, 1981, pp. 21–45.

Weidenbaum, Murray. "Are Drug Prices Too High?" *The Public Interest* 112 (summer 1993), pp. 84–89.

Welsch, Jonathan. "American Home Used a Blitz for Orudis." *The Wall Street Journal* (December 4, 1995), p. B3.

Wiggins, Steven N., and Robert Maness. "Price Competition in Pharmaceutical Markets." Mimeo, Department of Economics, Texas A&M University (June 1994).

## CEBS Questions

CEBS Sample Question on Subject Matter from CEBS Course IX Study Manual

1. List and define the methods used by third-party payers to control pharmaceutical costs. (pages 515 and 517)

CEBS Sample Exam Questions

1. Which of the following statements is the safest conclusion regarding the relationship between firm size and the innovation process in the pharmaceutical industry?
   A. Large firms are the best innovators because they have the financial resources to conduct effective research and development
   B. Large firms are the best innovators because they can advertise more effectively
   C. Small firms are the best innovators because there is less bureaucratic red tape in smaller firms
   D. Small firms are the best innovators because they have more creative talent
   E. A mixture of firm sizes is most favorable for fostering pharmaceutical innovation

2. Which of the following is (are) correct statements regarding the economic performance of the pharmaceutical industry in recent years?
   I. Drug prices have increased more rapidly than general prices
   II. The average profit rate is higher than that in the manufacturing sector

    III. The risk of the pharmaceutical industry is less than of the manufacturing
        sector
        A. I only
        B. II only
        C. I and II only
        D. II and III only
        E. I and III only

3. All the following statements regarding a patent for a pharmaceutical drug are
correct EXCEPT:
    A. The legal maximum number of years for a patent is 14 years
    B. The effective life of a patent is often less than the legal maximum because
       the FDA takes a number of years to approve a product for commercial
       introduction
    C. A pharmaceutical patent is granted for a drug's chemical composition, not
       its therapeutic novelty
    D. A legal patent does not guarantee a monopoly position
    E. The Waxman-Hatch Act quickened the approval process for generic drugs

*Answer to Sample Question from Study Manual*
The methods used are formularies, drug utilization review, and required generic
substitution. A formulary is a required list of selected pharmaceutical products that
physicians are required to prescribe for the third-party payers' patients. A drug
utilization review monitors the actions of physicians and identifies physicians who
inappropriately prescribe medicines. Generic substitution requires that pharmacists
substitute lower-priced generic products for higher priced brand-names whenever
possible.

*Answers to Sample Exam Questions*
1. E is the answer. See pages 534–535 of the text.
2. C is the answer. Statement III is incorrect. The pharmaceutical industry faces
high risks in product innovations and product liability. Statements I and II are
correct. See pages 545 and 548 of the text.
3. A is the answer. The legal patent period was changed from 17 years to 20 years
in 1996. See pages 518–519 of the text.

# 17

# An Overview of Health Care Reform

Hospital Fees Hit the Middle Class Hard: Present System Favors the Rich and the Poor—Medical Men Suggest Ways to Lower the Cost of Illness—*The New York Times*

**M**any people today are dissatisfied with the performance of the U.S. health care system. The cost of health care in the United States is alleged to be higher and rising faster than in any other country. Many worry that the health care monster will continue to devour an increasingly large slice of the economic pie. Moreover, at any one point in time, critics note that one out of every six nonelderly citizens lacks insurance coverage for acute care. Many others in the United States are seriously underinsured or lack proper long-term care insurance coverage.

The title of the newspaper article above captures the U.S. health care system's failure to provide universal coverage and contain health care costs. One indeed might argue (perhaps wrongly) that poor people either receive free care at public institutions or are provided with medical and long-term care coverage through the Medicaid program, while rich individuals can afford to self-insure. Middle-income individuals, then, are hit hardest by hospital fees because they face the prospects of rising copayments, reduced wage income, benefit denial, job lock, or other problems pertaining to private health insurance coverage.

The fascinating thing about the newspaper article cited above is that it originally appeared in *The New York Times* 75 years ago, proving that the more things change, the more they remain the same.[1] Private health insurance was just barely in its embryo stage in 1924 when the article was first published.

---

[1] See Chenery (1924). Incidentally, the next article on the same page was titled "When Russian Empire Tottered—An Inside Picture." Go figure!

Without health insurance, a large fraction of a middle-class family's income was subject to the vagaries of health status. In fact, at a well-known hospital, the cost of maintaining one patient for one day rose from $2.65 in 1919 to $4.71 in 1929, an average annual increase of nearly 9 percent.[2] The quest for financial security in the 1920s most likely resulted in the eventual birth and growth of private health insurance in the United States. Interestingly enough, William Chenery, the journalist who wrote the *New York Times* article, suggested that the United States copy the private health insurance system with which Cuba was experimenting at the time rather than the British or German social health insurance systems. The U.S. private health insurance industry, in fact, began to emerge about five years later, in 1929, as discussed at the beginning of Chapter 13.

Today the health care crisis has taken on a different shape. Only a small percentage of the population is currently uninsured compared to the 1920s. However, everyone is affected by the rising cost of health care services, not just the middle-income class. A rising share of compensation going toward health insurance premiums affects employers and employees alike. The poor and elderly populations, as well as the state and federal governments, are affected by Medicaid and Medicare budgets that are being squeezed due to escalating medical costs. Health care analysts and policymakers are searching for ways to improve the American health care system.

Not surprisingly, various groups have advanced a large number of health care reform plans. The plans differ in a number of respects, especially concerning the role the individual, employer, and government play in the financing of medical insurance and the functions the government and marketplace serve in the allocation of health care resources. To help us better understand what health care reform is all about, this chapter

- Summarizes the performance of the U.S. health care system and conducts an international comparison.

- Examines the various proposals for health care reform at the national level.

- Analyzes the health care reforms currently being adopted in various states.

- Briefly reviews President Clinton's National Health Security Act of 1993.

---

[2]Caldwell (1930), as cited by Stevens (1987). According to Stevens, the 1920s represented the flowering of consumerism in the hospital services industry. Stevens notes that "there was a running joke in the late 1920s that there were two classes of people in hospitals, those who entered poor and those who left poor" (p. 134). Apparently, the joke is still running!

# The Performance of the U.S. Health Care System: A Summary and an International Comparison

Thus far, the structure, conduct, and performance of the U.S. health care system has been examined in piecemeal fashion. Chapter 13 analyzed the private health insurance industry, and Chapters 14, 15, and 16 discussed the individual markets for physician services, hospital services, and pharmaceutical products. In this section, we summarize what is known about the structure, conduct, and performance of each individual medical care market. After the summary of the individual markets, the aggregate performance of the entire health care economy is assessed and compared to the performance of a select group of health care systems around the world.

## Summarizing the Structure, Conduct, and Performance of the Various Medical Care Markets

**Private Health Insurance Industry**   The structure of the private health insurance industry is highly competitive largely because it contains many firms, each serving only a small portion of the market. Recently, however, competitive pressure has brought about a wave of mergers as insurance firms try to capture a competitive edge in the marketplace. As a result, antitrust officials might want to keep a watchful eye on future organizational developments in this market. Barriers to entry appear low so potential competition must be considered by the existing firms, and products appear to be reasonably homogeneous. Consumer information in the group buyer market is relatively complete; however, some information imperfections exist in the market for individual insurance.

As economic theory suggests, the conduct of the insurance industry reflects its highly competitive structure. The price of medical insurance has tended to decline over the long run, and some firms in the industry have followed undesirable practices because of the intense competition. Benefit denial, cherry-picking, and high prices charged to the medically indigent are among some of the undesirable practices observed. On the performance side, a large percentage of people remain uninsured in the United States, even after allowing for Medicaid and Medicare coverage. A family without health insurance coverage faces substantial financial insecurity. Overinsurance, underinsurance, and job lock are other problems in the private health insurance industry that impose cost on society.

**Physician Services Industry**   Because convenience is valued by consumers (and thus the individual demand curves are downward sloping) and given the vast number of sellers in the market, the physician services industry can be considered monopolistically competitive with relatively low barriers to entry. Medical licensure represents the primary barrier to entry into the physician market. The question, from a societal point of view, is whether the benefits of quality improvements resulting from medical licensing outweigh the higher prices from entry restrictions. With the development of large, institutional suppliers of physician services, the necessity of medical licensing may diminish in the future as enterprise liability plays a greater role. The limited nature of the entry barrier has meant that the number of physicians per capita has grown substantially over time. One important structural issue is whether there are too many specialists and not enough primary care givers in the United States. It should not be forgotten that any ability of physicians to raise prices has been seriously compromised, both by MCOs and by the government, which have increasingly used their monopsonistic powers to extract price concessions from physicians.

The prevalence of an asymmetry of information between patients and physicians has influenced conduct in the physician services market. Health economists continue to analyze if physicians play on the asymmetry of information, especially in competitive markets, by unnecessarily inducing the demand for their services. This type of behavior was developed and analyzed within the context of the supplier-induced-demand model. Practice variations have also been observed across geographic regions of the United States (and in other countries as well). Policy analysts continue to sort out the reasons behind practice variations. In terms of performance, the growth in physician prices and expenditures continues to outpace the growth in the general price level and the overall economy, although the differential has moderated in recent years. However, in real terms, physician income growth has stabilized in recent years, and the rate of return of physician education is reasonably close to the rates of return observed on comparable types of educational investments.

**Hospital Services Industry**    Because economies of scale are exhausted at about the 200–bed level, most areas in the United States cannot support more than two or three hospitals. Moreover, people are reluctant to travel far distances for hospital services, so most markets tend to be local in nature. The huge sunk costs of building a hospital and learning curve effects cause substantial barriers to entry into the hospital services industry. While most hospitals tend to offer standardized products, some large teaching hospitals are often perceived as offering better quality. Given that the out-of-pocket price for hospital services is less than 3 cents on the dollar, most patient/consumers tend to be relatively uninformed about price and have little incentive to comparison shop for hospital services. Countervailing these monopoly-like characteristics is the fact that institutional buyers, like MCOs and the government, have taken on a greater buyer role in the hospital services industry. All these considerations suggest that the hospital services industry can best be described structurally as a mild or loose (standardized) oligopoly.

Conduct issues pertaining to the hospital services industry include the effects of ownership and competition on pricing and the charitable function of hospitals. Earlier studies, prior to the 1980s, found that increased competition caused hospitals, especially nonprofit hospitals, to increase quality by adopting new cost-enhancing technologies and thus raising prices. This type of behavior was referred to as the Medical Arms Race. Newer studies based on more recent data have tended to find that greater competition has not led to higher hospital prices and, in some cases, has led to lower prices, especially among for-profit hospitals. Given the many complex factors affecting hospital pricing, more careful studies on the effects of competition in this industry are needed before we can comfortably conclude that competition leads to lower hospital prices, however.

The effect of MCOs on the cost of hospital services and the growth of integrated delivery systems (IDSs) are two other important conduct issues concerning the hospital services industry. Studies conclude that MCOs tend to lower hospital costs by about 15 to 20 percent compared to otherwise identical fee-for-service insurance plans. Quality of care in MCOs and in fee-for-service insurance plans is very similar, although some evidence indicates that MCOs may provide poor individuals with inferior care. This is another important area where additional research is required. IDSs, in which physicians, hospitals, and other medical organizations integrate their organizations either legally or by contract, have been evolving over time. These integrated systems have been developing in large part to counteract the powerful institutional buyer side (e.g., MCOs and the government) in the hospital services market. IDSs may offer cost savings and quality of care improvements, but studies have not consistently provided evidence for these benefits.

As far as performance is concerned, hospital expenditures make up a large percentage of GDP. While hospital care expenditures exploded from 1.8 percent of GDP in 1960 to 4.9 percent in 1992, the good news is that the rate has stabilized in recent years and was 4.7 percent in 1996. The hospital price inflation rate continues to outstrip the general price inflation rate, although recent years have witnessed a narrowing of the gap. Staffing ratios at hospitals continue to burgeon, most likely reflecting the more severe case-mix associated with inpatient services, as more people are directed toward outpatient services. Any dramatic attempts at further cost reductions for inpatient hospital services may be futile as a smaller and smaller percentage of critically ill patients account for an increasingly greater fraction of costs. Most likely, only rationing of care to the severely ill will further reduce the cost of hospital inpatient services in the future.

**Pharmaceutical Industry**    Substantial barriers to entry brought on by patents and promotion expenditures, differentiated products resulting from promotion expenditures, and a few dominant firms in the therapeutic markets are the key structural characteristics associated with the pharmaceutical industry. The demand side of the pharmaceutical market has become more concentrated over time due to institutional buyers, but their ability to affect the operation and performance of the industry is still somewhat limited. Recall that consumers' out-of-pocket expenditures currently stand at about 55 percent for drugs compared to less than 3 percent for hospital services. All these characteristics lead to the conclusion that the pharmaceutical industry can be roughly labeled as a tight, differentiated oligopoly.

Despite its oligopolistic nature, there are ample signs of price competition in the pharmaceutical industry. During the patent period, branded drugs often compete against other branded drugs treating the same illness but based on different chemical compositions. After the legal patent period, branded drugs face considerable competition from generic drugs, and generic drugs compete among themselves, as well. Although the price competition is not perfect, it has tended to be much more rigorous since the passing of the Waxman-Hatch Act in 1984. The high promotion expenditures of pharmaceutical companies simultaneously play both an informative and a persuasive role. For example, studies suggest that the promotion expenditures of leading firms tend to preserve their market shares while the promotion expenditures of follower firms reduce the leaders' market shares. Research and development expenditures, the source of product competition among pharmaceutical companies, have been found to depend on cash flows. It appears from the literature that an assortment of firm sizes, some relatively large and some relatively small, are desirable for innovation purposes.

At first blush, the U.S. pharmaceutical industry appears to allocate resources inefficiently. Since the late 1970s, real drug prices have risen, although once again the gap between the drug price inflation rate and the general price inflation rate has narrowed in recent years. In addition, pharmaceutical profit rates are much greater than the manufacturing industry average even after allowing for the amortization of promotion and R&D expenditures. It is interesting to note that these high profits may be financing new drug discoveries because the innovation and commercial introduction of new drugs tend to be risky endeavors. Most pharmaceutical companies have a series of costly misses before a commercial hit. Rather than signal a misallocation of society's resources, the high profits may reflect the high risks and provide the source of financing for R&D ventures. New drug discoveries have increased tremendously in the United States since the late 1970s as a result.

**Overall Health Care Economy**   The preceding discussion suggests that the prices and expenditures on various medical services continue to rise, albeit at a slower rate than in the past. The transition to a managed-care health care system has helped to promote some cost savings in various medical care markets but has also resulted in some rationing of care. Choice of physician, physician autonomy and income, hospital inpatient admissions, and selection among pharmaceutical products have all been greatly limited by the movement to a managed-care health care system in the United States. The limitations pertain not only to private managed-care insurance plans but also to managed-care plans under the auspices of the Medicare and Medicaid programs. Whether MCOs have properly curbed the excesses brought on by the unlimited fee-for-service indemnity plans of the past or have unnecessarily and unfairly denied care remains a heated issue and an important area for future research. Another issue currently debated is whether the cost savings that can be attributed to the growth in managed care are a one-time phenomenon or the beginning of a long-term trend of lower rates of growth in health care expenditures.

From the discussion above, it also seems that competition in the health care sector may have sown the seeds of its own destruction. For example, benefit denial and cherry-picking behavior take place in the private health insurance industry because of competition. Induced demand in the physician services industry and the medical arms race in the hospital industry are argued to occur because of competition. Indeed, a theory X'er, one who thinks medical care is unique, would certainly subscribe to that opinion. A theory Y'er might argue, however, that competition cannot function properly until more medical firms are organized on a for-profit basis and consumers pay a greater proportion of the price of medical services, two properties of perfect competition that were described at the beginning of Chapter 8.

About the only thing that is clear from this discussion is that the debate over the relative merits of competition in the health care industry is likely to continue in the future. A portion of that debate is taken up in the remainder of the chapter. Before we tackle that issue, however, let us examine how the U.S. health care system stacks up against other health care systems around the world. For example, we saw in Chapter 2 that the health care systems in Canada, Germany, and the United Kingdom involve a single-payer system rather than a multiple-payer system like that of the United States. Also, their health care systems provide nearly universal access to medical care services and involve a greater financing and regulatory role for the federal government and less reliance on competition in health care matters. Thus it would be interesting and informative to examine how the United States compares to these and other countries in terms of health care expenditures, the utilization of medical care, and health care outcomes. To that we now turn our attention.

### The U.S. Health Care Economy: An International Comparison

Table 17–1 compares health care spending, medical utilization, and health outcome data for the so-called group of seven or G-7 countries: Canada, France, Germany, Italy, Japan, the United Kingdom, and the United States. These G-7 countries possess highly developed market economies and share many similar circumstances. (Like the other G-7 countries, with the exception of the United States, France and Italy provide nearly universal access to medical services and have a single-payer system.) Data for health care spending as a percentage of GDP are shown in column 1 of the table. The next three columns contain comparative data on the age distribution of the population, income per capita, and the availability of technology, three important determinants of health care spending. Data for the hospital admission rate and per capita physician consultations are reported in the fifth and sixth columns and are intended as measures of medical utilization. The infant mortality rate, listed in the last column, serves as a comparative measure of health outcomes. All these data are collected and based on definitions established by the Organization for Economic Cooperation and Development (OECD).

Before discussing the figures in the table, we should point out that data from different countries may not be directly comparable for several reasons and, therefore, should be accepted with some skepticism. For example, no standard taxonomy exists across countries. Medical authorities in, say, France might distinguish among inpatient and outpatient services differently than do their counterparts in the United States. Also, in practice, it is often very difficult to draw a line separating medical services, such as acute and long-term care services. In addition, monetary values for health care expenditures and gross domestic product must be converted to a common denominator, such as U.S. dollars, before meaningful comparisons can be made. Any conversion factor, such as purchasing power parities or currency exchange rates, is not without measurement error. Nevertheless, many comparative system analysts believe these data paint a reasonable picture of the health care situation in various countries.

The figures in column 1 suggest that the United States spends more on medical care as a fraction of GDP than do the other G-7 countries (as defined by the OECD). In fact, as a fraction of GDP, the United States spends slightly over 35 percent more

| TABLE 17–1 | COMPARATIVE HEALTH CARE SYSTEM STATISTICS FOR THE G-7 COUNTRIES | | | | | | |
|---|---|---|---|---|---|---|---|
| | Health Care Spending as a Percentage of GDP (1996) | Percent of Population Greater Than 65 Years (1996) | GDP per Capita (1995) | MRIs per Million Persons (1995) | Hospital Admissions Percent of Population (1995) | Per Capita Physician Consultations (1993) | Infant Mortality (1995) |
| **Canada** | 9.2% | 12.1% | $21,252 | 1.3 | 12.5% | 6.8 | 6.0 |
| **France** | 9.6 | 15.4 | 19,953 | 2.1 | 22.7 | 6.3 | 5.0 |
| **Germany** | 10.5 | 15.3 | 20,470 | 4.8 | 20.7 | 5.9 | 5.3 |
| **Italy** | 7.6 | 16.4 | 19,487 | 3.1(1994) | 16.0(1994) | 11.0(1988) | 6.2 |
| **Japan** | 7.2(1995) | 14.7 | 21,912 | 20.1 | 8.9 | 16.3 | 4.3 |
| **United Kingdom** | 6.9 | 15.8 | 17,923 | 3.4 | 20.8 | 5.8 | 6.0 |
| **United States** | 14.2 | 12.2 | 25,635 | 15.5 | 12.4 | 6.0 | 8.0 |

SOURCE: Gerard F. Anderson, "In Search of Value: An International Comparison of Cost, Access, and Outcomes," *Health Affairs* 16 (November/December 1997), Exhibits 1–6.

than Germany, the next biggest spender. Per capita health care spending in the United States ($3,708) was more than double the average ($1,768) for the other G-7 countries in 1995 (not shown in the table).

The data in the next three columns provide some explanation for the higher health care spending in the United States. While the percentage of the population greater than 65 years of age is relatively low and therefore cannot account for the high health care spending in the United States, the figures on income and magnetic resonance imagers (MRIs) per million persons do offer some explanation. As discussed in Chapters 4 and 8, the income elasticity of demand in the aggregate is greater than one, indicating that health care spending is highly responsive to income at the aggregate level. Income (GDP) per capita in the United States is about 27 percent higher than the average of the other G-7 countries and, therefore, supports a greater proportion of health care spending.

In addition, we saw in Chapter 8 that a greater availability of cost-enhancing medical technologies raises the demand and also reduces the supply of medical services. The shifts in demand and supply both lead to a greater amount of spending on health care services, provided both curves are inelastic with respect to price. According to the data in the table, the United States has more MRIs per million persons than all the G-7 countries other than Japan. In fact, the United States has about 167 percent more MRIs per million persons than the average of the other G-7 countries. Data elsewhere suggest that there are also 30 percent more scanners per person in the United States compared to the average of the other G-7 countries (Anderson, 1997). If the availability of technology offers the complete explanation, Japan should also experience high health care costs as there are both more MRIs and scanners in Japan than in the United States. That is not the case, however.

Columns 5 and 6 provide information on medical utilization to see what health dollars may buy besides medical technology. Perhaps the high health care spending in the United States shows up in a relatively large amount of inpatient and physician office visits. An examination of the medical utilization data in the table suggests just the opposite, however. In particular, only 12.4 percent of the population in the United States is admitted into hospitals, compared to an average of 17 percent for the other G-7 countries. The data for physician contacts allows us to draw a similar conclusion; medical utilization does not explain the high health care costs in the United States.

Comparatively high health care expenditures coupled with low medical utilization rates have led some analysts to believe that medical prices must be significantly higher in the United States than in the other countries. Others argue, however, that this may not be a legitimate conclusion to draw from these data due to quality differences in medical services across countries. Specifically, the quality of medical services may be higher in the United States and account for the alleged higher medical prices. Unfortunately, good indicators of the quality of care are unavailable because of measurement issues. Anecdotal evidence does suggest that waiting times are shorter for most medical services in the United States.

The last column in the table provides an indication of the level of health in the United States relative to the other G-7 countries. The infant mortality rate (deaths per thousand live births) is thought to be highly correlated with other measures of health status, making it a reasonable benchmark for the general state of health of all population segments (Goldman and Grossman, 1988). The data in the table imply that all the other G-7 countries have an infant mortality rate much lower than that of the United States. The discrepancy is not a trivial one. In the United States, about 2.5 more infants out of every 1,000 children born alive never get a chance to blow out the candles on their first birthday cake. Think about that!

In summary, almost 16 percent of the U.S. population is without health insurance coverage at a point in time. In contrast, nearly universal health insurance coverage exists in the other G-7 countries. Government in the United States is responsible for financing about 44 percent of all health care spending. The comparable figure for the other G-7 countries is well over 90 percent (Anderson, 1997). Health care spending as a fraction of GDP is higher, medical utilization rates are lower, and the infant mortality rate is higher in the United States than in the typical G-7 country. Many analysts have concluded from such data that health care costs and infant mortality are lower in other countries because the government plays a more dominant role in the health care sector and because there is universal access to health insurance. In fact, many health care policy analysts believe that a similar approach can produce better results in the United States.[3]

## An Overview of Health Care Reform in the United States

The debate over health care reform in the United States has been heated, and the volume of the discussion attests to the liveliness of the issue. Facing a bewildering number of proposals and counterproposals from every interest group imaginable, health care professionals and consumers alike have a difficult time keeping abreast of the issues. The debate is further complicated by the vast array of new terminology. Terms with which many of us are unfamiliar, such as *global budgeting, health alliances,* and *play-or-pay,* are bandied about regularly. This section attempts to help you sort through this maze by reviewing the efficiency and equity implications of four generic health care reform proposals: medical savings accounts, individual mandates, managed competition, and national health insurance. These four proposals were chosen primarily because they include the basic elements of the majority of the proposals typically considered.

Following this discussion, we examine health care reform at the state level. State governments are a frequently overlooked player in the health care debate. We review the health care reform packages of four states to get a flavor of the various strategies currently under consideration at the state level. Finally, we examine the basic features of the Clinton health care plan, or the National Health Security Act of 1993.

---

[3]However, see Santerre, Grubaugh, and Stollar (1991) and Grubaugh and Santerre (1994) for some evidence contrary to the view that increased government involvement leads to better performance of the U.S. health care system.

# Health Care Reform at the Federal Level

To bring some consistency to the discussion, each plan is evaluated using four economic criteria:

1. *Universal coverage:* Does the plan achieve universal coverage, and, if so, how?

2. *Financing and budgetary implications:* How is the plan financed, and to what extent does it affect the federal deficit?

3. *Cost containment:* How does the plan contain the growth of medical care expenditures over time?

4. *Employment:* To what extent does the plan influence overall employment opportunities?

Note that the first criterion deals with the issue of vertical equity, while the last two concern efficiency. A summary of how each plan measures up to the four criteria appears in table 17–2, which the reader is urged to consult throughout the discussion. In addition, the discussion refers to the generalized model of a health care system discussed in Chapter 2.

## Medical Savings Accounts

This plan takes a distinctly market-oriented approach to reforming health care by calling for the development of individual tax-free medical savings accounts (MSAs) to pay for routine medical care. Proponents claim that routine care accounts for a significant fraction of medical expenditures.[4] The program is purely voluntary in that individuals have the option to make yearly contributions to their MSAs up to a specified amount, and any funds left in the account at the end of the year can be carried over to the next year and earn interest. Catastrophic health insurance plans to finance major medical expenses can also be purchased with pretax income. Premiums for the catastrophic plans are generally cheap due to the high deductibles involved.

An example may help to clarify the structure of the MSA proposal. Suppose your employer presently pays $7,000 for your family's major medical and routine care insurance coverage. Under the MSA plan, your employer would purchase catastrophic health insurance coverage worth, say, $3,500 for your family. The catastrophic plan covers expensive major illnesses and has a sizable deductible. In addition, the employer deposits the remaining $3,500 into a tax-free MSA. Your family can use the funds in the MSA to pay for routine care or to finance the deductible on major medical illnesses during the year. The routine care services could be purchased as needed or on a prepaid basis through a health care provider like an HMO. Your family makes the choice by considering relative prices, income, health status, degree of risk aversion, and other demand-side factors. Any unused funds in the MSA are rolled over and used for similar purposes in future years.

---

[4]This discussion is based on Goodman and Musgrave (1992) and Tripoli (1993).

| **TABLE 17–2** | A SUMMARY OF THE FOUR HEALTH CARE PLANS | | | |
| --- | --- | --- | --- | --- |
| | **Medical Savings Accounts** | **Individual Mandates** | **Managed Competition** | **National Health Insurance** |
| **Universal coverage** | This program is not designed to achieve universal coverage. However, health insurance premiums should become more affordable when they become tax deductible and apply mainly to catastrophic plans. Tax credits and subsidies are used to make health insurance more affordable for poor individuals. | The plan is implemented through mandated insurance coverage and a guarantee by the government that basic medical coverage is available across the country. Tax credits and subsidies are available to make coverage affordable to all. Near-universal coverage is attainable. | Employers are required to provide medical coverage to all full-time workers. Subsidies are provided to low-income families to purchase medical insurance. Medicaid and Medicare are maintained. Near-universal coverage is possible. | Universal coverage is achieved through a national health insurance plan that covers all citizens. |
| **Financing** | The plan is financed primarily out of individual contributions to medical savings accounts. Because government expenditures on Medicare and Medicaid end, the deficit should diminish. | The plan is financed largely by premium payments by consumers either directly or through employers. A tax increase is necessary, which negatively affects the budget deficit. Medicare and Medicaid programs are ended. | Medical coverage is financed primarily through employer mandates so employees most likely pay through forgone wages. Government expenditures are paid through a payroll tax. The impact on the deficit should not be too significant. | Medical coverage is financed out of an income tax. Also, funds for Medicare and Medicaid are diverted to partially offset the cost of the plan. An employer tax equal to the cost of employer-financed medical insurance is also levied. |

| | | | | |
|---|---|---|---|---|
| **Cost containment** | Because consumers pay for most health care expenditures out of their own Medisave accounts, they have the incentive to minimize waste and shop around for competitive prices. A reduction in administrative expenses also translates into cost savings. | Costs are contained through the maintenance of a highly competitive medical insurance market. Private insurance vendors are disciplined by the marketplace to provide competitive prices to consumers. | Cost containment results from the maintenance of a highly competitive private insurance market. A uniform benefit package is offered, and employers are required to pay for 80 percent of the representative plan. The remaining 20 percent provides an incentive for consumers to shop wisely. | Costs are contained through the utilization of a single-payer system that decreases the administration and billing costs that are the by-product of a multipayer system. Also, global budgeting is used to establish a constant relation between gross domestic product and health care expenditures. |
| **Employment** | Minimal impact because labor market distortions are kept to a minimum. | Minor impact because labor market distortions are kept to a minimum. | Likely to have a significant effect because employer mandates may create substantial distortions in labor markets, especially among low-wage workers. | Employment effects will be concentrated in the private insurance market and health care administration. |

The MSA plan does not call for universal health care coverage, but it does give the public freedom of choice. A person can elect to create an MSA and contribute as much as desired up to a present limit. Because contributions to the MSAs are tax deductible, the price of medical care is reduced, making it affordable for more people. Tax credits also further reduce the price for low-income families, and government subsidies are available for truly needy individuals. Horizontal equity is achieved because all premiums or contributions to the MSAs are tax deductible whether paid by the employee or the employer.[5] Elderly individuals finance health care expenditures with the introduction of medical IRAs. Like traditional IRAs, these accounts grow tax free and can be used to cover medical expenses during retirement. Eventually they will take the place of Medicare.

Under this plan, consumers individually finance a major proportion of medical expenditures by drawing from the MSAs. The impact on the federal deficit is minimal because the current Medicare and Medicaid programs are ended. The increase in the deficit results primarily from forgone tax revenues due to tax credits and subsidies to needy individuals.

Cost containment is achieved through enhanced price competition. Since consumers are directly responsible for payment of most medical care out of their MSAs, they have the incentive to reduce waste and comparison shop. Realizing this, health care providers, such as physicians and hospitals, are forced to provide high-quality, competitively priced medical care. This point is made clear if we look at this plan in terms of the generalized model of a health care system presented in Chapter 2. It is apparent that this plan minimizes the impact of third-party payers because most transactions take place directly between consumers and health care providers. As a result, fewer market distortions occur because third-party payers play a less influential role in the MSA plan. In addition, costs are reduced due to administrative savings. With high deductibles on catastrophic health care plans, insurance companies are no longer bogged down with thousands of small claims that are relatively expensive to process. Managed care is likely to thrive under the MSA plan as health care providers and insurance companies strive to control costs and remain competitive. The employment effect of this plan is minimal because it relies heavily on the market mechanism.

Several criticisms of MSAs have been raised (Tanner, 1995). First, critics claim that consumers are not sufficiently informed to make cost-conscious decisions regarding medical treatments. Opponents argue that due to the lack of information, physicians will continue to induce the demand for their services and health care costs will continue to rise.

Second, critics argue that consumers will forgo necessary or preventive care to save money in the MSAs for other purposes. Less medical care, in turn, will lead to poorer health and higher health care costs in the long run.

Third, opponents allege that the plan will lead to adverse selection as healthy people select MSAs while sick individuals choose conventional insurance. Eventually, the

---

[5]If only medical premiums paid by employers are tax deductible, horizontal inequities exist because the price of medical coverage depends on employment status rather than income.

price of insurance will increase and create financial access problems as more and sicker members enroll in conventional insurance plans.

Fourth, critics point out that the deductible on catastrophic insurance will be insufficient to control expenditures on high-cost, low-benefit medicine. That is, once a person is hospitalized for a major illness, the size of the deductible will not matter. Since critically sick patients account for most of the spending on health care, the MSA plan will be ineffective in containing health care costs.

Finally, critics argue that an MSA plan is regressive since the benefits will accrue primarily to wealthy individuals.

The advocates of medical saving accounts have responded to each of these criticisms (Tanner, 1995). Basically, proponents point to demand studies showing that consumers are conscious of health care prices, even very small out-of-pocket prices. MSAs will make consumers more responsive and cost conscious, since they will consider the full price of medical services. Further, proponents point to the success of MSA plans currently in use in producing medical cost savings and preventing adverse selection. Finally, advocates claim the current tax break for employer-provided insurance is far more regressive than an MSA plan available for all.

The MSA plan has recently become a hot item as the Health Insurance Portability and Accountability Act of 1996 establishes an experiment with MSA plans.

## Individual Mandates[6]

Like the MSA plan, the individual mandate plan places the responsibility for medical coverage squarely on the shoulders of consumers. Individuals are required by law to purchase a basic medical insurance plan as defined by the government. They still have the option to purchase more comprehensive coverage, and nothing precludes employers from providing medical insurance to their employees.

Universal coverage is achieved through a combination of mandated medical coverage and the government's guarantee that basic medical coverage is available at a competitive price for those unable to pay for a private plan. Tax credits are offered to ensure affordability, and for those who still cannot afford insurance, government vouchers are available. The Medicaid and Medicare programs are eventually phased out.

To make sure competitively priced medical coverage for the basic plan is available to all, the government solicits bids from private insurance vendors throughout the country. At least one basic plan is offered in every geographic region of the country to serve as "fallback" coverage for any consumer who did not purchase a plan in the private market. The plan also moves toward achieving horizontal equity because tax credits depend on income status rather than employment status.

The plan is financed primarily by individual contributions; however, tax credits and subsidies are available. Although Pauly, Danzon, Feldstein, and Hoff (1991) do not provide figures, they believe a modest tax increase is necessary to extend medical

---

[6]This overview is based on Pauly, Danzon, Feldstein, and Hoff (1991).

coverage to the uninsured. The extent of the increase depends on the magnitude of the tax credits and subsidies provided.

Cost containment is ensured through the maintenance of a highly competitive medical insurance market. Private insurance companies find it in their self-interest to provide high-quality, low-cost insurance to consumers who must purchase and pay for their own medical coverage. Competition is also enhanced because the government plays no role as a third-party insurer since the market for medical insurance is completely private. Employment ramifications are likely to be kept to a minimum. In this type of market environment, managed care is likely to be relied on extensively to control costs.

As with the MSA plan, critics of the individual mandate argue that consumers lack the necessary information to shop wisely. Medical insurance plans contain numerous complex terms and conditions, and therefore are difficult for the average person to comprehend. In addition, some argue that the individual mandate provides less incentive than the MSA plan for consumers to consider the full price of the medical services they buy because third-party payers continue to play an influential role under the individual mandate plan. Finally, critics claim that the individual mandate imposes a serious restraint on an individual's freedom of choice (although it should be kept in mind that Social Security and car insurance in many states are presently mandatory).

## Managed Competition[7]

The managed-competition plan has received tremendous publicity primarily because it has been used as the basis for the Clinton health care plan. The attractive feature of the plan is that it builds on the existing system of employer-provided medical coverage. Employers are mandated to provide medical coverage for basic medical services and pay, for example, an 8 percent payroll tax on the first $22,500 of wages for employees not covered.[8] Self-employed individuals and early retirees must pay for health care coverage with an 8 percent tax on adjusted income up to a preset maximum. The tax is collected through the income tax system.

The most novel portion of this plan is the creation across the country of government insurance buyer organizations called **health alliances.** These public or non-profit agencies use their monopsony power to negotiate competitive prices for health insurance from private insurance companies. Individuals without employer-provided insurance and small employers may purchase competitively priced health insurance through one of these alliances. The alliances also serve as brokers that collect premiums, manage enrollment, and carry out other administrative duties. The intent is to have each alliance offer a number of competing plans to their enrollees.

Universal coverage is ensured through employer mandates and subsidies provided to low-income families to pay for medical coverage. Medicaid and Medicare are maintained and eventually take advantage of the alliances to provide medical coverage. The

---

[7]This discussion is based on Enthoven and Kronick (1989) and Enthoven (1993).

[8]Other health care proposals give employers the option to pay a tax in lieu of providing medical coverage to full-time employees. In the popular literature, this is referred to as the "pay-or-play" option.

plan is financed primarily with employer-mandated health insurance premiums and consumer payments. Government expenditures are financed primarily by the payroll tax and other revenues resulting from the plan. The impact on the deficit is not likely to be significant.

Cost containment results from competition among private insurers as they vie for customers through the alliances. This is why the term *managed competition* was coined. The health alliances "manage" the various health care plans to ensure there is sufficient "competition" at the insurance end of the medical care market. To simplify matters for consumers and intensify competition, all plans must offer a uniform benefit package. This puts consumers in a better position to make informed choices. As further encouragement for cost-conscious behavior, employers are required to make a fixed contribution toward medical coverage for each employee equal to 80 percent of the average plan's cost in the area. The remaining 20 percent is the employee's responsibility. A limit is also placed on the tax deduction employees can take for premium payments. This encourages consumers to pick less expensive health plans that provide less generous benefits, since they must pay for more costly plans with after-tax dollars.

One criticism of managed competition is that rural areas may lack enough private insurance companies. The scarcity of suppliers may make it difficult to promote price competition (Kronick, Goodman, Wennberg, and Wagner 1993). Another complaint is that the government-sponsored health alliances may result in "one-size-fits-all" health insurance plans, and, as a result, consumers will lose the benefits of variety. Finally, one of the more controversial elements of employer mandates is the fact that they create labor market distortions of the type discussed in Insight 13–1. Economic theory suggests that mandated benefits may inhibit employment, particularly among low- or minimum-wage workers, and that the costs of benefits are shared by both employees and employers. Employees pay for mandated benefits through wage reductions.

## National Health Insurance[9]

The national health insurance plan calls for the implementation of a national health insurance system very similar to the one presently existing in Canada. As such, the current multipayer system in the United States is replaced by a single-payer public medical insurance program. In terms of the generalized model of a health care system, this means the role of third-party payer is completely taken over by the government sector, and the private market for medical insurance is almost completely eliminated (some specific services, such as dental and optical care, may continue to be covered by private insurance).

Universal coverage is guaranteed with this plan because everyone is covered for all necessary medical services, with no copayments or deductibles. The plan achieves vertical equity because it is financed out of general taxes, with a heavy reliance on the

---

[9]This discussion is based on Himmelstein and Woolhandler (1989).

income tax system. A tax increase is necessary to provide the additional funding needed to broaden coverage to uninsured individuals. Since currently funded medical programs, such as Medicare and Medicaid, are no longer needed, funds earmarked for these programs would be used to finance a national health insurance program. Employer taxes increase by the amount currently spent on health care benefits. The implication is that employer-provided funds are diverted from the private insurance market to a publicly run health insurance program.

Cost containment is based primarily on the efficiencies associated with using a single-payer system. Billing and administration costs are reduced because health care providers no longer need to contend with the complex set of insurance forms and billing procedures that result from a multipayer system. In addition, overall expenditures are controlled by establishing a link between gross domestic product and health care costs. Once the proportion between the two is established, overall health care costs are allowed to grow only as fast as the overall economy. Global budgets and simplified fee schedules are utilized to compensate health care providers, such as hospitals and physicians, for services provided. The role of managed care with a national insurance plan is difficult to determine, because most of the impetus for managed care comes from the private health insurance market, which the plan eliminates.

Finally, the employment effects are likely to be most noticeable in the private health insurance market and health care administration. With the elimination of the private health insurance market and the decrease in administrative waste, some job displacement is likely to occur, particularly in the short run.

While the national health insurance plan comes closest to providing universal health insurance, a general criticism has been levied against the plan. The extensive involvement of government and the elimination of private insurers alarm those who believe that government enterprise is monopoly enterprise. Critics claim that the creation of financial innovations to control medical costs would be weakened in a government-run health insurance program. Critics also argue that because a competitive incentive is missing, a public monopoly insurer may offer little variety and be unresponsive to consumer wants.

## Health Care Reform at the State Level

Unlike most countries, the United States follows a more decentralized approach to health care policy that allows individual states a certain degree of latitude in developing their own health care policies. The reason is largely historic and has its roots in our federalist form of government, which provides states with limited discretion to govern. Coupled with this tradition has been the general belief in the United States that issues relating to health, education, and poverty are best addressed at the local or community level. A case in point is the Medicaid program, which is jointly financed by the federal and state governments. Since states foot a portion of the bill, they have been given some say as to how those tax dollars are spent. As a result, vastly different Medicaid programs have developed across states over time.

Advocates for a decentralized approach to health care reform point out that this approach is more democratic. This is because states are in a better position than the federal government to address the unique needs of the local population. Another advantage is that states can be seen as "laboratories" or "guinea pigs" where alternative policies can be tried out to see whether they should be adopted at the national level or in other states. Finally, advocates of the decentralized approach are fond of pointing out that the issue of whether health care reform should take place at the state or federal level is largely moot because our system of government allows states to block any major reforms if they desire. All this suggests that states are likely to continue playing a critical role in the formation of U.S. health care policy for years to come.

Confronted with the burden of rising health care costs, a growing number of individuals who lack health care coverage, and a citizenry in no mood for further tax increases, most states have been forced to reexamine their health care programs. Many states are aggressively investigating various policy options aimed at reforming the financing and delivery of medical care. During the 1993 legislative session, every state except Nevada and Wyoming considered some type of health care reform (Rogal and Helms, 1993). As Iglehart (1994) writes, "The legislation ranges from comprehensive plans with the goal of providing all citizens with health insurance through public subsidies and coverage financed jointly by employers and employees to less ambitious laws that reform the small-group insurance market, establish new cost-containment mechanisms, or create study commissions" (p. 75).

Naturally, space limitations prohibit a discussion of the health care reform taking place in each state. With this constraint in mind, we now provide a brief overview of the health care reform packages adopted or under serious consideration in Hawaii, Maryland, Minnesota, and Oregon. These states were chosen because they represent the broad spectrum of policies currently under consideration in other states.

## Hawaii: The Case of Employer Mandates

Hawaii's health care system has achieved a certain level of recognition over the years, primarily because it has succeeded in achieving near universal health care coverage. Estimates indicate that in 1995 only 5.8 percent of full-time workers between the ages of 18 and 64 years and their dependents were without health insurance. That was the lowest rate in the country (AARP, 1997). Many years before other states began taking the notion of health care reform seriously, Hawaii passed the Prepaid Health Act of 1974, which mandated, with few exceptions, that employers provide health insurance to all employees.[10] Each medical plan must provide a minimum number of benefits, and the employee's premium contribution is limited to 1.5 percent of total wages.

Because a significant proportion of the population remained without medical insurance despite the employer mandate, the State Health Insurance Program of Hawaii

---

[10]As Iglehart (1994) points out, the Employer Retirement Income Security Act (ERISA) prevents states from requiring employers to provide health insurance benefits. To mandate employer health benefits, states must obtain a congressional exemption from ERISA. Hawaii passed its Prepaid Health Care Act before ERISA became law.

(SHIP) was created in 1989. Individuals without insurance who were not eligible for Medicaid or Medicare were able to purchase medical insurance through SHIP. The SHIP program was later rolled into the Hawaii Health QUEST Program that was designed to provide medical insurance for those individuals with incomes up to 300 percent of the poverty level. The premium was based on a sliding scale, with those individuals with incomes at or below the poverty level paying nothing for coverage. In addition, this program provided a standard package of medical benefits. MCOs compete with one another for QUEST contracts (Intergovernment Health Policy Project, 1995).

Unfortunately, the high cost of the QUEST program has forced the state in recent years to scale back the eligibility requirements. For example, beginning in August 1995, only individuals with incomes up to 200 percent of the poverty level qualify for the program. Other changes were also made in the program to restrict eligibility, such as increasing the share of the health premium paid by the self-employed.

Because Hawaii has succeeded in achieving nearly universal coverage, the case has been made for transporting the system to the U.S. mainland. Whether this is advisable is open for debate. There is no doubt, however, that much of the success of the program lies in circumstances unique to Hawaii. Unlike in most other states, the market for health insurance is dominated by two insurance companies: Blue Cross/Blue Shield and Kaiser Permanente. That makes it much easier for the state to manage the system because any negotiations that must take place between the state and the insurance industry are confined to a small group.

In addition, given Hawaii's location, firms must incur high costs if they wish to relocate to avoid the insurance mandates. States in the continental United States do not have the luxury of a captive private sector (Tanner, 1993).

Finally, the private business sector accepted the mandates because it has always felt an obligation to provide health insurance to employees. The acceptance is an offshoot of the policy long followed by plantation owners to provide for the health care needs of their workers (Neubauer, 1993).

## *Maryland: The Case of Regulation*

Over the years, the state of Maryland has taken a decidedly regulatory approach to health care policy. Beginning in 1977, it was the first state to implement an all-payer hospital payment system.[11] Maryland's all-payer payment system regulates the price paid by all buyers of hospital services. Even price discounts to MCOs are limited by the regulation (McDonough, 1997). Maryland also has one of the more restrictive sets of CON laws that require health care providers to obtain state approval before they introduce any new medical technologies or facilities (Snyder, 1998).

Legislation that took effect in 1993 created the Maryland Health Care Access and Cost Commission (HCACC). The HCACC is responsible, among other things, for

---

[11]A number of other states have implemented a hospital-rate-setting system over the years. However, most have since abandoned their efforts, and Maryland and West Virginia are currently the only states that continue to rely on some type of hospital-rate-setting system (McDonough, 1997).

developing and maintaining a database on health care services and for developing a standardized payment system for care practitioners and payers in the state.[12] For example, a new payment system for physicians similar to the resource-based relative value scale (RBRVS) system used by Medicare is currently being developed.

The legislated changes in the health insurance market are directed at improving access to medical insurance for small firms. Any health insurance company doing business in Maryland must offer a standard health insurance package to all businesses employing 50 or fewer workers. Coverage cannot be denied for any medical precondition or frequency of claims submitted. In addition, a community-based rating system has been adopted that allows for only minor adjustments in premiums. To control costs, the average community-rated premium can be no greater than 12 percent of the average wage in the state. However, this legislation does not mandate that employers finance health insurance. The hope is that once employers with few workers have access to reasonably priced medical insurance, they will voluntarily provide it to their employees (Anderson, Heyssel, and Dickler, 1993).

## *Minnesota: The Case of Regulated Competition*

In contrast to Maryland, Minnesota had taken a more free market approach to health care through the years. However, beginning in 1992, Minnesota approved MinnesotaCare (originally called HealthRight) that addressed the issues of cost containment and access. The cost containment plan places great emphasis on competition along with some degree of regulation (Blewett, 1994). The competitive aspect focuses on integrated service networks (ISNs), which are prepaid health plans that compete on the basis of price and quality. Competition is made possible by the mandatory disclosure of price and quality information and standardization of health benefits coverage.

The regulatory component calls for the state commissioner of health to set a cap on the growth of ISN premiums and control fees of out-of-network providers through an all-payer rate-setting system. Other cost containment mechanisms include targets for health care expenditure growth, statewide and regional limits on health care spending, health care planning, retrospective review of capital expenditures for new technologies that cost more than $500,000, restrictions on physician referrals, and a ban on balance billing for Medicare charges (Leichter, 1993).

The act addresses the problem of uninsured persons primarily by offering state-subsidized coverage based on a sliding-fee scale to children, their parents, and eventually others not covered by Medicaid. The subsidized insurance is financed through a variety of taxes on health care providers and a 5-cent-per-pack increase in the state cigarette tax. The legislation also calls for significant changes in the small-group insurance market similar to those adopted in Maryland. Any insurance company offering health insurance policies in Minnesota must guarantee coverage regardless of health conditions, and policies cannot be canceled due to excessive claims or health reasons. In addition, a modified community rating system is now in place, and small

---

[12]This information can be found on the Maryland Health Care Access and Cost Commission Web page at http://www.hcacc.state.md.us.

businesses are being offered low-cost insurance plans that do not include selected high-cost medical services (Intergovernment Health Policy Project, 1993).

In 1995, the Minnesota legislature began to repeal or modify many of the reforms enacted earlier. For example, the legislature repealed the all-payer rate-setting regulations. In addition, the state curtailed the expansion of MinnesotaCare subsidies to childless households with incomes up to 275 percent of the poverty level (Intergovernment Health Policy Project, 1995). In 1997, the legislature repealed other health care reforms contained in MinnesotaCare. In particular, the state repealed revenue limits placed on health care providers and changed the growth limits on health care expenditures to cost containment goals that are now voluntary (Minnesota Department of Health, 1998).

## Oregon: The Case of Rationing Medicaid Services

Confronted with the conflicting problems of rising Medicaid expenditures and a growing number of people without medical insurance. Oregon has developed one of the more controversial health care reform packages. At issue is a plan that rations medical care to those on Medicaid. The Oregon Health Plan is troubling to many because it represents the first time a government authority has taken such an active role in the explicit rationing of medical services in the United States.

The focal point of the program is a prioritized list of approximately 740 medical procedures. The list was developed after an exhaustive process that measured the relative value of each medical procedure. Each medical procedure was ranked based on its ability to improve health, its cost, and perceived community value. Based on the list, treatment for a severe head injury with loss of consciousness was ranked number one, medical therapy of rheumatic fever was ranked 386, and medical therapy for infectious mononucleosis was ranked 637.[13]

Once the legislature has determined the level of funding for the program, the health services commission determines the number of medical procedures the state can finance. According to recent estimates, the state would cover 574 out of 743 illnesses or disorders. A lack of funds precludes coverage for the remaining 169 (O'Neill, 1998). For example, any Medicaid recipient in need of a liver transplant (ranked number 617) would be denied coverage under the Oregon plan.

Proponents of the Oregon plan argue that the state is trading off comprehensive coverage for a few to make greater access available to many. Prior to the plan, the Oregon Medicaid program covered only individuals with incomes at or below 58 percent of the poverty level as established by the federal government. Currently, individuals with incomes at or below 100 percent of the poverty level are eligible for Medicaid coverage. In addition, pregnant women and children below age 6 can also qualify if family income does not exceed 133 percent of the poverty level. For a fixed budget, greater coverage can be achieved only by denying services to a relatively few individuals who need very costly medical care relative to the benefits received.

---

[13]This information is available on the Oregon Health Plan Web site at http://www.ohppr.das.state.or.us.

The Oregon Plan also controls cost through the use of managed care. Most new Medicaid recipients are now required to enroll in one of 13 managed-care plans offered by the state. At the moment, 87 percent of all Medicaid recipients in Oregon are enrolled in a Medicaid managed-care plan (Bodenheimer, 1997).

As you can imagine, criticisms of the program have emanated from all corners of the health care field. From an economic perspective, the program can be criticized on both efficiency and equity grounds. Regarding efficiency, there is concern about whether the state can objectively determine the relative values of alternative medical procedures. Tanner (1993) believes that such determinations may be better left to the marketplace.

Because only 13 percent of all Medicaid recipients have their medical benefits confined to the list of approved medical procedures, the Oregon Health Plan has also been criticized on equity grounds. The other 87 percent who are enrolled in managed-care plans may receive benefits in excess of the list of approved benefits supplied by the state. This raises all sorts of equity questions regarding the distribution of medical services as some individuals experience a reduction in benefits while others receive additional benefits (Bodenheimer, 1997).

According to Bodenheimer (1997), the state has estimated that the medical procedures not on the approved list in the traditional Medicaid plan account for approximately 10 percent of all medical expenses. As a result, the state subtracts 10 percent from the capitation payments to managed-care plans to contain costs. While it is up to each managed-care vendor to determine which medical procedures should be covered in the plan, every managed-care plan must, at the very minimum, provide insurance coverage for all those medical procedures on the approved list. Bodenheimer notes that many of the managed-care plans provide medical benefits in addition to those on the approved list because they are deemed "medically necessary." As a result, it is possible for those Medicaid recipients in managed-care plans to receive more benefits than those enrolled in the traditional fee-for-service plan.

### What Can Be Gained from State Attempts at Health Care Reform?

After reviewing the tremendous diversity in the strategies adopted by states to reform health care, one is left to question what knowledge can be gained from all of this. Barrand and Schroeder (1994) suggest that four basic lessons can be gleaned from health care reform at the state level. First, the tremendous diversity in health care reform reflects the diversity in our health care system across states and the differing views concerning the appropriate role of government. Reform at the national level must be broad enough to consider diversity. Second, attempts at state health care reform reveal that the political process is as complicated at the state level as it is at the federal level. It appears that the political gridlock impeding health care reform at the federal level is also present at the state level. Third, "implementing" health care reform may be more difficult than "designing" reform. With the implementation of such items as new billing procedures, price controls, and quality reviews, states face an enormous set of practical problems in getting the reform up and running. These problems should be kept in mind when changes are made at the federal level. Finally, the need for public education is paramount. Confusion on the part of the public concerning various policies under review only clouds the issue and makes the task of reforming health care even more difficult.

## An Overview of the Clinton Health Care Plan

The National Health Security Act proposed by President Bill Clinton drew extensively on the managed-competition model of health care reform. Each region of the country would be represented by one not-for-profit health alliance that would utilize its monopsony power to negotiate premiums for health insurance with private insurance companies. Employers and individuals would be able to purchase health insurance through these alliances at rates that would be lower than those under the present decentralized, fragmented system. Large firms with more than 5,000 employees would be able to form their own corporate alliances.[14]

Universal coverage was to be accomplished primarily through employer-mandated health insurance. Each employer would be required to provide health insurance to its full-time employees and finance at least 80 percent of the premium of the average plan in the health alliance. The remaining portion would be the responsibility of the employee. To make the cost affordable for employers, total premium contributions would be capped at 3.5 to 7.9 percent of total payroll. Additional reductions in premiums would be made available to small firms. Also, adjustments in premiums would be made for unemployed persons, part-time workers, and self-employed individuals.

The plan would be financed from a combination of savings from existing public health insurance programs and additional taxes. Savings from Medicaid would result as that program is merged into the Clinton plan. Presumably, the rate of growth of expenditures for the Medicaid program would diminish over time as the cost containment policies of the Clinton plan take hold. Savings in the Medicare program would emanate from a variety of sources, including more extensive use of managed care and a reduction in payments to providers. There would also be savings from other federal medical programs as they are integrated into the system. Additional taxes would include an increase in the cigarette tax of 75 cents per pack and a 1 percent payroll tax on all corporate alliances.

Cost containment would be achieved primarily through the creation of a national health board. Among other duties, that agency would be responsible for determining the maximum rate of growth of health insurance premiums from year to year.

---

[14]The notion of one alliance per region differs slightly from the managed-competition plan developed by Enthoven and Kronick (1989). Under that plan, multiple alliances would be set up in different regions. The argument against multiple alliances is that such an arrangement would add unwanted complexity to the structure. Enthoven and Singer (1995) counter with the argument that health alliances would become too strong under the Clinton plan. Health alliances are meant "to be market makers, not regulating agencies" (p. 89). With only one alliance per region, power may become too concentrated on the demand side and result in numerous mergers on the supply side of the market. The result would be less competition, not more. In addition, with only one health alliance, it may become too easy for interest groups to exert political pressure on the system.

Indirectly, that would give the national health board control over the growth of health care expenditures by allowing it to establish global budgets for each health alliance.

## The Collapse of the Clinton Health Care Plan

When President Clinton unveiled his plan to reform the U.S. health care system on September 22, 1993, public support was initially strong.[15] Early public opinion polls reported twice as many people supporting than opposing the Clinton plan (Rockman, 1995). By the summer of 1994, support for the Clinton plan had dipped to about 40 percent, and it was highly unlikely that any comprehensive health care package would be enacted. The final blow was the election of November 1994, which gave the Republican party control of the House of Representatives. The question now becomes: Why did support for the Clinton health care reform plan erode so rapidly?

The most obvious explanation is that the Clinton health care plan lacked the necessary political support in Congress. Brady and Buckley (1995) utilized the median voter hypothesis to address that possibility. The median position is the middle position at which an equal number is above or below it. As a result, the median position represents the decisive or swing position under a simple majority voting rule (i.e., 51 percent agreement). By observing the characteristics of the median voter, we can identify whether a policy under consideration is likely to pass or fail.

Brady and Buckley ranked each member of the 103d Congress from most to least liberal (or most to least conservative) and argued that the Clinton plan would pass only if it mustered the support of the median voter in each house of Congress. Without the support of those members of Congress, the Clinton health care plan had little or no chance of becoming law. After reviewing the voting records of those legislators at or near the 50th position in the Senate and the 218th position in the House (there are 435 representatives), Brady and Buckley pointed out that the median voters in both the House of Representatives and the Senate represented conservative constituents primarily from southern and border states. Based on the median voter hypothesis, Brady and Buckley concluded that the Clinton plan was politically to the left of the median voter in both houses of Congress and therefore would not be enacted.

Other analysts attribute the demise of the plan to its complexity and the failure of the Clinton administration to articulate the plan to the public in clear and precise terms. Many people found it difficult to understand, and, as debate over reform progressed, they began to worry more about its ill effects than the problem of health care reform. As a result, public support dwindled out of a fear of the unknown.

Steinman and Watts (1995) point to the political institutions in the United States that are biased against reform. Our political system is based on the federalist model, in which political power is fragmented and shared among many groups. This situation "yields enormous power to intransigent interest groups and thus makes efforts" at reform extremely difficult (p. 329). Along similar lines, Morone (1995) states that the

---

[15]For a more comprehensive look at why the Clinton plan failed, consult the spring 1995 issues of either *Health Affairs* or the *Journal of Health Politics, Policy and Law*.

U.S. political process is devised "to produce a stalemate" (p. 394). With our system of government, political interest groups had the ability to put pressure on the political process to effectively block any meaningful reform. Also, because the period of debate was so protracted, opponents of reform had time to muster a public relations campaign to turn public opinion against the plan. (Remember the infamous Harry and Louise commercials?)

Navarro (1995) looks at the entire episode from the perspective of class relations. The corporate or capitalist class in the United States rejected the Clinton reform package because it would weaken their hold over the working class. Any program that guarantees universal medical coverage infringes on the ability of the corporate class to dictate the terms of employment to the working class. To maintain a strong hold, it is preferable that the working class depend on the corporate class for medical coverage rather than on a government entity.

These are just a few of the many reasons being offered to explain why the Clinton health care plan collapsed. It is safe to say that a multitude of social, political, and economic factors contributed to the failure of the plan. Yankelovich (1995) summarizes the entire process best: "Technical experts designed it, special interests argued it, political leaders sold it, journalists more interested in the political ramifications than its contents kibitzed it, and advertising attacked it. There was no way for the average American to understand what it meant for them" (p. 9).

## SUMMARY

The advanced state of technology is the greatest strength of the U.S. health care system. Premature babies, sometimes weighing much less than 2 pounds, face a relatively good chance of surviving if they are born in the United States because of the state of technology. A relatively high life expectancy after age 80 is another reflection of the advanced state of health care technology in the United States (OECD, 1990). That is, people 80 years and older in the U.S. tend to live longer than their counterparts in most other countries because of the abundance of advanced medical technologies. Also, the United States continues to be the world leader in pharmaceutical innovation. As mentioned in the text, pharmaceutical products save, extend, and improve the quality of lives.

Unfortunately, the U.S. health care system is not without weaknesses. Its most glaring weakness is exemplified by the fact that nearly 16 percent of the population is without health insurance. The lack of health insurance creates medical access problems and subjects a family's income to the vagaries of health status. The inability to successfully control costs is another major weakness of the U.S. health care system. The growth of health care costs continues unabated, although the pace has slowed in recent years mostly due to the influence of managed-care organizations. Whether managed care can continue to slow the growth of health care costs remains questionable.

Eliminating the weaknesses while maintaining the strengths is a challenge faced by any plan for changing the U.S. health care system. Indeed, much of the debate on health care reform reflects that dilemma. This chapter presented four generic health care reform plans to provide insight into the health care reform debate in the United States. The MSA plan is the most market oriented of the four plans. With this plan, consumers are allowed to contribute to medical savings accounts with pretax income to pay for routine medical expenses. Low-cost catastrophic medical insurance with high deductibles is also available to pay for major medical expenses.

The individual mandate plan also relies heavily on the market mechanism to allocate medical resources. Consumers are required to purchase a private medical insurance plan that covers basic medical care. To make this possible, the government guarantees that basic insurance coverage is available throughout the country at a competitive price through a government-sponsored fallback plan. In addition, tax credits and subsidies are available to further lower the price for those who cannot afford health insurance.

The managed-care plan calls for more government intervention than the previous two plans. The key to this plan is the formation of health alliances, government-sponsored organizations that negotiate with private insurance companies for competitively priced medical insurance. Also, employers are mandated to provide health insurance to employees.

Finally, the national health insurance plan calls for the most extensive level of government involvement in medical markets. With this plan, the government replaces the private insurance market by offering a national health insurance plan that covers all citizens for medical expenses. Furthermore, global budgets and price controls are utilized to contain the growth of medical costs over time.

These four plans capture the essence of the vast majority of the health care reform plans currently being considered. The vast differences among the plans indicate the many opinions that exist concerning what ails the U.S. health care system and what needs to be done to correct those ailments.

We also saw that the states have taken a very active role in health care reform. Almost every state has initiated, or is contemplating, health care reform. Despite the fact that the policies vary immensely across states, the goal is always the same: to simultaneously contain the growth of health care costs while improving access to quality care.

The chapter closed with a basic blueprint of the Clinton health care plan. The Clinton health care plan represents the sixth time during the 20th century that the United States has debated a greatly expanded role for government in health care. Previous debates took place in the late 1910s, the 1930s, the late 1940s, the 1960s, the 1970s, and the 1990s. Only once—during the 1960s, when the Medicaid and Medicare programs were instituted—were proponents of government involvement in medical care successful (Skocpol, 1995).

## Review Questions and Problems

1. Discuss the four generic plans for health care reform in terms of the general model of a health care system presented in Chapter 2. Pay particular attention to the role third-party payers play in each plan.

2. Discuss each of the four generic plans for health care reform in terms of theories X and Y as discussed in Chapter 1.

3. Which one of the four generic plans of health care reform appeals to you the most? Substantiate your opinion using economic theory.

4. Which generic health care plan would best correct moral hazard? Why? Which generic plan would best achieve scale economies in health insurance administration? Why? Which plan would provide the most variety? Why?

5. Choose a state other than one of the four discussed in the chapter, and research any basic changes in health care policy that have been made or are currently being considered.

6. Discuss the main features of the Clinton health care reform plan, and provide some reasons why it was not enacted.

## References

American Association of Retired Persons. *Reforming the Health Care System: State Profiles 1997.* Washington, DC: 1997.

Anderson, Gerald, Robert Heyssel, and Robert Dickler. "Competition versus Regulation: Its Effect on Hospitals." *Health Affairs* 12 (spring 1993), pp. 70–80.

Anderson, Gerard F. "In Search of Value: An International Comparison of Cost, Access, and Outcomes." *Health Affairs* 16 (November/December 1997), pp. 163–71.

Barrand, Nancy L., and Steven Schroeder. "Lessons from the States." *Inquiry* 31 (spring 1994), pp. 10–13.

Blewett, Lynn A. "Reforms in Minnesota: Forging the Path." *Health Affairs* 13 (fall 1994), pp. 200–9.

Bodenheimer, Thomas. "The Oregon Health Plan—Lessons for the Nation." *New England Journal of Medicine* 337 (August 28, 1997), pp. 651–55.

Brady, David W., and Kara M. Buckley. "Health Care Reform in the 103d Congress: A Predictable Failure." *Journal of Health Politics, Policy and Law* 20 (spring 1995), pp. 447–84.

Caldwell, Bert W. "The Cost of Medical Care from the Viewpoint of the Hospital." In *Hospitals and the Cost of Medical Care.* Papers of the American Conference of Hospital Services. Chicago: American Hospital Association, February 18, 1930.

Chenery, William L. "Hospital Fees Hit the Middle Class Hard." *The New York Times,* November 9, 1924, p. 7.

Enthoven, Alain C. "The History and Principles of Managed Competition." *Health Affairs* (supplement 1993), pp. 24–48.

Enthoven, Alain C., and Richard Kronick. "A Consumer-Choice Health Plan for the 1990s." Parts 1 and 2. *New England Journal of Medicine* 320 (January 5, 1989), pp. 29–37; (January 12, 1989), pp. 94–101.

Enthoven, Alain C., and Sara J. Singer. "Market-Based Reform: What to Regulate and by Whom?" *Health Affairs* 14 (spring 1995), pp. 105–19.

Goodman, John C., and Gerald L. Musgrave. *Patient Power: Solving America's Health Care Crisis.* Washington, DC: Cato Institute, 1992.

Grubaugh, Stephen G., and Rexford E. Santerre. "Comparing the Performance of Health Care Systems: An Alternative Approach." *Southern Economic Journal* 60 (April 1994), pp. 1030–42.

Himmelstein, David, and Steffie Woolhandler. "A National Health Program for the United States." *New England Journal of Medicine* 320 (January 12, 1989), pp. 102–08.

Iglehart, John K. "Health Care Reform—The States." *New England Journal of Medicine* 330 (January 6, 1994), pp. 75–79.

Intergovernment Health Policy Project. *Profiles of the States and Health Care Reform.* Washington, DC: George Washington University, July 1993.

———. *Profiles of the States and Health Care Reform.* Washington, DC: George Washington University, October 1995.

Kronick, Richard, David C. Goodman, John Wennberg, and Edward Wagner. "The Marketplace in Health Care Reform: The Demographic Limitations of Managed Competition." *New England Journal of Medicine* 328 (January 14, 1993), pp. 148–52.

Leichter, Howard M. "Minnesota: The Trip from Acrimony to Accommodation." *Health Affairs* 12 (summer 1993), pp. 48–57.

Maryland Health Care Access and Cost Commission, http://www.hcacc.state.md.us.

Minnesota Department of Health. *MinnesotaCare Interim Growth Limits Changed to Cost Containment.* February 1998.

McDonough, John E. "Tracking the Demise of State Hospital Rate Setting." *Health Affairs* 16 (January/February 1997), pp. 142–49.

Morone, James A. "Nativism, Hollow Corporations and Managed Competition: Why the Clinton Health Care Reform Failed." *Journal of Health Politics, Policy and Law* 20 (spring 1995), pp. 394–98.

Navarro, Vincente. "Why Congress Did Not Enact Health Care Reform." *Journal of Health Politics, Policy and Law* 20 (spring 1995), pp. 455–62.

Neubauer, Deane. "Hawaii: A Pioneer in Health System Reform." *Health Affairs* 12 (summer 1993), pp. 31–39.

Oregon Health Plan, http://www.ohppr.das.state.or.us.

Organization for Economic Cooperation and Development. *Health Care Systems in Transition: The Search for Efficiency.* Paris: OECD, 1990.

O'Neill, Patrick. "State Health Plan Studies Three Changes in Services Offered." *The Oregonian*, July 7, 1998.

Pauly, Mark, Patricia Danzon, Paul Feldstein, and John Hoff. "A Plan for Responsible National Health Insurance." *Health Affairs* 10 (spring 1991), pp. 5–25.

Rockman, Bert A. "The Clinton Presidency and Health Care Reform." *Journal of Health Politics, Policy and Law* 20 (spring 1995), pp. 399–402.

Rogal, Deborah L., and W. David Helms. "State Models: Tracking States' Efforts to Reform Their Health Systems." *Health Affairs* 12 (summer 1993), pp. 27–30.

Santerre, Rexford E., Stephen G. Grubaugh, and Andrew J. Stollar. "Government Intervention in Health Care Markets and Health Care Outcomes: Some International Evidence." *Cato Journal* 11 (spring-summer, 1991), pp. 1–12.

Skocpol, Theda. "The Rise and Resounding Demise of the Clinton Plan." *Journal of Health Politics, Policy and Law* 19 (spring 1995), pp. 86–98.

Snyder, Dale. "Building Bureaucracy and Invading Patient Privacy: Maryland's Health Care Regulations." *The Heritage Foundation Backgrounder*, http://www.heritage.org (April 16, 1998).

Steinman, Sven, and Jon Watts. "It's the Institutions, Stupid! Why Comprehensive National Health Insurance Always Fails in America." *Journal of Health Politics, Policy and Law* 19 (spring 1995), pp. 329–72.

Stevens, Rosemary. *In Sickness and in Wealth.* New York: Basic Books, 1987.

Tanner, Michael. "Medical Savings Accounts: Answering the Critics." *Policy Analysis*, no. 228. Washington, DC: Cato Institute, May 25, 1995.

———. "Laboratory Failures: States Are No Model for Health Care Reform." *Policy Analysis*, no. 207. Washington, DC: Cato Institute, September 23, 1993.

Tripoli, Leigh. "Agoraphobia: What Ails Most of the Conservative Proposals to Reform Health Care." *Business Economics* (April 1993), pp. 30–35.

Yankelovich, Daniel. "The Debate That Wasn't: The Public and the Clinton Plan." *Health Affairs* 14 (spring 1995), pp. 7–23.

# A Brief Exposure to Econometrics[1]

Economics is a social science. As a science, the development of economic principles follows the two main tenets of the scientific method. First, we build models that adequately describe the conceptual elements of our theory. In the construction process, strict adherence to the rules of deductive reasoning and mathematics is critical. We then typically examine the predicted results more deeply—for instance, by analyzing the comparative static effects caused by changes in the *ceteris paribus* conditions. Second, we test the model against known facts, the data, with logical reasoning and statistics leading the way. If the model is correctly specified, the empirical investigation will strongly support our hypotheses, whereas weak empirical results will suggest an incorrect model specification.[2] In the latter event, we must be willing and able to reexamine the theoretical model and test the revised specification.

Suppose that recently enacted federal legislation provides a subsidy to households for purchasing primary health care services. This new government program has sparked your interest, and you decide to investigate. Economic theory tells you that the quantity demanded of a good depends on the good's price as well as other influences—the all-else-the-same condition. As you think about your specific problem, you realize that quantity demanded can be measured as visits to a primary health care provider, with the unit price being simply the patient's out-of-pocket charge per visit. You would anticipate that as the price of a visit rises, the typical household makes fewer visits to the primary health care facility—that is, the quantity demanded falls. With this demand function, the federal subsidy can be viewed as a simple reduction in the

---

[1]We are indebted to Bruce Carpenter of Mansfield University for composing this appendix.

[2]One must be very careful in interpreting positive empirical evidence. Observed data cannot prove a theory: They can only support the theory.

price of a primary health care visit. Therefore, direct assessment of the subsidy's market impacts is possible.[3]

What other influences would be important in the determination of demand? Surely a family's income has an influence on the level of primary health care demanded. In fact, a natural assumption would be that primary health care is a normal good. Perhaps the market structure is important. In an area where one facility is the sole provider of primary health care services, you might expect demand to differ significantly from the demand arising in an area characterized by vigorous competition.

In total, then, you expect a household's demand for primary health care services to be dependent on the price of a visit, the household's income, and the number of primary care facilities available. Furthermore, you can implement and investigate the consequences of the federal subsidy simply by reducing the price of a visit. However, as the subsidy is introduced, various questions immediately come to mind: How responsive is quantity demanded to the subsidy? Does household spending on primary health care rise, fall, or stay the same? Does total spending on primary health care rise, fall, stay the same? Will there be "room" for more providers? Is health care a normal good as assumed? Just how important is the number of medical care facilities? As you can see, the conceptual, theoretical model provides a description of the general demand framework and a methodology for analyzing implications given the assumptions. Yet it also generates an enormous set of additional questions that theory cannot answer. Indeed, the answers lie within the everyday workings of the market. To properly address these questions, we need to employ an additional tool: econometrics. **Econometrics** is the application of statistical techniques to the problems of economics. Through econometric models we quantify a general equation, estimate its specific numerical parameters, and then address the numerical analysis.

This appendix

- Briefly introduces the major concepts of econometrics.

- Examines initial definitions, the population regression function, and functional forms.

- Offers a few comments concerning data.

- Illustrates the process of estimation and testing.

## The Population Regression Function and Sampling

As economists, we generally are not satisfied simply with the theoretical demand for primary health care services. More important to us is a deeper understanding of the market mechanism responsible for generating the observed data. We want to know why those data were observed, what variables influence the market, and the strength of their influence.

---

[3]Note, however, that this is a partial equilibrium analysis. It neglects the important cross-impacts the subsidy has in the markets for physicians, nurses, facilities, and so on.

Quantitative analysis of this sort is important for at least two reasons. First, the methodology allows us to test the cause-and-effect relationships the theory suggests and thus guides us in our search for accurate and useful theoretical models. In this sense, empirical investigation should be looked at as being complementary to theoretical research. Second, given sound and well-tested theoretical models, we can utilize the theory in conjunction with the empirical applications to predict the impact of policy initiatives or of any other change affecting the market.

As we will soon see, the method we use for this investigation, regression analysis, is similar in many ways to sample averages. However, since we ask the data to give us more than the simple average, the method of estimation is slightly more complicated. We begin our investigation with an examination of the population regression function.

Suppose we believe that for a typical individual, the quantity demanded of primary health care services ($Q$) is inversely related to the out-of-pocket price of health care services ($P$) and positively affected by the individual's income level ($Y$). This hypothesis establishes the cause-and-effect flows in the model; that is, changes in either price or income affect the level of health care services demanded. In more mathematical terminology, we take the variable $Q$ as the dependent variable[4] and the variables $P$ and $Y$ as the independent variables.[5] Furthermore, we might predict that a linear relationship exists between the independent and dependent variables. Mathematically, we assume that

**(A-1)**   $Q = \beta_1 + \beta_2 P + \beta_3 Y,$

where $\beta_2 < 0$ and $\beta_3 > 0$.

With fixed income, quantity demanded changes as price changes, and we trace out a demand curve similar to $D_1$ in figure A-1. More specifically, as the price of a visit changes by \$1, the number of visits demanded falls by $\beta_2$. $\beta_2$, then, is the slope of the demand curve.[6] Similarly, $\beta_3$ measures the impact of a change in income. To see this, suppose price is fixed and income increases. Since we've assumed that primary health care is a normal good, the number of visits rises, and the demand curve rises vertically by $\beta_3 \cdot \Delta Y$ (the character $\Delta$ means "change in"), as shown in figure A-1. Strictly speaking, $\beta_1$ is the number of visits a typical household would make to a primary care facility when the household has no income and the visit is free. Of course, a demand equation must be more applicable than that, and thus $\beta_1$ is viewed as a base level of quantity demanded. As income rises, we expect the demand for a normal good to rise, and so should the base quantity demanded. Furthermore, at any income level, the vertical intercept, the maximum quantity demanded of a free good, is $\beta_1 + \beta_3 Y$. This suggests

---

[4]The dependent variable is often referred to as the *endogenous* variable. Here we take *endogenous* to mean the variable whose value is determined within the model.

[5]Independent variables are often called *exogenous* variables, or variables whose value is determined outside of the model. That is, these variables are determined by an economic process other than the one currently under investigation.

[6]Notice that in figure A-1, quantity is on the vertical axis while price is on the horizontal axis—the exact opposite from the traditional graph. The reason for this departure from tradition is that figure A-1 depicts what we believe to be the cause-and-effect relationship of demand as discussed above.

---

**FIGURE A–1**   PARAMETERS IN A DEMAND EQUATION

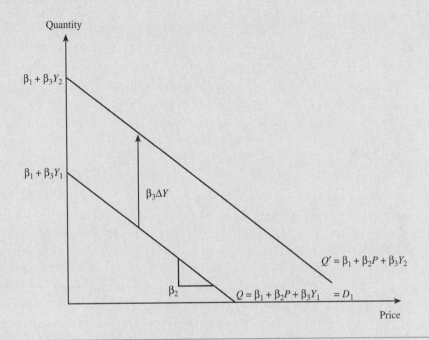

---

that the consumer becomes satiated at some level of consumption and will not consume any more, since doing so would lead to reduced satisfaction.

Let us return for a moment to the slope parameter on price, $\beta_2$. Certainly we see that $\beta_2$ is the absolute change in quantity demanded due to a change in price, and as such it should figure prominently in the own-price elasticity. In fact, given a level of income $Y_1$, a price $P_1$, and the corresponding quantity demanded, $Q_1$, the own-price elasticity of demand is

**(A-2)**   $E_D = \dfrac{\% \, \Delta Q}{\% \, \Delta P}$

$= \beta_2 \dfrac{P_1}{Q_1}$

Similarly, the income elasticity of demand is

**(A-3)**   $E_Y = \dfrac{\% \, \Delta Q}{\% \, \Delta Y}$

$= \beta_3 \dfrac{Y_1}{Q_1}$

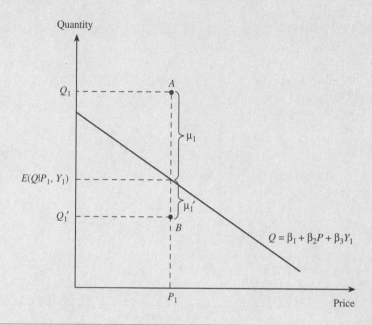

FIGURE A-2    A POPULATION REGRESSION FUNCTION

## The Error Structure

One more modification is required, however, to make this a workable econometric model. As we begin to think of our demand model as a statistical representation, we must also begin to think of data. In our model, a data point consists of three measurements for the same person: a price of health care, the individual's income level, and the resulting quantity of health care demanded. As we look at our data, it is quite possible that we witness two data points similar to $A$ and $B$ in figure A-2. Notice that in this case, the same level of income ($Y_1$) and the same price level ($P_1$) have resulted in two different levels of health care demanded ($Q_1$ and $Q_1'$). In fact, we can envision an entire *continuum* of possible $Q$s associated with each price and income pair. The reason for this might be due to differing tastes and preferences among individuals, or perhaps because of random shocks. Regardless of the source, the proper representation of our demand model must take these discrepancies into consideration.

We do this by incorporating an error term, u, into our model and rewriting equation A-1 as

**(A-4)**   $Q = \beta_1 + \beta_2 P + \beta_3 Y + u,$

where $\beta_2 < 0$ and $\beta_3 > 0$.[7] The error term, u, is the source of random behavior in our model.

So where does this leave us with our mathematical theory of demand? Suppose we assume that *on average*, the observed error at a given value of $P$ and $Y$ is zero, that is, $E[u|P_1, Y_1] = 0$.[8] As a result, equation A-4 can be interpreted as the relationship among price, income, and an actual level of health care services demanded and equation A-1 can be interpreted as the relationship among price, income, and the *average* level of health care services demanded. As we can see in figure A-2 given an income level of $Y_1$ and a price of $P_1$, we can expect, on average, to observe a quantity demanded of $E[Q|P_1, Y_1]$, which is a point on the demand curve. The amount by which $Q_1$ exceeds $E[Q|P_1, Y_1]$ is the level of error $u_1 > 0$. Similarly, the amount by which $Q_1'$ falls short of the average is the level of error $u_1' < 0$.

We now define the population regression function (PRF) as the generalized average level of health care demanded, or

**(A-5)**  $E[Q|P, Y] = \beta_1 + \beta_2 P + \beta_3 Y.$

Our job as applied economists, then, is to estimate the unknown parameters $\beta_1$, $\beta_2$, and $\beta_3$ and thus describe the average demand structure.

At this juncture, we need to examine the error term introduced in equation A-4 more closely. In particular, we need to impose a set of assumptions describing the error term's behavior and discuss their relevance. Conceptually, an infinite number of possible error values exist at any given level of $P$ and $Y$ (i.e., there is an entire continuous domain from which to select an error's value). Furthermore, an entirely different population of errors may correspond to each $P$ and $Y$ pair. The purpose of the error assumptions is to standardize these various populations into one typical population. Whether or not the assumptions are valid should always be explored by the applied economist.

The first error assumption is by now familiar: We assume the average error at any given level of $P$ and $Y$ is zero. Such an assumption assures us that the average value of $Q$ is determined solely by explanatory factors and places the central value of the dependent variable's distribution directly on the PRF. Suppose for a moment that the average error were different from zero. In that case, the average value of $Q$ would be determined by the explanatory factors *plus* unobservable error. In fact, the PRF would be meaningless, and any hopes of accurate prediction would be dashed! This assumption, along with the implied effect on the dependent variable, is formally presented in the first row of table A-1.

---

[7]In the following discussion, we will continue to use this illustrative model. However, the reader should be aware that the general regression model with $(k - 1)$ explanatory variables is expressed as

$$Y = \beta_1 + \beta_2 X_2 + \beta_3 X_3 + \ldots + \beta_k X_k + u.$$

[8]The symbol $E[\ldots]$ is the expected value, or average, operator, and the vertical bar refers to holding the values of $P$ and $Y$ fixed at the given levels. Taken together, the expression is read "the expected (average) value of u given $P = P_1$ and $Y = Y_1$ is zero."

| TABLE A-1 | ERROR ASSUMPTIONS |
|-----------|-------------------|

Model: $Y = \beta_1 + \beta_2 X_2 + \beta_3 X_3 + \ldots + \beta_k X_k + u$

| Error Assumptions | Dependent Variable Assumptions |
|-------------------|-------------------------------|
| $E[u \mid X_1, \ldots, X_k] = 0$ | $E[Y \mid X_1, \ldots, X_k] = \beta_1 + \beta_2 X_2 + \ldots + \beta_k X_k$ |
| $\text{var}(u) = \sigma_u^2$ | $\text{var}(Y) = \sigma_y^2$ |
| $\text{cov}(u_i, u_j) = 0$ for $i \neq j$ | $\text{cov}(Y_i, Y_j) = 0$ for $i \neq j$ |

In practice, we might commonly face violations of this assumption, for any true explanatory variable that happens to be excluded from the proposed model leads to $E[u \mid \ldots] \neq 0$. Given the web of cause-and-effect relationships that bind markets together, it seems somewhat naive to expect every model to be in full compliance with this assumption. Yet it is not unreasonable to believe that the most important explanatory variables have been included and only variables of marginal explanatory importance excluded.[9]

The second assumption controls another aspect of the errors: the error variance. We can think of variance as the dispersion of the errors around their mean, or average, value.[10] In instances where the errors are very concentrated about zero (and thus show very little variability), the variance is small. Our purpose here is not to assume anything about the amount of variation but to address the uniformity of that variation. Specifically, we assume the error variance at each possible level of $P$ and $Y$ is the same, or

**(A-6)**  $\text{var}(u \mid P, Y) = \text{var}(u)$

$$= \sigma_u^2,$$

where $\sigma_u^2$ is a constant value at all levels of $P$ and $Y$. The second row of table A-1 presents this assumption, as well as its implications for the dependent variable.

On occasion this assumption will be violated, in which case the errors are said to be *heteroskedastic*,[11] or unequally dispersed. While this error variance behavior might be independent of any model influence, it often arises in association with an included independent variable, and then almost exclusively in cross-sectional models. Suppose for a moment that our illustrative health care model is based on individual household measurements. Families with very low incomes have very limited ability to purchase health care and most likely have very little flexibility in these purchases; that is, we will

---

[9]The omission of important explanatory variables is an issue in what is known as *specification error*. See Gujarati (1995), Chapters 6 and 13, for an excellent presentation of this problem.

[10]The square root of the variance is defined as the *standard deviation*.

[11]Again, Gujarati (1995), Chapter 11, serves as a good reference.

find that most families with low incomes will purchase an amount of health care very close to the mean. Higher-income families have greater ability to buy health care and consequently have greater flexibility in these purchases, which is reflected in a wider dispersion of purchases about the mean.

Finally, we ask that the errors be independently drawn so that one observed value neither influences nor is influenced by any other error observation. To accomplish this, we assume the covariance[12] between error terms is zero, or

**(A-7)**   $cov(u_i, u_j) = 0$ for all $i \neq j$.

Any violation of this assumption is taken to mean that a systematic, functional relationship exists among successive observations of the error random variables. For instance, it might be the case that a positive (negative) error in one time period would most likely be followed by a positive (negative) error in the next time period. As we can see, the value an error takes on is not an independent event but is dependent on an earlier observation. In this instance, the two errors vary together in a positive way. Alternatively, we can easily imagine an instance where a positive (negative) error in one time period would most likely bring about a negative (positive) error in the succeeding period. Here we have an instance of negative covariation. This relationship, generally referred to as an *autocorrelated process,*[13] is most problematic in time series models in which the observational units come from successive periods of time. Row three of table A-1 provides us with a formal statement of this assumption, as well as its implications for the dependent variable.

We summarize all the regression model assumptions and impose an additional assumption describing the exact probability distribution generating the errors by saying that for the sample of size $n$,

**(A-8)**   $u_i \sim$ i.i.d $N(0, \sigma_u^2)$ for $i = 1, 2, \ldots, n$,

which is read "the $n$ observations are realizations of $n$ random variables that are *i*ndependent (no autocorrelation) and *i*dentically (same mean and variance) *d*istributed as a *n*ormal random variable having zero mean and a variance $\sigma_u^2$." Normally distributed errors are not needed for estimation but are required for hypothesis testing. Henceforth, we assume equation A-8 holds.

---

[12]The covariance between two random variables is a measure of the variables' independence. If the covariance is zero, the random variables are independent; the value taken on by one random variable does not influence, and is not influenced by, the value taken on by the other random variable. A positive covariance indicates a positive relationship between the random variables, whereas a negative covariance indicates an inverse relationship. A related concept is *correlation*, which is the covariance between two random variables relative to their standard deviations. The usefulness of the correlation coefficient comes from the fact that it is a standardized index measuring the degree of covariability, whereas the covariance is not. A correlation value of 1 indicates a perfect positive linear relationship between the two random variables, and values close to 1 indicate a strong, but not perfect, positive linear relationship. Similarly, a correlation coefficient of $-1$ means that a perfect inverse linear relationship exists between the two random variables, while a value close to $-1$ indicates a strong, but not perfect, inverse linear relationship. No analogous interpretation is possible from covariances alone.

[13]See Gujarati (1995), Chapter 12.

## An Alternative Functional Form

We have represented the PRF as a linear relationship between the dependent and independent variables. This formulation is not a requirement. Indeed, we often find it advantageous to utilize nonlinear functional forms. Perhaps the most common nonlinear form is the log-log specification, in which all variables in the PRF are entered in their natural log (Ln) values. The underlying belief when we use such a functional form is that the independent variables exert a multiplicative, as opposed to an additive, influence on the dependent variable. An additional benefit of this model specification is that the parameters are elasticities. Thus, our original specification of the population regression function would be

**(A-9)** $\quad Q = \beta_1' P^{\beta_2} Y^{\beta_3} u'$

As it stands, this model specification is not compatible with the estimation techniques discussed shortly. However, if we take the natural log of both sides of the equation, the result is a form we can estimate:[14]

**(A-10)** $\quad \mathrm{Ln}Q = \mathrm{Ln}\beta_1' + \beta_2\mathrm{Ln}P + \beta_3\mathrm{Ln}Y + \mathrm{Ln}u'$

$$= \beta_1 + \beta_2\mathrm{Ln}P + \beta_3\mathrm{Ln}Y + u.$$

Notice that although the functional form is nonlinear, the parameters still enter the equation in a linear fashion. This linearity of the parameters is essential for the techniques described next to be useful.

# Data

Ideally, at this point we would design an experiment to examine what we believe to be the true demand for health care as expressed in equation A-4. We would select a diverse collection of $P$ and $Y$ values, and the experiment would then generate the corresponding values of $Q$. If need be, we could repeat the experiment again and again, using the same independent variable measurements to guard against spurious results. This is precisely the methodology that physicists and chemists follow in their laboratories.

Unfortunately, applications in economics are far from the ideal. First, we are unable to set the levels of the independent variables. The very market process we seek to explain may generate some of our data—for instance, the levels of health care prices. Other independent variables, such as income, may not be generated in the market of interest, but are certainly generated within the economic system. Second, the notion of independent variables implies that no functional relationship exists between the observed values. In the purest of settings, we would not expect to see the level of income

---

[14]The reader should be aware that the data we collect are not in their natural log form. Therefore, before we can utilize them in a log-log model, we must first use statistical software to transform the original data into natural log form.

in a county exert any influence over the price consumers pay (i.e., we would not expect to observe any correlation between the independent variables). Yet these values are all determined within the economic system, and thus income does influence price somewhat and we do observe a correlation between the independent variables. Finally, we can never hope to replicate the experiment.

Of course, we must initially proceed under the assumption that the independent variables are truly independent. At some later date, we can examine the exogenous variables in light of the first two observations above. If the results warrant further action, we can pursue advanced correction procedures.

## Data Types

Now we collect our data: $n$ observations for each variable in the model, for a total of $n$ data points. *It is extremely important that we maintain the internal consistency of each data point.* As the data were generated, the $i$th observation of price occurred in conjunction with the $i$th observation of income and the $i$th observed quantity of health care services demanded. Since the model predicts that price and income jointly determine health care demand, we must ensure that all observational units stay together. In practice, this is easily accomplished, although it does occupy some of our time.

The data sets we will encounter are either time series or cross-sectional. Time series data are generated at progressive points through time—for instance, from the first quarter of 1980 through the third quarter of 1995. Other possibilities include annual, monthly, weekly, or daily observations. Cross-sectional data, on the other hand, are measurements on different economic units (e.g., individual households or states) within the same time period.

## The Data Set: An Example

Earlier we assumed the demand for primary health care is a linear function of price and income, given as

**(A-11)**  $\text{Quantity} = \beta_1 + \beta_2\text{Price} + \beta_3\text{Income} + u.$

We then collect (hypothetical) data for the price of health care, quantity of health care demanded, and income for the year 1995 in 25 counties throughout the Northeast. This cross-sectional data set represents a sample of size $n = 25$ and is displayed in table A-2. The price variable is the average price a household paid for a primary health care visit, the quantity variable is the average number of visits made by a household per year, and income is the average household income measured in thousands of dollars per year.

The first thing we should always do when starting an empirical investigation is get to know the data. First, we should print a table of the entire data set, such as table A-2. For simplicity, each row should correspond to one data point. This practice accomplishes at least two important functions. First, since a row corresponds to one observation, maintaining internal consistency is now a trivial task. If, for instance, the

| TABLE A–2 | HYPOTHETICAL PRIMARY HEALTH CARE DATA SET | | |
|---|---|---|---|
| County | Quantity | Price | Income |
| 1 | 14.353 | 46.588 | 12.205 |
| 2 | 13.553 | 51.808 | 11.837 |
| 3 | 13.282 | 50.870 | 14.302 |
| 4 | 13.391 | 51.169 | 13.485 |
| 5 | 12.927 | 51.114 | 13.302 |
| 6 | 13.730 | 47.106 | 10.258 |
| 7 | 13.577 | 50.359 | 10.381 |
| 8 | 13.281 | 48.358 | 12.170 |
| 9 | 13.062 | 50.008 | 23.297 |
| 10 | 13.374 | 50.482 | 26.035 |
| 11 | 13.588 | 49.731 | 27.293 |
| 12 | 13.150 | 50.727 | 26.502 |
| 13 | 13.594 | 49.443 | 23.901 |
| 14 | 13.730 | 50.649 | 25.283 |
| 15 | 13.782 | 49.780 | 25.669 |
| 16 | 13.751 | 49.975 | 23.908 |
| 17 | 13.757 | 50.139 | 39.142 |
| 18 | 14.343 | 50.445 | 39.979 |
| 19 | 13.511 | 49.205 | 40.788 |
| 20 | 14.280 | 48.751 | 40.014 |
| 21 | 13.902 | 50.847 | 39.947 |
| 22 | 13.576 | 52.885 | 42.052 |
| 23 | 13.777 | 50.079 | 41.881 |
| 24 | 13.756 | 52.328 | 43.100 |
| 25 | 13.339 | 51.570 | 38.953 |

tenth row of the data table corresponds to Fairfield County in Connecticut, all entries in that row should indeed be from Fairfield County. Any deviations can be quickly and easily corrected. Second, this procedure gives us the opportunity to clean up the database, correcting any mistyped entries.

Another extremely useful exercise is to look at a simple scatterplot of the price and quantity data, such as that shown in figure A-3. Any irregularities certainly stand out

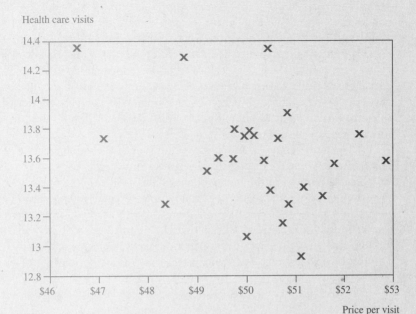

**FIGURE A–3**     A SCATTER DIAGRAM

now. Notice, for instance, the data point along the northwestern edge of figure A-3. Although we may not have seen this in our perusal of the data table, we certainly see it in the diagram. Again, we would investigate our data entry accuracy, but under no circumstances should we omit these observations.

Scatterplots can also tell us what to expect from the estimated model. Our earlier discussion concerning the nature of sampling and the error term suggests that the sample will most certainly *not* lie on a straight line. Yet economic theory leads us to believe that the slope of a demand curve is negative. Together, these two observations indicate that we should see the data cluster about a negative line. Put slightly differently, the data should form a group that is, for the most part, negatively sloped. As we look at figure A-3, we see the vague image of a negatively sloped group. However, the group is quite plump, which is indicative of considerable error.

# Estimation and Testing

Now it is time to actually estimate the parameters of the model. First, glance at figure A-3 again. We have already decided that a straight line is the appropriate way to describe the model. But as you can see, there are many possible straight lines that could pass through the scatter diagram. Which one is the best? Any choice of coefficients yields a different straight line—that is, a different *predicted* value of quantity demanded given observed *P* and *Y*. Now we define predicted error as the difference between actual and predicted quantity demanded. Note that this is the estimated counterpart of population error shown in figure A-2. We define the best set of coefficients as those that yield the smallest sum of squared predicted error. This procedure is known as *ordinary least squares (OLS)* or, as it is often called, *linear regression*.[15] Many statistical packages are available that perform OLS, and each one has its strong points and weaknesses.[16] For a beginner, the choice of econometrics software isn't critical. Whatever software we end up using should be used as often as possible so that we can learn what the software can and cannot do for us.

We do find some commonalities among all the econometric software packages. For instance, we need to provide the software with the name of the dependent (*Y*) variable, the name(s) of the independent (*X*) variable(s),[17] the number of observations, and whether we want the estimated model to contain an intercept term. After we have successfully passed this information along to the software, we get a stream of output similar to that in table A-3. Notice that the output first includes some general information: the name we gave to the dependent variable (Quantity in our example), the number of observations, and some overall statistics (the degrees of freedom, $R^2$, $\bar{R}^2$ and $F^*$).

We will return to the overall statistics, but for now let us turn to the information at the bottom of table A-3. Under the column labeled *Name* are the names we have given the independent variables: CONSTANT refers to the intercept term, PRICE refers to the independent variable price of health care, and INCOME refers to the independent variable income. In the next column, labeled *Coefficient*, we find the parameter estimates. As we can see, the estimated intercept term is 19.9886. From this we infer that if price and income were both zero, the estimated level of health care demanded would be 19.9886 visits per household per year.

The following row gives us the estimated coefficient for the price variable, or −.1353. Recall that this value is our estimate of the demand curve's slope and the negative value indicates that the estimated demand function is indeed negatively sloped, as we would expect from theory. Furthermore, this estimate tells us that as the price of a visit increases by $1, the quantity demanded declines by .1353 visits.

Finally, we see that the coefficient attached to the income variable is .0155. Prior to estimation, our intuition would lead us to believe that health care is a normal good; that is, as income rises, the amount of health care demanded increases as well. This a priori belief is supported by the empirical results, particularly the positive sign attached to the estimated coefficient.[18] Care must be taken when interpreting the

---

[15]A formal presentation of the OLS estimator is not necessary for the purposes of this appendix. The reader who is interested in the theoretical development of the estimators should consult Gujarati (1995), Chapter 2.

[16]Some of the more common software packages are EVIEWS, RATS, MINITAB, SAS, and SPSS. If you don't already have access to econometrics software, ask your instructor for assistance in acquiring some.

[17]A suggestion: Always choose names that are (1) easy to remember and (2) reflective of the data they represent.

[18]Had this sign been negative, the data would lead us to believe that health care is an inferior good.

| TABLE A-3 | INITIAL REGRESSION RESULTS |
|---|---|

Dependent Variable: Quantity
Total Observations: 25
$R^2 = .3654$
$F^*(2.22) = 6.33$

Degrees of Freedom: 22
$\bar{R}^2 = .3077$

| Name | Coefficient | Standard Error | t-Statistic |
|---|---|---|---|
| CONSTANT | +19.9886 | +2.2415 | +8.9175 |
| PRICE | −.1353 | +.0456 | −2.9693 |
| INCOME | +.0155 | +.0054 | +2.8557 |

numerical value of this estimate. It should be clear at this point that a one-unit increase in income will generate an estimated .0155 additional visits, all else being the same. But just what is a one-unit increase in income? As we constructed the database, we decided to measure income in thousands of dollars. Thus, for instance, the first income observation of 12.2052 (see table A-2) indicates an income level of $12,205. Therefore, a one-unit increase in income actually means a $1,000 increase in income.[19]

The estimated demand parameters give us the opportunity to predict the mean level of health care visits demanded under various possible scenarios. For instance, suppose we believe income in county 1 will rise to $12,500 and the price of a visit will rise to $47 next year. If we assume no major structural changes occur, it is reasonable to use the estimated demand function to predict next year's quantity demanded. To do this, we simply apply the assumed income and price values to the estimated model and calculate the estimate of $Q$ to be $\hat{Q} = 19.9886 − (.1353)(47) + (.0155)(12.5) = 13.8233$ visits. As long as no major structural changes occur in the underlying health care market and the assumed values for price and income do not differ too drastically from the data set, the predicted value for $Q$ is quite reliable.

Estimates for elasticities are easily obtained as well. Recall from equation A-2 that own-price elasticity is dependent on a price and income level, the corresponding quantity demanded, and the value of $\beta_2$. Since we are now working with an estimated model, we use the estimated parameters, together with the assumed values for the independent variables and the corresponding predicted value for $Q$. We then use

---

[19]Our interpretations are in no way restricted to $1,000 units. For instance, suppose we want to know the impact of a $1 increase in income. Since a $1,000 increase in income leads to an estimated .0155 increase in the quantity demanded of health care, a $1 (= $l,000/1,000) increase in income leads to an estimated .0155/1,000 = .0000155 increase in the quantity demanded of health care. Likewise, a $10,000 increase in income is predicted to lead to a .155 (= 10 · .0155) unit increase in the demand for health care services.

equation A-2.[20] Let us assume price and income remain the same as above, in which case the estimated own-price elasticity is

$$(\text{A-12}) \quad E_D = \frac{\hat{\beta}_2 P}{\hat{Q}}$$

$$= -.1353 \left( \frac{47}{13.8233} \right)$$

$$= -.46$$

The reader may wish to verify that the estimated income elasticity when price is $47 and income is $12,500 is $E_Y = .014$.

### Hypothesis Testing

As with all estimation procedures, the results we obtain are *not* the population parameters we seek but are one observation from an entire population of possibilities, indicating our best guess at their values. Our next step, then, is to gauge the goodness of these estimates. Under no circumstances should we ever refer to $-.1353$ (the estimated coefficient on the price variable) as the population parameter, the mean value of the estimator's distribution, the central value of the estimates, or anything other than what it really is: our best estimate of a population parameter.

What do we mean, then, by hypothesis testing? Quite simply, we try to see whether the data we have collected and the estimates we have obtained support the theoretical hypotheses we developed at the outset of the investigation. Does it seem likely that the data we observe were generated by a population similar to the one we hypothesized? This is the question to which we now turn.

A typical hypothesis test consists of five very well-defined steps: (1) state the null and alternative hypotheses, (2) state the confidence level of the test, (3) calculate the test statistic, (4) record the critical *t*-value, and (5) state the conclusion of the test. Until you are very comfortable with testing, you should strictly adhere to these five steps. A discussion of these steps follows.

**State the Null and Alternative Hypotheses**  The null hypothesis (symbolically designated as $H_o$) is the estimator's *assumed* mean value, and until the data tell us otherwise, it is as good a mean as any other. Since $H_o$ is an assumed mean, it must be an equality. We should look at the null hypothesis as a challenge to the data and, in most instances, hope the data suggest rejection of the null hypothesis in favor of the

---

[20]Often researchers choose to estimate elasticities at the "point of means." They do this for two reasons. First, by using the sample averages, they are in essence asking. "What is the own-price elasticity of demand *on average?*" Thus, they learn more about the central tendencies of the data. Second, a well-known property of OLS regressions is that when the sample averages are the assumed values for the independent variables, the estimated value for the dependent variable is the same as its sample average, or the estimated regression goes through the "point of means." This, of course, makes it extremely convenient to use. As the above example illustrates, however, we are not limited to the point of means.

alternative hypothesis (symbolically designated as $H_A$). Keep in mind that empirical evidence can never prove; it can only disprove. Whereas the null hypothesis must be an equality, the alternative is an inequality reflecting the researcher's a priori beliefs about the parameter's true value.

For example, as we begin the estimation work, we may have no preconceived idea about the impact of income on health care demand; health care could be a normal or an inferior good. Of course, we do believe it has *some* impact. If $\beta_3$ is the income variable's coefficient, the appropriate null and alternative hypotheses are $H_o: \beta_3 = 0$ versus $H_A: \beta_3 \neq 0$. This type of test, in which the null hypothesis is zero, is referred to as a *significance test*. Rejection of the null hypothesis suggests that the true value of $\beta_3$ is not zero but is indeed some other value. An alternative expression is that our estimate is significantly different from zero. With $H_A$ expressed in terms of a "not equals," we refer to this as a *two-tailed test*. As we will see shortly, estimates of $\beta_3$ either far above or far below zero will give us sufficient cause to reject $H_o$. With two-tailed tests, there are two rejection regions.

Economic theory suggests that the slope of a demand curve is negative. As a result, we expect that the coefficient on the price variable is not zero but is in fact negative. Thus, with $\beta_2$ being the coefficient of the price of health care variable, the appropriate null and alternative hypotheses are $H_o: \beta_2 = 0$ versus $H_A: \beta_2 < 0$. This too is a significance test, but it is tempered by a priori expectations as to the numerical sign of the coefficient. This is an example of a one-tailed test, since only significantly negative estimates lead to rejection of the null hypothesis. A one-tailed test has only one rejection region.

Of course, we are not restricted to tests against zero. Suppose previous empirical work suggests that the slope of demand is $\beta_2^*$. We would like to know whether our results support or refute these prior findings. The appropriate test would then be a two-tailed test expressed as $H_o: \beta_2 = \beta_2^*$ versus $H_A: \beta_2 \neq \beta_2^*$. It bears repeating that our convictions concerning the true value of $\beta_2$ aren't very strong here. Similarly, if we believe that $\beta_2$ is smaller than some $\beta_2^*$, the appropriate test is $H_o: \beta_2 = \beta_2^*$ versus $H_A: \beta_2 < \beta_2^*$, whereas we would use $H_o: \beta_2 = \beta_2^*$ versus $H_A: \beta_2 > \beta_2^*$ when we believe $\beta_2$ is larger than $\beta_2^*$.

**State the Confidence Level of the Test**   Even when the null hypothesis is correct, it is possible to obtain an estimate that seems to support rejection of the null hypothesis. That is, we might obtain an extreme sample that yields an estimate that is either very large or very small relative to the mean and be led to reject a hypothesis that is in fact true. The confidence level of the test predetermines the probability of such an occurrence. We define $\alpha$ as the probability of rejecting a true null hypothesis. An $\alpha = .01$ suggests that we are willing to accept that 1 percent of the time we will reject an otherwise true null hypothesis, while an $\alpha = .05$ means we are willing to accept rejection of the null hypothesis 5 percent of the time when it is in fact true. The smaller $\alpha$ is, the harder it is to reject $H_o$ and the stricter we say the test is. Traditionally, $\alpha$s of 1 percent, 5 percent, and 10 percent are used.

**Calculate the Test Statistic**   The null hypothesis assumes that the mean value of $\hat{\beta}_2$'s distribution is $\beta_2^*$. In table A-3 the estimate of $\hat{\beta}_2$ is found in the column labeled *coefficient*, while the estimate of $\hat{\beta}_2$'s standard deviation ($\hat{\sigma}_{\hat{\beta}_2}$) is found in the column labeled *standard error*. We now calculate the test statistic as

$$(\text{A-13}) \quad t^* = \frac{\hat{\beta}_2 - \beta_2^*}{\hat{\sigma}_{\hat{\beta}_2}}$$

**Record the Critical *t* Value**   The critical *t*-value is like a border: It determines whether an estimate is "close to" or "faraway from" its hypothesized value. As such, it relies on three factors: the degrees of freedom, the α level of the test, and whether the test is one-tailed or two-tailed. The degrees of freedom are determined as the number of observations (*n*) minus the total number of regression coefficients estimated in our equation inclusive of the intercept term (*k*). The number of observations, the total number of coefficients estimated, and the degrees of freedom are all obtainable from our computer output. If we look at a *t*-table,[21] we notice that the critical *t*s are in the body of the table, with row and column headings describing it. The rows are determined by the degrees of freedom, calculated as $n - k$ (or total observations minus all parameters estimated). The correct column comes from a combination of the α-level of the test and the type of test. Now recall that the α-level of the test is the probability of rejecting a true null hypothesis. This is interpreted as the area under the *t*-curve in the tail(s) or rejection region(s). If the test is one-tailed, there is only one rejection region and its area is α. If the test is two-tailed, there are two rejection regions, each with area α/2 for a total area of α. Where the correct row and column meet, we find the desired critical *t*-value.[22]

Suppose we have $n = 25$ and we have estimated three parameters so that there are 22 degrees of freedom. First, let's find the critical *t*-value for a two-tailed test with $\alpha = .05$, or $\alpha/2 = .025$. The critical *t*-value, then, is the one that has 22 degrees of freedom and 2.5 percent of the area to the right of it, or 2.074. We see this graphically depicted in panel *a* of figure A-4. Because the curve is symmetrical, we immediately know that 2.5 percent of the area is to the left of $-2.074$ as well. Together these two tails comprise 5 percent of the area under the curve and identify the rejection region. Instead of a two-tailed test, imagine a one-tailed test in which the alternative is "greater than." In this case, all 5 percent of the area is in one tail, and the critical value is 1.717. Since large estimates lead to rejection, the rejection region is the right tail as depicted in panel *b* of figure A-4. If the one-tailed test is of the "less than" type, we tend to reject for small values of the estimate, and thus the critical value is $-1.171$, with the left tail being the rejection region (see panel *c* of figure A-4).

**State the Conclusion of the Test**   If the calculated *t* falls in the rejection region, then we reject $H_o$ in favor of $H_A$; otherwise, we do not reject the test. Notice that we

---

[21]We can find the *t*-tables at the back of any statistics or econometrics textbook.

[22]Care must be exercised here, because the formats of *t*-tables differ. Some will have two sets of column headings, one for one-tailed tests and the other for two-tailed tests. Others have only one set of column headings, with the α-values for *either* one-tailed or two-tailed tests. In these cases, it is assumed that the user can make the transition between one- and two-tailed tests. No matter how the table is constructed, there will always be instructions for use.

**FIGURE A–4**     REJECTION REGIONS

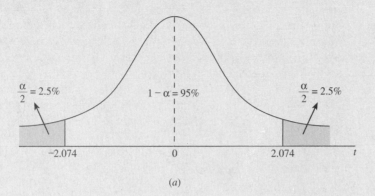

$\frac{\alpha}{2} = 2.5\%$     $1 - \alpha = 95\%$     $\frac{\alpha}{2} = 2.5\%$

−2.074     0     2.074     *t*

(*a*)

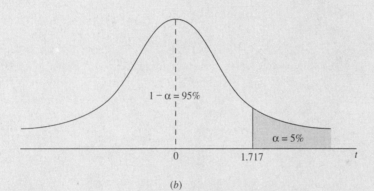

$1 - \alpha = 95\%$

0     1.717     *t*

$\alpha = 5\%$

(*b*)

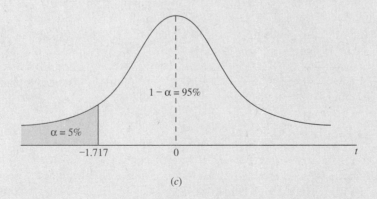

$1 - \alpha = 95\%$

$\alpha = 5\%$

−1.717     0     *t*

(*c*)

do not ever "accept" the results of the test; all the data can ever do is reject (or refute) a null hypothesis.

Let us return to our estimated regression function in table A-3 and consider hypothesis testing. The first thing to notice is the last column, labeled t-*Statistic*. As we shall see, these are the calculated $t$-values for a test with a null hypothesis of zero; the software does some of our work! The first time through, however, let's formally conduct the test of $\beta_2$ (the coefficient on the price variable) against zero:

1. $H_o$: $\beta_2 = 0$

   $H_A$: $\beta_2 < 0$.

   Notice that we have imposed our a priori belief as to the negativity of $\beta_2$, which results in a one-tailed test.

2. $\alpha = .05$.

   The probability of rejecting a true null hypothesis is 5 percent.

3. $t* \dfrac{-.1353 - 0}{0.0456}$

   $= -2.9693$.

   Notice that this comes directly from column 4 of table A-3.

4. $t^c_{.05.22} = -1.717$.

   Here we find df = $n - k = 22$. If we look at table A-3, we see that econometric software often gives us the degrees of freedom as well. The usual notation for the critical $t^c$ is $t^c_{\alpha.df}$ if a one-tailed test and $t_{\alpha/2.df}$ if a two-tailed test.

5. Reject $H_o$ since $|t*| > |t^c_{.05,22}|$.

   Using absolute values simply eliminates the sometimes confusing algebraic signs.

The reader may wish to verify that the estimate of $\beta_3$ in table A-3 is significantly different from zero at the 5 percent level.

While conducting our preliminary regression work, we often find that the $t$-tables aren't handy. Luckily, we have a rule of thumb to aid us. If the $t$-statistic is greater than 2 in absolute value, we can feel comfortable that the estimate is significantly different from 0 at the 5 percent level (for a two-tailed test). A $t$-statistic of 3 or greater most likely means the estimate is significantly different from 0 at the 1 percent level. However, be aware that these are rules of thumb and are not intended to replace the proper test procedure.

## Goodness of Fit and More Tests

A descriptive statistic on which researchers often focus is $R^2$, the coefficient of multiple determination. As we look at our data set, it is quite obvious that the dependent variable (quantity of health care demanded) is not a constant but instead exhibits some variability. Econometricians measure the total variation as the sum of squared deviations away from the dependent variable's mean. We refer to it as the *total sum of squares*. Recall that the variability comes from exactly two causes. Part of the variation can be attributed to the explanatory power of the model and is aptly named the *explained sum of squares* (although *regression sum of squares* is often used as well). The remainder of the total sum of squares is unexplained by the model and is attributable to error. The introduction of a population random disturbance term implies that the regression model cannot perfectly explain all the dependent variable's variation and gives rise to this error sum of squares. It is also possible that we incorrectly omitted a variable as we constructed the model. Such an omission would most certainly dilute the explanatory power of the model. A famous theorem in statistics tells us that the total sum of squares is equal to the explained sum of squares plus the unexplained sum of squares. Stated as sums of squares, these values are quite meaningless individually. However, if we express them as the ratio of explained to total sum of squares, we have something very useful. This ratio, otherwise known as $R^2$, yields the percentage of the dependent variable's variation about its mean that is explained by our regression model.

Many researchers believe their success or failure hinges on the size of $R^2$. Much of the effort involved in improving their results is in reality a series of exercises aimed at maximizing $R^2$. A large $R^2$ is, of course, desirable. After all, the purpose of a regression model is to explain the average behavior of the dependent variable, and the larger $R^2$ is, the larger is the percentage of the dependent variable's variation that has been explained. But are we to infer that a small $R^2$ implies poor models? Such an approach might lead us to dismiss valuable economic models. Consider our example in table A-3. There we find that $R^2$ is .3654, or that 36.54 percent of the dependent variable's variation about its mean is explained by the regression model. At first blush this may seem "small," but when viewed together with all coefficients being significantly different from zero, we can hardly claim this model is poor.

Here we have a perfect example of a cross-sectional model. Often these models yield a small $R^2$ (40 percent or less), yet have strongly significant coefficients. The very nature of the data is the culprit here. Cross-sectional models employ small individual observational units, perhaps with considerably unique characteristics. That translates into considerable random error, which translates into small $R^2$. On the other hand, we most generally find time series models with $R^2$ in excess of 90 percent. Again, the cause lies with the data. Time series data either track an individual unit through time, in which case the dependent variable's variation does not come from unique characteristic differences among observational units, or track aggregate data through time, in which case the aggregation process has obscured any idiosyncratic characteristics of the data.

One other problem is associated with a strategy of maximizing $R^2$. The addition of any variable whatsoever to the regression model will cause $R^2$ to increase. For instance, suppose we add a new independent variable, based on the price of electricity in London, to our health care model. A *t*-test of the estimated coefficient most certainly would tell us that the coefficient is not significantly different from zero, but $R^2$ will go up nonetheless. In response to this dilemma, the adjusted $R^2$, or $\overline{R}^2$ (pronounced "*R* bar squared"), was developed.[23] $\overline{R}^2$ has the property that it will increase

---

[23]For the interested reader, we calculate the adjusted $R^2$ as

$$\overline{R}^2 = R^2 - \left(\frac{k-1}{n-k}\right)(1 - R^2).$$

only when an additional independent variable makes a meaningful addition to the explanatory power of the model.

Let's go back to the notion of a "small" $R^2$. Suppose we know that in our health care model, $\beta_2$ and $\beta_3$ are in fact zero. As a result, our model really doesn't explain anything, and $R^2$ is zero. Now suppose that $\beta_2$ and $\beta_3$, while not exactly zero, are both indistinguishably different from zero. In this instance, we expect to find that almost all the dependent variable's variation is due to error, with precious little explained by the model. A "small" $R^2$ would no doubt result. Thus, you can see that a correspondence exists between $R^2$ and all the explanatory coefficients considered simultaneously. If all $\beta$s are simultaneously zero or jointly indistinguishable from zero, $R^2$ is small. However, having just one of the $\beta$s different from zero implies that $R^2$ is no longer small. We can test $R^2$ against zero, then, as a means of testing jointly the significance of all explanatory coefficients. This procedure is referred to as the $F$-test,

To conduct the $F$-test, let us assume the following general model:

**(A-14)** $Y_i = \beta_1 + \beta_2 X_{2,i} + \beta_3 X_{3,i} + \ldots + \beta_k X_{k,i} + u_i.$

Once we have estimated this model, we can proceed with the $F$-test as follows:

1. $H_o: \beta_2 = \beta_3 = \ldots = \beta_k = 0$   The null hypothesis states that all parameters
   $H_A$: at least one $\beta_i \neq 0$.   except the intercept term are zero and have no
   influence on the dependent variable.

2. Set the $\alpha$-level of the test,   The choice of $\alpha$ dictates the $F$-table to use.
   either $\alpha = .01$, or $\alpha = .05$,
   or $\alpha = .10$

3. Many packages automat-   Recall that $k$ is the total number of parameters
   ically give the calculated   estimated.
   $F$-statistic, but in case yours
   doesn't, we calculate

$$F^* (k - 1, n - k) = \frac{R^2}{(1 - R^2)}\left(\frac{n - k}{k - 1}\right).$$

4. Retrieve $F^c_\alpha(k - 1, n - k)$.   Finding the critical $F$-value in the table
   requires two parameters: $k - 1$ (numerator
   degrees of freedom) typically identifies the
   correct row, and $n - k$ (or denominator
   degrees of freedom) identifies the correct
   column. Where the row and column meet, we
   find the critical $F$-value.

5. Make a decision: Reject $H_o$
   in favor of $H_A$ for $F^* > F^c_\alpha$
   $(k - 1, n - k)$; otherwise,
   do not reject $H_o$.

Once again, let us demonstrate this test using the health care example:

1. $H_o$: $\beta_2 = \beta_3 = 0$
   $H_A$: $\beta_2 \neq 0$, or $\beta_3 \neq 0$,
   or both.

2. Set $\alpha = .05$.

3. Calculate                    Notice that we could have simply taken this
                                 from our output in table A-3.

$$F^*(3 - 1, 25 - 3) = \frac{.3654}{(1 - .3654)}\left(\frac{25 - 3}{3 - 1}\right) = 6.33.$$

4. Find $F_\alpha^c(2,22) = 3.44$.

5. Reject $H_o$ since $F^* > F^c$ and
   conclude that a relationship
   does exist; that is, $R^2$ is not
   small.

Recall when we first looked at the scatterplot of the price and quantity data in figure A-3. We described it as "plump" and indicative of a lot of error. Table A-4 shows the results of a simple regression with only the price of health care as the independent variable. In it we see the statistical manifestation of "plump." This result is marginally acceptable at best. Notice that the intercept is significantly different from zero at virtually any $\alpha$-level. However, the coefficient on the price variable is significant at the $\alpha = .05$ level but not at the $\alpha = .01$ level (one-tailed).[24] The same conclusion holds for $R^2$; it is significantly different from zero at the $\alpha = .05$ level, but not at the $\alpha = .01$ level. As the income variable is added (refer to table A-3), the price coefficient becomes strongly negative, the income coefficient becomes strongly positive, and $R^2$ becomes significant at all levels of $\alpha$. These dramatic changes are all symptomatic of a good additional variable. To see *why* these changes occurred, refer to figure A-5. This diagram is simply a revised version of the original scatterplot in figure A-3. Instead of all data points being marked with an X, if a price–quantity pair corresponds to an income level in the lowest third, it is marked with an X; if it corresponds to an income level in the middle third, it is marked with a square; and if it corresponds to an income level in the top third, it is marked with a triangle. We see that for the most part, each subgroup forms a much thinner grouping of data. Such graphical depiction is the characteristic mark of a variable that adds appreciable explanatory power to the model. Why these variables are often called control variables should be clear.

---

[24]As an exercise, you should set up and conduct the appropriate *t*-tests to verify the accuracy of these statements.

| TABLE A–4 | SIMPLE REGRESSION RESULTS |
|---|---|

Dependent Variable: Quantity
Total Observations: 25
$R^2 = .1302$
$F^*(1.23) = 3.44$

Degrees of Freedom: 23
$\overline{R}^2 = .0924$

| Name | Coefficient | Standard Error | *t*-Statistic |
|---|---|---|---|
| CONSTANT | +18.1812 | +2.4622 | +7.3843 |
| PRICE | −.0910 | +.0491 | −1.8553 |

| FIGURE A–5 | INFLUENCE OF INCOME |
|---|---|

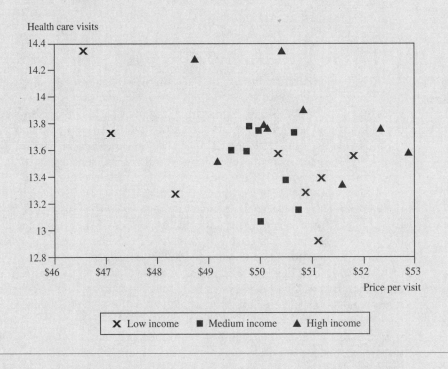

*Dummy Variables*

Up to now, the variables we have used are quantitative in nature. However, there are times when we would like to introduce some qualitative information, such as the distinction between male or female, young or old, and so on. We use this qualitative information by creating a dummy variable, a variable that has two values: 0 in the

| TABLE A–5 | DUMMY VARIABLES | | |
|:---:|:---:|:---:|:---:|
| County | Price | NHCF | NHCFPRICE |
| 1 | 46.588 | 1.000 | 46.588 |
| 2 | 51.808 | .000 | .000 |
| 3 | 50.870 | 1.000 | 50.870 |
| 4 | 51.169 | .000 | .000 |
| 5 | 51.114 | 1.000 | 51.114 |
| 6 | 47.106 | 1.000 | 47.106 |
| 7 | 50.359 | .000 | .000 |
| 8 | 48.358 | .000 | .000 |
| 9 | 50.008 | .000 | .000 |
| 10 | 50.482 | .000 | .000 |
| 11 | 49.731 | .000 | .000 |
| 12 | 50.727 | .000 | .000 |
| 13 | 49.443 | .000 | .000 |
| 14 | 50.649 | 1.000 | 50.649 |
| 15 | 49.780 | 1.000 | 49.780 |
| 16 | 49.975 | 1.000 | 49.975 |
| 17 | 50.139 | 1.000 | 50.139 |
| 18 | 50.445 | 1.000 | 50.445 |
| 19 | 49.205 | .000 | .000 |
| 20 | 48.751 | 1.000 | 48.751 |
| 21 | 50.848 | 1.000 | 50.848 |
| 22 | 52.885 | .000 | .000 |
| 23 | 50.079 | 1.000 | 50.079 |
| 24 | 52.328 | 1.000 | 52.328 |
| 25 | 51.570 | .000 | .000 |

absence of an attribute and 1 in the presence of the attribute. How we define the attribute and how we define presence or absence is not important; the results will be the same. We then incorporate this dummy variable into the regression estimation procedure as we would any other variable. The interpretation of the results, however, is best shown by an example.

In the health care model, it turns out that some counties have only one health care facility, while other municipalities have more than one (see table A-5). One possible

| TABLE A–6 | REGRESSION RESULTS WITH DUMMY VARIABLE |
|-----------|----------------------------------------|

Dependent Variable: Quantity
Total Observations: 25
$R^2 = .4982$
$F^*(3.21) = 6.95$

Degrees of Freedom: 21
$\overline{R}^2 = .4265$

| Name | Coefficient | Standard Error | t-*Statistic* |
|------|-------------|----------------|---------------|
| CONSTANT | +18.5031 | +2.1353 | +8.6653 |
| PRICE | −.1069 | +.0432 | −2.4769 |
| INCOME | +.0126 | +.0051 | +2.4661 |
| NHCF | +.2732 | +.1159 | +2.3571 |

argument might be that as health providers are more readily available, some induced demand occurs.[25] If this hypothesis is true, we would expect the demand for health care to be higher in counties with more than one health care facility. What we would like to do is analyze this hypothesis. Examination of the counties reveals that counties 1, 3, 5, 6, 14, 15, 16, 17, 18, 20, 21, 23, and 24 all have more than one health care facility. Let us define the dummy variable NHCF (standing for *n*umber of *h*ealth *c*are *f*acilities) as taking on the value 1 if the county has more than one health care facility and 0 otherwise.

We now treat this dummy variable as we would any other independent variable. The results of this regression are shown in table A-6. Notice that the introduction of the dummy variable has increased both $R^2$ and $\overline{R}_2$. When corrected for the degrees of freedom, the model now explains 42.7 percent of Quantity's variation about its mean. Furthermore, the $F$ test suggests that $R^2$ is different from zero at the $\alpha = .01$ level. We see also that the coefficient on NHCF is significantly different from zero at the $\alpha = .01$ level.[26] While the introduction of NHCF has altered the magnitudes of the other estimates, it has not done so in a particularly exaggerated way. Certainly, it has not diminished the significance of the estimates. All in all, this exercise strongly supports the hypothesis that two demand structures exist, one for counties with only one health care facility and a higher demand for counties with more than one health care facility. Figure A-6 lend graphical support to this conclusion. The price–quantity pairs associated with multifacility counties are marked with an X, while the pairs associated with the single-facility counties are marked with a square. Without a doubt, the X group lies at a higher level.

Just how much higher is the estimated demand in the multifacility counties? The answer lies in the interpretation of the estimated coefficients. In single-facility counties,

---

[25]See Chapter 10 for a discussion concerning the supplier-induced demand model.

[26]Once again, an excellent exercise is to verify the validity of these claims.

| FIGURE A–6 | SINGLE VERSUS MULTIPLE FACILITIES |
| --- | --- |

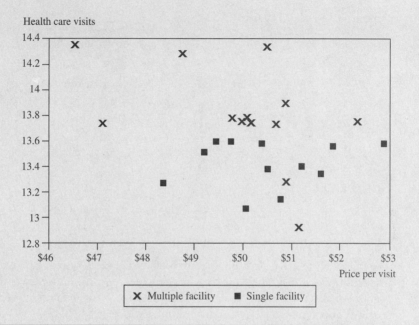

NHCF is zero and that variable drops out of consideration. The estimated constant term for these counties is 18.5031. In multifacility counties, NHCF takes on the value 1, so the constant term becomes 18.5031 (the value in single-facility counties) *plus* .2732 (the change in the intercept term due to being in a multifacility county) for a value of 18.7763. Hence, we see that the roles of some coefficients change considerably when we introduce a dummy variable. First, the estimated constant term assumes the role of a constant term where the attribute is missing (the dummy variable is zero). Second, the estimated coefficient on the dummy variable measures the *incremental* impact the presence of the attribute has on the constant term. To find the estimated constant term when the attribute is present, we simply add the two estimates.

As a more concrete application, consider a county with an average income of $20,000. If this county is a single-facility county, our estimate of the demand function is $\hat{Q} = 18.5031 + .0126(20) + .2732(0) - .1069PRICE$, or $\hat{Q} = 18.7551 - .1069PRICE$. On the other hand, if the county is a multifacility county, the estimated demand function is $\hat{Q} = 18.5031 + .0126(20) + .2732(1) - .1069PRICE$, or $\hat{Q} = 19.0283 - .1069PRICE$. What we see, then, is that, all else being the same, the demand for health care in multifacility counties is .2732 visits per household higher than the corresponding demand in single-facility counties, or the amount of NHCF's estimated coefficient. Finally, the imposition of NHCF affects only the level of demand; it does not address potential differences in price responsiveness.

| TABLE A-7 | REGRESSION RESULTS WITH INTERACTION DUMMY |
|---|---|

Dependent Variable: Quantity
Total Observations: 25
$R^2$ = .5858      Degrees of Freedom: 20
$F^*(4.20)$ = 7.07      $\overline{R}^2$ = .5029

| Name | Coefficient | Standard Error | $t$-Statistic |
|---|---|---|---|
| CONSTANT | +13.5068 | +3.139 | +4.3027 |
| PRICE | −.0084 | +.0625 | −.1340 |
| INCOME | +.0135 | +.0048 | +2.822 |
| NHCF | +8.2740 | +3.8912 | +2.1260 |
| NHCFPRICE | −.1593 | +.0774 | −2.0566 |

Let's look at figure A-6 once again. Notice that the group of data representing the multifacility counties (those data points represented with an X) seem to not only lie higher but also form a somewhat different shape than the data points representing the single-facility counties. This might indicate a difference between the two data groups in their reaction to prices. To test this possibility, we again turn to our dummy variable, NHCF. However, this time we ask NHCF to identify any marginal differences in pricing behavior that might exist. In this context, we use the dummy variable information in conjunction with the price information by defining the new variable NHCFPRICE = NHCF · PRICE. NHCFPRICE takes on the value of PRICE in multifacility counties (since NHCF = 1 and PRICE · 1 = PRICE) and takes on the value zero in single-facility counties (since NHCF = 0 and PRICE · 0 = 0). Table A-5 shows the results of the variable construction. We then use NHCFPRICE as we would any other variable.

The results of this regression appear in table A-7. First, you should verify that all the estimated coefficients, except the estimated price coefficient, are significantly different from zero at the $\alpha$ = .05 level (two-tailed) and that $R^2$ is significantly different from zero at the $\alpha$ = .01 level. Notice also that both $R^2$ and $\overline{R}^2$ have increased.

Interaction dummy variables (dummy variables created as the product of two variables) are interpreted in much the same manner that intercept dummies are. In the absence of the attribute, the estimated price coefficient is simply the coefficient on the price variable. From table A-7 we find the estimated coefficient on PRICE to be −.0084, which is not significantly different from zero. Thus, it would seem that our data suggest that demand in single-facility counties is consistent with a perfectly inelastic demand structure. The coefficient on NHCFPRICE measures the change in price responsiveness (the slope of demand) due to a county offering more than one health care facility. As table A-7 indicates, this change is −.1593, which is significantly different from zero, suggesting that demand in multifacility counties is not perfectly inelastic. The slope of demand in these counties is estimated as the sum of the two individual estimates, or $-.1677$. Our overall conclusion seems to be that individuals not only consume more health care when it is more readily available but are also more sensitive to price changes in counties with multiple facilities. Could it be that they comparison shop?

## SUMMARY

As we look back on all the changes brought on as the illustrative model evolved, we come to the question: What is truth? Which is the correct model? Of course, we don't know with certainty. Most of the discussion centered on the slope coefficient on price, since that is where the most economic interest lies. Questions concerning the magnitude and sign of the slope coefficient on price are of paramount interest. Each version brought with it changes in the estimated parameters, but changes well within the realm of both statistical and economic reason. Equally important, but often overlooked, was the lack of change taking place with the slope coefficient on the income variable. The income coefficient started out mildly positive, and in the very last version it remains mildly positive. Finally, each new version resulted in higher values for $\bar{R}^2$. The most important lesson we can learn is that empirical investigations can never uncover truth! Looking back, we conclude that while the last version isn't truth, it is closer to it than the first version. Until additional information becomes available, this represents our best attempt at estimating the demand for health care.

Two final observations are in order. The development of this particular example followed a path where only a linear function was considered and two different kinds of dummy variable applications were useful. Not all models will follow such a path. Perhaps some version of a nonlinear model is appropriate. Certainly dummy variables are not always applicable. When should we use them? It may take some time for, say, an income change, to affect demand. Thus, you might want to consider using income lagged one period instead of the current income value. Or should it be lagged two periods? Should current as well as lagged income be used? What if past values of demand influence current demand? Rest assured, there is no stock answer. You need to explore the possibilities. Let the data talk to you.

In our discussion, we used a demand model to illustrate the usefulness of econometrics, but don't get the idea that econometric modeling can be applied only to demand. Any functional relationship that exists in economics is a candidate for econometric analysis. Production functions, cost functions, supply functions, input demand functions, and input supply functions are all excellent sources for econometric applications. Just let economic theory and your imagination be your guide.

The purpose of this appendix was to introduce you to the vocabulary of econometrics. It presented a rudimentary discussion of the nature of estimation, testing, and model building. We have neglected far more than we covered. We have yet to contend with the detection and correction of autocorrelated and heteroskedastic errors. Multicollinearity is always a problem in econometric applications. And when was the last time you analyzed a market with only a demand curve? From the beginning of our economic training, we are told that it takes two blades of the scissors to cut; likewise, it takes demand and supply to properly describe the workings of a market. In econometrics, this translates into the estimation of a system of equations. These topics are well beyond the scope of this appendix. However, the interested reader is encouraged to explore these topics.

## References

Berndt, Ernst. *The Practice of Econometrics: Classic and Contemporary.* Reading, MA: Addison-Wesley, 1991.

Griffiths, William, R. Carter Hill, and George Judge. *Learning and Practicing Econometrics.* New York: John Wiley & Sons, 1993.

Gujarati, Damodar. *Basic Econometrics.* 3d ed. New York: McGraw-Hill, 1995.

Judge, George G., R. Carter Hill, William E. Griffiths, Helmut Lutkepohl, and Tsoung-Chao Lee. *Introduction to the Theory and Practice of Econometrics.* 2d ed. New York: John Wiley & Sons, 1988.

Maddala, G. S. *Introduction to Econometrics.* New York: Macmillan, 1992.

Wallace, T. D., and J. Lew Silver. *Econometrics: An Introduction.* New York: Addison-Wesley, 1988.

# Glossary

**adverse selection**  Occurs when an individual with poor health acquires low-risk medical insurance meant for healthy consumers. Results when an asymmetry of information develops between the insurer and the subscriber concerning the subscriber's true health status.

**advertising**  Promotional activities undertaken by a firm to either manipulate the demand for its product or provide more information to consumers. (See *informational advertising, persuasive advertising,* and *reminder advertising.*)

**Agency for Health Policy Research**  A government agency established to develop outcomes research and medical care guidelines for physician services.

**agency theory**  A theory that views relationships as a contract between a principal and agents. The proper design of the compensation package is an important consideration in agency theory since the interests of the agent are very likely to differ from those of the principal.

**allocative efficiency**  The condition in which the optimal amount of output is produced given the underlying structure of social benefits and costs. (See *production possibilities curve.*)

**American Medical Association (AMA)**  A national organization founded in 1897 that represents the collective interests of physicians.

**antitrust laws**  A body of legislation aimed at promoting competition in the U.S. economy.

**applied research**  See *technology.*

**assignment**  A policy under Medicare whereby physicians agree to accept a guaranteed payment for their services and in return forgo the right to balance-bill Medicare patients.

**asymmetry of information**  The situation where two economic agents in a market transaction have different amounts of relevant information. Asymmetry may allow the agent with more information to practice opportunistic behavior.

**average fixed costs**  Total fixed costs divided by the quantity of output.

**average product**  Total output divided by the level of a factor input, such as labor.

**average total costs**  Total costs divided by the quantity of output.

**average variable costs**  Total variable costs divided by the quantity of output.

**balance billing**  A situation where medical care providers bill patients in excess of the price established by a third-party payer.

**Balanced Budget Act of 1997**  An act passed by Congress in 1997 that significantly expands the role of managed care in the Medicare Program. (See also *Medicare + Choice*.)

**barrier to entry** An obstacle that prevents firms from costlessly entering a particular market. In the health care field, barriers can exist because of cost structure or legal restrictions.

**basic research** See *technology*.

**Blue Cross/Blue Shield** A traditionally not-for-profit insurance company that provides medical insurance for hospital (Blue Cross) and physician (Blue Shield) services.

**bounded rationality** The notion that people, in general, have a limited ability to formulate and solve problems at a point in time.

**boycotting** An agreement among competitors in a given input or output market not to do business with a particular supplier or customer. Boycotting is prohibited by the Sherman Antitrust Act.

**brand loyalty advantage** See *first mover*.

**capitation payment** A method of payment for medical services whereby medical care providers receive a fixed payment per person in return for providing medical care services regardless of the quantity of medical care delivered.

**certificate of need (CON) laws** State laws requiring health care providers to receive permission from a state agency before making a capital purchase above a stipulated amount.

*ceteris paribus* A Latin phrase meaning "all other factors remaining constant."

**cherry picking** A practice by private insurance companies of offering medical insurance to individuals they believe to be healthy while denying coverage to those they believe to be unhealthy.

**Children's Health Insurance Program** An act passed by Congress in 1997 that significantly expands medical insurance coverage to children through the Medicaid program.

**clinical investigation** See *technology*.

**clinical need** The quantity of medical care that a clinical expert prescribes as though medical care were a free good.

**coinsurance** A component of a medical insurance plan whereby consumers pay a fixed percentage of the cost of medical care.

**collusive oligopoly** An oligopolistic-type market structure where all the firms in the industry jointly maximize profits as if they all acted collectively as a monopolist.

**community rating** A method used by third-party payers to establish insurance premiums based on the average benefits paid out for the total population served. In this case, premiums reflect the average health risk factors for the entire population served.

**comparative static analysis** A comparison of the initial and new equilibrium points after an external change alters the model.

**compensating wage differential** The increase in wages needed to attract the marginal worker to a given occupation because there is an added cost to entering the occupation, such as a professional license.

**complements** Two goods that are used together in consumption. Two goods are complements in consumption if an increase in the price of one good causes a decrease in the demand for the other.

**constant returns to scale** Exist when a percentage increase in all factor inputs leads to a proportionately equal increase in output. The long-run cost curve is horizontal if constant returns to scale exist.

**consumer price index (CPI)** A price index that measures the cost of purchasing a fixed market basket of consumer goods and services over time. The CPI is used to measure the consumer price inflation rate from one period to the next.

**consumer surplus** The difference between what consumers are willing to pay for a product and the market clearing price. As such, consumer surplus is represented by the area under the demand curve but above market price.

**cost-benefit analysis** A method of analysis used for decision making that estimates the total costs and benefits of an activity.

**cost effectiveness analysis** A method of analysis used for decision making that estimates the total costs of achieving a defined health care objective, such as a life-year saved, from a medical treatment or health behavior.

**cost identification study**   A study that measures the total costs of a particular medical condition. Cost identification considers direct medical costs, direct nonmedical costs and indirect costs.

**cost shifting**   The practice of charging a higher price for a medical service in one market to compensate for a lower price received for the same product in another market.

**credence attributes**   Those characteristics of a good or service that can be assessed only after repeated purchases. Most medical care products possess credence characteristics.

**cross-price elasticity**   An elasticity measure of the extent to which the quantity demanded of one product changes with respect to a change in the price of an alternative product. In precise terms, it equals the percentage change in the quantity demanded of one product divided by the percentage change in the price of another product. If the value of the coefficient is negative, the two products are complements; if the coefficient is positive, the two products are substitutes.

**customary, prevailing, and reasonable rate**   See *usual, customary, and reasonable rate.*

**deadweight loss**   The social surplus not realized because resources are misallocated.

**decreasing returns to scale**   Exist when a percentage increase in all factor inputs leads to a less than proportional increase in output.

**deductible**   An annual out-of-pocket, lump-sum payment for medical services that a consumer must pay before medical insurance provides reimbursement.

**demand**   The quantities of a good or service that a consumer is willing and able to purchase at various prices at a specific point in time. The **market demand** for a product equals the total demand for an entire population.

**demand curve**   A graphical depiction of the relationship between quantity demanded and the price of a good or service. The **market demand** curve equals the horizontal summation of consumers' individual demand curves.

**demand function**   A mathematical expression containing the various factors that influence the quantity demanded of a given product.

**dependent variable**   A variable whose value is influenced by the value of one or more independent variables.

**diagnosis related group (DRG)**   A reimbursement system developed under Medicare used to compensate hospitals based on the patient's primary diagnosis. (See *prospective payment system.*)

**diffusion**   See *technology.*

**discount rate**   The rate of interest used to discount a future stream of payments. (See *present value.*)

**discovery by design**   The use of scientific knowledge to discover and develop new drugs.

**diseconomies of scale**   Exist when the average cost of production increases with the level of output.

**disproportionate share hospital payments**   Additional reimbursement payments received by states from the federal government for the Medicaid program to defer the high cost of providing medical care to a large number of low-income individuals.

**distributive justice**   (See *horizontal equity* and *vertical equity.*)

**drug utilization review**   Programs that control costs by reviewing the prescribing behavior of physicians to ensure that formularies are followed and inappropriate medicines are not prescribed.

**economic model**   A simplified depiction of a complex economic phenomenon used by economists to examine economic behavior.

**economic profit**   Total revenues minus total costs, including both explicit and implicit costs.

**economies of scale**   Exist when the average cost of production decreases with the quantity of output.

**economies of scope**   Exist when the total cost of jointly producing two or more products is cheaper than the total cost of producing each product individually.

**elastic** Describes a situation where the absolute value of the elasticity is greater than 1. This means the percentage change in the dependent variable is greater than the percentage change in the independent variable in absolute value terms.

**elasticity** A measure economists use to gauge the extent to which one variable changes in response to a change in another variable. It equals the percentage change in a dependent variable divided by the percentage change in an independent variable.

**elasticity of input substitution** An elasticity measure of the extent to which two inputs can be substituted for each other in the production process. In precise terms, it equals the percentage change in the input rate divided by the percentage change in the marginal products of the two inputs.

**employer mandates** A health care reform plan that requires employers to provide medical care insurance to employees.

**endogenous** Describes factors that are determined in the economic model, such as price and quantity in the supply and demand model.

**enthusiasm hypothesis** The hypothesis that geographic variations in the utilization of certain types of medical procedures reflect differences in medical preferences among physicians.

**equilibrium** When there is no tendency for further change. **Market equilibrium** occurs in the supply-and-demand model when quantity demanded equals quantity supplied at the market clearing price.

**exclusive provider organization (EPO)** A type of preferred provider organization that provides zero reimbursement to enrollees who acquire medical care from health care providers not included in the network.

**exogenous** Describes factors that are determined outside the economic model, such as buyer income or tastes and preferences in the supply and demand model.

**experience attributes** Those characteristics of a good or service that can be assessed only after the product has been purchased.

**experience rating** A method used by third-party payers to establish insurance premiums based on the expected benefits paid out as a result of individual health risk factors.

**explicit costs** Payments made to nonowners of the firm.

**externality** Exists when the actions of a market participant affect another participant in either an adverse or a beneficial fashion and no financial compensation takes place. An externality can emanate from either the demand or the supply side of the market.

**fee-for-service payment** A method of payment for medical care services whereby a medical care provider receives an individual payment for each medical service provided.

**firm** An organization that is responsible for coordinating the transformation of inputs, such as land, labor, capital, and entrepreneurship, into some final output or outputs.

**first dollar coverage** A health insurance plan that reimburses an individual for all medical care expenses, beginning with the first dollar spent on medical care.

**first mover** A firm that poses a barrier to entry by being the first to introduce a product to a given market. Potential competitors must overcome the problem of name recognition if they wish to enter the market.

**fixed costs** Costs of production that remain constant regardless of the level of production.

**fixed payment** A payment that is independent of the actual costs or quantity of medical services delivered.

**Flexner Report** A report published in 1910 that was highly critical of the medical training physicians received in the United States and Canada. As a result, numerous changes were made in the education and training of physicians.

**Food and Drug Administration (FDA)** A government agency that regulates the introduction of new drugs in the United States.

**formulary** A list of low-cost pharmaceutical products that physicians are required to prescribe whenever possible. Hospitals and other health care providers use formularies to control costs.

**for-profit organization** An organization owned by private individuals. Ownership gives the individuals a claim on any residual profits.

**function** A mathematical expression that establishes a relationship between the value of a dependent variable and a set of values for the independent variables.

**fuzzy demand curve** A demand curve for medical care reflecting the possibility that the relationship between the price and quantity demanded of medical care may not be exact or precisely known.

**gag rules** Rules that prohibit a physician in a managed-care plan from discussing alternative treatment options not covered by the health insurance plan, providing information on the limitations of the plan, and commenting negatively about the plan to patients.

**global budgeting** A method used by third-party payers to control medical care costs by establishing total expenditure limits for medical services over a specified period of time.

**group-model health maintenance organization** A health maintenance organization (HMO) that contracts with group physician practices. (See *health maintenance organization.*)

**health** The condition of being of sound body and mind and free of any disease or physical pain.

**health alliance** A public agency that uses its monopsony power to negotiate competitive prices for health insurance from the private insurance market. (See *managed competition.*)

**Health Care Financing Administration (HCFA)** An agency of the U.S. Department of Health and Human Services that is responsible for overseeing the financing and quality control programs for Medicare and the federal portion of Medicaid.

**health care system** The organizational and institutional structures through which an

economy makes choices regarding the production, consumption, and distribution of health care services.

**health economics** A field of economics that uses economic theory to study how an economy utilizes scarce health care resources to provide and distribute medical care.

**Health Insurance Portability and Accountability Act of 1996** An act of Congress that addresses the nonportability of health insurance by making it more difficult for insurers to segment markets and deny individuals or groups health insurance based on health status.

**health maintenance organization (HMO)** A health care delivery system that combines the insurer and producer functions. HMOs are prepaid and in return provide comprehensive services to enrollees.

**Herfindahl-Hirschman index** An index used to measure the degree of industry concentration in a given market.

**horizontal equity** Equity that is achieved when, for example, individuals with similar incomes pay equal amounts of taxes and receive the same amounts of subsidies; in other words, equals are treated equally.

**horizontal merger** A merger between two firms in the same market.

**human capital approach** Equates the value of a human life to the market value of the output produced by an individual over an expected lifetime.

**image differentiation** The use by a firm of promotional activities to differentiate consumers' perceptions of its product relative to other products in the market.

**imperfect consumer information** The assumption that consumers lack all the information necessary to make informed decisions concerning the appropriate quantity and type of medical care to consume.

**implicit costs** Costs that measure the opportunity cost of utilizing resources owned by the firm.

**income effect**   The increase (decrease) in quantity demanded brought about by an increase (a decrease) in real income when the price of a product decreases (increases). The concept is used to derive a downward-sloping demand curve.

**income elasticity of demand**   An elasticity measure of the extent to which the quantity demanded changes with a change in income. In precise terms, it equals the percentage change in the quantity demanded divided by the percentage change in income.

**inconsistency**   See *service.*

**increasing returns to scale**   Exist when a percentage increase in all factor inputs leads to a greater percentage increase in output.

**indemnity insurance**   Medical insurance that reimburses the insured a fixed amount for each type of medical service consumed.

**independent provider association (IPA)**   A type of health maintenance organization that contracts with a number of independent medical care providers to deliver medical services at a discounted price or on a capitation basis.

**independent variable**   A variable whose values are predetermined and influence the value of a dependent variable.

**individual mandates**   A health care reform plan that requires individuals to purchase their own medical insurance. Tax credits and subsidies would be available to those who cannot afford to purchase medical insurance.

**inelastic**   Describes a situation where the absolute value of the elasticity is less than 1, or the percentage change in the dependent variable is less than the percentage change in the independent variable.

**inferior good**   A good for which demand decreases when consumers experience an increase in income.

**informational advertising**   Advertising that provides information to consumers.

**inseparability**   See *service.*

**insurance premium**   The cost of medical insurance. In the private insurance market, it equals the sum of expected benefits paid out,

administrative costs, taxes, and profits. (See also *experience rating* and *community rating.*)

**intangibility**   See *service.*

**integrated delivery system (IDS)**   A legal or contractual combination of buyers and suppliers, such as medical organizations producing different medical services, like physician groups, hospitals, and nursing homes.

**inventory**   See *service.*

**job lock**   The situation where an individual cannot change jobs without potentially losing medical care insurance for a given period of time.

**kinked demand curve**   The demand curve faced by an oligopolist based on the assumption that competitors will match a decrease but not an increase in the price of the product.

**law of demand**   An economic principle stating that the quantity demanded of a good or service is inversely related to its price.

**law of diminishing marginal product**   An economic principle stating that as more and more units of an input are used in production, a point is eventually reached where output increases by a continually smaller and smaller amount. In other words, the **marginal product** of the factor input begins to fall in value.

**law of diminishing marginal utility**   An economic principle stating that as units of a product are consumed, a point is eventually reached where total utility increases at a smaller and smaller rate. In other words, the **marginal utility** of the product begins to fall.

**law of increasing opportunity cost**   An economic principle stating that the **opportunity cost** of an activity increases as more of that activity is undertaken.

**law of supply**   An economic principle stating that the quantity supplied of a good or service increases with its price.

**learning-by-doing**   The economies that result from knowledge or experience gained through the cumulative production of a product.

**limit pricing**   The practice of pricing a product just below the break-even point of a potential entrant as a way to discourage entry.

**loading fee**   That portion of medical insurance premiums in excess of expected benefits paid out. Its value depends on such items as administrative costs, taxes, and the intensity of competition in the insurance market.

**long run**   A time horizon over which all inputs in the production process are variable.

**long-run average cost curve**   An envelope curve comprising the cost-minimizing points from a series of short-run average cost curves. It represents the lowest cost of producing each unit of output in the long run.

**managed-care organization (MCO)**   An organization that controls the utilization and cost of medical care by reviewing and monitoring the appropriateness, extensiveness, and costs of medical services.

**managed competition**   A health care reform plan that calls for the establishment of health alliances that would use their monopsony power to negotiate competitively priced medical coverage from a number of alternative private insurance companies.

**managerial expense preference model**   A model of firm behavior positing that managers utilize a portion of the firm's profits to maximize their own utility.

**marginal cost**   The change in total costs brought about by a one-unit change in the production of a product.

**marginal product**   The change in total output brought about by a one-unit change in a factor input.

**marginal rate of technical substitution**   The rate at which one input can be substituted for another in the production process. In precise terms, it equals the ratio of the marginal products of two inputs.

**marginal revenue**   The addition to total revenue brought about by the sale of one more unit of output.

**marginal social benefit**   The change in total social benefit brought about by a one-unit change in the consumption of a good or service.

**marginal social cost**   The change in total social costs resulting from a one-unit change in the production of a good or service.

**marginal utility**   The change in total utility or satisfaction brought about by a one-unit change in the consumption of a good or service.

**market allocation**   A collusive agreement among rival firms not to compete with one another in a given geographical market. This activity is prohibited by the Sherman Antitrust Act.

**market failure**   The situation where a market outcome fails to produce the socially optimal quantity of output or distribute income fairly.

**Medicaid**   A jointly financed program between federal and state governments that provides medical insurance to certain segments of the poor population without private health insurance.

**medical care**   Those goods and services that maintain, improve, or restore an individual's physical or mental well-being.

**medical savings accounts**   A health care reform plan that allows individuals to establish tax-free savings accounts to finance primary medical care.

**Medicare**   A federally financed program that provides medical insurance primarily to elderly individuals.

**Medicare + Choice**   Part of the Balanced Budget Act of 1997 that significantly increases the number of insurance plans available to Medicare recipients, along with altering the method in which Medicare pays for those plans.

**medigap insurance policies**   Private insurance policies purchased by elderly individuals to cover some or all of their medical expenses not paid for by Medicare.

**merger**   The combining of two or more firms.

**microeconomics**   A field of economics that uses economic theory to study how individual consumers and firms make economic decisions.

**molecule manipulation**   A method of drug discovery whereby pharmaceutical companies utilize trial and error to determine the therapeutic value of a large number of chemical entities.

**monopolistic competition**   A product market characterized by numerous sellers, moderate product differentiation, no barriers to entry, and some imperfections in consumer information.

**monopoly**   A product market characterized by one seller and perfect barriers to entry.

**monopoly power**   The ability a firm has in a given market to control the price of its product. The degree of monopoly power any firm possesses is inversely related to the level of competition in the market.

**monopsony**   A market characterized by a single buyer that has the ability to influence market price.

**moral hazard**   The situation where individuals alter their behavior after they have purchased medical insurance because they are no longer liable for the full cost of their actions.

**morbidity rate**   The rate at which a given disease is present in a population.

**mortality rate**   The death rate for a given population measured by the ratio of the number of deaths divided by the average size of the population during a given period.

**multihospital system**   An organization that is made up of two or more hospitals and is managed by a single corporation.

**multipayer system**   A system in which health care providers are reimbursed by numerous third-party payers.

**multiple regression**   A statistical technique used by economists to estimate the relation between a dependent variable and one or more independent variables.

**multisource drug**   A drug that is no longer under patent protection and is available from alternative suppliers.

**national health insurance (NHI)**   A government-sponsored health insurance system covering the entire population and financed by tax revenues. Such a system exists in Canada.

**national health system (NHS)**   A health care system directly run by the government and financed by general taxes. Such a system exists in Great Britain.

**natural monopoly**   A firm that faces long-run economies of scale over the entire market demand curve.

**net benefit calculus**   The optimizing rule used by economic agents that looks at the expected net benefits of a given activity, defined as the expected benefits minus the expected costs. When net benefits are greater than zero, the economic agent's well-being is enhanced by choosing the activity in question.

**net marginal social benefit**   The difference between marginal social benefit and marginal social cost.

**network health maintenance organization**   An HMO that provides physician services by contracting with more than one physician group practice.

**nominal**   Describes an economic measure that is expressed in terms of current market prices.

**normal good**   A good for which demand increases when consumers experience an increase in income.

**normative economic analysis**   The use of economic theory and empirical analysis to justify whether an economic outcome is desirable.

**not-for-profit**   An organization that is prohibited from distributing profits.

**oligopoly**   A product market that is characterized by a few dominant sellers and substantial barriers to entry.

**Omnibus Budget Reconciliation Act of 1989**   An act passed by Congress significantly reforming the method by which physicians are compensated under the Medicare program.

**opportunistic behavior**   The situation where a health care provider takes advantage of an asymmetry of information and provides medical care to advance his or her own economic self-interests.

**opportunity cost** The value of what is given up by not pursuing the next best alternative.

**Orphan Drug Act** An act providing incentives to pharmaceutical companies to develop drugs to treat rare diseases that are otherwise unprofitable to develop because the potential demand is low.

**outcome quality** The quality of medical care as measured by its end result, such as patient satisfaction or postcare morbidity or mortality.

**out-of-pocket price** The price consumers pay for medical care after all third-party payments have been considered.

**output maximization** See *quantity maximization.*

**over-the-counter drug** A drug that consumers can purchase without a prescription from a physician.

**own-price elasticity of demand** An elasticity measure of the responsiveness of quantity demanded to changes in a product's own price. In precise terms, it equals the percentage change in quantity demanded divided by the percentage change in price.

**own-price elasticity of supply** An elasticity measure of the responsiveness of quantity supplied to changes in price. In precise terms, it equals the percentage change in quantity supplied divided by the percentage change in price.

**patent** A government document that grants the legal right to an innovating firm to be the sole producer of a product for up to 20 years (in the United States).

**patient dumping** The situation where a private hospital fails to admit a very sick patient because it fears that the medical bills will exceed a preset limit established by a third-party payer. As a result, the patient is forced to acquire medical care services from a public hospital.

**per capita** Per unit of the population.

**perfect competition** A product market characterized by numerous buyers and sellers, a homogeneous product, no barriers to entry, and perfect consumer information.

**perfectly elastic** The special case where there is an infinite change in the value of the dependent variable when the independent variable changes in value.

**perfectly inelastic** The special case where the value of the dependent variable is unresponsive to changes in the value of the independent variable.

**personal health care expenditures** Total expenditures by individuals on medical care goods and services.

**persuasive advertising** Advertising that aims to convince consumers to purchase the product.

**physician control model** A model of hospital behavior that hypothesizes that physicians exert influence on hospitals to employ more than the profit-maximizing level of all other inputs to enhance their own productivity and income.

**physician payment review commission (PPRC)** A commission established in 1985 to advise and make recommendations to Congress regarding physician payment reform. PPRC was replaced by MedPAC.

**physician practice hypothesis** A hypothesis stating that per capita variations in the use of medical care are explained by systematic differences in clinical opinions concerning the proper type and amount of medical care to prescribe.

**physician profiling** The process by which a managed-care organization selects and monitors the performance of physicians.

**positive economic analysis** The analysis of economic behavior that uses economic theory along with empirical analysis to explain what is or what happened.

**practice guideline** A statement concerning the known costs, benefits, and risks of using a particular medical intervention to bring about a given medical outcome.

**preferred provider organization (PPO)** A third-party payer that offers financial incentives, such as low out-of-pocket prices, to enrollees who acquire medical care from a preset list of physicians and hospitals. A PPO is a prepaid type of MCO that combines the insurer and producer functions.

**prescription drug** A drug that can be purchased only with a physician's prescription.

**present value**   A technique used to determine today's value of a future stream of cash payments.

**price ceiling**   A government-imposed limit on the price of a product.

**price discrimination**   The practice of charging a different price for the same product in two or more markets.

**price fixing**   The practice by rival firms in the same market of acting in a collusive manner and setting prices for the purpose of increasing profits. This practice is prohibited by the Sherman Antitrust Act.

**price leadership model**   An oligopolistic-type market structure where the firms in a given industry agree that one firm will serve as the price leader and the others will follow its pricing and output actions.

**primary care**   Medical care services that deal with the prevention, early detection, and treatment of disease.

**primary care physician**   A physician specializing in family practice, general practice, internal medicine, obstetrics/gynecology, or pediatrics.

**process quality**   The quality of medical care as measured by the quality of treatment.

**product differentiation**   A situation where firms within a given market sell slightly different products.

**production efficiency**   Achieved when one activity (production or consumption) cannot be increased without a reduction in another activity because the maximum level of output is being produced from a finite amount of inputs. (See *production possibilities curve*.)

**production function**   A mathematical expression that shows the maximum level of output that a firm can produce using various quantities of factor inputs.

**production possibilities curve (PPC)**   An economic model that shows the various combinations of goods an economy can produce when **production efficiency** is achieved. **Allocative efficiency** is obtained when society chooses that point on the curve that maximizes overall satisfaction. The model illustrates the economic concepts of scarcity, choice, and opportunity costs.

**professional licensure**   The requirement that a health care professional, such as a doctor or a nurse, obtain a license from the government before being allowed to practice medicine.

**profit maximization**   A situation where sellers strive to attain the greatest amount of economic profits.

**progressive redistribution scheme**   The situation where net taxes as a fraction of income increase with income.

**property rights model**   A model hypothesizing that for-profit organizations are more efficient than their not-for-profit counterparts because the owners of for-profit organizations force managers to act in a cost-efficient manner and strive to maximize profits. Managers of not-for-profit organizations do not face such pressure and are free to pursue other objectives, such as quality maximization.

**proportional redistribution scheme**   The situation where net taxes as a fraction of income remain constant with income.

**prospective payment system (PPS)**   A method of payment used by third-party payers in which payments are made on a case-by-case basis. Congress adopted a prospective payment system in 1983 when it introduced the DRG system for classifying Medicare patients.

**public choice model**   A model postulating that public organizations are less efficient than private organizations because bureaucrats and special interest groups cause public organizations to behave inefficiently and overproduce.

**public contracting model**   A health insurance model whereby the government contracts with various health care providers for medical services on behalf of the general population.

**public enterprise**   A medical care organization operated by a government authority.

**public good**   A product has the properties of a public good if it can be consumed simultaneously by more than one consumer and it is costly to exclude nonpayers from consuming the good. Public goods are generally provided by a government entity and funded out of tax revenues.

**public interest group theory**   A theory of government behavior that hypothesizes that governments intervene in a market-based economy to advance the general interest of its citizens.

**quality and quantity maximization**   The assumption that a medical care provider jointly determines what quality and quantity of output to produce that maximize utility.

**quality differentiation**   The situation where firms attempt to differentiate their products based on quality.

**quality maximization**   Occurs when medical care providers maximize the quality of output produced at the expense of economic profits.

**quantity maximization**   Occurs when medical care providers maximize the amount of output produced at the expense of economic profits.

**quaternary-level care**   State-of-the-art medical care.

**rationality**   The notion that consumers will never purposely make themselves worse off and have the ability to rank preferences and allocate income in a fashion that derives the maximum level of utility.

**rationally ignorant**   The situation where consumers have less than perfect information concerning a good or service due to the high cost of acquiring additional information.

**real**   Describes an economic measure that is expressed in base-year prices.

**regressive redistribution scheme**   The situation where net taxes as a fraction of income decrease with income.

**reminder advertising**   Advertising that reinforces consumers' knowledge about the product.

**required generic substitution**   Cost control policies that require physicians and pharmacists to use lower-priced generic drugs whenever medically possible.

**resource-based relative value system**   A method to compensate physicians that bases the payment on the time and effort of physician services necessary to produce the medical service.

This system is currently used by the Medicare program.

**risk adjustment**   The process of setting the capitation rate for an insurance policy based on the health status and expected medical costs of an individual or group purchasing the plan.

**risk assessment**   The process of modeling and estimating the expected medical costs of a person or group of people.

**risk aversion**   The quality of preferring less risk to more, all other things held equal.

**risk selection**   Occurs when a greater share of individuals with either higher or lower expected medical costs enroll in or select a particular medical insurance plan.

**rule of reason**   States that courts should weigh the social desirability of a business practice, such as a merger, when determining if that practice should be allowed to take place. Thus, both the procompetitive and anticompetitive aspects of the business practice are considered.

**search attributes**   Those characteristics of a good or service that are easily evaluated prior to its purchase, such as size, color, or design.

**secondary care**   Medical care that consists of more sophisticated treatments than primary care services.

**second opinions**   A utilization review program in which each decision made by a physician concerning the need for surgery is routinely reviewed by another physician.

**selective contracting**   Occurs when a third-party contracts exclusively with a preselected set of medical care providers.

**service**   A product that exhibits the four characteristics of intangibility, inseparability, inventory, and inconsistency. **Intangibility** means that a medical service cannot be evaluated by the five senses. **Inseparability** means that production takes place at the time of consumption. **Inventory** refers to the fact that it is impossible for health care providers to maintain an inventory of medical services. **Inconsistency** reflects the fact that the composition and quality of medical services vary greatly across points of consumption.

**Sherman Antitrust Act** A law passed in 1890 prohibiting certain forms of anticompetitive behavior. This act is considered the centerpiece of antitrust legislation in the United States.

**short run** A time horizon over which the quantity of at least one factor input is fixed in the production process. In this case, output can be altered only by changing the quantity of one or more of the variable inputs utilized in the production process.

**short-run economies of scale** Exist when average variable costs decline with the level of output.

**sickness funds** Private, not-for-profit insurance companies in Germany that collect premiums from employees and employers. (See *socialized health insurance.*)

**single payer** The situation where only one third-party payer is responsible for paying health care providers for medical services.

**single-source drug** A drug covered by patent protection.

**socialized health insurance (SHI)** A German-style health care system in which the government mandates that employers and employees jointly finance the cost of medical care insurance.

**spatial differentiation** The situation where firms attempt to differentiate themselves based on location.

**special interest group theory** A theory of government behavior that hypothesizes that governments intervene in a market-based economy for the purpose of advancing the economic self-interests of a particular interest group.

**staff-model health maintenance organization** An HMO that directly employs physicians on a salary basis.

**Standard Industrial Classification (SIC) system** A system, designed by the U.S. Census Bureau, to categorize and code the output of firms into various classes. The code can contain up to seven digits. The four-digit SIC code is considered to represent the industry level. The first digit in the coding system identifies the sector of the economy (0 for agriculture, 2 for manufacturing, 5 for trade). The second digit

defines the commodity group in that sector. For example, the two-digit code 28 represents the "chemicals and allied products" group of the manufacturing sector. The third digit represents an industry group. For example, 283 represents the "drugs" industry group and 282 stands for the "plastic materials and synthetics" industry group. The fourth digit identifies a specific segment of an industry group. For example, the four-digit code 2834 represents the "pharmaceutical preparations" industry, and the 2833 stands for the "medicinal chemicals and botanical products" industry.

**structural quality** The quality of medical services as measured by the quality of the inputs used in production, such as credentials of physicians, education of nurses, and vintage and variety of equipment.

**structure-conduct-performance paradigm** A model used by economists when conducting an industry analysis. It predicts that market structure influences firm conduct, which determines market performance.

**substitutes** Two goods that are replacements in consumption and fulfill a similar purpose. Two goods are substitutes in consumption if an increase in the price of one good causes an increase in demand for the other.

**substitution effect** The increase (decrease) in quantity demanded brought about by a relative decrease (increase) in the price of a product. The concept is used to derive a downward-sloping demand curve.

**supplier-induced demand model** A model of firm behavior that hypothesizes that physicians take advantage of the asymmetry of information about medical care to convince their patients to consume more medical care than is necessary to further their own economic self-interests.

**supply** The quantity of output a firm is willing and able to produce at various prices during a specific time period. The **market supply** equals the total amount supplied in a given market.

**supply curve** The short-run supply curve for an individual firm facing a perfectly competitive market equals that part of the short-run marginal cost curve that lies above the average variable cost curve. The **market supply curve** equals the horizontal summation of the individual firms' supply curves, with adjustments made for factor price changes.

**survivor theory** Categorizes firms based on size and hypothesizes that any category that includes a growing number of firms over time represents the most efficient producers in comparison to those categories where the number of firms is decreasing.

**technical efficiency** Achieved when the maximum level of output is produced from a given mix of inputs at a point in time.

**technology** The development and diffusion of medical technology takes place in four stages. During the **basic research** stage, the investigation of new knowledge is without commercial purpose. In the **applied research** stage, new scientific knowledge is applied to the solution of a medical problem. The **clinical investigation** stage occurs with testing of new medical technologies on human subjects. The **diffusion** stage marks the commercial introduction and adoption of a new medical technology.

**tertiary care** Highly complex medical care that involves more sophisticated medical treatments than primary or secondary medical care.

**theory X of health economics** An economic theory stating that health and disease occur randomly and that economic incentives cannot be called upon to provide quality medical care at low cost. Government intervention is needed to ensure individuals have access to quality medical care.

**theory Y of health economics** An economic theory stating that individuals have significant control over health through lifestyle choices and that the market mechanism will discipline health care providers to provide high-quality medical care at low cost. There is little need for government intervention in health care markets.

**third-party payer** An organization that provides medical care insurance to individuals in return for tax or premium payments.

**total costs** The sum of **fixed** and **variable** costs associated with the production of a given quantity of output.

**total product curve** A curve showing the quantity of output produced by different levels of a specific input, such as labor, given that all other inputs are held constant.

**total social benefit** The total of the benefits a society receives from the consumption of a particular product. (See *total social surplus*.)

**total social cost** The total of the costs resulting from the production of a particular product. (See *total social surplus*.)

**total social surplus** The *total social benefit* minus the *total social cost* of producing a given quantity of a good or service.

**transaction cost economics** The view that contracts may be incomplete and therefore costly to engage in. Transaction costs include the costs of searching out the best price, and the cost associated with the negotiating, writing, and enforcing of contracts.

**type I error** Occurs when an outcome is rejected as false when it is true. For example, the FDA rejects an application of a drug even though the drug is truly safe and effective.

**type II error** Occurs when an outcome is accepted as true when it is false. For example, the FDA accepts an application of a drug even though the drug is unsafe or ineffective.

**unitary elasticity** An elasticity with a value of 1 such that the percentage change in the dependent variable equals the percentage change in the independent variable in absolute value terms.

**universal coverage** Achieved when an entire population has medical insurance coverage.

**usual, customary, and reasonable rate (UCR)** A cost control method utilized by third-party payers to control the fees paid to medical care providers for medical goods and services. The UCR fee is limited to the lowest of the actual charge of the physician, the customary charge, or the prevailing charge in the local area.

**utility** The level of satisfaction or pleasure an individual or group receives from consuming a good or service.

**utility analysis**   A method of analysis used to make policy decisions that considers the quantity as well as the quality of a life saved from a medical intervention. (See also *cost effectiveness analysis*.)

**utility function**   A mathematical expression that shows the extent to which various factors affect total utility.

**utility maximization model**   An economic model that assumes people try to attain the highest possible level of satisfaction through their consumption decisions.

**utility maximization rule**   A rule stating that a consumer's utility is maximized when the marginal utility received from the last dollar spent on each commodity is equal across all goods and services purchased.

**utilization review**   Programs implemented to control medical costs by evaluating the medical decisions of hospitals and physicians. These programs can be carried out on a prospective, concurrent, or retrospective basis.

**value of life**   The monetary worth of a human life.

**variable costs**   Costs of production that vary directly with the quantity of output produced.

**variable payment**   Reimbursement that increases with higher costs incurred or a greater quantity of services supplied.

**vertical equity**   Achieved when unequal individuals are treated unequally. For example, people with higher incomes pay higher taxes.

**vertical merger**   A merger between two firms in a supplier–purchaser relationship.

**virtual integration**   A contractual combination of buyers and suppliers.

**voluntary performance standard**   A target rate of growth for physician expenditures financed by the Medicare program. This rate is established by Congress to control the cost of Medicare over time. This cost control method ended in 1997.

**Waxman-Hatch Act of 1984**   The Drug Price Competition and Patent Term Restoration Act, which extended the effective life of a new drug product and shortened the approval process for generic drugs.

**willingness-to-pay approach**   Determines the value of a human life based on a person's willingness to pay for relatively small reductions in the chance of dying.

# Credits

American Academy of Pediatrics: Table 2 from "Physician Reimbursement by Salary on Fee-for-Service: Effect on Physician Practice Behavior in a Randomized Practice Study" by Gerald B. Hickson, William A. Altemeier, and James M. Perrin from Pediatrics, 80, September 1987. © 1987 by the American Academy of Pediatrics.

American Economic Review: Table 2 from "Health Insurance and the Demand for Medical Care: Evidence from a Randomized Experiment" by Willard G. Manning et al., from American Economic Review, 77, June 1987. © 1987 by American Economic Review.

American Enterprise Institute: Table 20 from Competition in the Pharmaceutical Industry: The Declining Profitability of Drug Innovation by Meir Statman. © 1983 by the American Enterprise Institute.

American Enterprise Institute: Figure 1 from The Regulation of Pharmaceuticals: Balancing the Benefits and Risks by Henry G. Grabowski and John M. Vernon. © 1983 by the American Enterprise Institute.

American Hospital Association: Table 1 and Table 2 from Hospital Statistics. © by the American Hospital Association.

American Medical Association: Tables 1, A-1, A-2, A-3, and A-17 from Physician Characteristics and Distribution in the U.S., 1997/1998 edition. © 1998 by the American Medical Association.

American Medical Association: Tables 51-52 from Physician Marketplace Statistics, 1990 edition. © 1990 by the American Medical Association.

American Medical Association: Tables 96, 97, 98, 99, 111, and 115 from Physician Marketplace Statistics,

1997/1998 edition. © 1998 by the American Medical Association.

American Medical Association: Tables 24, 26, 30, and 46 from Socioeconomic Characteristics of Medical Practice 1997/98. © 1998 by the American Medical Association.

Boston Consulting Group: Figure 2-25 from The Changing Environment for U.S. Pharmaceuticals. © 1993 by the Boston Consulting Group.

Leslie S. Cutler: "Why Governments Should Pay for Medical Students' Education" by Leslie S. Cutler from Hartford Courant, January 27, 1993, p. D13. © 1993 by Leslie S. Cutler.

Dow Jones & Company, Inc.: Adapted from "Prescription to Stop Drug Companies' Profiteering" by Suzanne Tregarthen from The Wall Street Journal, March 5, 1992, p. A12. © 1992 by Dow Jones & Company, Inc. All rights reserved worldwide. Reprinted by permission of Dow Jones & Company, Inc.

Dow Jones & Company, Inc.: "A Growing Economy Can Pay Its Bills" by William J. Baumol from The Wall Street Journal, May 18, 1992, p. A16. © 1992 by Dow Jones & Company, Inc. All rights reserved worldwide. Reprinted by permission of Dow Jones & Company, Inc.

Dow Jones & Company, Inc.: "Take Two Tablespoons of Mustard and Call If You Don't Feel Better" by Larry M. Greenberg from The Wall Street Journal, February 22, 1994, p. 81. © 1994 by Dow Jones & Company, Inc. All rights reserved worldwide. Reprinted by permission of Dow Jones & Company, Inc.

Dow Jones & Company, Inc.: "Price of Pleasure: New Legal Theorists Attach a Dollar Value to the Joys of